*CHILTON*

REPAIR MANUAL

CHEVROLET LUMINA PONTIAC GRAND PRIX OLDS CUTLASS SUPREME BUICK REGAL 1988-90

All U.S. and Canadia   ET LUMINA •
OLDSMOBILE CUTLASS SUPR   DATE DUE   RIX

629.2872
L971
1990

President GARY R. INGERSOLL
Senior Vice President, Book Publishing and Research RONALD A. HOXTER
Vice President and General Manager JOHN P. KUSHNERICK
Editor-in-Chief KERRY A. FREEMAN, S.A.E.
Managing Editor DEAN F. MORGANTINI, S.A.E.
Senior Editor RICHARD J. RIVELE, S.A.E.
Senior Editor W. CALVIN SETTLE, JR., S.A.E.
Editor JAMES B. STEELE

CHILTON BOOK COMPANY
Radnor, Pennsylvania
19089

7

CONTENTS

1 GENERAL INFORMATION and MAINTENANCE

2 ENGINE PERFORMANCE and TUNE-UP

3 ENGINE and ENGINE OVERHAUL

4 EMISSION CONTROLS

5 FUEL SYSTEM

6 CHASSIS ELECTRICAL

RN

7 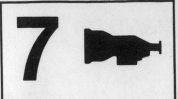 DRIVE TRAIN

8  SUSPENSION and STEERING

9 BRAKES

10 BODY

11 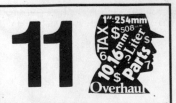 MECHANIC'S DATA

SAFETY NOTICE

Proper service and repair procedures are vital to the safe, reliable operation of all motor vehicles, as well as the personal safety of those performing repairs. This book outlines procedures for servicing and repairing vehicles using safe, effective methods. The procedures contain many NOTES, CAUTIONS and WARNINGS which should be followed along with standard safety procedures to eliminate the possibility of personal injury or improper service which could damage the vehicle or compromise its safety.

It is important to note that repair procedures and techniques, tools and parts for servicing motor vehicles, as well as the skill and experience of the individual performing the work vary widley. It is not possible to anticipate all of the conceivable ways or conditions under which vehicles may be serviced, or to provide cautions as to all of the possible hazards that may result. Standard and accepted safety precautions and equipment should be used during cutting, grinding, chiseling, prying, or any other process that can cause material removal or projectiles

Some procedures require the use of tools specially designed for a specific purpose. Before substituting another tool or procedure, you must be completly satisfied that neither your personal safety, nor the performance of the the vehicle will be endangered.

Although the information in this guide is based on industry sources and is as complete as possible at the time of publication, the possibility exists that the manufacturer made later changes which could not be included here. While striving for total accuracy, Chilton Book Company cannot assume responsibility for any errors, changes, or omissions that may occur in the compilation of this data.

PART NUMBERS

Part numbers listed in this reference are not recommendations by Chilton for any product by brand name. They are references that can be used with interchange manuals and aftermarket supplier catalogs to locate each brand supplier's discrete part number.

SPECIAL TOOLS

Special tools are recommended by the vehicle manufacturer to perform their specific job. Use has been kept to a minimum, but where absolutely necessary, they are referred to in the text by the part number of the tool manufacturer. These tools can be purchased, under the appropriate part number, from the Service Tool Division, Kent-Moore Corporation, 29784 Little Mac, Roseville, MI 48066-2298, or an equivalent tool can be purchased locally from a tool supplier or parts outlet. Before substituting any tool for the one recommended, read the SAFETY NOTICE at the top of this page.

ACKNOWLEDGMENTS

Chilton Book Company expresses appreciation to the General Motors Corporation for their generous assistance.

Copyright © 1990 by Chilton Book Company
All Rights Reserved
Published in Radnor, Pennsylvania 19089, by Chilton Book Company

Manufactured in the United States of America
1234567890   9876543210

Chilton's Repair Manual: Lumina, Grand Prix, Cutlass, Regal 1988-1990
ISBN 0-8019-7950-1 pbk.
Libary of Congress Catalog Card No. 88-43194

General Information and Maintenance

1

HOW TO USE THIS BOOK

Chilton's Repair Manual for the Chevrolet Lumina, Buick Regal, Oldsmobile Cutlass Supreme, and Pontiac Grand Prix is intended to teach you about the inner workings of your car and save you money on its upkeep.

The first two chapters will be the most used, since they contain maintenance and tune-up information and procedures. Studies have shown that a properly tuned and maintained car can get at least 10% better gas mileage (which translates into lower operating costs) and periodic maintenance will catch minor problems before they turn into major repair bills. The other chapters deal with the more complex systems of your car. Operating systems from engine through brakes are covered to the extent that the average do-it-yourselfer becomes mechanically involved. This book will not explain such things as rebuilding the differential for the simple reason that the expertise required and the investment in special tools make this task impractical and uneconomical. It will give you the detailed instructions to help you change your own brake pads and shoes, tune-up the engine, replace spark plugs and filters, and do many more jobs that will save you money, give you personal satisfaction and help you avoid expensive problems.

A secondary purpose of this book is a reference guide for owners who want to understand their car and/or their mechanics better. In this case, no tools at all are required. Knowing just what a particular repair job requires in parts and labor time will allow you to evaluate whether or not you're getting a fair price quote and help decipher itemized bills from a repair shop.

Before attempting any repairs or service on your car, read through the entire procedure outlined in the appropriate chapter. This will give you the overall view of what tools and supplies will be required. There is nothing more frustrating than having to walk to the bus stop on Monday morning because you were short one gasket on Sunday afternoon. So read ahead and plan ahead. Each operation should be approached logically and all procedures thoroughly understood before attempting any work. Some special tools that may be required can often be rented from local automotive jobbers or places specializing in renting tools and equipment. Check the yellow pages of your phone book.

All chapters contain adjustments, maintenance, removal and installation procedures, and overhaul procedures. When overhaul is not considered practical, we tell you how to remove the failed part and then how to install the new or rebuilt replacement. In this way, you at least save the labor costs. Backyard overhaul of some components (such as the alternator or water pump) is just not practical, but the removal and installation procedure is often simple and well within the capabilities of the average car owner.

Two basic mechanic's rules should be mentioned here. First, whenever the LEFT side of the car or engine is referred to, it is meant to specify the DRIVER'S side of the car. Conversely, the RIGHT side of the car means the PASSENGER'S side. Second, all screws and bolts are removed by turning counterclockwise, and tightened by turning clockwise.

Safety is always the most important rule. Constantly be aware of the dangers involved in working on or around an automobile and take proper precautions to avoid the risk of personal injury or damage to the vehicle. See the section in this chapter, Servicing Your Vehicle Safely, and the SAFETY NOTICE on the acknowledgment page before attempting any service procedures and pay attention to the instructions provided. There are 3 common mistakes in mechanical work:

1. Incorrect order of assembly, disassembly or adjustment. When taking something apart or putting it together, doing things in the wrong order usually just costs you extra time; however it CAN break something. Read the entire procedure before beginning disassembly. Do everything in the order in which the instructions say you should do it, even if you can't immediately see a reason for it. When you're taking apart something that is very intricate (for example a carburetor), you might want to draw a picture of how it looks when assembled at one point in order to make sure you get everything back in its proper position. We will supply exploded views whenever possible, but sometimes the job requires more attention to detail than an illustration provides. When making adjustments (especially tune-up adjustments), do them in order. One adjustment often affects another and you cannot expect satisfactory results unless each adjustment is made only when it cannot be changed by any other.

2. Overtorquing (or undertorquing) nuts and bolts. While it is more common for overtorquing to cause damage, undertorquing can cause a fastener to vibrate loose and cause serious damage, especially when dealing with aluminum parts. Pay attention to torque specifications and utilize a torque wrench in assembly. If a torque figure is not available remember that, if you are using the right tool to do the job, you will probably not have to strain yourself to get a fastener tight enough. The pitch of most threads is so slight that the tension you put on the wrench will be multiplied many times in actual force on what you are tightening. A good example of how critical torque is can be seen in the case of spark plug installation, especially where you are putting the plug into an aluminum cylinder head. Too little torque can fail to crush the gasket, causing leakage of combustion gases and consequent overheating of the plug and engine parts. Too much torque can damage the threads or distort the plug, which changes the spark gap at the electrode. Since more and more manufacturers are using aluminum in their engine and chassis parts to save weight, a torque wrench should be in any serious do-it-yourselfer's tool box.

There are many commercial chemical products available for ensuring that fasteners won't come loose, even if they are not torqued just right (a very common brand is Loctite®). If you're worried about getting something together tight enough to hold, but loose enough to avoid mechanical damage during assembly, one of these products might offer substantial insurance. Read the label on the package and make sure the product is compatible with the materials, fluids, etc. involved before choosing one.

3. Crossthreading. This occurs when a part such as a bolt is screwed into a nut or casting at the wrong angle and forced, causing the threads to become damaged. Crossthreading is more likely to occur if access is difficult. It helps to clean and lubricate fasteners, and to start threading with the part to be installed going straight in, using your fingers. If you encounter resistance, unscrew the part and start over again at a different angle until it can be inserted and turned several times without much effort. Keep in mind that many parts, especially spark plugs, use tapered threads so that gentle turning will automatically bring the part you're threading to the proper angle if you don't force it or resist a change in angle. Don't put a wrench on the part until it's been turned in a couple of times by hand. If you suddenly encounter resistance and the part has not seated fully, don't force it. Pull it back out and make sure it's clean and threading properly.

Always take your time and be patient; once you have some experience, working on your car will become an enjoyable hobby.

TOOLS AND EQUIPMENT

Naturally, without the proper tools and equipment it is impossible to properly service your vehicle. It would be impossible to catalog each tool that you would need to perform each or every operation in this book. It would also be unwise for the amateur to rush out and buy an expensive set of tools and the theory that he may need one or more of them at sometime.

The best approach is to proceed slowly, gathering together a good quality set of those tools that are used most frequently. Don't be misled by the low cost of bargain tools. It is far better to spend a little more for better quality. Forged wrenches, 6- or 12-point sockets and fine tooth ratchets are by far preferable to their less expensive counterparts. As any good mechanic can tell you, there are few worse experiences than trying to work on a car with bad tools. Your monetary savings will be far outweighed by frustration and mangled knuckles.

Certain tools, plus a basic ability to handle tools, are required to get started. A basic mechanics tool set, a torque wrench, and a Torx bits set. Torx bits are hexagonal drivers which fit both inside and outside on special Torx head fasteners used in various places on some cars.

Begin accumulating those tools that are used

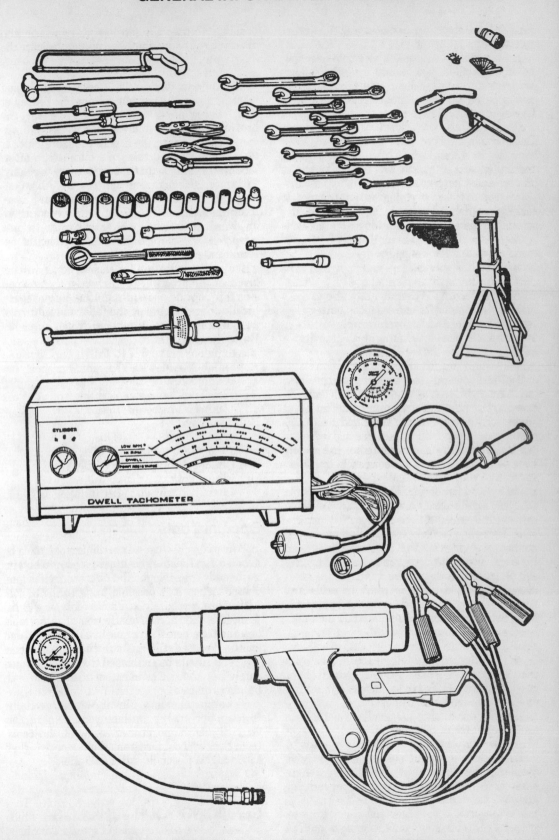

You need only a basic assortment of hand tools for most maintenance and repair jobs

most frequently; those associated with routine maintenance and tune-up.

In addition to the normal assortment of screwdrivers and pliers you should have the following tools for routine maintenance jobs (your car, depending on the model year, uses both SAE and metric fasteners).

1. SAE/Metric wrenches, sockets and combination open end/box end wrenches in sizes from $1/8$ in. (3mm) to $3/4$ in. (19mm), and a spark plug socket ($13/16$ in. or $5/8$ in.). If possible, buy various length socket drive extensions. One break in this department is that the metric sockets available in the U.S. will all fit the ratchet handles and extensions you may already have ($1/4$, $3/8$, and $1/2$ in. drive).

2. Jackstands for support.
3. Oil filter wrench.
4. Oil filler spout or funnel.
5. Grease gun for chassis lubrication.
6. Hydrometer for checking the battery.
7. A low flat pan for draining oil.
8. Lots of rags for wiping up the inevitable mess.

In addition to the above items there are several others that are not absolutely necessary, but handy to have around. These include oil-dry, a transmission fluid funnel and the usual supply of lubricants, antifreeze and fluids, although these can be purchased as needed. This is a basic list for routine maintenance, but only your personal needs and desires can accurately determine your list of necessary tools.

The second list of tools is for tune-ups. While the tools involved here are slightly more sophisticated, they need not be outrageously expensive. There are several inexpensive tach/dwell meters on the market that are every bit as good for the average mechanic as a $100.00 professional model. Just be sure that it goes to at least 1,200–1,500 rpm on the tach scale and that it works on 4, 6 and 8 cylinder engines. A basic list of tune-up equipment could include:

1. Tach-dwell meter
2. Spark plug wrench
3. Timing light (a DC light that works from the car's battery is best, although an AC light that plugs into 110V house current will suffice at some sacrifice in brightness)
4. Wire spark plug gauge/adjusting tools
5. Set of feeler blades.

Here again, be guided by your own needs. A feeler blade will set the point gap as easily as dwell meter will read dwell, but slightly less accurately. And since you will need a tachometer anyway ... well, make your own decision.

In addition to these basic tools, there are several other tools and gauges you may find useful. These include:

1. A compression gauge. The screw-in type

is slower to use, but eliminates the possibility of a faulty reading due to escaping pressure
2. A manifold vacuum gauge
3. A test light
4. An induction meter. This is used for determining whether or not there is current in a wire. These are handy for use if a wire is broken somewhere in a wiring harness.

As a final note, you will probably find a torque wrench necessary for all but the most basic work. The beam type models are perfectly adequate, although the newer click (breakaway) type are more precise, and you don't have to crane your neck to see a torque reading in awkward situations. The breakaway torque wrenches are more expensive and should be recalibrated periodically.

Torque specification for each fastener will be given in the procedure in any case that a specific torque value is required. If no torque specifications are given, use the following values as a guide, based upon fastener size:

Bolts marked 6T
6mm bolt/nut – 5–7 ft. lbs.
8mmbolt/ nut – 12–17 ft. lbs.
10mm bolt/nut –23–34 ft. lbs.
12mm bolt/nut – 41–59 ft.lbs.
14mm bolt/nut – 56–76 ft. lbs.

Bolts marked 8T
6mm bolt/nut – 6–9 ft. lbs.
8mmbolt/nut – 13–20 ft. lbs.
10mm bolt/nut –27–40 ft. lbs.
12mm bolt/nut – 46–69 ft.lbs.
14mm bolt/nut – 75–101 ft. lbs.

Special Tools

Normally, the use of special factory tools is avoided for repair procedures, since these are not readily available for the do-it-yourselfer mechanic. When it is possible to perform the job with more commonly available tools, it will be pointed out, but occasionally, a special tool was designed to perform a specific function and should be used. Before substituting another tool, you should be convinced that neither your safety nor the performance of the vehicle will be compromised.

Some special tools are available commercially from major tool manufacturers. Others for your car can be purchased from you dealer or from Special Tool Division, Kent-Moore 29784 Little Mack, Roseville, MI 48066-2298.

SERVICING YOUR VEHICLE SAFELY

It is virtually impossible to anticipate all of the hazards involved with automotive maintenance and service but care and common sense will prevent most accidents.

The rules of safety for mechanics range from "don't smoke around gasoline," to "use the proper tool for the job." The trick to avoiding injuries is to develop safe work habits and take every possible precaution.

Do's

• Do keep a fire extinguisher and first aid kit within easy reach.

• Do wear safety glasses or goggles when cutting, drilling, grinding, prying or recharging the A/C system. If you wear glasses for the sake of vision, then they should be made of hardened glass that can serve also as safety glasses, or wear safety goggles over your regular glasses.

• Do shield your eyes whenever you work around the battery. Batteries contain sulfuric acid. In case of contact with the eyes or skin, flush the area with water or a mixture of water and baking soda and get medical attention immediately.

• Do use safety stands (jackstands) for any under-car service. Jacks are for raising vehicles; safety stands are for making sure the vehicle stays raised until you want it to come down. Whenever the vehicle is raised, block the wheels remaining on the ground and set the parking brake.

• Do use adequate ventilation when working with any chemicals. Asbestos dust resulting from brake lining wear causes cancer.

• Do disconnect the negative (–) battery cable when working on the electrical system.

• Do follow manufacturer's directions whenever working with potentially hazardous materials. Both brake fluid and antifreeze are poisonous if taken internally.

• Do properly maintain your tools. Loose hammerheads, mushroomed punches and chisels, frayed or poorly grounded electrical cords, excessively worn screwdrivers, spread wrenches (open end), cracked sockets, slipping ratchets, or faulty droplight sockets can cause accidents.

• Do use the proper size and type of tool for the job being done.

• Do when possible, pull on a wrench handle rather than push on it, and adjust you stance to prevent a fall.

• Do be sure that adjustable wrenches are tightly adjusted on the nut or bolt and pulled so that the face is on the side of the fixed jaw.

• Do select a wrench or socket that fits the nut or bolt. The wrench or socket should sit straight, not cocked.

• Do strike squarely with a hammer. avoid glancing blows.

• Do set the parking brake and block the wheels if the work requires that the engine be running.

Don'ts

• Don't run an engine in a garage or anywhere else without proper ventilation – EVER! Carbon monoxide is poisonous. It is absorbed by the body 400 times faster than oxygen. It takes a long time to leave the human body and you can build up a deadly supply of it in your system by simply breathing in a little every day. You may not realize you are slowly poisoning yourself. Always use power vents, windows, fans or open the garage doors.

• Don't work around moving parts while wearing a necktie or other loose clothing. Short sleeves are much safer than long, loose sleeves. Hard-toed shoes with neoprene soles protect your toes and give a better grip on slippery surfaces. Jewelry such as watches, fancy belt buckles, rings, beads, or body adornment of any kind is not safe while working around a car. Long hair should be hidden under a hat or cap.

• Don't use pockets for toolboxes. A fall or bump can drive a screwdriver deep into you body. Even a wiping cloth hanging from the back pocket can wrap around a spinning shaft or fan.

• Don't smoke when working around gasoline, cleaning solvent or other flammable material.

• Don't smoke when working around the battery. When the battery is being charged, it gives off explosive hydrogen gas.

• Don't use gasoline to wash your hands. There are excellent soaps available. Gasoline may contain lead, and lead can enter the body through a cut, accumulating in the body until you are very ill. Gasoline also removes all the natural oils from the skin so that bone dry hands will suck up oil and grease.

• Don't service the air conditioning system unless you are equipped with the necessary tools and training. The refrigerant (R-12) is extremely cold and when exposed to the air, will instantly freeze any surface it comes in contact with, including your eyes. Always wear safety glasses when servicing the A/C system. Although the refrigerant is normally non-toxic, R-12 becomes a deadly poisonous gas in the presence of an open flame. One good whiff of the vapors from burning refrigerant can be fatal.

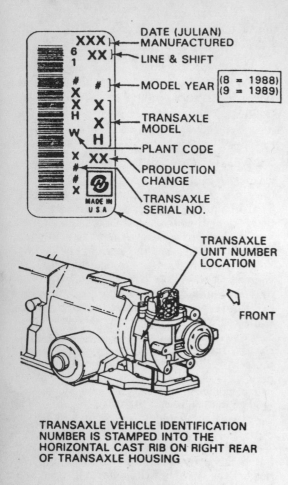

DATE (JULIAN) MANUFACTURED

LINE & SHIFT

MODEL YEAR (8 = 1988) (9 = 1989)

TRANSAXLE MODEL

PLANT CODE

PRODUCTION CHANGE

TRANSAXLE SERIAL NO.

TRANSAXLE UNIT NUMBER LOCATION

FRONT

TRANSAXLE VEHICLE IDENTIFICATION NUMBER IS STAMPED INTO THE HORIZONTAL CAST RIB ON RIGHT REAR OF TRANSAXLE HOUSING

Automatic transaxle code locations — 440 T4

VEHICLE IDENTIFICATION NUMBER (VIN)

Vehicle

The vehicle identification plate is located on the left upper instrument panel and is visible from outside the vehicle. Use this number when ordering specific parts because there can be many different component combinations for the same model.

Engine

The engine identification letter is the eighth digit in the vehicle identification number.

VIN A, D = 2.3L QUAD 4 (DOHC)
VIN R = 2.5L L4 (Lumina only)
VIN W = 2.8L V6
VIN T = 3.1L V6

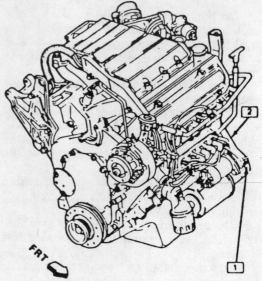

1. V.I.N Location
2. Engine Code Location

2.8L (VIN W) and 3.1L (VIN T) engine code location

Vehicle identification number (VIN) location

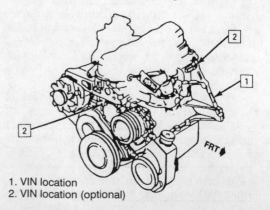

1. VIN location
2. VIN location (optional)

2.5L (VIN R) L4 engine code location — Lumina

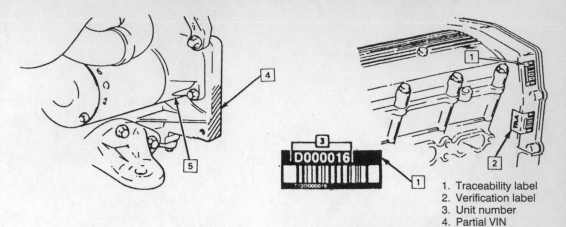

1. Traceability label
2. Verification label
3. Unit number
4. Partial VIN
5. Starter

Engine code location — 2.3 Quad 4 DOHC

Transaxle

For transaxle identification locations, see the accompanyng illustrations.

ROUTINE MAINTENANCE

Schedule I

Use maintenance schedule I if the following conditions exist.

1. When most trips are less than 4 miles.

2. When most trips are less than 10 miles and the outside temperature remains below freezing.

3. When most trips include extended idling and frequent low speed operation as in stop and go traffic.

4. Towing a trailer.

5. Operating in dusty areas.

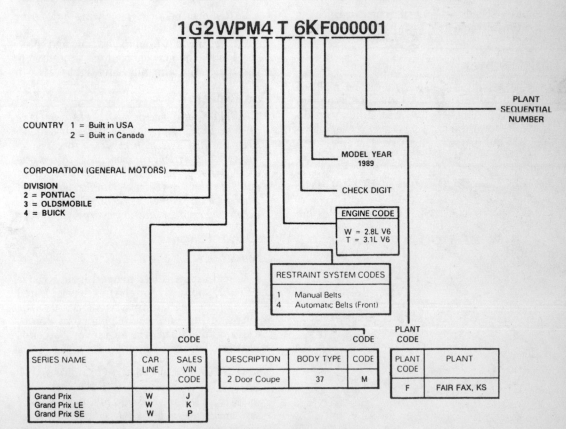

1G2WPM4 T 6K F000001

COUNTRY 1 = Built in USA
2 = Built in Canada

CORPORATION (GENERAL MOTORS)

DIVISION
2 = PONTIAC
3 = OLDSMOBILE
4 = BUICK

PLANT
SEQUENTIAL
NUMBER

MODEL YEAR
1989

CHECK DIGIT

ENGINE CODE

W = 2.8L V6
T = 3.1L V6

RESTRAINT SYSTEM CODES

1   Manual Belts
4   Automatic Belts (Front)

PLANT
CODE

SERIES NAME	CAR LINE	SALES VIN CODE
Grand Prix	W	J
Grand Prix LE	W	K
Grand Prix SE	W	P

DESCRIPTION	BODY TYPE	CODE
2 Door Coupe	37	M

PLANT CODE	PLANT
F	FAIR FAX, KS

Vehicle identification number chart

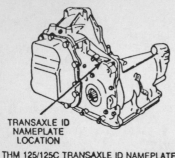

TRANSAXLE ID
NAMEPLATE
LOCATION

THM 125/125C TRANSAXLE ID NAMEPLATE
YPSILANTI, MICHIGAN

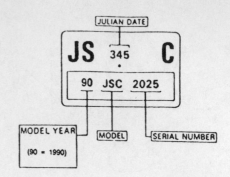

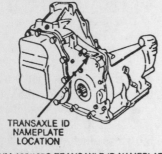

TRANSAXLE ID
NAMEPLATE
LOCATION

THM 125/125C TRANSAXLE ID NAMEPLATE
WINDSOR, CANADA

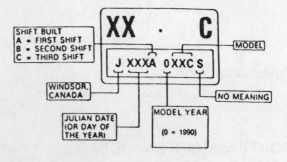

Automatic transaxle code location — Turbo Hydro-matic (THM 125C)

Schedule II

Follow schedule II only if none of the driving conditions in schedule I apply.

Air Cleaner

The air filter element should be replaced every 30,000 miles (50,000 km). Replace more often if the vehicle is operated in dusty conditions. Replace the air cleaners with the following part numbers.

- VIN A = 2.3L GUAD 4 (DOHC) – AC Type A974C
- VIN D = 2.3L GUAD 4 (DOHC) – AC Type A1088CC
- VIN R = 2.5L L4 (Lumina) – AC Type A785C
- VIN W = 2.8L V6 – AC Type A1129C
- VIN T = 3.1L V6 – AC Type A1129C

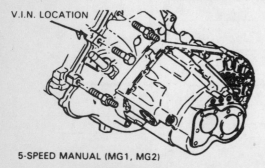

V.I.N. LOCATION

5-SPEED MANUAL (MG1, MG2)

Manual transaxle code locations

REMOVAL AND INSTALLATION

1. Remove the air cleaner wing nut, cover and element.
2. Clean any dirt from the housing and cover.
3. Install the new element, cover and wing nut. Tighten the wing nut hand tight.

Fuel Filter

CAUTION: *To reduce the risk of fire and personal injury, it is necessary to relieve the fuel system pressure before servicing any fuel system component. If this procedure is not performed, fuel may be sprayed out of the connection under pressure. Always keep a dry chemical (Class B) fire extinguisher near the work area.*

2.5L L4 TBI Engines

LUMINA ONLY

Fuel pressure relief procedures: remove the Fuel Pump fuse from the fuse block located in the passenger compartment. Start the engine and run until the engine stops due to the lack of fuel. Crank the engine for 3 seconds to ensure all pressure is relieved.

2.3L QUAD 4, 2.8L and 3.1L PFI Engines

CAUTION: *To reduce the risk of fire and personal injury, it is necessary to relieve the fuel system pressure before servicing any fuel system component. If this procedure is not performed, fuel may be sprayed out of the con-*

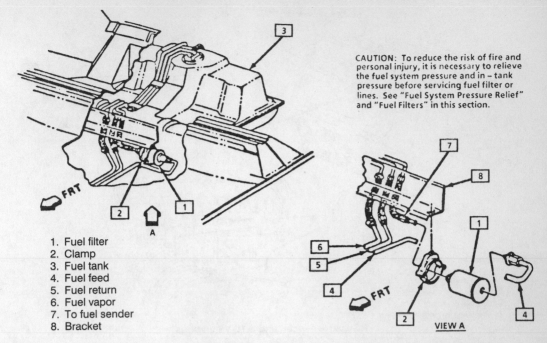

CAUTION: To reduce the risk of fire and personal injury, it is necessary to relieve the fuel system pressure and in – tank pressure before servicing fuel filter or lines. See "Fuel System Pressure Relief" and "Fuel Filters" in this section.

1. Fuel filter
2. Clamp
3. Fuel tank
4. Fuel feed
5. Fuel return
6. Fuel vapor
7. To fuel sender
8. Bracket

VIEW A

Fuel filter location

nection under pressure. *Always keep a dry chemical (Class B) fire extinguisher near the work area.*

Fuel pressure relief procedures:

a. Disconnect the negative (–) battery cable.

b. Loosen the fuel filler cap to relieve tank vapor pressure.

c. Connect a fuel pressure gauge J–34730–1 or equivalent to the fuel pressure relief connection at the fuel rail.

d. Wrap a shop towel around the fittings while connecting the gauge to prevent fuel spillage.

e. Install a bleed hose into an approved container and open the valve to bleed the system pressure. The system is safe for servicing.

REMOVAL AND INSTALLATION

The fuel filter is located in the fuel feed line attached to the left frame rail, at the rear of the vehicle.

1. Disconnect the negative (–) battery cable.

2. Raise the vehicle and support with jackstands.

3. Disconnect the fuel lines from the filter. To reduce fuel spillage, place a shop towel over the fuel lines before disconnecting.

4. Remove the clamp and filter from the vehicle.

5. Loosely install the new filter. Using new O-ring seals, install the fuel lines to the filter. Use a backup wrench to prevent the filter from turning and O-ring damage. Torque the fittings to 22 ft. lbs. (30 Nm).

6. Secure the filter to the vehicle. Reconnect the negative (–) battery cable. Lower the vehicle and start the engine to check for fuel leaks.

PCV Valve

The PCV valve should be inspected every 30,000 miles (50,000 km) to check for proper

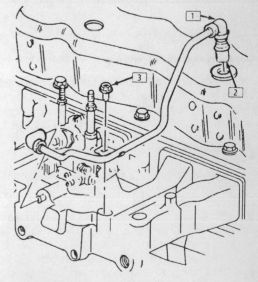

1. Tube assembly
2. PCV valve
3. Bolt (14–25 ft. lbs.)

PCV valve – 2.5L L4 (Lumina only)

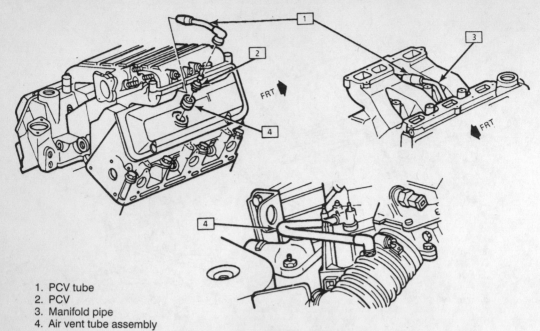

1. PCV tube
2. PCV
3. Manifold pipe
4. Air vent tube assembly

PCV valve — 2.8L and 3.1L V6 engines

operation. A rough idle may result from improper operation or vacuum leak.

NOTE: *The 2.3L QUAD 4 (VIN A, D) is not equipped with a PCV valve.*

To maintain proper idle control, the PCV valve restricts the flow when the intake manifold vacuum is high. The system is designed to allow excess blow by gases to be vented into the intake manifold to be burned, reducing hydrocarbon emissions.

To remove the PCV valve, pull the valve out of the rocker arm cover and disconnect the rubber hose. Insert the new valve into the hose and the rocker cover.

Evaporative Canister

The evaporative canister has a filter located in the bottom of the unit. This filter is not serviceable and has to replaced with the canisters. Refer to the "Evaportive System" in Chapter 4.

Battery

It is not possible to check the specific gravity in this manner on sealed (maintenance free) batteries. Instead, the indicator built into the top of the case must be relied on to display any signs of battery deterioration. If the indicator is dark, the battery can be assumed to be OK. If the indicator is light, the specific gravity is low, and the battery should be charged or replaced.

CABLES AND CLAMPS

Once a year, the battery terminals and the cable clamps should be cleaned. Loosen the clamps and remove the cables, negative cable first. On batteries with posts on top, the use of a puller specially made for the purpose is recommended. These are inexpensive, and available in auto parts stores. Side terminal battery cables are secured with a bolt.

Clean the cable lamps and the battery terminal with a wire brush, until all corrosion, grease, etc., is removed and the metal is shiny. It is especially important to clean the inside of the clamp thoroughly, since a small deposit of foreign material or oxidation there will prevent a sound electrical connection and inhibit either

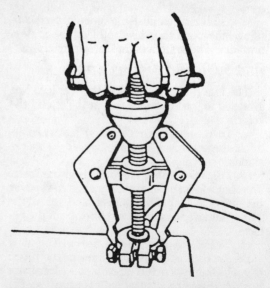

Use a puller to remove the battery cable

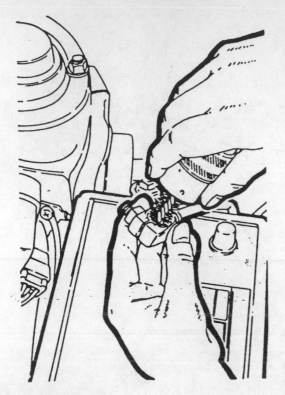

Clean battery cable clamps with a wire brush

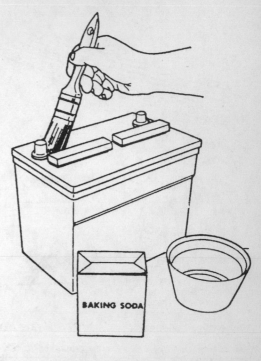

Cleaning the battery with baking soda and water

starting or charging. Special tools are available for cleaning these parts, one type for conventional batteries and another type for side terminal batteries.

Before installing the cables, loosen the battery hold down clamp or strap, remove the battery and check the battery tray. Clear it of any debris, and check it for soundness. Rust should be wire brushed away, and the metal given a coat of anti-rust paint. Replace the battery and tighten the hold down clamp or strap securely, but be careful not to overtighten, which will crack the battery case.

After the clamps and terminals are clean, reinstall the cables, negative cable last; do not hammer on the clamps to install. Tighten the clamps securely, but do not distort them. Give the clamps and terminals a thin external coat of grease after installation, to retard corrosion.

Check the cables at the same time that the terminals are cleaned. If the cable insulation is cracked or broken, or if the ends are frayed, the cable should be replaced with a new cable of the same length and gauge.

CAUTION: *Keep flame or sparks away from the battery; it gives off explosive hydrogen gas. Battery electrolyte contains sulphuric acid. If you should splash any on your skin or in your eyes, flush the affected area with plenty of clear water. If it lands in your eyes, get medical help immediately.*

Belts

Once a year or at 12,000 mile intervals, the tension (and condition) of the alternator, power steering (if so equipped), air conditioning (if so equipped), and Thermactor air pump drive belts should be checked, and, if necessary, adjusted. Loose accessory drive belts can lead to poor engine cooling and diminish alternator, power steering pump, air conditioning compressor or Thermactor air pump output. A belt that is too tight places a severe strain on the water pump, alternator, power steering pump, compressor or air pump bearings.

Replace any belt that is so glazed, worn or stretched that it cannot be tightened sufficiently.

NOTE: *The material used in late model drive belts is such that the belts do not show wear. Replace belts at least every three years.*

On vehicles with matched belts, replace both belts. New $1/2$ in., $3/8$ in. and $15/16$ in. wide belts are to be adjusted to a tension of 140 lbs.; $1/4$ in. wide belts are adjusted to 80 lbs., measured on a belt tension gauge. Any belt that has been operating for a minimum of 10 minutes is considered a used belt. In the first 10 minutes, the belt should stretch to its maximum extent. After 10 minutes, stop the engine and recheck

6-rib "V" belt

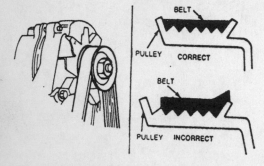

Proper V-belt alignment

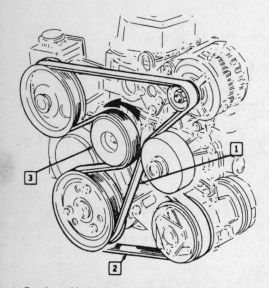

1. Routing without air conditioning
2. Routing with air conditioning
3. Tensioner — rotate drive belt tensioner in direction of arrow to install or remove drive belt.

Serpentine belt routing — 2.5L L4 (Lumina only)

Belt tension gauge J–23600–B

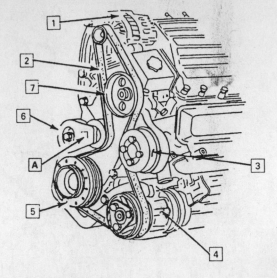

A. Insert breaker bar here
1. Generator
2. Serpentine belt
3. Water pump
4. Air conditioning compressor
5. Crankshaft
6. Belt tensioner
7. Power steering pump

Serpentine belt routing — 2.8L and 3.1L V6 engines

the belt tension. Belt tension for a used belt should be maintained at 110 lbs. (all except $^1/4$ in. wide belts) or 60 lbs. ($^1/4$ in. wide belts). If a belt tension gauge is not available, the following procedures may be used.

Serpentine Belt

A single serpentine belt is used to drive all engine accessories formerly driven by multiple drive belts. The accessories are rigidly mounted with the belt tension maintained automatically by a spring loaded tensioner (all engines except the 2.8L and 3.1L with manual transaxle). The manual transaxle engines use a separate belt to drive the thermactor air pump.

The The 2.3L QUAD 4 engine uses two drive belts, one to drive the power steering pump and the second to drive the A/C compressor and alternator. The power steering belt is not self-adjusting and has to be adjusted manually. The A/C and alternator belt is automatically adjusted by a spring loaded belt tensioner, requiring no periodic adjustment. QUAD 4 engine without air conditioning has an idler pulley in place of the compressor, consequently the A/C and no–A/C belts are the same.

INSPECTION

Inspection of the belt may reveal cracks in the belt ribs. The cracks will not impair belt per-

HOW TO SPOT WORN V-BELTS

V-Belts are vital to efficient engine operation—they drive the fan, water pump and other accessories. They require little maintenance (occasional tightening) but they will not last forever. Slipping or failure of the V-belt will lead to overheating. If your V-belt looks like any of these, it should be replaced.

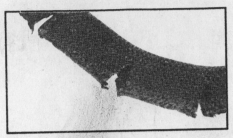

Cracking or weathering

This belt has deep cracks, which cause it to flex. Too much flexing leads to heat build-up and premature failure. These cracks can be caused by using the belt on a pulley that is too small. Notched belts are available for small diameter pulleys.

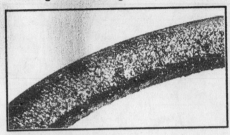

Softening (grease and oil)

Oil and grease on a belt can cause the belt's rubber compounds to soften and separate from the reinforcing cords that hold the belt together. The belt will first slip, then finally fail altogether.

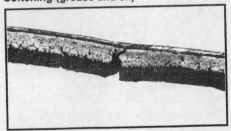

Glazing

Glazing is caused by a belt that is slipping. A slipping belt can cause a run-down battery, erratic power steering, overheating or poor accessory performance. The more the belt slips, the more glazing will be built up on the surface of the belt. The more the belt is glazed, the more it will slip. If the glazing is light, tighten the belt.

Worn cover

The cover of this belt is worn off and is peeling away. The reinforcing cords will begin to wear and the belt will shortly break. When the belt cover wears in spots or has a rough jagged appearance, check the pulley grooves for roughness.

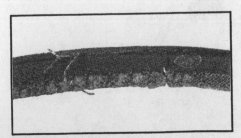

Separation

This belt is on the verge of breaking and leaving you stranded. The layers of the belt are separating and the reinforcing cords are exposed. It's just a matter of time before it breaks completely.

formance and should not considered a problem requiring belt replacement.

The belt should be replaced if sections of the belt ribs are missing or the belt is outside the tensioners operating range.

NOTE: *The belt tension is maintained by the automatic tensioner and is NOT adjustable (except the QUAD 4 power steering and the 3.1L V6 air pump belts).*

1. **Tension Measurement:** run the engine with no accessories ON until the engine is warmed up. Shut the engine OFF. Using a belt tension gauge No. J–23600–B or equivalent, measure tension between the alternator and power steering pump. Note the reading.

2. With the accessories OFF, start the engine and allow to stabilize for 15 seconds. Turn the engine OFF. Using a 15mm socket, apply clockwise force to the tensioner pulley bolt. Release the tension and record the tension.

3. Using the 15mm socket, apply counterclockwise force to the tensioner pulley bolt and raise the pulley to eliminate all tension. Slowly lower the pulley to the belt and take a tension reading without disturbing the belt tensioner position.

4. Average the three readings. If the average is not between 50–70 lbs. (225–315 N) and the belt is within the tensioner's operating range, replace the belt.

BELT ADJUSTMENT

2.8L and 3.1L V6 Air Pump Belt

1. Loosen the air pump mounting bolts.
2. Using a suitable pry bar, move the air pump to get the proper belt adjustment. Be care-

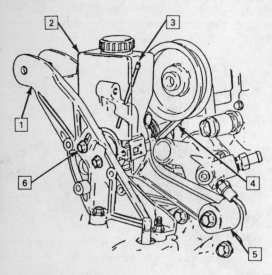

AIR pump adjustment — 2.8 and 3.1L with manual transaxle

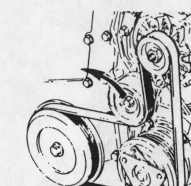

Serpentine belt routing — 2.3L Quad 4. Rotate tensioner in direction of arrow to remove or install the belt

THE INDICATOR MARK ON THE STATIONARY PORTION OF THE TENSIONER MUST BE WITHIN THE LIMITS OF THE SLOTTED AREA ON THE MOVEABLE PORTION OF THE TENSIONER. ANY READING OUTSIDE THESE LIMITS INDICATES EITHER A FAULTY BELT OR TENSIONER.

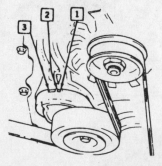

1. Engine torque strut bracket
2. Power steering pump
3. Belt tensioner
4. Drive belt
5. Rear bracket
6. Adjusting bolt

Power steering belt adjustment — 2.3L Quad 4

1. Minimum belt length
2. Nominal belt length
3. Maximum belt length

Belt tensioner adjustment positions — 2.3L Quad 4

ful not to damage the aluminum pump housing.

3. Tighten the air pump bolts.

2.3L QUAD 4 (VIN A,D)

POWER STEERING BELT

1. Place a belt tension gauge J–36018 or equivalent onto the pump belt.

2. Loosen the two pump-to-rear bracket adjustment bolts.

3. Torque the engine-to-front bracket bolts to 44 inch lbs. (5 Nm).

4. (VI–D), using a 1/2 inch drive handle in the tab, move the pump to the proper adjustment lbs. (VI–A), tighten the adjustment stud to the proper adjustment. Adjustment to 110 lbs (500 N).

5. Torque the pump adjusting bolts to 67 ft. lbs. (92 Nm).

REMOVAL AND INSTALLATION

1. Disconnect the negative (–) battery cable.

2. Remove the belt guard, if so equipped.

3. Lift or rotate the tensioner using a 1/2 in. breaker bar. Use a 13mm wrench on the 2.3L QUAD 4 engines.

NOTE: *Loosen the pump-to-engine bracket bolts and adjusting stud to remove the power steering pump belt on the 2.3L QUAD 4 engines.*

4. Remove the belt.

5. **To install:** lift the tensioner using the breaker bar, install the belt onto pulleys as shown in the "Serpentine Belt Routing" illustrations in this section and install the belt guard.

6. If the tensioner was removed, torque the retaining bolts to 40 ft. lbs. (54 Nm).

Hoses

CAUTION: *On models equipped with an electric cooling fan, disconnect the negative battery cable, or fan motor wiring harness connector before replacing any radiator/heater hose. The fan may come on, under certain circumstances, even though the ignition is Off.*

REPLACEMENT

Inspect the condition of the radiator and heater hoses periodically. Early spring and at the beginning of the fall or winter, when you are performing other maintenance, are good times. Make sure the engine and cooling system are cold. Visually inspect for cracking,

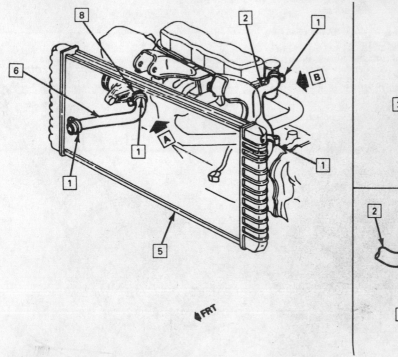

1. Clamp
2. Inlet hose
3. Align arrow on hose to arrow on inlet
4. Water inlet
5. Radiator
6. Outlet hose
7. Align arrow on hose to bead on outlet
8. Water pump inlet

2.5L L4 radiator hoses (Lumina only)

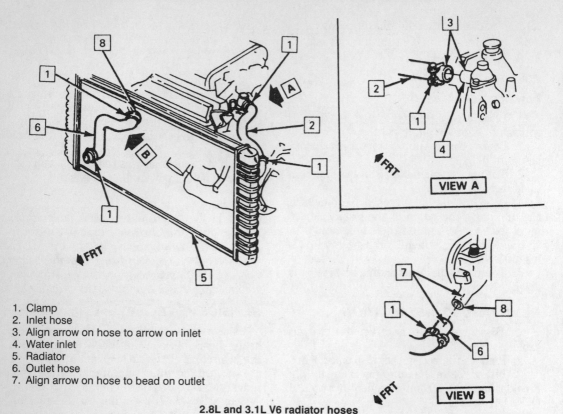

1. Clamp
2. Inlet hose
3. Align arrow on hose to arrow on inlet
4. Water inlet
5. Radiator
6. Outlet hose
7. Align arrow on hose to bead on outlet

2.8L and 3.1L V6 radiator hoses

rotting or collapsed hoses, replace as necessary. Run your hand along the length of the hose. If a weak or swollen spot is noted when squeezing the hose wall, replace the hose.

1. Drain the cooling system into a suitable container (if the coolant is to be reused).

CAUTION: *When draining the coolant, keep in mind that cats and dogs are attracted by the ethylene glycol antifreeze, and are quite likely to drink any that is left in an uncovered container or in puddles on the ground. This will prove fatal in sufficient quantity. Always drain the coolant into a sealable container. Coolant should be reused unless it is contaminated or several years old.*

2. Loosen the hose clamps at each end of the hose that requires replacement.

3. Twist, pull and slide the hose off the radiator, water pump, thermostat or heater connection.

4. Clean the hose mounting connections. Position the hose clamps on the new hose.

5. Coat the connection surfaces with a water resistant sealer and slide the hose into position. Make sure the hose clamps are located beyond the raised bead of the connector (if equipped) and centered in the clamping area of the connection.

6. Tighten the clamps to 20–30 inch lbs. Do not overtighten.

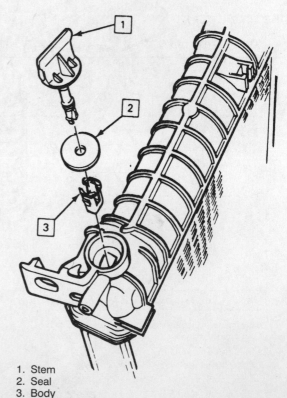

1. Stem
2. Seal
3. Body

Radiator drain plug

HOW TO SPOT BAD HOSES

Both the upper and lower radiator hoses are called upon to perform difficult jobs in an inhospitable environment. They are subject to nearly 18 psi at under hood temperatures often over 280°F., and must circulate nearly 7500 gallons of coolant an hour—3 good reasons to have good hoses.

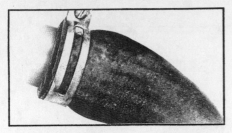

A good test for any hose is to feel it for soft or spongy spots. Frequently these will appear as swollen areas of the hose. The most likely cause is oil soaking. This hose could burst at any time, when hot or under pressure.

Swollen hose

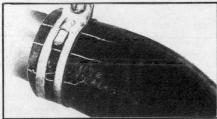

Cracked hoses can usually be seen but feel the hoses to be sure they have not hardened; a prime cause of cracking. This hose has cracked down to the reinforcing cords and could split at any of the cracks.

Cracked hose

Weakened clamps frequently are the cause of hose and cooling system failure. The connection between the pipe and hose has deteriorated enough to allow coolant to escape when the engine is hot.

Frayed hose end (due to weak clamp)

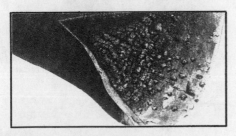

Debris, rust and scale in the cooling system can cause the inside of a hose to weaken. This can usually be felt on the outside of the hose as soft or thinner areas.

Debris in cooling system

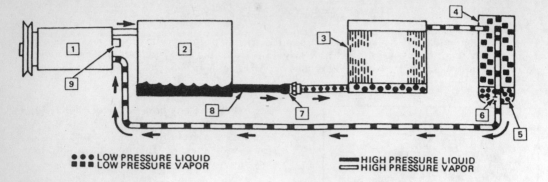

● ● ● LOW PRESSURE LIQUID
■ ■ ■ LOW PRESSURE VAPOR

▬▬▬ HIGH PRESSURE LIQUID
▭▭▭ HIGH PRESSURE VAPOR

1. Compressor
2. Condenser
3. Evaporator
4. Accumulator
5. Dessicant bag

6. Oil bleed hole
7. Expansion tube (orifice)
8. Liquid line
9. Pressure relief valve

Air conditioning system flow chart

7. Fill the cooling system.

8. Start the engine and allow it to reach normal operating temperature. Check for leaks.

Air Conditioning System

GENERAL SERVICING PROCEDURES

The most important aspect of air conditioning service is the maintenance of pure and adequate charge of refrigerant in the system. A refrigeration system cannot function properly if a significant percentage of the charge is lost. Leaks are common because the severe vibration encountered in an automobile can easily cause a sufficient cracking or loosening of the air conditioning fittings. As a result, the extreme operating pressures of the system force refrigerant out.

The problem can be understood by considering what happens to the system as it is operated with a continuous leak. Because the orifice tube regulates the flow of refrigerant to the evaporator, the level of refrigerant there is fairly constant. The accumulator-drier stores any excess of refrigerant, and so a loss will first appear there as a reduction in the level of liquid. As this level nears the bottom of the vessel, some refrigerant vapor bubbles will begin to appear in the stream of liquid supplied to the orifice tube. This vapor decreases the capacity of the orifice tube very little as the valve opens to compensate for its presence. As the quantity of liquid in the condenser decreases, the operating pressure will drop there and throughout the high side of the system. As the R-12 continues to be expelled, the pressure available to force the liquid through the orifice tube will continue to decrease, and, eventually,

the orifice will prove to be too much of a restriction for adequate flow.

At this point, low side pressure will start to drop, and severe reduction in cooling capacity, marked by freeze-up of the evaporator coil, will result. Eventually, the operating pressure of the evaporator will be lower than the pressure of the atmosphere surrounding it, and air will be drawn into the system wherever there are leaks in the low side.

Because all atmospheric air contains at least some moisture, water will enter the system and mix with the R-12 and the oil. Trace amounts of moisture will cause sludging of the oil, and corrosion of the system. Saturation and clogging of the accumulator-drier, and freezing of the orifice will eventually result. As air fills the system to a greater and greater extend, it will interfere more and more with the normal flows of refrigerant and heat.

A list of general precautions that should be observed while doing this follows:

1. Keep all tools as clean and dry as possible.

2. Thoroughly purge the service gauges and hoses of air and moisture before connecting them to the system. Keep them capped when not in use.

3. Thoroughly clean any refrigerant fitting before disconnecting it, in order to minimize the entrance of dirt into the system.

4. Plan any operation that requires opening the system beforehand in order to minimize the length of time it will be exposed to open air. Cap or seal the open ends to minimize the entrance of foreign material.

5. When adding oil, pour it through an extremely clean and dry tube or funnel. Keep the

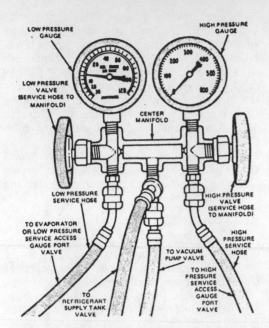

Air conditioning manifold gauge set

High pressure gauge port valve adapters

oil capped whenever possible. Do not use oil that has not been kept tightly sealed.

6. Use only refrigerant 12 (R-12). Purchase refrigerant intended for use in only automotive air conditioning system. Avoid the use of refrigerant 12 that may be packaged for another use, such as cleaning, or powering a horn, as it is impure.

7. Completely evacuate any system that has been opened to replace a component, other than when isolating the compressor, or that has leaked sufficiently to draw in moisture and air. This requires evacuating air and moisture with a good vacuum pump for at least one hour. If a system has been open for a considerable length of time it may be advisable to evacuate the system for up to 12 hours (overnight).

8. Use a wrench on both halves of a fitting that is to be disconnected, so as to avoid placing torque on any of the refrigerant lines.

ADDITIONAL PREVENTIVE MAINTENANCE CHECKS

Antifreeze

In order to prevent heater core freeze-up during A/C operation, it is necessary to maintain permanent type antifreeze protection of +15° F (–9° C) or lower. A reading of –15° F (–26° C) is ideal since this protection also supplies sufficient corrosion inhibitors for the protection of the engine cooling system.

WARNING: *Do not use antifreeze longer than specified by the manufacturer.*

Radiator Cap

For efficient operation of an air conditioned car's cooling system, the radiator cap should have a holding pressure which meets manufacturer's specifications. A cap which fails to hold these pressure should be replaced.

Condenser

Any obstruction of or damage to the condenser configuration will restrict the air flow which is essential to its efficient operation. It is therefore, a good rule to keep this unit clean and in proper physical shape.

NOTE: *Bug screens are regarded as obstructions.*

Condensation Drain Tube

This single molded drain tube expels the condensation, which accumulates on the bottom of the evaporator housing, into the engine compartment.

If this tube is obstructed, the air conditioning performance can be restricted and condensation buildup can spill over onto the vehicle's floor.

SAFETY PRECAUTIONS

Because of the importance of the necessary safety precautions that must be exercised when working with air conditioning systems and R-12 refrigerant, a recap of the safety precautions are outlined.

1. Avoid contact with a charged refrigeration system, even when working on another part of the air conditioning system or vehicle. If a heavy tool comes into contact with a section of copper tubing or a heat exchanger, it can easily cause the relatively soft material to rupture.

2. When it is necessary to apply force to a fitting which contains refrigerant, as when checking that all system couplings are securely

tightened, use a wrench on both parts of the fitting involved, if possible. This will avoid putting torque on the refrigerant tubing. (It is advisable, when possible, to use tube or line wrenches when tightening these flare nut fittings.)

3. Do not attempt to discharge the system by merely loosening a fitting, or removing the service valve caps and cracking these valves. Precise control is possibly only when using the service gauges. Place a rag under the open end of the center charging hose while discharging the system to catch any drops of liquid that might escape. Wear protective gloves when connecting or disconnecting service gauge hoses.

4. Discharge the system only in a well ventilated area, as high concentrations of the gas can exclude oxygen and act as an anesthetic. When leak testing or soldering this is particularly important, as toxic gas is formed when R-12 contacts any flame.

5. Never start a system without first verifying that both service valves are backseated, if equipped, and that all fittings are throughout the system are snugly connected.

6. Avoid applying heat to any refrigerant line or storage vessel. Charging may be aided by using water heated to less than 125° F (52° C) to warm the refrigerant container. Never allow a refrigerant storage container to sit out in the sun, or near any other source of heat, such as a radiator.

7. Always wear safety goggles when working on a system to protect the eyes. If refrigerant contacts the eye, it is advisable in all cases to see a physician as soon as possible.

8. Frostbite from liquid refrigerant should be treated by first gradually warming the area with cool water, and then gently applying petroleum jelly. A physician should be consulted.

9. Always keep refrigerant can fittings capped when not in use. Avoid sudden shock to the can which might occur from dropping it, or from banging a heavy tool against it. Never carry a refrigerant can in the passenger compartment of a car.

10. Always completely discharge the system before painting the vehicle (if the paint is to be baked on), or before welding anywhere near the refrigerant lines.

TEST GAUGES

Most of the service work performed in air conditioning requires the use of a set of two gauges, one for the high (head) pressure side of the system, the other for the low (suction) side.

The low side gauge records both pressure and vacuum. Vacuum readings are calibrated from 0 to 30 inches Hg and the pressure graduations read from 0 to no less than 60 psi.

The high side gauge measures pressure from 0 to at last 600 psi.

Both gauges are threaded into a manifold that contains two hand shut-off valves. Proper manipulation of these valves and the use of the attached test hoses allow the user to perform the following services:

1. Test high and low side pressures.
2. Remove air, moisture, and contaminated refrigerant.
3. Purge the system (of refrigerant).
4. Charge the system (with refrigerant).

RELATIVE HUMIDITY (%)	AMBIENT AIR TEMP		MAXIMUM LOW SIDE PRESSURE		ENGINE SPEED (rpm)	MAXIMUM RIGHT CENTER AIR OUTLET TEMPERATURE		MAXIMUM HIGH SIDE PRESSURE	
	°F	°C	PSIG	kPaG		°F	°C	PSIG	kPaG
20	70	21	32	221	2000	43	6	175	1207
	80	27	32	221		44	7	225	1551
	90	32	32	221		50	10	275	1896
	100	38	33	228		51	11	275	1896
30	70	21	32	221	2000	45	7	190	1310
	80	27	32	221		47	8	235	1620
	90	32	34	234		54	12	290	2000
	100	38	38	262		57	14	310	2137
40	70	21	32	221	2000	46	8	210	1448
	80	27	32	221		50	10	255	1758
	90	32	37	255		57	14	305	2103
	100	38	44	303		63	17	345	2379
50	70	21	32	221	2000	48	9	225	1551
	80	27	34	234		53	12	270	1862
	90	32	41	283		60	16	325	2241
	100	38	49	338		69	21	380	2620
60	70	21	32	221	2000	50	10	240	1655
	80	27	37	255		56	13	290	2000
	90	32	44	303		63	17	340	2344
	100	38	55	379		75	24	395	2724
70	70	21	32	221	2000	52	11	255	1758
	80	27	40	276		59	15	305	2103
	90	32	48	331		67	19	355	2448
80	70	21	36	248	2000	53	12	270	1862
	80	27	43	296		62	17	320	2206
	90	32	52	356		70	21	370	2551
90	70	21	40	276	2000	55	13	285	1965
	80	27	47	324		65	18	335	2310

Air conditioning performance test chart

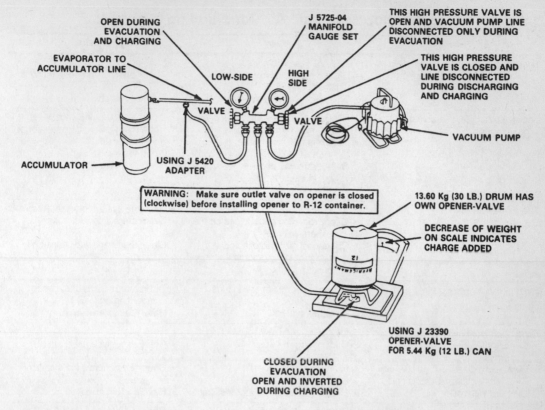

OPEN DURING
EVACUATION
AND CHARGING

J 5725-04
MANIFOLD
GAUGE SET

THIS HIGH PRESSURE VALVE IS
OPEN AND VACUUM PUMP LINE
DISCONNECTED ONLY DURING
EVACUATION

EVAPORATOR TO
ACCUMULATOR LINE

LOW-SIDE

HIGH
SIDE

THIS HIGH PRESSURE
VALVE IS CLOSED AND
LINE DISCONNECTED
DURING DISCHARGING
AND CHARGING

VALVE

VALVE

VACUUM PUMP

ACCUMULATOR

USING J 5420
ADAPTER

WARNING: Make sure outlet valve on opener is closed
(clockwise) before installing opener to R-12 container.

13.60 Kg (30 LB.) DRUM HAS
OWN OPENER-VALVE

DECREASE OF WEIGHT
ON SCALE INDICATES
CHARGE ADDED

USING J 23390
OPENER-VALVE
FOR 5.44 Kg (12 LB.) CAN

CLOSED DURING
EVACUATION
OPEN AND INVERTED
DURING CHARGING

Evacuating and recharging the air conditioning system

The manifold valves are designed so that they have no direct effect on gauge readings, but serve only to provide for, or cut off, flow of refrigerant through the manifold. During all testing and hook-up operations, the valves are kept in a close position to avoid disturbing the refrigeration system. The valves are opened only to purge the system or refrigerant or to charge it.

INSPECTION

CAUTION: *The compressed refrigerant used in the air conditioning system expands into the atmosphere at a temperature of -21.7° F (-30° C) or lower. This will freeze any surface, including your eyes, that it contacts. In addition, the refrigerant decomposes into a poisonous gas in the presence of a flame. Do not open or disconnect any part of the air conditioning system.*

NOTE: *If your vehicle is equipped with an aftermarket air conditioner, the following system check may not apply. You should contact the manufacturer of the unit for instructions on systems checks.*

1. Place the automatic transmission in Park or the manual transmission in Neutral. Set the parking brake.
2. Run the engine at a fast idle (about 1,500 rpm) either with the help of a friend or by temporarily readjusting the idle speed screw.
3. Set the controls for maximum cold with the blower on High.
4. If equipped, locate the sight glass in one of the system lines. Usually it is on the left alongside the top of the radiator, if so equipped.
5. If you see bubbles, the system must be recharged. Very likely there is a leak at some point.
6. If there are no bubbles, there is either no refrigerant at all or the system is fully charged. Feel the two hoses going to the belt-driven compressor. If they are both at the same temperature, the system is empty and must be evacuated and recharged.
7. If one hose (high pressure) is warm and the other (low pressure) is cold, the system may be all right. However, you are probably making these tests because you think there is something wrong, so proceed to the next step.
8. Have an assistant in the car turn the fan control on and off to operate the compressor clutch. Watch the sight glass, if so equipped.
9. If bubbles appear when the clutch is disengaged and disappear when it is engaged, the system is properly charged.
10. If the refrigerant takes more than 45 seconds to bubble when the clutch is disengaged,

Troubleshooting Basic Air Conditioning Problems

Problem	Cause	Solution
There's little or no air coming from the vents (and you're sure it's on)	• The A/C fuse is blown • Broken or loose wires or connections • The on/off switch is defective	• Check and/or replace fuse • Check and/or repair connections • Replace switch
The air coming from the vents is not cool enough	• Windows and air vent wings open • The compressor belt is slipping • Heater is on • Condenser is clogged with debris • Refrigerant has escaped through a leak in the system • Receiver/drier is plugged	• Close windows and vent wings • Tighten or replace compressor belt • Shut heater off • Clean the condenser • Check system • Service system
The air has an odor	• Vacuum system is disrupted • Odor producing substances on the evaporator case • Condensation has collected in the bottom of the evaporator housing	• Have the system checked/repaired • Clean the evaporator case • Clean the evaporator housing drains
System is noisy or vibrating	• Compressor belt or mountings loose • Air in the system	• Tighten or replace belt; tighten mounting bolts • Have the system serviced

Sight glass condition
  Constant bubbles, foam or oil streaks
  Clear sight glass, but no cold air
  Clear sight glass, but air is cold
  Clouded with milky fluid
	• Undercharged system
	
	• No refrigerant at all
	• System is OK
	• Receiver drier is leaking dessicant
		• Charge the system
		
		• Check and charge the system
		
		• Have system checked

Large difference in temperature of lines	• System undercharged	• Charge and leak test the system
Compressor noise	• Broken valves • Overcharged • Incorrect oil level • Piston slap • Broken rings • Drive belt pulley bolts are loose	• Replace the valve plate • Discharge, evacuate and install the correct charge • Isolate the compressor and check the oil level. Correct as necessary. • Replace the compressor • Replace the compressor • Tighten with the correct torque specification
Excessive vibration	• Incorrect belt tension • Clutch loose • Overcharged • Pulley is misaligned	• Adjust the belt tension • Tighten the clutch • Discharge, evacuate and install the correct charge • Align the pulley
Condensation dripping in the passenger compartment	• Drain hose plugged or improperly positioned • Insulation removed or improperly installed	• Clean the drain hose and check for proper installation • Replace the insulation on the expansion valve and hoses
Frozen evaporator coil	• Faulty thermostat • Thermostat capillary tube improperly installed • Thermostat not adjusted properly	• Replace the thermostat • Install the capillary tube correctly • Adjust the thermostat
Low side low—high side low	• System refrigerant is low • Expansion valve is restricted	• Evacuate, leak test and charge the system • Replace the expansion valve
Low side high—high side low	• Internal leak in the compressor—worn	• Remove the compressor cylinder head and inspect the compressor. Replace the valve plate assembly if necessary. If the compressor pistons, rings or

Troubleshooting Basic Air Conditioning Problems (cont.)

Problem	Cause	Solution
Low side high—high side low (cont.)		cylinders are excessively worn or scored replace the compressor
	• Cylinder head gasket is leaking	• Install a replacement cylinder head gasket
	• Expansion valve is defective	• Replace the expansion valve
	• Drive belt slipping	• Adjust the belt tension
Low side high—high side high	• Condenser fins obstructed	• Clean the condenser fins
	• Air in the system	• Evacuate, leak test and charge the system
	• Expansion valve is defective	• Replace the expansion valve
	• Loose or worn fan belts	• Adjust or replace the belts as necessary
Low side low—high side high	• Expansion valve is defective	• Replace the expansion valve
	• Restriction in the refrigerant hose	• Check the hose for kinks—replace if necessary
	• Restriction in the receiver/drier	• Replace the receiver/drier
	• Restriction in the condenser	• Replace the condenser
Low side and high side normal (inadequate cooling)	• Air in the system	• Evacuate, leak test and charge the system
	• Moisture in the system	• Evacuate, leak test and charge the system

the system is overcharged. This usually causes poor cooling at low speeds.

CAUTION: *If it is determined that the system has a leak, it should be corrected as soon as possible. Leaks may allow moisture to enter and cause a very expensive rust problem.*

NOTE: *Exercise the air conditioner for a few minutes, every two weeks or so, during the cold months. This avoids the possibility of the compressor seals drying out from lack of lubrication.*

TESTING THE SYSTEM

CAUTION: *Always wear safety goggles when working on a system to protect the eyes. If refrigerant contacts the eye, it is advisable in all cases to see a physician as soon as possible.*

1. Connect a gauge set (engine not running). The LOW side gauge hose to the suction line near the accumulator and the HIGH side gauge hose to the liquid line or muffler. The muffler is a round shaped can about three times larger than the liquid line.

2. Close (clockwise) both gauge set valves.

3. Park the car in the shade, at least 5 feet from any walls. Start the engine, set the parking brake, place the transmission in NEUTRAL and establish an idle of 1,100–2,000 rpm.

4. Run the air conditioning system for full cooling, in the MAX or COLD mode.

5. The low pressure gauge should read 5–20

psi; the high pressure gauge should indicate 120–180 psi. Refer to the "A/C Performance Test Chart" illustration in this section for optimum pressure and temperature specifications.

WARNING: *These pressures are the norm for an ambient temperature of 70–80° F (21–27° C). Higher air temperatures along with high humidity will cause higher system pressures. At idle speed and an ambient temperature of 110° F (43° C), the high pressure reading can exceed 300 psi.*

Under these extreme conditions, you can keep the pressures down by directing a large electric floor fan through the condenser.

DISCHARGING THE SYSTEM

CAUTION: *Always wear safety goggles when working on a system to protect the eyes. If refrigerant contacts the eye, it is advisable in all cases to see a physician as soon as possible.*

1. Remove the caps from the high and low pressure charging valves in the high and low pressure lines.

2. Turn both manifold gauge set hand valves to the fully closed (clockwise) position.

3. Connect a gauge set (engine not running). The LOW side gauge hose to the suction line near the accumulator and the HIGH side gauge hose to the liquid line or muffler. The muffler is a round shaped can about three times larger than the liquid line.

4. Place the end of the center hose away

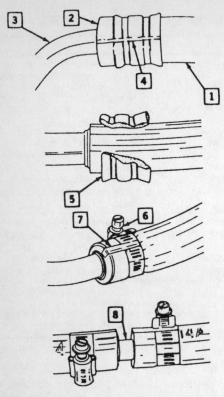

1. Hose
2. Original hose clamp
3. Fitting
4. Groove made by fine-tooth hacksaw
5. Band after splitting
6. Special screw-type service clamp
7. Locator lug in proper position
8. Splicer fitting

Air conditioning hose repair — always lubricate connections with refrigerant oil only

from you and the car and into a suitable container.

5. Open the low pressure gauge valve slightly and allow the system pressure to bleed off.

6. When the system is just about empty, open the high pressure valve very slowly to avoid losing an excessive amount of refrigerant oil. Allow any remaining refrigerant to escape.

EVACUATING THE SYSTEM

NOTE: *This procedure requires the use of a vacuum pump.*

1. Connect a gauge set (engine not running). The LOW side gauge hose to the suction line near the accumulator and the HIGH side gauge hose to the liquid line or muffler. The muffler is a round shaped can about three times larger than the liquid line.

2. Discharge the system.

3. Make sure that the low pressure gauge set hose is connected to the low pressure service gauge port on the top center of the accumulator/drier assembly or in the suction line and the high pressure hose connected to the high pressure service gauge port on the compressor discharge (liquid) line.

4. Connect the center service hose to the inlet fitting of the vacuum pump.

5. Turn both gauge set valves to the wide open position.

6. Start the pump and note the low side gauge reading.

7. Operate the pump until the low pressure gauge reads 25–30 inch Hg. Continue running the vacuum pump for 10 minutes more. If you have replaced some component in the system, run the pump for an additional 20–30 minutes.

8. Leak test the system. Close both gauge set valves. Turn off the pump. The needle should remain stationary at the point at which the pump was turned off. If the needle drops to zero rapidly, there is a leak in the system which must be repaired.

LEAK TESTING

Some leak tests can be performed with a soapy water solution. There must be at least a $1/2$ lb. charge in the system for a leak to be detected. The most extensive leak tests are performed with either a Halide flame type leak tester or the more preferable electronic leak tester.

In either case, the equipment is expensive, and, the use of a Halide detector can be **extremely** hazardous!

CHARGING THE SYSTEM
(MAXIMUM R–12 CHARGE IS 2.25 LBS)

CAUTION: *NEVER OPEN THE HIGH PRESSURE SIDE WITH A CAN OF REFRIGERANT CONNECTED TO THE SYSTEM! OPENING THE HIGH PRESSURE SIDE WILL OVERPRESSURIZE THE CAN, CAUSING IT TO EXPLODE! Always wear safety goggles when working on a system to protect the eyes. If refrigerant contacts the eye, it is advisable in all cases to see a physician as soon as possible.*

1. Connect a gauge set (engine not running). The LOW side gauge hose to the suction line near the accumulator and the HIGH side gauge hose to the liquid line or muffler. The muffler is a round shaped can about three times larger than the liquid line.

2. Close (clockwise) both gauge set valves.

3. Connect the center hose to the refrigerant can opener valve.

4. Make sure the can opener valve is closed, that is, the needle is raised, and connect the

valve to the can. Open the valve, puncturing the can with the needle.

5. Loosen the center hose fitting at the pressure gauge, allowing refrigerant to purge the hose of air. When the air is bled, tighten the fitting.

CAUTION: *IF THE LOW PRESSURE GAUGE SET HOSE IS NOT CONNECTED TO THE ACCUMULATOR/DRIER, KEEP THE CAN IN AN UPRIGHT POSITION!*

6. Disconnect the wire harness snap-lock connector from the clutch cycling pressure switch and install a jumper wire across the two terminals of the connector.

7. Open the low side gauge set valve and the can valve.

8. Allow refrigerant to be drawn into the system.

9. When no more refrigerant is drawn into the system, start the engine and run it at about 1,500 rpm. Turn on the system and operate it at the full high position. The compressor will operate and pull refrigerant gas into the system.

NOTE: *To help speed the process, the can may be placed, upright, in a pan of warm water, not exceeding 125° F (52° C).*

10. If more than one can of refrigerant is needed, close the can valve and gauge set low side valve when the can is empty and connect a new can to the opener. Repeat the charging process until the sight glass (if equipped) indicates a full charge. The frost line on the outside of the can will indicate what portion of the can has been used. **Maximum R-12 charge is 2.25 lbs.**

CAUTION: *NEVER ALLOW THE HIGH PRESSURE SIDE READING TO EXCEED 240 psi.*

11. When the charging process has been completed, close the gauge set valve and can valve. Remove the jumper wire and reconnect the cycling clutch wire. Run the system for at least five minutes to allow it to normalize. Low pressure side reading should be 4–25 psi; high pressure reading should be 120–210 psi at an ambient temperature of 70–90° F (21–32° C).

12. Turn the engine OFF before removing the manifold gauges.

13. Loosen both service hoses at the gauges to allow any refrigerant to escape. Remove the gauge set and install the dust caps on the service valves.

NOTE: *Multi-can dispensers are available which allow a simultaneous hook-up of up to four 14 oz. cans of R-12.*
CAUTION: *The maximum charge for these systems is 2.25 lbs. Never exceed the recommended maximum charge for the system.*

REFRIGERANT OIL CAPACITIES

The V-5 compressor system requires a total of **8 fluid ounces (240ml)** of 525 viscosity refrigerant oil.

New oil quantities must be added to the system during component replacement and excessive leaks. Refer to the following for specific oil quantities.

1. No signs of excessive oil leaks, add:

a. COMPRESSOR–remove, drain oil, measure if less than 1 oz. (30ml) add 2 oz. (60ml). If the measurement is more, add the same amount of new oil.

b. EVAPORATOR – add 3 oz. (90ml).

c. CONDENSER – add 1 oz. (30ml).

d. ACCUMULATOR – add 3.5 oz. (105ml).

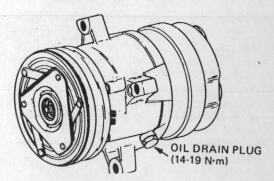

OIL DRAIN PLUG (14-19 N·m)

V–5 compressor oil drain plug

2. Refrigerant oil leak due to a large leak, add:

a. When the defective component has been replaced and the lead has been repaired, add 3 oz. (90ml) plus the required amount of oil for the particular component as previously outlined.

b. Up to 4 oz. (120ml) of oil can collect in the compressor crankcase. When replacing the compressor, drain the oil from the drain plug and measure the amount. New replacement compressors will be shipped with about 8 oz. (240ml) of oil. Drain the oil from the new compressor and add the same amount as drained from the old one.

Orifice Tube Service

The orifice tube can be cleaned with solvent and compressed air. Replace the tube if the plastic frame is broken, brass orifice tube is damaged or plugged, screen material is torn and screen is plugged with fine gritty material.

REMOVAL AND INSTALLATION

1. Discharge the A/C system as previously outlined in this section.

2. Loosen the fitting at the liquid line to the evaporator inlet pipe and remove the tube care-

Orifice tube removing tool — J-26549-C

fully with a needle nosed pliers or orifice tube removing tool J-26549-C or equivalent.

3. **To install:** lubricate with refrigerant oil and insert the new orifice tube with the shorter screen end in first.

4. Install the liquid line and torque to 11 ft. lbs. (17 Nm).

5. Evacuate and recharge the A/C system.

NOTE: *If the orifice tube can not be removed easily because of impacted residue, perform the following: Clean out as much residue as possible. Carefully apply heat to the area with a heat gun or hair dryer 1/4 inch from the dimples on the inlet pipe. Using the orifice removing tool J-26549-C, carefully turn with a push-pull motion to loosen the impacted tube. Swab the inside of the inlet pipe with R-11 or equivalent to remove any residue. Install the new orifice tube as previously outlined.*

Windshield Wipers

For maximum effectiveness and longest element lift, the windshield and wiper blades should be kept clean. Dirt, tree sap, road tar and so on will cause streaking, smearing and blade deterioration if left on the glass. It is advisable to wash the windshield carefully with a commercial glass cleaner at least once a month. Wipe off the rubber blades with the wet rag afterwards. Do not attempt to move the wipers by hand; damage to the motor and drive mechanism will result.

If the blades are found to be cracked, broken or torn, they should be replaced immediately. Replacement intervals will vary with usage, although ozone deterioration usually limits blade life to about one year. If the wiper pattern is smeared or streaked, or if the blade chatters across the glass, the elements should be replaced. It is easiest and most sensible to replace the elements in pairs.

There are basically three different types of refills, which differ in their method of replacement. One type has two release buttons, approximately 1/3 of the way up from the ends of the blade frame. Pushing the buttons down releases a lock and allows the rubber filler to be removed from the frame. The new filler slides back into the frame and locks in place.

The second type of refill has two metal tabs which are unlocked by squeezing them together. The rubber filler can then be withdrawn from the frame jaws. A new refill is installed by inserting the refill into the front frame jaws and sliding it rear ward to engage the remaining frame jaws. There are usually four jaws. Be certain when installing that the refill is engaged in all of them. At the end of its travel, the tabs will lock into place on the front jaws of the wiper blade frame.

The third type is a refill made from polycarbonate. The refill has a simple locking device at one end which flexes downward out of the groove into which the jaws of the holder fit, allowing easy release. By sliding the new refill through all the jaws and pushing through the slight resistance when it reaches the end of its travel, the refill will lock into position.

Regardless of the type of refill used, make sure that all of the frame jaws are engaged as the refill is pushed into place and locked. The metal blade holder and frame will scratch the glass if allowed to touch it.

Tires and Wheels

Inspect the tires regularly for wear and damage. Remove stones or other foreign particles which may be lodged in the tread. If tread wear is excessive or irregular it could be a sign of front end problems, or simply improper inflation.

The inflation should be checked at least once per month and adjusted if necessary. The tires must be cold (driven less than one mile) or an inaccurate reading will result. Do not forget to check the spare.

The correct inflation pressure for your vehicle can be found on a decal mounted to the car. Depending upon model and year, the decal can be located at the driver's door, the passenger's door or the glove box. If you cannot find the decal a local automobile tire dealer can furnish you with information.

Inspect tires for uneven wear that might indicate the need for front end alignment or tire rotation. Tires should be replaced when a tread wear indicator appears as a solid band across the tread.

When you buy new tires, give some thought to these points, especially if you are switching to larger tires or to another profile series (50, 60, 70, 78):

1. The wheels must be the correct width for the tire. Tire dealers have charts of tire and rim compatibility. A mismatch can cause sloppy handling and rapid tread wear. The old rule of thumb is that the tread width should match the rim width (inside bead to inside bead)

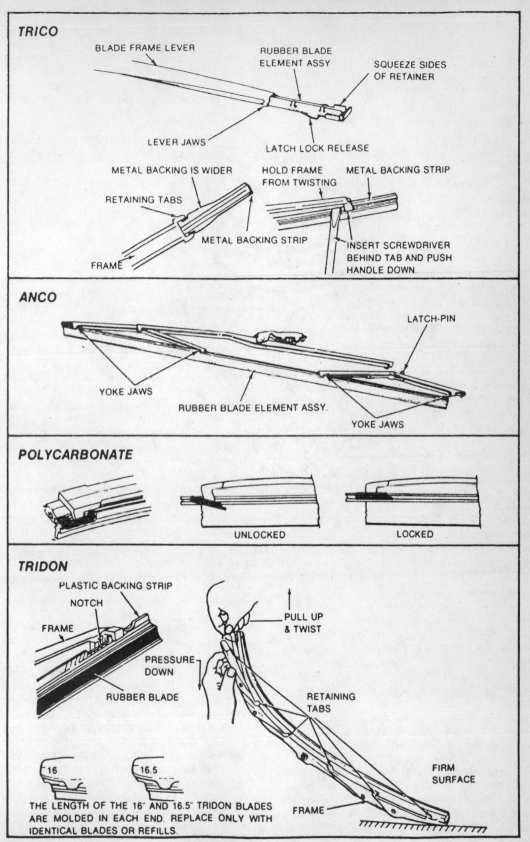

TRICO

BLADE FRAME LEVER

RUBBER BLADE ELEMENT ASSY

SQUEEZE SIDES OF RETAINER

LEVER JAWS

LATCH LOCK RELEASE

METAL BACKING IS WIDER

HOLD FRAME FROM TWISTING

METAL BACKING STRIP

RETAINING TABS

METAL BACKING STRIP

FRAME

INSERT SCREWDRIVER BEHIND TAB AND PUSH HANDLE DOWN.

ANCO

LATCH-PIN

YOKE JAWS

RUBBER BLADE ELEMENT ASSY.

YOKE JAWS

POLYCARBONATE

UNLOCKED

LOCKED

TRIDON

PLASTIC BACKING STRIP

NOTCH

FRAME

PULL UP & TWIST

PRESSURE DOWN

RUBBER BLADE

RETAINING TABS

16

16.5

FIRM SURFACE

FRAME

THE LENGTH OF THE 16" AND 16.5" TRIDON BLADES ARE MOLDED IN EACH END. REPLACE ONLY WITH IDENTICAL BLADES OR REFILLS.

Wiper insert replacement

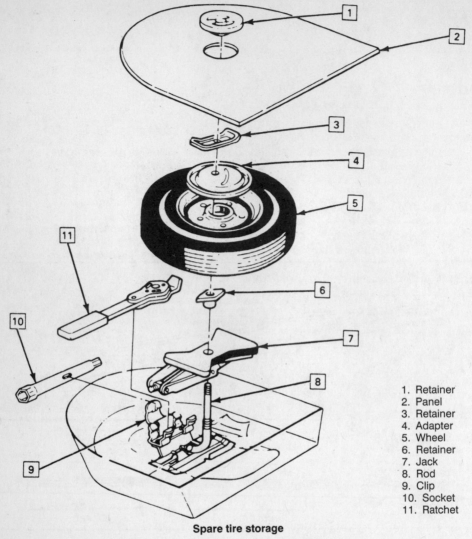

1. Retainer
2. Panel
3. Retainer
4. Adapter
5. Wheel
6. Retainer
7. Jack
8. Rod
9. Clip
10. Socket
11. Ratchet

Spare tire storage

within an inch. For radial tires, the rim width should be 80% or less of the tire (not tread) width.

2. The height (mounted diameter) of the new tires can greatly change speedometer accuracy, engine speed at a given road speed, fuel mileage, acceleration, and ground clearance. Tire makers furnish full measurement specifications. Speedometer drive gears are available from GM dealers for correction.

NOTE: *Dimensions of tires marked the same size may vary significantly, even among tires from the same maker.*

3. The spare tire should be usable, at least for low speed operation, with the new tires.

4. There should not be any body interference when loaded, on bumps, or in turning.

The only sure way to avoid problems with these points is to stick to tire and wheel sizes available as factory options.

TIRE ROTATION

Tire wear can be equalized by switching the position of the tires about every 6000 miles. Including a conventional spare in the rotation pattern can give up to 20% more tire life. If front end problems are suspected have them corrected before rotating the tires.

CAUTION: *Do not include the new "Spacesaver" spare tire in the rotation pattern.*

CAUTION: *Tires should be rotated periodically to get the maximum tread lift available. A good time to do this is when changing over from regular tires to snow tires, or about once per year. If front end problems are suspected have them corrected before rotating the tires. Torque the lug nuts to 100 ft. lbs. (136 Nm).*

NOTE: *Mark the wheel position or direction of rotation on radial, or studded snow tires before removing them.*

CAUTION: *Avoid overtightening the lug nuts to prevent damage to the brake disc or drum. Alloy wheels can also be cracked by overtightening. Use of a torque wrench is highly recommended. Torque the lug nuts in a criss-cross sequence shown to 100 ft. lbs. (136 Nm).*

TREAD DEPTH

All tires have 8 built-in tread wear indicator bars that show up as $\frac{1}{2}$ inch wide smooth bands across the tire when $\frac{1}{2}$ inch of tread remains. The appearance of tread wear indicators means that the tires should be replaced. In fact, many states have laws prohibiting the use of tires with less than $\frac{1}{16}$ inch tread.

You can check your own tread depth with an inexpensive gauge or by using a Lincoln head penny. Slip the Lincoln penny into several tread grooves. If you can see the top of Lincoln's head in 2 adjacent grooves, the tires have less than $\frac{1}{2}$ inch tread left and should be replaced. You can measure snow tires in the same manner by using the "tails" side of the Lincoln penny. If you can see the top of the Lincoln memorial, it's time to replace the snow tires.

TIRE STORAGE

Store the tires at proper inflation pressure if they are mounted on wheels. All tires should be kept in a cool, dry place. If they are stored in the garage or basement, do not let them stand on a concrete floor, set them on strips of wood.

Care For Aluminum Wheels

Aluminum wheels should be cleaned and waxed regularly. Do not use abrasive cleaners because they may damage the protective coating.

FLUIDS AND LUBRICANTS

Engine Oil Recommendations

Engine oils are labeled on the containers with various API (American Petroleum Institute) designations of quality. Always use SF/CC or SF/CD quality energy conserving oils of the proper viscosity. A new quality designation, SG will protect the engine even better than the previous oils. The SG designation may be shown alone or in combination with other designations such as SG/CC, SG/CD, SF, SG or CC.

Oil Viscosity

Engine oil viscosity (thickness) has an effect on fuel economy and cold weather starting. The lower viscosity oil can provide better fuel economy and cold weather performance, but if used

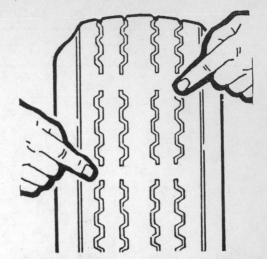

Replace a tire that shows the built-in 'bump strip'

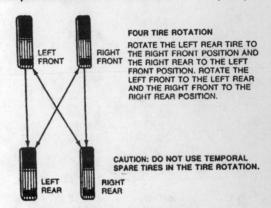

FOUR TIRE ROTATION
ROTATE THE LEFT REAR TIRE TO THE RIGHT FRONT POSITION AND THE RIGHT REAR TO THE LEFT FRONT POSITION. ROTATE THE LEFT FRONT TO THE LEFT REAR AND THE RIGHT FRONT TO THE RIGHT REAR POSITION.

CAUTION: DO NOT USE TEMPORAL SPARE TIRES IN THE TIRE ROTATION.

Tire rotation pattern

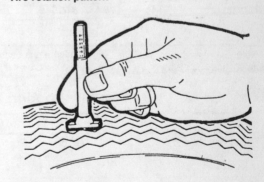

Tire tread depth gauge

in hot weather condition, may not provide adequate engine lubrication.

CAUTION: *Using oils of any viscosity other than those recommended, may cause engine damage.*

CAUTION: *When choosing an engine oil, consider the range of temperature the vehicle will be operated in before the next oil change.*

Tire Size Comparison Chart

"Letter" sizes			Inch Sizes	Metric-inch Sizes		
"60 Series"	"70 Series"	"78 Series"	1965–77	"60 Series"	"70 Series"	"80 Series"
		Y78-12	5.50-12, 5.60-12 6.00-12	165/60-12	165/70-12	155-12
		W78-13	5.20-13	165/60-13	145/70-13	135-13
		Y78-13	5.60-13	175/60-13	155/70-13	145-13
			6.15-13	185/60-13	165/70-13	155-13, P155/80-13
A60-13	A70-13	A78-13	6.40-13	195/60-13	175/70-13	165-13
B60-13	B70-13	B78-13	6.70-13 6.90-13	205/60-13	185/70-13	175-13
C60-13	C70-13	C78-13	7.00-13	215/60-13	195/70-13	185-13
D60-13	D70-13	D78-13	7.25-13			
E60-13	E70-13	E78-13	7.75-13			195-13
			5.20-14	165/60-14	145/70-14	135-14
			5.60-14	175/60-14	155/70-14	145-14
			5.90-14			
A60-14	A70-14	A78-14	6.15-14	185/60-14	165/70-14	155-14
	B70-14	B78-14	6.45-14	195/60-14	175/70-14	165-14
	C70-14	C78-14	6.95-14	205/60-14	185/70-14	175-14
D60-14	D70-14	D78-14				
E60-14	E70-14	E78-14	7.35-14	215/60-14	195/70-14	185-14
F60-14	F70-14	F78-14, F83-14	7.75-14	225/60-14	200/70-14	195-14
G60-14	G70-14	G77-14, G78-14	8.25-14	235/60-14	205/70-14	205-14
H60-14	H70-14	H78-14	8.55-14	245/60-14	215/70-14	215-14
J60-14	J70-14	J78-14	8.85-14	255/60-14	225/70-14	225-14
L60-14	L70-14		9.15-14	265/60-14	235/70-14	
	A70-15	A78-15	5.60-15	185/60-15	165/70-15	155-15
B60-15	B70-15	B78-15	6.35-15	195/60-15	175/70-15	165-15
C60-15	C70-15	C78-15	6.85-15	205/60-15	185/70-15	175-15
	D70-15	D78-15				
E60-15	E70-15	E78-15	7.35-15	215/60-15	195/70-15	185-15
F60-15	F70-15	F78-15	7.75-15	225/60-15	205/70-15	195-15
G60-15	G70-15	G78-15	8.15-15/8.25-15	235/60-15	215/70-15	205-15
H60-15	H70-15	H78-15	8.45-15/8.55-15	245/60-15	225/70-15	215-15
J60-15	J70-15	J78-15	8.85-15/8.90-15	255/60-15	235/70-15	225-15
	K70-15		9.00-15	265/60-15	245/70-15	230-15
L60-15	L70-15	L78-15, L84-15	9.15-15			235-15
	M70-15	M78-15				255-15
		N78-15				

Note: Every size tire is not listed and many size comparisons are approximate, based on load ratings. Wider tires than those supplied new with the vehicle, should always be checked for clearance.

Troubleshooting Basic Tire Problems

Problem	Cause	Solution
The car's front end vibrates at high speeds and the steering wheel shakes	• Wheels out of balance • Front end needs aligning	• Have wheels balanced • Have front end alignment checked
The car pulls to one side while cruising	• Unequal tire pressure (car will usually pull to the low side) • Mismatched tires • Front end needs aligning	• Check/adjust tire pressure • Be sure tires are of the same type and size • Have front end alignment checked
Abnormal, excessive or uneven tire wear See "How to Read Tire Wear"	• Infrequent tire rotation • Improper tire pressure • Sudden stops/starts or high speed on curves	• Rotate tires more frequently to equalize wear • Check/adjust pressure • Correct driving habits
Tire squeals	• Improper tire pressure • Front end needs aligning	• Check/adjust tire pressure • Have front end alignment checked

Troubleshooting Basic Wheel Problems

Problem	Cause	Solution
The car's front end vibrates at high speed	• The wheels are out of balance • Wheels are out of alignment	• Have wheels balanced • Have wheel alignment checked/ adjusted
Car pulls to either side	• Wheels are out of alignment • Unequal tire pressure • Different size tires or wheels	• Have wheel alignment checked/ adjusted • Check/adjust tire pressure • Change tires or wheels to same size
The car's wheel(s) wobbles	• Loose wheel lug nuts • Wheels out of balance • Damaged wheel • Wheels are out of alignment • Worn or damaged ball joint • Excessive play in the steering link-age (usually due to worn parts) • Defective shock absorber	• Tighten wheel lug nuts • Have tires balanced • Raise car and spin the wheel. If the wheel is bent, it should be replaced • Have wheel alignment checked/ adjusted • Check ball joints • Check steering linkage • Check shock absorbers
Tires wear unevenly or prematurely	• Incorrect wheel size • Wheels are out of balance • Wheels are out of alignment	• Check if wheel and tire size are compatible • Have wheels balanced • Have wheel alignment checked/ adjusted

Refer to the "Engine Oil Viscosity Recommendations" chart in this section.

Fuel Recommendations

It is important to use fuel of the proper octane rating in your car. Octane rating is based on the quantity of anti-knock compounds added to the fuel and it determines the speed at which the gas will burn. The lower the octane rating, the faster it burns. The higher the octane, the slower the fuel will burn and a greater percentage of compounds in the fuel prevent spark ping (knock), detonation and preignition (dieseling).

As the temperature of the engine increases, the air/fuel mixture exhibits a tendency to ignite before the spark plug is fired. If fuel of an octane rating too low for the engine is used, this will allow combustion to occur before the piston has completed its compression stroke, thereby creating a very high pressure very rapidly.

Using leaded gasoline can damage the emis-10.0sion control system by decreasing the effectiveness of the catalyst in the catalytic converter and by damaging the oxygen sensor which is part of the "Computer Command Control System". UNLEADED GASOLINE ONLY must be used in your vehicle to prevent damage to these components.

Do not use gasolines containing more than 5 percent methanol even if they contain cosolvents and corrosion inhibitors.

Although gasolines containing 5 percent or less methanol and appropriate cosolvents and inhibitors for methanol may be suitable for use in your car, General Motors does not endorse their use, at this time.

The 2.5L L4, 2.8L and 3.1L V6 engines are designed to use only unleaded gasoline, with an Research Octane Number (RON) rating of at least 91, or an Antiknock Index of 87. The 2.3L QUAD 4 and 3.1L Turbo is designed to use only unleaded gasoline with an Antiknock Index of 91.

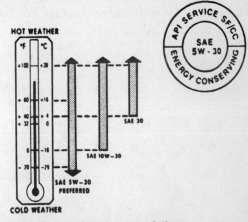

Engine oil viscosity recommendations

Engine

OIL LEVEL CHECK

The engine oil level should be checked frequently. For instance, at each refueling stop. Be sure that the vehicle is parked on a level surface with the engine off. Also, allow a few minutes after turning off the engine for the oil to drain into the pan or an inaccurate reading will result.

1. Open the hood and remove the engine oil dipstick.

2. Wipe the dipstick with a clean, lint-free rag and reinsert it. Be sure to insert it all the way.

3. Pull out the dipstick and note the oil level. It should be between the SAFE (MAX) mark and the ADD (MIN) mark.

4. If the level is below the lower mark, replace the dipstick and add fresh oil to bring the level within the proper range. Do not overfill.

50 5. Recheck the oil level and close the hood.

NOTE: *Use a multi-grade oil with API classification SF.*

OIL AND FILTER CHANGE

NOTE: *The engine oil and oil filter should be changed at the same time, at the recommended intervals on the maintenance schedule chart. If your vehicle is being driven under dusty, polluted, or off road conditions, cut the mileage intervals in half. The same thing goes for cars driven in stop-and-go traffic or for only short distances.*

Always drain the oil after the engine has been running long enough to bring it to operating temperature. Hot oil will flow easier and more contaminants will be removed along with the oil than if it were drained cold. You will need a large capacity drain pan (2 gallons) which you can purchase at any auto store. Another necessity is containers for used oil. You

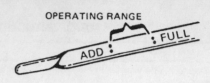

Oil level dipstick

will find that plastic bottles such as those used for detergents, bleaches etc., make excellent storage jugs. One ecologically desirable solution to the used oil disposal problem is to find a cooperative gas station owner who will allow you to dump your used oil into his tank.

General Motors recommends changing both the oil and filter during the first oil change and the filter every other oil change thereafter. For the small price of an oil filter, its cheap insurance to replace the filter at every oil change. One of the larger filter manufacturers points out in its advertisements that not changing the filter leaves a quantity of dirty oil in the engine, which could be as much as a quart on some models. This claim is true and should be kept in mind when changing your oil. Change your oil as follows:

1. Run the engine to normal operating temperature.

2. after the engine has reached operating temperature, shut it off, firmly apply the parking brake, and block the wheels.

3. Raise and support the front end on jackstands.

4. Place a drip pan beneath the oil pan and remove the drain plug.

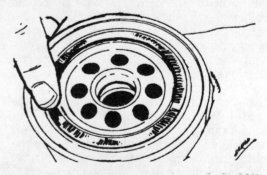

Lubricate the gasket on the new filter with clean engine oil. A dry gasket may not make a good seal and will allow the filter to leak.

CAUTION: *The oil can be very hot! Protect yourself by using rubber gloves if necessary.*

5. Allow the engine to drain thoroughly.

6. While the oil is draining, replace the filter as described below.

7. When the oil has completely drained, clean the threads of the plug and coat them

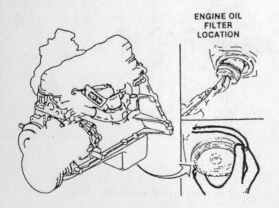

Oil filter location — 2.5L L4 Lumina

ENGINE OIL
FILTER
LOCATION

with non-hardening sealer or Teflon tape and install the plug. Tighten it snugly.

WARNING: *The threads in the oil pan are easily stripped! Do not overtighten the plug! Torque to 25 ft. lbs. (34 Nm).*

8. Fill the crankcase with the proper amount of oil shown in the Capacities Chart in this chapter.

9. Start the engine and check for leaks.

REPLACING THE OIL FILTER

Gasoline Engines

1. Place the drip pan beneath the oil filter.

2. Using a strap wrench for the 2.8L and 3.1L V6 engine, remove the oil filter. Keep in mind that it's holding dirty, hot oil. Remove the oil filter through the hole in the oil pan directly above the oil drain plug on the 2.5L L4 Lumina engines. Pull the filter through with a pliers. Refer to the "Force Balancer Assembly" in Chapter 3 for filter location.

3. Using an oil filter wrench, turn the filter counterclockwise to remove it (2.3L QUAD 4, 2.8L and 3.1L V6 engine).

CAUTION: *The oil could be very hot! Protect yourself by using rubber gloves if necessary.*

4. Wipe the contact surface of the new filter clean and coat the rubber gasket with clean engine oil.

5. Clean the mating surface of the adapter on the block.

6. Screw the new filter into position on the block using hand pressure only. Do not use a strap wrench to install the filter! Then hand-turn the filter 1/2-3/4 additional turn. Do not overtighten or you may squash the gasket and cause it to leak.

7. Refill the engine with a correct amount of fresh oil.

   a. 2.3L QUAD 4 (VIN A,D) – 4 Quarts (with filter)

   b. 2.5L L4 engine (VIN R) – 4 Quarts (with filter)

   c. 2.8L and 3.1L V6 engine (VIN W and T) – 4 Quarts (with filter)

8. Check the oil level on the dipstick. It is normal for the level to be a bit above the full mark. Start the engine and allow it to idle a few minutes.

CAUTION: *Do not run the engine above idle speed until it has built up oil pressure, indicated when the oil light goes out.*

9. Shut off the engine, allow the oil to drain for a minute, and check the oil level. Check around the filter and drain plug for any leaks, and correct as necessary.

Automatic Transaxle

FLUID RECOMMENDATION AND LEVEL CHECK

The automatic transaxle fluid level should be checked at each engine oil change. When adding or changing the automatic transaxle fluid use only fluid labeled Dexron® II.

1. Set the parking brake and start the engine with the transaxle in "P" (Park).

2. With the service brakes applied, move the shift lever through all the gear ranges, ending in "P" (Park).

NOTE: *The fluid level must be checked with the engine running at slow idle, the car level and the fluid at least at room temperature. The correct fluid level cannot be read if you have just driven the car for a long time at high speed, city traffic in hot weather or if the car has been pulling a trailer. In these cases, wait at least 30 minutes for the fluid to cool down.*

3. Remove the dipstick located at the rear end of the engine compartment, wipe it clean, then push it back in until the cap seats.

4. Pull the dipstick out and read the fluid level. The level should be in the cross-hatched area of the dipstick.

5. Add fluid using a long plastic funnel in the dipstick tube. Keep in mind that it only takes one pint of fluid to raise the level from "ADD" to "FULL" with a hot transaxle.

WARNING: *Damage to the automatic transaxle may result if the fluid level is above the "FULL" mark. Remove excess fluid by threading a small rubber hose into the dipstick tube and pump the fluid out with a syphon pump.*

FLUID DRAIN AND REFILL

According to General Motors, under normal operating conditions the automatic transmis-

1 FLUID LEVEL INDICATOR (125C)
2 LEVEL TO BE IN CROSS-HATCHED AREA ON FLUID LEVEL INDICATOR BLADE. CHECK AT OPERATING TEMPERATURE.
3 COLD LEVEL ENGINE OFF

Automatic transaxle fluid check — THM 125C

1 FLUID LEVEL INDICATOR (440-T4)
2 LEVEL TO BE IN CROSS-HATCHED AREA ON FLUID LEVEL INDICATOR BLADE. CHECK AT OPERATING TEMPERATURE.
3 COLD LEVEL ENGINE OFF

Automatic transaxle fluid check — THM 440-T4

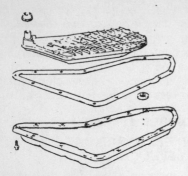

Automatic transaxle filter change — THM 125C (3T40)

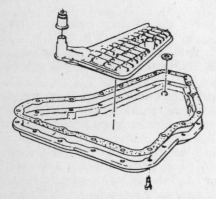

Automatic transaxle filter change — THM 440–T4 (4T60)

sion fluid only needs to be changed every 100,000 miles unless one or more of the following driving conditions is encountered. In the following cases the fluid and filter should be changed every 15,000 miles:

a. Driving in heavy traffic when the outside temperature reaches 90° F.

b. Driving regularly in hilly or mountainous areas.

c. Towing a trailer.

d. Using a vehicle as a taxi or police car or for delivery purposes.

Remember, these are factory recommendations and are considered to be minimum. You must determine a change interval which fits your driving habits. If your vehicle is never subjected to these conditions, a 100,000 mile change interval is adequate. If you are a normal driver, a two-year/30,000 mile interval will be more than sufficient to maintain the long life for which your automatic transaxle was designed.

NOTE: *Use only fluid labeled Dexron® II. Use of other fluids could cause erratic shifting and transaxle damage.*

1. Jack up your vehicle and support it safely with jackstands.

2. Disconnect the negative (–) battery cable.

3. Remove the bottom pan bolts.

4. Loosen the rear bolts about four turns.

5. Carefully pry the oil pan loose and allow the fluid to drain.

6. Remove the remaining bolts, the pan, and the gasket or RTV sealant. Discard the old gasket.

7. Clean the pan with solvent and dry it thoroughly, with compressed air.

8. Remove the filter and O-ring seal.

9. Install a new transaxle filter and O-ring seal, locating the filter against the dipstick stop.

NOTE: *Always replace the filter with a new one. Do not attempt to clean the old one.*

10. Install a new gasket or RTV sealant then tighten the pan bolts to 12 ft. lbs. (15 Nm).

11. Lower the car and add about 4 quarts of Dexron® II transmission fluid.

12. Start the engine and let idle. Block the wheels and apply the parking brake.

13. At idle, move the shift lever through the ranges. With the lever in "PARK", check the fluid level and add as necessary. The drain and refill capacity is 6 quarts.

NOTE: *The transmission fluid currently being used may appear to be darker and have a strong odor. This is normal and not a sign of required maintenance or transmission failure.*

Manual Transaxle

FLUID RECOMMENDATION

According to General Motors, manual transaxle fluid should be checked every 15,000 miles to make sure the level is full. The tran-

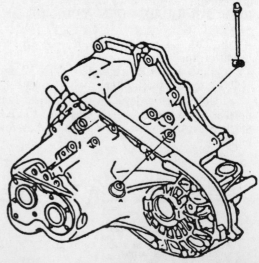

Manual transaxle fluid level dipstick — HM–282 (5TM40)

saxle fluid does not have to be changed at a regular interval. The manufacturer recommends no need manual transaxle fluid change, but after 100,000 miles the fluid should be changed.

The proper manual transaxle fluid for the HM–282 transaxle is Synchromesh Transaxle Fluid No. 12345349 or equivalent. Do NOT use any other fluid because damage may occur.

FLUID LEVEL CHECK

To check for proper fluid level in the HM–282 manual transaxle, remove the fluid level dipstick located on the driver's side (left) in the transaxle case. With the engine warn, add enough fluid to bring the level to the FULL line.

DRAIN AND REFILL

1. Raise the vehicle and support with jackstands.

2. Position a drain pan under the transaxle drain plug. Remove the drain plug and allow to drain completely.

3. Install the drain plug and torque to 18 ft. lbs. (24 Nm).

4. Using a long thin funnel, refill the transaxle with 2.1 qts. (2.0 Liters) of Synchromesh transaxle fluid No. 12345349 or equivalent.

5. Check the fluid level and add if neccessary.

6. Install the fluid level dipstick. Drive the vehicle for a mile and stop and check for leaks.

Differential

The differential assembly is part of the transaxle assembly and is lubricated by the transaxle fluid.

Engine Cooling System

The engine is kept cool by a liquid circulating through the engine to a radiator. In the radiator, the liquid is cooled by air passing through the radiator tubes. The the coolant is circulated by a rotating water pump driven by the engine crankshaft. The complete engine cooling system consists of a radiator, recovery system, cooling fan, thermostat, water pump and serpentine belt.

FLUID RECOMMENDATION AND LEVEL CHECK

A see-through plastic reservoir called a coolant recovery bottle, is located in the front compartment near the radiator assembly. This bottle is connected to the radiator by a hose. As the car is driven, the coolant is heated and expands, the portion of the fluid displaced by this expansion flows from the radiator into the recovery bottle. When the car is stopped and the coolant cools and contracts, the displaced coolant is drawn back into the radiator by vacuum. Thus, the radiator is kept filled with coolant to the desired level at all times. The coolant level should be between the "ADD" and "FULL" marks on the recovery bottle. If coolant is needed, add it to the recovery bottle not the radiator. The "ADD" and "FULL" marks on the recovery bottle are approximately one quart apart so that a 50/50 mixture can be added.(50% ethylene glycol antifreeze and 50% water).

CAUTION: *Do not remove the radiator cap or the thermostat housing cap while the engine and radiator are still hot. This also includes the recovery bottle cap if coolant in the recovery bottle is boiling. Scalding fluid and steam can be blown out under pressure if any cap is taken off too soon. The engine cooling fan is electric and can come on whether or not the engine is running. The fan can start automatically in response to a heat sensor when the ignition is in "Run". Remember to keep hands, tools and clothing away from the cooling fan when working under the compartment lid.*

DRAIN AND REFILL

CAUTION: *When draining the coolant, keep in mind that cats and dogs are attracted by the ethylene glycol antifreeze, and are quite likely to drink any that is left in an uncovered container or in puddles on the ground. This will prove fatal in sufficient quantity. Always drain the coolant into a sealable container. Coolant should be reused unless it is contaminated or several years old.*

CAUTION: *The cooling system should be drained and refilled every 24 months or 30,000 miles. Please read the Cautions above then perform the following procedure:*

NOTE: *Use a good quality antifreeze with water pump lubricants, rust inhibitors and other corrosion inhibitors along with acid neutralizers. Use a permanent type coolant that meets manufacturer's specifications.*

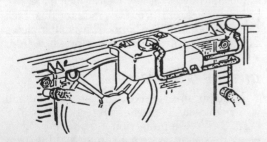

Coolant recovery bottle

1. When the engine is cool, open the engine compartment lid and turn the thermostat housing cap slowly counter-clockwise until it reaches a stop.

NOTE: *Do not press down while turning the cap.*

2. Wait until any remaining pressure is released, then press down on the cap and continue turning it counter-clockwise. Remove the cap.

3. Open the radiator drain valve and air bleed vent on the thermostat housing and bypass pipe.

4. Allow the system to drain completely, then CLOSE the radiator drain valve tightly.

5. Remove the coolant recovery bottle and clean with tap water. Reinstall the recovery bottle.

6. Using a 50/50 solution of antifreeze and water, fill the radiator through the radiator neck until the coolant reaches the neck.

7. Start the engine and let idle for five minutes, keep adding coolant until the coolant lever is to the radiator neck.

8. Install the radiator cap. Add coolant to the recovery bottle after the engine has warmed up. The coolant level should be at the HOT mark.

NOTE: *The low coolant light may come on after this procedure. after operating the vehicle so that the engine heats up and cools down two times, if the low coolant indicator light does not go out, check and refill the recovery bottle.*

SYSTEM INSPECTION

Most permanent antifreeze/coolant have a colored dye added which makes the solution an excellent leak detector. When servicing the cooling system, check for leakage at:

• All hoses and hose connections
• Radiator seams, radiator core, and radiator drain plug
• All engine block and cylinder head freeze (core) plugs, and drain plugs
• Edges of all cooling system gaskets (head gaskets, thermostat gasket)

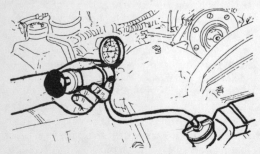

Pressure testing the cooling system

Radiator drain valve

• Transaxle fluid cooler
• Heating system components, water pump
• Check the engine oil dipstick for signs of coolant in the engine oil. Will turn the oil a white color
• Check the coolant in the radiator for signs of oil in the coolant

Investigate and correct any indication of coolant leakage.

Check the Radiator Cap

While you are checking the coolant level, check the radiator cap for a worn or cracked gasket. If the cap does not seal properly, fluid will be lost and the engine will overheat.

A worn cap should be replaced with a new one with the proper pressure rating.

Clean Radiator of Debris

Periodically clean any debris such as leaves, paper, insects, etc., from the radiator fins. Pick the large pieces off by hand. The smaller pieces can be washed away with water pressure from a hose.

CHECKING SYSTEM PROTECTION

A 50/50 mix of coolant concentrate and water will usually provide protection to –35° F (–37° C). Freeze protection may be checked by using a cooling system hydrometer. Inexpensive hydrometers (floating ball types) may be obtained from a local department store (auto-motive section) or an auto supply store. Follow the directions packaged with the coolant hy-drometer when checking protection.

COOLING SYSTEM PRESSURE TESTING

CAUTION: *When draining the coolant, keep in mind that cats and dogs are attracted by the ethylene glycol antifreeze, and are quite likely to drink any that is left in an uncov-ered container or in puddles on the ground. This will prove fatal in sufficient quantity. Always drain the coolant into a sealable con-tainer. Coolant should be reused unless it is contaminated or several years old.*

1. Tighten the radiator and heater hose clamps.

CAUTION: *To avoid being burned, do not remove the radiator cap while the engine is at normal operating temperature. The scald-ing coolant is under pressure and may be forced out of the filler neck, causing personal injury. Allow the engine to cool down and use a large shop towel to turn the cap.*

2. Remove the radiator cap.
3. Fill the system to the base of the filler neck with antifreeze.
4. Connect a cooling system pressure tester J–24460–01 or equivalent, to the filler neck.
5. Build up pressure to NO more than 20 psi (138 kPa). The system should hold the pres-sure for at least two minutes.
6. If the system will not hold the pressure, check for leaks.
7. Repair the leak and recheck the system.

FLUSHING AND CLEANING

CAUTION: *Do not remove the radiator cap or the thermostat housing cap while the engine and radiator are still hot. This also includes the recovery bottle cap if coolant in the recovery bottle is boiling. Scalding fluid and steam can be blown out under pressure if any cap is taken off too soon. The engine cool-ing fan is electric and can come on whether or not the engine is running. The fan can start automatically in response to a heat sensor when the ignition is in "Run." Remem-ber to keep hands, tools and clothing away from the cooling fan when working under the compartment lid.*

1. Drain the existing antifreeze and cool-ant. Open the radiator and engine drain pet-cocks (models equipped), or disconnect the bot-tom radiator hose, at the radiator outlet. Set the heater temperature controls to the full HOT position.

NOTE: *Before opening the radiator drain plug, spray it with some penetrating lubri-cant.*

2. Close the drain plug or reconnect the lower hose and fill the system with water.
3. Add a can of quality radiator flush. Make sure the flush is safe to use in engines having aluminum components.
4. Idle the engine until the upper radiator hose gets hot.
5. Drain the system again.
6. Repeat this process until the drained water is clear and free of scale.
7. Close all drain plugs and connect all the hoses.
8. If equipped with a coolant recovery system, flush the reservoir with water and leave empty.
9. Determine the capacity of your cooling system (see capacities chart). Add a 50/50 mix of quality antifreeze (ethylene glycol) and water to provide the desired protection.

Brake Master Cylinder

FLUID RECOMMENDATION

CAUTION: *Use only Heavy Duty Brake Fluid meeting DOT3 specifications. Do NOT use any other fluid because severe brake system damage will result.*

LEVEL CHECK

The brake fluid in the master cylinder should be checked every 6 months/6,000 miles.

Check the fluid level on the side of the reser-voir. If fluid is required, remove the screw on filler cap and gasket from the master cylinder. Fill the reservoir to the full line in the reservoir with Heavy Duty Brake Fluid meeting DOT3 specifications ONLY. Install the filler cap, making sure the gasket is properly seated in the cap. Make sure no dirt enters the system when adding fluid.

If fluid has to be added frequently, the system should be checked for a leak. Check for leaks at the master cylinder, calipers, propor-tioning valve and brake lines. If a leak is found,

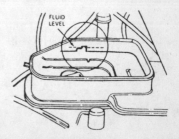

Brake master cylinder fluid level

replace the component and bleed the system as outlined in Chapter 9.

Clutch Master Cylinder

FLUID RECOMMENDATION

CAUTION: *Use only Heavy Duty Brake Fluid meeting DOT3 specifications. Do NOT use any other fluid because severe clutch system damage will result.*

LEVEL CHECK

The clutch system fluid in the master cylinder should be checked every 6 months/6,000 miles.

The clutch master cylinder reservoir is located on top of the left (driver) strut tower. Check the fluid level on the side of the reservoir. If fluid is required, remove the screw on filler cap and gasket from the master cylinder. Fill the reservoir to the full line in the reservoir with Heavy Duty Brake Fluid meeting DOT3 specifications ONLY. Install the filler cap, making sure the gasket is properly seated in the cap. Make sure no dirt enters the system when adding fluid.

If fluid has to be added frequently, the system should be checked for a leak. Check for leaks at the master cylinder, slave cylinder and hose. If a leak is found, replace the component and bleed the system as outlined in Chapter 7.

Power Steering

FLUID RECOMMENDATIONS

When adding fluid or making a complete fluid change, always use GM P/N 1050017 power steering fluid or equivalent. Do NOT use automatic transmission fluid. Failure to use the proper fluid may cause hose and seal damage and fluid leaks.

LEVEL CHECK

The power steering fluid reservoir is directly above the steering pump. The pump is located on top of the engine on the right (passenger) side.

Power steering fluid level is indicated either by marks on a see through reservoir or by marks on a fluid level indicator on the reservoir cap.

If the fluid is warmed up (about 150° F), the level should be between the HOT and COLD marks.

If the fluid is cool (about 70° F), the level should be between the ADD and COLD marks.

Chassis Greasing

Lubricate the chassis lubrication points every 7,500 miles or 12 months. If your vehicle is equipped with grease fittings, lubricate the

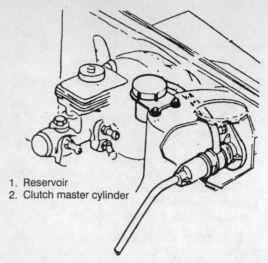

1. Reservoir
2. Clutch master cylinder

Clutch master cylinder

suspension and steering linkage with heavy duty chassis grease. Lubricate the transaxle shift linkage, parking cable guides, under body contact points and linkage with white lithium grease.

Body Lubrication

Lock Cylinders

Apply graphite lubricant sparingly thought the key slot. Insert the key and operate the lock several times to be sure that the lubricant is worked into the lock cylinder.

Door Hinges and Hinge Checks

Spray a silicone lubricant on the hinge pivot points to eliminate any binding conditions. Open and close the door several times to be sure that the lubricant is evenly and thoroughly distributed.

Trunk lid or Tailgate

Spray a silicone lubricant on all of the pivot and friction surfaces to eliminate any squeaks or binds. Work the tailgate to distribute the lubricant

Body Drain Holes

Be sure that the drain holes in the doors and rocker panels are cleared of obstruction. A small screwdriver can be used to clear them of any debris.

Wheel bearings (Rear)

CAUTION: *Some brake pads contain asbestos, which has been determined to be a cancer causing agent. Never clean the brake surfaces with compressed air! Avoid inhaling any dust from any brake surface! When clean-*

SEALED WHEEL BEARING DIAGNOSIS

WHEEL BEARING ASSEMBLY LOOSENESS DIAGNOSIS

Free the shoes from the disc, or remove calipers.
Reinstall 2 wheel nuts to secure disc to bearing.
Mount dial indicator as shown below.
Grasp disc and use a push-pull movement.

If looseness exceeds 0.1270 mm (0.005 in.).
Replace hub and bearing assembly.

WHEEL BEARING ASSEMBLY NOISE DIAGNOSIS

If a Road Test indicates noise, it could be wheels, bearings or tires, check the following:

1. Check tires for proper pressure and uneven wear.
2. Raise car on a hoist and spin wheels; check for out-of-round tires, out-of-balance tires, bent rims, loose and/or rough wheel bearings.

OTHER NOISE
(CORRECT AS REQUIRED)

SUSPECT BEARING NOISE

FRONT WHEEL BEARING ASSEMBLY

Hoist Car and Support Lower Control Arm and Spin Wheel with Engine.

NOISE OR ROUGHNESS CAN BE HEARD FROM DRIVER'S SEAT

Replace hub and bearing assembly

REAR WHEEL BEARING ASSEMBLY

Hoist Car Spin Wheel with Wheel Spinner

NOISE OR ROUGHNESS CAN BE HEARD FROM DRIVER'S SEAT

Replace hub and bearing assembly

NOISE OR ROUGHNESS CANNOT BE HEARD

Noise is not Wheel Bearing Assembly

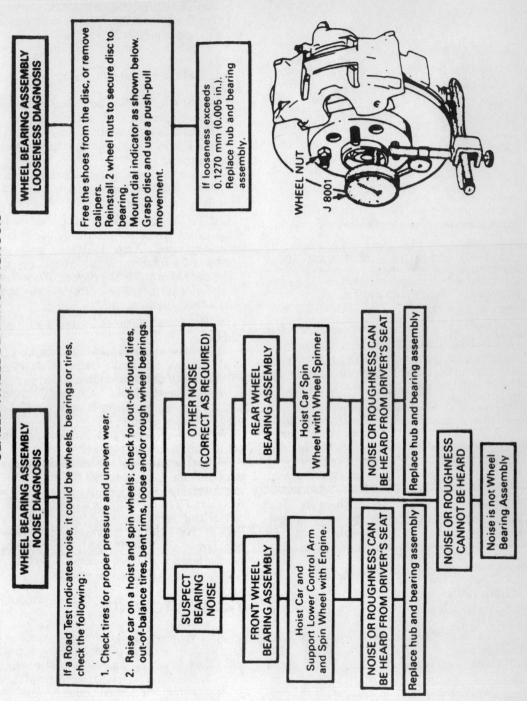

WHEEL NUT

J 8001

Sealed wheel bearing diagnosis chart

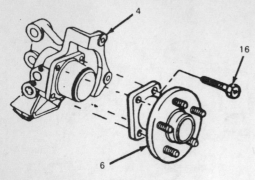

4. Knuckle assembly
6. Hub and bearing assembly
16. Bolt (Torx head)

Rear wheel bearing and hub assembly

ing brake surfaces, use a commercially available brake cleaning fluid.

REMOVAL, PACKING AND INSTALLATION

The W body models are equipped with sealed hub and bearing assemblies. The hub and bearing assemblies are non–serviceable. If the assembly is damaged, the complete unit must be replaced. Refer to the "Sealed Wheel Bearing Diagnosis Chart" in this section.

NOTE: *Sodium-based grease is not compatible with lithium-based grease. Read the package labels and be careful not to mix the two types. If there is any doubt as to the type of grease used, completely clean the old grease from the bearing and hub before replacing.*

Before handling the bearings, there are a few things that you should remember to do and not to do. **Remember to DO the following:**

• Remove all outside dirt from the housing before exposing the bearing.
• Treat a used bearing as gently as you would a new one.
• Work with clean tools in clean surroundings.
• Use clean, dry canvas gloves, or at least clean, dry hands.
• Clean solvents and flushing fluids are a must.
• Use clean paper when laying out the bearings to dry.
• Protect disassembled bearings from rust and dirt. Cover them up.
• Use clean rags to wipe bearings.
• Keep the bearings in oil-proof paper when they are to be stored or are not in use.
• Clean the inside of the housing before replacing the bearing.
Do NOT do the following:
• Don't work in dirty surroundings.

• Don't use dirty, chipped or damaged tools.
• Try not to work on wooden work benches or use wooden mallets.
• Don't handle bearings with dirty or moist hands.
• Do not use gasoline for cleaning; use a safe solvent.
• Do not spin-dry bearings with compressed air. They will be damaged.
• Do not spin dirty bearings.
• Avoid using cotton waste or dirty cloths to wipe bearings.
• Try not to scratch or nick bearing surfaces.
• Do not allow the bearing to come in contact with dirt or rust at any time.

CAUTION: *Some brake pads contain asbestos, which has been determined to be a cancer causing agent. Never clean the brake surfaces with compressed air! Avoid inhaling any dust from any brake surface! When cleaning brake surfaces, use a commercially available brake cleaning fluid.*

1. Raise the vehicle and support with jackstands.
2. Remove the wheel and tire assembly.
3. Remove the brake caliper and support with a wire to the surrounding body.
4. Remove the brake hose bracket, caliper and rotor assembly. Refer to the "Brake Caliper" section in Chapter 9.
5. Remove the four hub and bearing assembly-to-knuckle attaching bolts.
6. **To install:** place the hub and bearing assembly on the knuckle. Install the hub and bearing assembly-to-knuckle attaching bolts and torque to 52 ft. lbs. (70 Nm). Install the brake caliper and torque the mounting bolts to 79 ft. lbs. (107 Nm). Install the wheel and tire assembly. Lower the vehicle and pump the brake pedal a few times before moving the vehicle.

TRAILER TOWING

Your vehicle is designed and intended to be used mainly to carry people. Towing a trailer will affect handling, durability and economy. Your safety and satisfaction depend upon proper use of correct equipment. Also, you should avoid overloads and other abusive use.

Factory trailer towing packages are available on most cars. However, if you are installing a trailer hitch and wiring on your car, there are a few thing that you ought to know.

Information on trailer towing, special equipment and optional equipment is available at your local dealership. You can write to Oldsmobile Customer Service Department, P.O. Box 30095, Lansing, MI 48909. In Canada, General

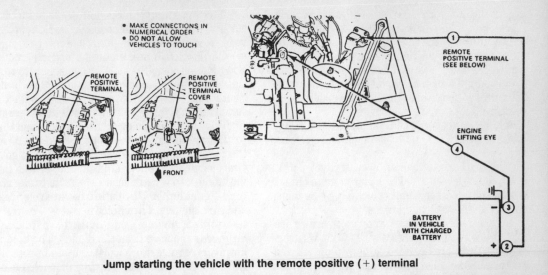

- MAKE CONNECTIONS IN NUMERICAL ORDER
- DO NOT ALLOW VEHICLES TO TOUCH

REMOTE POSITIVE TERMINAL

REMOTE POSITIVE TERMINAL COVER

FRONT

REMOTE POSITIVE TERMINAL (SEE BELOW)

ENGINE LIFTING EYE

BATTERY IN VEHICLE WITH CHARGED BATTERY

Jump starting the vehicle with the remote positive (+) terminal

Motors of Canada Limited, Customer Service Department, Oshawa, Ontario L1J 5Z6.

Trailer Weight

Trailer weight is the first, and most important, factor in determining whether or not your vehicle is suitable for towing the trailer you have in mind. The horsepower-to-weight ratio should be calculated. The basic standard is a ratio of 35:1. That is, 35 pounds of GVW (gross vehicle weight) for every horsepower.

To calculate this ratio, multiply you engine's rated horsepower by 35, then subtract the weight of the vehicle, including passengers and luggage. The resulting figure is the ideal maximum trailer weight that you can tow. One point to consider: a numerically higher axle ratio can offset what appears to be a low trailer weight. If the weight of the trailer that you have in mind is somewhat higher than the weight you just calculated, you might consider changing your rear axle ratio to compensate.

Hitch Weight

There are three kinds of hitches: bumper mounted, frame mounted, and load equalizing.

Bumper mounted hitches are those which attach solely to the vehicle's bumper. Many states prohibit towing with this type of hitch, when it attaches to the vehicle's stock bumper, since it subjects the bumper to stresses for which it was not designed. aftermarket rear step bumpers, designed for trailer towing, are acceptable for use with bumper mounted hitches.

CAUTION: *Do NOT attach any hitch to the bumper bar on the vehicle. A hitch attachment may be made through the bumper*

mounting locations, but only if an additional attachment is also made.

CAUTION: *Frame mounted hitches can be of the type which bolts to two or more points on the frame, plus the bumper, or just to several points on the frame. Frame mounted hitches can also be of the tongue type, for Class I towing, or, of the receiver type, for classes II and III.*

Load equalizing hitches are usually used for large trailers. Most equalizing hitches are welded in place and use equalizing bars and chains to level the vehicle after the trailer is hooked up.

The bolt-on hitches are the most common, since they are relatively easy to install.

Check the gross weight rating of your trailer. Tongue weight is usually figured as 10% of gross trailer weight. Therefore, a trailer with a maximum gross weight of 2,000 lbs. will have a maximum tongue weight of 200 lbs. Class I trailers fall into this category. Class II trailers are those with a gross weight rating of 2,000–3,500 lbs., while Class III trailers fall into the 3,500–6,000 lbs. category. Class IV trailers are those over 6,000 lbs. and are for use with fifth wheel trucks, only.

When you have determined the hitch that you'll need, follow the manufacturer's installation instructions, exactly, especially when it comes to fastener torques. The hitch will subjected to a lot of stress and good hitches come with hardened bolts. Never substitute an inferior bolt for a hardened bolt.

Wiring

Wiring the car for towing is fairly easy. There are a number of good wiring kits available and these should be used, rather than trying to design your own. All trailers will need brake lights and turn signals as well as tail lights and side marker lights. Most states require extra marker lights for overly wide trailers. Also, most states have recently required back-up lights for trailers, and most trailer manufacturers have been building trailers with back-up lights for several years.

Additionally, some Class I, most Class II and just about all Class III trailers will have electric brakes.

Add to this number an accessories wire, to operate trailer internal equipment or to charge the trailer's battery, and you can have as many as seven wires in the harness.

Determine the equipment on your trailer and buy the wiring kit necessary. The kit will contain all the wires needed, plus a plug adapter set which included the female plug, mounted on the bumper or hitch, and the male plug, wired into, or plugged into the trailer harness.

When installing the kit, follow the manufacturer's instructions. The color coding of the wires is standard throughout the industry.

One point to note, some domestic vehicles, and most imported vehicles, have separate turn signals. On most domestic vehicles, the brake lights and rear turn signals operate with the same bulb. For those vehicles with separate turn signals, you can purchase an isolation unit so that the brake lights won't blink whenever the turn signals are operated, or, you can go to your local electronics supply house and buy four diodes to wire in series with the brake and turn signal bulbs. Diodes will isolate the brake and turn signals. The choice is yours. The isolation units are simple and quick to install, but far more expensive than the diodes. The diodes, however, require more work to install properly, since they require the cutting of each bulb's wire and soldering in place of the diode.

One final point, the best kits are those with

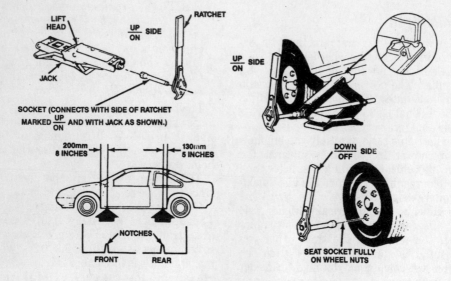

Jacking the vehicle with the service jack

Capacities

Years	Engines	Crankcase including Filter (qts.)	Transmission (pts.) ▲		Fuel Tank (gals.)	Cooling System (qts.)	
			MT	AT		with A/C	without A/C
1988	6-173	4.0	5.0	16.0	16.0	12.6	12.3
1989	6-173	4.0	5.4	12.0	16.0	12.6	12.6
	6-191	4.0	5.4	12.0	16.0	12.6	12.6
1990	4-138	4.0	4.6	12.0	16.5	9.2	9.2
	4-151	4.0	—	12.0	16.5	9.4	9.4
	6-173	4.0	5.4	12.0	16.5	12.6	12.6
	6-191	4.0	5.4	12.0	16.5	12.6	12.6

▲ Drain and refill only

a spring loaded cover on the vehicle mounted socket. This cover prevents dirt and moisture from corroding the terminals. Never let the vehicle socket hang loosely. Always mount it securely to the bumper or hitch.

PUSHING AND TOWING

WARNING: *Push starting is not recommended for cars equipped with a catalytic converter. Raw gas collecting in the converter may cause damage. Jump starting is recommended.*

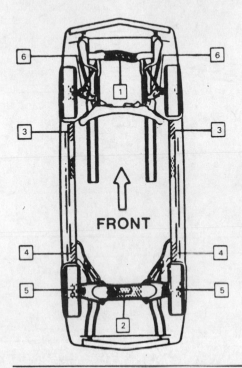

FRONT

NOTICE: When jacking or lifting a vehicle at the frame side rails or other prescribed lift points, be certain that lift pads do not contact the catalytic converter, brake pipes or cables, or fuel lines. Such contact may result in damage or unsatisfactory vehicle performance.

The centerline of gravity on front wheel drive vehicles is further forward than on rear-wheel-drive vehicles. Therefore, whenever removing major components from the rear of a front-wheel-drive vehicle, while supported on a hoist, it is mandatory to support the vehicle in a manner to prevent the possibility of the vehicle tipping forward.

CAUTION: To help avoid personal injury when a vehicle is on a hoist, provide additional support for the vehicle at the opposite end from which components are being removed. This will reduce the possibility of the vehicle falling off of the hoist.

When supporting the vehicle with jack stands, the supports should be placed under the body side rail pinchwelds or similar strong and stable structure.

CAUTION: Use jacking pad only for raising the vehicle with a floor jack. Do not use rods, trailing arm or jacking pad for pulling or towing the vehicle.

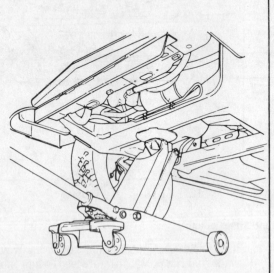

1 WHEN USING FLOOR JACK, LIFT ON CENTER OF FRONT CROSSMEMBER

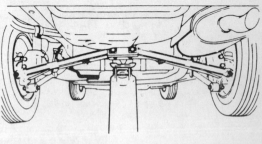

2 WHEN USING FLOOR JACK, LIFT ON REAR JACK PAD

Vehicle jacking and lifting points

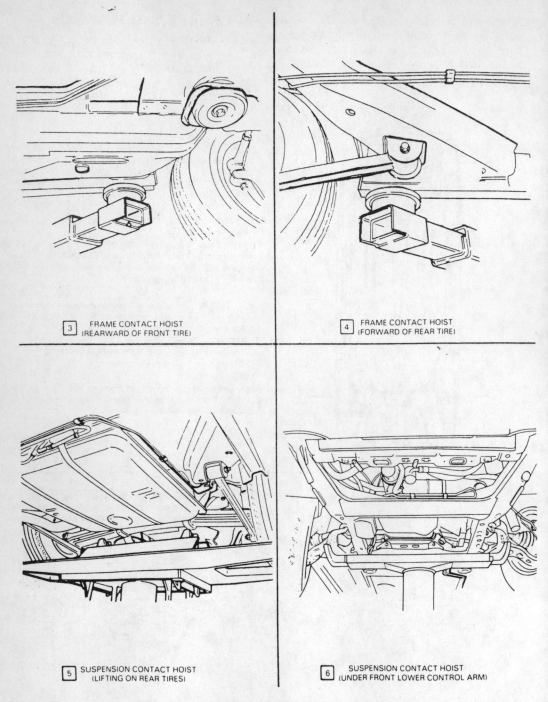

3 FRAME CONTACT HOIST
(REARWARD OF FRONT TIRE)

4 FRAME CONTACT HOIST
(FORWARD OF REAR TIRE)

5 SUSPENSION CONTACT HOIST
(LIFTING ON REAR TIRES)

6 SUSPENSION CONTACT HOIST
(UNDER FRONT LOWER CONTROL ARM)

Vehicle jacking and lifting points

To push start your manual transmission equipped car (automatic transmission models cannot be push started), make sure of bumper alignment. If the bumper of the car pushing does not match with your car's bumper, it would be wise to tie an old tire either on the back of your car, or on the front of the pushing car. Switch the ignition to **ON** and depress the clutch pedal. Shift the transaxle to third gear

and hold the accelerator pedal about halfway down. signal the push car to proceed, when the car speed reaches about 10 mph, gradually release the clutch pedal. The car engine should start, if not have the car towed.

If the transaxle is in proper working order, the car can be towed with the front wheels on the ground for distances under 15 miles at speeds no greater then 30 mph. If the transaxle

Follow Schedule I if the the car is mainly operated under one or more of the following conditions:

- When most trips are less than 4 miles (6 kilometers).
- When most trips are less than 10 miles (16 kilometers) and outside temperatures remain below freezing.
- When most trips include extended idling and/or frequent low-speed operation as in stop-and-go traffic.
- Towing a trailer**
- Operating in dusty areas.

Schedule I should also be followed if the car is used for delivery service, police, taxi or other commercial applications.

The services shown in this schedule up to 48,000 miles (80 000 km) are to be performed after 48,000 miles at the same intervals

ITEM NO.	TO BE SERVICED	WHEN TO PERFORM Miles (Kilometers) or Months, Whichever Occurs First — MILES (000)	3	6	9	12	15	18	21	24	27	30	33	36	39	42	45	48
		KILOMETERS (000)	5	10	15	20	25	30	35	40	45	50	55	60	65	70	75	80
1	Engine Oil & Oil Filter Change*	Every 3,000 mi (5 000 km) or 3 mos.	•	•	•	•	•	•	•	•	•	•	•	•	•	•	•	•
2	Chassis Lubrication	Every other oil change		•		•		•		•		•		•		•		•
3	Carb. Choke & Hose Insp.* (If Equipped)††	At 6,000 mi. (10 000 km) and then every 30,000 mi. (50 000 km)		•										•				
4	Carb. or Throttle Body Mount Bolt Torque (Some Models)	At 6,000 mi. (10 000 km) only		•														
5	Eng. Idle Speed Adj. (Some Models)*			•								•						
6	Tire & Wheel Insp. and Rotation	At 6,000 mi. (10,000 km) and then every 15,000 mi. (25,000 km)		•					•					•				
7	Vac. or Air Pump Drive Belt Insp.*	Every 30,000 mi. (50 000 km) or 24 mos.										•						
8	Cooling System Service*											•						
9	Wheel Brg. Repack (Rear-Wheel-Drive Cars Only)	See explanation for service interval																
10	Transmission/Transaxle Service																	
11	Spark Plug Replacmen*											•						
12	Spark Plug Wire Insp. (Some Models)*	Every 30,000 mi. (50 000 km)										•						
13	PCV Valve Insp. (Some Models)*††											•						
14	EGR System Insp.*††	Every 30,000 mi. (50 000 km) or 36 mos.										•						
15	Air Cleaner & PCV Filter Repl.*											•						
16	Eng. Timing Check (Some Models)*											•						
17	Fuel Tank, Cap & Lines Insp.*††	Every 30,000 mi. (50 000 km)										•						
18	Thermostatically Controlled Air Cleaner Insp. (Some Models)*											•						

FOOTNOTES: * An Emission Control Service

†† The U.S. Environmental Protection Agency has determined that the failure to perform this maintenance item will not nullify the emission warranty or limit recall liability prior to the completion of vehicle useful life. General Motors, however, urges that all recommended maintenance services be performed at the indicated intervals and the maintenance be recorded in section C of the owner's maintenance schedule.

** Trailoring is not recommended for some models. See the Owner's Manual for details.

Follow Schedule II only if none of the driving conditions specified in Schedule I apply.

The services shown in this schedule up to 45,000 miles (75,000 km) are to be performed after 45,000 miles at the same intervals.

ITEM NO.	TO BE SERVICED	WHEN TO PERFORM — Miles (Kilometers) or Months, Whichever Occurs First	MILES (000) 7.5 / KM (000) 12.5	15 / 25	22.5 / 37.5	30 / 50	37.5 / 62.5	45 / 75
1	Engine Oil Change*	Every 7,500 mi. (12 500 km) or 12 mos.	•	•	•	•	•	•
	Filter Change*	At first and every other oil change or 12 mos.	•		•		•	
2	Chassis Lubrication	Every 7,500 mi. (12 500 km) or 12 mos.	•	•	•	•	•	•
3	Carb. Choke & Hose Insp.* (If Equipped)††	At 7,500 mi. (12 500 km) and then at each 30,000 mi. (50 000 km) interval	•				•	
4	Carb. or Throttle Body Mount Bolt Torque (Some Models)*		•					
5	Eng. Idle Speed Adj. (Some Models)*	At 7,500 mi. (12 500 km) only	•					
6	Tire & Wheel Insp. and Rotation	At 7,500 mi. (12 500 km) and then every 15,000 mi. (25 000 km)	•		•		•	
7	Vac. or Air Pump Drive Belt Insp.*	Every 30,000 mi. (50 000 km) or 24 mos.				•		
8	Cooling System Service*	Every 30,000 mi. (50 000 km)				•		
9	Wheel Brg. Repack (Rear-Wheel-Drive Cars Only)	Every 30,000 mi. (50 000 km)				•		
10	Transmission/Transaxle Service	See explanation for service interval						
11	Spark Plug Replacement*					•		
12	Spark Plug Wire Insp. (Some Models)*	Every 30,000 mi. (50 000 km)				•		
13	PCV Valve Insp. (Some Models)*††					•		
14	EGR System Insp.*††					•		
15	Air Cleaner & PCV Filter Repl.*	Every 30,000 mi. (50 000 km) or 36 mos.				•		
16	Eng. Timing Check (Some Models)*					•		
17	Fuel Tank, Cap & Lines Insp.††	Every 30,000 mi. (50 000 km)				•		
18	Thermostatically Controlled Air Cleaner Insp. (Some Models)*					•		

FOOTNOTES: * An Emission Control Service

†† The U.S. Environmental Protection Agency has determined that the failure to perform this maintenance item will not nullify the emission warranty or limit recall liability prior to the completion of vehicle useful life. General Motors, however, urges that all recommended maintenance services be performed at the indicated intervals and the maintenance be recorded in section C of the owner's maintenance schedule.

is known to be damaged or if the car has to be towed over 15 miles or over 30 mph the car must be dollied or towed with the rear wheels raised and the steering wheel secured so that the front wheels remain in the straight-ahead position. The steering wheel must be clamped with a special clamping device designed for towing service. If the key controlled lock is used damage to the lock and steering column may occur.

JACKING

CAUTION: *The jack that is furnished with the vehicle is ONLY to be used in an emergency to remove a flat tire. Never get beneath the car or, start or run the engine while the vehicle is supported by the jack. Personal injury may result if these procedures are not followed exactly.*

CHANGING A FLAT TIRE

1. Park on a level surface and apply the parking brake firmly.
2. Turn the 4-way hazard flashers ON.
3. Shift the transaxle gear selector into the PARK position.
4. Remove the jacking tools and spare tire from the stowage area.
5. Connect the socket with side of ratchet marked UP/ON . Raise the jack slowly. NOT under vehicle.
6. Position the jack head under the vehicle closest to the tire to be changed.
7. Raise the jack until the lift head mates with the vehicle notches as shown in the jacking previous illustration. Do NOT raise the vehicle.
8. Remove the wheel cover using the wedge end of ratchet. Connect the DOWN/OFF side of the ratchet to the socket and loosen, but do not remove the wheel nuts.
9. Connect the UP/ON side of the ratchet to the jack as shown in the illustration.
10. Raise the vehicle so the inflated spare will clear the surface when installed.
11. Remove the wheel nuts and wheel.

To install:
12. Install the spare tire and loosely tighten the wheel nuts.
13. Connect the UP/ON side of the ratchet to the socket and tighten the wheel nuts in a criss-cross sequence.
14. Lower the vehicle and remove the jack.
15. Retighten the wheel nuts securely.
16. Install the wheel cover and securely store all jacking equipment.
17. Start driving the vehicle slowly to see if everything is secure.

Engine Performance and Tune-Up

2

TUNE-UP PROCEDURES

In order to extract the full measure of performance and economy from your engine it is essential that it be properly tuned at regular intervals. A regular tune-up will keep your vehicle's engine running smoothly and will prevent the annoying minor breakdowns and poor performance associated with an untuned engine.

A complete tune-up should be performed every 30,000 miles. This interval should be halved if the vehicle is operated under severe conditions, such as trailer towing, prolonged idling, continual stop and start driving, or if starting or running problems are noticed. It is assumed that the routine maintenance described in Chapter 1 has been kept up, as this will have a decided effect on the results of a tune-up. All of the applicable steps of a tune-up should be followed in order, as the result is a cumulative one.

If the specifications on the tune-up sticker in the engine compartment disagree with the Tune-Up Specifications chart in this chapter, the figures on the sticker must be used. The sticker often reflects changes made during the production run.

Spark Plugs

A typical spark plug consists of a metal shell surrounding a ceramic insulator. A metal electrode extends downward through the center of the insulator and protrudes a small distance. Located at the end of the plug and attached to the side of the outer metal shell is the side electrode. The side electrode bends in at a 90° angle so that its tip is even with, and parallel to, the tip of the center electrode. The distance between these two electrodes (measured in thousandths of an inch) is called the spark plug gap. The spark plug in no way produces a spark but merely provides a gap across which the current can arc. The coil produces anywhere from 20,000 to 40,000 volts or more, which travels from the coils, through the spark plug wires to the spark plugs. The current passes along the center electrode and jumps the gap to the side electrode, and, in so doing, ignites the air/fuel mixture in the combustion chamber.

SPARK PLUG HEAT RANGE

Spark plug heat range is the ability of the plug to dissipate heat. The longer the insulator (or the farther it extends into the engine), the hotter the plug will operate; the shorter the insulator the cooler it will operate. A plug that

Tune-up Specifications

| Engine | Years | Spark Plugs | | Ignition Timing (deg.) | | Idle Speed | |
		Type	Gap (in.)	Man. Trans.	Auto. Trans.	Man. Trans.	Auto. Trans.
4-138	1990	FR3L8	0.035	Not adjustable		Not adjustable	
4-151	1990	R43CTS6	0.060	Not adjustable		Not adjustable	
6-173	1988–90	R43-LTSE	0.045	Not adjustable		Not adjustable	
6-191	1989–90	R43-LTSE	0.045	Not adjustable		Not adjustable	

Troubleshooting Engine Performance

Problem	Cause	Solution
Hard starting (engine cranks normally)	• Binding linkage, choke valve or choke piston	• Repair as necessary
	• Restricted choke vacuum diaphragm	• Clean passages
	• Improper fuel level	• Adjust float level
	• Dirty, worn or faulty needle valve and seat	• Repair as necessary
	• Float sticking	• Repair as necessary
	• Faulty fuel pump	• Replace fuel pump
	• Incorrect choke cover adjustment	• Adjust choke cover
	• Inadequate choke unloader adjustment	• Adjust choke unloader
	• Faulty ignition coil	• Test and replace as necessary
	• Improper spark plug gap	• Adjust gap
	• Incorrect ignition timing	• Adjust timing
	• Incorrect valve timing	• Check valve timing; repair as necessary
Rough idle or stalling	• Incorrect curb or fast idle speed	• Adjust curb or fast idle speed
	• Incorrect ignition timing	• Adjust timing to specification
	• Improper feedback system operation	• Refer to Chapter 4
	• Improper fast idle cam adjustment	• Adjust fast idle cam
	• Faulty EGR valve operation	• Test EGR system and replace as necessary
	• Faulty PCV valve air flow	• Test PCV valve and replace as necessary
	• Choke binding	• Locate and eliminate binding condition
	• Faulty TAC vacuum motor or valve	• Repair as necessary
	• Air leak into manifold vacuum	• Inspect manifold vacuum connections and repair as necessary
	• Improper fuel level	• Adjust fuel level
	• Faulty distributor rotor or cap	• Replace rotor or cap
	• Improperly seated valves	• Test cylinder compression, repair as necessary
	• Incorrect ignition wiring	• Inspect wiring and correct as necessary
	• Faulty ignition coil	• Test coil and replace as necessary
	• Restricted air vent or idle passages	• Clean passages
	• Restricted air cleaner	• Clean or replace air cleaner filler element
	• Faulty choke vacuum diaphragm	• Repair as necessary
Faulty low-speed operation	• Restricted idle transfer slots	• Clean transfer slots
	• Restricted idle air vents and passages	• Clean air vents and passages
	• Restricted air cleaner	• Clean or replace air cleaner filter element
	• Improper fuel level	• Adjust fuel level
	• Faulty spark plugs	• Clean or replace spark plugs
	• Dirty, corroded, or loose ignition secondary circuit wire connections	• Clean or tighten secondary circuit wire connections
	• Improper feedback system operation	• Refer to Chapter 4
	• Faulty ignition coil high voltage wire	• Replace ignition coil high voltage wire
	• Faulty distributor cap	• Replace cap
Faulty acceleration	• Improper accelerator pump stroke	• Adjust accelerator pump stroke
	• Incorrect ignition timing	• Adjust timing
	• Inoperative pump discharge check ball or needle	• Clean or replace as necessary
	• Worn or damaged pump diaphragm or piston	• Replace diaphragm or piston

Troubleshooting Engine Performance (cont.)

Problem	Cause	Solution
Faulty acceleration (cont.)	• Leaking carburetor main body cover gasket	• Replace gasket
	• Engine cold and choke set too lean	• Adjust choke cover
	• Improper metering rod adjustment (BBD Model carburetor)	• Adjust metering rod
	• Faulty spark plug(s)	• Clean or replace spark plug(s)
	• Improperly seated valves	• Test cylinder compression, repair as necessary
	• Faulty ignition coil	• Test coil and replace as necessary
	• Improper feedback system operation	• Refer to Chapter 4
Faulty high speed operation	• Incorrect ignition timing	• Adjust timing
	• Faulty distributor centrifugal advance mechanism	• Check centrifugal advance mechanism and repair as necessary
	• Faulty distributor vacuum advance mechanism	• Check vacuum advance mechanism and repair as necessary
	• Low fuel pump volume	• Replace fuel pump
	• Wrong spark plug air gap or wrong plug	• Adjust air gap or install correct plug
	• Faulty choke operation	• Adjust choke cover
	• Partially restricted exhaust manifold, exhaust pipe, catalytic converter, muffler, or tailpipe	• Eliminate restriction
	• Restricted vacuum passages	• Clean passages
	• Improper size or restricted main jet	• Clean or replace as necessary
	• Restricted air cleaner	• Clean or replace filter element as necessary
	• Faulty distributor rotor or cap	• Replace rotor or cap
	• Faulty ignition coil	• Test coil and replace as necessary
	• Improperly seated valve(s)	• Test cylinder compression, repair as necessary
	• Faulty valve spring(s)	• Inspect and test valve spring tension, replace as necessary
	• Incorrect valve timing	• Check valve timing and repair as necessary
	• Intake manifold restricted	• Remove restriction or replace manifold
	• Worn distributor shaft	• Replace shaft
	• Improper feedback system operation	• Refer to Chapter 4
Misfire at all speeds	• Faulty spark plug(s)	• Clean or replace spark plug(s)
	• Faulty spark plug wire(s)	• Replace as necessary
	• Faulty distributor cap or rotor	• Replace cap or rotor
	• Faulty ignition coil	• Test coil and replace as necessary
	• Primary ignition circuit shorted or open intermittently	• Troubleshoot primary circuit and repair as necessary
	• Improperly seated valve(s)	• Test cylinder compression, repair as necessary
	• Faulty hydraulic tappet(s)	• Clean or replace tappet(s)
	• Improper feedback system operation	• Refer to Chapter 4
	• Faulty valve spring(s)	• Inspect and test valve spring tension, repair as necessary
	• Worn camshaft lobes	• Replace camshaft
	• Air leak into manifold	• Check manifold vacuum and repair as necessary
	• Improper carburetor adjustment	• Adjust carburetor
	• Fuel pump volume or pressure low	• Replace fuel pump
	• Blown cylinder head gasket	• Replace gasket
	• Intake or exhaust manifold passage(s) restricted	• Pass chain through passage(s) and repair as necessary
	• Incorrect trigger wheel installed in distributor	• Install correct trigger wheel

Troubleshooting Engine Performance (cont.)

Problem	Cause	Solution
Power not up to normal	• Incorrect ignition timing	• Adjust timing
	• Faulty distributor rotor	• Replace rotor
	• Trigger wheel loose on shaft	• Reposition or replace trigger wheel
	• Incorrect spark plug gap	• Adjust gap
	• Faulty fuel pump	• Replace fuel pump
	• Incorrect valve timing	• Check valve timing and repair as necessary
	• Faulty ignition coil	• Test coil and replace as necessary
	• Faulty ignition wires	• Test wires and replace as necessary
	• Improperly seated valves	• Test cylinder compression and repair as necessary
	• Blown cylinder head gasket	• Replace gasket
	• Leaking piston rings	• Test compression and repair as necessary
	• Worn distributor shaft	• Replace shaft
	• Improper feedback system operation	• Refer to Chapter 4
Intake backfire	• Improper ignition timing	• Adjust timing
	• Faulty accelerator pump discharge	• Repair as necessary
	• Defective EGR CTO valve	• Replace EGR CTO valve
	• Defective TAC vacuum motor or valve	• Repair as necessary
	• Lean air/fuel mixture	• Check float level or manifold vacuum for air leak. Remove sediment from bowl
Exhaust backfire	• Air leak into manifold vacuum	• Check manifold vacuum and repair as necessary
	• Faulty air injection diverter valve	• Test diverter valve and replace as necessary
	• Exhaust leak	• Locate and eliminate leak
Ping or spark knock	• Incorrect ignition timing	• Adjust timing
	• Distributor centrifugal or vacuum advance malfunction	• Inspect advance mechanism and repair as necessary
	• Excessive combustion chamber deposits	• Remove with combustion chamber cleaner
	• Air leak into manifold vacuum	• Check manifold vacuum and repair as necessary
	• Excessively high compression	• Test compression and repair as necessary
	• Fuel octane rating excessively low	• Try alternate fuel source
	• Sharp edges in combustion chamber	• Grind smooth
	• EGR valve not functioning properly	• Test EGR system and replace as necessary
Surging (at cruising to top speeds)	• Low carburetor fuel level	• Adjust fuel level
	• Low fuel pump pressure or volume	• Replace fuel pump
	• Metering rod(s) not adjusted properly (BBD Model Carburetor)	• Adjust metering rod
	• Improper PCV valve air flow	• Test PCV valve and replace as necessary
	• Air leak into manifold vacuum	• Check manifold vacuum and repair as necessary
	• Incorrect spark advance	• Test and replace as necessary
	• Restricted main jet(s)	• Clean main jet(s)
	• Undersize main jet(s)	• Replace main jet(s)
	• Restricted air vents	• Clean air vents
	• Restricted fuel filter	• Replace fuel filter
	• Restricted air cleaner	• Clean or replace air cleaner filter element
	• EGR valve not functioning properly	• Test EGR system and replace as necessary
	• Improper feedback system operation	• Refer to Chapter 4

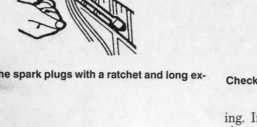

Remove the spark plugs with a ratchet and long extension

Check the spark plug gap with a wire feeler gauge

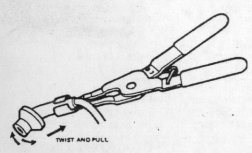

TWIST AND PULL

Special pliers used to remove the boots and wire from the spark plug

absorbs little heat and remains too cool will quickly accumulate deposits of oil and carbon since it is not hot enough to burn them off. This leads to plug fouling and consequently to misfiring. A plug that absorbs too much heat will have deposits also, but due to the excessive heat, the electrodes will burn away quickly and in some instances, pre-ignition may result. Pre-ignition takes place when plug tips get so hot that they glow sufficiently to ignite the fuel/air mixture before the actual spark occurs. This early ignition will usually cause pinging during low speeds and heavy loads.

The general rule of thumb for choosing the correct heat range when picking a spark plug is, if most of your driving is long distance, high speed travel, use a colder plug; if most of your driving is stop and go, use a hotter plug. Original equipment plugs are compromise plugs, but most people never have occasion to change their plugs from the factory recommended heat range. The best rule of thumb is to use the factory recommended spark plug.

REPLACING SPARK PLUGS

WARNING: *To avoid engine damage, do NOT remove spark plugs when the engine is warm.*

A set of spark plugs usually requires replacement after about 30,000 miles on cars with electronic ignition, depending on your style of driv-

ing. In normal operation, plug gap increases about 0.001 inch (0.0254mm) for every 1,000–2,500 miles. As the gap increases, the plug's voltage requirement also increases. It requires a greater voltage to jump the wider gap and about two to three times as much voltage to fire a plug at high speeds than at idle.

NOTE: *On 1990 Luminas equipped with the 4 cyl. engine, the spark plugs are located on the front of the engine just below the valve cover. It may be necessary to remove the air cleaner, and set it to one side, without disconnecting any tubing or wiring.*

On the vehicles equipped with the 6 cyl. engine, the spark plugs are located on both sides of the engine. The air induction hose has to removed and set aside.

The 2.3L QUAD 4 (VIN A, D) spark plugs are located under the ignition coil and module assembly. To gain access to the spark plugs, the coil and module assembly has to be removed. Refer to the "Spark Plug" section in this chapter.

When you're removing spark plugs, you should work on one at a time. Don't start by removing the plug wires all at once, because unless you number them, they may become mixed up. Take a minute before you begin and number the wires with tape. The best location for numbering is near where the wires come out of the cap.

WARNING: *To avoid engine damage, do NOT remove spark plugs when the engine is hot. The spark plug threads may be stripped if removed on a hot engine.*

Mark each spark plug wire with tape to ensure proper wire reinstallation. Only replace one spark plug at a time.

All Engines (Except 2.3L QUAD4)

1. Twist the spark plug boot and remove the boot and wire from the plug. Do not pull on the wire itself as this may damage the wire.

2. If possible, use a brush or rag to clean the area around the spark plug. Make sure that all the dirt is removed so that none will enter the cylinder after the plug is removed.

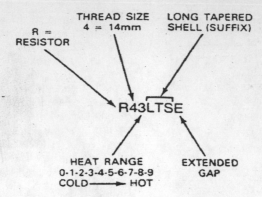

```
                 THREAD SIZE      LONG TAPERED
                   4 = 14mm       SHELL (SUFFIX)
      R =
    RESISTOR


                      R43LTSE


                HEAT RANGE          EXTENDED
              0-1-2-3-4-5-6-7-8-9      GAP
               COLD ----> HOT
```

• = COPPER CORE
L = LONG REACH
S = EXTENDED TIP   SUFFIXES ARE COMBINED TO FORM SUCH
T = TAPERED SEAT SHELL DESIGN   DESIGNATIONS AS: LS, LTS, TS, ETC.
TSE = TAPERED SEAT WITH EXTENDED TIP
X = WIDE GAP
Z = SPECIAL GAP (USUALLY DENOTES WIDE GAP) ALSO EUROPEAN
6 = 1.5mm (0.60 IN.) GAP
8 = 2.0mm (0.80 IN.) GAP

Spark plug specifications

3. Remove the spark plug using the proper size socket. Either a $5/8$ inch or $13/16$ inch size socket depending on the engine. Turn the socket counterclockwise to remove the plug. Be sure to hold the socket straight on the plug to avoid breaking the plug, or rounding off the hex on the plug.

4. Once the plug is out, check it against the plugs shown in the Color section in this book to determine engine condition. This is crucial since plug readings are vital signs of engine condition.

5. Use a round wire feeler gauge to check the plug gap. The correct size gauge should pass through the electrode gap with a slight drag. If you're in doubt, try one size smaller and one larger. The smaller gauge should go through easily while the larger one should not go through at all. If the gap is incorrect, use the electrode bending tool on the end of the gauge to adjust the gap. When adjusting the gap, always bend the side electrode. The center electrode is non-adjustable.

6. Apply a drop of penetrating oil or anti-seize compound on the threads of the new plug and install it. Don't oil the threads too heavily. Turn the plug in clockwise by hand until it is snug.

7. When the plug is finger tight, tighten it with a wrench. Take care not to overtighten. Torque the plug to 18 ft. lbs. (24 Nm).

8. Install the plug boot firmly over the plug. Proceed to the next plug.

2.3L QUAD 4 (VIN A,D)

NOTE: *The 2.3L QUAD 4 (VIN A, D) engine has aluminum cylinder heads. Allow the engine to cool before removing the spark plugs or the engine may be damaged.*

1. Disconnect the negative (–) battery cable.
2. Remove the air cleaner assembly.
3. Remove the four ignition cover-to-cylinder head bolts.
4. If the spark plug boot sticks, use a spark plug connector removing tool J-36011 or equivalent to remove with a twisting motion.
5. Remove the ignition cover and set aside.
6. Clean any dirt away from the spark plug recess area.
7. Remove the spark plugs with a spark plug socket.

To install:

1. The 2.3L engine uses AC Type FR3LS and the gap is 0.035 inch (0.89mm).
2. Gap and install the four spark plugs. Torque the plugs to 17 ft. lbs. (23 Nm), do not overtighten.
3. If removed, install the plug boots and retainers-to-ignition cover.
4. Apply dielectric compound to the plug boot.
5. Install the ignition cover-to-engine while carefully aligning the boots with the spark plug terminals.
6. Apply thread locking compound Locktite or equivalent to the ignition cover bolts. Install the bolts and torque to 15 ft. lbs. (20 Nm).

Spark plug connector tool J–36011 — 2.3L Quad 4

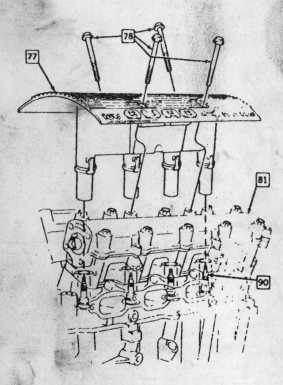

77. Ignition coil and module assembly
78. Mounting bolts
81. Camshaft housing cover
90. Spark plug

Spark plug removal — 2.3L Quad 4

7. If removed, connect the ignition cover electrical connectors.

8. Install the air cleaner and connect the negative battery cable.

CHECKING AND REPLACING SPARK PLUG CABLES

Your vehicle is equipped with an electronic ignition system which utilizes 8mm wires to conduct the hotter spark produced (except 2.3L QUAD 4 (VIN A, D). The boots on these wires are designed to cover the spark plug cavities on the cylinder head.

NOTE: *The 2.3L QUAD 4 (VIN A, D) does NOT us spark plug wires. The coil assembly is connected directly to the spark plug with rubber connectors.*

Visually inspect the spark plug cables for burns, cuts, or breaks in the insulation. Check the spark plug boots and the nipples on the distributor cap and coil. Replace any damaged wiring. If no physical damage is obvious, the wires can be checked with an ohmmeter for excessive resistance. (See the tune-up and troubleshooting section).

When installing a new set of spark plug cables, replace the cables one at a time so there will be no mix-up. Start by replacing the longest cable first. Install the boot firmly over the spark plug. Route the wire exactly the same as the original. Insert the nipple firmly into the tower on the distributor cap. Repeat the process for each cable.

NOTE: *Always coat the terminals of any wire removed or replaced with a thin layer of dielectric compound.*

When installing a wire be sure it is firmly mounted over or on the plug, distributor cap connector or coil terminal.

FIRING ORDERS

NOTE: *To avoid confusion, tag using a piece of tap, and remove the spark plug wire one at a time, for replacement.*

NOTE: *The 2.3L QUAD 4 (VIN A,D) do NOT have spark plug wires.*

If new wires have been installed (original wires are marked for cylinder location) and are not identified, or the wires have been removed from the distributor cap, the firing order is, 1–3–4–2 on the 2.5L 4 cyl. engine and 1–2–3–4–5–6 on the 2.8L and 3.1L 6 cyl. engines.

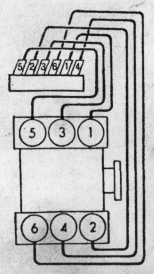

**2.8L and 3.1L distributorless firing order:
1–2–3–4–5–6**

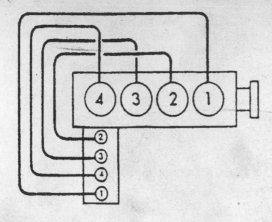

GM (Pontiac) 2.5 engine with Direct Ignition System (DIS) Firing order 1-3-4-2 Distributorless

Electronic Ignition System

Your car uses an electronic ignition system. The purpose of using an electronic ignition system is: To eliminate the deterioration of spark quality which occur in the breaker point ignition system as the breaker points wore. To extend maintenance intervals. To provide a more intense and reliable spark at every firing impulse in order to ignite the leaner gas mixtures necessary to control emissions.

The Direct Ignition System (DIS) is a distributorless ignition system installed on all 1988–90 "W" body engines. The (DIS) system uses individual coils (2 for L4 and 3 for V6), crankshaft sensor, ignition module and electronic control module (ECM) to directly transfer spark to the spark plugs without the use of a distributor assembly. No vacuum or mechanical advances are used. The 1990 2.3L QUAD 4 engine uses the Integrated Direct Ignition (IDI) system. This system is the same as the (DIS) system except the (DIS) uses three coils and the (IDI) system uses two coils.

The (DIS) and (IDI) systems uses a "Waste Spark" method of spark distribution. Each cylinder is paired with its opposing cylinder in the firing order, so that one cylinder fires on the compression stroke and the other on the exhaust stroke. Most of the voltage is used for the compression stroke because little voltage is needed on the exhaust stroke. This dual firing helps reduce exhaust emissions.

CAUTION: *Never ground the TACH terminal; serious module and ignition coil damage will result. If there is any doubt as to the correct tachometer hook-up, check with the tachometer manufacturer. Do not come in contact with any spark plug wires while the*

engine is running. 20,000–30,000 volts are passing to the spark plugs with engine running.

Ignition Timing

The Direct Ignition System (DIS) does NOT require any timing or crankshaft sensor adjustments.

Valve Lash

All the engines in this book are equipped with hydraulic valve lifters that require NO valve lash adjustment. The adjustment to zero lash is maintained automatically by hydraulic pressure in the lifter. If disassembly is required, refer to the "Rocker Arm" removal and installation procedures in Chapter 3.

Idle Speed

ADJUSTMENT

2.5L (Lumina Only) VIN R

NOTE: *The following procedures explain setting the idle speed. They should not be attempted by the Do-it-Yourself mechanic because expensive equipment is required and is not practical to purchase this equipment for one time usage.*

These adjustments are controlled by the Electronic Control Module (ECM). No adjustments are necessary unless the throttle body assembly has been replaced. Below is the procedure for adjusting the idle speed.

NOTE: *The throttle stop screw is used for regulating minimum idle speed and the adjustment is factory set. The screw is covered with a plug to discourage unauthorized adjustments. However, if it is necessary to gain access to the idle stop screw, the following procedures eliminate the need to remove the throttle body from the manifold.*

CAUTION: *To prevent the engine from running at high rpm, make sure the ignition is OFF and the vehicle is in NEUTRAL before connecting the IAC (Idle Air Control) valve. Failure to do so may result in the vehicle moving.*

1. Start the engine and run until it reaches normal operating temperature. Then turn the ignition OFF.
2. Remove the air cleaner and gasket. Block the front wheels and apply the parking brake.
3. Pierce the idle stop screw plug with an awl and apply leverage to remove it.
4. Turn the ignition to the ON position. Connect a SCAN tool to the ALDL (assembly line diagnostic link) connector in the computer harness under the dash panel on the driver's side.

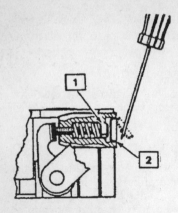

1. Idle speed adjustment screw
2. Idle stop screw plug

Idle speed adjustment screw — 2.5L L4 throttle body injection (TBI)

5. Select the field service mode on the SCAN tool. This will cause the IAC (idle air control) valve to seat in the throttle the ignition ON, but do NOT start the engine. Wait at least 45 seconds.

6. Disconnect the IAC valve electrical connector.

7. Start the engine and place the transaxle in the PARK position. The throttle plate may have to be kept open to maintain an idle.

8. Select "Engine rpm" on the SCAN tool and read engine rpm.

a. No accessories or cooling fan should be on.

b. Make sure the cruise control is not holding the throttle plates open.

c. Idle speed should be 600 ± 50 rpm.

9. Adjust the idle stop screw to obtain 600 ± 50 rpm. Turn the ignition OFF and reconnect the IAC valve electrical connector.

10. Apply silicone sealant or equivalent to cover the idle stop screw.

11. Reset the IAC valve as follows:

a. Select"Engine rpm" on the SCAN tool.

b. Start the engine and hold the speed to 200 rpm.

c. Select the "Field Service Mode" on the SCAN tool. This will reset the IAC valve pintle position.

d. Exit the "Field Service Mode" and allow the engine to idle.

12. Disconnect the SCAN tool and install the air cleaner assembly.

13. Remove the blocks from the wheels and road test to check for proper operation.

2.3L QUAD 4, 2.8L and 3.1L Engines

Multi-Port Injection

IDLE LEAN PROCEDURE

NOTE: *The following procedures explain setting the idle speed. They should not be attempted by the Do-it-Yourself mechanic because expensive equipment is required and is not practical to purchase this equipment for one time usage.*

The Multi-Port Injection system idle speed is controlled by the Electronic Control Module (ECM) and should not be adjusted unless the throttle body is removed or the battery is disconnected.

Any time the battery is disconnected, the programmed position of the IAC (idle air control) valve pintle is lost and replaced with a default value. This condition may cause the engine idle to fluctuate for approximately seven minutes. To return the IAC valve pintle to the proper position, perform the following.

1. Reconnect the battery and place the A/C controls on OFF.

2. Set the parking brake and block the wheels.

3. Start the engine and place the automatic transaxle in "Drive" and "Neutral" for manual transaxles.

4. Run the engine until it reaches normal operating temperature. This will allow the ECM (electronic control module) memory to be updated with the correct IAC valve pintle position. The idle should stabilize after this procedure is performed.

Engine and Engine Overhaul

3

ENGINE ELECTRICAL

Understanding the Engine Electrical System

The engine electrical system can be broken down into three separate and distinct systems:

1. The starting system.
2. The charging system.
3. The ignition system.

BATTERY AND STARTING SYSTEM

Basic Operating Principles

The battery is the first link in the chain of mechanisms which work together to provide cranking of the automobile engine. In most modern cars, the battery is a lead/acid electrochemical device consisting of six 2V subsections connected in series so the unit is capable of producing approximately 12V of electrical power. Each subsection, or cell, consists of a series of positive and negative plates held a short distance apart in a solution of sulfuric acid and water. The two types of plates are of dissimilar metals. This causes a chemical reaction to be set up, and it is this reaction which produces current flow from the battery when its positive and negative terminals are connected to an electrical appliance such as a lamp or motor. The continued transfer of electrons would eventually convert the sulfuric acid in the electrolyte to water, and make the two plates identical in chemical composition. As electrical energy is removed from the battery, its voltage output tends to drop. Thus, measuring battery voltage and battery electrolyte composition are two ways of checking the ability of the unit to supply power. During the starting of the engine, electrical energy is removed from the battery. However, if the charging circuit is in good condition and the operating conditions are normal, the power removed from the battery will be replaced by the generator (or alternator) which will force electrons back through the battery, reversing the normal flow, and restoring the battery to its original chemical state.

The battery and starting motor are linked by very heavy electrical cables designed to minimize resistance to the flow of current. Generally, the major power supply cable that leaves the battery goes directly to the starter, while other electrical system needs are supplied by a smaller cable. During starter operation, power flows from the battery to the starter and is grounded through the car's frame and the battery's negative (–) ground strap.

The starting motor is a specially designed, direct current electric motor capable of producing a very great amount of power for its size. One thing that allows the motor to produce a great deal of power is its tremendous rotating speed. It drives the engine through a tiny pinion gear (attached to the starter's armature), which drives the very large flywheel ring gear at a greatly reduced speed. Another factor allowing it to produce so much power is that only intermittent operation is required of it. This, little allowance for air circulation is required, and the windings can be built into a very small space.

The starter solenoid is a magnetic device which employs the small current supplied by the starting switch circuit of the ignition switch. This magnetic action moves a plunger which mechanically engages the starter and electrically closes the heavy switch which connects it to the battery. The starting switch circuit consists of the starting switch contained within the ignition switch, a transmission neutral safety switch or clutch pedal switch, and the wiring necessary to connect these in series with the starter solenoid or relay.

A pinion, which is a small gear, is mounted to a one-way drive clutch. This clutch is splined to the starter armature shaft. When the ignition switch is moved to the **START** position, the solenoid plunger slides the pinion toward the flywheel ring gear via a collar and spring. If the teeth on the pinion and flywheel match properly, the pinion will engage the flywheel immediately. If the gear teeth butt one another, the spring will be compressed and will force the gears to mesh as soon as the starter turns far enough to allow them to do so. As the solenoid plunger reaches the end of its travel, it closes the contacts that connect the battery and starter and then the engine is cranked.

As soon as the engine starts, the flywheel ring gear begins turning fast enough to drive the pinion at an extremely high rate of speed. At this point, the one-way clutch begins allowing the pinion to spin faster than the starter shaft so that the starter will not operate at excessive speed. When the ignition switch is released from the starter position, the solenoid is de-energized, and a spring contained within the solenoid assembly pulls the gear out of mesh and interrupts the current flow to the starter.

Some starters employ a separate relay, mounted away from the starter, to switch the motor and solenoid current on and off. The relay thus replaces the solenoid electrical switch, but does not eliminate the need for a solenoid mounted on the starter used to mechanically engage the starter drive gears. The relay is used to reduce the amount of current the starting switch must carry.

THE CHARGING SYSTEM

Basic Operating Principles

The automobile charging system provides electrical power for operation of the vehicle's ignition and starting systems and all the electrical accessories. The battery services as an electrical surge or storage tank, storing (in chemical form) the energy originally produced by the engine driven alternator. The system also provides a means of regulating alternator output to protect the battery from being overcharged and to avoid excessive voltage to the accessories.

The storage battery is a chemical device incorporating parallel lead plates in a tank containing a sulfuric acid/water solution. Adjacent plates are slightly dissimilar, and the chemical reaction of the two dissimilar plates produces electrical energy when the battery is connected to a load such as the starter motor. The chemical reaction is reversible, so that when the alternator is producing a voltage (electrical pressure) greater than that produced by the battery, electricity is forced into the battery, and the battery is returned to its fully charged state.

The vehicle's alternator is driven mechanically, through serpentine belts, by the engine crankshaft. It consists of two coils of fine wire, one stationary (the stator), and one movable (the rotor). The rotor may also be known as the armature, and consists of fine wire wrapped around an iron core which is mounted on a shaft. The electricity which flows through the two coils of wire (provided initially by the battery in some cases) creates an intense magnetic field around both rotor and stator, and the interaction between the two fields creates voltage, allowing the alternator to power the accessories and charge the battery.

Newer automobiles use alternating current generators or alternators, because they are more efficient, can be rotated at higher speeds, and have fewer brush problems. In an alternator, the field rotates while all the current produced passes only through the stator winding. The brushes bear against continuous slip rings rather than a commutator. This causes the current produced to periodically reverse the direction of its flow. Diodes (electrical one-way switches) block the flow of current from traveling in the wrong direction. A series of diodes is wired together to permit the alternating flow of the stator to be converted to a pulsating, but unidirectional flow at the alternator output. The alternator's field is wired in series with the voltage regulator.

The regulator consists of several circuits. Each circuit has a core, or magnetic coil of wire, which operates a switch. Each switch is connected to ground through one or more resistors. The coil of wire responds directly to system voltage. When the voltage reaches the required level, the magnetic field created by the winding of wire closes the switch and inserts a resistance into the generator field circuit, thus reducing the output. The contacts of the switch cycle open and close many times each second to precisely control voltage.

While alternators are self-limiting as far as maximum current is concerned, DC generators employ a current regulating circuit which responds directly to the total amount of current flowing through the generator circuit rather than to the output voltage. The current regulator is similar to the voltage regulator except that all system current must flow through the energizing coil on its way to the various accessories.

Alternator

The alternator charging system consists of the alternator, voltage regulator, warning light, battery, and fuse link wire.

A failure of any component of the charging system can cause the entire system to stop functioning. Because of this, the charging system can be very difficult to troubleshoot when problems occur.

When the ignition key is turned on, current flows from the battery, through the charging system indicator light on the instrument panel, to the voltage regulator, and to the alternator. Since the alternator is not producing any current, the alternator warning light comes on. When the engine is started, the alternator begins to produce current and turns the alternator light off. As the alternator turns and produces current, the current is divided in two ways: part to the battery to charge the battery and power the electrical components of the vehicle, and part is returned to the alternator to enable it to increase its output. In this situation, the alternator is receiving current from the battery and from itself. A voltage regulator is wired into the current supply to the alternator to prevent it from receiving too much current which would cause it to put out too much current. Conversely, if the voltage regulator does not allow the alternator to receive enough current, the battery will not be fully charged and will eventually go dead.

The battery is connected to the alternator at all times, whether the ignition key is turned on or not. If the battery were shorted to ground, the alternator would also be shorted. This would damage the alternator. To prevent this, a fuse link is installed in the wiring between the battery and the alternator. If the battery is shorted, the fuse link will melt, protecting the alternator.

ALTERNATOR PRECAUTIONS

Several precautions must be observed with alternator equipped vehicles to avoid damaging the unit. They are as follows:

1. If the battery is removed for any reason, make sure that it is reconnected with the correct polarity. Reversing the battery connections may result in damage to the one-way rectifiers.

2. When utilizing a booster battery as a starting aid, always connect it as follows: positive to positive, and negative (booster battery) to a good ground on the engine of the car being started.

3. Never use a fast charger as a booster to start cars with alternating current (AC) circuits.

4. When servicing the battery with a fast charger, always disconnect the car battery cables.

5. Never attempt to polarize an alternator.

6. Avoid long soldering times when replacing diodes or transistors. Prolonged heat is damaging to alternators.

7. Do not use test lamps of more than 12 volts (V) for checking diode continuity.

Troubleshooting Basic Charging System Problems

Problem	Cause	Solution
Noisy alternator	• Loose mountings • Loose drive pulley • Worn bearings • Brush noise • Internal circuits shorted (High pitched whine)	• Tighten mounting bolts • Tighten pulley • Replace alternator • Replace alternator • Replace alternator
Squeal when starting engine or accelerating	• Glazed or loose belt	• Replace or adjust belt
Indicator light remains on or ammeter indicates discharge (engine running)	• Broken fan belt • Broken or disconnected wires • Internal alternator problems • Defective voltage regulator	• Install belt • Repair or connect wiring • Replace alternator • Replace voltage regulator
Car light bulbs continually burn out— battery needs water continually	• Alternator/regulator overcharging	• Replace voltage regulator/alternator
Car lights flare on acceleration	• Battery low • Internal alternator/regulator problems	• Charge or replace battery • Replace alternator/regulator
Low voltage output (alternator light flickers continually or ammeter needle wanders)	• Loose or worn belt • Dirty or corroded connections • Internal alternator/regulator problems	• Replace or adjust belt • Clean or replace connections • Replace alternator or regulator

8. Do not short across or ground any of the terminals on the alternator.

9. The polarity of the battery, alternator, and regulator must be matched and considered before making any electrical connections within the system.

10. Never separate the alternator on an open circuit. Make sure that all connections within the circuit are clean and tight.

11. Disconnect the battery terminals when performing any service on the electrical system. This will eliminate the possibility of accidental reversal of polarity.

12. Disconnect the battery ground (–) cable if arc welding is to be done on any part of the car.

CHARGING SYSTEM TROUBLESHOOTING

There are many possible ways in which the charging system can malfunction. Often the source of a problem is difficult to diagnose, requiring special equipment and a good deal of experience. This is usually not the case, however, where the charging system fails completely and causes the dash board warning light to come on or the battery to become dead. To troubleshoot a complete system failure only two pieces of equipment are needed: a test light, to determine that current is reaching a certain point; and a current indicator (ammeter), to determine the direction of the current flow and its measurement in amps. This test works under three assumptions:

a. The battery is known to be good and fully charged.

b. The alternator belt is in good condition and adjusted to the proper tension.

c. All connections in the system are clean and tight.

NOTE: *In order for the current indicator to give a valid reading, the car must be equipped with battery cables which are of the same gauge size and quality as original equipment battery cables.*

1. Turn off all electrical components on the car. Make sure the doors of the car are closed. If the car is equipped with a clock, disconnect the clock by removing the lead wire from the rear of the clock. Disconnect the positive battery cable from the battery and connect the ground wire on a test light to the disconnected positive battery cable. Touch the probe end of the test light to the positive battery post. The test light should not light. If the test light does light, there is a short or open circuit on the car.

2. Disconnect the voltage regulator wiring harness connector at the voltage regulator. Turn on the ignition key. Connect the wire on a test light to a good ground (engine bolt).

Touch the probe end of a test light to the ignition wire connector into the voltage regulator wiring connector. This wire corresponds to the **I** terminal on the regulator. If the test light goes on, the charging system warning light circuit is complete. If the test light does not come on and the warning light on the instrument panel is on, either the resistor wire, which is parallel with the warning light, or the wiring to the voltage regulator, is defective. If the test light does not come on and the warning light is not on, either the bulb is defective or the power supply wire form the battery through the ignition switch to the bulb has an open circuit. Connect the wiring harness to the regulator.

3. Examine the fusible link wire in the wiring harness from the starter relay to the alternator. If the insulation on the wire is cracked or split, the fuse link may be melted. Connect a test light to the fuse link by attaching the ground wire on the test light to an engine bolt and touching the probe end of the light to the bottom of the fuse link wire where it splices into the alternator output wire. If the bulb in the test light does not light, the fuse link is melted.

4. Start the engine and place a current indicator on the positive battery cable. Turn off all electrical accessories and make sure the doors are closed. If the charging system is working properly, the gauge will show a draw of less than 5 amps. If the system is not working properly, the gauge will show a draw of more than 5 amps. A charge moves the needle toward the battery, a draw moves the needle away from the battery. Turn the engine off.

5. Disconnect the wiring harness from the voltage regulator at the regulator at the regulator connector. Connect a male spade terminal (solderless connector) to each end of a jumper wire. Insert one end of the wire into the wiring harness connector which corresponds to the **A** terminal on the regulator. Insert the other end of the wire into the wiring harness connector which corresponds to the **F** terminal on the regulator. Position the connector with the jumper wire installed so that it cannot contact any metal surface under the hood. Position a current indicator gauge on the positive battery cable. Have an assistant start the engine. Observe the reading on the current indicator. Have your assistant slowly raise the speed of the engine to about 2,000 rpm or until the current indicator needle stops moving, whichever comes first. Do not run the engine for more than a short period of time in this condition. If the wiring harness connector or jumper wire becomes excessively hot during this test, turn off the engine and check for a grounded wire in the regulator wiring harness. If the current indica-

tor shows a charge of about three amps less than the output of the alternator, the alternator is working properly. If the previous tests showed a draw, the voltage regulator is defective. If the gauge does not show the proper charging rate, the alternator is defective.

Ignition Coil

TESTING

2.5L L4 (Lumina) VIN R

CAUTION: *When handling secondary spark plug leads with the engine running, insulated pliers MUST be used and care exercised to prevent a possible electrical shock.*

Two separate ignition coils are mounted to the ignition module assembly. Each coil provides the spark for two spark plugs simultaneously. The primary cylinder fires on the compression stroke and the secondary cylinder fires on the exhaust stroke. Firing on the exhaust stroke requires a minimal amount of voltage leaving the remainder to fire the compressed air/fuel mixture. Each coil can also be replaced separately and interchanged with the other coil assembly.

MISFIRE AT IDLE

1. Engine rpm should drop equally on all spark plug leads.
2. A spark tester tool ST-125 must be used because it is essential to verify adequate available secondary voltage at the spark plug (25,000 volts).

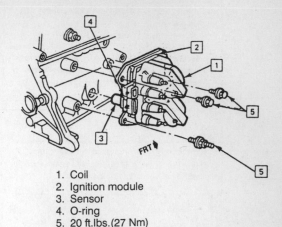

1. Coil
2. Ignition module
3. Sensor
4. O-ring
5. 20 ft.lbs.(27 Nm)

Direct ignition system (DIS) — 2.5L L4 Lumina

3. If the spark jumps the gap after grounding the opposite plug wire, there is excessive resistance in the plug which was bypassed. Check for poor connections at the plug and carbon tracking inside the spark plug boot.
4. If there is carbon tracking in the spark plug boot, replace the coil and be sure the plug wires to that coil are clean and tight. Excessive wire resistance may cause the coil to be damaged.
5. If no spark conditions follows the suspected coil, that coil is faulty. The ignition module may cause a no spark condition. This test could also be performed by substituting a

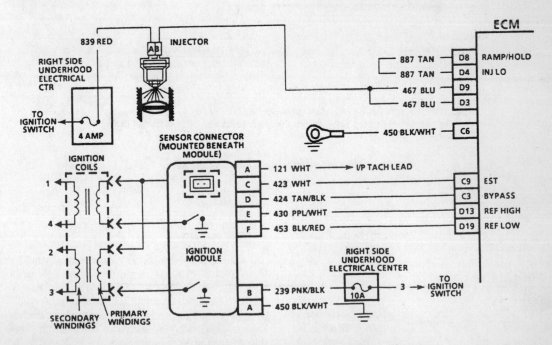

Direct ignition system (DIS) wiring diagram — 2.5L L4 (Lumina)

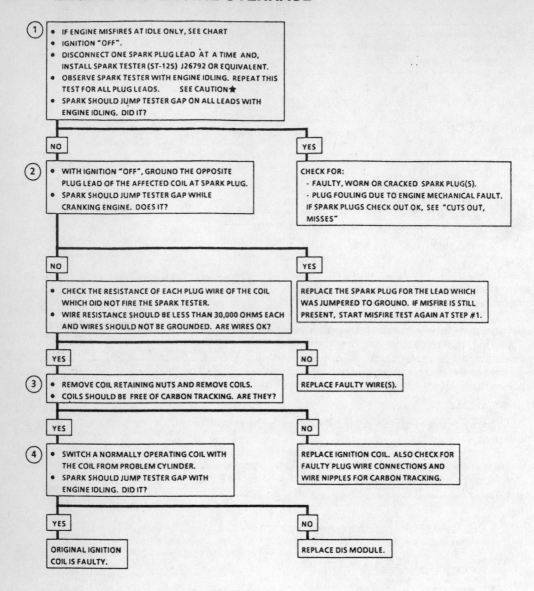

① • IF ENGINE MISFIRES AT IDLE ONLY, SEE CHART
   • IGNITION "OFF".
   • DISCONNECT ONE SPARK PLUG LEAD AT A TIME AND, INSTALL SPARK TESTER (ST-125) J26792 OR EQUIVALENT.
   • OBSERVE SPARK TESTER WITH ENGINE IDLING. REPEAT THIS TEST FOR ALL PLUG LEADS.   SEE CAUTION★
   • SPARK SHOULD JUMP TESTER GAP ON ALL LEADS WITH ENGINE IDLING. DID IT?

NO   YES

② • WITH IGNITION "OFF", GROUND THE OPPOSITE PLUG LEAD OF THE AFFECTED COIL AT SPARK PLUG.
   • SPARK SHOULD JUMP TESTER GAP WHILE CRANKING ENGINE. DOES IT?

CHECK FOR:
   - FAULTY, WORN OR CRACKED SPARK PLUG(S).
   - PLUG FOULING DUE TO ENGINE MECHANICAL FAULT.
   IF SPARK PLUGS CHECK OUT OK, SEE "CUTS OUT, MISSES"

NO   YES

• CHECK THE RESISTANCE OF EACH PLUG WIRE OF THE COIL WHICH DID NOT FIRE THE SPARK TESTER.
• WIRE RESISTANCE SHOULD BE LESS THAN 30,000 OHMS EACH AND WIRES SHOULD NOT BE GROUNDED. ARE WIRES OK?

REPLACE THE SPARK PLUG FOR THE LEAD WHICH WAS JUMPERED TO GROUND. IF MISFIRE IS STILL PRESENT, START MISFIRE TEST AGAIN AT STEP #1.

YES   NO

③ • REMOVE COIL RETAINING NUTS AND REMOVE COILS.
   • COILS SHOULD BE FREE OF CARBON TRACKING. ARE THEY?

REPLACE FAULTY WIRE(S).

YES   NO

④ • SWITCH A NORMALLY OPERATING COIL WITH THE COIL FROM PROBLEM CYLINDER.
   • SPARK SHOULD JUMP TESTER GAP WITH ENGINE IDLING. DID IT?

REPLACE IGNITION COIL. ALSO CHECK FOR FAULTY PLUG WIRE CONNECTIONS AND WIRE NIPPLES FOR CARBON TRACKING.

YES   NO

ORIGINAL IGNITION COIL IS FAULTY.

REPLACE DIS MODULE.

★CAUTION: When handling secondary spark plug leads with engine running, insulated pliers must be used and care exercised to prevent a possible electrical shock.

Misfire under load diagnosis; — 2.5L L4 Lumina

known good coil for the one causing the no spark condition.

6. Use the following procedures in conjunction with the diagnostic charts in this section.

2.3L QUAD 4 (VIN A, D)
2.8L and 3.1L V6 (VIN W, T)

CAUTION: *When handling secondary spark plug leads with the engine running, insulated pliers MUST be used and care exercised to prevent a possible electrical shock.*

NOTE: *Refer to the "Misfire" diagnostic and wiring diagrams in this chapter for testing procedures.*

Two separate ignition coils are mounted to the ignition module assembly. Each coil provides the spark for two spark plugs simultaneously. The primary cylinder fires on the compression stroke and the secondary cylinder fires on the exhaust stroke. Firing on the exhaust stroke requires a minimal amount of voltage leaving the remainder to fire the com-

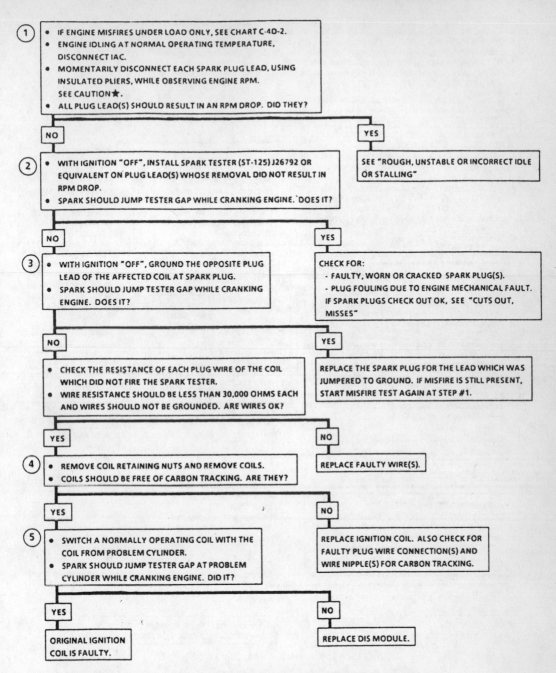

1.
- IF ENGINE MISFIRES UNDER LOAD ONLY, SEE CHART C-4D-2.
- ENGINE IDLING AT NORMAL OPERATING TEMPERATURE, DISCONNECT IAC.
- MOMENTARILY DISCONNECT EACH SPARK PLUG LEAD, USING INSULATED PLIERS, WHILE OBSERVING ENGINE RPM. SEE CAUTION ★.
- ALL PLUG LEAD(S) SHOULD RESULT IN AN RPM DROP. DID THEY?

NO → 2.
- WITH IGNITION "OFF", INSTALL SPARK TESTER (ST-125) J26792 OR EQUIVALENT ON PLUG LEAD(S) WHOSE REMOVAL DID NOT RESULT IN RPM DROP.
- SPARK SHOULD JUMP TESTER GAP WHILE CRANKING ENGINE. DOES IT?

YES → SEE "ROUGH, UNSTABLE OR INCORRECT IDLE OR STALLING"

NO → 3.
- WITH IGNITION "OFF", GROUND THE OPPOSITE PLUG LEAD OF THE AFFECTED COIL AT SPARK PLUG.
- SPARK SHOULD JUMP TESTER GAP WHILE CRANKING ENGINE. DOES IT?

YES → CHECK FOR:
- FAULTY, WORN OR CRACKED SPARK PLUG(S).
- PLUG FOULING DUE TO ENGINE MECHANICAL FAULT.
IF SPARK PLUGS CHECK OUT OK, SEE "CUTS OUT, MISSES"

NO →
- CHECK THE RESISTANCE OF EACH PLUG WIRE OF THE COIL WHICH DID NOT FIRE THE SPARK TESTER.
- WIRE RESISTANCE SHOULD BE LESS THAN 30,000 OHMS EACH AND WIRES SHOULD NOT BE GROUNDED. ARE WIRES OK?

YES → REPLACE THE SPARK PLUG FOR THE LEAD WHICH WAS JUMPERED TO GROUND. IF MISFIRE IS STILL PRESENT, START MISFIRE TEST AGAIN AT STEP #1.

YES → 4.
- REMOVE COIL RETAINING NUTS AND REMOVE COILS.
- COILS SHOULD BE FREE OF CARBON TRACKING. ARE THEY?

NO → REPLACE FAULTY WIRE(S).

YES → 5.
- SWITCH A NORMALLY OPERATING COIL WITH THE COIL FROM PROBLEM CYLINDER.
- SPARK SHOULD JUMP TESTER GAP AT PROBLEM CYLINDER WHILE CRANKING ENGINE. DID IT?

NO → REPLACE IGNITION COIL. ALSO CHECK FOR FAULTY PLUG WIRE CONNECTION(S) AND WIRE NIPPLE(S) FOR CARBON TRACKING.

YES → ORIGINAL IGNITION COIL IS FAULTY.

NO → REPLACE DIS MODULE.

★CAUTION: When handling secondary spark plug leads with engine running, insulated pliers must be used and care exercised to prevent a possible electrical shock.

Misfire at idle diagnosis; — 2.5L L4 Lumina

pressed air/fuel mixture. Each coil can also be replaced separately and interchanged with the other coil assembly.

MISFIRE

1. A spark tester tool ST-125 must be used because it is essential to verify adequate availa-ble secondary voltage at the spark plug (25,000 volts). The tester needs at least 25,000 volts to jump the gap.

2. If the spark jumps the gap on all wires, the ignition system may be considered to be in good working condition. If the spark plugs show no signs of wear, damage or fouling, an

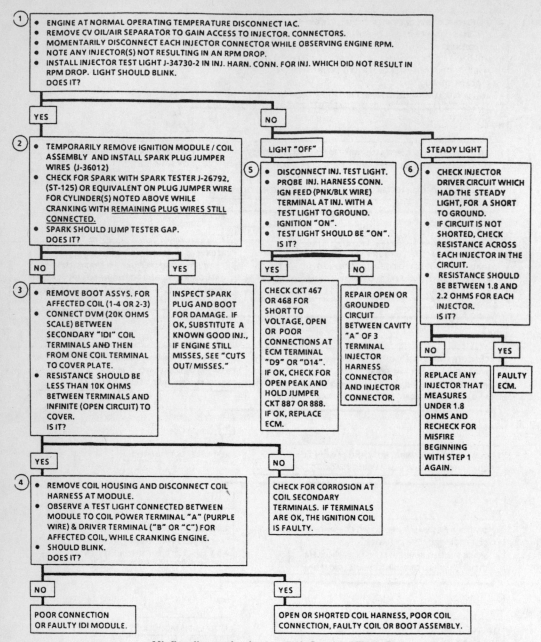

Misfire diagnosis chart — 2.3L Quad 4 (VIN A, D)

engine mechanical fault should be checked. Also, check for poor connections at the plug and carbon tracking inside the spark plug boot.

3. If the spark jumps the gap after grounding the opposite plug wire, there is excessive resistance in the plug which was bypassed. Check for poor connections at the plug and carbon tracking inside the spark plug boot.

4. If there is carbon tracking in the spark plug boot, replace the coil and be sure the plug wires to that coil are clean and tight. Excessive

wire resistance may cause the coil to be damaged.

5. If no spark conditions follows the suspected coil, that coil is faulty. The ignition module may cause a no spark condition. This test could also be performed by substituting a known good coil for the one causing the no spark condition.

6. Use the following procedures in conjunction with the diagnostic chart for the 2.8L and 3.1L V6 engines in this section.

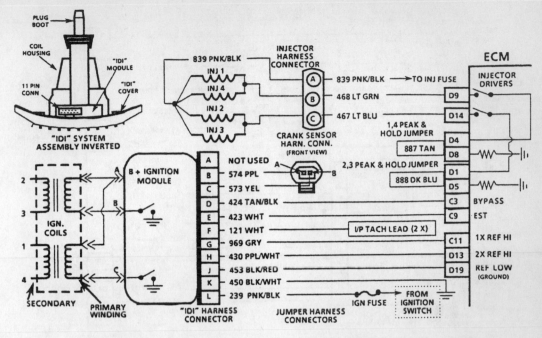

Integrated Direct Ignition system (IDI) wiring diagram — 2.3L Quad 4 (VIN A,D)

REMOVAL AND INSTALLATION

2.3L QUAD 4 (VIN A,D)

1. Disconnect the negative (–) battery cable.
2. Disconnect the 11 pin (IDI) harness connector at the ignition cover.
3. Remove the four ignition cover assembly-to-cylinder head bolts.
4. Remove the ignition assembly from the vehicle.

5. Remove the four coil housing-to-cover screws.

CAUTION: *Be careful not to damage the module terminals when pulling the coil assemblies from the module. Pull slowly and carefully away from the ignition assembly.*

6. Disconnect the coil harness connectors.
7. Remove the coils, contacts and seals from the cover.

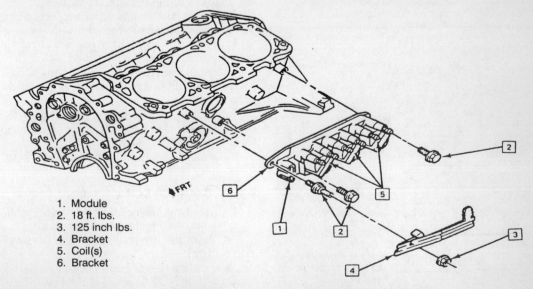

1. Module
2. 18 ft. lbs.
3. 125 inch lbs.
4. Bracket
5. Coil(s)
6. Bracket

Direct Ignition System coil and module — 2.8L and 3.1L V6 (VIN W,T)

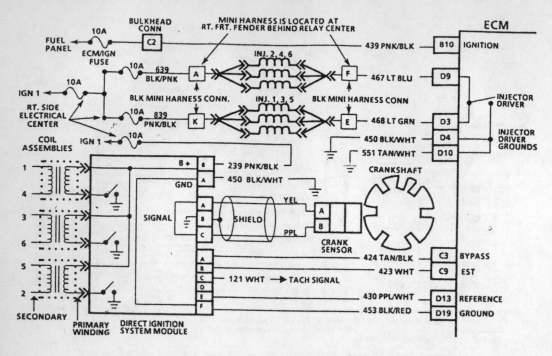

Direct Ignition System (DIS) wiring diagram — 2.8L and 3.1L V6 (VIN W,T)

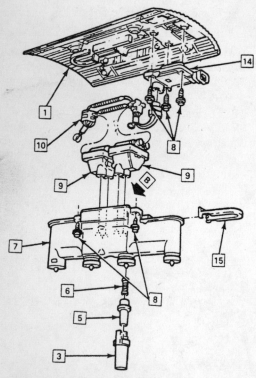

1. Ignition cover	8. 35 inch lbs.
3. Retainer	9. Coils
5. Boot	10. Harness assembly
6. Spring	14. Module
7. Housing	15. Retainer

Ignition coil assembly — 2.3L Quad 4 (VIN A, D)

NOTE: *If the spark plug boots stick, use a spark plug connector removing tool J–36011 or equivalent to remove with a twisting motion.*

To install:

1. Install the coils-to-cover.

2. Connect the coil harness.

3. Using new seals, install the seals into the housing.

4. Install the contacts-to-housing. use petroleum jelly to retain the contact in place.

5. Install the housing cover, retaining screws and torque to 35 inch lbs. (4 Nm).

6. Install the spark plug boots and retainers-to-ignition cover.

7. Install the ignition assembly-to-cylinder heads. Carefully align the boots to the spark plug terminals.

8. Apply thread locking compound to the bolts. Install the four retaining bolts and torque to 19 ft. lbs. (26 Nm).

9. Connect the 11 pin connector and negative battery cable.

2.5L L4 (Lumina) VIN R

1. Disconnect the negative (–) battery cable.

2. Rotate the engine as follows:

a. Block the wheels and put the transaxle in Neutral.

b. Position the coolant reservoir out of the way, but do NOT disconnect the hoses.

c. Remove the torque strut-to-engine bracket nut and bolt.

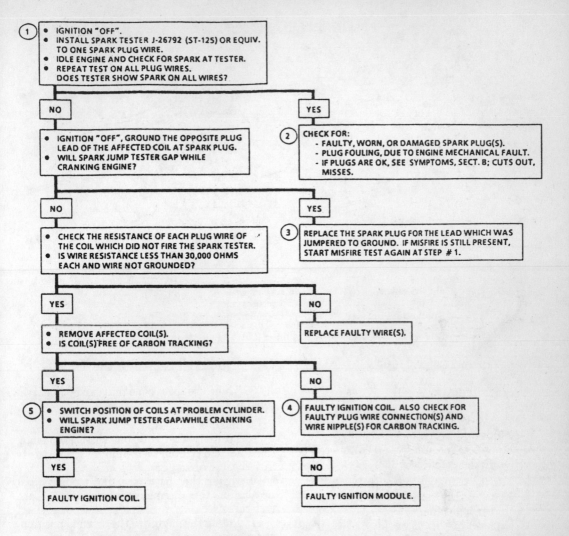

1. • IGNITION "OFF".
   • INSTALL SPARK TESTER J-26792 (ST-125) OR EQUIV. TO ONE SPARK PLUG WIRE.
   • IDLE ENGINE AND CHECK FOR SPARK AT TESTER.
   • REPEAT TEST ON ALL PLUG WIRES. DOES TESTER SHOW SPARK ON ALL WIRES?

NO

• IGNITION "OFF", GROUND THE OPPOSITE PLUG LEAD OF THE AFFECTED COIL AT SPARK PLUG.
• WILL SPARK JUMP TESTER GAP WHILE CRANKING ENGINE?

YES

2. CHECK FOR:
   - FAULTY, WORN, OR DAMAGED SPARK PLUG(S).
   - PLUG FOULING, DUE TO ENGINE MECHANICAL FAULT.
   - IF PLUGS ARE OK, SEE SYMPTOMS, SECT. B; CUTS OUT, MISSES.

NO

• CHECK THE RESISTANCE OF EACH PLUG WIRE OF THE COIL WHICH DID NOT FIRE THE SPARK TESTER.
• IS WIRE RESISTANCE LESS THAN 30,000 OHMS EACH AND WIRE NOT GROUNDED?

YES

3. REPLACE THE SPARK PLUG FOR THE LEAD WHICH WAS JUMPERED TO GROUND. IF MISFIRE IS STILL PRESENT, START MISFIRE TEST AGAIN AT STEP # 1.

YES

• REMOVE AFFECTED COIL(S).
• IS COIL(S) FREE OF CARBON TRACKING?

NO

REPLACE FAULTY WIRE(S).

YES

5. • SWITCH POSITION OF COILS AT PROBLEM CYLINDER.
   • WILL SPARK JUMP TESTER GAP WHILE CRANKING ENGINE?

NO

4. FAULTY IGNITION COIL. ALSO CHECK FOR FAULTY PLUG WIRE CONNECTION(S) AND WIRE NIPPLE(S) FOR CARBON TRACKING.

YES

FAULTY IGNITION COIL.

NO

FAULTY IGNITION MODULE.

Direct Ignition System (DIS) diagnostic chart — 2.8L and 3.1L V6 (VIN W,T)

d. Using a suitable pry bar at the torque strut bracket, rotate the engine and transaxle assembly forward.

e. Align the slave hole in the torque strut with the engine bracket hole.

f. Retain the engine in this position using the torque strut-to-engine bracket bolt.

3. Label each spark plug wire for proper installation.

4. Remove the spark plug and module electrical connectors from the ignition coils.

5. Remove the two coil-to-module attaching screws.

CAUTION: *Be careful not to damage the module terminals when pulling the coil assemblies from the module. Pull slowly and carefully away from the engine.*

6. Gently pull the coil assemblies from the module.

7. There are two coils that can be replaced separately.

To install:

8. Position the coil on the base plate (module) and tighten the retaining screws to 45 inch lbs. (5 Nm).

9. Install the spark plug and module electrical connectors. Reconnect the negative (–) battery cable.

10. Rotate the engine to the original position as follows:

a. Pull the pry bar forward to release the engine weight and remove the bolt from the torque strut slave hole and then remove the engine bracket.

b. Allow the engine and transaxle to rotate back to its original position.

c. Remove the pry bar.

d. Install the torque strut-to-engine

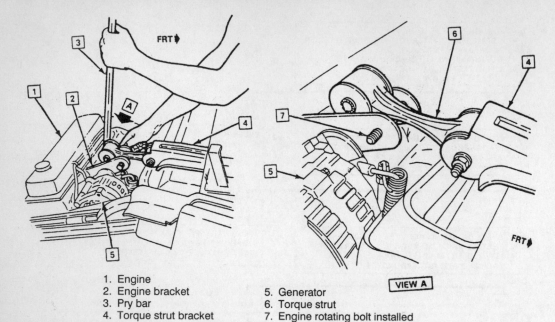

1. Engine
2. Engine bracket
3. Pry bar
4. Torque strut bracket
5. Generator
6. Torque strut
7. Engine rotating bolt installed

VIEW A

Rotating the engine — 2.5L L4 Lumina

bracket bolt and nut and torque to 37 ft. lbs. (51 Nm).

e. Reposition the coolant resevoir.

2.8L and 3.1L V6 (VIN W, T)

1. Remove the air cleaner assembly.
2. Disconnect the negative (–) battery cable.
3. Rotate the engine as follows:

a. Put the transaxle in Neutral.

b. Remove the strut-to-engine bracket bolts and swing the strut aside.

c. Replace the passenger side torque strut-to-engine bracket bolt in the engine bracket.

d. Remove the coolant reservoir bolts and move to the side, but do NOT disconnect the hoses.

e. Place a pry bar in the bracket so that it contacts the bracket and the bolt.

f. Rotate the engine by pulling forward on the pry bar.

g. Align the slave hole in the driver side torque strut-to-engine bracket hole.

h. Retain the engine in this position using the torque strut-to-engine bracket bolt.

4. Label each spark plug wire for proper installation.

5. Remove the spark plug and module electrical connectors from the ignition coils.

6. Remove the two coil-to-module attaching screws.

CAUTION: *Be careful not to damage the module terminals when pulling the coil assemblies from the module. Pull slowly and carefully away from the engine.*

7. Gently pull the coil assemblies from the module.

8. There are three coils that can be replaced separately.

To install:

9. Position the coil on the base plate (module) and tighten the retaining screws to 45 inch lbs. (5 Nm).

10. Install the spark plug and module electrical connectors. Reconnect the negative (–) battery cable.

11. Rotate the engine to the original position as follows:

a. Pull the pry bar forward to release the engine weight and remove the bolt from the torque strut slave hole and engine bracket.

b. Allow the engine and transaxle to rotate back to its original position.

c. Remove the pry bar.

d. Install the torque strut-to-engine bracket bolt and nut and torque to 37 ft. lbs. (51 Nm).

e. Reposition the coolant reservoir.

Ignition Module

REMOVAL AND INSTALLATION

2.3L QUAD 4 (VIN A,D)

1. Refer to the "Ignition Coil Assembly" illustration in this section for ignition module location.

2. Disconnect the negative (–) battery cable.

3. Remove the electrical harness, four retaining bolts and ignition cover assembly from the vehicle.

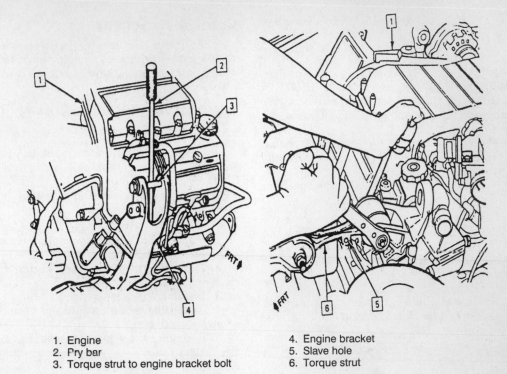

1. Engine
2. Pry bar
3. Torque strut to engine bracket bolt
4. Engine bracket
5. Slave hole
6. Torque strut

Rotating the engine — 2.8L and 3.1L V6 (VIN W,T)

4. Remove the four housing screws, coil housing and coil harness connectors.

5. Remove the three module-to-housing cover screws and module.

To install:

1. If replacing the module or a coil, the new unit should come with a package of silicone grease with it, if not, purchase a tube at your local parts distributor. Spread the grease on the metal face of the module and on the cover where the module seats. The grease MUST be used for module cooling.

2. Install the module-to-cover, module screws and torque to 35 inch lbs. (4 Nm).

3. Install the coil harness-to-module and housing cover screws. Torque the screws to 35 inch lbs. (4 Nm).

4. Install the spark plug boots and retainers.

5. Install the ignition system-to-cylinder head while carefully aligning the spark plug boots with the terminals.

6. Apply thread locking compound to the bolts. Install the four retaining bolts and torque to 19 ft. lbs. (26 Nm).

7. Connect the 11 pin connector and negative battery cable.

2.5L L4 (Lumina) VIN R

1. Disconnect the negative (–) battery cable.
2. Rotate the engine as follows:

a. Block the wheels and put the transaxle in Neutral.

b. Position the coolant reservoir out of the way, but do NOT disconnect the hoses.

c. Remove the torque strut-to-engine bracket nut and bolt. Refer to the "Rotating the Engine" illustration in the ignition coil section.

d. Using a suitable pry bar at the torque strut bracket, rotate the engine and transaxle assembly forward.

e. Align the slave hole in the torque strut with the engine bracket hole.

f. Retain the engine in this position using the torque strut-to-engine bracket bolt.

3. Label each spark plug wire for proper installation.

4. Remove the spark plug and module electrical connectors from the DIS assembly.

5. Remove the three DIS assembly-to-engine attaching bolts.

WARNING: *Be careful not to damage the crankshaft sensor and module terminals when pulling the DIS assemblies from the engine. Pull slowly and carefully away from the engine.*

6. Remove the DIS assembly from the engine. Remove the DIS assembly from the bracket.

7. Remove the coils from the DIS assembly.

To install:

1. Install the module to the bracket.
2. Install the coil assemblies to the module and torque the screws to 45 inch lbs. (5 Nm).
3. Install the DIS assembly and attaching bolts to the engine and torque to 20 ft. lbs. (27 Nm).
4. Reconnect the spark plugs and module electrical connectors to their original positions as removed.
5. Rotate the engine to its original position as follows:

a. Pull the pry bar forward to release the engine weight and remove the bolt from the torque strut slave hole and engine bracket.
b. Allow the engine and transaxle to rotate back to its original position.
c. Remove the pry bar.
d. Install the torque strut-to-engine bracket bolt and nut and torque to 37 ft. lbs. (51 Nm).
e. Reposition the coolant reservoir.

2.8L and 3.1L V6 (VIN W, T)

1. Remove the air cleaner assembly
2. Disconnect the negative (–) battery cable.
3. Raise the vehicle and support with jackstands.
4. Label each spark plug wire for proper installation.
5. Remove the spark plug and module electrical connectors from the DIS assembly.
6. Remove the three DIS assembly-to-engine attaching bolts.

WARNING: *Be careful not to damage the crankshaft sensor and module terminals when pulling the DIS assemblies from the engine. Pull slowly and carefully away from the engine.*

7. Remove the DIS assembly from the engine. Remove the DIS assembly from the bracket.
8. Remove the coils from the DIS assembly.
To install:

1. Install the module to the bracket.
2. Install the coil assemblies to the module and torque the screws to 45 inch lbs. (5 Nm).
3. Install the DIS assembly and attaching bolts to the engine and torque to 20 ft. lbs. (27 Nm).
4. Reconnect the spark plugs and module electrical connectors to their original positions as removed.
5. Install the air cleaner and reconnect the negative (–) battery cable.

Crankshaft Sensor

The reluctor is an integral part of the crankshaft and the crankshaft sensor is mounted in a fixed position, timing adjustment is NOT possible.

REMOVAL AND INSTALLATION

2.3L QUAD 4 (VIN A,D)

1. Disconnect the negative (–) battery cable and sensor harness connector above the oil filter.
2. Remove the one sensor retaining bolts and sensor from the engine.
To install:

1. Inspect the sensor O-ring for damage and replace if necessary.
2. Lubricate the new sensor O-ring with clean engine oil.
3. Install the sensor-to-engine.
4. Install the retaining bolt and torque to 88 inch lbs. (10 Nm).
5. Reconnect the sensor harness and negative battery cable.

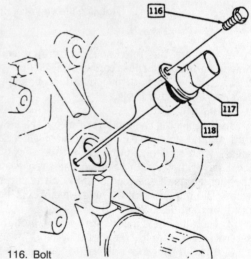

116. Bolt
117. Crankshaft sensor
118. Sensor O-ring — lubricate with engine oil

Crankshaft sensor removal — 2.3L Quad 4

2.5L L4 (Lumina) VIN R

1. Disconnect the negative (–) battery cable.
2. Remove the DIS (Direct Ignition System) assembly as outlined in the "Ignition Module or Coil" procedures in this section.
3. After the DIS assembly has been removed from the vehicle, remove the two crankshaft retaining screws.

CAUTION: *Be careful not to damage the crankshaft and module terminals when pull-*

ing the coil assemblies from the engine. Pull slowly and carefully away from the engine.

4. Remove the crankshaft sensor from the DIS assembly.

To install:

1. Inspect the sensor O-ring for wear, leakage or cracks. Replace if necessary.

2. Lubricate the new O-ring seal with engine oil before installing.

3. Install the crankshaft sensor onto the DIS assembly and torque the two attaching screws to 20 inch lbs. (2.3 Nm).

NOTE: *Use extreme care when installing the crankshaft sensor on the DIS assembly so the sensor terminals are not damaged.*

4. Position the coil pack assembly onto the engine. Be careful to position the crankshaft sensor properly into the engine. Torque the three coil-to-engine attaching bolts to 9 ft. lbs. (12.2 Nm).

5. Refer to the "Ignition Coil" removal and installation procedures in this section for engine rotating procedures that can be very helpful.

6. Reconnect the spark plug wires and module electrical connectors in their original positions. Reconnect the negative (–) battery cable.

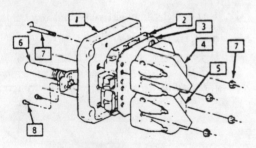

1. Base plate
2. Module
3. Shield
4. 2–3 Coil
5. 1–4 Coil
6. Sensor
7. Studs and nuts (40 inch lbs.)
8. Screws (20 inch lbs.)

Removing the crankshaft sensor — 2.5L L4 Lumina

2.8L and 3.1L V6 (VIN W, T)

1. Disconnect the negative (–) battery cable.

2. Remove the sensor electrical connector.

3. Remove the sensor attaching bolts and sensor from the engine.

To install:

4. Inspect the sensor O-ring for wear, cracks or leakage. Replace if necessary.

5. Lubricate the new O-ring seal with engine oil before installing.

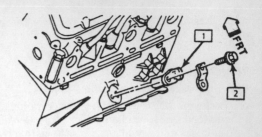

1. Crankshaft sensor
2. Bolt (71 inch lbs.)

Removing the crankshaft sensor — 2.8L and 3.1L V6 engines

6. Install the sensor and attaching bolt, torque the bolt to 88 inch lbs. (10 Nm).

7. Reconnect the sensor electrical connector and negative (–) battery cable.

Alternator

ALTERNATOR PRECAUTIONS

To prevent damage to the alternator and regulator, the following precautions should be taken when working with the electrical system.

1. Never reverse the battery connections.

2. Booster batteries for starting must be connected properly: positive-to-positive (+) and negative-to-negative (–).

3. Disconnect the battery cables before using a fast charger; the charger has a tendency to force current through the diodes in the opposite direction for which they were designed. This burns out the diodes.

4. Never use a fast charger as a booster for starting the vehicle.

5. Never disconnect the voltage regulator while the engine is running.

6. Avoid long soldering times when replacing diodes or transistors. Prolonged heat is damaging to AC (alternating current) generators.

7. Do not use test lamps of more than 12 volts (V) for checking diode continuity.

8. Do not short across or ground any of the terminals on the AC (alternating current) generator.

9. The polarity of the battery, generator, and regulator must be matched and considered before making any electrical connections within the system.

10. Never operate the alternator on an open circuit. Make sure that all connections within the circuit are clean and tight.

11. Disconnect the battery terminals when performing any service on the electrical system. This will eliminate the possibility of accidental reversal of polarity.

12. Disconnect the battery ground cable if arc welding is to be done on any part of the car.

REMOVAL AND INSTALLATION

Testing or replacing individual components in the alternator is not practical or economical for a do-it-yourself mechanic. The tools needed are expensive and would not be practical to purchase to use only a few times. Complete rebuilt units can be purchased through your local parts distributor for a fraction of the cost of a new unit.

2.3L QUAD 4 (VIN A,D)

1. Disconnect the negative (–) battery cable.
2. Remove the electrical center fuse block shield.
3. Remove the serpentine belt as outlined in Chapter 1.
4. Label and remove the alternator electrical connectors.

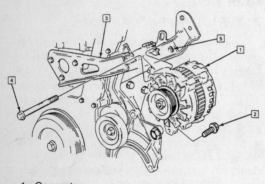

1. Generator
2. 19 ft. lbs.
3. Bracket
4. 40 ft. lbs.
5. Tighten strut bolt after tightening pivot bolt

Alternator mounting — 2.3L Quad 4

5. Remove the alternator brace bolt, rear bolt and front bolt.

NOTE: *Use extreme care when removing the alternator, not to damage the air conditioning compressor and condensor hose.*

6. Lift the alternator out between the engine lifting eyelet and the air conditioning compressor.
To install:
1. Install the alternator, front, rear and brace retaining bolts.
2. Torque the long bolt to 40 ft. lbs. (54 Nm), the short bolt to 19 ft. lbs. (26 Nm) and the brace bolt to 18 ft. lbs. (25 Nm).
3. Connect the alternator electrical connec-

tors, serpentine belt and fuse block shield.
4. Connect the negative battery cable and check for proper operation.

2.5L L4 (Lumina) VIN R

1. Disconnect the negative (–) battery cable. CAUTION: *Failure to observe this step may cause personal injury from a hot battery lead at the alternator.*
2. Remove the serpentine belt as outlined in the "Belt" section in Chapter 1.
3. Remove the electrical connectors from the back of the alternator.
4. Remove the rear (first), front attaching bolts and heat shield.
5. Remove the alternator assembly carefully making sure all wires are disconnected.
6. **To install:** position the alternator into the mounting bracket.
7. Install the front and rear mounting bolts, but do not tighten.
8. Install the heat shield with the rear mounting bolts.
9. Install the electrical connectors and tighten the battery cable nut.
10. Torque the mounting bolts to 18 ft. lbs. (25 Nm).
11. Install the serpentine belt as outlined in Chapter 1.
12. Reconnect the negative (–) battery cable.

2.8L and 3.1L V6 (VIN W, T)

1. Disconnect the negative (–) battery cable. CAUTION: *Failure to observe this step may cause personal injury from hot battery lead at the alternator.*

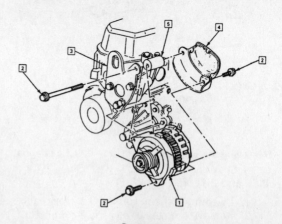

1. Generator
2. 18 ft. lbs.
3. Bracket
4. Heat shield
5. Spacer

Alternator mounting — 2.5L L4 Lumina

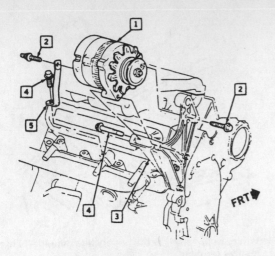

1. Generator
2. 18 ft. lbs.
3. Bracket
4. 37 ft. lbs.
5. Brace

Alternator mounting — 2.8L and 3.1L V6 (VIN W,T)

2. Remove the air cleaner assembly.
3. Remove the serpentine belt as outlined in the "Belt" section.
4. Remove the electrical connectors from the back of the alternator.
5. Remove the rear (first), front attaching bolts and heat shield.
6. Remove the alternator assembly carefully making sure all wires are disconnected.

To install:

7. Position the alternator into the mounting bracket.
8. Install the front and rear mounting bolts, but do not tighten.
9. Install the heat shield with the rear mounting bolts.
10. Install the electrical connectors and tighten the battery cable nut.
11. Torque the mounting bolts as follows:

   a. Long bolt to 35 ft. lbs. (47 Nm)
   b. Short bolt to 18 ft. lbs. (25 Nm)
   c. Bracket bolt to 18 ft. lbs. (25 Nm)

12. Install the serpentine belt as outlined in Chapter 1.
13. Install the air cleaner and negative (–) battery cable.

ALTERNATOR BENCH TEST (OFF THE VEHICLE)

Testing or replacing individual components in the alternator is not practical or economical for a do-it-yourself mechanic. The tools needed are expensive and would not be practical to purchase to use only a few times. Complete rebuild units can be purchased through your local parts distributor for a fraction of the cost of a new unit.

1. Remove the alternator from the vehicle as outlined in the previous section.
2. Make all connections as outlined in the "Alternator Bench Test" illustration in this section, EXCEPT do NOT hock-up the carbon pile yet.
3. The battery must be fully charged. Use a 30–500Ω resistor between the battery and "L" terminal.
4. Rotate the alternator pulley in a clockwise direction. Slowly increase the speed and observe the voltage.
5. If the voltage is uncontrolled and increases above 16.0 volts, replace the alternator.
6. If the voltage is below 16.0 volts, increase the speed and adjust the carbon pile to obtain the maximum amperage output. Maintain voltage above 13.0 volts.
7. If the output is within 15 amperes of rated output, the alternator is functioning properly.
8. If the output is not within 15 amperes of rated output, replace the alternator.

NOTE: *The CS–130 alternator can NOT be disassembled, and must be serviced as a complete unit.*

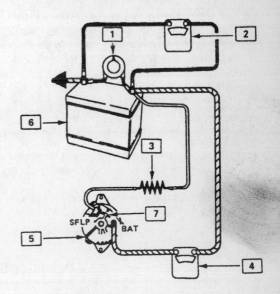

1. Carbon pile
2. Voltmeter
3. Resistor
4. Test ammeter
5. Generator
6. Battery
7. Connect resistor to "L" terminal

Alternator bench test — CS–130 models

Voltage Regulator

No periodic maintaince on the alternator is required. The CS–130 is serviced as a complete unit only. No internal repair parts, including the regulator, are available at this time.

Battery

The original equipment Delco Freedom® battery is a completely sealed unit that never requires the addition of water or acid. The only openings in the battery are vent holes located on the sides of the battery case. The vents allow the small amount of gas produced in the battery to escape.

The automotive battery has three functions: first, it provides a source of energy to crank the engine; second, it acts as a voltage stabilizer for the electrical system; and third, it provides energy for a limited time when the electrical load used exceeds the output of the alternator.

The original equipment battery has a Reserve Capacity of 90 amperes and a Cold Cranking rating of 630 amperes. When replacing the battery, a battery equal or higher than the original rating is recommended.

REMOVAL AND INSTALLATION

WARNING: *Always turn the ignition switch to the OFF position when connecting or disconnecting the battery cables or battery chargers. Failure to follow this procedures may cause damage to the ECM or other electronic components.*

1. Remove the air cleaner assembly.
2. Remove the negative (–) battery cable.
3. Remove the positive (+) battery cable.
4. Remove the bolts from the cross brace and cross brace.
5. Remove the battery heat shield by grasping the fasteners with your fingers and pull up and out.
6. Remove the battery hold down, retainer and battery.

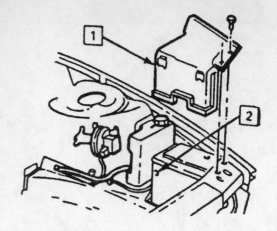

Battery removal. (1) is the battery heat shield; (2) is positive terminal

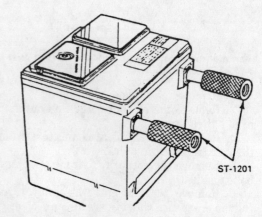

ST-1201

Battery removing tool

To install:
1. Position the battery into the holding tray.
2. Install the retainer and battery hold down. Torque the bolt to 71 inch lbs. (8 Nm).
3. Install the battery heat shield.
4. First, install the positive (+) battery

Alternator Specifications

Engine	Years	Manufacturer	Field Current @ 12v (amps)	Output (amps)
4-138	1990	Delco	5.4–6.4	36
4-151	1989–90	Delco	5.4–6.4	30
6-173	1988–90	Delco	5.4–6.4	30
6-191	1989–90	Delco	5.4–6.4	36

cable and torque the terminal to 13 ft. lbs. (17 Nm).

5. Install the cross brace and bolts.

6. Install the negative (–) battery cable and torque the terminal to 13 ft. lbs. (17 Nm).

7. Install the air cleaner assembly.

BUILT-IN HYDROMETER

The original equipment Delco Freedom® battery has a temperature-compensated hydrometer in the top of the battery. This hydrometer can tell your the condition of the vehicles battery. Refer to the following for color designation:

1. **GREEN DOT VISIBLE** – If any green can be seen in the hydrometer eye, the battery may be tested.

2. **DARK GREEN DOT NOT VISIBLE** – If no green dot is present and there is a cranking complaint, test the battery for a low charge condition.

3. **CLEAR OR LIGHT YELLOW** – If the hydrometer looks clear or light yellow, the fluid level is below the level of the hydrometer. This can indicate excessive or prolonged charging, a broken case, excessive tipping or a normally worn out battery. Check the charging system for an over-charge condition.

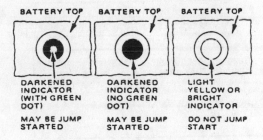

Built-in hydrometer — Delco Freedom battery

CURRENT DRAIN TEST

If the battery discharges or goes very low after sitting overnight, there may be an excessive electrical drain. Check the electrical system as follows:

1. Remove the air cleaner assembly. (2.8L and 3.1L V6)

2. Disconnect the negative (–) battery cable.

3. Install an adapter kit ST-1201, or equivalent. Refer to the "Current Drain Test" illustration in this section. Connect the adapter kit into the negative (–) battery cable.

4. Install a 3/8–16 nut with standard threads on the battery negative (–) terminal screw.

Current drain test circuit

5. Set the Multimeter part No. J–34029–A to DC, MA (milliamps), and at the 2,000 range.

6. With all lamps, accessories and ignition switch OFF, connect the Multimeter J–34029–A in series with the battery.

7. The current drain of 25 milliamps or less indicates that all lamps and accessories are OFF and there is not an unexplained current drain.

8. A possible cause may be misadjusted rear compartment lamp switch, glove compartment lamp or a grounded or pinched wire.

Starter

WARNING: *Never operate the starter motor more than 30 seconds at a time without pausing to allow it to cool for at least two minutes. Overheating, caused by excessive cranking, will seriously damage the starter motor.*

REMOVAL AND INSTALLATION

2.3L QUAD 4 (VIN A,D)

1. Disconnect the negative (–) battery cable.

2. Remove the air cleaner and inlet hose from the throttle body.

3. Remove and plug the coolant reservoir hose at the radiator filler neck.

4. Remove the coolant reservoir.

5. Remove the intake manifold brace bolts.

6. Place a drain pan under the oil filter and remove the filter.

7. Remove the starter retaining bolts, lower the starter onto the frame member and disconnect the starter electrical connectors.

8. The starter motor is heavy, so be careful not to drop the starter when removing.

To install:

1. Position the starter into the vehicle, connect the electrical connectors and torque the retaining bolts to 32 ft. lbs. (43 Nm).

2. Install a new oil filter. This may be a

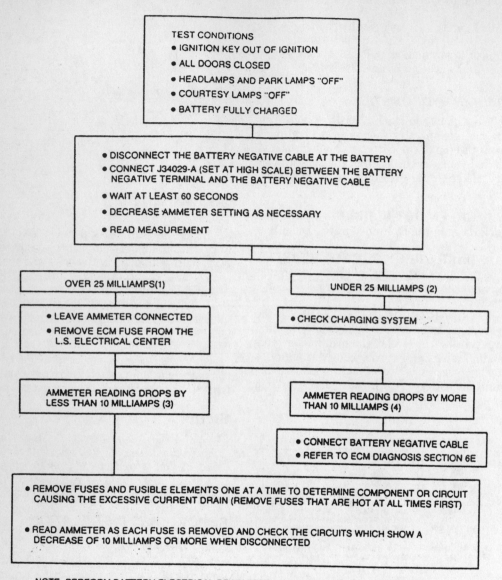

TEST CONDITIONS
- IGNITION KEY OUT OF IGNITION
- ALL DOORS CLOSED
- HEADLAMPS AND PARK LAMPS "OFF"
- COURTESY LAMPS "OFF"
- BATTERY FULLY CHARGED

- DISCONNECT THE BATTERY NEGATIVE CABLE AT THE BATTERY
- CONNECT J34029-A (SET AT HIGH SCALE) BETWEEN THE BATTERY NEGATIVE TERMINAL AND THE BATTERY NEGATIVE CABLE
- WAIT AT LEAST 60 SECONDS
- DECREASE AMMETER SETTING AS NECESSARY
- READ MEASUREMENT

OVER 25 MILLIAMPS(1)

UNDER 25 MILLIAMPS (2)

- LEAVE AMMETER CONNECTED
- REMOVE ECM FUSE FROM THE L.S. ELECTRICAL CENTER

- CHECK CHARGING SYSTEM

AMMETER READING DROPS BY LESS THAN 10 MILLIAMPS (3)

AMMETER READING DROPS BY MORE THAN 10 MILLIAMPS (4)

- CONNECT BATTERY NEGATIVE CABLE
- REFER TO ECM DIAGNOSIS SECTION 6E

- REMOVE FUSES AND FUSIBLE ELEMENTS ONE AT A TIME TO DETERMINE COMPONENT OR CIRCUIT CAUSING THE EXCESSIVE CURRENT DRAIN (REMOVE FUSES THAT ARE HOT AT ALL TIMES FIRST)
- READ AMMETER AS EACH FUSE IS REMOVED AND CHECK THE CIRCUITS WHICH SHOW A DECREASE OF 10 MILLIAMPS OR MORE WHEN DISCONNECTED

NOTE: PERFORM BATTERY ELECTRICAL DRAIN TEST AGAIN AFTER MAKING ANY REPAIRS

Battery current should be less than 25 milliamps with no circuits active. This test determines the value of battery current with all systems off.

(1) A current drain over 25 milliamps indicates a fault.

(2) A current drain under 25 milliamps is OK.

(3) A current drain drop under 10 milliamps indicates the problem is not ECM related.

(4) A current drain drop over 10 milliamps indicates the problem is ECM related.

Current drain diagnostic chart

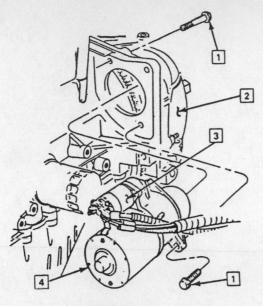

1. 32 ft. lbs.
2. Engine
3. Solenoid
4. Starter motor

Starter mounting — 2.3L Quad 4

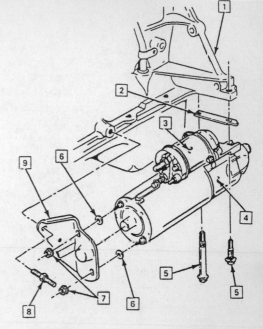

1. Engine
2. Shim
3. Solenoid
4. Starter motor
5. 32 ft. lbs.
6. Washer
7. Nut
8. 18 ft. lbs.
9. Bracket

Starter motor mounting — 2.5L L4 Lumina

good time to change the engine oil and filter at the same time.

3. Install the intake manifold brace, coolant reservoir and hoses.

4. Add coolant if needed.

5. Install the air cleaner and inlet hose.

6. Connect the negative battery cable and check for proper operation.

2.5L L4 (Lumina) VIN R

Testing or replacing individual components in the alternator is not practical or economical for a do-it-yourself mechanic. The tools needed are expensive and would not be practical to purchase to use only a few times. Complete rebuilt units can be purchased through your local parts distributor for a fraction of the cost of a new unit.

1. Disconnect the negative (–) battery cable.

CAUTION: *Failure to observe this step may cause personal injury from hot battery lead at the starter motor.*

2. Raise the vehicle and support with jackstands.

3. Remove the flywheel inspection cover bolts and cover.

4. Remove the stud from the starter support bracket.

5. Remove the two starter mounting bolts and shim if equipped.

6. Remove the starter motor. Be careful not

to damage the starter wires by letting the starter hang down.

7. While holding the starter motor, disconnect the starter electrical connectors from the starter solenoid.

8. Remove the starter from the rear bracket.

To install:

1. Install the support bracket to the starter.

2. Install the starter adjustment shims, if so equipped.

3. Position the starter to the engine mounting flange and torque the bolts to 32 ft. lbs. (43 Nm).

4. Install the bracket-to-engine and torque the stud to 18 ft. lbs. (25 Nm).

5. Install the inspection cover.

6. Lower the vehicle and connect the starter electrical wires. Reconnect the negative (–) battery cable.

2.8L and 3.1L V6 (VIN W, T)

1. Remove the air cleaner.

2. Disconnect the negative (–) battery cable.

CAUTION: *Failure to observe this step may cause personal injury from hot battery lead at the starter motor.*

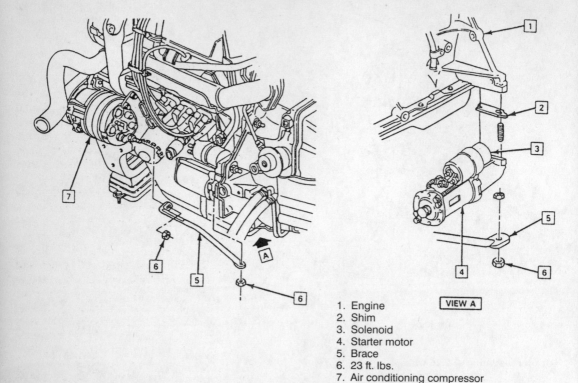

1. Engine
2. Shim
3. Solenoid
4. Starter motor
5. Brace
6. 23 ft. lbs.
7. Air conditioning compressor

VIEW A

Starter motor mounting — 2.8L and 3.1L V6 (VIN W,T)

3. Raise the vehicle and support with jackstands.

4. If the engine is equipped with an engine oil cooler, remove the engine oil, oil filter and position the hose next to the starter motor to the side.

5. Remove the nut from the brace at the air conditioning compressor, nut from the brace at the engine and the brace.

6. Remove the flywheel inspection cover.

7. Remove the starter bolts and shims (if equipped). Do not let the starter hang from the starter wires.

8. Remove the starter wires from the solenoid and remove the starter.

To install:

1. While supporting the starter, connect the starter wires at the solenoid.

2. Install the starter motor-to-engine mount with the shims (if equipped) and the mounting bolts. Torque the bolts to 32 ft. lbs. (43 Nm).

3. If equipped with an engine oil cooler, reposition the hose next to the starter motor, install the oil filter and refill the engine with the proper amount of engine oil.

4. Install the flywheel inspection cover and tighten the bolts.

5. Install the starter support brace to the air conditioning compressor and torque the nut to 23 ft. lbs. (31 Nm).

6. Lower the vehicle, reconnect the negative (−) battery cable and install the air cleaner assembly.

STARTER ALIGNMENT

While the starter is engaged, if a high pitch whine, low pitch whoop or rumble occurs, the starter may have to be aligned or serviced with the proper shims that can be purchased at the

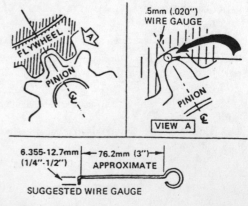

Starter motor alignment

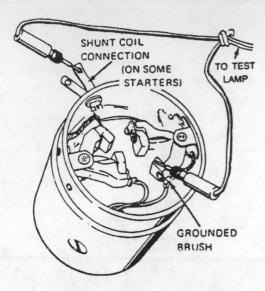

Checking the starter motor brush continuity

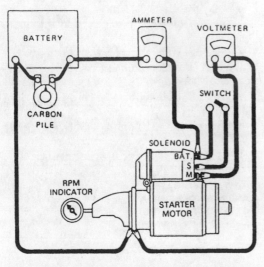

Make the connections as shown and compare rpm, current and voltage readings with specifications

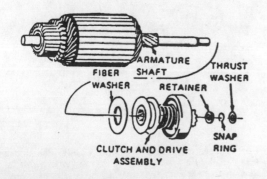

Armature shaft exploded view

dealer or local parts distributor. Measure the distance between the pinion gear and the flywheel ring gear as shown in the following illustration.

STARTER OVERHAUL

1. To remove the solenoid, remove the screw from the field coil connector and solenoid mounting screws. Rotate the solenoid 90° and remove it along with the plunger return spring.

2. For further service, remove the two through-bolts, then remove the commutator end frame and washer.

3. To replace the clutch and drive assembly proceed as follows:

a. Remove the thrust washer or the collar from the armature shaft.

b. Slide a $5/8$ inch deep socket or a piece of pipe of suitable size over the shaft and against the retainer as a driving tool. Tap the tool to remove the retainer off the snap ring.

c. Remove the snap ring from the groove in the shaft. Check and make sure the snap ring is not distorted. If it is, it will be necessary to replace it with a new one upon reassembly.

d. Remove the retainer and clutch assembly from the armature shaft.

4. The shift lever may be disconnected from the plunger at this time by removing the roll pin.

5. On models with the standard starter, the brushes may be removed by removing the brush holder pivot pin which positions one insulated and one grounded brush. Remove the brush and spring and replace the brushes as necessary.

6. On models with the smaller 5MT starter, remove the brush and holder from the brush support, then remove the screw from the brush holder and separate the brush and holder. Replace the brushes as necessary.

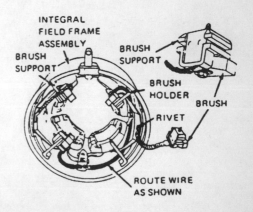

Brush replacement

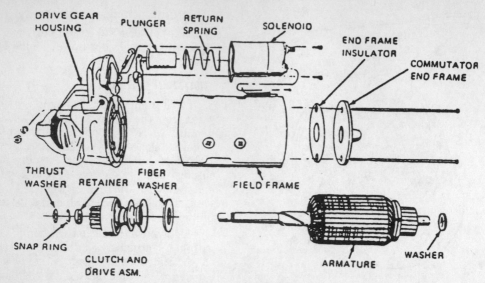

DRIVE GEAR HOUSING   PLUNGER   RETURN SPRING   SOLENOID   END FRAME INSULATOR   COMMUTATOR END FRAME

THRUST WASHER   RETAINER   FIBER WASHER   FIELD FRAME

SNAP RING   CLUTCH AND DRIVE ASM.   ARMATURE   WASHER

Starter motor exploded view

To assemble:

1. Lubricate the drive end of the armature shaft and slide the clutch assembly onto the armature shaft with the pinion away from the armature.

2. Slide the retainer onto the shaft with the cupped side facing the end of the shaft.

3. Install the snap ring into the groove on the armature shaft.

4. Install the thrust washer on the shaft.

5. Position the retainer and thrust washer with the snap ring in between. Using two pliers, grip the retainer and thrust washer or collar and squeeze until the snap ring is forced

into the retainer and is held securely in the groove in the armature shaft.

6. Lubricate the drive gear housing bushing.

7. Engage the shift lever yoke with the clutch and slide the complete assembly into the drive gear housing.

8. Install the shift lever pivot bolt and tighten.

9. Install the solenoid assembly and apply

TESTING SERIES COIL FOR GROUND

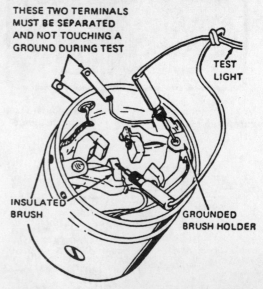

THESE TWO TERMINALS MUST BE SEPARATED AND NOT TOUCHING A GROUND DURING TEST

TEST LIGHT

INSULATED BRUSH   GROUNDED BRUSH HOLDER

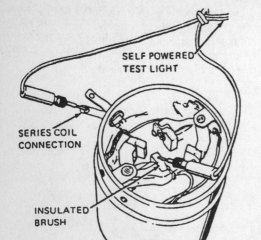

SELF POWERED TEST LIGHT

SERIES COIL CONNECTION

INSULATED BRUSH

Series coil test - place one lead on the insulated brush and the other on the series terminal. The light should light; if not, repair or replace the coil

For starters equipped with shunt coils, use a test lamp with one lead on the grounded brush holder and the other on an insulated brush. If the lamp lights, the coil is grounded and must be repaired or replaced

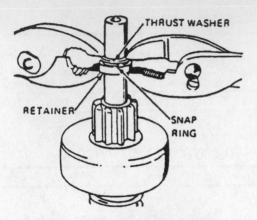

Installing the retainer and thrust washer

CHECKING PINION CLEARANCE

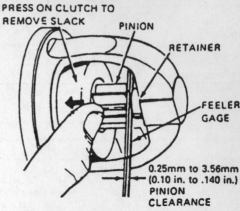

Checking pinion clearance

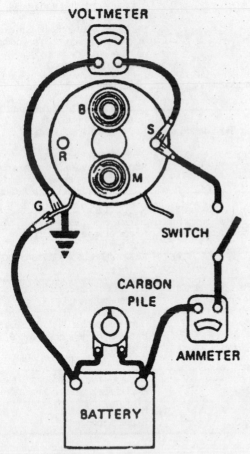

Solenoid current draw - check the draw of the windings as shown. The reading should be 14.5-16.5 amps at 10 volts. The secondary winding is checked in the same manner. The reading should be 41-47 amps at 10 volts

sealer to the solenoid flange where the field frame contacts it.

10. Position the field frame against the drive gear housing on the alignment pin using care to prevent damage to the brushes.

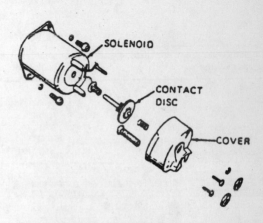

Starter solenoid disassembly

11. Lubricate the commutator end frame and install the washer on the armature shaft. Slide the end frame onto the shaft and tighten the bolts. Make sure the bolts pass through the holes in the insulator.

12. Connect the field coil connector to the solenoid terminal.

NOTE: *When the starter motor has been disassembled or the solenoid has been replaced, it is necessary to check the pinion clearance. Pinion clearance must be correct to prevent the buttons on the shift lever yoke from rubbing on the clutch collar during cranking.*

13. Check **pinion clearance** as follows:

a. Disconnect the motor field coil connector from the solenoid motor terminal and insulate it carefully.

b. Connect the (+) 12 volt battery lead to the solenoid motor terminal and the (-) lead to the motor frame.

c. Flash a jumper lead momentarily from the solenoid motor terminal to the starter

Starter Specifications

Engine	Years	Manufacturer	No-Load Test		
			Amps	Volts	rpm
4-cylinder	1989–90	Delco	50	10	6,000–11,900
6-cylinder	1989–90	Delco	52	10	6,000–12,000

Troubleshooting Basic Starting System Problems

Problem	Cause	Solution
Starter motor rotates engine slowly	• Battery charge low or battery defective	• Charge or replace battery
	• Defective circuit between battery and starter motor	• Clean and tighten, or replace cables
	• Low load current	• Bench-test starter motor. Inspect for worn brushes and weak brush springs.
	• High load current	• Bench-test starter motor. Check engine for friction, drag or coolant in cylinders. Check ring gear-to-pinion gear clearance.
Starter motor will not rotate engine	• Battery charge low or battery defective	• Charge or replace battery
	• Faulty solenoid	• Check solenoid ground. Repair or replace as necessary.
	• Damage drive pinion gear or ring gear	• Replace damaged gear(s)
	• Starter motor engagement weak	• Bench-test starter motor
	• Starter motor rotates slowly with high load current	• Inspect drive yoke pull-down and point gap, check for worn end bushings, check ring gear clearance
	• Engine seized	• Repair engine
Starter motor drive will not engage (solenoid known to be good)	• Defective contact point assembly	• Repair or replace contact point assembly
	• Inadequate contact point assembly ground	• Repair connection at ground screw
	• Defective hold-in coil	• Replace field winding assembly
Starter motor drive will not disengage	• Starter motor loose on flywheel housing	• Tighten mounting bolts
	• Worn drive end busing	• Replace bushing
	• Damaged ring gear teeth	• Replace ring gear or driveplate
	• Drive yoke return spring broken or missing	• Replace spring
Starter motor drive disengages prematurely	• Weak drive assembly thrust spring	• Replace drive mechanism
	• Hold-in coil defective	• Replace field winding assembly
Low load current	• Worn brushes	• Replace brushes
	• Weak brush springs	• Replace springs

frame. This will shift the pinion into the cranking position and will remain until the battery is disconnected.

d. Push the pinion back as far as possible to take up any movement and check the clearance with a feeler gauge. The clearance should be 0.010 in. to 0.140 in.

e. Means for adjusting pinion clearance is not provided on the starter motor. If the clear-ance is not within specifications, check for im-proper installation or worn parts.

ENGINE MECHANICAL

This section contains the needed informa-tion to overhaul your 2.3L QUAD 4, 2.5L L4, 2.8L and 3.1L V6 engines. The main components of the overhaul are cylinder block, cylinder head, crankshaft, valve train, pistons, camshaft and oiling system.

Engine Overhaul Tips

Most engine overhaul procedures are fairly standard. In addition to specific parts replacement procedures and complete specifications for your individual engine, this chapter also is a guide to assist rebuilding procedures. Examples of standard rebuilding practice are shown and should be used along with specific details concerning your particular engine.

Competent and accurate machine shop services will ensure maximum performance, reliability and engine life.

In most instances it is more profitable for the do-it-yourself mechanic to remove, clean and inspect the component, buy the necessary parts and deliver these to a shop for actual machine work.

On the other hand, much of the rebuilding work (crankshaft, block, bearings, piston rods, and other components) is well within the scope of the do-it-yourself mechanic.

TOOLS

The tools required for an engine overhaul or parts replacement will depend on the depth of your involvement. With a few exceptions, they will be the tools found in a mechanic's tool kit (see Chapter 1). More in-depth work will require any or all of the following:
- dial indicator (reading in thousandths) mounted on a universal base
- micrometers and telescope gauges
- jaw and screw-type pullers
- scraper
- valve spring compressor
- ring groove cleaner
- piston ring expander and compressor
- ridge reamer
- cylinder hone or glaze breaker
- Plastigage®
- engine hoist and stand

The use of most of these tools is illustrated in this chapter. Many can be rented for a one-time use from a local parts jobber or tool supply house specializing in automotive work.

Occasionally, the use of special tools is called for. See the information on Special Tools and Safety Notice in the front of this book before substituting another tool.

INSPECTION TECHNIQUES

Procedures and specifications are given in this chapter for inspecting, cleaning and assessing the wear limits of most major components. Other procedures such as Magnaflux® and Zyglo® can be used to locate material flaws and stress cracks. Magnaflux® is a magnetic process applicable only to ferrous materials. The Zyglo® process coats the material with a fluorescent dye penetrant and can be used on any material Check for suspected surface cracks can be more readily made using spot check dye. The dye is sprayed onto the suspected area, wiped off and the area sprayed with a developer. Cracks will show up brightly.

OVERHAUL TIPS

Aluminum has become extremely popular for use in engines, due to its low weight. Observe the following precautions when handling aluminum parts:
- Never hot tank aluminum parts (the caustic hot tank solution will disintegrate the aluminum.
- Remove all aluminum parts (identification tag, etc.) from engine parts prior to the tanking.
- Always coat threads lightly with engine oil or anti-seize compounds before installation, to prevent seizure.
- Never overtorque bolts or spark plugs especially in aluminum threads.

Stripped threads in any component can be repaired using any of several commercial repair kits (Heli-Coil®, Microdot®, Keenserts®, etc.).

When assembling the engine, any parts that will be frictional contact must be prelubed to provide lubrication at initial start-up. Any product specifically formulated for this purpose can be used, but engine oil is not recommended as a prelube.

When semi-permanent (locked, but removable) installation of bolts or nuts is desired, threads should be cleaned and coated with Loctite® or other similar, commercial non-hardening sealant.

REPAIRING DAMAGED THREADS

Several methods of repairing damaged threads are available. Heli-Coil® (shown here), Keenserts® and Microdot® are among the most widely used. All involve basically the same principle—drilling out stripped threads, tapping the hole and installing a prewound insert—making welding, plugging and oversize fasteners unnecessary.

Two types of thread repair inserts are usually supplied: a standard type for most Inch Coarse, Inch Fine, Metric Course and Metric Fine thread sizes and a spark lug type to fit most spark plug port sizes. Consult the individual manufacturer's catalog to determine exact applications. Typical thread repair kits will contain a selection of prewound threaded inserts, a tap (corresponding to the outside diameter

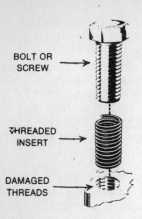

Damaged bolt holes can be repaired with thread repair inserts

Standard thread repair insert (left) and spark plug thread insert (right)

Drill out the damaged threads with the specified drill. Drill completly through the hole or to the bottom of a blind hole

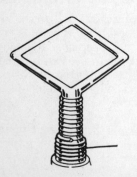

Screw the threaded insert onto the installation tool until the tang engages the slot. Screw the insert into the tapped hole until it is 1/4-1/2 turn below the top surface. After installation break off the tang with a hammer and punch

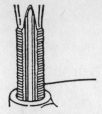

With the tap supplied, tap the hole to receive the thread insert. Keep the tap well oiled and back it out frequently to avoid clogging the threads

threads of the insert) and an installation tool. Spark plug inserts usually differ because they require a tap equipped with pilot threads and a combined reamer/tap section. Most manufacturers also supply blister-packed thread repair inserts separately in addition to a master kit containing a variety of taps and inserts plus installation tools.

Before effecting a repair to a threaded hole, remove any snapped, broken or damaged bolts or studs. Penetrating oil can be used to free frozen threads. The offending item can be removed with locking pliers or with a screw or stud extractor. After the hole is clear, the thread can be repaired, as shown in the series of accompanying illustrations.

Checking Engine Compression

A noticeable lack of engine power, excessive oil consumption and/or poor fuel mileage measured over an extended period are all indicators of internal engine wear. Worn piston rings, scored or worn cylinder bores, blown head gaskets, sticking or burnt valves and worn valve seats are all possible culprits here. A check of each cylinder's compression will help you locate the problems.

As mentioned in the Tools and Equipment section of Chapter 1, a screw-in type compression gauge is more accurate that the type you simply hold against the spark plug hole, although it takes slightly longer to use. It's worth it to obtain a more accurate reading. Follow the procedures below.

Gasoline Engines

1. Warm up the engine to normal operating temperature.
2. Mark the spark plug wires and remove all the spark plugs.
3. Disconnect the BAT terminal from the ignition module.
4. Remove the air cleaner assembly and fully open the throttle plates by operating the throttle linkage by hand or by having an assistant floor the accelerator pedal.
5. Coat the gauge threads with oil and

The screw in type compression gauge is more accurate

screw the compression gauge into the no.1 spark plug hole until the fitting is snug.

WARNING: *Be careful not to crossthread the plug hole. On aluminum cylinder heads use extra care, as the threads in these heads are easily ruined.*

6. Ask an assistant to depress the accelerator pedal fully on both carbureted and fuel injected vehicles. Then, while you read the compression gauge, ask the assistant to crank the engine two or three times in short bursts using the ignition switch. There should be four puffs per cylinder.

7. Read the compression gauge at the end of each series of cranks, and record the highest of these readings. Repeat this procedure for each of the engine's cylinders. Compare the highest reading of each cylinder to the compression pressure specification of **100 psi (689 kPa) minimum.** The lowest cylinder reading should not be less than **70 percent** of the highest reading.

NORMAL – Compression builds up quickly and evenly to the specified compression on each cylinder.

PISTON RINGS – Compression low on the first stroke, tends to build up on the following strokes, but does not reach normal. This reading should be tested with the addition of a few shots of engine oil into the cylinder. If the compression increases considerably, the rings are leaking compression.

VALVES – Low on the first stroke, does not tend to build up on following strokes. This reading will stay around the same with a few shots of engine oil.

HEAD GASKET – The compression reading is low between two adjacent cylinders. The head gasket between the two cylinders may be blown. If there is the sign of white smoke coming from the exhaust while the engine is running may indicate water leaking into the cylinder.

A cylinder's compression pressure is usually acceptable if it is not less than 70 percent of maximum. The difference between any two cylinders should be no more than 12–14 pounds.

8. If a cylinder is unusually low, shoot about a tablespoon of clean engine oil into the cylinder through the spark plug hole and repeat the compression test. If the compression comes up after adding the oil, it appears that the cylinder's piston rings or bore are damaged or worn. If the pressure remains low, the valves may not be seating properly (a valve job is needed), or the head gasket may be blown near that cylinder. If compression in any two adjacent cylinders is low, and if the addition of oil does not help the compression, there is leakage past the head gasket. Oil and coolant water in the combustion chamber can result from this problem. There may be evidence of water droplets on the engine dipstick when a head gasket has blown.

Engine

REMOVAL AND INSTALLATION

2.3L QUAD 4 (VIN A,D)

1. Disconnect the negative (–) battery cable. CAUTION: *To reduce the risk of fire and personal injury, it is necessary to relieve the fuel system pressure before servicing any fuel system component. If this procedure is not performed, fuel may be sprayed out of the connection under pressure. Always keep a dry chemical (Class B) fire extinguisher near the work area.*

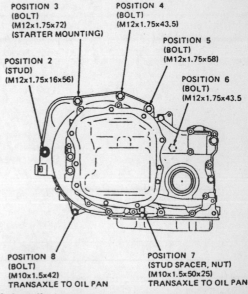

POSITION 3
(BOLT)
(M12x1.75x72)
(STARTER MOUNTING)

POSITION 4
(BOLT)
(M12x1.75x43.5)

POSITION 5
(BOLT)
(M12x1.75x58)

POSITION 2
(STUD)
(M12x1.75x16x56)

POSITION 6
(BOLT)
(M12x1.75x43.5

POSITION 8
(BOLT)
(M10x1.5x42)
TRANSAXLE TO OIL PAN

POSITION 7
(STUD SPACER, NUT)
(M10x1.5x50x25)
TRANSAXLE TO OIL PAN

Automatic transaxle–to–engine mounting. Manual similar

Troubleshooting Engine Mechanical Problems

Problem	Cause	Solution
External oil leaks	· Fuel pump gasket broken or improperly seated	· Replace gasket
	· Cylinder head cover RTV sealant broken or improperly seated	· Replace sealant; inspect cylinder head cover sealant flange and cylinder head sealant surface for distortion and cracks
	· Oil filler cap leaking or missing	· Replace cap
	· Oil filter gasket broken or improperly seated	· Replace oil filter
	· Oil pan side gasket broken, improperly seated or opening in RTV sealant	· Replace gasket or repair opening in sealant; inspect oil pan gasket flange for distortion
	· Oil pan front oil seal broken or improperly seated	· Replace seal; inspect timing case cover and oil pan seal flange for distortion
	· Oil pan rear oil seal broken or improperly seated	· Replace seal; inspect oil pan rear oil seal flange; inspect rear main bearing cap for cracks, plugged oil return channels, or distortion in seal groove
	· Timing case cover oil seal broken or improperly seated	· Replace seal
	· Excess oil pressure because of restricted PCV valve	· Replace PCV valve
	· Oil pan drain plug loose or has stripped threads	· Repair as necessary and tighten
	· Rear oil gallery plug loose	· Use appropriate sealant on gallery plug and tighten
	· Rear camshaft plug loose or improperly seated	· Seat camshaft plug or replace and seal, as necessary
	· Distributor base gasket damaged	· Replace gasket
Excessive oil consumption	· Oil level too high	· Drain oil to specified level
	· Oil with wrong viscosity being used	· Replace with specified oil
	· PCV valve stuck closed	· Replace PCV valve
	· Valve stem oil deflectors (or seals) are damaged, missing, or incorrect type	· Replace valve stem oil deflectors
	· Valve stems or valve guides worn	· Measure stem-to-guide clearance and repair as necessary
	· Poorly fitted or missing valve cover baffles	· Replace valve cover
	· Piston rings broken or missing	· Replace broken or missing rings
	· Scuffed piston	· Replace piston
	· Incorrect piston ring gap	· Measure ring gap, repair as necessary
	· Piston rings sticking or excessively loose in grooves	· Measure ring side clearance, repair as necessary
	· Compression rings installed upside down	· Repair as necessary
	· Cylinder walls worn, scored, or glazed	· Repair as necessary
	· Piston ring gaps not properly staggered	· Repair as necessary
	· Excessive main or connecting rod bearing clearance	· Measure bearing clearance, repair as necessary
No oil pressure	· Low oil level	· Add oil to correct level
	· Oil pressure gauge, warning lamp or sending unit inaccurate	· Replace oil pressure gauge or warning lamp
	· Oil pump malfunction	· Replace oil pump
	· Oil pressure relief valve sticking	· Remove and inspect oil pressure relief valve assembly
	· Oil passages on pressure side of pump obstructed	· Inspect oil passages for obstruction

Troubleshooting Engine Mechanical Problems (cont.)

Problem	Cause	Solution
No oil pressure (cont.)	• Oil pickup screen or tube obstructed	• Inspect oil pickup for obstruction
	• Loose oil inlet tube	• Tighten or seal inlet tube
Low oil pressure	• Low oil level	• Add oil to correct level
	• Inaccurate gauge, warning lamp or sending unit	• Replace oil pressure gauge or warning lamp
	• Oil excessively thin because of dilution, poor quality, or improper grade	• Drain and refill crankcase with recommended oil
	• Excessive oil temperature	• Correct cause of overheating engine
	• Oil pressure relief spring weak or sticking	• Remove and inspect oil pressure relief valve assembly
	• Oil inlet tube and screen assembly has restriction or air leak	• Remove and inspect oil inlet tube and screen assembly. (Fill inlet tube with lacquer thinner to locate leaks.)
	• Excessive oil pump clearance	• Measure clearances
	• Excessive main, rod, or camshaft bearing clearance	• Measure bearing clearances, repair as necessary
High oil pressure	• Improper oil viscosity	• Drain and refill crankcase with correct viscosity oil
	• Oil pressure gauge or sending unit inaccurate	• Replace oil pressure gauge
	• Oil pressure relief valve sticking closed	• Remove and inspect oil pressure relief valve assembly
Main bearing noise	• Insufficient oil supply	• Inspect for low oil level and low oil pressure
	• Main bearing clearance excessive	• Measure main bearing clearance, repair as necessary
	• Bearing insert missing	• Replace missing insert
	• Crankshaft end play excessive	• Measure end play, repair as necessary
	• Improperly tightened main bearing cap bolts	• Tighten bolts with specified torque
	• Loose flywheel or drive plate	• Tighten flywheel or drive plate attaching bolts
	• Loose or damaged vibration damper	• Repair as necessary
Connecting rod bearing noise	• Insufficient oil supply	• Inspect for low oil level and low oil pressure
	• Carbon build-up on piston	• Remove carbon from piston crown
	• Bearing clearance excessive or bearing missing	• Measure clearance, repair as necessary
	• Crankshaft connecting rod journal out-of-round	• Measure journal dimensions, repair or replace as necessary
	• Misaligned connecting rod or cap	• Repair as necessary
	• Connecting rod bolts tightened improperly	• Tighten bolts with specified torque
Piston noise	• Piston-to-cylinder wall clearance excessive (scuffed piston)	• Measure clearance and examine piston
	• Cylinder walls excessively tapered or out-of-round	• Measure cylinder wall dimensions, rebore cylinder
	• Piston ring broken	• Replace all rings on piston
	• Loose or seized piston pin	• Measure piston-to-pin clearance, repair as necessary
	• Connecting rods misaligned	• Measure rod alignment, straighten or replace
	• Piston ring side clearance excessively loose or tight	• Measure ring side clearance, repair as necessary
	• Carbon build-up on piston is excessive	• Remove carbon from piston

Troubleshooting Engine Mechanical Problems (cont.)

Problem	Cause	Solution
Valve actuating component noise	• Insufficient oil supply	• Check for: (a) Low oil level (b) Low oil pressure (c) Plugged push rods (d) Wrong hydraulic tappets (e) Restricted oil gallery (f) Excessive tappet to bore clearance
	• Push rods worn or bent	• Replace worn or bent push rods
	• Rocker arms or pivots worn	• Replace worn rocker arms or pivots
	• Foreign objects or chips in hydraulic tappets	• Clean tappets
	• Excessive tappet leak-down	• Replace valve tappet
	• Tappet face worn	• Replace tappet; inspect corresponding cam lobe for wear
	• Broken or cocked valve springs	• Properly seat cocked springs; replace broken springs
	• Stem-to-guide clearance excessive	• Measure stem-to-guide clearance, repair as required
	• Valve bent	• Replace valve
	• Loose rocker arms	• Tighten bolts with specified torque
	• Valve seat runout excessive	• Regrind valve seat/valves
	• Missing valve lock	• Install valve lock
	• Push rod rubbing or contacting cylinder head	• Remove cylinder head and remove obstruction in head
	• Excessive engine oil (four-cylinder engine)	• Correct oil level

Valve Specifications

Engine	Years	Seat Angle (deg.)	Face Angle (deg.)	Spring Test Pressure (lbs. @ in.)	Spring Installed Height (in.)	Stem to Guide Clearance (in.) Intake	Stem to Guide Clearance (in.) Exhaust	Stem Diameter Intake	Stem Diameter Exhaust
4-138	1990	45	①	79 @ 1.440	1.0040	0.0010–0.0027	0.0015–0.0032	0.2744–0.2751	0.2740–0.2747
4-151	1989–90	46	45	75 @ 1.680	1.6800	0.0010–0.0026	0.0013–0.0041	0.3421–0.3423	0.3421–0.3423
6-173	1988–90	46	45	90 @ 1.701	1.5748	0.0010–0.0027	0.0010–0.0027	0.3410–0.3416	0.3410–0.3416
6-191	1988–90	46	45	90 @ 1.701	1.5748	0.0010–0.0027	0.0010–0.0027	0.3410–0.3416	0.3410–0.3416

① Intake: 44
   Exhaust: 44.5

2. **Fuel pressure relief procedures:**

a. Disconnect the negative (–) battery cable.

b. Loosen the fuel filler cap to relieve tank vapor pressure.

c. Connect a fuel pressure gauge J-34730-1 or equivalent to the fuel pressure relief connection at the fuel rail.

d. Wrap a shop towel around the fittings while connecting the gauge to prevent fuel spillage.

e. Install a bleed hose into an approved container and open the valve to bleed the system pressure. The system is safe for servicing.

3. Mark the hood hinges and remove the hood with an assistant. Drain the engine coolant into a suitable drain pan.

4. Remove the heater hoses at the heater core and thermostat housing.

5. Remove the radiator upper hose.

6. Remove the air cleaner and inlet hose from the vehicle.

Troubleshooting the Cooling System

Problem	Cause	Solution
High temperature gauge indication—overheating	• Coolant level low	• Replenish coolant
	• Fan belt loose	• Adjust fan belt tension
	• Radiator hose(s) collapsed	• Replace hose(s)
	• Radiator airflow blocked	• Remove restriction (bug screen, fog lamps, etc.)
	• Faulty radiator cap	• Replace radiator cap
	• Ignition timing incorrect	• Adjust ignition timing
	• Idle speed low	• Adjust idle speed
	• Air trapped in cooling system	• Purge air
	• Heavy traffic driving	• Operate at fast idle in neutral intermittently to cool engine
	• Incorrect cooling system component(s) installed	• Install proper component(s)
	• Faulty thermostat	• Replace thermostat
	• Water pump shaft broken or impeller loose	• Replace water pump
	• Radiator tubes clogged	• Flush radiator
	• Cooling system clogged	• Flush system
	• Casting flash in cooling passages	• Repair or replace as necessary. Flash may be visible by removing cooling system components or removing core plugs.
	• Brakes dragging	• Repair brakes
	• Excessive engine friction	• Repair engine
	• Antifreeze concentration over 68%	• Lower antifreeze concentration percentage
	• Missing air seals	• Replace air seals
	• Faulty gauge or sending unit	• Repair or replace faulty component
	• Loss of coolant flow caused by leakage or foaming	• Repair or replace leaking component, replace coolant
	• Viscous fan drive failed	• Replace unit
Low temperature indication—undercooling	• Thermostat stuck open	• Replace thermostat
	• Faulty gauge or sending unit	• Repair or replace faulty component
Coolant loss—boilover	• Overfilled cooling system	• Reduce coolant level to proper specification
	• Quick shutdown after hard (hot) run	• Allow engine to run at fast idle prior to shutdown
	• Air in system resulting in occasional "burping" of coolant	• Purge system
	• Insufficient antifreeze allowing coolant boiling point to be too low	• Add antifreeze to raise boiling point
	• Antifreeze deteriorated because of age or contamination	• Replace coolant
	• Leaks due to loose hose clamps, loose nuts, bolts, drain plugs, faulty hoses, or defective radiator	• Pressure test system to locate source of leak(s) then repair as necessary
	• Faulty head gasket	• Replace head gasket
	• Cracked head, manifold, or block	• Replace as necessary
	• Faulty radiator cap	• Replace cap
Coolant entry into crankcase or cylinder(s)	• Faulty head gasket	• Replace head gasket
	• Crack in head, manifold or block	• Replace as necessary
Coolant recovery system inoperative	• Coolant level low	• Replenish coolant to FULL mark
	• Leak in system	• Pressure test to isolate leak and repair as necessary
	• Pressure cap not tight or seal missing, or leaking	• Repair as necessary
	• Pressure cap defective	• Replace cap
	• Overflow tube clogged or leaking	• Repair as necessary
	• Recovery bottle vent restricted	• Remove restriction

Troubleshooting the Cooling System (cont.)

Problem	Cause	Solution
Noise	• Fan contacting shroud	• Reposition shroud and inspect engine mounts
	• Loose water pump impeller	• Replace pump
	• Glazed fan belt	• Apply silicone or replace belt
	• Loose fan belt	• Adjust fan belt tension
	• Rough surface on drive pulley	• Replace pulley
	• Water pump bearing worn	• Remove belt to isolate. Replace pump.
	• Belt alignment	• Check pulley alignment. Repair as necessary.
No coolant flow through heater core	• Restricted return inlet in water pump	• Remove restriction
	• Heater hose collapsed or restricted	• Remove restriction or replace hose
	• Restricted heater core	• Remove restriction or replace core
	• Restricted outlet in thermostat housing	• Remove flash or restriction
	• Intake manifold bypass hole in cylinder head restricted	• Remove restriction
	• Faulty heater control valve	• Replace valve
	• Intake manifold coolant passage restricted	• Remove restriction or replace intake manifold

NOTE: *Immediately after shutdown, the engine enters a condition known as heat soak. This is caused by the cooling system being inoperative while engine temperature is still high. If coolant temperature rises above boiling point, expansion and pressure may push some coolant out of the radiator overflow tube. If this does not occur frequently it is considered normal.*

Crankshaft and Connecting Rod Specifications
(All specifications in inches)

Engine	Years	Crankshaft				Connecting Rod		
		Main Bearing Journal Diameter	Main Bearing Oil Clearance	Shaft End Play	Thrust on No.	Journal Diameter	Oil Clearance	Side Clearance
4-138	1990	2.0470–2.0480	0.0005–0.0023	0.0034–0.0045	3	1.8887–1.8897	0.0005–0.0020	0.006–0.018
4-151	1989–90	2.3000	0.0005–0.0022	0.0050–0.0180	5	2.0000	0.0005–0.0030	0.006–0.024
6-173	1988–90	2.6473–2.6483	0.0016–0.0032	0.0024–0.0083	3	1.9944–1.9983	0.0013–0.0026	0.006–0.017
6-191	1989–90	2.6473–2.6483	0.0012–0.0027	0.0024–0.0083	3	1.9944–1.9983	0.0014–0.0036	0.014–0.027

Troubleshooting the Serpentine Drive Belt

Problem	Cause	Solution
Tension sheeting fabric failure (woven fabric on outside circumference of belt has cracked or separated from body of belt)	• Grooved or backside idler pulley diameters are less than minimum recommended • Tension sheeting contacting (rubbing) stationary object • Excessive heat causing woven fabric to age • Tension sheeting splice has fractured	• Replace pulley(s) not conforming to specification • Correct rubbing condition • Replace belt • Replace belt
Noise (objectional squeal, squeak, or rumble is heard or felt while drive belt is in operation)	• Belt slippage • Bearing noise • Belt misalignment • Belt-to-pulley mismatch • Driven component inducing vibration • System resonant frequency inducing vibration	• Adjust belt • Locate and repair • Align belt/pulley(s) • Install correct belt • Locate defective driven component and repair • Vary belt tension within specifications. Replace belt.
Rib chunking (one or more ribs has separated from belt body)	• Foreign objects imbedded in pulley grooves • Installation damage • Drive loads in excess of design specifications • Insufficient internal belt adhesion	• Remove foreign objects from pulley grooves • Replace belt • Adjust belt tension • Replace belt
Rib or belt wear (belt ribs contact bottom of pulley grooves)	• Pulley(s) misaligned • Mismatch of belt and pulley groove widths • Abrasive environment • Rusted pulley(s) • Sharp or jagged pulley groove tips • Rubber deteriorated	• Align pulley(s) • Replace belt • Replace belt • Clean rust from pulley(s) • Replace pulley • Replace belt
Longitudinal belt cracking (cracks between two ribs)	• Belt has mistracked from pulley groove • Pulley groove tip has worn away rubber-to-tensile member	• Replace belt • Replace belt
Belt slips	• Belt slipping because of insufficient tension • Belt or pulley subjected to substance (belt dressing, oil, ethylene glycol) that has reduced friction • Driven component bearing failure • Belt glazed and hardened from heat and excessive slippage	• Adjust tension • Replace belt and clean pulleys • Replace faulty component bearing • Replace belt
"Groove jumping" (belt does not maintain correct position on pulley, or turns over and/or runs off pulleys)	• Insufficient belt tension • Pulley(s) not within design tolerance • Foreign object(s) in grooves • Excessive belt speed • Pulley misalignment • Belt-to-pulley profile mismatched • Belt cordline is distorted	• Adjust belt tension • Replace pulley(s) • Remove foreign objects from grooves • Avoid excessive engine acceleration • Align pulley(s) • Install correct belt • Replace belt
Belt broken (Note: identify and correct problem before replacement belt is installed)	• Excessive tension • Tensile members damaged during belt installation • Belt turnover • Severe pulley misalignment • Bracket, pulley, or bearing failure	• Replace belt and adjust tension to specification • Replace belt • Replace belt • Align pulley(s) • Replace defective component and belt

Troubleshooting the Serpentine Drive Belt (cont.)

Problem	Cause	Solution
Cord edge failure (tensile member exposed at edges of belt or separated from belt body)	• Excessive tension • Drive pulley misalignment • Belt contacting stationary object • Pulley irregularities • Improper pulley construction • Insufficient adhesion between tensile member and rubber matrix	• Adjust belt tension • Align pulley • Correct as necessary • Replace pulley • Replace pulley • Replace belt and adjust tension to specifications
Sporadic rib cracking (multiple cracks in belt ribs at random intervals)	• Ribbed pulley(s) diameter less than minimum specification • Backside bend flat pulley(s) diameter less than minimum • Excessive heat condition causing rubber to harden • Excessive belt thickness • Belt overcured • Excessive tension	• Replace pulley(s) • Replace pulley(s) • Correct heat condition as necessary • Replace belt • Replace belt • Adjust belt tension

General Engine Specifications

Engine	Years	Fuel System Type	SAE net Horsepower @ rpm	SAE net Torque ft. lb. @ rpm	Bore × Stroke	Comp. Ratio	Oil Press. (psi.) @ 2000 rpm
4-138	1990	MFI	160 @ 6200	155 @ 5200	3.62 × 3.35	10.0:1	30
4-151	1989–90	TBI	98 @ 4500	134 @ 2800	4.00 × 3.00	8.3:1	35
6-173	1988–90	MFI	130 @ 4500	170 @ 3600	3.50 × 2.99	8.9:1	50
6-191	1988–90	MFI	140 @ 4500	185 @ 3600	3.50 × 3.31	8.8:1	50

MFI—Multi-port Fuel Injection
TBI—Throttle Body Fuel Injection

Piston and Ring Specifications

(All specifications in inches)

Engine	Years	Ring Gap			Ring Side Clearance			Piston Clearance
		#1 Compr.	#2 Compr.	Oil Control	#1 Compr.	#2 Compr.	Oil Control	
4-138	1990	0.0138–0.0236	0.0157–0.0256	0.016–0.055	0.0027–0.0047	0.0016–0.0032	0.016–0.021	0.0007–0.0020
4-151	1989–90	0.0010–0.0020	0.0010–0.0020	0.020–0.060	0.0020–0.0030	0.0020–0.0030	0.015–0.055	0.0014–0.0022
6-173	1988–90	0.0010–0.0020	0.0010–0.0020	0.020–0.055	0.0010–0.0030	0.0010–0.0030	0.008	0.0020–0.0028
6-191	1989–90	0.0010–0.0020	0.0010–0.0020	0.020–0.055	0.0020–0.0035	0.0020–0.0035	0.008	0.0020–0.0028

Torque Specifications

(All specifications in ft. lbs.)

Engine	Years	Cyl. Head	Conn. Rod	Main Bearing	Crankshaft Damper	Flywheel	Manifold	
							Intake	Exhaust
4-138	1990	③	④	⑤	⑥	⑦	18	⑧
4-151	1989–90	②	29	65	162	55	25	⑨
6-173	1988–90	①	39	70	76	46	⑩	18
6-191	1989–90	①	39	70	76	46	⑩	18

① 33 ft. lbs. plus a 90 degree turn
② Step 1: 18 ft. lbs.
   Step 2:
      Bolts, a, b, c, d, e, f, g, h, j: 26 ft. lbs.;
      Bolt i: 18 ft. lbs.
   Step 3: All bolts and additional 90 degree turn
③ Head bolts numbered 93: 26 ft. lbs. plus a 110 degree turn
   Bolts numbered 111: 26 ft. lbs. plus a 100 degree turn
④ 18 ft. lbs. plus an 80 degree turn
⑤ 15 ft. lbs. plus a 90 degree turn
⑥ 74 ft. lbs. plus a 90 degree turn
⑦ 22 ft. lbs. plus a 45 degree turn
⑧ Studs: 106 inch lbs.
   Nuts: 27 ft. lbs.
⑨ Step 1: 15 ft. lbs.
   Step 2: 24 ft. lbs.
⑩ Inner bolts: 37 ft. lbs.
   Outer bolts: 26 ft. lbs.

7. Discharge the air conditioning system as outlined in the "Discharging the Air Conditioning System" procedures in Chapter 1. If equipped with Air Conditioning.

8. Remove the air conditioning compressor and condenser hose at the compressor, if so equipped. Refer to the "Air Conditioning Compressor" section in this chapter.

9. Disconnect and label engine the vacuum lines.

10. Disconnect and label the electrical connectors from the alternator, air conditioning compressor, fuel injection harness, starter solenoid, engine ground strap, ignition assembly, coolant sensor, oil pressure sensor, knock sensor, oxygen sensor, IAC (idle air control valve) and TPS (throttle position sensor). The last two sensors are located at the throttle body.

11. Disconnect the power brake vacuum hose and throttle cable.

12. Remove the power steering pump and position aside. Do NOT remove the pump hoses unless necessary.

13. Release the fuel pressure, if not already done and remove the fuel lines.

14. Remove the engine torque strut mounts.

15. Remove the transaxle fill tube (Auto Trans only).

16. Remove the exhaust heat shield and exhaust pipe-to-manifold.

17. Remove the upper transaxle-to-engine bolts.

18. Raise the vehicle and support with jackstands.

19. Remove the remaining transaxle-to-engine bolts (lower).

20. Remove the upper exhaust-to-transaxle bracket.

21. Remove the lower radiator hose.

22. Remove the flywheel or converter cover.

23. Scribe a mark on the torque converter and flywheel. Remove the torque converter nuts.

24. Remove the transaxle-to-engine bracket.

25. Lower the vehicle.

26. Install the engine lifting fixture and remove the engine. Place the engine on a suitable workstand.

To install:

NOTE: *Make sure all the engine mounting bolts are in their correct location to prevent transaxle and engine damage.*

1. Install the engine to a lifting fixture and position the engine in the vehicle. With an assistant, align the engine-to-transaxle.

2. Raise the vehicle and support with jackstands.

3. Install the transaxle-to-engine bracket and bolts. Torque the engine-to-transaxle bolts to:

   a. Positions 2,3,4,5,6 – 71 ft. lbs. (96 Nm).

   b. Positions 7,8 – 41 ft. lbs. (56 Nm).

4. Apply thread locking compound and install the torque converter-to-flywheel bolts. Torque the bolts to 46 ft. lbs. (63 Nm). Install the flywheel cover.

5. At the right side of the vehicle, install the engine mount bolt.

6. Install the lower radiator hose and engine ground wires.

7. Install the air conditioning compressor and condensor hose. Connect the compressor and alternator electrical harnesses.

8. Install the heater hoses at the heater core and throttle body.

9. Install the exhaust-to-transaxle bracket.

10. Lower the vehicle.

11. Install the exhaust pipe-to-manifold and heat shield. Torque the exhaust bolts to 22 ft. lbs. (30 Nm).

12. Install the upper engine mounts.

13. Connect the fuel lines.

14. Install the power steering pump, lines and drive belt.

15. Install the throttle cable and power brake vacuum hose.

16. Connect the electrical connectors to the oxygen sensor, knock sensor, oil pressure sensor, coolant sensor, ignition assembly, TPS sensor, IAC sensor and starter solenoid.

17. Connect all engine vacuum hoses.

18. Install the upper radiator hose and fill the radiator with the specified amount of antifreeze.

19. Refill the engine with the specified amount of engine oil.

20. Evacuate and recharge the air conditioning system as outlined in the "Air Conditioning System" section in Chapter 1.

21. Install the air cleaner and inlet hose.

22. Install the hood assembly with the help of an assistant.

23. Recheck all procedures for completion of repair.

24. Recheck all fluid levels.

25. Connect the negative battery cable. Start the engine and check for fluid leaks.

2.5L L4 (Lumina) VIN R

1. Disconnect the negative (–) battery cable. CAUTION: *When draining the coolant, keep in mind that cats and dogs are attracted by the ethylene glycol antifreeze, and are quite likely to drink any that is left in an uncovered container or in puddles on the ground. This will prove fatal in sufficient quantity. Always drain the coolant into a sealable container. Coolant should be reused unless it is contaminated or several years old.*

2. Place a suitable drain pan under the radiator drain valve and drain the engine coolant.

3. Remove the air cleaner assembly.

4. Mark the hood hinges with a scribe and remove the hood assembly. Refer to the "Body" section in Chapter 10 for assistance.

5. Mark and remove all engine wiring. Place all the wire assemblies out of the way.

6. Remove the vacuum, heater and radiator hoses.

7. Remove the air conditioning compressor from the engine and place to the side with a piece of rope or wire. Do NOT disconnect the hoses from the compressor.

8. Remove the alternator and bracket as outlined in the "Alternator" section in this chapter.

9. Remove the engine torque strut.

10. Remove the throttle and transaxle linkage.

11. Remove the transaxle-to-engine bolts except the two upper bolts.

12. Raise the vehicle and support with jackstands.

13. Remove the engine mount-to-frame bolts.

14. Remove the exhaust pipe from the manifold.

15. Remove the torque converter-to-flywheel bolts.

16. Remove the starter motor as outlined in the "Starter Motor" section in this chapter.

17. Remove the power steering pump and attach to the inner fender with a piece of rope or wire. Do NOT disconnect the hoses.

18. Release fuel pressure and remove the fuel lines at the throttle body assembly.

CAUTION: *To reduce the risk of fire and personal injury, it is necessary to relieve the fuel system pressure before servicing any fuel system component. If this procedure is not performed, fuel may be sprayed out of the connection under pressure. Always keep a dry chemical (Class B) fire extinguisher near the work area.*

Fuel pressure relief procedures:

a. Remove the fuel filler cap.

b. Remove the Fuel pump fuse from the fuse block located in the passenger compartment.

c. Start the engine and run until the engine stops due to the lack of fuel.

d. Crank the engine for 3 seconds to ensure all pressure is relieved.

e. Make sure the negative (–) battery cable is disconnected.

19. Remove the rear engine support bracket.

20. Support the transaxle assembly with a transaxle holding fixture.

21. Disconnect the transaxle from the engine and support with a jack.

22. Attach an suitable engine lifting device.

23. Remove the engine assembly. Use care not to get under the engine assembly in case of lift failure.

24. Place the engine on a suitable work stand.

To install:

1. Place the engine assembly onto a suitable lifting device.

2. With an assistant, install the engine into the vehicle.

3. Position the engine into the engine mounts and engage the transaxle with the engine.

4. Remove the engine lifting device.

5. Install the torque converter bolts and engine-to-transaxle mounting bolts. Torque the torque converter bolts to 55 ft. lbs. (75 Nm).

6. Remove the transaxle holding fixture.

7. Install the rear support bracket bolts.

8. Install the engine mount nuts and torque to 32 ft. lbs. (43 Nm).

9. Install the rear transaxle mount bracket bolts and torque to 35 ft. lbs. (47 Nm).

10. Install the fuel lines to the throttle body assembly.

11. Install the power steering pump.

12. Install the starter motor assembly.

13. Install the flywheel cover plate.

14. Install the exhaust pipe-to-manifold.

15. Install the engine torque strut.

16. Install the alternator and bracket as outlined in the "Alternator" section in this chapter.

17. Install the air conditioning compressor.

18. Install the heater, radiator and vacuum hoses.

19. Install the throttle and transaxle linkages.

20. Install and reconnect all engine wiring harnesses.

21. Install the hood assembly to its original position with an assistant.

22. Refill the cooling system with engine coolant.

23. Reconnect the negative (–) battery cable.

24. Install the air cleaner assembly.

25. Inspect for proper fluid levels.

26. Recheck every procedure for proper reinstallation.

27. Start the vehicle and check for any fluid leaks.

2.8L and 3.1L V6 (VIN W, T)

FROM THE BOTTOM

1. Remove the air cleaner assembly.

2. Disconnect the negative (–) battery cable.

CAUTION: *When draining the coolant, keep in mind that cats and dogs are attracted by the ethylene glycol antifreeze, and are quite likely to drink any that is left in an uncovered container or in puddles on the ground. This will prove fatal in sufficient quantity. Always drain the coolant into a sealable container. Coolant should be reused unless it is contaminated or several years old.*

3. Drain the engine coolant into a suitable drain pan.

4. Remove the battery remote jump start terminal from the body, but leave the cables attached.

5. Disconnect the cooling fan electrical connectors.

6. Remove the transaxle cooler lines at the radiator and the fluid level indicator.

7. Remove the upper and lower radiator hoses.

8. Remove the heater inlet and outlet hoses.

9. Release the fuel pressure as outlined below.

CAUTION: *To reduce the risk of fire and personal injury, it is necessary to relieve the fuel system pressure before servicing any fuel system component. If this procedure is not performed, fuel may be sprayed out of the connection under pressure. Always keep a dry chemical (Class B) fire extinguisher near the work area.*

Fuel pressure relief procedures:

a. Disconnect the negative (–) battery cable.

b. Loosen the fuel filler cap to relieve tank vapor pressure.

c. Connect a fuel pressure gauge J–34730–1 or equivalent to the fuel pressure relief connection at the fuel rail.

d. Wrap a shop towel around the fittings while connecting the gauge to prevent fuel spillage.

e. Install a bleed hose into an approved container and open the valve to bleed the system pressure. The system is safe for servicing.

10. Remove the serpentine belt from the engine as outlined in the "Belt" section in Chapter 1.

11. Remove the shift cable linkage and cable from the mounting bracket.

12. Remove the accelerator and cruise control from the throttle linkage, if so equipped.

13. Remove the air conditioning pressure switch wire connector.

14. Remove the vacuum check valve from the power brake booster.

15. Remove the canister purge vacuum line at the engine.

16. Remove the torque struts from the engine.

17. Remove all electrical connectors at the right side cowl.

18. Remove the upper bolts securing the wiring harness plastic bracket-to-body side rail.

19. Remove the ECM and fuse block and set on top of the engine.

20. Remove the strut-to-body mounting nuts.

21. Remove the vacuum hose from the vacuum reservoir.

22. Raise the vehicle and support with jackstands.

23. Remove the front wheel and tire assemblies.

24. Remove the right side splash shield.

25. Remove the oil filter.

26. Remove the air conditioning compressor and hang from the body with the hoses still connected. Do NOT disconnect the refrigerant hoses.

27. Remove the exhaust crossover pipe from the manifold.

28. Remove Steering gear pinch bolt as outlined in Chapter 8.

29. Remove the brake hose from the strut.

30. Remove the brake calipers as outlined in the "Brake Caliper" section in Chapter 9.

CAUTION: *Some brake pads contain asbestos, which has been determined to be a cancer causing agent. Never clean the brake surfaces with compressed air! Avoid inhaling any dust from any brake surface! When cleaning brake surfaces, use a commercially available brake cleaning fluid.*

31. Lower the vehicle far enough to place the engine/transaxle table under the frame.

32. Remove the frame bolts.

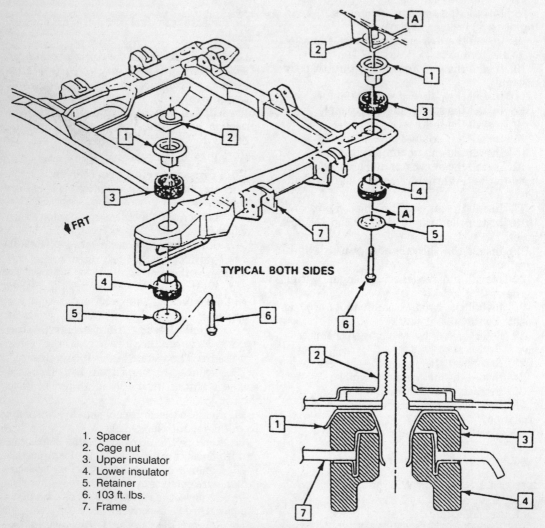

TYPICAL BOTH SIDES

1. Spacer
2. Cage nut
3. Upper insulator
4. Lower insulator
5. Retainer
6. 103 ft. lbs.
7. Frame

Frame removal

33. Lower the table with the engine/transaxle attached.

34. Raise the vehicle and remove the engine/transaxle from the vehicle.

35. Seperate the engine from the transaxle and place the engine on a suitable work stand.

To install:

1. Attach the transaxle and engine together and tighten. Slowly lower the body onto the drivetrain.

2. Install the strut bolts to the shock towers.

3. Install the frame bolts.

4. Remove the engine/transaxle table from under the vehicle.

5. Install the brake calipers as outlined in Chapter 9.

6. Install the brake hose at the strut.

7. Install the steering pinch bolt as outlined in Chapter 8.

8. Install the exhaust crossover pipe-to-manifold.

9. Install the air conditioning compressor as outlined in this chapter.

10. Install the oil filter and right side splash shield.

11. Install the tire and wheel assemblies and torque the lug nuts to 100 ft. lbs. (136 Nm).

12. Install the wiring harness bracket to body side rail.

13. Lower the vehicle.

14. Install the vacuum hose at the vacuum reservoir.

15. Install the ECM and the fuse block.

16. Install the remaining bolts securing the wiring harness bracket to the body side rail.

17. Install the torque struts at engine.

18. Reconnect the canister purge vacuum line and vacuum check valve at the power brake booster.

19. Reconnect the air conditioning pressure switch electrical connector.

20. Reconnect the accelerator and cruise control cables to the mounting bracket.

21. Install the serpentine belt as outlined in the "Belt" section in Chapter 1.

22. Install the heater inlet and outlet hoses.

23. Install the radiator upper and lower hoses.

24. Install the transaxle fluid indicator and cooler lines at the radiator.

25. Reconnect the cooling fan electrical connectors.

26. Install the battery remote jump start terminal to body.

27. Refill all necessary fluids (engines oil, coolant, transaxle fluid).

28. Install the battery cables.

29. Install the air cleaner assembly.

30. Recheck all procedures for proper reinstallation.

31. Start the engine and check for any fluid leaks.

2.8L and 3.1L V6 (VIN W, T)

FROM THE TOP

1. Remove the air cleaner and duct assembly.

2. Disconnect the negative (–) battery cable.

3. Mark the hood hinges with a marker or a scripe to ensure proper reinstallation. With an assistant, remove the hood assembly.

4. Mark and remove all necessary engine wiring and place the harnesses out of the way.

5. Remove the throttle, T.V. and cruise control (if equipped) from the throttle body assembly.

6. Release the fuel pressure and remove the fuel lines at the throttle body.

CAUTION: *To reduce the risk of fire and personal injury, it is necessary to relieve the fuel system pressure before servicing any fuel system component. If this procedure is not performed, fuel may be sprayed out of the connection under pressure. Always keep a dry chemical (Class B) fire extinguisher near the work area.*

Fuel pressure relief procedures:

a. Disconnect the negative (–) battery cable.

b. Loosen the fuel filler cap to relieve tank vapor pressure.

c. Connect a fuel pressure gauge J–34730–1 or equivalent to the fuel pressure relief connection at the fuel rail.

d. Wrap a shop towel around the fittings while connecting the gauge to prevent fuel spillage.

e. Install a bleed hose into an approved container and open the valve to bleed the system pressure. The system is safe for servicing.

7. Remove the AIR pump and serpentine belt as outlined in the "Belt" section in Chapter 1.

8. Position a suitable drain pan under the radiator drain valve and drain the engine coolant.

CAUTION: *When draining the coolant, keep in mind that cats and dogs are attracted by the ethylene glycol antifreeze, and are quite likely to drink any that is left in an uncovered container or in puddles on the ground. This will prove fatal in sufficient quantity. Always drain the coolant into a sealable container. Coolant should be reused unless it is contaminated or several years old.*

9. Remove the upper and lower radiator hoses.

10. Remove the air conditioning compressor mounting bolts at the front mounting bracket. Refer to the "Compressor" section in this chapter for assistance.

11. Remove the power steering pump and move to the side. Attach to the body with a piece of wire or rope. Do NOT disconnect the pump hoses.

12. Remove the heater hoses from the engine and move out of the way.

13. Remove the brake booster vacuum hose.

14. Remove the EGR hose from the exhaust manifold.

15. Raise the vehicle and support with jackstands.

16. Remove the air conditioning compressor from the engine and attach to the body with a piece of rope or wire. Do NOT disconnect the refrigerant hoses.

17. Remove the flywheel cover, starter motor and torque converter bolts.

18. Remove the transaxle bracket and front engine mount nuts.

19. Remove the exhaust pipe at the crossover pipe.

20. Lower the vehicle.

21. Remove the torque struts and coolant recovery bottle.

22. Remove the left crossover pipe-to-manifold clamp.

23. Pull the engine forward and support with a piece of rope.

24. Disconnect the bulkhead electrical connector.

25. Remove the right crossover pipe-to-manifold clamp.

26. Remove the engine support and allow the engine to move to the normal position.

27. Support the transaxle with a suitable floor jack or equivalent.

28. Remove the remaining transaxle-to-engine bolts.

29. Attach an engine lifting device and remove the engine from the vehicle. Check for connected wires and hoses as the engine is coming out of the body.

30. Place the engine on a suitable work stand.

To install:

1. With an assistant, install a lifting device onto the engine and position into the vehicle.

2. Remove the lifting device.

3. Install the transaxle-to-engine bolts.

4. Remove the transaxle support.

5. Pull the engine assembly forward and support with a piece of rope.

6. Reconnect the right crossover pipe-to-manifold clamp.

7. Reconnect the bulkhead electrical connector.

8. Remove the engine support and allow the engine to roll to the normal position.

9. Install the left crossover pipe-to-manifold clamp.

10. Install the coolant recovery bottle and torque struts.

11. Raise the vehicle and support with jackstands.

12. Install the crossover-to-exhaust pipe.

13. Install the front engine mount retaining nuts and torque to 32 ft. lbs. (43 Nm).

14. Install the transaxle bracket, torque converter bolts and starter motor.

15. Install the flywheel cover.

16. Install the air conditioning compressor-to-engine as outlined in the "Compressor" section in this chapter.

17. Lower the vehicle.

18. Install the EGR valve to exhaust manifold.

19. Reconnect the brake booster vacuum supply, heater hoses and power steering pump.

20. Install the air conditioning compressor front mounting bracket bolts.

21. Install the radiator hoses, serpentine and AIR pump belts. Refer to the "Belt" section in Chapter 1 for assistance.

22. Reconnect the fuel lines to the throttle body assembly.

23. Install the throttle, TV and cruise control linkage to the throttle body.

24. Reconnect all necessary engine electrical wiring.

25. Install the hood assembly with an assistant.

26. Reconnect the battery cables.

27. Install the air cleaner and duct assembly.

28. Recheck all procedures for proper reinstallation and correct if necessary.

29. Refill the engine with engine oil, coolant and transaxle fluid if needed.

30. Inspect vehicle for fluid leaks before and after starting the engine.

31. Road test the vehicle and recheck for fluid leaks.

Engine Mount

REMOVAL AND INSTALLATION

2.5L L4 (Lumina) VIN R

1. Disconnect the negative battery cable.

2. Raise and safely support the vehicle

3. Remove the engine-to-chassis nuts.

4. Disconnect the engine torque struts.

5. Install an engine support fixture J–28467–A or equivalent.

6. Remove the upper mount-to-engine bracket nuts and remove the mount.

7. Install the mount and mount-to-engine bracket. Tighten the nuts to 32 ft. lbs. (43 Nm).

8. Install and tighten the torque strut nuts to 32 ft. lbs. (43 Nm).

9. Lower the vehicle and remove the engine support fixture.

2.3L QUAD 4, 2.8L and 3.1L

1. Disconnect the negative battery cable. Raise and safely support the vehicle.

2. Remove the engine mount retaining nuts from below the cradle mounting bracket.

3. Raise the engine slightly to provide clearance and remove the engine mount- to-bracket nuts.

4. Remove the engine mount.

5. Install the mount in position and tighten the mount-to-bracket nuts to 32 ft. lbs. Lower the engine into position.

6. Install the mounting bracket-to-cradle nuts and tighten to 63 ft. lbs.

7. Lower the vehicle and connect the negative battery cable.

Rocker Arm Cover

REMOVAL AND INSTALLATION

2.3L QUAD 4 (VIN A,D)

INTAKE COVER

NOTE: *The camshaft housing and cylinder head use the same retaining bolts. When the bolts are removed to service the camshaft cover, the cylinder head gasket MUST be replaced also. When valve components are removed, mark each part for proper reinstallation.*

1. Disconnect the negative (–) battery cable.

2. Remove the ignition coil and module assembly as outlined in this chapter. Use a spark plug boot remover tool J–36011 or equivalent.

3. Disconnect the idle speed power steering pressure switch, remove the power steering belt, retaining bolts and position the pump aside out of the way. Do NOT disconnect the pump hoses. Remove the pump bracket.

4. Remove the power steering pump drive pulley using a three jaw puller or steering wheel puller with backup nuts.

5. Remove the oil/air separator but leave the hoses attached.

CAUTION: *To reduce the risk of fire and personal injury, it is necessary to relieve the fuel system pressure before servicing any fuel system component. If this procedure is not performed, fuel may be sprayed out of the connection under pressure. Always keep a dry chemical (Class B) fire extinguisher near the work area.*

6. **Fuel pressure relief procedures:**

a. Disconnect the negative (–) battery cable.

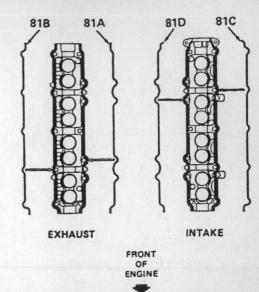

81A. Inner seal (exhaust, red)
81B. Outer seal (exhaust, red)
81C. Outer seal (intake, blue)
81D. Inner seal (intake, blue)

Camshaft housing seals — 2.3L Quad 4

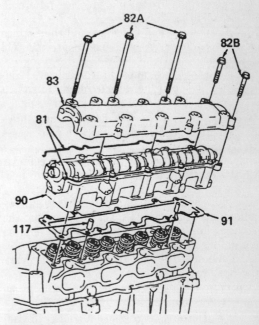

81. Housing to cover seals. Each seal is different
82A. Bolts
82B. Bolts
83. Camshaft cover
90. Camshaft housing (intake shown)
91. Cylinder head to camshaft housing gasket
117. Dowel pin

Camshaft housing covers — 2.3L Quad 4

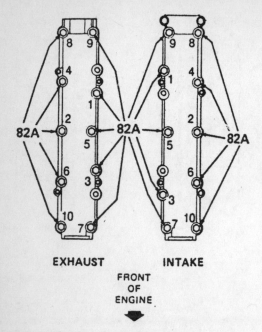

EXHAUST   INTAKE

FRONT
OF
ENGINE

Camshaft housing torque sequence

b. Loosen the fuel filler cap to relieve tank vapor pressure.

c. Connect a fuel pressure gauge J-34730-1 or equivalent to the fuel pressure relief connection at the fuel rail.

d. Wrap a shop towel around the fittings while connecting the gauge to prevent fuel spillage.

e. Install a bleed hose into an approved container and open the valve to bleed the system pressure. The system is safe for servicing.

7. Disconnect the fuel lines, vacuum lines and engine electrical connectors to gain access to the housing cover.

8. Remove the fuel rail from the cylinder head. Cover injector openings and injector nozzles.

9. Disconnect the timing chain cover and position out of the way. Do not remove from the vehicle. For assistance, refer to the "Timing Chain" procedures in this chapter.

10. Remove the camshaft housing and cylinder head retaining bolts.

NOTE: *Use the reverse of the torquing sequence to loosen the retaining bolts.*

11. Push the cover off the housing by threading four housing bolts into the tapped holes in the cover. Tighten the bolts in an even sequence so the cover does not bind on the dowel pins and remove the cover.

To install:

1. Clean all gasket mating surfaces with a gasket scraper and solvent. RTV sealant is NOT needed on the gaskets. The gaskets are different, refer to the "Camshaft Housing Seals" illustration in this section.

2. Using new gaskets, position the cover onto the camshaft housing.

3. Apply pipe sealant GM 1052080 or equivalent to the housing and cover retaining bolts.

4. Install the bolts and torque in sequence to the specified torque in the specification chart in the beginning of this chapter. Also, refer to the "Cylinder Head" installation procedures for torque sequence.

5. Install the timing chain housing.

6. Uncover the injectors and install new O-rings. Install the fuel rail-to-cylinder head and tighten.

7. Connect electrical connectors, vacuum lines and fuel hoses.

8. Install the oil/air separator, power steering drive pulley using installer J-36015 and power steering pump assembly.

9. Install the steering pump drive belt and adjust to specifications in Chapter 1.

10. Install the ignition assembly and connect the negative battery cable.

11. Recheck all procedures to ensure completion of repair, start the engine and check for fluid leaks.

EXHAUST COVER

NOTE: *The camshaft housing and cylinder head use the same retaining bolts. When the bolts are removed to service the camshaft cover, the cylinder head gasket MUST be replaced also. When valve components are removed, mark each part for proper reinstallation.*

1. Disconnect the negative (–) battery cable.

2. Remove the ignition coil and module assembly as outlined in this chapter. Use a spark plug boot remover tool J-36011 or equivalent.

3. Disconnect the oil pressure switch and remove the transaxle level dipstick (automatic).

4. Remove the oil/air separator but leave the hoses attached.

5. Disconnect vacuum lines and engine electrical connectors to gain access to the housing cover.

6. Disconnect the timing chain cover and position out of the way. Do not remove from the vehicle. For assistance, refer to the "Timing Chain" procedures in this chapter.

7. Remove the camshaft housing and cylinder head retaining bolts.

NOTE: *Use the reverse of the torquing sequence to loosen the retaining bolts.*

8. Push the cover off the housing by threading four housing bolts into the tapped holes in the cover. Tighten the bolts in an even sequence so the cover does not bind on the dowel pins and remove the cover.

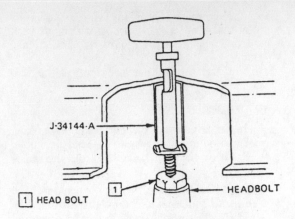

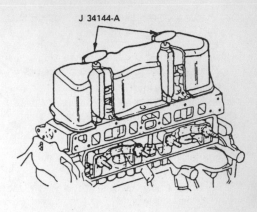

Rocker arm cover removal — 2.5L L4 Lumina

To install:

1. Clean all gasket mating surfaces with a gasket scraper and solvent. RTV sealant is NOT needed on the gaskets. The gaskets are different, refer to the "Camshaft Housing Seals" illustration in this section.

2. Using new gaskets, position the cover onto the camshaft housing.

3. Apply pipe sealant GM 1052080 or equivalent to the housing and cover retaining bolts.

4. Install the bolts and torque in sequence to the specified torque in the specification chart in the beginning of this chapter. Also, refer to the "Cylinder Head" installation procedures for torque sequence.

5. Install the timing chain housing.

6. Connect electrical connectors and vacuum lines.

7. Install the oil/air separator.

8. Install the ignition assembly and connect the negative battery cable.

9. Recheck all procedures to ensure completion of repair, start the engine and check for fluid leaks.

2.5L L4 (Lumina) VIN R

1. Remove the air cleaner assembly. (Refer to Chapter 1).

2. Remove the PCV valve and hose.

3. Remove the accelerator and throttle valve TV cables.

4. Remove the valve cover bolts.

5. Disconnect and mark the wires from the spark plugs and clips.

6. Remove the valve cover by using the Rocker Arm Cover Removing tool No. J34144–A or equivalent and lightly tap with a rubber hammer.

NOTE: *Prying on the cover could cause damage to the sealing surfaces.*

7. Remove the rocker arm bolt and ball.

8. If replacing the push rod only, loosen the rocker arm bolt and swing the arm clear of the push rod.

9. Remove the rocker arm and pushrod. If removing more than one, label each part to ensure the part is placed in its original location.

To install:

10. Clean the rocker arm cover with solvent and dry with a clean rag.

11. Install the push rod into the same hole as removed. Place the guide, rocker arm, ball and nut over the stud and finger tighten the nut.

12. Make sure the camshaft is on the base of the cam lob (valve in the closed position) before tightening the rocker arm nut. Torque the rocker arm nut to 24 ft. lbs. (32 Nm).

13. Apply a continuous $\frac{3}{16}$ in. diameter bead of RTV sealant or equivalent around the cylinder head sealing surfaces inboard at the bolt holes.

NOTE: *Keep the sealant out of the bolt holes.*

14. Install the rocker arm cover and torque the attaching bolts to 80 inch lbs. (9 Nm).

15. Install the spark plug wires and clips,

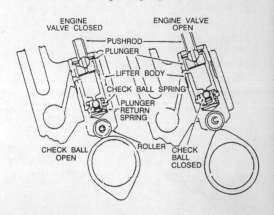

Roller valve lifters — 2.5L L4 Lumina

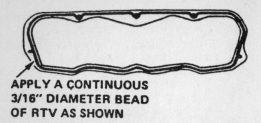

**APPLY A CONTINUOUS
3/16" DIAMETER BEAD
OF RTV AS SHOWN**

Camshaft housing cover installation

PCV valve and hose, accelerator and TV cable and air cleaner assembly.

2.8L and 3.1L V6 (VIN W, T)
FRONT ROCKER COVER

1. Remove the air cleaner assembly.
2. Disconnect the negative (–) battery cable.
3. Drain the engine coolant from the radiator.

CAUTION: *When draining the coolant, keep in mind that cats and dogs are attracted by the ethylene glycol antifreeze, and are quite likely to drink any that is left in an uncovered container or in puddles on the ground. This will prove fatal in sufficient quantity. Always drain the coolant into a sealable container. Coolant should be reused unless it is contaminated or several years old.*

4. Remove the ignition wire clamps and guide from the coolant tube.
5. Remove the coolant tube mount at the cylinder head, coolant tube at each end, coolant tube at the water pump and coolant tube.
6. Remove the tube from the rocker cover-to-air inlet.
7. Remove the four rocker cover retaining bolts and remove the cover.

NOTE: *Prying on the cover could cause damage to the sealing surfaces.*

To install:
1. Clean all sealing surfaces on the cylinder head and rocker cover with degreaser and a gasket scraper.
2. Install a new gasket and bolt grommets. Make sure the gasket is properly seated in the rocker cover groove.
3. Apply a continuous $\frac{3}{16}$ in. diameter bead of RTV sealant or equivalent around the cylinder head sealing surfaces inboard at the bolt holes.
NOTE: *Keep the sealant out of the bolt holes.*
4. Install the rocker cover and torque the retaining bolts to 89 inch lbs. (10 Nm).
5. Install the ignition wire guide.
6. Install the tube from the rocker arm cover-to-air inlet.

7. Reconnect the coolant tube, coolant tube hose at the water pump, coolant tube at each end and coolant tube mount at the cylinder head.
8. Install the ignition wire clamp at the coolant tube.

REAR ROCKER COVER

1. Remove the air cleaner assembly.
2. Disconnect the negative (–) battery cable.
3. Drain the engine coolant from the radiator.

CAUTION: *When draining the coolant, keep in mind that cats and dogs are attracted by the ethylene glycol antifreeze, and are quite likely to drink any that is left in an uncovered container or in puddles on the ground. This will prove fatal in sufficient quantity. Always drain the coolant into a sealable container. Coolant should be reused unless it is contaminated or several years old.*

4. Remove the vacuum hoses at the intake plenum.
5. Remove the EGR tube at the crossover pipe.
6. Remove the ignition wire guide and harness at the intake plenum and at spark plugs.
7. Remove the coolant hoses at the throttle base and electrical wiring from the intake plenum.
8. Remove the throttle, TV and cruise control cables from the throttle body assembly.
9. Remove the bracket from the right side of the intake plenum.
10. Remove the brake booster vacuum hose from the plenum.
11. Remove the serpentine belt as outlined in the "Belt" section in Chapter 1.

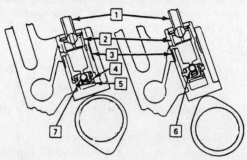

1. Pushrod
2. Plunger
3. Lifter body
4. Check ball spring
5. Plunger return spring
6. Check ball (closed)
7. Check ball (open)

Conventional valve lifters — 2.8L and 3.1L V6 engines

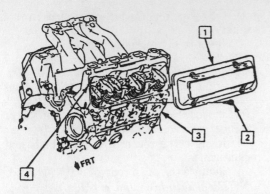

1. Rocker arm cover
2. 89 inch lbs.
3. Cylinder head
4. Sealer

Rocker arm cover removal — 2.8L and 3.1L V6 engines

12. Remove the coolant recovery bottle, exhaust pipe at the crossover and engine struts at the engine.

13. Rotate the engine as outlined in the "Ignition Coil" section in this chapter.

14. Remove the alternator and set aside.

15. Remove the PCV valve from the rocker cover.

16. Remove the four rocker cover retaining bolts and remove the cover.

NOTE: *Prying on the cover could cause damage to the sealing surfaces.*

To install:

1. Clean all sealing surfaces on the cylinder head and rocker cover with degreaser and a gasket scraper.

2. Install a new gasket and bolt grommets. Make sure the gasket is properly seated in the rocker cover groove.

3. Apply a continuous ³⁄₁₆ in. diameter bead of RTV sealant or equivalent around the cylinder head sealing surfaces inboard at the bolt holes.

NOTE: *Keep the sealant out of the bolt holes.*

4. Install the rocker cover and torque the retaining bolts to 89 inch lbs. (10 Nm).

5. Install the PCV valve to the rocker cover.

6. Install the alternator.

7. Return the engine to the proper position. Refer to the "Igntion Coil and Engine Rotating" section in this chapter.

8. Install the torque struts to the engine, exhaust pipe at the crossover and the coolant recovery bottle.

9. Install the serpentine belt as outlined in the "Belts" section in Chapter 1.

10. Reconnect the brake booster vacuum hose and support bracket at the intake plenum.

11. Reconnect the throttle, TV and cruise control linkage to the intake plenum.

12. Reconnect all necessary electrical wiring to the intake plenum.

13. Install the coolant hoses to the throttle base and ignition wire harness.

14. Install the EGR tube at the crossover pipe.

15. Refill the cooling system with the specified engine coolant.

16. Reconnect the negative (–) battery cable.

17. Install the air cleaner assembly.

18. Recheck all procedures to ensure proper reinstallation.

19. Start the vehicle and check for oil, coolant, vacuum and exhaust leaks.

Pushrod Cover
REMOVAL AND INSTALLATION
2.5L L4 (Lumina) VIN R

1. Disconnect the negative (–) battery cable.

2. Remove the intake manifold as outlined in the "Intake Manifold" procedures in this chapter.

CAUTION: *When draining the coolant, keep in mind that cats and dogs are attracted by the ethylene glycol antifreeze, and are quite likely to drink any that is left in an uncovered container or in puddles on the ground. This will prove fatal in sufficient quantity. Always drain the coolant into a sealable container. Coolant should be reused unless it is contaminated or several years old.*

3. Remove the four push rod cover attaching nuts.

NOTE: *Do not pry on the cover or damage to the sealing surface may result.*

4. To remove the push rod cover, proceed as follows:

a. Unscrew the four nuts from the cover attaching studs, reverse the two nuts so the washers face outward and screw them back onto the inner two studs. Assemble the remaining nuts to the same two inner studs with washers facing inward.

b. Using a small wrench on the inner nut, on each stud, jam the two nuts tightly together. Again using the small wrench, on the inner nut, unscrew the studs until the cover breaks loose.

c. After breaking the cover loose, remove the jammed nuts from each stud. Remove the cover from the studs. Examine the stud and rubber washer assembly and replace if either stud or washer is damaged.

To install:

5. Clean the sealing surfaces on the cover and cylinder block.

6. Apply a continuous ³⁄₁₆ inch (5mm) bead

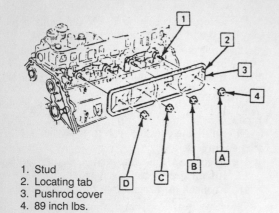

1. Stud
2. Locating tab
3. Pushrod cover
4. 89 inch lbs.

Pushrod cover — 2.5L L4 Lumina

of RTV sealer or equivalent around the push rod cover.

7. Install the cover and torque the bolts to 90 inch lbs. (10 Nm).

8. Install the intake manifold as outlined in the "Intake Manifold" installation procedures in this chapter.

Rocker Arm and Push Rod

REMOVAL AND INSTALLATION

2.5L L4 (Lumina) VIN R

1. Disconnect the negative (–) battery cable.
2. Remove the rocker arm cover as outlined in the "Rocker Arm Cover" procedures in this section.
3. Remove the rocker arm bolt and ball.
4. If replacing the push rod only, loosen the rocker arm bolt and swing the arm clear of the push rod.
5. If replacing the rocker arm or guide, remove the rocker arm and guide.

NOTE: *Mark all components so they are reinstalled in their original location. The push rod guide are different and MUST be replaced in their original location. Coat all bearing surfaces with Molykote® or equivalent before installing valve components.*

6. Install the push rod through the cylinder head and into the lifter seat.
7. Install the guide, rocker arm, ball and bolt. Torque the rocker arm bolts to 24 ft. lbs. (32 Nm).
8. Install the rocker arm cover as outlined in the "Rocker Arm Cover" procedures in this section.

2.8L and 3.1L V6 (VIN W, T)

1. Disconnect the negative (–) battery cable.
2. Remove the rocker arm cover as outlined

in the "Rocker Arm Cover" procedures in this section.

3. Remove the rocker arm nuts.

NOTE: *Mark all components so they are reinstalled in their original location. The push rod guide are different and MUST be replaced in their original location. Coat all bearing surfaces with Molykote® or equivalent before installing valve components.*

4. Remove the rocker arm pivot balls and rocker arms.
5. Remove the push rods.

NOTE: *The intake and exhaust push rods are different lengths. The intake push rods are marked orange. The exhaust push rods are marked blue.*

To install:

6. Position the correct length push rod into the cylinder head (intake = orange and exhaust = blue). Make sure the push rods are seated in the lifter.
7. Coat the rocker arm balls with Molykote® or equivalent. Install the rocker arms and pivot balls over the push rod.
8. Torque the rocker arm nuts to 18 ft. lbs. (25 Nm).
9. Install the rocker arm cover as outlined in the "Rocker Arm Cover" procedures in this section.

Thermostat

The thermostat is used to control the flow of engine coolant. When the engine is cold, the thermostat is closed to prevent coolant from circulating through the engine. As the engine begins to warm up, the thermostat opens to allow the coolant to flow through the radiator and cool the engine to its normal operating temperature. Fuel economy and engine durability is increased when operated at normal operating temperature.

REMOVAL AND INSTALLATION

2.3L QUAD 4 (VIN A,D)

CAUTION: *When draining the coolant, keep in mind that cats and dogs are attracted by the ethylene glycol antifreeze, and are quite likely to drink any that is left in an uncovered container or in puddles on the ground. This will prove fatal in sufficient quantity. Always drain the coolant into a sealable container. Coolant should be reused unless it is contaminated or several years old.*

1. Remove the air cleaner assembly and partially drain the engine coolant into a drain pan.
2. Remove the radiator and heater hoses from the coolant outlet.
3. Remove the electrical connectors from the coolant outlet.

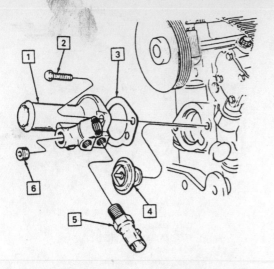

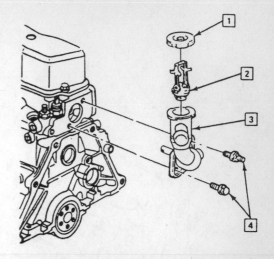

1. Water outlet
2. 19 ft. lbs.
3. Gasket
4. Thermostat
5. Coolant sensor
6. Plug

1. Cap
2. Thermostat
3. Housing assembly
4. 17 ft. lbs.

Thermostat assembly — 2.5L L4Lumina

Thermostat assembly — 2.3L Quad 4

4. Remove the pipe and retaining bolts from the outlet.

5. Remove the outlet and thermostat.

To install:

1. Clean the gasket mating surfaces with a gasket scraper and solvent.

2. Using a new gasket and RTV sealant, install the thermostat and outlet.

3. Torque the bolts to 19 ft. lbs. (26 Nm).

4. Install the pipe, electrical connectors and hoses to the coolant outlet.

5. Refill the radiator with the specified amount of engine coolant, connect the negative battery cable and install the air cleaner.

6. Start the engine and check for leaks.

2.5L L4 (Lumina) VIN R

CAUTION: *When draining the coolant, keep in mind that cats and dogs are attracted by the ethylene glycol antifreeze, and are quite likely to drink any that is left in an uncovered container or in puddles on the ground. This will prove fatal in sufficient quantity. Always drain the coolant into a sealable container. Coolant should be reused unless it is contaminated or several years old.*

To avoid being burned, do NOT remove the thermostat housing cap while the engine is at normal operating temperature. The cooling system will release scalding fluid and steam under pressure if the cap is removed while the engine is still hot.

1. Drain about a $1/2$ gallon of engine coolant from the radiator.

2. Remove the thermostat housing cap.

3. Remove the thermostat by using the wire handle to lift it out of the housing.

4. **To install:** insert the thermostat and seal into the housing. Install the thermostat housing cap. Refill the engine with the proper amount of engine coolant.

2.8L and 3.1L V6 (VIN W, T)

1. Drain about a $1/2$ gallon of engine coolant from the radiator.

2. Remove the radiator hose from the water outlet.

3. Remove the water outlet attaching bolts and water outlet.

4. Remove the thermostat.

5. Clean the manifold water inlet and water outlet mating surfaces with solvent and a gasket scraper.

To install:

6. Position the thermostat into the intake manifold.

7. Apply a 0.125 inch (3mm) bead of RTV sealer to the thermostat housing.

8. Install the water outlet to the intake manifold. Torque the attaching bolts to 17 ft. lbs. (23 Nm).

9. Install the radiator hose to the water outlet housing.

10. Refill the engine with the specified engine coolant. Start the engine and check for coolant leaks.

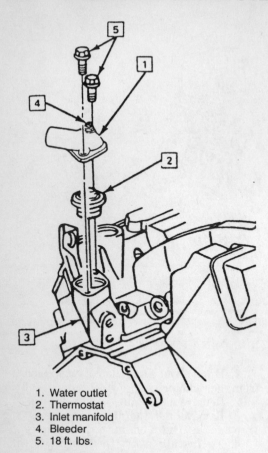

1. Water outlet
2. Thermostat
3. Inlet manifold
4. Bleeder
5. 18 ft. lbs.

Thermostat assembly — 2.8L and 3.1L V6 engines

Intake Manifold

REMOVAL AND INSTALLATION

2.3L QUAD 4 (VIN A,D)

1. Disconnect the negative (–) battery cable.
2. Drain the engine coolant from the radiator.
3. Remove the vacuum hoses and electrical connectors from the intake manifold. Position the harnesses aside out of the way.
4. Remove the air cleaner and inlet air duct.
5. Remove the throttle cable, power brake vacuum hose, throttle body coolant lines and the oil/air separator from the oil filler.
6. Remove the oil fill tube and cap. Rotate the tube after removing the retaining screw.
7. Remove the intake manifold support bracket, manifold retaining bolts and nuts. Remove the manifold and gasket.

To install:

1. Clean the gasket mating surfaces with a gasket scraper and solvent.
2. Install the new gasket so the numbers on the gasket face are turned toward the manifold surface.
3. Install the manifold and torque the retain-

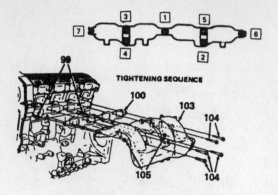

TIGHTENING SEQUENCE

99. Stud
100. Intake manifold gasket
103. Intake manifold
104. Bolt
105. Nut

Intake manifold — 2.3L Quad 4

ing bolt/nuts in sequence to specifications located in the beginning of this chapter.
4. Install the intake manifold bracket and retainer.
5. Install the oil fill tube with a new O-ring. Rotate as necessary to gain clearance.
6. Install the oil/air separator-to-fill cap.
7. Install the throttle body-to-intake manifold using a new gasket.
8. Connect the vacuum hoses, electrical connectors and coolant hoses.
9. Refill the radiator with the specified amount of engine coolant.
10. Install the air cleaner and inlet tube, connect the negative battery cable and recheck each operation for completion of repair.
11. Start the engine and check for fluid leaks.

2.5L L4 (Lumina) VIN R

1. Disconnect the negative (–) battery cable.
2. Remove the air cleaner assembly.
3. Remove the PCV valve and hose at the throttle body assembly.
4. Drain the engine coolant at the radiator.
CAUTION: *When draining the coolant, keep in mind that cats and dogs are attracted by the ethylene glycol antifreeze, and are quite likely to drink any that is left in an uncovered container or in puddles on the ground. This will prove fatal in sufficient quantity. Always drain the coolant into a sealable container. Coolant should be reused unless it is contaminated or several years old.*
5. Release the fuel pressure and remove the fuel lines from the throttle body.
CAUTION: *To reduce the risk of fire and personal injury, it is necessary to relieve the fuel system pressure before servicing any fuel*

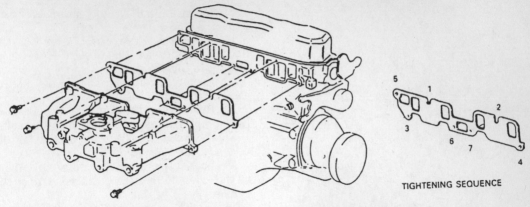

Intake manifold assembly and tightening sequence — 2.5L L4 Lumina. Tighten the bolts to 25 ft. lbs.

system component. If this procedure is not performed, fuel may be sprayed out of the connection under pressure. Always keep a dry chemical (Class B) fire extinguisher near the work area.

Fuel pressure relief procedures:

a. Remove the fuel filler cap.

b. Remove the Fuel pump fuse from the fuse block located in the passenger compartment.

c. Start the engine and run until the engine stops due to the lack of fuel.

d. Crank the engine for 3 seconds to ensure all pressure is relieved.

e. Make sure the negative (–) battery cable is disconnected.

6. Remove the vacuum lines and brake booster hose from the throttle body.

7. Remove all linkage and wiring from the TBI assembly.

8. Rotate the engine as outlined in the "Ignition Coil" section in this chapter.

9. Remove the heater hose.

10. Remove the seven intake manifold retaining bolts and remove the manifold.

To install:

1. Clean all gasket surfaces on the cylinder head and intake manifold with solvent and a gasket scraper.

2. Install the intake manifold with a new gasket.

3. Install all the retaining bolts and washers hand tight.

4. Torque the bolts in proper sequence, as shown in the "Intake Manifold" illustration in this section, to 25 ft. lbs. (34 Nm).

5. Rotate the engine to the original position as outlined in the "Ignition Coil" section in this chapter.

6. Install all heater hoses, vacuum hoses, throttle linkages and wiring.

7. Install the fuel lines.

8. Refill the engine with the specified engine coolant.

9. Install the PCV valve and hose to the TBI assembly.

10. Install the air cleaner assembly and reconnect the negative (–) battery cable.

11. Start the engine and check for fuel, oil, vacuum and coolant leaks.

2.8L and 3.1L V6 (VIN W, T)

1. Disconnect the negative (–) battery cable.

2. Remove the air cleaner assembly.

3. Remove all cables from the throttle body.

4. Remove the brake vacuum, cable bracket, air intake duct and throttle body from the intake plenum.

5. Remove the EGR, wiring harness, intake plenum bolts and the plenum assembly.

6. Release the fuel pressure and remove the fuel lines.

CAUTION: *To reduce the risk of fire and personal injury, it is necessary to relieve the fuel system pressure before servicing any fuel system component. If this procedure is not performed, fuel may be sprayed out of the connection under pressure. Always keep a dry chemical (Class B) fire extinguisher near the work area.*

Fuel pressure relief procedures:

a. Disconnect the negative (–) battery cable.

b. Loosen the fuel filler cap to relieve tank vapor pressure.

c. Connect a fuel pressure gauge J–34730-1 or equivalent to the fuel pressure relief connection at the fuel rail.

d. Wrap a shop towel around the fittings while connecting the gauge to prevent fuel spillage.

e. Install a bleed hose into an approved container and open the valve to bleed the system pressure. The system is safe for servicing.

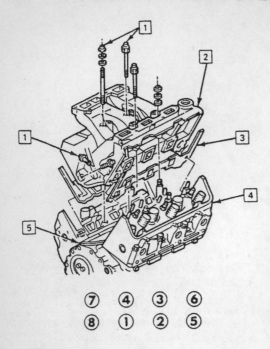

1. Tighten in proper sequence
   to 15 ft. lbs., then
   retighten to 24 ft. lbs.
2. Intake manifold
3. Gasket
4. Cylinder head
5. Sealer

**Intake manifold assembly and tightening
sequence — 2.8L and 3.1L V6 engines**

7. Remove the serpentine belt as outlined in the "Belts" section in Chapter 1.

8. Remove the alternator and move to the side.

9. Remove the power steering hoses at the alternator bracket. Remove the power steering pump and move to the side. Refer to the "Power Steering Pump" procedures in Chapter 8.

10. Remove the wire connectors from the fuel injectors.

11. Drain the cooling system at the radiator. CAUTION: *When draining the coolant, keep in mind that cats and dogs are attracted by the ethylene glycol antifreeze, and are quite likely to drink any that is left in an uncovered container or in puddles on the ground. This will prove fatal in sufficient quantity. Always drain the coolant into a sealable container. Coolant should be reused unless it is contaminated or several years old.*

12. Remove the heater hose at the water pump and cylinder head.

13. Remove the front rocker arm cover as outlined in the "Rocker Arm Cover (FRONT)" procedures in this chapter.

14. Remove the PCV hose, alternator brace and bracket.

15. Remove the rear rocker arm cover as outlined in the "Rocker Arm Cover (REAR)" procedures in this chapter.

16. Remove the upper radiator hose, all necessary wiring and coolant sensor.

17. Remove the throttle body heater hose, heater pipe to intake and intake manifold bolts. NOTE: *Retain the Belleville washers in the same orientation on the four center bolts.*

18. Loosen the rocker arm nuts, move them to the side and pull the push rods out of the engine. NOTE: *The intake and exhaust push rods are different lengths. The intake push rods are marked orange. The exhaust push rods are marked blue.*

19. Remove the intake manifold and gasket from the engine.

To install:

1. Inspect the inlet flanges for flatness with a straight edge and a feeler gauge. Refer to "Cylinder Head" flatness inspection for assistance.

2. Clean the gasket material from all mating surfaces. Remove any excess RTV sealant from the front and rear ridges of the cylinder block. Clean the sealing surfaces with solvent and a gasket scraper.

3. Place a bead of RTV sealer or equivalent on each ridge where the front and rear of the intake manifold contact the cylinder block. Refer to the "Intake Manifold" illustration in this section.

4. Install the intake manifold with a new gasket onto the engine.

5. Install the push rods in their original locations. (Intake rods are marked ORANGE) and (Exhaust rods are marked BLUE). Make sure the push rods are seated in the lifter.

6. Reposition the rocker arms over the push rods and torque the rocker arm nuts to 18 ft. lbs. (25 Nm).

7. Torque the intake manifold in proper sequence and in two steps as outlined in the "Intake Manifold" illustration in this section.

8. Install the heater pipe-to-manifold.

9. Install the throttle body heater hose, coolant sensor and any necessary wiring.

10. Install the upper radiator hose.

11. Install the rear rocker arm cover as outlined in the "Rocker Arm Cover (REAR)" procedures in this section.

12. Install the alternator bracket and brace.

13. Install the PCV hose.

14. Install the front rocker arm cover as outlined in the "Rocker Arm Cover (FRONT) procedures in this section.

15. Install the heater pipe at the water pump and cylinder head.

16. Install the spark plug wires to their original locations.

17. Install the fuel rail assembly. Refer to the "Fuel Rail" assembly in Chapter 5.

18. Reconnect the wires to the fuel injectors.

19. Install the power steering pump, power steering line to alternator bracket and the alternator.

20. Install the fuel lines to the fuel rail.

21. Install the serpentine belt as outlined in the "Belts" section in Chapter 1.

22. Install the intake plenum and plenum bolts. Torque the bolts to 16 ft. lbs. (21 Nm) in a criss-cross pattern.

23. Install the plug harness, EGR valve, throttle body and air intake duct.

24. Install the cable bracket, brake vacuum pipe and cables to throttle body.

25. Refill the engine cooling system with the specified amount and strength anti-freeze.

26. Install the air cleaner and the negative (–) battery cable.

27. Recheck all procedures for proper reinstallation.

28. Start the engine and check for oil, fuel, coolant and vacuum leaks. Correct immediately if a problem is found.

Exhaust Manifold

REMOVAL AND INSTALLATION

2.3L QUAD 4 (VIN A,D)

1. Disconnect the negative (–) battery cable.

2. Remove the oxygen sensor connector, exhaust heat shield and raise the vehicle supported by jackstands.

3. Remove the manifold-to-pipe spring loaded nuts.

4. Pull the pipe from the manifold and lower the vehicle.

5. Remove the exhaust manifold nuts and manifold.

To install:

1. Clean the gasket mating surfaces.

2. Apply Anti-seize compound to the oxygen sensor and install.

3. Install the manifold with a new gasket. Torque the manifold in sequence to the specification in the beginning of the chapter.

4. Install the exhaust bracket and raise the vehicle safely supported with jackstands.

5. Install exhaust pipe with a new gasket. Torque the spring loaded nuts to 22 ft. lbs. (37 Nm). Turn the nuts in evenly until fully seated.

6. Lower the vehicle.

7. Install the heat shield, oxygen sensor connector and connect the negative battery cable. Start the engine to check for exhaust leaks.

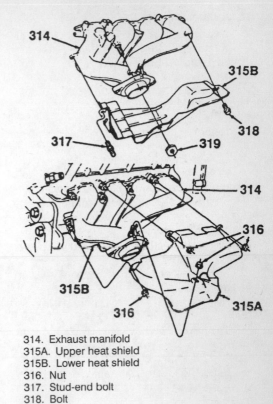

314. Exhaust manifold
315A. Upper heat shield
315B. Lower heat shield
316. Nut
317. Stud-end bolt
318. Bolt
319. Nut

Exhaust manifold heat shields — 2.3L Quad 4

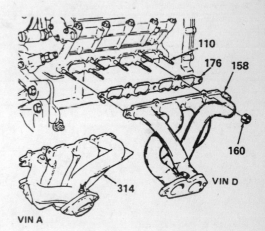

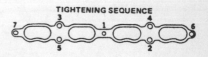

110. Stud
158. Manifold assembly (VIN D)
160. Nut
176. Gasket
314. Manifold assembly (VIN A)

Exhaust manifold — 2.3L Quad 4

2.5L L4 (Lumina) VIN R

1. Disconnect the negative (–) battery cable.
2. Remove the torque strut bolts at the radiator panel and cylinder head.
3. Remove the oxygen sensor and the oil level indicator tube.
4. Raise the vehicle and support with jackstands.
5. Remove the exhaust pipe from the manifold.
6. Lower the vehicle.
7. Bend rocking tabs away from the bolts and remove the retaining bolts and washers.
8. Remove the exhaust manifold and gasket.

To install:

1. Clean the sealing surfaces of the cylinder head and manifold.
2. Lubricate the bolt threads with anti-seize compound.
3. Install the exhaust manifold with a new gasket.
4. Torque the bolts in sequence and torque as outlined in the "Exhaust Manifold (2.5L)" illustration in this section.
5. Bend the locking tabs against the bolts.
6. Raise the vehicle and support with jackstands.

7. Install the exhaust pipe to the manifold.
8. Lower the vehicle.
9. Install the oil level indicator tube, oxygen sensor and torque rod bracket at the cylinder head and radiator support.
10. Start the engine and check for exhaust leaks.

2.8L and 3.1L V6 (VIN W, T)

FRONT MANIFOLD

1. Disconnect the negative (–) battery cable.
2. Remove the air cleaner assembly.
3. Remove the coolant recovery bottle.
4. Remove the serpentine belt as outlined in the "Belts" section in Chapter 1.
5. Remove the air conditioning compressor and move to the side. Attach to the body with a piece of wire or rope. Do NOT disconnect the refrigerant hoses. For further assistance, refer to the "Compressor" section in this chapter.
6. Remove the right side torque strut, air conditioning and torque strut mounting bracket and the heat shield.
7. Remove the exhaust crossover pipe at the manifold.
8. Remove the exhaust manifold bolts, manifold and gasket.

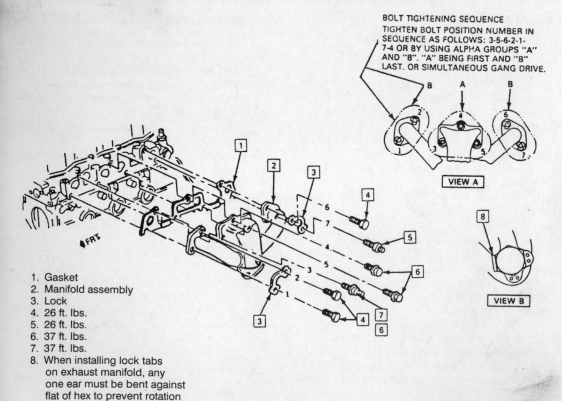

BOLT TIGHTENING SEQUENCE
TIGHTEN BOLT POSITION NUMBER IN SEQUENCE AS FOLLOWS: 3-5-6-2-1-7-4 OR BY USING ALPHA GROUPS "A" AND "B". "A" BEING FIRST AND "B" LAST. OR SIMULTANEOUS GANG DRIVE.

VIEW A

VIEW B

1. Gasket
2. Manifold assembly
3. Lock
4. 26 ft. lbs.
5. 26 ft. lbs.
6. 37 ft. lbs.
7. 37 ft. lbs.
8. When installing lock tabs on exhaust manifold, any one ear must be bent against flat of hex to prevent rotation

Exhaust manifold assembly — 2.5L L4 Lumina

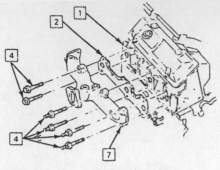
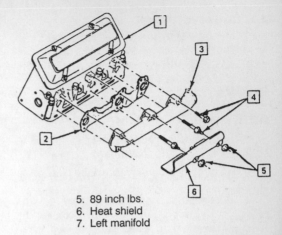

1. Cylinder head
2. Gasket
3. Right manifold
4. 18 ft. lbs.

5. 89 inch lbs.
6. Heat shield
7. Left manifold

Exhaust manifold assembly — 2.8L and 3.1L V6 engines

To install:

1. Clean the mating surfaces on the cylinder head and manifold.

2. Install the manifold, new gasket and retaining bolts.

3. Loosely tighten the retaining bolts.

4. Install the exhaust crossover pipe to the manifold.

5. Torque the manifold and crossover bolts to 18 ft. lbs. (25 Nm).

6. Install the heat shield and torque the nuts to 89 inch lbs. (10 Nm).

7. Install the air conditioning and torque strut mounting bracket.

8. Install the right side torque strut and air conditioning compressor.

9. Install the serpentine belt as outlined in the "Belts" section in Chapter 1.

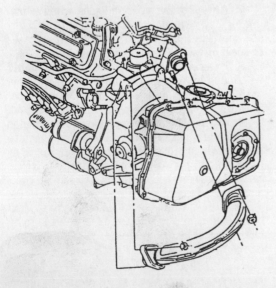

Exhaust crossover pipe assembly — 2.8L and 3.1L V6 engines. Tighten the nuts to 18 ft. lbs.

10. Install the coolant recovery bottle, negative (–) battery cable and air cleaner assembly.

11. Start the vehicle and check for exhaust and air conditioning leaks.

REAR MANIFOLD

1. Disconnect the negative (–) battery cable.

2. Remove the air cleaner assembly.

3. Raise the vehicle and support with jackstands.

4. Remove the exhaust pipe at crossover.

5. Lower the vehicle.

6. Remove the coolant recovery bottle and the torque struts at engine.

7. Rotate the engine as outlined in the "Ignition Coil" procedures in this chapter.

8. Remove the heat shield, crossover at the manifold and throttle body cables.

9. Remove the throttle body cable bracket from the intake plenum.

10. Remove the exhaust manifold bolts, manifold and gasket.

To install:

1. Clean the mating surfaces on the cylinder head and exhaust manifold.

2. Install the manifold, new gasket and retaining bolts.

3. Loosely tighten the manifold retaining bolts.

4. Install the crossover pipe to the manifold.

5. Torque the manifold and crossover bolts to 18 ft. lbs. (25 Nm).

6. Install all throttle body cables and bracket to the intake plenum.

7. Return the engine to its original position.

8. Install the coolant recovery bottle and torque struts.

9. Raise the vehicle and support with jackstands.

10. Install the exhaust pipe to the crossover.

11. Lower the vehicle.

12. Install the negative (–) battery cable and air cleaner assembly.

13. Recheck all procedures for proper reinstallation. Start the vehicle and check for exhaust leaks.

Air Conditioning Compressor

A list of general precautions that should be observed while doing this follows:

1. Keep all tools as clean and dry as possible.

2. Thoroughly purge the service gauges and hoses of air and moisture before connecting them to the system. Keep them capped when not in use.

3. Thoroughly clean any refrigerant fitting before disconnecting it, in order to minimize the entrance of dirt into the system.

4. Plan any operation that requires opening the system beforehand in order to minimize the length of time it will be exposed to open air. Cap or seal the open ends to minimize the entrance of foreign material.

5. When adding oil, pour it through an extremely clean and dry tube or funnel. Keep the oil capped whenever possible. Do not use oil that has not been kept tightly sealed.

6. Use only refrigerant 12. Purchase refrigerant intended for use in only automotive air conditioning system. Avoid the use of refrigerant 12 that may be packaged for another use, such as cleaning, or powering a horn, as it is impure.

7. Completely evacuate any system that has been opened to replace a component, other than when isolating the compressor, or that has leaked sufficiently to draw in moisture and air. This requires evacuating air and moisture with a good vacuum pump for at least one hour.

If a system has been open for a considerable length of time it may be advisable to evacuate the system for up to 12 hours (overnight).

8. Use a wrench on both halves of a fitting that is to be disconnected, so as to avoid placing torque on any of the refrigerant lines.

SAFETY PRECAUTIONS

Because of the importance of the necessary safety precautions that must be exercised when working with air conditioning systems and R-12 refrigerant, a recap of the safety precautions are outlined.

1. Avoid contact with a charged refrigeration system, even when working on another part of the air conditioning system or vehicle. If a heavy tool comes into contact with a section of copper tubing or a heat exchanger, it can easily cause the relatively soft material to rupture.

2. When it is necessary to apply force to a fitting which contains refrigerant, as when checking that all system couplings are securely tightened, use a wrench on both parts of the fitting involved, if possible. This will avoid putting torque on the refrigerant tubing. (It is advisable, when possible, to use tube or line wrenches when tightening these flare nut fittings.)

3. Do not attempt to discharge the system by merely loosening a fitting, or removing the service valve caps and cracking these valves. Precise control is possibly only when using the service gauges. Place a rag under the open end of the center charging hose while discharging the system to catch any drops of liquid that might escape. Wear protective gloves when connecting or disconnecting service gauge hoses.

4. Discharge the system only in a well ventilated area, as high concentrations of the gas can exclude oxygen and act as an anesthetic. When leak testing or soldering this is particularly important, as toxic gas is formed when R-12 contacts any flame.

5. Never start a system without first verifying that both service valves are backseated, if equipped, and that all fittings are throughout the system are snugly connected.

6. Avoid applying heat to any refrigerant line or storage vessel. Charging may be aided by using water heated to less than 125°F (52°C) to warm the refrigerant container. Never allow a refrigerant storage container to sit out in the sun, or near any other source of heat, such as a radiator.

7. Always wear safety goggles when working on a system to protect the eyes. If refrigerant contacts the eye, it is advisable in all cases to see a physician as soon as possible.

8. Frostbite from liquid refrigerant should be treated by first gradually warming the area with cool water, and then gently applying petroleum jelly. A physician should be consulted.

9. Always keep refrigerant can fittings capped when not in use. Avoid sudden shock to the can which might occur from dropping it, or from banging a heavy tool against it. Never carry a refrigerant can in the passenger compartment of a car.

10. Always completely discharge the system before painting the vehicle (if the paint is to be baked on), or before welding anywhere near the refrigerant lines.

REMOVAL AND INSTALLATION

1. Disconnect the negative (–) battery cable.

2. Discharge the air conditioning system as

outlined in the "Air Conditioning" section in Chapter 1.

3. Loosen the serpentine belt at the adjustment pulley.

4. Remove the coolant recovery bottle.

5. Disconnect the suction and discharge hoses from the compressor.

NOTE: *Always plug all disconnected refrigerant lines to prevent moisture from entering the system. If the system is not plugged, the moisture will cause severe damage to the air conditioning system.*

6. Disconnect the compressor clutch and switch wires.

7. Remove the two front and rear bracket bolts.

8. Remove the compressor assembly from the vehicle.

To install:

1. Install the bracket, if removed, to the compressor and torque to 18 ft. lbs. (25 Nm).

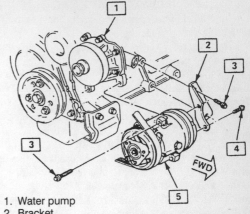

1. Water pump
2. Bracket
3. 37 ft. lbs.
4. 20 ft. lbs.
5. Compressor assembly

Air conditioning compressor assembly — 2.5L L4 Lumina

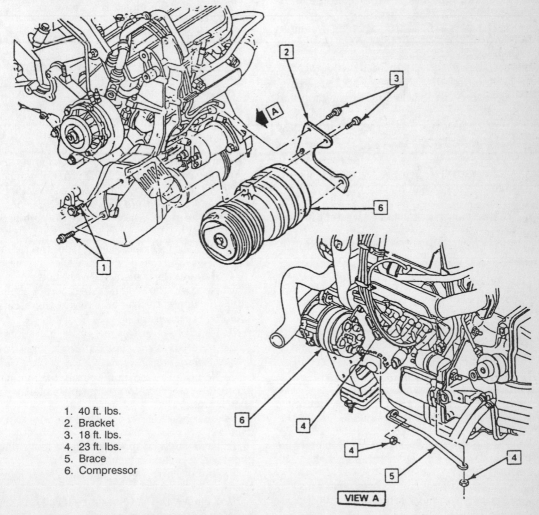

1. 40 ft. lbs.
2. Bracket
3. 18 ft. lbs.
4. 23 ft. lbs.
5. Brace
6. Compressor

Air conditioning compressor assembly — 2.8L and 3.1L V6 engines

2. Install the compressor assembly.

3. Install the front and rear bracket bolts and torque to 23 ft. lbs. (31 Nm).

4. Connect the compressor clutch and switch wires.

5. Reconnect the discharge and suction hoses. Lubricate the sealing surfaces with refrigerant oil before assembly.

6. Install the coolant recovery bottle, serpentine belt and negative (–) battery cable.

7. Evacuate the air conditioning system for at least one hour with an evacuation pump. Refer to the "Evacuating the Air Conditioning System" section in Chapter 1.

8. After the evacuation, charge and leak check the system as outlined in Chapter 1.

Air Conditioning Condenser

REMOVAL AND INSTALLATION

1. Disconnect the negative (–) battery cable.

2. Remove the air cleaner assembly, mounting stud and air cleaner duct.

3. Discharge the air conditioning system as outlined in the "Air Conditioning" section in Chapter 1.

4. Remove the coolant recovery bottle.

5. Remove the engine strut brace bolts from the upper tie bar and rotate the strut and brace rearward.

NOTE: *To prevent shearing of the rubber bushing, loosen the bolts on the engine strut before swinging the struts.*

6. Remove the air intake resonator mounting nut, upper radiator mounting panel bolts and clamps.

7. Remove the condenser refrigerant line fittings.

8. Remove the upper radiator mounting panel bolts and clamps.

9. Disconnect the cooling fan electrical connectors.

10. Remove the upper radiator mounting panel with the fans attached.

11. Tilt the radiator rearward and hold.

12. Remove the condenser.

To install:

1. Install the condenser and reposition the radiator into the original position.

2. Install the upper radiator mounting panel with the fans attached and connect the fan wires.

3. Install the mounting panel bolts and clamps. Torque the bolts to 89 inch lbs. (10 Nm).

4. Install the coolant recovery bottle.

5. Swing the engine strut to the proper position and tighten the bolts.

6. Evacuate, recharge and leak test the air

conditioning system as outlined in Chapter 1 and 3.

7. Install the air cleaner and negative (–) battery cable. Start the engine and check for air conditioning system and coolant leaks.

Radiator

The radiator assembly is made of a aluminum core and two plastic side tanks. Repairs on the aluminum tubes can be made using the hot melt adhesive method.

The side tanks are made of high pressure plastic. The tanks are attached to the core by the use of clinched tabs. The tanks can be removed by benting back the tabs. A high temperature rubber gasket is used to seal the tanks and core together. The gasket MUST be replaced any time a tank is removed.

REMOVAL AND INSTALLATION

1. Disconnect the negative (–) battery cable.

2. Remove the air cleaner, mounting stud and duct.

CAUTION: *When draining the coolant, keep in mind that cats and dogs are attracted by the ethylene glycol antifreeze, and are quite likely to drink any that is left in an uncovered container or in puddles on the ground. This will prove fatal in sufficient quantity. Always drain the coolant into a sealable container. Coolant should be reused unless it is contaminated or several years old. To avoid beign burned, do NOT remove the thermostat housing cap while the engine is at normal operating temperature. The cooling system will release scalding fluid and steam under pressure if the cap is removed while the engine is still hot.*

3. Drain the engine coolant from the radiator.

4. Remove the coolant recovery bottle.

5. Remove the engine strut brace bolts from the upper tie bar and rotate the struts and brace rearward.

NOTE: *To prevent shearing of the rubber bushing, loosen the bolts on the engine strut before swinging the struts.*

6. Remove the air intake resonator mounting nut, upper radiator mounting panel bolts and clamps.

7. Disconnect the cooling fan electrical connectors.

8. Remove the upper radiator mounting panel with the fans attached.

9. Remove the upper and lower radiator hoses.

10. Remove the automatic transaxle cooler lines from the radiator.

11. Remove the radiator.

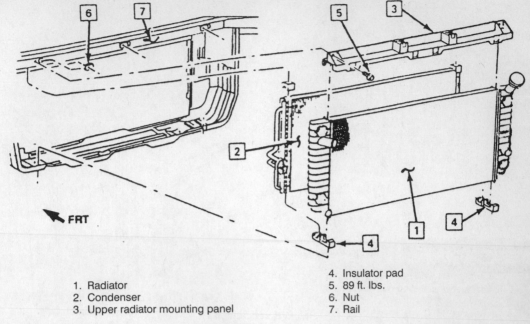

1. Radiator
2. Condenser
3. Upper radiator mounting panel
4. Insulator pad
5. 89 ft. lbs.
6. Nut
7. Rail

Radiator mounting

To install:

If a new radiator is being used, transfer all necessary fittings from the old radiator to the new one.

1. Position the radiator into the lower insulator pads

2. Install the automatic transaxle cooler lines to radiator.

3. Install the upper and lower radiator hoses and tighten the clamps.

4. Install the upper radiator mounting panel with the fans attached and connect the fan wires.

5. Install the mounting panel bolts and clamps. Torque the bolts to 89 inch lbs. (10 Nm).

6. Install the coolant recovery bottle.

7. Swing the engine strut to the proper position and tighten the bolts.

8. Refill the engine with the specified amount of engine coolant.

9. Install the air cleaner and negative (–) battery cable. Start the engine and check for coolant leaks.

RADIATOR REPAIR

1. Remove the radiator from the vehicle as outlined earlier.

2. For damaged area that are between the cooling fins, it may be necessary to remove some of the fins. Do not remove more fins than necessary. Remove about 1/4 inch beyond the leak.

3. A severely damaged tube can be blocked off all together. Do NOT block more than two tubes in the radiator.

4. If the area is not clean, the adhesive will not stick to the aluminum surface. Clean the area with solvent and a soft wire brush or steel wool. Clean all grease, road dirt and paint off the area.

5. Position the core so the repair area is accessible.

6. Apply a wet cloth if you are working near the plastic tanks or the joints between the core tubes.

CAUTION: *Always wear safety glasses and gloves when working with heated material.*

7. Heat the area slightly with a small torch or heat gun to be sure it is dry. Do NOT use a blow torch.

8. Brush the area to be repaired with a small steel brush supplied in the repair kit.

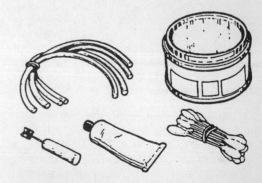

Hot melt adhesive kit

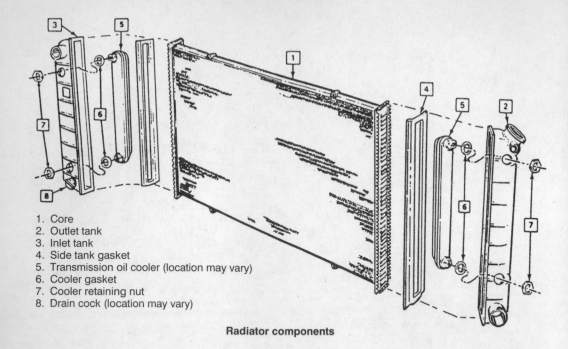

1. Core
2. Outlet tank
3. Inlet tank
4. Side tank gasket
5. Transmission oil cooler (location may vary)
6. Cooler gasket
7. Cooler retaining nut
8. Drain cock (location may vary)

Radiator components

CAUTION: *If the primer contacts your eyes, do NOT rub the eyes. Splash the area with large amounts of water and seek medical attention. Use the primer with adequate ventilation. Do NOT mix the primer with water.*

9. Scrub the repair area with a cotton swab and primer until a fresh swab stays clean. The clear yellow/brown coating does NOT have to be removed.

10. Heat the repair area with a heat gun or small torch.

11. Withdraw the torch and rub the adhesive stick on the repair area. The adhesive will flow at a temperature of approximately 500°F (260°C).

12. If the stick will not melt, remove the stick and reheat.

13. Continue heating until the adhesive flows and wets the entire repair area and fills the joint.

14. Heat the repair area until the adhesive is bubble-free and smooth. Curing is not required.

15. Test the radiator for leaks, when the repair is cool. Refer to the "Leak Testing" procedure in Chapter 1.

TANK AND SEAL REPLACEMENT

1. Sometimes a tank seal can be mistaken for a header or core leak. Before replacing the tank and or seal, tighten the clinch tabs using a slip tool No. J–33419–A or locking pliers. If this does not stop the leak and the tank seal is the problem, the tank will have to be removed.

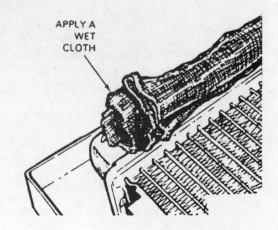

APPLY A WET CLOTH

Step 1

Step 2 — Clean area to be repaired with soft wire brush

Step 3 — Scrub the area with primer

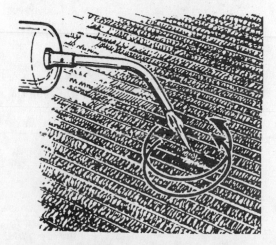

Step 4 — Heat the area but do not overheat

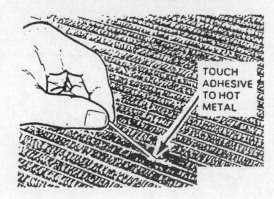

TOUCH
ADHESIVE
TO HOT
METAL

Step 5

2. Pry open all the clinch tabs, except those under the inlet, outlet and filler neck with a tool J–33419–A or a screwdriver.

3. Lift the tabs far enough the remove the tank. Do NOT overbend the tabs, breakage may occur.

4. Lift the tank and slide it out from under

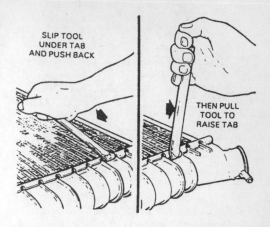

SLIP TOOL
UNDER TAB
AND PUSH BACK

THEN PULL
TOOL TO
RAISE TAB

Tank removal — opening clinch tabs

the remaining tabs. If the tank will not move, tap the tank with your hand to dislodge the gasket.

5. Lift the remaining tabs with a pliers.

6. Remove the old gasket and discard.

7. Clean the header, gasket groove and plastic tank of dirt and old rubber.

8. **Auto Transaxle Only:** if the tank is being replaced, remove the oil cooler and install into new tank.

9. Coat the tank and new gasket in clean engine coolant. Position the tank and gasket on the header surface.

10. Clinch the two end tabs and two in the middle only.

11. Clinch the remaining clinch tabs in the sequence shown using tool J–33419–A or pliers.

12. Replace the core if there are more than three tabs broken on one side or two adjacent tabs are broken.

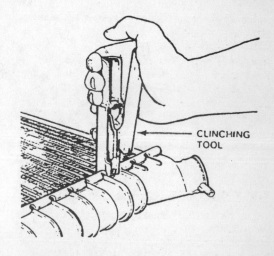

CLINCHING
TOOL

Tank installation — closing clinch tabs

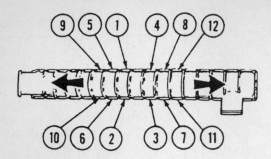

Clinching sequence

13. Pressure test the radiator before installation as outlined in the "Leak Testing" section in Chapter 1.

Water Pump

REMOVAL AND INSTALLATION

2.3L QUAD 4 (VIN A,D)

1. Disconnect the negative (–) battery cable.
2. Disconnect the upper engine torque strut and rotate the engine rearward.
3. Disconnect and remove the oxygen sensor, if needed.
4. Remove the exhaust heat shield and EGR valve, if so equipped.
5. Remove the exhaust pipe from manifold.
6. Remove the exhaust manifold as outlined in this chapter.
7. Partially drain the engine coolant.
8. Remove the coolant return hose and lower coolant pipe from the pump.

9. Remove the pump retaining bolts and pump.

To install:

1. Clean the gasket mating surfaces with a gasket scraper and solvent.
2. Install the pump, retaining bolts and torque to 19 ft. lbs. (26 Nm).
3. Install the lower coolant pipe and torque to 124 inch lbs. (14 Nm).
4. Install the coolant return hose.
5. Install the exhaust manifold, oxygen sensor, EGR valve and heat shield as outlined in this chapter.
6. Return the engine to its proper position and install the torque strut.
7. Refill the engine with coolant, connect the negative battery cable, start the engine and check for coolant leaks.

2.5L L4 (Lumina) VIN R

1. Disconnect the negative (–) battery cable.
2. Remove the alternator as outlined in the "Alternator" section in this chapter.
3. Remove the convenience center heat shield.
4. Drain about a gallon of engine coolant from the radiator. Enough to be below the water pump level.

CAUTION: *When draining the coolant, keep in mind that cats and dogs are attracted by the ethylene glycol antifreeze, and are quite likely to drink any that is left in an uncovered container or in puddles on the ground. This will prove fatal in sufficient quantity.*

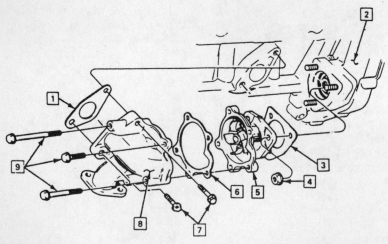

1. Gasket
2. Timing chain housing
3. Gasket
4. 19 ft. lbs.
5. Water pump body
6. Gasket
7. 19 ft. lbs.
8. Water pump cover
9. 125 inch lbs.

Water pump mounting — 2.3L Quad 4

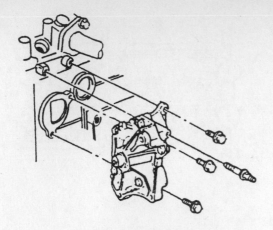

Water pump mounting — 2.5L L4 Lumina. Tighten the bolts to 24 ft. lbs.

Always drain the coolant into a sealable container. Coolant should be reused unless it is contaminated or several years old. To avoid beign burned, do NOT remove the thermostat housing cap while the engine is at normal operating temperature. The cooling system will release scalding fluid and steam under pressure if the cap is removed while the engine is still hot.

5. Remove the four water pump-to-engine attaching bolts.
6. Remove the water pump and gasket.
7. Remove the pulley from the old pump if a new pump is being installed.

To install:
8. Clean the water pump mating surfaces with solvent and a gasket scraper.
9. Install the pump and pulley assembly onto the engine with a new gasket.
10. Install the water pump attaching bolts and torque to 24 ft. lbs. (33 Nm).
11. Install the convenience center heat shield, alternator and negative (–) battery cable.
12. Refill the cooling system with the specified amount of engine coolant.
13. Start the engine and check for coolant leaks.

2.8L and 3.1L V6 (VIN W, T)

1. Disconnect the negative (–) battery cable.
2. Remove the air cleaner assembly.
3. Drain about a gallon of engine coolant from the radiator. Enough to be below the water pump level.

CAUTION: *When draining the coolant, keep in mind that cats and dogs are attracted by the ethylene glycol antifreeze, and are quite likely to drink any that is left in an uncovered container or in puddles on the ground. This will prove fatal in sufficient quantity. Always drain the coolant into a sealable container. Coolant should be reused unless it is contaminated or several years old. To avoid beign burned, do NOT remove the thermostat housing cap while the engine is at normal operating temperature. The cooling system will release scalding fluid and steam under pressure if the cap is removed while the engine is still hot.*

4. Remove the serpentine belt as outlined in the "Belts" section in Chapter 1.
5. Remove the pulley.
6. Remove the water pump attaching bolts (5).
7. Remove the water pump and gasket.

To install:
8. Clean the water pump mounting surfaces with solvent and a gasket scraper.
9. Install the water pump with a new gasket.
10. Install the attaching bolts and torque to 89 inch lbs. (10 Nm).
11. Install the pulley and serpentine belt.
12. Refill the cooling system with the specified amount of engine coolant.
13. Install the air cleaner and negative (–) battery cable.
14. Start the engine and check for coolant leaks.

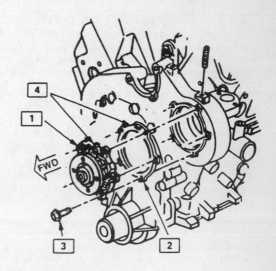

1. Water pump
2. Gasket
3. 89 inch lbs.
4. Locator — must be vertical

Water pump mounting — 2.8L and 3.1L V6 engines

Cylinder Head

REMOVAL AND INSTALLATION

2.3L QUAD 4 (VIN A,D)

1. Disconnect the negative (–) battery cable.
CAUTION: *When draining the coolant, keep in mind that cats and dogs are attracted by the ethylene glycol antifreeze, and are quite likely to drink any that is left in an uncovered container or in puddles on the ground. This will prove fatal in sufficient quantity. Always drain the coolant into a sealable container. Coolant should be reused unless it is contaminated or several years old.*

2. Drain the cooling system.
3. Remove the heater inlet and throttle body heater hoses from the water inlet.
4. Remove the exhaust manifold as outlined in this chapter.
5. Remove the intake and exhaust camshaft housing as outlined "Rocker Arm Cover" section in this chapter.
6. Remove the oil fill cap, tube and retainer. Pull the tube up and out of the block.
7. Disconnect and move the fuel injector harness.
CAUTION: *To reduce the risk of fire and personal injury, it is necessary to relieve the fuel system pressure before servicing any fuel system component. If this procedure is not performed, fuel may be sprayed out of the connection under pressure. Always keep a dry chemical (Class B) fire extinguisher near the work area.*

8. **Fuel pressure relief procedures:**
a. Disconnect the negative (–) battery cable.
b. Loosen the fuel filler cap to relieve tank vapor pressure.
c. Connect a fuel pressure gauge J-34730-1 or equivalent to the fuel pressure relief connection at the fuel rail.
d. Wrap a shop towel around the fittings while connecting the gauge to prevent fuel spillage.
e. Install a bleed hose into an approved container and open the valve to bleed the system pressure. The system is safe for servicing.
9. Remove the throttle body and air inlet tube with the hoses and cables still connected. Position the assembly out of the way.
10. Remove the power brake booster hose and throttle cable bracket.
11. Remove the MAP sensor vacuum hose and all electrical connectors from the intake manifold and cylinder head.
12. Remove the radiator inlet hose and coolant sensor connectors.
13. In the reveres order of installation,

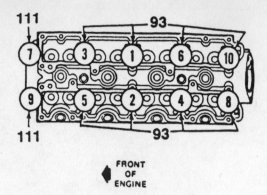

93. 26 ft. lbs. plus
110° rotation
111. 26 ft. lbs. plus
100° rotation

Cylinder head bolt tightening sequence — 2.3L Quad 4

remove the cylinder head-to-block retaining bolts.

14. Gently tap the outer edges of the cylinder head with a rubber hammer to dislodge the head gasket. Do NOT pry a screwdriver between the two surfaces.
15. Remove the cylinder head and intaket manifold as an assembly.

To install:
1. Clean all gasket mating surfaces with a plastic scraper and solvent. Remove all dirt from the bolts with a wire brush.
2. Clean and inspect the oil flow check valve, but do NOT remove the valve.
3. Check the cylinder head mating surface for flatness using a straight edge and a feeler gauge. Resurface the head if the warpage exceeds 0.010 inch (0.25mm).
4. Check to see if the dowel pins are installed properly, replace if necessary.
NOTE: *To avoid damage, install new spark plugs after the cylinder head has been installed on the engine. In the mean time, plug the holes to prevent dirt from entering the combustion chamber during reinstallation.*

5. Do NOT use any sealing compounds on the new cylinder head gasket. Match the new gasket with the old one to ensure a perfect match.
6. Install the cylinder head and camshaft housing covers.
7. Torque the (93) bolts to 26 ft. lbs. (35 Nm) plus 110 degrees. Torque the (111) bolts to 26 ft. lbs. (35 Nm) plus 100 degrees. Refer to the torquing sequence illustration in this section.
8. Install the throttle body heater hoses, upper radiator hose and intake manifold bracket.

9. Install cylinder head and intake manifold electrical connectors and vacuum hoses.

10. Install the throttle body-to-intake manifold with a new gasket. Install the throttle cable, MAP sensor vacuum hose and air cleaner duct.

11. Lubricate the new oil fill tube O-ring and install the fill tube. Make sure the tube is fully seated in the block.

12. Install and torque the exhaust manifold as previously outlined in this chapter.

13. Fill the radiator with the specified amount of engine coolant.

14. Recheck all procedures to ensure completion of repair.

15. Connect the negative battery cable, start the engine and check for fluid leaks.

2.5L L4 (Lumina) VIN R

1. Disconnect the negative (–) battery cable.

2. Drain the cooling system at the radiator into a suitable drain pan.

3. Raise the vehicle and support it safely with jack stands.

4. Remove the exhaust pipe and oxygen sensor.

5. Lower the vehicle.

6. Remove the oil level indicator tube and auxiliary ground cable.

7. Remove the air cleaner assembly.

8. Disconnect the EFI electrical connections and vacuum hoses.

9. From the throttle body; remove the wiring connectors, throttle linkage and fuel lines.

CAUTION: *To reduce the risk of fire and personal injury, it is necessary to relieve the fuel system pressure before servicing any fuel system component. If this procedure is not performed, fuel may be sprayed out of the connection under pressure. Always keep a dry chemical (Class B) fire extinguisher near the work area.*

Fuel pressure relief procedures:

a. Remove the fuel pump fuse from the fuse block located in the passenger compartment.

b. Start the engine and run until the engine stops due to the lack of fuel.

c. Crank the engine for 3 seconds to ensure all pressure is relieved.

10. Remove the heater hose from the intake manifold.

11. Remove the wiring connectors from the manifold and cylinder head.

12. Remove the vacuum hoses, serpentine belt and alternator bracket.

13. Remove the radiator hoses.

14. Remove the rocker arm cover as outlined in this chapter.

15. Loosen the rocker arm nuts and move the rocker arms to the side enough to remove the push rods.

16. Mark each push rod and remove from the engine. Refer to the "Rocker Arm" section in this chapter for assistance.

NOTE: *Mark each valve component to ensure that they are replaced in the same location as removed. This is very important because each component will follow different wear patterns.*

17. Remove the cylinder head bolts.

18. Tap the sides of the cylinder head with a plastic hammer to dislodge the gasket. Remove the cylinder head with the intake and exhaust manifold still attached.

19. If the cylinder head has to be serviced or replaced, remove the intake manifold, exhaust manifold and remaining hardware.

To install:

1. Before installing, clean the gasket surfaces of the head and block with solvent and a gasket scraper.

2. Check the cylinder head for warpage using a straight edge. Refer to the "Cylinder Head Resurfacing" procedures in this section.

3. Make sure the retaining bolt threads and the cylinder block threads are clean since dirt could affect bolt torque.

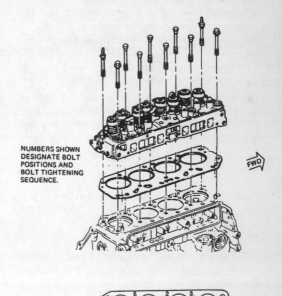

NUMBERS SHOWN DESIGNATE BOLT POSITIONS AND BOLT TIGHTENING SEQUENCE.

Cylinder head torquing sequence — 2.5L L4 Lumina. Tighten all bolts in 3 steps: Step 1 Tighten all bolts to 18 ft. lbs. (25 Nm). Step 2 Tighten all bolts EXCEPT No. 9 to 26 ft. lbs. (35 Nm); tighten No. 9 to 18 ft. lbs. Step 3 Tighten all bolts in sequence an additional 90° (1/4 turn)

4. Match up the old head gasket with the new one to ensure the holes are EXACT. Install a new gasket over the dowel pins in the cylinder block.

5. Install the cylinder head in place over the dowel pins.

6. Coat the cylinder head bolt threads with sealing compound and install finger tight.

7. Torque the cylinder head bolts gradually in the sequence shown in the illustration. Refer to the "Torque Specifications" chart in the beginning of this chapter for instructions.

8. Install the push rods, rocker arms and nuts (or bolts) in the same location as removed. Torque the nuts (or bolts) to 24 ft. lbs. (32 Nm).

9. Install the rocker arm cover as outlined in the "Rocker Arm Cover" removal and installation procedures in this chapter.

10. Install the radiator hoses, alternator bracket and serpentine belt.

11. Connect all intake manifold and cylinder head wiring.

12. Install the vacuum hoses and heater hose at manifold.

13. Install the wiring, throttle linkage and fuel lines to the throttle body assembly.

14. Install the oil level indicator tube-to-exhaust manifold.

15. Install the air cleaner assembly.

16. Refill the engine cooling system with the specified amount of engine coolant.

17. Raise the vehicle and support with jackstands.

18. Install the exhaust pipe and oxygen sensor.

19. Lower the vehicle.

20. Connect the negative (–) battery cable.

21. Recheck each operation for completion of the repair.

22. Start the engine and check for coolant, fuel, oil and vacuum leaks.

2.8L and 3.1L V6 (VIN W, T)

FRONT

1. Disconnect the negative (–) battery cable.

2. Drain the cooling system at the radiator into a suitable drain pan.

CAUTION: *When draining the coolant, keep in mind that cats and dogs are attracted by the ethylene glycol antifreeze, and are quite likely to drink any that is left in an uncovered container or in puddles on the ground. This will prove fatal in sufficient quantity. Always drain the coolant into a sealable container. Coolant should be reused unless it is contaminated or several years old.*

3. Remove the air cleaner assembly.

4. Remove the rocker arm cover as outlined in that section in this chapter.

5. Remove the intake plenum and manifold as outlined in those sections in this chapter.

6. Remove the exhaust crossover pipe and front exhaust manifold.

7. Remove the oil level indicator and spark plug wires from the front head.

8. Loosen the rocker arm nuts and move to the side or remove.

9. Mark each push rod and remove from the engine. Refer to the "Rocker Arm" section in this chapter for assistance. The intake push rods are marked (orange) and the exhaust push rods are marked (blue).

NOTE: *Mark each valve component to ensure that they are replaced in the same location as removed. This is very important because each component will follow different wear patterns.*

10. Remove the cylinder head bolts.

11. Tap the sides of the cylinder head with a plastic hammer to dislodge the gasket. Remove the cylinder.

12. If the cylinder head has to be serviced or replaced, remove all remaining hardware.

To install:

1. Before installing, clean the gasket surfaces of the head and block with solvent and a gasket scraper.

2. Check the cylinder head for warpage using a straight edge. Refer to the "Cylinder Head Resurfacing" procedures in this section.

3. Make sure the retaining bolt threads and the cylinder block threads are clean since dirt could affect bolt torque.

4. Match up the old head gasket with the new one to ensure the holes are EXACT. Install a new gasket over the dowel pins in the cylinder block with the "This Side Up" mark facing UP.

5. Install the cylinder head in place over the dowel pins.

6. Coat the cylinder head bolt threads with sealing compound and install finger tight.

7. Torque the cylinder head bolts gradually in the sequence shown in the illustration. Refer to the "Torque Specifications" chart in the beginning of this chapter for instructions.

8. Install the intake gasket.

9. Install the valve mechanisms and rocker arms over the valves. Torque the rocker arm nuts to 18 ft. lbs. (25 Nm).

10. Install the intake manifold and plenum as outlined in the appropriate section in this chapter.

11. Install the rocker arm covers as outlined in the appropriate section in this chapter.

12. Install the oil level indicator and front exhaust manifold.

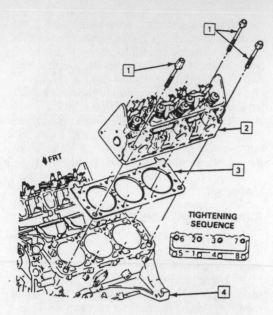

1. Coat threads with sealer. Tighten in proper sequence to 33 ft.lbs.(45 Nm), then tighten an additional 90° (¹/₄ turn)
2. Cylinder head
3. Gasket
4. Cylinder block

Cylinder head tightening sequence — 2.8L and 3.1L V6 engines

13. Install the exhaust crossover pipe and oxygen sensor (if removed).

14. Install the air cleaner assembly.

15. Refill the engine cooling system with the specified amount of engine coolant.

16. Connect the negative (–) battery cable.

17. Recheck each operation for completion of the repair.

18. Start the engine and check for coolant, fuel, oil and vacuum leaks.

REAR

1. Disconnect the negative (–) battery cable.

2. Drain the cooling system at the radiator into a suitable drain pan.

CAUTION: *When draining the coolant, keep in mind that cats and dogs are attracted by the ethylene glycol antifreeze, and are quite likely to drink any that is left in an uncovered container or in puddles on the ground. This will prove fatal in sufficient quantity. Always drain the coolant into a sealable container. Coolant should be reused unless it is contaminated or several years old.*

3. Remove the air cleaner assembly.

4. Raise the vehicle and support with jackstands.

5. Remove the exhaust crossover pipe and rear exhaust manifold.

6. Lower the vehicle.

7. Remove the torque struts at the engine.

8. Remove the coolant recovery bottle.

9. Rotate the engine as outlined in the "Ignition Coil" section in this chapter.

10. Remove the exhaust crossover heat shield and crossover from the rear manifold.

11. Remove rear exhaust manifold.

12. Remove the spark plug wires from the rear head.

13. Remove the rocker arm cover as outlined in that section in this chapter.

14. Remove the intake plenum and manifold as outlined in those sections in this chapter.

15. Loosen the rocker arm nuts and move to the side or remove.

16. Mark each push rod and remove from the engine. Refer to the "Rocker Arm" section in this chapter for assistance. The intake push rods are marked (orange) and the exhaust push rods are marked (blue).

NOTE: *Mark each valve component to ensure that they are replaced in the same location as removed. This is very important because each component will follow different wear patterns.*

17. Remove the cylinder head bolts.

18. Tap the sides of the cylinder head with a plastic hammer to dislodge the gasket. Remove the cylinder.

19. If the cylinder head has to be serviced or replaced, remove all remaining hardware.

To install:

1. Before installing, clean the gasket surfaces of the head and block with solvent and a gasket scraper.

2. Check the cylinder head for warpage using a straight edge. Refer to the "Cylinder Head Resurfacing" procedures in this section.

3. Make sure the retaining bolt threads and the cylinder block threads are clean since dirt could affect bolt torque.

4. Match up the old head gasket with the new one to ensure the holes are EXACT. Install a new gasket over the dowel pins in the cylinder block with the "This Side Up" mark facing UP.

5. Install the cylinder head in place over the dowel pins.

6. Coat the cylinder head bolt threads with sealing compound and install finger tight.

7. Torque the cylinder head bolts gradually in the sequence shown in the illustration. Refer to the "Torque Specifications" chart in the beginning of this chapter for instructions.

8. Install the intake gasket.

9. Install the valve mechanisms and rocker arms over the valves. Torque the rocker arm nuts to 18 ft. lbs. (25 Nm).

10. Install the intake manifold and plenum

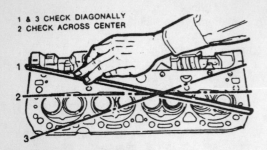

1 & 3 CHECK DIAGONALLY
2 CHECK ACROSS CENTER

Check the cylinder head for warpage

as outlined in the appropriate section in this chapter.

11. Install the rocker arm covers as outlined in the appropriate section in this chapter.

12. Install the spark plug wires and rear exhaust manifold.

13. Install the exhaust crossover pipe, oxygen sensor (if removed) and crossover heat shield.

14. Rotate the engine to its original position and install the torque strut.

15. Refill the engine cooling system with the specified amount of engine coolant.

16. Raise the vehicle and support with jackstands.

17. Install the exhaust pipe at the crossover and lower the vehicle.

18. Connect the negative (–) battery cable.

19. Recheck each operation for completion of the repair.

20. Start the engine and check for coolant, fuel, oil and vacuum leaks.

CLEANING AND INSPECTION

CAUTION: *To avoid personal injury ALWAYS wear safety glasses when using a power drill and wire brush.*

1. Remove all traces of carbon from the head, using a decarbon-type wire brush

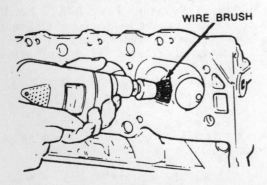

WIRE BRUSH

Remove the carbon from the cylinder head with a wire brush and electric drill

mounted in an electric drill. Do not use a motorized brush on any gasket mating surface.

2. Lay a straight edge across the cylinder head face and check between the straight edge and the head with feeler gauges. Make the check at six points minimum. Cylinder head flatness should be within 0.003–0.006 inch. These surfaces may be reconditioned by parallel grinding. This procedure must be done by a qualified machine shop. If more than 10% must be removed, the head should be replaced.

Valves

REMOVAL AND INSPECTION

1. Remove the cylinder head(s) from the vehicle as previously outlined in the "Cylinder Head" removal and installation procedures.

2. Using a suitable valve spring compressor, compress the valve spring and remove the valve keys using a magnetic retrieval tool.

3. Slowly release the compressor and remove the valve spring caps (or rotors) and the valve springs.

CAUTION: *The valve springs are under high spring load, always wear safety glasses when removing valve springs. Decompressing a valve spring quickly may cause personal injury.*

4. Fabricate a valve arrangement board (piece of cardboard with holes punched through) to use when you remove the valves, which will indicate the port in which each valve was originally installed (and which cylinder head on V6 models). Also note that the valve keys, rotators, caps, etc. should be arranged in a manner which will allow you to install them on the valve on which they were originally removed.

5. Remove and discard the valve seals. On models using the umbrella type seals, note the location of the large and small seals for assembly purposes.

6. Thoroughly clean the valves on the wire wheel of a bench grinder, then clean the cylinder head mating surface with a soft wire wheel, a soft wire brush, or a wooden scraper. Avoid using a metallic scraper, since this can cause damage to the cylinder head mating surface, especially on models with aluminum heads.

7. Using a valve guide cleaner chucked into a drill, clean all of the valve guides.

8. Install each valve into its respective port (guide) of the cylinder head.

9. Mount a dial indicator so that the stem is at 90° to the valve stem, as close to the valve guide as possible.

10. Move the valve off its seat, and measure the valve guide-to-stem clearance by rocking

the stem back and forth to actuate the dial indicator.

11. Measure the valve stems using a micrometer, and compare to specifications, to determine whether stem or guide wear is responsible for excessive clearance. *Consult the machine shop for valve guide reconditioning.*

NOTE: *Consult the Specifications tables earlier in this chapter.*

REFACING

Using a valve grinder, resurface the valves according to specifications in this chapter.
NOTE: *All machine work should be performed by a competent, professional machine shop.*

CAUTION: *Valve face angle is not always identical to valve seat angle. Consult the specifications chart in this chapter.*

A minimum margin of $\frac{1}{32}$ inch. should remain after grinding the valve. The valve stem top should also be squared and resurfaced, by placing the stem in the V-block of the grinder, and turning it while pressing lightly against the grinding wheel. Be sure to chamfer the edge of the tip so that the squared edges don't dig into the rocker arm.

LAPPING

This procedure should be performed after the valves and seats have been machined, to ensure that each valve mates to each seat precisely.

1. Invert the cylinder head, lightly lubricate the valve stems, and install the valves in the head as numbered.

2. Coat valve seats with fine grinding compound, and attach the lapping tool suction cup to a valve head.
NOTE: *Moisten the suction cup.*

3. Rotate the tool between your palms, changing position and lifting the tool often to prevent grooving.

4. Lap the valve until a smooth and uniform wear pattern exists.

5. Remove the valve and tool, and rinse away all traces of grinding compound.

Valve Guide Service

The valve guides used in these engines are integral with the cylinder head, that is, they cannot be replaced.
NOTE: *Refer to the previous "Valves— Removal and Installation" to check the valve guides for wear.*

Valve guides are most accurately repaired using the bronze wall rebuilding method. In

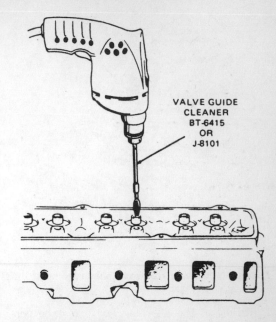

VALVE GUIDE
CLEANER
BT-6415
OR
J-8101

Cleaning valve guides

this operation, "threads" are cut into the bore of the valve guide and bronze wire is turned into the threads. The bronze "wall" is then reamed to the proper diameter. This method is well received for a number of reasons: it is relatively inexpensive, it offers better valve lubrication (the wire forms channels which retain oil), it offers less valve friction, and it preserves the original valve guide-to-seat relationship.

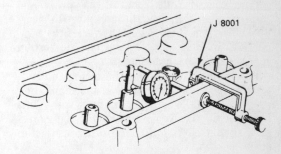

J 8001

Checking valve guide clearance

Another popular method of repairing valve guides is to have the guides "knurled." The knurling entails cutting into the bore of the valve guide with a special tool The cutting action "raises" metal off of the guide bore which actually narrows the inner diameter of the bore, thereby reducing the clearance between the valve guide bore and the valve stem. This method offers the same advantages as the bronze wall method, but will generally wear faster.

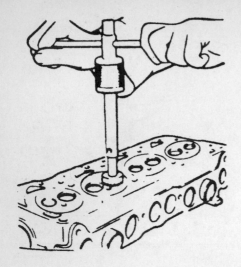

Reaming the valve seat with a hand reamer

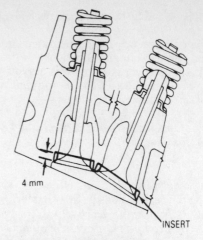

Checking valve seat clearance

Either of the above services must be performed by a professional machine shop which has the specialized knowledge and tools necessary to perform the service.

Valve Seat Service

The valve seats are integral with the cylinder head on all engines. On all engines the seats are machined into the cylinder head casting itself.

Valve Spring Testing

Place the spring on a flat surface next to a square. Measure the height of the spring, and rotate it against the edge of the square to measure distortion. If spring height varies (by comparison) by more than $\frac{1}{16}$ in. or if distortion exceeds $\frac{1}{16}$ in., replace the spring.

In addition to evaluating the spring as above, test the spring pressure at the installed and compressed (installed height minus valve lift) height using a valve spring tester. Spring pressure should be ± 1 lb. of all other springs in either position.

VALVE AND SPRING INSTALLATION

NOTE: *Be sure that all traces of lapping compound have been cleaned off before the valves are installed.*

1. Lubricate all of the valve stems with a light coating of engine oil, then install the valves into the proper ports/guides.

2. If the umbrella-type valve seals are used, install them at this time. Be sure to use a seal protector to prevent damage to the seals as they are pushed over the valve keeper grooves. If O-ring seals are used, don't install them yet.

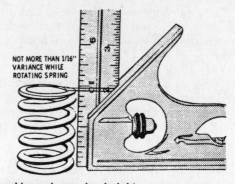

Checking valve spring height

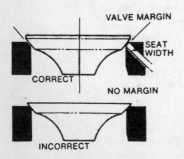

Valve seat width and centering

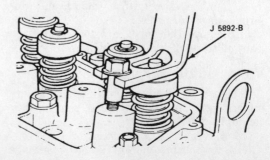

Compressing the valve spring

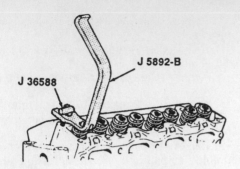

Valve spring removal — 2.3L Quad 4

C–type valve spring compressor

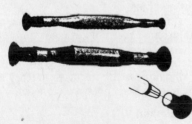

Hand-held valve lappping tool

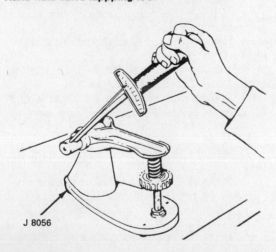

J 8056

Checking valve spring tension

3. Install the valve springs and the spring retainers (or rotators), and using the valve compressing tool, compress the springs.

4. If umbrella-type seals are used, just install the valve keepers (white grease may be used to hold them in place) and release the pressure on the compressing tool. If O-ring type seals are used, carefully work the seals into the second groove of the valve (closest to the head), install the valve keepers and release the pressure on the tool.

NOTE: *If the O-ring seals are installed BEFORE the springs and retainers are compressed, the seal will be destroyed.*

5. After all of the valves are installed and retained, tap each valve spring retainer with a rubber mallet to seat the keepers in the retainer.

Valve Oil Seal

WITHOUT REMOVING THE CYLINDER HEAD

1. Disconnect the negative (–) battery cable.
2. Remove the rocker arm cover as previously outlined in this chapter.
3. Remove the rocker arm assembly at the valve being serviced.
4. Remove the spark plug at the cylinder being serviced.
5. 2.3L QUAD 4, remove the camshaft over the valve being serviced.
6. Install a spark plug port adapter tool No. J–23590 into the spark plug hole. Apply compressed air to the cylinder to keep the valve in the closed position.
7. Using a valve spring compressor tool J–

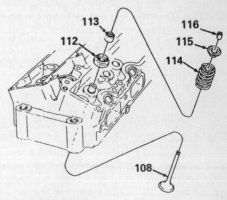

108. Valve (intake shown)
112. Rotator assembly
113. Valve stem seal
114. Spring
115. Retainer
116. Keys

Valve components — 2.3L Quad 4

Valve spring compressor — cylinder head installed

5892–B or equivalent, remove the valve keepers, cap, keepers and seal.

To install:

8. Position the valve seal over the end of the valve.

9. Install the spring, cap and keepers using the spring compressor. Carefully release the spring compressor and make sure the keepers are in the proper position.

10. Release the air pressure from the cylinder and remove the spark plug port adapter.

11. Install the spark plug and wire.

12. Install the rocker arm assembly as previously outlined in this chapter. Reconnect the negative (–) battery cable. Start the engine and check for oil leaks.

Oil Pan

REMOVAL AND INSTALLATION

2.3L QUAD 4 (VIN A,D)

NOTE: *The oil pan is of aluminum construction. Use care not to damage the casting by overtorquing during installation.*

1. Disconnect the negative (–) battery cable.
2. Drain the engine oil.

Oil pan assembly — 2.3L Quad 4. The 12 bolts to the cylinder block are different in length and width from the others.

3. Remove the splash shield-to-suspension support bolt.

4. Remove the exhaust manifold bracket (manual only).

5. Remove the radiator outlet pipe-to-oil pan bolt.

6. Remove the transaxle-to-oil pan nut.

7. Gently pry out the spacer between the oil pan and transaxle.

8. Remove the oil pan-to-transaxle bolt, oil pan bolts, oil pan and pan gasket. The crankshaft may have to be rotated to gain clearance.

To install:

1. Clean the gasket mating surfaces with a plastic gasket scraper and solvent.

2. Apply RTV sealer to the strips across the top of the carrier at the oil pan at the three way joint. Use only enough sealer to restore the silicone strip to its original dimension if using the old seal.

3. Using new seals and gaskets, install the oil pan and gaskets. The gaskets do not need any sealer.

4. Refer to the oil pan illustration. Torque the bolts (39A,C) to 106 inch lbs. (12 Nm) and the bolts 39B to 17 ft. lbs. (24 Nm). Do NOT overtorque.

5. Position the spacer to its original position and install stud.

6. Install and tighten the oil pan-to-transaxle nut and bolt.

7. Install the splash shield, radiator outlet pipe and exhaust manifold bracket (manual).

8. Install the flywheel cover.

9. Refill the engine with the specified engine oil, connect the negative battery cable, start the engine and check for oil leaks.

2.5L L4 (Lumina) VIN R

1. Disconnect the negative (–) battery cable.

2. Remove the coolant recovery bottle and engine torque strut.

3. Remove the air cleaner assembly and the air inlet.

4. Remove the serpentine belt as outlined in the "Belts" section in Chapter 1.

5. Loosen and move the air conditioning compressor from the bracket. Use a piece of wire or rope to hold the compressor out of the way.

6. Remove the oil level indicator and fill tube.

7. Support the engine using an engine support tool J–28467–A and J–36462.

8. Raise the vehicle and support with jackstands.

9. Drain the engine oil into a suitable drain pan.

10. Remove the starter motor and move aside.

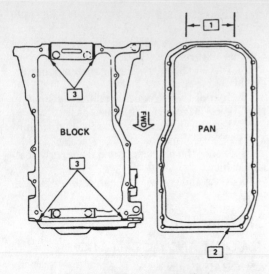

Apply RTV Sealant as specified:
1. ³/₈″ wide x ³/₁₆″ thick
2. ³/₁₆″ wide x ¹/₈″ thick
3. ¹/₈″ bead in areas shown

Oil pan sealer locations — 2.5L L4 Lumina

11. Remove the flywheel cover.
12. Turn the front wheels to full right.
13. Remove the engine wiring harness retainers under the oil pan on the right and left sides.
14. Remove the right engine splash shield.
15. Remove the front engine mount bracket bolts and nuts.
16. Remove the transaxle mount nuts.
17. Using the engine support fixture tool J–28467–A and J–36462, raise the engine about two inches.
18. Remove the front engine mount and bracket.
19. Loosen the frame bolts.
20. Remove the oil pan retaining bolts and oil pan.

To install:
1. Clean all engine and oil pan gasket sur-

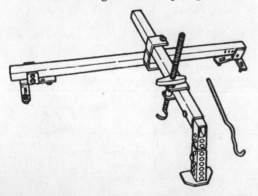

Engine support fixture J–28467–A

faces with solvent and a gasket scraper.
2. Apply RTV sealer to the oil pan and engine surfaces as illustrated in this section.
3. Install the oil pan and retaining bolts. Torque the bolts to 89 inch lbs. (10 Nm).
4. Install the frame bolts and torque to 103 ft. lbs. (140 Nm).
5. Install the engine mount and bracket.
6. Lower the engine into position and install the transaxle mount nuts.
7. Install the engine mount nuts and bracket bolts.
8. Install the engine splash shield.
9. Install the engine wiring harness to the oil pan.
10. Install the flywheel cover and reinstall the starter motor.
11. Lower the vehicle.
12. Remove the engine support fixtures.
13. Install the oil level indicator and tube assembly.
14. Reinstall the air conditioning compressor to its original location.
15. Install the serpentine belt as outlined in the "Belts" section in Chapter 1.
16. Install the air inlet and air cleaner assembly.
17. Install the engine torque strut and coolant recovery bottle.
18. Reconnect the negative (–) battery cable.
19. Fill the engine with the proper amount of engine oil.
20. Start the engine and check for oil leaks.

2.8L and 3.1L V6 (VIN W, T)

1. Remove the air cleaner assembly.
2. Disconnect the negative (–) battery cable.
3. Remove the serpentine belt as outlined in the "Belts" section in Chapter 1.
4. Remove the serpentine belt tensioner.
5. Install the engine support fixture tool J–28467–A and J–36462 or equivalent.
6. Raise the vehicle and support with jackstands.
7. Drain the engine oil into a suitable drain pan.
8. Remove the right front tire and wheel assembly.
9. Remove the right engine splash shield.
10. Remove the steering gear pinch bolt.
11. Remove the transaxle mount retaining nuts.
12. Remove the engine-to-frame mount retaining nuts.
13. Remove the front engine horse collar bracket from the cylinder block.
14. Remove the flywheel cover.
15. Remove the starter motor and move out of the way.

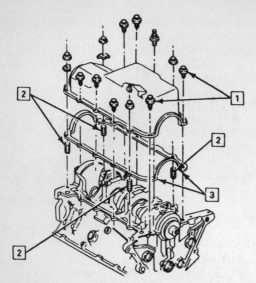

1. 18 ft. lbs.
2. 13 ft. lbs. ALL OTHERS—89 inch lbs.
3. Sealer

Oil pan assembly — 2.8L and 3.1L V6 engines

16. Place a jackstand under the frame front center crossmember.

17. Loosen the rear frame bolts, but do NOT remove.

18. Remove the front frame bolts and lower the front of the frame.

19. Remove the oil pan retaining bolts and nuts.

20. Remove the oil pan by gently prying on the corners with a gasket scraper.

To install:

1. Clean all gasket surfaces clean of any gasket material with solvent and a gasket scraper.

2. Install a new gasket, oil pan and the pan retaining bolts and nuts.

3. Torque the oil pan retaining nuts to 89 inch lbs. (10 Nm), rear bolts to 18 ft. lbs. (25 Nm), and the remaining bolts to 89 inch lbs. (10 Nm).

4. Install new frame-to-body bolts and torque to 103 ft. lbs. (140 Nm).

5. Remove the jackstands.

6. Install the starter motor.

7. Install the flywheel medal and plastic shields.

8. Install the front engine horse collar bracket from the cylinder block.

9. Install the engine-to-frame mount retaining nuts.

10. Install the transaxle-to-frame mount retaining nuts.

11. Install the steering gear pinch bolt.

12. Install the right splash shield.

13. Install the front wheel and tire assembly and torque the lug nuts to 100 ft. lbs. (136 Nm).

14. Lower the vehicle and remove the engine support fixtures.

15. Install the serpentine belt tensioner assembly.

16. Install the serpentine belt as outlined in the "Belts" section in Chapter 1.

17. Fill the engine with the specified amount and viscosity of engine oil.

18. Install the air cleaner and negative (–) battery cable.

19. Start the engine and check for engine oil leaks.

Oil Pump

REMOVAL AND INSTALLATION

2.3L QUAD 4 (VIN A,D)

1. Disconnect the negative (–) battery cable.

2. Remove the oil pan as previously outlined in this section.

3. Remove the four oil pump retaining bolts and oil pump.

4. Remove the pump screen, gerotor cover and relief pressure valve. Cut the top of the valve with side cutters and pry out the remaining bottom half of valve with a suitable prybar.

5. Remove the cover, but do NOT remove the drive gear and shaft.

To install:

1. Clean all parts in cleaning solvent to remove varnish and sludge.

2. Inspect parts for cracks, scoring, excessive wear or physical damage. Replace if necessary.

3. Lubricate the gears with clean engine oil.

4. Install the gerotor gear into the housing, housing cover and retaining bolts. Torque cover bolts to 106 inch lbs. (12 Nm).

5. Install the pressure relief valve by seating the valve with a $\frac{9}{16}$ inch deep socket.

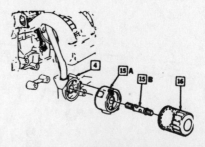

4. Cylinder block MDFL™ MDNM™
15A. Oil cooler adapter
15B. Oil cooler connecter
16. Oil filter

Engine oil cooler adapter — 2.3L Quad 4 (VIN A)

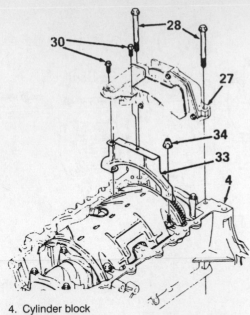

4. Cylinder block
27. Oil pump assembly
28. Bolt
30. Bolt
33. Pump to block brace
34. Nut

Oil pump assembly — 2.3L Quad 4

6. Install the pump cover bolts and torque to 106 inch lbs. (12 Nm).

7. Make sure the pump screen is clean and install.

8. Install the oil pump and torque the retaining bolts to 33 ft. lbs. (45 Nm).

9. Install the oil pan with a new gasket, new oil filter and fill the engine with clean engine oil.

10. Connect the negative battery cable, start the engine and check for leaks.

2.5L L4 (Lumina) VIN R

NOTE: *The force balancer assembly does NOT have to be removed to service the oil pump or pressure regulator assemblies.*

1. Drain the crankcase oil and remove the oil pan and filter as outlined in the "Oil Pan" removal procedures in this chapter.

2. Remove the oil pump cover, oil pump gears and pressure regulator valve.

CAUTION: *The pressure regulator valve spring is under pressure. Use care when unscrewing the plug, or removing the pin.*

To install:

• 3. Clean all sludge, oil and varnish from the pump assembly with carburetor cleaner or equivalent.

4. Lubricate all parts with engine oil.

WARNING: *To avoid engine damage, all pump cavities must be packed with petro-leum jelly BEFORE installing the gears to ensure priming.*

5. Install the pump gears, pump cover and pressure regulator. Torque the pump cover bolts to 7 ft. lbs. (10 Nm).

6. Install the plug and pin and make sure the pin is properly seated.

7. Clean and install the oil pump inlet screen, oil pan and new filter. Torque the oil pan bolts to 20 ft. lbs. (27 Nm).

8. Refill the crankcase with the specified engine oil. Start the engine and check for oil pressure and leaks.

2.8L and 3.1L V6 (VIN W, T)

1. Disconnect the negative (–) battery cable and drain the engine oil.

2. Remove the oil pan assembly as previously outlined in this chapter.

3. Remove the oil pump and drive shaft extension.

4. Clean the pump pickup with solvent and a stiff brush.

5. **To install:** position the oil pump and drive shaft extension onto the mounting area. Make sure the drive shaft extension is engaged with the pump drive and the pump is flush with the rear main bearing cap.

6. Torque the pump mounting bolts to 30 ft. lbs. (41 Nm).

7. Install the oil pan assembly as previously outlined in this chapter.

8. Refill the engine with the specified amount and viscosity of engine oil.

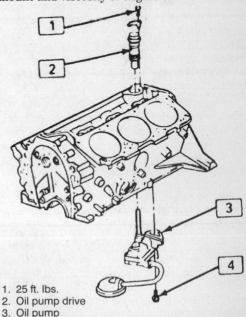

1. 25 ft. lbs.
2. Oil pump drive
3. Oil pump
4. 30 ft. lbs.

Oil pump assembly — 2.8L and 3.1L V6 engines

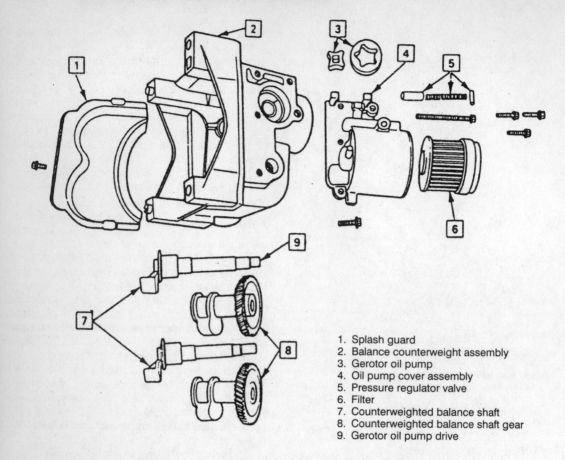

1. Splash guard
2. Balance counterweight assembly
3. Gerotor oil pump
4. Oil pump cover assembly
5. Pressure regulator valve
6. Filter
7. Counterweighted balance shaft
8. Counterweighted balance shaft gear
9. Gerotor oil pump drive

Oil pump and force balancer assembly — 2.5L L4 Lumina

9. Reconnect the negative (–) battery cable.
10. Start the engine and check for oil leaks and oil pressure.

NOTE: *If the oil pressure does NOT increase to specifications withing about ten seconds, turn OFF the engine. Restart and allow to run for no more than five seconds. If there is no increase in oil pressure, turn off the engine and remove oil pump to recheck for improper installation.*

Force Balancer Assembly

The 2.5L L4 engine uses a force balancer assembly that is driven directly from the crankshaft. Two eccentrically weighted shafts and gears are counter rotated by a concentric gear on the crankshaft at twice the crankshaft speed. The balancer helps dampen engine vibration and includes a sump pick-up screen, a gerotor-type oil pump and an oil filter. The filter is serviced through an opening in the bottom of the oil pan.

REMOVAL AND INSTALLATION

2.5L L4 Lumina Engine

1. Disconnect the negative (–) battery cable.
2. Drain the engine oil and remove the oil filter assembly.
3. Remove the oil pan assembly as outlined in the "Oil Pan" removal procedures in this chapter.
4. Remove the four force balancer attaching bolts and remove the balancer assembly. Refer to the force balancer illustrations in this section.
5. **Important:** before installation, perform the following procedures:

NOTE: *When installing the balancer, the end of the housing without the dowel pins MUST remain in contact with the block surface. If it loses contact, gear engagement may be lost and permanent damage to either the crank or balancer gears may result.*

a. Rotate the engine to Top Dead Center (TDC) on the No. 1 and No. 4 cylinders.
b. Position the balancer assembly onto the crankshaft with the balancer weights at BTC

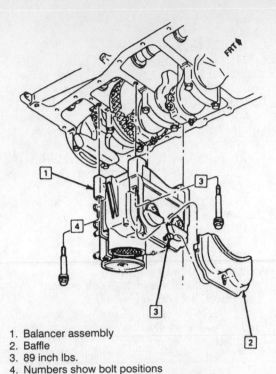

1. Balancer assembly
2. Baffle
3. 89 inch lbs.
4. Numbers show bolt positions

Force balancer tightening sequence — 2.5L L4 Lumina

(bottom dead center), plus or minus one half of a gear tooth.

  c. Torque the bolts in the following sequence in two steps, 3–1–2–4. Refer to the "Force Balancer Torquing Sequence" illustration in this section.

  d. The first torque step to 107 inch lbs. (12 Nm). The second torque step to 11 ft. lbs. (15 Nm) plus 75 degrees (1 flat) for the short bolts. And 11 ft. lbs. (15 Nm) plus 90 degrees ($1\frac{1}{2}$ flats) for the long bolts.

6. Install the oil pan assembly as outlined in the "Oil Pan" installation procedures in this chapter.

7. Refill the crankcase with the specified engine oil. Start the engine and check for oil leaks.

Timing Gear Cover

REMOVAL AND INSTALLATION

2.5L L4 (Lumina) VIN R

1. Disconnect the negative (–) battery cable.
2. Remove the torque strut bolt at the cylinder head bracket and move the strut out of the way.
3. Remove the serpentine belt as outlined in the "Belts" section in Chapter 1.
4. Install the engine support fixture tool J–28467–A and J–36462.

5. Raise the vehicle and support with jackstands.

6. Remove the right front tire assembly.

7. Disconnect the right lower ball joint from the knuckle as outlined in the "Ball Joint" section in Chapter 8.

8. Support the engine using the engine support fixture previously installed.

9. Remove the two right hand frame attaching bolts.

10. Loosen the two left hand frame attaching bolts, but do NOT remove.

11. Lower the vehicle.

12. Lower the engine on the right hand side.

13. Raise the vehicle and support with jackstands.

14. Remove the engine vibration dampener using a dampener puller.

WARNING: *Do NOT use a jaw puller to remove the engine dampener. If a vibration dampener puller is not used to remove the dampener, damage may result to the dampener.*

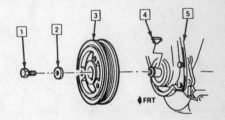

1. 162 ft. lbs.
2. Washer
3. Crankshaft balancer
4. Key
5. Front cover

Crankshaft damper assembly — 2.5L L4 Lumina

15. Remove the timing cover retaining bolts.

16. Remove the cover by gently prying the cover away from the block with gasket scaper. Be careful not to distort the cover or oil pan sealing surfaces.

17. Remove the old timing cover oil seal.

To install:

1. Clean all gasket mating surfaces with solvent and a gasket scraper.

2. Apply a $\frac{3}{8}$ inch wide by $\frac{3}{16}$ inch thick bead of RTV sealer to the joint at the oil pan and timing cover.

3. Apply a $\frac{1}{4}$ in. wide by $\frac{1}{8}$ in. thick bead of RTV sealer to the timing cover at the block mating surface.

4. Install a new timing cover oil seal using a timing cover seal installer tool J–34995 or equivalent.

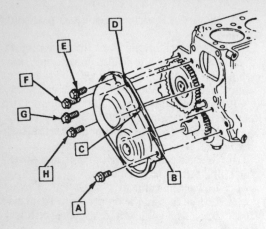

Timing gear cover and tightening sequence — 2.5L L4 Lumina. Tighten bolts A and G to 89 inch lbs.

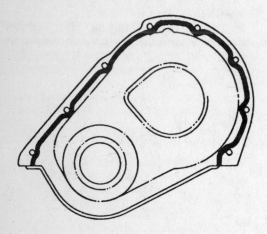

RTV Sealant application — 2.5L L4 Lumina

5. Install the cover onto the block and install the retaining bolts loosely.

6. Install the timing cover seal installer tool J-34995 to align the timing cover.

7. Tighten two opposing bolts to hold the cover in place.

8. Torque the bolts in sequence as shown in the illustration (A-H) to 89 inch lbs. (10 Nm). Remove the timing cover oil seal installer tool.

9. Install the crankshaft vibration dam-

Vibration damper puller

pener and torque the bolt to 162 ft. lbs. (220 Nm).

10. Lower the vehicle.e

11. Raise the engine to its proper position using the support fixture.

12. Raise the vehicle and support with jackstands.

13. Raise the frame and install the removed frame bolts. Torque the bolts to 103 ft. lbs. (140 Nm).

14. Install the right ball joint and torque the nut. Refer to the "Ball Joint" section in chapter 8.

15. Install the right front tire and torque the lug nuts to 100 ft. lbs. (136 Nm).

16. Lower the vehicle.

17. Remove the engine support fixture.

18. Install the torque strut and bolt to the cylinder head bracket.

19. Install the serpentine belt as outlined in the "Belts" section in Chapter 1.

20. Reconnect the negative (–) battery cable and recheck the following procedures to ensure completion of repairs.

21. Start the engine and check for oil leaks.

Timing Chain Cover

REMOVAL AND INSTALLATION

2.3L QUAD 4 (VIN A,D)

NOTE: *The timing chain and cam housing gaskets can be replaced without removing the timing chain cover from the vehicle.*

1. Disconnect the negative (–) battery cable.

2. Drain the engine coolant from the radiator.

CAUTION: *When draining the coolant, keep in mind that cats and dogs are attracted by the ethylene glycol antifreeze, and are quite likely to drink any that is left in an uncovered container or in puddles on the ground. This will prove fatal in sufficient quantity. Always drain the coolant into a sealable container. Coolant should be reused unless it is contaminated or several years old.*

3. Remove the serpentine belt as outlined in Chapter 1.

4. Disconnect the oxygen sensor connector, remove the exhaust manifold heat shields and manifold bracket.

5. Loosen the exhaust manifold-to-pipe spring loaded nuts.

6. Raise the vehicle and support with jackstands.

7. Remove the right front wheel, lower splash shield and engine balancer bolt. Use a crankshaft balancer puller tool J-38122 to prevent the balancer from turning during bolt removal. Remove the balancer.

8. Remove lower front cover bolts and nut.

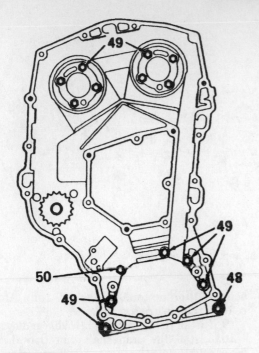

48. Stud-end bolt
49. Chain housing bolts (13)
50. Housing to block stud; also pivot for timing chain tensioner shoe

Timing chain cover — 2.3L Quad 4

9. Remove the exhaust manifold-to-pipe nuts. Pull the pipe out of the way.
10. If removing the timing cover from the vehicle, remove the exhaust manifold, water pump and hoses as outlined in this chapter..
11. Remove the front cover upper bolts, oil/air separator hose and timing cover.
12. If removing the inner timing cover, remove the timing chain and inner cover retaining bolts, disconnect the motor mounts and raise with a floor jack to remove.

To install:
1. Inspect the oil pan inner silicone bead and aluminum carrier at the oil pan. Use RTV sealer to repair these if damaged.
2. Clean the gasket mating surfaces with a scraper and solvent.
3. Install the timing cover with new gaskets, no sealer needed on new gaskets.
4. Lower the engine into position and tighten the motor mounts.

WARNING: *Do NOT install the timing chain tensioner shoe pivot stud until after the timing chain is in place.*

5. Install the oil pan-to-timing cover retaining bolts hand tight.
6. Torque the timing cover-to-block bolts, if removed, to 19 ft. lbs. (26 Nm).

7. Torque the timing cover-to-oil pan bolts to 17 ft. lbs. (24 Nm).
8. If removed, install the timing chain and tensioner as outlined in the "Timing Chain" section in this chapter.
9. Install the front cover with new gaskets and hand tighten the bolts.
10. Install the oil/air separator hose.
11. Raise the vehicle and support with jackstands.
12. If removed, install the water pump and hoses.
13. Install the crankshaft balancer. Torque the bolt to 74 ft. lbs. (100 Nm) + 90 degrees. Hold the crankshaft still with the balancer puller tool.
14. If removed, install the exhaust manifold, pipe and shields.
15. Install the right splash shield, front tire and lower the vehicle.
16. Install the serpentine belt, oxygen sensor connector and refill the radiator with engine coolant.
17. Recheck each procedure to ensure completion of repair.
18. Connect the negative battery cable, start the engine and check for oil and coolant leaks.

2.8L and 3.1L V6 (VIN W, T)

1. Disconnect the negative (–) battery cable.
2. Remove the air cleaner assembly.
3. After the engine is cool, drain the engine coolant into a suitable container.

CAUTION: *When draining the coolant, keep in mind that cats and dogs are attracted by the ethylene glycol antifreeze, and are quite likely to drink any that is left in an uncovered container or in puddles on the ground. This will prove fatal in sufficient quantity. Always drain the coolant into a sealable container. Coolant should be reused unless it is contaminated or several years old.*

4. Remove the serpentine belt as outlined in the "Belts" section in Chapter 1.
5. Remove the alternator and move out of the way.
6. Remove the power steering pump and support out of the way with a piece of wire or rope. Do NOT disconnect the pump hoses.
7. Raise the vehicle and support with jackstands.
8. Remove the inner splash shield and flywheel covers.
9. Remove the starter motor and support out of the way with wire. Make sure the negative (–) battery cable is disconnected first.
10. Remove the crankshaft vibration dampener with a dampener puller.

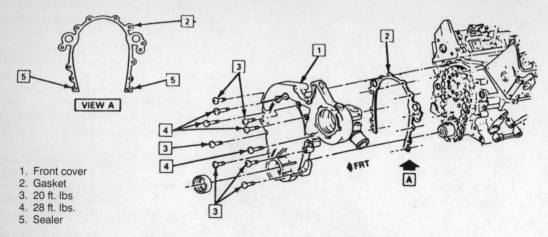

1. Front cover
2. Gasket
3. 20 ft. lbs
4. 28 ft. lbs
5. Sealer

Timing chain cover — 2.8L and 3.1L V6 engines

WARNING: *Do NOT use a jaw puller to remove the engine dampener. If a vibration dampener puller is not used to remove the dampener, damage may result to the dampener.*

11. Remove the serpentine belt idler pulley.
12. Remove the oil pan as outlined in this chapter.
13. Remove the lower timing cover bolts.
14. Lower the vehicle.
15. Remove the radiator hose at the water pump.
16. Remove the heater hose from the system fill pipe and the bypass and overflow hoses.
17. Remove the evaporator canister purge hose.
18. Remove the upper timing cover retaining bolts and cover.
19. Remove the old timing cover oil seal.

To install:

1. Clean all mating surfaces free of gasket material with solvent and a gasket scraper.
2. Install a new timing cover oil seal with a oil seal installer tool J–35468 or equivalent. Use this tool to align the cover also.
3. Apply RTV sealer to both sides of the cover mating surfaces and install a new gasket.
4. Position the cover onto the engine and loosely install the upper retaining bolts. Make sure the gasket is in proper position before going any further, if it is not, it may be a long day.
5. Torque the bolts according to the illustration in this section. The #3 bolts to 20 ft. lbs. (27 Nm) and the #4 bolts to 28 ft. lbs. (38 Nm).
6. Raise the vehicle and support with jackstands.
7. Install the oil pan as outlined in this chapter.
8. Install the lower timing cover retaining bolts and torque to 20 ft. lbs. (27 Nm). Also, refer to the illustration.
9. Install the serpentine belt idler pulley.
10. Install the crankshaft vibration dampener and torque the bolt to 66–85 ft. lbs. (90–115 Nm).
11. Install the starter motor, flywheel covers and inner splash shield.
12. Lower the vehicle.
13. Install the radiator hose, heater hose, bypass and overflow hoses and canister purge hose.
14. Install the power steering pump and alternator.
15. Install the belt tensioner and serpentine belt.
16. Refill the cooling system with the specified amount of anti-freeze.
17. Install the air cleaner assembly.
18. Reconnect the negative (–) battery cable.
19. Recheck all procedures for completion of repair. Check for proper fluid levels.
20. Start the engine and check for oil, coolant and vacuum leaks.

Camshaft and Timing Gears

REMOVAL AND INSTALLATION

2.3L QUAD 4 (VIN A,D)

NOTE: *The camshaft housing and cylinder head use the same retaining bolts. When the bolts are removed to service the camshaft cover, the cylinder head gasket MUST be replaced also. When valve components are removed, mark each part for proper reinstallation.*

INTAKE CAMSHAFT

1. Disconnect the negative (–) battery cable.
2. Remove the ignition coil and module as-

sembly as outlined in this chapter. Use a spark plug boot remover tool J–36011 or equivalent.

3. Disconnect the idle speed power steering pressure switch, remove the power steering belt, retaining bolts and position the pump aside out of the way. Do NOT disconnect the pump hoses. Remove the pump bracket.

4. Remove the power steering pump drive pulley using a three jaw puller or steering wheel puller with backup nuts.

5. Remove the oil/air separator but leave the hoses attached.

6. Remove the camshaft housing and cylinder head retaining bolts.

NOTE: *Use the reverse of the torquing sequence to loosen the retaining bolts.*

7. Push the cover off the housing by threading four housing bolts into the tapped holes in the cover. Tighten the bolts in an even sequence so the cover does not bind on the dowel pins and remove the cover.

8. Remove the camshaft from the camshaft housing. Be careful not to damage the camshaft bearing journals

To install:

1. Clean all gasket mating surfaces with a gasket scraper and solvent. RTV sealant is NOT needed on the gaskets. The gaskets are different, refer to the "Camshaft Housing Seals" illustration in this chapter.

2. Position the camshaft into the journals.

3. Using new gaskets, position the cover onto the camshaft housing.

4. Apply pipe sealant GM 1052080 or equivalent to the housing and cover retaining bolts.

5. Install the bolts and torque in sequence to the specified torque in the specification chart in the beginning of this chapter. Also, refer to the "Cylinder Head" installation procedures for torque sequence.

6. Connect electrical connectors and vacuum lines.

7. Install the oil/air separator, power steering drive pulley using installer J–36015 and power steering pump assembly.

8. Install the steering pump drive belt and adjust to specifications in Chapter 1.

9. Install the ignition assembly and connect the negative battery cable.

10. Recheck all procedures to ensure completion of repair, start the engine and check for fluid leaks.

EXHAUST CAMSHAFT

NOTE: *The camshaft housing and cylinder head use the same retaining bolts. When the bolts are removed to service the camshaft cover, the cylinder head gasket MUST be replaced also. When valve components are re-moved, mark each part for proper reinstallation.*

1. Disconnect the negative (–) battery cable.

2. Remove the ignition coil and module assembly as outlined in this chapter. Use a spark plug boot remover tool J–36011 or equivalent.

3. Disconnect the oil pressure switch and remove the transaxle level dipstick (automatic).

4. Remove the oil/air separator but leave the hoses attached.

5. Disconnect vacuum lines and engine electrical connectors to gain access to the housing cover.

6. Remove the timing cover and position out of the way. For assistance, refer to the "Timing Chain" procedures in this chapter.

7. Remove the camshaft housing and cylinder head retaining bolts.

NOTE: *Use the reverse of the torquing sequence to loosen the retaining bolts.*

8. Push the cover off the housing by threading four housing bolts into the tapped holes in the cover. Tighten the bolts in an even sequence so the cover does not bind on the dowel pins and remove the cover.

9. Remove the camshaft from the housing. Be careful not to damage the camshaft journals.

To install:

1. Clean all gasket mating surfaces with a gasket scraper and solvent. RTV sealant is NOT needed on the gaskets. The gaskets are different, refer to the "Camshaft Housing Seals" illustration in this section.

2. Lubricate the camshaft journals and position the camshaft into the housing.

3. Using new gaskets, position the cover onto the camshaft housing.

4. Apply pipe sealant GM 1052080 or equivalent to the housing and cover retaining bolts.

5. Install the bolts and torque in sequence to the specified torque in the specification chart in the beginning of this chapter. Also, refer to the "Cylinder Head" installation procedures for torque sequence.

6. Install the timing chain housing.

7. Connect electrical connectors and vacuum lines.

8. Install the oil/air separator.

9. Install the ignition assembly and connect the negative battery cable.

10. Recheck all procedures to ensure completion of repair, start the engine and check for fluid leaks.

2.5L L4 (Lumina) VIN R

The camshaft has to be removed from the engine to remove the timing gear. The gear is pressed onto the camshaft and has to be be pressed off. The camshaft uses a thrust plate

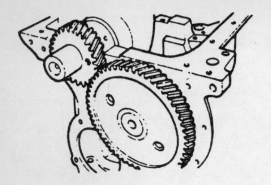

Timing gear alignment—2.5L

that can be removed by inserting a screwdriver through the two holes in the timing gear and removing the two screws.

1. Disconnect the negative (–) battery cable.
2. Remove the engine assembly from the vehicle as outlined in the "Engine Assembly" section in this chapter.
3. Remove the rocker arm cover and pushrods as outlined in the "Rocker Arm Cover" section in this chapter.
4. Remove the pushrod cover and valve lifters as outlined in the "Pushrod Cover" section in this chapter.
5. Remove the serpentine belt, crankshaft pulleys and vibration dampener.
6. Remove the front cover as outlined earlier in this section.
7. Remove the two camshaft thrust plate screws.

NOTE: *The camshaft journals are the same diameter. Care must be taken when removing the camshaft to avoid damage to the cam bearings.*

8. Carefully slide the camshaft and gear through the front of the block.
9. To remove the camshaft gear, use a arbor press and adapter. Position the thrust plate to avoid damage to the woodruff key as the gear is removed.

To install:

1. Old and new camshafts should be cleaned with solvent and compressed air before being installed.
2. Support the camshaft at the back of the front journal in the arbor press using the press adapter.
3. Position the spacer ring, thrust plate and woodruff key over the end of the shaft.
4. Press the gear onto the camshaft.
5. Measure the end clearance with a feeler gauge between the cam journal and thrust plate. The measurement should be between 0.0015 in. to 0.0050 in. If the measurement is LESS than 0.0015, replace the spacer ring. If

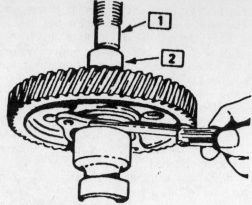

1. Arbor press
2. J–21474–13 or J–21795–1

Installing camshaft gear with an arbor press — 2.5L L4 Lumina

the measurement is MORE than 0.0050, replace the thrust plate.

WARNING: *Always apply Assembly Lube (GM E.O.S 1052367 or equivalent) to the cam journals and lobes. If this procedures is not done, cam damage may result.*

6. Carefully install the camshaft into the engine block by rotating and pushing forward until seated.
7. Install the thrust plate screws and torque to 89 inch lbs. (10 Nm).
8. Install the front cover, vibration dampener and serpentine belt.
9. Install the valve lifter and pushrod cover.
10. Install the pushrods and rocker arm cover as outlined in the "Rocker Arm" section in this chapter.

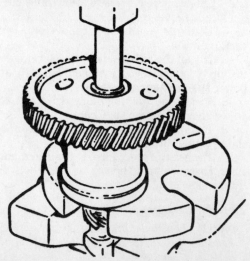

Removing camshaft gear with an arbor press 2.5L L4 Lumina

Camshaft thrust plate screw removal — 2.5L L4 Lumina

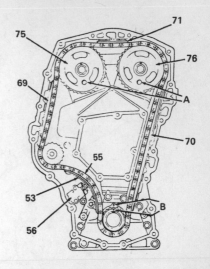

11. Install the engine into the vehicle.

12. Refill all necessary fluids.

13. Recheck every procedure to ensure completion of repair.

14. Start the engine and check for oil, vacuum, coolant and exhaust leaks.

Timing Chain and Sprockets

REMOVAL AND INSTALLATION

2.3L QUAD 4 (VIN A,D)

NOTE: *Before attempting to remove the timing chain, completely read the procedures for "Timing Chain Cover" and "Timing Chain".*

1. Disconnect the negative (–) battery cable.

2. Remove the timing chain cover as outlined in this chapter.

3. Remove the crankshaft oil slinger.

4. Rotate the crankshaft clockwise until the camshaft sprocket's dowel pin holes line up with the holes in the timing chain housing.

5. The mark on the crankshaft sprocket should line up with the mark on the cylinder block and the sprocket keyway should point upwards with the centerline of the cylinder bores. This is the timed position as in the "Timing Chain Alignment" illustration in this section.

6. Remove the timing chain guides.

7. Raise the vehicle and support with jackstands.

8. Remove the timing chain tensioner and spring. Use eye protection to guard against spring tension.

9. Make sure all the slack in the chain is above the tensioner assembly, then remove the tensioner shoe. Slide a small prybar under the timing chain while pulling on the shoe.

10. If the tensioner shoe will NOT come out proceed as follows.

　a. Lower the vehicle.

　b. Hold the intake camshaft sprocket with the sprocket removing tool J–36013. remove the sprocket bolt and washer.

A. Cam timing alignment pin locations
B. Crankshaft gear timing marks
53. Chain tensioner shoe assembly
55. Timing chain
56. Timing chain tensioner
69. Right timing chain guide
70. Left timing chain guide
71. Upper timing chain guide
75. Exhaust cam sprocket
76. Intake cam sprocket

Timing chain alignment — 2.3L Quad 4

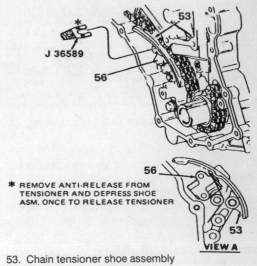

53. Chain tensioner shoe assembly
56. Timing chain tensioner

Retaining timing chain spring tension — 2.3L Quad 4

　c. Rethread the bolt into the camshaft by hand. Without the washer, the bolt provides a surface to push against.

　d. Remove the intake camshaft sprocket

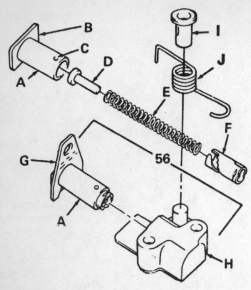

56. Timing chain tensioner assembly
A. Plunger assembly
B. Long end
C. Peg
D. Nylon plug
E. Spring
F. Restraint cylinder
G. J–36589 anti-release device
H. Tensioner body
I. Sleeve
J. Spring

Timing chain tensioner assembly

using a three jaw puller in the three relief holes.

WARNING: *Do NOT attempt to pry the sprocket off the camshaft, sprocket or chain housing damage may occur.*

11. Remove the tensioner retaining bolts and tensioner.

12. Remove the timing chain from the sprockets.

To install:

1. Inspect the parts for wear and replace if needed. Follow the steps without deviation.

2. Apply thread locking compound to the bolt. Install the intake camshaft sprocket, washer and bolt. Torque to 40 ft. lbs. (55 Nm).

3. Install the guide tools J–36008 through the holes in the camshaft sprockets and timing cover for correct timing.

4. **VERY IMPORTANT**.

   a. If the camshafts are out of position and must be rotated more than ⅛ turn in order to align the guide pins.

   b. The crankshaft MUST be rotated 90° degrees clockwise off of TDC (top dead center) in order to give the valves adequate clearance to open.

   c. Once the camshafts are in position and

guide pins installed, rotate the crankshaft COUNTER CLOCKWISE back to TDC.

5. Install the timing chain over the exhaust camshaft sprocket, around idler sprocket and around crankshaft sprocket.

6. Remove the sprocket guide pin from the intake sprocket. Rotate the intake camshaft sprocket counter clockwise enough to slide the timing chain over the sprocket. The length of the timing chain between the two sprockets will tighten.

7. Recheck to see if the guide pins slide into the holes freely. If not, the chain may have to be repositioned.

8. Leave the pins installed.

9. Raise the vehicle and support with jackstands.

10. Remove the slack from the chain between the intake and crankshaft sprockets. The crankshaft timing marks should be in alignment. If not, move the chain one tooth forward or rearward to remove the slack and recheck.

11. Install the chain housing-to-block stud and tensioner. The stud should be under the timing chain.

12. Reload the tensioner to its zero position as follows.

   a. Assemble the restraint cylinder, spring and nylon plug into the plunger. While rotating the restraint cylinder clockwise, push the restraint cylinder into the plunger until it bottoms. The pin in the plunger will lock the restraint in the loaded position.

   b. Install the tensioner spacer tool J–36589 onto the plunger.

   c. Install the plunger assembly into the tensioner body with the long end toward the crankshaft when installed.

13. Install the tensioner assembly to the chain housing. Torque the bolts to 115 inch lbs. (13 Nm).

14. Install the tensioner shoe, spring and sleeve. Remove the spacer tool and squeeze the plunger into the tensioner body to unload the plunger.

15. Lower the vehicle enough to remove the alignment guide pins.

16. Rotate the crankshaft clockwise two full rotations and recheck timing mark alignment. The guide pins should slide in freely.

WARNING: *If the timing marks are not aligned properly, severe engine damage may occur.*

17. Remove the timing chain guide pins.

18. Install the crankshaft oil slinger, front timing cover and balancer.

19. Start the engine and check for fluid leaks.

2.8L and 3.1L V6 (VIN W, T)

1. Disconnect the negative (–) battery cable.

2. Remove the serpentine belt, crankshaft pulleys and front timing cover as outlined previously in this chapter.

3. Place #1 piston at TDC (top dead center) with the marks on the camshaft and crankshaft sprockets aligned (#4 firing position).

4. Remove the camshaft sprocket and chain.

NOTE: *If the sprocket does not slide off the camshaft easily, tap on the lower edge of the sprocket with a plastic or rubber mallet. Also, spray some penetrating oil on the camshaft-to-sprocket area and let soak for a few minutes.*

5. Remove the crankshaft sprocket with a three jaw puller if it does not come off by hand.

To install:

6. Position the crankshaft sprocket into position with the woodruff key in the proper position.

7. Apply Assembly Lube to the thrust surfaces of the cam and crankshaft.

8. If the engine is out of valve timing, install both sprockets and align the marks as shown in the illustration without the chain installed. Remove the camshaft sprocket after the marks are lined up.

9. Hold the cam sprocket with the chain hanging down and align the marks on the camshaft and crankshaft sprockets.

10. Align the dowel pin in the camshaft with the dowel hole in the sprocket.

11. Draw the camshaft sprocket onto the camshaft using the retaining bolts. Torque the retaining bolts to 18 ft. lbs. (25 Nm).

12. Lubricate the chain and sprockets with engine oil.

13. Install the timing cover, vibration dampener, pulleys and serpentine belt.

14. Recheck every procedures for completion of repair.

15. Start the engine and check for oil, coolant and vacuum leaks.

Camshaft

REMOVAL AND INSTALLATION

2.8L and 3.1L V6 (VIN W, T)

1. Disconnect the negative (–) battery cable.

2. Remove the engine assembly from the vehicle as outlined in the "Engine Assembly" section in this chapter.

3. Remove the intake manifold as outlined in the "Intake Manifold" section in this chapter.

4. Remove the rocker arm covers as outlined in this chapter.

5. Loosen the rocker arms far enough to remove the pushrods. Mark each valve component to ensure installation is in the same location as removal.

6. Remove each valve lifter and place next to the corresponding lifter bore.

7. Remove the front timing cover as previously outlined.

8. Remove the timing chain and cam sprocket.

NOTE: *If the sprocket does not slide off the camshaft easily, tap on the lower edge of the sprocket with a plastic or rubber mallet. Also, spray some penetrating oil on the camshaft-to-sprocket area and let soak for a few minutes.*

9. With a long bolt threaded into the sprocket bolt hole, slowly turn the camshaft while pulling it out of the block.

NOTE: *The camshaft journals are the same diameter. Care must be taken when removing*

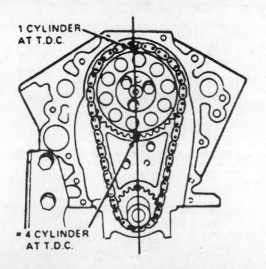

Timing chain adjustments — 2.8L and 3.1L V6 engines

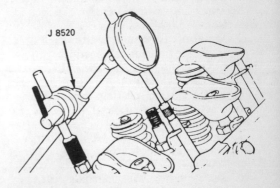

Measuring camshaft with a dial indicator

the camshaft to avoid damage to the cam bearings.

To install:

1. Old and new camshafts should be cleaned with solvent and compressed air before being installed.

2. Apply Assembly Lube (GM E.O.S 1052367 or equivalent) to the camshaft journals and lobes before installation.

WARNING: *Always apply Assembly Lube (GM E.O.S 1052367 or equivalent) to the cam journals and lobes. If this procedures is not done, cam damage may result.*

3. Carefully install the camshaft into the block until seated in the rear bearing.

4. Install the timing chain and sprockets as previously outlined in this chapter.

5. Install the front timing cover as outlined earlier in this chapter.

6. Install the lifters into their original locations.

7. Install the rocker arms over the pushrods and adjust as specified in the "Rocker Arm" section in this chapter.

8. Install the intake manifold and rocker arm covers.

9. Install the engine assembly into the vehicle as outlined in the "Engine Assembly" section in this chapter.

10. Refill the engine with the proper amount of coolant and engine oil. Also recheck the transaxle fluid.

11. Recheck each procedure to ensure the proper completion of repair.

12. Start the engine and check for fluid leaks.

INSPECTION

1. Check the camshaft sprocket, keyway and threads, bearing journals and lobes for wear, galling, gouges or overheating. If any of these conditions exist, replace the camshaft.

NOTE: *Do NOT attempt to repair the camshaft. Always replace the camshaft and lifters as an assembly. Old valve lifters will destroy a new camshaft in less time than it took you to replace the camshaft.*

2. **Camshaft Lift Measurement:**

   a. Lubricate the camshaft bearings with Assembly Lube 1051396 or equivalent.

   b. Carefully install the camshaft into the block. If the cam bearings are damaged badly, set the camshaft on "V" blocks instead.

   c. Install a dial indicator J–8520 and measure the camshaft lift as shown in the illustration in this section.

   d. Measure the bearing journals with a micrometer. Take measurements for run-out and diameter. If not within specification in

the "Camshaft" chart in the beginning of this chapter, replace the camshaft.

WARNING: *Always apply Assembly Lube (GM E.O.S 1052367 or equivalent) to the cam journals and lobes. If this procedures is not done, cam damage may result.*

Camshaft Bearings

REMOVAL AND INSTALLATION

2.5L L4 Lumina engine

NOTE: *Camshaft bearing removal and installation should be done by a qualified machine shop because the tools needed are expensive and would not be economical to purchase for a one time usage.*

1. Remove the engine from the vehicle as previously outlined.

2. Remove the camshaft from the engine as previously outlined.

3. Unbolt and remove the engine flywheel.

4. Drive the rear camshaft expansion plug out of the engine block from the inside using a long pry bar.

5. Using a camshaft bearing service tool No. J33049 or equivalent, drive the front camshaft bearing towards the rear and the rear bearing towards the front.

6. Install the appropriate extension on the service tool and drive the center bearing out towards the rear.

7. Drive all of the new bearings into place in the opposite direction of which they were removed, making sure to align the oil holes in the engine block bores.

CAUTION: *Never reuse camshaft bearings. Always use new bearings.*

NOTE: *The front camshaft bearing must be driven approximately $1/8$ in. behind the front*

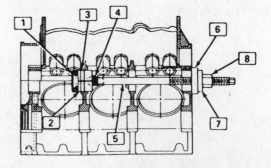

1. Back-up nut
2. Expanding collet
3. Bearing
4. Expanding mandrel
5. 2 piece puller screw
6. Pulling plate
7. Thrust bearing
8. Pulling nut

Removing and installing camshaft bearings — all engines

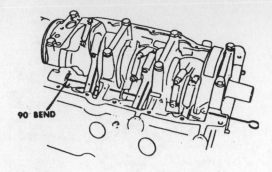

Checking cam bearing oil hole alignment with brass rod. Make rod as shown, using $^3\!/_{32}$″ rod about 30 in. long. (1) indicates 90° bend

of the cylinder block to uncover the oil hole to the timing gear oiling nozzle.

To install:

8. Install the camshaft bearings so that the oil holes in the bearing is aligned with the hole in the block.

9. Install the camshaft and timing gear as outlined in the "Camshaft" installation procedures.

10. Install the timing gear cover, vibration dampener, all accessaries and install the engine into the vehicle as outlined in the "Engine" installation procedures in this chapter.

2.8L and 3.1L V6 engine

NOTE: *Camshaft bearing removal should be done by a qualified machine shop because the tools needed are expensive and would not be economical to purchase for a one time usage.*

Camshaft bearings can be replaced with engine completely or partially disassembled. To replace bearings without complete disassembly remove the camshaft and crankshaft leaving cylinder heads attached and pistons in place. Before removing crankshaft, install two inch pieces of rubber hose to the threads of connecting rod bolts to prevent damage to crankshaft. Fasten connecting rods against sides of engine so they will not be in the way while replacing camshaft bearings.

1. Remove the timing chain front cover and camshaft rear cover as outlined in the "Timing Chain Cover and Camshaft" removal procedures.

2. Using a camshaft bearing Tool J–33049 or its equivalent, with the nut and thrust washer installed to the end of the threads, index the pilot in the camshaft front bearing and install the puller screw through the pilot.

3. Install the remover and installer tool with the shoulder toward the bearing, making

sure a sufficient number of threads are engaged.

4. Using two wrenches, hold the puller screw while turning the nut. When the bearing has been pulled from the bore, remove the remover and installer tool and bearing from the puller screw.

5. Remove the remaining bearings (except front and rear) in the same manner. It will be necessary to index the pilot in the camshaft rear bearing to remove the rear intermediate bearing.

6. Assemble the remover and installer tool on the driver handle and remove the camshaft front and rear bearings by driving towards the center of the cylinder block.   The camshaft front and rear bearings should be installed first. These bearings will act as guides for the pilot, and center the remaining bearings being pulled into place.

7. Assemble the remover and installer tool on the driver handle and install the camshaft front and rear bearings by driving them towards the center of the cylinder block. Make sure the oil holes in the bearing line up with the holes in the block.

8. Using Tool Set J–6098, or its equivalent with the nut and thrust washer installed to end of the threads, index the pilot into the camshaft front bearing and install the puller screw through the pilot.

9. Index the camshaft bearing into the bore (with oil hole aligned as outlined below), then install the remover and installer tool on the puller screw with the shoulder toward the bearing.

10. Using two wrenches, hold the puller screw while turning the nut. After the bearing has been pulled into the bore, remove the remover and installer tool from the puller screw and check the alignment of the oil holes in the camshaft bearings.

11. Install the remaining bearings in the same manner. It will be necessary to index the pilot in the camshaft rear bearing to install the rear intermediate bearing.

12. Clean the rear cover mating surfaces and apply a $^1\!/_8$ in. bead of RTV to the cover. Install the rear cover using a the appropriate size core plug installer.

13. Install the camshaft as outlined in the "Camshaft" installation procedures. Install the timing gear cover, all accessaries and install the engine into the vehicle.

Pistons and Connecting Rods

REMOVAL AND INSTALLATION

The engine does not have to be removed to remove a piston and connecting rod assembly.

The cylinder head and oil pan has to be removed to access the connecting rod bolts. If more than one assembly needs to be serviced, it is easier to remove the engine from the vehicle.

1. Remove the engine assembly from the vehicle, see "Engine" removal and installation procedures.

2a. **6 cylinder:** remove the intake manifold and the cylinder head over piston assembly being removed.

2b. **4 cylinder:** remove the cylinder head and manifolds as an assembly.

3. Drain the oil and remove the oil pan.

4. Remove the oil pump and sump assembly. Remove the force balancer assembly as outlined in the "Forced Balancer" removal procedures (2.5L L4).

5. Stamp the cylinder number on the machine surfaces of the bolt bosses of the connecting rod and cap for identification when reinstalling. If the pistons are to be removed from the connecting rod, mark the cylinder number on the piston with a silver pencil or quick drying paint for proper cylinder identification and cap-to-rod location. The 2.5L L4 engine is numbered 1–4 from front to back; the 2.8L and 3.1L V6 engine is numbered 1–3–5 on the right bank, 2–4–6 on the left bank.

NOTE: *If the pistons or connecting rods are not marked from the factory, mark each assembly by scratching the number in the part with a scribe.*

6. Examine the cylinder bore above the ring travel. If a ridge exists, remove the ridge with a ridge reamer before attempting to remove the piston and rod assembly. This tool can be purchased as your local parts distributor or rented at a tool rental.

7. Remove the rod bearing cap and bearing. Tap on the lower cap to dislodge it from the connecting rod.

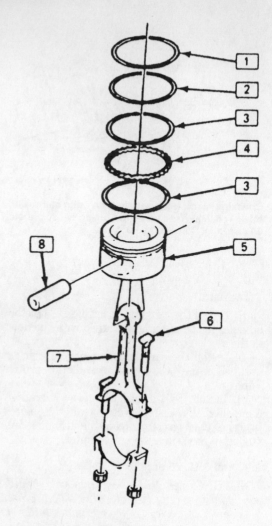

1. Upper compression ring
2. Lower compression ring
3. Oil control ring segment
4. Oil control ring spacer
5. Piston assembly
6. Bolt screw
7. Connecting rod
8. Piston pin

Piston, rings and connecting rod assembly

8. Install a guide hose over threads of rod bolts. This is to prevent damage to bearing journal and rod bolt threads. Use two pieces of ³/₈ in. fuel hose.

9. Remove the rod and piston assembly through the top of the cylinder bore by lightly tapping the connecting rod with a wooden hammer handle. Do NOT use any metal tools to remove the piston and connecting rod assembly.

NOTE: *If the piston rings will not clear the top of the cylinder, check to see if the ridge is completely removed.*

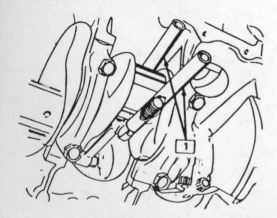

Protect the connecting rod journal. Use short pieces of ³/₈″ hose as shown (1)

10. Remove all other rod and piston assemblies in the same manner.

CLEANING AND INSPECTION

Connecting Rods

Wash connecting rods in cleaning solvent and dry with compressed air. Check for twisted or bent rods and inspect for nicks or cracks. Also check the length of the rods and replace connecting rods that are damaged.

Pistons

Clean varnish from piston skirts and pins with a cleaning solvent. DO NOT WIRE BRUSH ANY PART OF THE PISTON. Clean the carbon out of the ring grooves with a ring groove cleaner or break a old ring in half. Make sure oil ring holes and slots are clean.

Inspect the piston for cracked ring lands, skirts or pin bosses, wavy or worn ring lands, scuffed or damaged skirts, eroded areas at the top of the piston. Replace pistons that are damaged or show signs of excessive wear. Inspect the grooves for nicks or burrs that might cause the rings to hang up.

Measure piston skirt (across center line of piston pin) and check piston clearance.

PISTON PIN REMOVAL AND INSTALLATION

Use care at all times when handling and servicing connecting rods and pistons. To prevent possible damage to these units, do not clamp the rod or piston in a vise since they may become distorted. Do not allow the pistons to strike against one another, against hard objects or bench surfaces, since distortion of the piston contour or nicks in the soft aluminum material may result.

WARNING: *Removing the piston from the connecting rod requires the use of expensive tools that would not be practical to purchase for a one time basis (except 2.3L QUAD 4). This procedure should be performed by a qualified engine machine shop.*

2.3L QUAD 4 (VIN A,D)

The piston pin is held in by retaining clips on either side of the pin, requiring no special tools to remove. Remove the retaining clips and push out the piston pin. Reuse the old retainers if not damaged. Make sure the clips are fully seated before installing into cylinder block.

All Other Engines

1. Remove the piston rings using a suitable piston ring remover.
2. Install the guide bushing of the piston pin removing and installing tool.

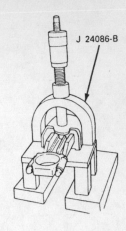

Installing piston to connecting rod

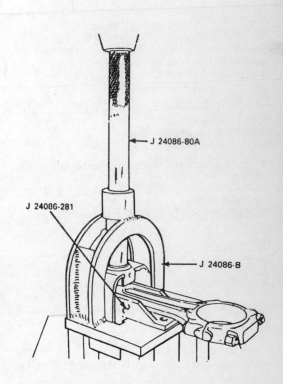

Removing piston from connecting rod

3. Install the piston and connecting rod assembly on a support, and place the assembly in an arbor press. Press the pin out of the connecting rod, using the appropriate piston pin tool.

4. When installing the new piston, apply clean engine oil to the pin and press in with a piston pin installing tool. Make sure the connecting rod moves freely without binding after pin is installed. If not, reaming the pin hole may have to be performed.

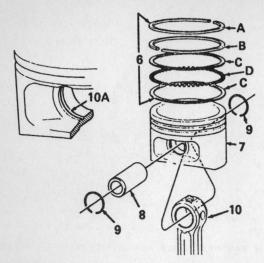

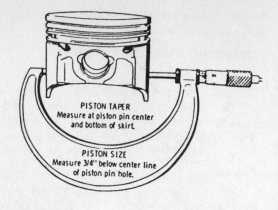

Measuring piston taper

6. Piston rings
A. Upper compression ring (top groove)
B. Lower compression ring (middle groove) must be installed with vendor identification mark toward top of piston.
C. Oil rails (lower groove)
D. Oil spacers (lower groove)
8. Pin
9. Retainers
10. Connecting rod
10A.Retainer groove

Piston, rings and connecting rod assembly — 2.3L Quad 4

MEASURING THE OLD PISTONS

Check used piston-to-cylinder bore clearance as follows:

1. Measure the cylinder bore diameter with a telescope gauge.

2. Measure the piston diameter. When measuring the pistons for size or taper, measurements must be made with the piston pin removed.

3. Subtract the piston diameter from the cylinder bore diameter to determine piston-to-bore clearance.

4. Compare the piston-to-bore clearances obtained with those clearances recommended in the "Piston and Connecting Rod" chart in the beginning of this chapter. Determine if the piston-to-bore clearance is in the acceptable range.

5. When measuring taper, the largest reading must be at the bottom of the skirt.

6. If the measurement is not within specifications, the cylinders should be bored and new oversize pistons should be installed.

SELECTING NEW PISTONS

1. If the used piston is not acceptable, check the service piston size and determine if a new piston can be selected. (Service pistons are available in standard, high limit and standard 0.254mm (0.010 in.) oversize.).

2. If the cylinder bore must be reconditioned, measure the new piston diameter, then hone the cylinder bore to obtain the preferred clearance.

3. Select a new piston and mark the piston to identify the cylinder for which it was fitted. (On some cars, oversize pistons may be found. These pistons will be 0.254mm (0.010 in.) oversize). After market piston manufactures supply oversized pistons 0.030 in., 0.040 in., and 0.060 in. in most cases.

4. After the cylinder has been reconditioned and new pistons purchased, remeasure bore and piston to ensure proper piston fit.

CYLINDER HONING

1. When cylinders are being honed, follow the manufacturer's recommendations for the use of the hone.

2. Occasionally during the honing operation, the cylinder bore should be thoroughly cleaned and the selected piston checked for correct fit.

3. When finish-honing a cylinder bore, the hone should be moved up and down at a sufficient speed to obtain a very fine uniform surface finish in a cross-hatch pattern of approximately 45–65 degrees included angle. The finish marks should be clean but not sharp, free from imbedded particles and torn or folded metal.

4. Permanently mark the piston for the cylinder to which it has been fitted and proceed to hone the remaining cylinders.

NOTE: *Handle pistons with care. Do not attempt to force pistons through cylinders until the cylinders have been honed to correct size. Pistons can be distorted through careless handling.*

5. Thoroughly clean the bores with hot water and detergent. Scrub well with a stiff bristle brush and rinse thoroughly with hot water. It is extremely essential that a good cleaning operation be performed. If any of the abrasive material is allowed to remain in the cylinder bores, it will rapidly wear the new rings and cylinder bores. The bores should be swabbed several times with light engine oil with a clean cloth and then wiped with a clean dry cloth. CYLINDERS SHOULD NOT BE CLEANED WITH KEROSENE OR GASOLINE. Clean the remainder of the cylinder block to remove the excess material spread during the honing operation.

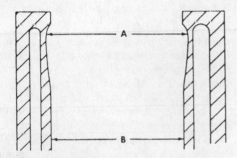

Cylinder bore wear pattern

Measuring cylinder bore

CHECKING CYLINDER BORE

Cylinder bore size can be measured with inside micrometers or a cylinder gauge. The most wear will occur at the top of the ring travel.

Reconditioned cylinder bores should be held to not more than 0.025mm (0.001 in.) taper.

If the cylinder bores are smooth, the cylinder walls should not be deglazed. If the cylinder walls are scored, the walls may have to be honed before installing new rings. It is important that reconditioned cylinder bores be thoroughly washed with a soap and water solution to remove all traces of abrasive material to eliminate premature wear.

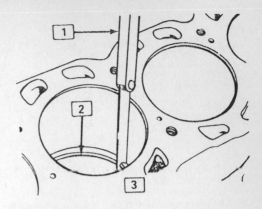

1. Feeler gauge
2. Piston ring
3. Measure ring gap clearance with ring positioned at bottom ring travel as shown

Measuring piston ring gap

Piston Rings

The pistons have three rings (two compression rings and one oil ring). The oil ring consists of two rails and an expander. Pistons have oil drain holes behind the oil rings.

RING TOLERANCES

When installing new rings, ring gap and side clearance should be checked as in the following illustrations. Check the measurements with the specifications in the "Piston and Rings" chart in the beginning of the chapter.

Piston Ring and Rail Gap

Each ring and rail gap must be measured with the ring or rail positioned squarely and at the bottom of the ring-travel area of the bore.

Side Clearance

Each ring must be checked for side clearance in its respective piston groove by inserting a

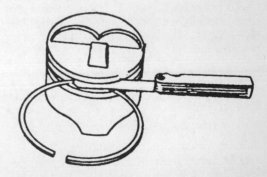

Measuring piston ring side clearance. Insert feeler gauge at top of ring groove to measure correctly.

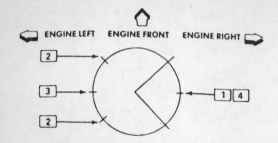

1. Oil ring spacer gap (tang in hole or slot with arc)
2. Oil ring rail gaps
3. 2nd compression ring gap
4. Top compression ring gap

Piston ring end-gap location

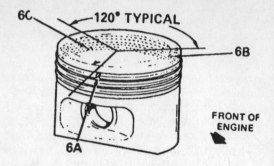

6A. Upper compression ring gap
6B. Lower compression ring gap
6C. Oil ring assembly gap

Positioning the piston ring gap — 2.3L Quad 4

feeler gauge between the ring and its upper land. The piston grooves must be cleaned before checking the ring for side clearance specifications. To check oil ring side clearance, the oil rings must be installed on the piston.

RING INSTALLATION

For service ring specifications and detailed installation productions, refer to the instructions furnished with the parts package. If oversized pistons are being used, make sure to select the proper oversize piston rings to fit the oversized pistons.

1. Using your fingers, install the oil expander.

NOTE: *Use care when installing the piston rings so not to scratch the piston skirt.*

2. Install the lower oil control ring and position the gaps as shown in the "Piston Ring Gap Location" illustration in this section. Install the upper oil control ring.

NOTE: *Use a piston ring expander to install the compression rings. Avoid expanding the rings more than necessary, which may cause ring damage or breakage.*

3. Using a piston ring installer (expander), install the second compression ring with manufacturers mark facing UP. Install the top compression ring with manufacturers mark facing UP. Position the gaps as shown in the ring gap illustration.

Connecting Rod Bearings

If you have already removed the connecting rod and piston assemblies from the engine, follow only Steps 3–7 of the following procedure.

REMOVAL, INSPECTION AND INSTALLATION

The connecting rod bearings are designed to have a slight projection above the rod and cap

faces to insure a positive contact. The bearings can be replaced without removing the rod and piston assemblies from the engine.

1. Drain the engine oil and remove the oil pan. See the "Oil Pan" removal procedures. It may be necessary to remove the oil pump to provide access to rear connecting rod bearings.

2. With the connecting rod journal at the bottom of the travel, stamp the cylinder number on the machined surfaces of the connecting rod and cap for identification when installing, then remove the rod nuts and caps.

3. Inspect journals for roughness and wear. Slight roughness may be removed with a fine grit polishing cloth saturated with engine oil. Burrs may be removed with a fine oil stone by moving the stone on the journal circumference. Do not move the stone back and forth across the journal. If the journals are scored or ridged, the crankshaft must be reconditioned or replaced.

4. The connecting rod journals should be checked for out-of-round and correct size with a micrometer.

NOTE: *Crankshaft rod journals will normally be standard size. If any undersized bearings are used, all will be 0.254mm undersize and 0.254mm will be stamped on the number 4 counterweight.*

If Plastigage® material is to be used:

5. Clean oil from the journal bearing cap, connecting rod and outer and inner surfaces of the bearing inserts. Position the insert so that the tang is properly aligned with the notch in the rod and cap.

6. Place a piece of Plastigage® material in the center of lower bearing shell as shown in the illustration.

7. Install the bearing cap onto the connecting rod and torque to specifications. Remove the bearing cap and determine the bearing clearances by comparing the width of the flattened

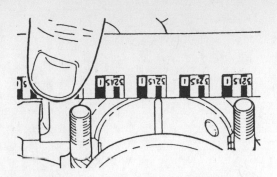

Measuring the bearing clearance with Plastigage®

plastic gauging material at its widest point with the graduation on the Plastigage® package. The number within the graduation on the envelope indicates the clearance in thousandths of an inch or millimeters. If this clearance is excessive, replace the bearing and recheck the clearance with the Plastigage® material. Lubricate the bearing with Assembly Lube or engine oil before installation. Repeat Steps 2–7 on the remaining connecting rod bearings.

NOTE: *All rods must be connected to their journals when rotating the crankshaft, to prevent engine damage.*

Piston and Connecting Rod Assembly

INSTALLATION

1. Make sure all parts are clean. Install some lengths of rubber tubing over the connecting rod bolts to prevent damage to the crankshaft journals.

2. Apply engine oil to the pistons, rings and cylinder walls, then install a piston ring compressing tool on the piston.

Main bearing insert markings. Amount undersize is stamped at either end. (Examples: 0.016, 0.032)

3. **Important:** install the assembly in its respective cylinder bore with the notch in the top of the piston facing towards the FRONT of the engine.

4. Lubricate the crankshaft journal with Assembly Lube and install the connecting rod bearing and cap, with the bearing index tang in rod and cap on same side.

NOTE: *When more than one rod and piston assembly is being installed, the connecting rod cap attaching nuts should be tightened only enough to keep each rod in position until all have been installed. This will aid installation of the remaining piston assemblies.*

5. Torque the rod cap nuts to the specifications in the "Torque Specifications" chart in the beginning of this chapter.

6. Install all other parts in reverse order of removal.

7. Install the engine in the vehicle. See "Engine" removal and installation.

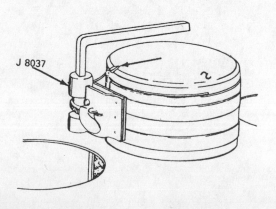

J 8037

Compressing piston rings for installation. Note that the notch points to the front of the engine

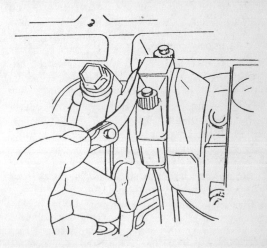

Measuring connecting rod side clearance with feeler gauge

Crankshaft

REMOVAL AND INSTALLATION

1. Remove the engine assembly as previously outlined in the "Engine" removal procedures.

2. Remove the engine front timing cover.

3. Remove the timing chain and sprockets.

4. Remove the oil pan as outlined in the "Oil Pan" removal procedures.

5. Remove the oil pump, (remove the force balancer assembly on the 2.5L L4 engine).

6. Stamp the cylinder number on the machined surfaces of the bolt boses of the connecting rods and caps, if not done by the factory, for identification when installing. If the pistons are to be removed from the connecting rod, mark the cylinder number on each piston with an indelible marker, silver pencil or quick drying paint for proper cylinder identification and cap to rod location.

7. Remove the connecting rod caps and store them so that they can be installed in their original positions. Put pieces of rubber fuel hose on the rod bolts before removal to protect the connecting rod journals.

8. Mark and remove all the main bearing caps.

9. Note the position of the keyway in the crankshaft so it can be installed in the same position.

10. With an assistant, lift the crankshaft out of the block. The rods will pivot to the center of the engine when the crankshaft is removed.

11. Remove both halves of the rear main oil seal.

INSTALLATION

1. Measure the crankshaft journals with a micrometer to determine the correct size rod and main bearings to be used. Whenever a new or reconditioned crankshaft is installed, new connecting rod bearings and main bearings must be installed. The bearing undersize are usually 0.010, 0.020 and 0.030 inch. Do not go any further undersize than 0.030 inch. See Main Bearings and Rod Bearings in the beginning of this chapter.

2. Clean all oil passages in the block (and crankshaft if it is being reused).

NOTE: *A new rear main seal should be installed any time the crankshaft is removed or replaced.*

3. Install sufficient oil pan bolts in the block to align with the connecting rod bolts. Use rubber bands between the bolts to position the connecting rods as required. Connecting rod position can be adjusted by increasing the tension on the rubber bands with additional turns around the pan bolts or thread protec-

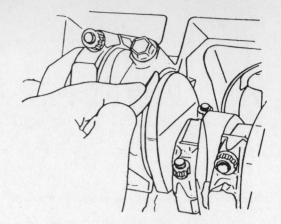

Measuring crankshaft end play with feeler gauge

tors. Install if not already done, pieces of rubber hose on the connecting rod bolts to protect the crankshaft journals during installation.

4. Position the upper half of main bearings in the block and lubricate them with Assembly Lube.

5. Position crankshaft keyway in the same position as removed, with an assistant, lower the crankshaft into the block. The connecting rods will follow the crank pins into the correct position as the crankshaft is lowered.

6. Lubricate the thrust flanges with Assembly Lube 10501609 or equivalent. Install rod caps with the lower half of the bearings lubricated with Assembly Lube. Lubricate the cap bolts with Assembly Lube and install, but do not tighten.

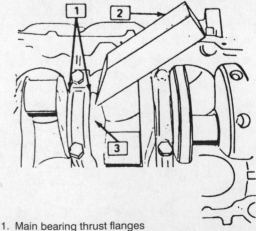

1. Main bearing thrust flanges
2. Wood block
3. Bump shaft rearward, then forward, to align thrust flanges of center main bearing

Setting crankshaft thrust bearing

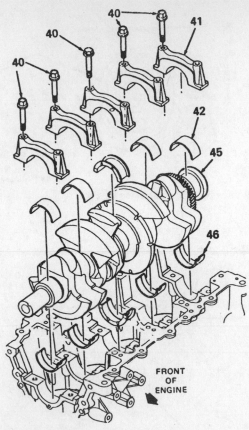

40. Bearing cap bolt
41. Crankshaft bearing cap
42. Lower bearings
   A. Nos. 1,2,4,5
   B. No. 3
45. Crankshaft
46. Upper bearings
   A. Nos. 1,2,4,5
   B. No. 3

Crankshaft and bearings — 2.3L Quad 4

7. With a block of wood, bump the crankshaft in each direction to align the thrust flanges of the main bearing. After bumping the shaft in each direction, wedge the shaft to the front and hold it while torquing the thrust bearing cap bolts.

NOTE: *In order to prevent the possibility of cylinder block and/or main bearing cap damage, the main bearing caps are to be tapped into their cylinder block cavity using a wood or rubber mallet before the bolts are installed. Do not use attaching bolts to pull the main bearing caps into their seats. Failure to observe this information may damage the cylinder block or a bearing cap.*

8. Torque all main bearing caps to specification in the "Torque Specifications" chart in this chapter.

9. Remove the connecting rod bolt thread protectors and lubricate the connecting rod bearings with Assembly Lube.

10. Install the connecting rod bearing caps in their original position. Torque the nuts to specifications in the "Torque Specifications" chart in this chapter.

11. Install the oil pump, oil pan, timing cover, accessaries and install the engine assembly into the vehicle as outlined in the "Engine" installation procedures.

Main Bearings

CHECKING BEARING CLEARANCE

1. Remove the bearing cap and wipe the oil from the crankshaft journal and the outer and inner surfaces of the bearing shell.

2. Place a piece of plastic gauging material (Plastigage®) in the center of the bearing.

3. Install the bearing cap and bearing. Place engine oil on the cap bolts and install. Torque the bolts to specification.

4. Remove the bearing cap and determine the bearing clearance by comparing the width of the flattened Plastigage® material at its widest point with the graduations on the Plastigage® container. The number within the graduation on the envelope indicates the clearance in millimeters or thousandths of an inch. If the clearance is greater than allowed, REPLACE BOTH BEARING SHELLS AS A SET. Recheck the clearance after replacing the shells. (Refer to Main Bearing Replacement).

REPLACEMENT

Main bearing clearances must be corrected by the use of selective upper and lower shells. UNDER NO CIRCUMSTANCES should the use of shims behind the shells to compensate for wear be attempted. To install the main bearing shells, proceed as follows:

1. Remove the oil pan as outlined below. On some models, the oil pump may also have to be removed.

2. Loosen all main bearing caps.

3. Remove the bearing caps and remove the lower shell.

4. Insert a flattened cotter pin or roll pin in the oil passage hole in the crankshaft, then rotate the crankshaft in the direction opposite to cranking rotation. The pin will contact the upper shell and roll it out.

5. The main bearing journals should be checked for roughness and wear. Slight roughness may be removed with a fine grit polishing cloth saturated with engine oil. Burrs may be removed with a fine oil stone. If the journals are scored or ridged, the crankshaft must be reconditioned or replaced.

Rear crankshaft oil seal installer

The journals can be measured for out-of-round with the crankshaft installed by using a crankshaft caliper and inside micrometer or a main bearing micrometer. The upper bearing shell must be removed when measuring the crankshaft journals. Maximum out-of-round of the crankshaft journals must not exceed 0.037mm (0.0015 inch).

6. Clean the crankshaft journals and bearing caps thoroughly for installing new main bearings.

7. Apply Assembly Lube, No. 1050169 or equivalent, to the thrust flanges and bearing inserts.

8. Place a new upper shell on the crankshaft journal with locating tang in the correct position and rotate the shaft to turn it into place using a cotter pin or roll pin as during removal.

9. Place a new bearing shell in the bearing cap.

10. Install a new oil seal in the rear main bearing cap and block.

11. Lubricate the main bearings with engine oil. Lubricate the thrust surface with Assembly Lube 1050169 or equivalent.

12. Lubricate the main bearing cap bolts with engine oil.

NOTE: *In order to prevent the possibility of cylinder block and/or main bearing cap damage, the main bearing caps are to be tapped into their cylinder block cavity using a wood or rubber mallet before the attaching bolts are installed. Do not use attaching bolts to pull the main bearing caps into their seats. Failure to observe this information may damage the cylinder block or a bearing cap.*

13. Torque the main bearing cap bolts to the specification in the "Torque Specifications" chart in the beginning of this chapter.

Rear Main Seal

REMOVAL AND INSTALLATION

All Engines

NOTE: *This is a one piece seal and can be replaced without removal of the oil pan or crankshaft.*

1. Support the engine with the engine support fixture J-28467-A or equivalent.

2. Remove the transaxle assembly as out-

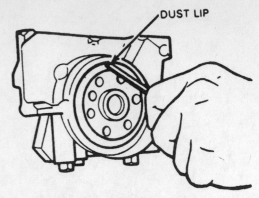

Removing rear main oil seal

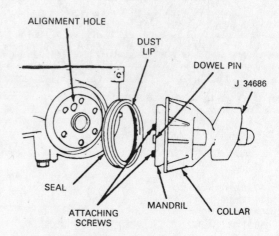

Installing rear main oil seal

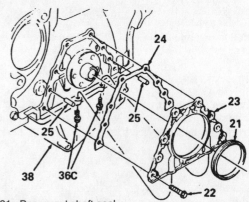

21. Rear crankshaft seal
22. Bolt
23. Rear seal housing
24. Gasket
25. Dowel pin
36C. Oil pan to housing bolt
38. Oil pan

Rear main oil seal — 2.3L Quad 4

lined in the "Transaxle" removal procedures in Chapter 7.

3. Remove the six flywheel attaching bolts and the flywheel (automatic).

4. If equipped with a (manual) transaxle, remove the pressure plate and disc.

5. Pry out the rear main seal with a screwdriver against the dust lip.

NOTE: *Do not damage the crankshaft or seal housing with the pry tool.*

To install:

6. Clean the block and crankshaft-to-seal mating surfaces.

7. Lubricate the outside of the seal for ease of installation and press into the block with your fingers.

8. Install the seal with a Seal Installer tool No. J34924–A or equivalent.

9. Install the flywheel and torque the bolts to the specification in the "Torque Specifications" chart in the beginning of the chapter.

10. Install the transaxle assembly.

Flywheel

REMOVAL AND INSTALLATION

All Engines

1. Disconnect the negative (–) battery cable.

2. Remove the transaxle assembly as outlined in the "Transaxle" removal procedures in Chapter 7.

3. Remove the six flywheel attaching bolts and remove the flywheel (automatic). Remove the pressure plate and disc before removing the six flywheel attaching bolts (manual).

4. **To install:** position the flywheel onto the crankshaft. Apply GM Thread Lock compound to the bolt threads and torque the bolts to the specifications in the "Torque Specifications" chart in this chapter. Install the pressure plate and clutch disc for a (manual) transaxle. Install the transaxle assembly as outlined in the "Transaxle" installation procedures in Chapter 7.

EXHAUST SYSTEM

Rubber straps, rubber rings and block type hangers are used to support the complete exhaust system. It is very important that they be installed properly to avoid annoying vibrations which are difficult to diagnose.

Catalytic Converter

The catalytic converter is an emission control device added to the exhaust system to reduce pollutants from the exhaust gas stream. The converter uses two types of catalysts to reduce three types of pollutants. The oxidation catalyst is coated with a material containing platinum and palladium which lowers the levels of hydrocarbons HC (unburned fuel) and carbon monoxide CO. The three way catalyst contains platinum and rhodium which lowers the levels of oxides of nitrogen NOx.

WARNING: *These catalysts will be damaged with the use of leaded fuels. ALWAYS USE UNLEADED FUEL IN YOUR GM VEHICLE.*

CAUTION: *Do NOT service the exhaust system while the engine is warm. Extreme heat is generated by engine and may cause severe burns if not allowed to completely cool before servicing.*

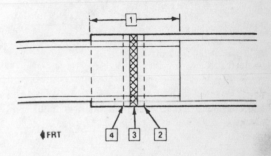

1. 88mm overlap
2. Converter cut
3. Weld
4. Exhaust pipe cut

Exhaust pipe cut location; cut as close to the weld as possible

Front Exhaust Pipe

REMOVAL AND INSTALLATION

1. Support the catalytic converter with a floor jack and a piece of wood.

2. Cut the front exhaust pipe at the manifold.

3. Remove the pipe.

To install:

4. Insert the front pipe into the converter and install a approved exhaust system clamp.

5. Torque the clamp nuts to 37 ft. lbs. (50 Nm).

Catalytic Converter

REMOVAL AND INSTALLATION

1. Cut the front exhaust pipe at the manifold.

2. Support the converter and cut the intermediate pipe as close to the weld as possible.

3. Remove the converter.

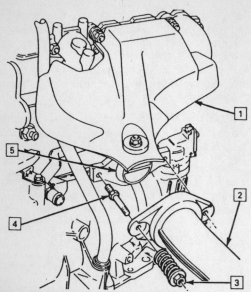

1. Heat shield
2. Front exhaust pipe
3. 19 ft. lbs.
4. Stud
5. Seal

Exhaust manifold–to–pipe attachment — 2.3L Quad 4

To install:

4. Place the clamps over the converter but do not tighten clamps.

5. Install the converter and torque the clamps to 37 ft. lbs. (50 Nm).

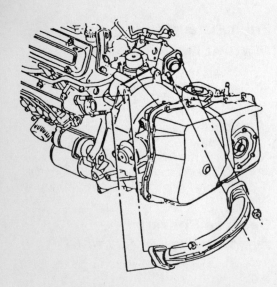

Exhaust crossover pipe — 2.8L and 3.1L engines. Tighten the nuts to 18 ft. lbs.

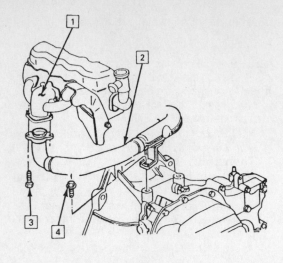

1. Manifold
2. Crossover pipe
3. 24 ft. lbs.
4. Bolt

Exhaust crossover pipe — 2.5L L4 Lumina

Intermediate Pipe

REMOVAL AND INSTALLATION

1. Support the muffler and catalytic converter with a floor jack and a piece of wood.
2. Cut the intermediate pipe at the muffler.
3. Support the intermediate pipe and cut the pipe at the converter.
4. Remove the pipe.

To install:

5. Position two clamps over the end of the pipe. Do not tighten.
6. Install the intermediate pipe and support.
7. Install the insulators, hangers and bolts as necessary. Torque the clamps to 37 ft. lbs. (50 Nm).

Muffler

REMOVAL AND INSTALLATION

1. Support the intermediate pipe and muffler.
2. Cut the intermediate pipe at the muffler in front of the weld.
3. Remove the hangers at the muffler.
4. Remove the muffler assembly.

To install:

5. Position two exhaust quality clamps onto the muffler. Do not tighten.
6. Install the muffler and hangers.
7. Torque the muffler clamps and hangers to 37 ft. lbs. (50 Nm).

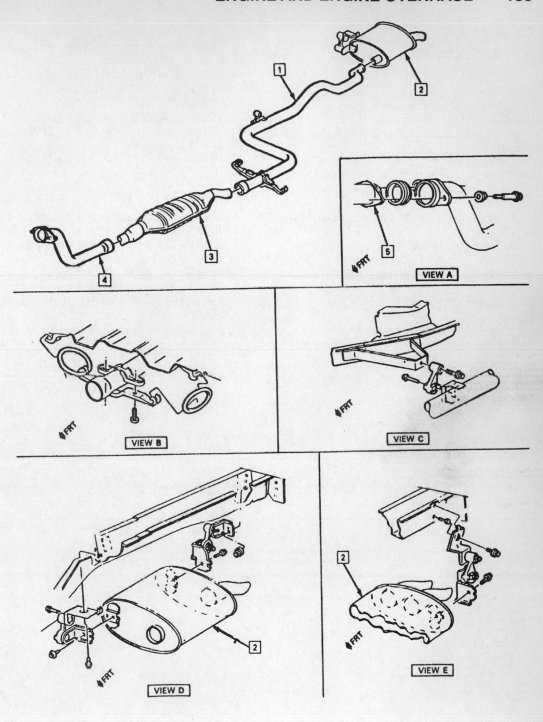

1. Intermediate pipe assembly
2. Muffler assembly
3. Converter

4. Front pipe assembly
5. Crossover pipe

Exhaust system components

Crossover Pipe

REMOVAL AND INSTALLATION

2.3L QUAD 4 (VIN A,D)

1. Disconnect the negative (–) battery cable.
2. Raise the vehicle and support with jack-stands.
3. Remove the spring loaded nuts from the exhaust manifold and pipe.
4. Support the catalytic converter. Cut the front pipe at the converter as close to the welds as possible to ensure an adequate overlap for clamping.
5. **To install:** position the front pipe to the manifold.
6. Torque the bolts to 19 ft. lbs. (26 Nm).
7. Insert the pipe into the converter and install a clamp. Torque the clamp to 37 ft. lbs. (50 Nm).
8. Lower the vehicle.

2.5L L4 (Lumina) VIN R

1. Disconnect the negative (–) battery cable.
2. Remove the bolts from the transaxle.
3. Raise the vehicle and support with jack-stands.
4. Remove the bolts from the exhaust manifold and pipe. Remove the crossover pipe.

To install:

5. Position the crossover to the manifold.
6. Torque the bolts to 24 ft. lbs. (32 Nm).
7. Lower the vehicle.
8. Install the bolt to transaxle and tighten.

2.8L and 3.1L V6 (VIN W, T)

1. Disconnect the negative (–) battery cable.
2. Remove the air cleaner assembly.
3. Remove the crossover mounting nuts.
4. Remove the crossover pipe.

To install:

5. Position the crossover to the manifold.
6. Install the mounting nuts and torque to 18 ft. lbs. (25 Nm).
7. Install the air cleaner and reconnect the negative battery cable.

Emission Controls

EMISSION CONTROLS

There are three basic sources of automotive pollution in the modern internal combustion engine. They are the crankcase with its accompanying blow-by vapors, the fuel system with its evaporation of unburned gasoline and the combustion chambers with their resulting exhaust emissions. Pollution arising from the incomplete combustion of fuel generally falls into three categories: hydrocarbons (HC) (unburned fuel), carbon monoxide (CO) and oxides of nitrogen (NOx).

The engines are equipped with an air pump system, positive crankcase ventilation, exhaust gas recirculation, electronic ignition, catalytic converter, thermostatically controlled air cleaner, or an evaporative emissions system depending on the model. Electronic engine controls are used on various engines, depending on model and year.

The belt driven air pump injects clean air either into the exhaust manifold, or downstream into the catalytic converter, depending on engine conditions. The oxygen contained in the injected air, supports continued combustion of the hot carbon monoxide (CO) and hydrocarbon (HC) gases, reducing their release into the atmosphere.

The back pressure modulated EGR valve is mounted next to the carburetor or upper intake manifold for fuel injected engines. Vacuum applied to the EGR diaphragm raises the pintle valve from its seat, allowing hot exhaust gases to be drawn into the intake manifold with the intake charge. The exhaust gases reduce peak combustion temperature; lower temperatures reduce the formation of oxides of nitrogen (NOx).

The dual brick catalytic converter is mounted in the exhaust system, ahead of the muffler. Catalytic converters use noble metals (platinum, palladium, and rhodium) and great heat — 1,200°F (650°C) — to catalytically oxidize HC and CO gases onto H_2O and CO_2. The Thermactor system is used as a fresh air (and therefore, oxygen) supply.

The thermostatically controlled air cleaner housing is able to draw fresh air from two sources: cool air from outside the car (behind the grille), or warm air obtained from a heat stove encircling the exhaust manifold. A warm air supply is desirable during cold engine operation. Because it promotes better atomization of the air/fuel mixture, while cool air promotes better combustion in a hot engine.

Instead of venting gasoline vapors from the carburetor float bowl or fuel tank into the atmosphere, an evaporative emission system captures the vapors and stores them in a charcoal filled canister, located ahead of the left front wheel arch. When the engine is running, a purge control solenoid allows fresh air to be drawn through the canister. The fresh air and vapors are then routed to the fuel injection system.

Crankcase Ventilation System

OPERATION

A Positive Crankcase Ventilation system (PCV) is used to provide more complete burning of the crankcase vapors. Fresh air from the air cleaner or intake duct (V6), is supplied to the crankcase, mixed with blow-by gases and then passed through a Positive Crankcase Ventilation valve (PCV) into the intake manifold (four cyl.) or the Air Plenum (V6). The system is used on all models but not controlled by the ECM (Electronic Engine Control Module). The primary control is through the PCV valve which meters the flow at a rate depending on manifold vacuum. To maintain engine idle qual-

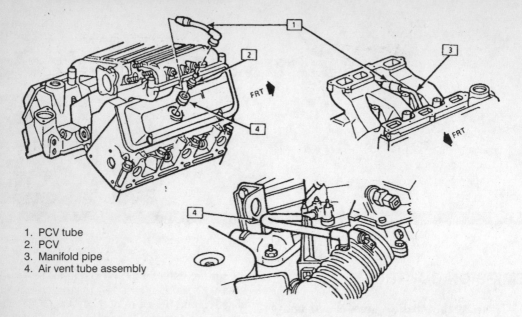

1. PCV tube
2. PCV
3. Manifold pipe
4. Air vent tube assembly

PCV valve location — 2.8L and 3.1L V6 engines

ity, the PCV valve restricts the flow when intake manifold vacuum is high.

INSPECTION AND SERVICE

A clogged PCV valve, oil/air separator or plugged hose could cause rough idling, stalling, oil leaks or sludge in the engine. A leaking valve or hose may cause rough idle, stalling or high idle speed. If the engine is operated without the the PCV valve installed properly, engine damage may result. Check the valve and hose as follows every 30,000 miles:

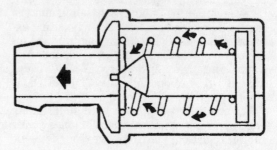

Typical PCV valve. Arrow points to the check valve

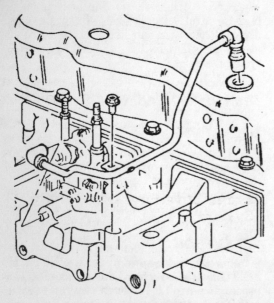

PCV valve location — 2.5L L4 Lumina

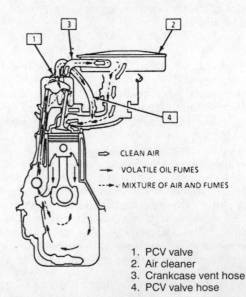

⇒ CLEAN AIR

→ VOLATILE OIL FUMES

--→ MIXTURE OF AIR AND FUMES

1. PCV valve
2. Air cleaner
3. Crankcase vent hose
4. PCV valve hose

PCV system — 2.5L L4 Lumina

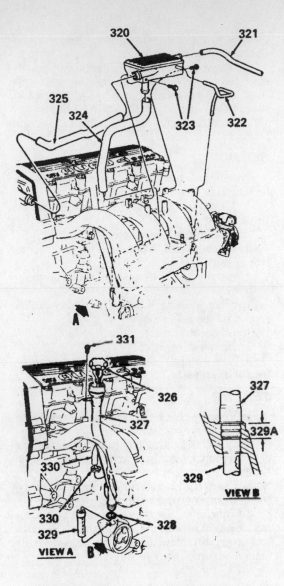

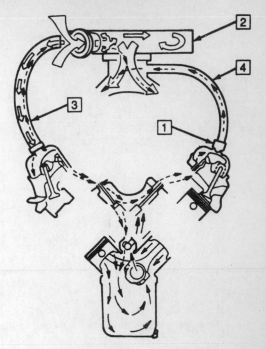

⇨ CLEAN AIR

→ VOLATILE OIL FUMES

---→ MIXTURE OF AIR AND FUMES

1. PCV valve
2. To throttle body
3. Crankcase vent hose
4. PCV valve hose
5. To intake manifold

PCV system — 2.8L and 3.1L V6 engines

320. Oil/air separator
321. Hose
322. Hose
323. Bolt
324. Hose
325. Hose
326. Oil fill cap and indicator
327. Oil fill tube
328. O-ring
329. Oil level indicator guide. Holes in
guide must face outboard 90° from
centerline of crankshaft
329A. Position top of guide 3/4" down from
surface of block
330. Clamp
331. Bolt

Crankcase ventilation system — 2.3L Quad 4

1. Remove the valve from the rocker arm
cover.
2. Apply the emergency brake and place the
auto transaxle in park, manual transaxle in neutral. Start the engine and run at idle.

3. Place your thumb over the end of the
valve to check for vacuum. If there is no
vacuum at the valve, check for plugged hoses at
manifold port or PCV valve. Replace plugged or
deteriorated hoses.

4. Turn off the engine and remove the PCV
valve. Shake the valve and listen for the rattle
of the check needle inside the valve. If the valve
does not rattle, replace the valve.

Evaporative Emission Control System

OPERATION

This method transfers fuel vapor from the
fuel tank to an activated carbon (charcoal) storage canister to hold the vapors when the vehicle is not operating. When the engine is running, the fuel vapor is purged from the carbon

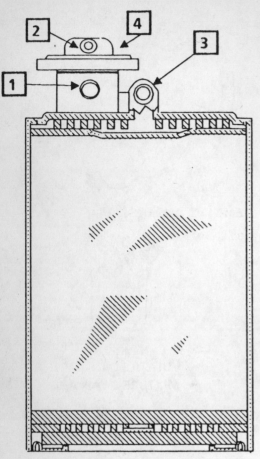

1. PCV
2. Control vacuum
3. Fuel tank
4. Purge valve

Vapor canister

element by intake air flow and consumed in the normal combustion process.

The vapor canister uses a integral diaphragm operated purge valve. When the engine is running, manifold vacuum is supplied to the top tube of the purge valve, the valve opens and the vapor is pulled into the throttle body or air plenum

SERVICE

Evidence of fuel loss or fuel vapor odor can be caused by the following:

1. Liquid fuel leaking from the fuel lines or throttle body.

2. Inoperative purge valve.

3. Disconnected or damaged vapor and control lines.

4. Air cleaner or cleaner gasket improperly seated.

Poor idle, stalling or poor driveability can be caused by the following:

1. Inoperative purge valve.

2. Damaged canister.

3. Hoses split, cracked, damaged or connected improperly.

TESTING

1. Visually check the canister for cracks or damage, replace canister.

2. If fuel is leaking from the bottom of the canister, replace canister and check for proper hose routing.

3. Check the filter at the bottom of the canister. If dirty, replace the filter.

4. Functional test the purge valve by installing a piece of hose to the lower tube of the valve and attempt to blow through it. Little or no air should pass into the canister.

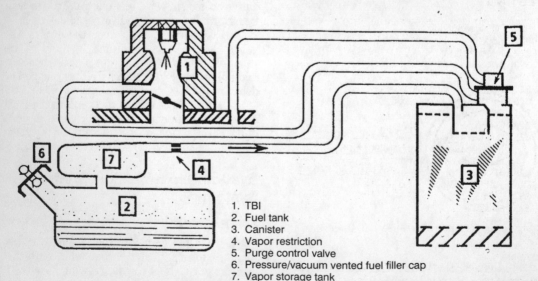

1. TBI
2. Fuel tank
3. Canister
4. Vapor restriction
5. Purge control valve
6. Pressure/vacuum vented fuel filler cap
7. Vapor storage tank

Evaporative control system — all models

5. Connect a vacuum pump and apply 15 Hg (51 kPa) of vacuum to the upper control valve tube. The diaphragm should hold vacuum for at least 20 seconds. If it does not hold vacuum, the canister must be replaced.

Fuel Vapor Canister

REMOVAL AND INSTALLATION

1. Disconnect the negative (–) battery cable.
2. Remove the hoses on the canister and mark them for installation.
3. Remove the canister bracket attaching bolt.
4. Install the canister and torque the attaching bolt to 6–9 ft. lbs. (8–12 Nm). Reconnect the hoses in their original locations.
5. Start the engine and check for proper operation and fuel leaks.

Exhaust Gas Recirculation System

The EGR System is used to lower the NOx (oxides of nitrogen) emission levels caused by high combustion temperature. It does that by decreasing combustion temperature. The main element of the system is the EGR valve mounted on the intake manifold (4 cyl.) and on the exhaust manifold (V6). The EGR valve feeds small amounts of exhaust gas back into the combustion chamber.

The EGR valve is opened by ported manifold vacuum to let exhaust gas flow into the intake manifold. The exhaust gas mixes with the air/fuel mixture as it moves into the combustion chamber. Very little exhaust gas is allowed to enter the valve, and none at idle.

TESTING

Too much (EGR) flow at idle, cruise or cold operation may cause the following conditions:
   a. Engine stops after cold start.
   b. Engine stops at idle after deceleration.

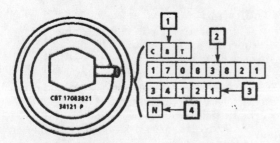

1. Assembly plant code
2. Part number
3. Date built
4. Type designation: P–Positive back pressure N–Negative back pressure Blank–Ported valve

EGR valve identification

   c. Vehicle surges during cruise.
   d. Rough idle.

Too little or no (EGR) flow allows combustion temperatures to get too high during acceleration and load conditions may cause the following conditions:
   a. Start knock (detonation).
   b. Engine overheating.
   c. Emission test failure.

NOTE: *The EGR valve on the 2.5L L4 (Lumina) VIN R is not controlled by the ECM (electronic control module). A Scan tool can not be used for diagnosis.*

REMOVAL AND INSTALLATION

2.3L QUAD 4 (VIN D)

The 2.3L QUAD 4 (VIN D) engine is equipped with a digital EGR valve. This type of valve is designed to operate independent of engine vacuum.

1. Disconnect the negative (–) battery cable and EGR valve connectors.
2. Remove the valve attaching nuts, valve and gasket.

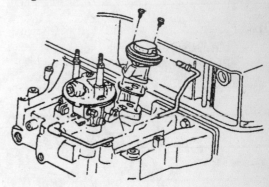

EGR valve location — 2.5L L4 Lumina

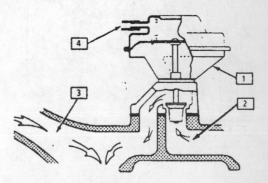

1. Valve assembly
2. Exhaust gas
3. Intake air
4. EGR vacuum port

EGR valve operation

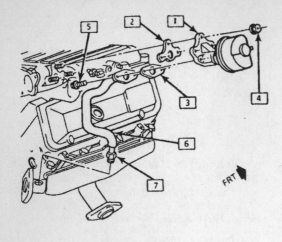

1. EGR valve
2. Valve gasket
3. Tube gasket
4. Nut
5. Bolt
6. EGR tube
7. Tube nut

EGR valve location — 2.8L and 3.1L V6 engines

To install:

1. Clean the gasket mating surface.
2. Install a new gasket, valve and nuts.
3. Torque the nuts to 18 ft. lbs. (26 Nm).
4. Connect the negative (–) battery cable.

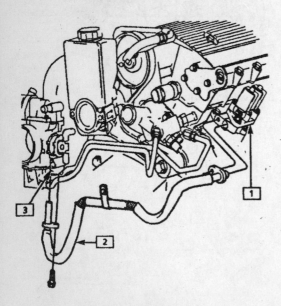

1. Digital EGR valve
2. EGR pipe
3. Intake manifold

EGR pipe — 2.3L Quad 4 (VIN D)

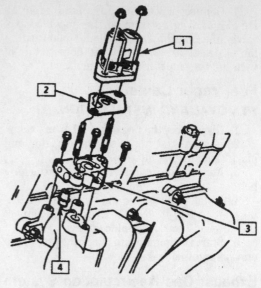

1. Digital EGR valve
2. EGR gasket
3. Adapter
4. Adapter seal

Digital EGR valve — 2.3L Quad 4 (VIN D only)

EGR PIPE

1. Disconnect the negative (–) battery cable.
2. Remove the air cleaner bracket and hose from the throttle body.
3. Remove the engine torque strut, power brake booster hose and throttle cable bracket.
4. Remove the emission canister purge hose retainer and EGR pipe retaining bolt.
5. Remove the throttle cable and bracket from the throttle body.
6. Remove the accessory vacuum hose from the top of the throttle body.
7. Remove the EGR pipe retaining bolts from the adapter and intake manifold.
8. Remove the pipe.

To install:

1. Install the pipe and retaining bolts. Torque the 8mm bolts to 19 ft. lbs. (26 Nm) and the 6mm bolts to 7 ft. lbs. (9 Nm).
2. Install the throttle cable, bracket, vacuum hoses, canister purge hose, brake booster hose and torque strut.
3. Install the air cleaner and duct.
4. Connect the negative (–) battery cable.

2.5L, 2.8L and 3.1L

1. Remove the air cleaner on the 4 cylinder engine.
2. Disconnect the vacuum line.
3. Remove the bolts and remove the valve from the manifold.

4. Before installation, start the engine for 5 seconds to blow out the carbon in the manifold.

5. Install the valve with a new gasket to the manifold and torque the attaching bolts on the 2.5L L4 engine to 16 ft. lbs. (22 Nm). Torque the three nuts on the 2.8L V6 engine to 15 ft. lbs. (20 Nm). Install the vacuum hose. Start the engine and check for exhaust leaks.

Valve Cleaning

1. Using a wire wheel, clean the carbon deposits from the mounting surface and around the valve.

2. Scrape any carbon deposits around the valve outlet with a suitable tool.

3. Clean all mounting surfaces.

Automatic Transmission Converter Clutch (TCC) System

OPERATION

The transmission converter clutch system is designed to eliminate power loss by the torque converter slippage. This system increases fuel efficiency because a more effective coupling to the flywheel is achieved. The converter clutch is operated by an ECM controlled solenoid within the automatic transaxle. The solenoid will not engage until the proper amount of fluid pressure is achieved.

INSPECTION

1. Install a tachometer.

2. Operate the vehicle until proper operating temperature.

3. Drive the vehicle at 50–55 mph (80–88 km/h) with light throttle.

4. Lightly touch the brake pedal and check for a slight bump when the TCC releases a slight increase in engine rpm.

5. Release the brake and check for a re-apply of the converter clutch and a slight decrease in engine rpm.

WARNING: *Do not apply 12-volts of battery current to test the TCC solenoid. Accidentally crossed wires will destroy the internal diodes of the TCC solenoid.*

REMOVAL AND INSTALLATION

1. Raise the vehicle and support with jackstands.

2. Disconnect the negative (–) battery cable.

3. Drain the transaxle fluid into a suitable drain pan. Refer to the "Transaxle Fluid Change" procedures in Chapter 7.

4. Remove the valve body side cover and drain excess fluid into the drain pan.

5. Disconnect the solenoid wires from the electrical connector and the pressure switch.

6. Remove the one solenoid attaching screw and pull the TCC solenoid out of the valve body.

To install:

7. Position a new O-ring seal onto the TCC solenoid. Lubricate the O-ring with Dexron®II and install the solenoid into the valve body. Tighten the one attaching screw and reconnect the electrical wires.

8. Install the valve body side cover with a new gasket and torque the bolts to 8 ft. lbs. (11 Nm).

9. Refill the transaxle with the proper amount of Dexron®II. Refer to the "Transaxle Fluid Change" procedures in Chapter 7.

10. Connect the negative (–) battery cable. Start the engine and wait till operating temperature has been reached. With the emergency brake applied, move the gear selector through the gears. Put the selector in PARK, check the

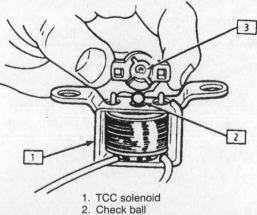

1. TCC solenoid
2. Check ball
3. Check ball seat

Torque converter clutch control solenoid (TCC) — automatic transaxle.

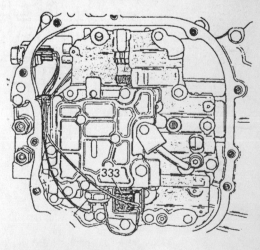

TCC solenoid location (333)

fluid level and fill to proper level with engine running.

Air Injection Reaction (AIR) System 3.1L V6 with Manual Transaxle Only

OPERATION

The Air Injection Reaction (AIR) system is used to reduce carbon monoxide (CO), hydrocarbon (HC) and oxides of nitrogen (NOx) emissions. The system also heats up the catalytic converter on engine start-up so the exhaust gases will be converted more quickly.

The system consists of an air pump, belt driven off the crankshaft. The pump has an in line filter to remove any foreign material. The control valve regulates air from the pump to the check valve at the exhaust ports. A check valve prevents back flow of exhaust into the pump in the event of an exhaust backfire.

AIR PUMP REMOVAL AND INSTALLATION

1. Disconnect the negative (–) battery cable.
2. Hold the pump pulley from turning by compressing the drive belt, then loosen the pump pulley bolts.
3. Loosen the pump mounting bracket bolts and release the tension from the belt.
4. Move the belt out of the way.
5. Remove the hoses, vacuum and electrical connections from the pump.

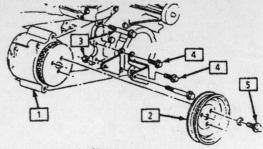

1. Air injection pump
2. Pulley
3. Nut/bolt–22 ft. lbs.
4. Bolt–60 ft. lbs.
5. Bolt–10 ft. lbs.

Air injection pump mounting — 3.1L V6 with manual transaxle

6. Remove the pulley from the pump.
7. If required, insert needle nose pliers and pull the filter fan from the hub.

To install:

1. Install the air pump to the mounting brackets and torque bolts as shown in the illustration.
2. Install the hoses, vacuum and electrical connections to the pump.
3. Install the control valve.
4. Install a new filter fan onto the pump hub.
5. Install the spacer and pump pulley against the centrifugal filter fan.

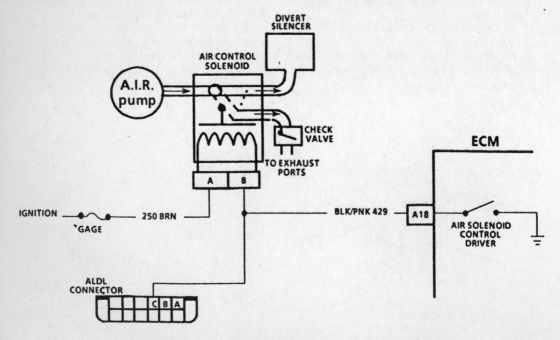

Air injection reactor (AIR) system — 3.1L V6 with manual transaxle

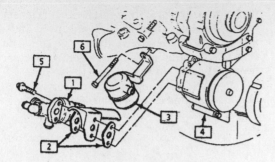

1. Air control diverter valve
2. Gasket
3. Diverter silencer
4. Air pump
5. Bolt—11 ft. lbs.
6. Bolt 25 ft. lbs.

AIR system control valve — 3.1L V6 with manual transaxle

6. Torque the pulley bolts to 10 ft. lbs. (13 Nm)

NOTE: *Number 6 procedure will compress the centrifugal filter fan onto the pump hole. Do NOT drive the filter fan on with a hammer. There might be a slight amount of interference with the housing bore, this is normal. After the new filter has been installed, it may squeal upon initial operation until the outside diameter sealing lip has worn in. This may require a short period of pump operation at various engine speeds.*

7. Install the pump drive belt and adjust.
8. Reconnect the negative (–) battery cable.
9. Start the engine and check for air injection system operation.

Oxygen (O_2) Sensor

The exhaust oxygen sensor is mounted in the exhaust system where it can monitor the oxygen content of the exhaust gases. The oxygen reacts to the oxygen sensor to produce a voltage output. The voltage ranges from 0.1 volts for lean mixtures to 0.9 volts for rich mixtures.

WARNING: *The oxygen sensor uses a permanently attached pigtail and connector. This pigtail should NOT be removed from the sensor. Damage to the oxygen sensor will result.*

REMOVAL AND INSTALLATION

NOTE: *The oxygen sensor may be difficult to remove when the engine temperature is below 120°F (48°C). Excessive force may damage*

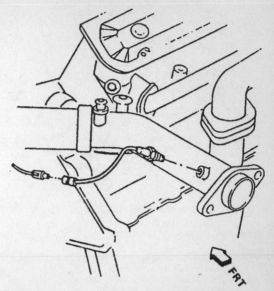

Oxygen sensor location — 2.8L and 3.1L V6 engines

the threads in the exhaust manifold or cross-over pipe.

1. Disconnect the negative (–) battery cable.
2. Disconnect the electrical connector at the plug.
3. Remove the sensor from the exhaust manifold or crossover pipe, being careful not to damage the manifold threads.

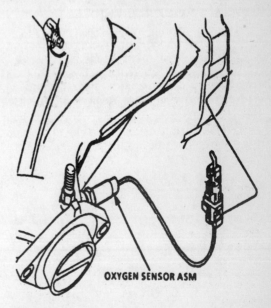

OXYGEN SENSOR ASM

SHOWN WITH HEAT SHIELD REMOVED FOR CLARITY DO NOT OPERATE CAR WITH HEAT SHIELD REMOVED.

Oxygen sensor — 2.3L Quad 4

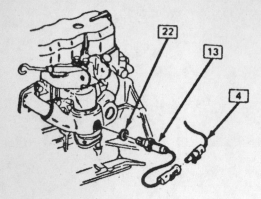

4. ECM harness — connector to O2 sensor
13. O2 sensor
22. O2 sensor seal

Oxygen sensor location — 2.5L L4 Lumina

NOTE: *A special anti-seize compound is used on the oxygen sensor threads to prevent thread seizure. The threads MUST be coated with anti-seize compound No. P/N 5613695 or equivalent before installation.*

4. **To install:** position the sensor and seal into the exhaust manifold. Torque the sensor to 30 ft. lbs. (41 Nm) and connect the electrical connector. Reconnect the negative (−) battery cable and start the engine to check for exhaust leaks.

Emission Service Light

The GM "W" body sold in the United States and some in Canada have the Computer Command Control systems. Vehicles with the Computer Command Control system include a **"Service Engine Soon"** light on 1988-90 models. This light is on the instrument panel to the right of the speedometer. The light will come ON during engine starting to let you know the bulb is working. Have the system serv-

iced by your dealer if the light does not come on during starting, intermittently or continuously while driving. These conditions may indicate that the Computer Command Control system needs servicing. In most cases, the vehicle will not have to be towed, but get to your General Motors dealer as soon as possible.

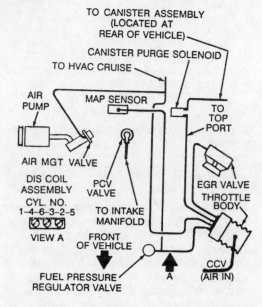

Vacuum hose routing — 2.8L and 3.1L engines with manual transaxle

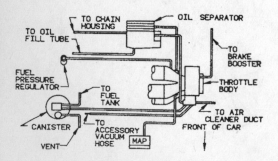

Vacuum hose routing — 2.3L Quad 4

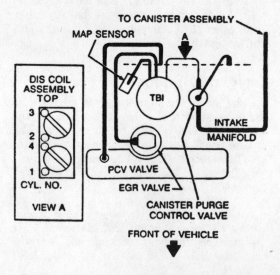

Vacuum hose routing — 1990 2.5L L4 engine

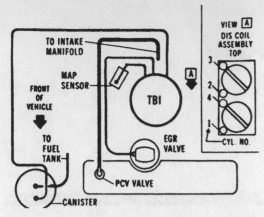

Vacuum hose routing — 1988–89 2.5L L4 engine

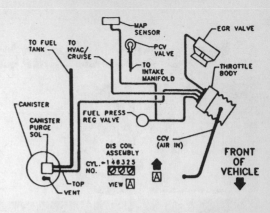

Vacuum hose routing — 2.8L and 3.1L V6 engines with automatic transaxle

GASOLINE FUEL INJECTION SYSTEM

NOTE: *This book contains testing and service procedures for your fuel injection system. More comprehensive testing and diagnosis procedures may be found in CHILTON'S GUIDE TO FUEL INJECTION AND FEEDBACK CARBURETORS, book part number 7488, available at Your local retailer.*

The 2.5L Lumina engine is equipped with a Throttle Body Injection (TBI) system. The throttle body is mounted on top of the intake manifold as a conventional carburetor would be. The throttle body has one main fuel injector to supply all four cylinder with the proper air/fuel mixture. The system is controlled by the ECM (electronic control module) which gets input from various sensors in the system. The ECM has the ability to detect problems in the system and store the problem (trouble code) in its memory. The **Service Engine Soon** light in the instrument panel, **ON** indicates that there may be a potential problem in the system.

The 2.3L, 2.8L and 3.1L engines are equipped with a Multi-port Fuel Injection (MFI) system. The throttle body is mounted in front of an air intake plenum that supplies air to fuel injectors mounted in the intake manifold over each cylinder. Each cylinder has its own fuel injector, controlled by the ECM assembly. The remainder of the system is basically the same as the throttle body injection system.

Electric Fuel Pump

These cars are equipped with electric fuel pumps mounted in the fuel tank. The fuel tank must be removed to access the fuel pump/level sensor assembly.

CAUTION: *To reduce the risk of fire and personal injury, it is necessary to relieve the fuel system pressure before servicing any fuel system component. If this procedure is not performed, fuel may be sprayed out of the connection under pressure. Always keep a dry chemical (Class B) fire extinguisher near the work area.*

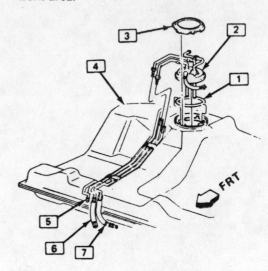

1. O-ring
2. Fuel level sender
3. Sender cam
4. Fuel tank
5. Fuel vapor
6. Fuel return
7. Fuel feed

Fuel pump and level sensor location

2.5L L4 Lumina

Fuel pressure relief procedures:

1. Remove the fuel filler cap.

2. Remove the Fuel pump fuse from the fuse block located in the passenger compartment.

3. Start the engine and run until the engine stops due to the lack of fuel.

4. Crank the engine for 3 seconds to ensure all pressure is relieved.

5. Make sure the negative (–) battery cable is disconnected.

2.3L QUAD 4 (VIN A, D)
2.8L and 3.1L V6 (VIN W, T)

Fuel Pressure Relief Procedures:

1. Disconnect the negative (–) battery cable.
2. Loosen the fuel filler cap to relieve tank vapor pressure.

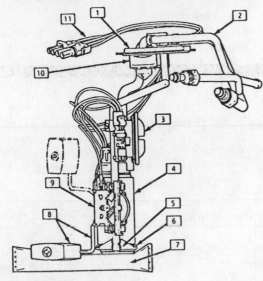

1. Fuel level sender cover
2. Fuel tubes
3. Pulsator
4. Rollervane fuel pump
5. Pump support bracket
6. Insulator
7. Strainer
8. Float and float arm
9. Fuel level sensor assembly
10. Pressure control/rollover valve
11. Wiring harness

Electric fuel pump and level sensor assembly

3. Connect a fuel pressure gauge J-34730-1 or equivalent to the fuel pressure relief connection at the fuel rail.
4. Wrap a shop towel around the fittings while connecting the gauge to prevent fuel spillage.
5. Install a bleed hose into an approved container and open the valve to bleed the system pressure. The system is safe for servicing.

REMOVAL AND INSTALLATION

1. Disconnect the negative (–) battery cable.
2. Relieve the fuel system pressure as outlined previously in this section.
3. Raise and safely support the vehicle with jackstands.
4. Drain and remove the fuel tank assembly as outlined in the "Fuel tank" removal procedures in this chapter.
5. Turn the fuel pump cam lock ring counterclockwise and lift the assembly out of the tank.
6. Remove the fuel pump from the level sensor unit as follows:

   a. Pull the pump up into the attaching hose or pulsator while pulling outward away from the bottom support.

   b. Take care to prevent damage to the rubber insulator and strainer during removal.

   c. When the pump assembly is clear of the bottom support, pull the pump out of the rubber connector for removal.

To install:

1. Replace any attaching hoses or rubber sound insulator that show signs of deterioration.
2. Push the fuel pump into the attaching hoses and install the pump/sensor assembly into the tank. Always use a new O-ring seal.

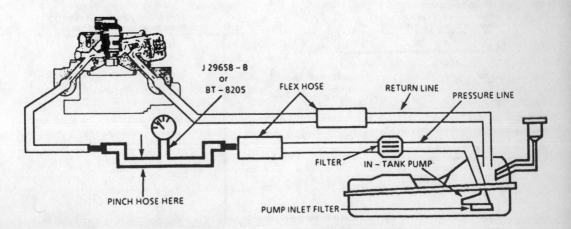

Fuel system diagram — 2.5L with TBI

NOTE: *Be careful not to fold over or twist the strainer when installing the sensor unit. Also, make sure the strainer does not block full travel of the float arm.*

3. Install the cam lock and turn clockwise to lock.

4. Install the fuel tank as outlined in this chapter.

5. Fill the tank with four gallons of gas and check for fuel leaks.

TESTING

The ECM will turn ON the fuel pump and will remain ON as long as the engine is crank-ing or running. The ECM will send the ON signal as long as it is receiving ignition reference pulses. If for some reason there are no ignition pulses, the ECM will shut the fuel pump OFF within two seconds after the key is ON. Consequently, a no fuel pressure condition may mean another problem then the fuel pump circuit.

2.5L L4 Lumina

1. With the ignition **OFF**, release the fuel pressure and check for fuel in the tank.

2. Connect a fuel pressure gauge J-29658-B or equivalent to the service fitting. Jump the

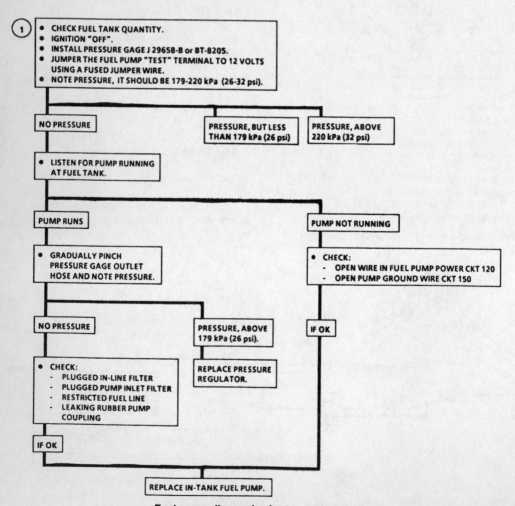

Fuel pump diagnosis chart — 2.5L with TBI

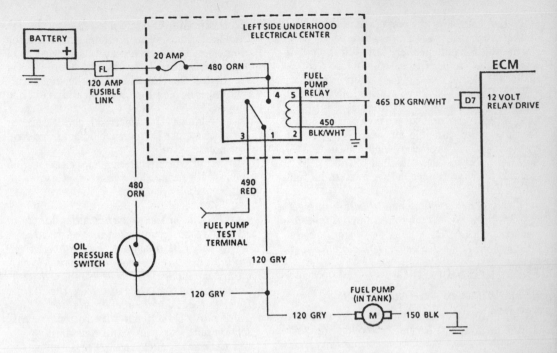

Fuel pump wiring schematic — 2.5L with TBI

fuel pump test terminal to 12 volts using a fused jumper wire.

3. With the key in the ON position and engine NOT running, the pressure should be **26–32 psi (179–220 kPa)**.

4. Listen to the pump running in the tank. If the pump is running, check for obstructed fuel filter, lines or pressure regulator. For further diagnosis, refer to the "Fuel Pump Diagnosis chart" in this section.

2.3L QUAD 4 (VIN A, D)
2.8L and 3.1L V6 (VIN W, T)

1. With the ignition **OFF**, release the fuel pressure and check for fuel in the tank.

2. Connect a fuel pressure gauge J-29658-B or equivalent to the service fitting.

3. With the ignition switch ON and engine NOT running, the fuel pump pressure should be **41–47 psi (280–325 kPa)** and hold steady when the engine is turned off.

4. If the pressure is not within specifications, refer to the "Fuel Pump Diagnosis chart" in this section.

Fuel Pump Relay

REMOVAL AND INSTALLATION

1. Disconnect the negative (–) battery cable.

2. The fuel pump relay is located in the engine compartment attached to the multi-use bracket on the upper dash panel extension.

3. Remove the electrical connector and two

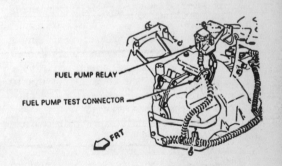

Fuel pump relay location(1) and pump test connector (2)

mounting nuts.

4. Install the relay, connect the electrical connector and torque the mounting nuts to 89 inch lbs. (10 Nm). Reconnect the negative (–) battery cable.

2.5L LUMINA (VIN R) THROTTLE BODY FUEL INJECTION SYSTEM

The TBI (Throttle Body Injection) system used by the 4-cylinder Lumina uses an electric fuel pump. The throttle body is placed on the intake manifold where the carburetor is normally mounted. The TBI unit is computer controlled and supplies the correct amount of fuel during all engine operating conditions.

The unit is made primarily of aluminum and consist of two major casting assemblies, a throttle body and fuel metering assembly.

With the TBI system, air is drawn into a single bore. The fuel is then injected into the air stream under pressure. The unit contains a pressure regulator, idle air control valve, and an electrically operated solenoid that activates the fuel injector. Also attached to the TBI is a throttle position sensor, a fuel inlet and a fuel return fitting.

NOTE: *The assembly identification number is stamped on the low mounting flange located on the TPS side of the throttle body, and should be noted before servicing the unit.*

Throttle Body Unit

REMOVAL AND INSTALLATION

CAUTION: *To reduce the risk of fire and personal injury, it is necessary to relieve the fuel system pressure before servicing any fuel system component. If this procedure is not performed, fuel may be sprayed out of the connection under pressure. Always keep a dry chemical (Class B) fire extinguisher near the work area.*

Fuel pressure relief procedures: remove the Fuel pump fuse from the fuse block located in the passenger compartment. Start the engine and run until the engine stops due to the lack of fuel. Crank the engine for 3 seconds to ensure all pressure is relieved.

1. Disconnect the negative (−) battery cable and air cleaner.
2. Release the fuel pressure.
3. Disconnect the electrical connectors to the idle air control, throttle position sensor and injector.
4. Remove the throttle linkage, return spring and cruise control linkage if so equipped.
5. Disconnect the vacuum hoses from the throttle body (mark the hose routing for proper connection during installation).
6. Disconnect the fuel supply and return steel lines from the throttle body using a flare nut and backup wrench. Discard the old O-rings.
7. Remove the three bolts securing the throttle body-to-engine. Remove the throttle body assembly from the engine.

To install:
1. Clean the throttle body and intake manifold sealing surfaces with solvent and a gasket scraper.
2. Install the throttle body with a new gasket onto the manifold and torque the two or three bolts to 13 ft. lbs. (17 Nm).

3. Inspect the O-ring seals for the inlet and return lines and replace if damaged. Install the fuel lines using a flare nut and backup wrench. Torque the lines to 17 ft. lbs. (23 Nm).
4. Install the throttle return spring, throttle linkage and cruise control linkage if so equipped.
5. Reconnect the electrical connectors to the throttle position sensor, idle air control motor and injector.
6. Install the air cleaner, start the engine and check for fuel leaks.

OVERHAUL

NOTE: *The procedures that follow apply to complete disassembly, cleaning and reassembly of the TBI assembly removed from the engine. In many cases, service repair of individual components may be completed without removing the entire unit from the engine. Refer to the "Model 700 Throttle Body Injection" parts breakdown illustrations in this section for disassembly and reassembly.*

1. Release the fuel pressure and remove the throttle body assembly. Refer to the "Throttle Body Assembly" removal procedures in this section.
2. Remove the five fuel meter cover screws and lockwashers while holding the cover on the fuel meter body.
3. Lift the fuel meter cover including the fuel pressure regulator assembly off the throttle body.
4. Discard the fuel outlet passage gasket only. Leave the fuel meter cover gasket on the fuel meter body.

CAUTION: *Do not remove the four screws securing the fuel pressure regulator assembly to the fuel meter cover. The regulator cover contains a large spring under heavy tension which, if accidentally released, could cause personal injury. The assembly is serviced as a complete unit.*

WARNING: *Do not immerse the fuel meter cover in any type of industrial cleaner because damage to the pressure regulator may result.*

5. Remove the sealing ring for the base of the fuel pressure regulator.
6. Clean the parts with carburetor cleaner or equivalent.

ASSEMBLY

1. Install a new dust seal for the fuel pressure regulator into the recess on the fuel meter body.
2. Install a new fuel return passage gasket on the fuel meter cover.
3. Install a new fuel meter gasket on the fuel meter body.

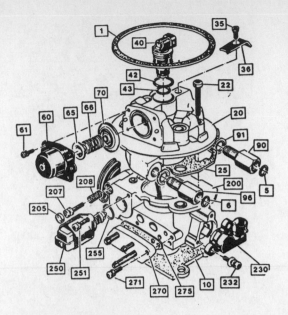

1. Air cleaner gasket
5. Fuel line inlet nut O-ring
6. Fuel line outlet nut O-ring
10. Gasket flange
20. Fuel meter assembly
22. Meter body to throttle body attaching screw
25. Gasket
35. Injector retaining screw
36. Injector retainer
40. Fuel injector
42. Injector upper O-ring
43. Injector lower O-ring
60. Pressure regulator cover
61. Screw
65. Spring seat
66. Pressure regulator spring
70. Pressure regulator diaphragm assembly
90. Fuel inlet nut
91. Fuel nut seal
96. Fuel outlet nut
200. Throttle body assembly
205. Idle stop screw plug
207. Idle stop screw and washer assembly
208. Idle stop screw spring
230. Throttle position sensor (TPS)
232. TPS screw and washer assembly
250. Idle air control valve (IACV)
251. IACV screw
255. IACV O-ring
270. Tube module assembly
271. Tube module assembly attaching screw
275. Tube module assembly gasket

Model 700 throttle body — exploded view

4. Install the fuel meter cover making sure the pressure regulator dust seal and cover gaskets are in place. Apply thread locking compound to the threads of the five fuel meter cover attaching screws. The two short screws go next to the fuel injector. Torque the five cover attaching screws to 28 inch lb. (3.0 Nm).

5. Install the throttle body assembly as outlined in the "Throttle Body Unit" installation.

Fuel Injector

REMOVAL AND INSTALLATION

CAUTION: *To reduce the risk of fire and personal injury, it is necessary to relieve the fuel system pressure before servicing any fuel system component. If this procedure is not performed, fuel may be sprayed out of the connection under pressure. Always keep a dry chemical (Class B) fire extinguisher near the work area.*

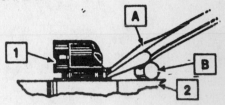

1. Fuel injector assembly   A. Small pry bar
2. Fuel meter body   B. Fulcrum

Fuel injector removal — 2.5L with TBI

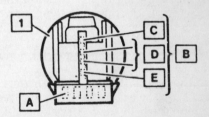

1. Fuel injector—top view   D. Day
A. Part number   E. Year
B. Build date code
C. Month (1–9, Jan–Dec; O–Oct., N–Nov., D–Dec.)

Fuel injector part number location — 2.5L Lumina with TBI

Fuel pressure relief procedures:
Connect a fuel gauge part No. J 34730-1 or equivalent to the fuel pressure valve on the fuel rail assembly. Wrap a towel around the fitting while connecting the gauge to prevent fuel spillage. Install the bleed hose into an approved container and open the valve to bleed the system pressure.

NOTE: *Use care in removing the injector to protect the electrical connector on top of the injector. Also, do NOT immerse the injector in any type of liquid solvent or cleaner.*

1. Disconnect the negative (–) battery cable.
2. Disconnect the electrical connector to

the fuel injector.

3. Remove the injector screw and retainer.

4. Using a fulcrum, place a small pry bar under the ridge opposite the connector end and carefully pry the injector out of the cavity. Refer to the following illustrations.

5. Remove the upper and lower O-rings from the injector and cavity.

6. Inspect the injector and fuel lines for dirt and contamination. If excess contamination is present, the fuel system will have to be flushed.

NOTE: *Make sure the replacement injector is an identical part No. The injectors from other model 700 systems may fit, but are calibrated for different flow rates. Check the part No. on the side of the throttle body.*

7. Lubricate the new upper and lower O-rings with automatic transmission fluid (ATF) and place them on the injector. (Make sure the upper O-ring is in the groove and the lower one is flush against the filter.

8. Install the injector into the cavity by pushing straight into the fuel injector cavity.

NOTE: *Make sure the electrical connector end on the injector is facing in the general direction of the cut out in the fuel meter body for the wire grommet.*

9. Install the injector retainer and coat the screw with thread locking compound. Torque the attaching screw to 27 inch lb. (3.0 Nm).

10. Reconnect the injector electrical connector.

11. Reconnect the negative (–) battery cable.

12. With the engine NOT running, turn the ignition switch to the ON position and check for fuel leaks at the throttle body area.

Fuel Pressure Regulator

CAUTION: *To reduce the risk of fire and personal injury, it is necessary to relieve the fuel system pressure before servicing any fuel system component. If this procedure is not performed, fuel may be sprayed out of the connection under pressure. Always keep a dry chemical (Class B) fire extinguisher near the work area.*

Fuel pressure relief procedures:

Connect a fuel gauge part No. J 34730-1 or equivalent to the fuel pressure valve on the fuel rail assembly. Wrap a towel around the fitting while connecting the gauge to prevent fuel spillage. Install the bleed hose into an approved container and open the valve to bleed the system pressure.

1. Cover assembly
2. Screw and washer
3. Spring seat
4. Spring
5. Diaphragm assembly
6. Fuel meter assembly

Fuel pressure regulator — 2.5L with TBI

1. Disconnect the negative (–) battery cable.

CAUTION: *The pressure regulator contains a large spring under heavy compression. Use care when removing the four screws to prevent personal injury.*

2. Remove the pressure regulator cover assembly (4 screws).

3. Remove the regulator spring, spring seat and diaphragm assembly.

NOTE: *To prevent leaks, the pressure regulator diaphragm MUST be replaced when the cover is removed.*

To install:

4. Position the new regulator diaphragm, spring, spring seat and cover on the throttle body assembly.

5. Coat the four attaching screws with thread locking compound. Install the four attaching screws and torque to 22 inch lb. (2.5 Nm).

6. Connect the negative (–) battery cable.

7. With the engine OFF, turn the ignition switch to the ON position and check for fuel leaks at the injector.

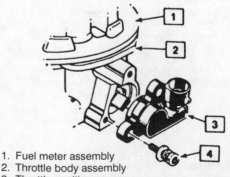

1. Fuel meter assembly
2. Throttle body assembly
3. Throttle position sensor
4. Screw and washer

Throttle position sensor (TPS)

Throttle Position Sensor (TPS)

The TPS is mounted on the side of the throttle body opposite the throttle lever assembly. The function of the TPS is to relay throttle valve position to the ECM (Electronic Control Module). The signal is needed to generate the proper injector controls (base pulse).

REMOVAL AND INSTALLATION

1. Disconnect the negative (–) battery cable.
2. Remove the air cleaner assembly.
3. Remove the electrical connector from the TP sensor.
4. Remove the two attaching screws and remove the sensor.

NOTE: *The throttle position sensor TPS is an electrical component and should not be immersed in any type of liquid solvent or cleaner.*

5. **To install:** position the TPS on the throttle body with the throttle valve normally closed. Install the sensor and rotate counter clockwise to align the mounting holes. Torque the two attaching screws to 18 inch lb. (2.0 Nm).
6. Connect the TPS electrical connector. Reconnect the negative (–) battery cable.

Idle Air Control Valve

The Idle Air Control valve (IAC) is mounted on the throttle body assembly and provides a constant idle speed regardless of engine loads or driving conditions. The IAC valve controls the amount of air that enters the engine by the way of a ECM signal.

REMOVAL AND INSTALLATION

NOTE: *The IAC valve is flange mounted, with a dual taper and 10mm diameter pintle. If replacement is necessary, only an IAC valve with the correct part No. having the correct pintle shape and size may be used.*

1. Disconnect the negative (–) battery cable.
2. Remove the IAC valve electrical connector.
3. Remove the two attaching screws and the IAC valve.

WARNING: *Under no circumstances should the valve pintle be tampered with by hand, screwed or pushed in, or pulled out because damage may result.*

To install:

4. Lubricate the new O-ring seal with automatic transmission fluid and install on the IAC valve.
5. Install the IAC valve to the throttle body.
6. Coat the two IAC valve attaching screws with thread locking compound and torque to 28 inch lb. (3.2 Nm).
7. Install the IAC electrical connector. Re-

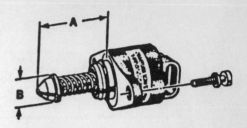

Idle air control (IAC) valve — 2.5L with TBI. Dimension A is pintle extension; dimension B is pintle diameter

connect the negative (–) battery cable.

8. Start the engine and allow to reach operating temperature. Check the idle speed with a tachometer.

ADJUSTMENT

Measure the distance between the tip of the IAC valve pintle and mounting flange. If the distance is greater than 28mm, use finger pressure to slowly retract the pintle. The force required to seat a new valve will not cause damage to the valve.

2.3L QUAD 4, 2.8L AND 3.1L V6 MULTI-PORT FUEL INJECTION (MFI) SYSTEM

All 1988 and later V6 and 1990 QUAD 4 models are equipped with a multi-port fuel injection (MFI) system. The MFI system is controlled by an electronic control module (ECM) which monitors engine operations and generates output signals to provide the correct air/fuel mixture, ignition timing and engine idle speed control. Input to the control unit is provided by an oxygen sensor, coolant temperature sensor, detonation sensor, hot film air mass sensor and throttle position sensor. The ECM also receives information concerning engine rpm, road speed, manifold air temperature, transmission gear position and air conditioning.

The main control sensor is the Oxygen (O_2) sensor, which is located in the exhaust manifold. The O_2 sensor tells the ECM how much oxygen is in the exhaust gas and the ECM changes the Air/Fuel mixture to the engine by controlling the fuel injectors. The best mixture for the engine to operate properly is a 14.7 to 1 ratio (air to fuel).

The ECM looks at the voltages from several sensors to determine how much fuel to give to each injector. The fuel is delivered under one of several conditions called "modes". All of the modes are controlled by the ECM. The modes

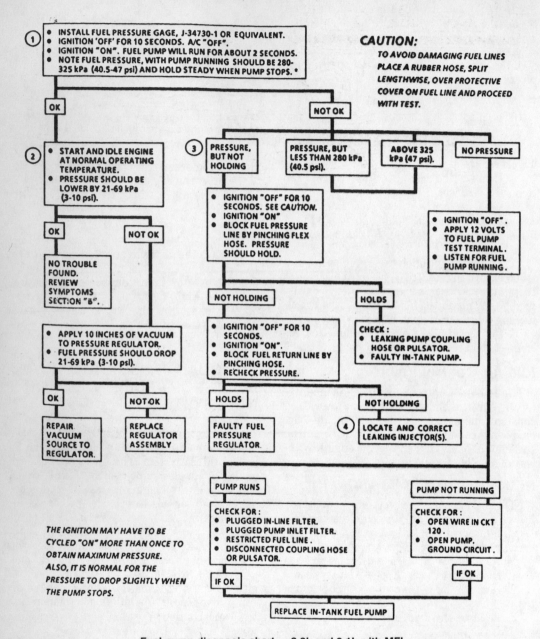

**THIS CHART ASSUMES
THERE IS NO CODE 54**

① • INSTALL FUEL PRESSURE GAGE, J-34730-1 OR EQUIVALENT.
 • IGNITION 'OFF' FOR 10 SECONDS. A/C "OFF".
 • IGNITION "ON". FUEL PUMP WILL RUN FOR ABOUT 2 SECONDS.
 • NOTE FUEL PRESSURE, WITH PUMP RUNNING SHOULD BE 280-
   325 kPa (40.5-47 psi) AND HOLD STEADY WHEN PUMP STOPS. •

CAUTION:

*TO AVOID DAMAGING FUEL LINES
PLACE A RUBBER HOSE, SPLIT
LENGTHWISE, OVER PROTECTIVE
COVER ON FUEL LINE AND PROCEED
WITH TEST.*

OK   NOT OK

② • START AND IDLE ENGINE
   AT NORMAL OPERATING
   TEMPERATURE.
 • PRESSURE SHOULD BE
   LOWER BY 21-69 kPa
   (3-10 psi).

③ PRESSURE, BUT NOT HOLDING

PRESSURE, BUT LESS THAN 280 kPa (40.5 psi).

ABOVE 325 kPa (47 psi).

NO PRESSURE

OK   NOT OK

NO TROUBLE
FOUND.
REVIEW
SYMPTOMS
SECTION "B".

• IGNITION "OFF" FOR 10
  SECONDS. SEE CAUTION.
• IGNITION "ON"
• BLOCK FUEL PRESSURE
  LINE BY PINCHING FLEX
  HOSE. PRESSURE
  SHOULD HOLD.

• IGNITION "OFF".
• APPLY 12 VOLTS
  TO FUEL PUMP
  TEST TERMINAL.
• LISTEN FOR FUEL
  PUMP RUNNING.

NOT HOLDING   HOLDS

• APPLY 10 INCHES OF VACUUM
  TO PRESSURE REGULATOR.
• FUEL PRESSURE SHOULD DROP
  21-69 kPa (3-10 psi).

• IGNITION "OFF" FOR 10
  SECONDS.
• IGNITION "ON".
• BLOCK FUEL RETURN LINE BY
  PINCHING HOSE.
• RECHECK PRESSURE.

CHECK :
• LEAKING PUMP COUPLING
  HOSE OR PULSATOR.
• FAULTY IN-TANK PUMP.

OK   NOT OK   HOLDS   NOT HOLDING

REPAIR
VACUUM
SOURCE TO
REGULATOR.

REPLACE
REGULATOR
ASSEMBLY.

FAULTY FUEL
PRESSURE
REGULATOR.

④ LOCATE AND CORRECT
  LEAKING INJECTOR(S).

PUMP RUNS   PUMP NOT RUNNING

*THE IGNITION MAY HAVE TO BE
CYCLED "ON" MORE THAN ONCE TO
OBTAIN MAXIMUM PRESSURE.
ALSO, IT IS NORMAL FOR THE
PRESSURE TO DROP SLIGHTLY WHEN
THE PUMP STOPS.*

CHECK FOR :
• PLUGGED IN-LINE FILTER.
• PLUGGED PUMP INLET FILTER.
• RESTRICTED FUEL LINE .
• DISCONNECTED COUPLING HOSE
  OR PULSATOR.

CHECK FOR :
• OPEN WIRE IN CKT
  120 .
• OPEN PUMP.
  GROUND CIRCUIT .

IF OK   IF OK

REPLACE IN-TANK FUEL PUMP

Fuel pump diagnosis chart — 2.8L and 3.1L with MFI

consist of starting, clear flood, run, acceleration and deceleration.

The system uses Bosch injectors, one at each intake port, rather than the single injector found on the throttle body system. The injectors are mounted on a fuel rail and are activated by a signal from the electronic control module (ECM). The injector is a solenoid-operated valve which remains open depending on the width of the electronic pulses (length of the signal) from the ECM; the longer the open time, the more fuel is injected. In this manner, the air/fuel mixture can be precisely controlled for maximum performance with minimum emissions.

Fuel is pumped from the tank by a high pressure fuel pump, located inside the fuel tank. It is a positive displacement roller vane pump. The impeller serves as a vapor separator and pre-charges the high pressure assembly.

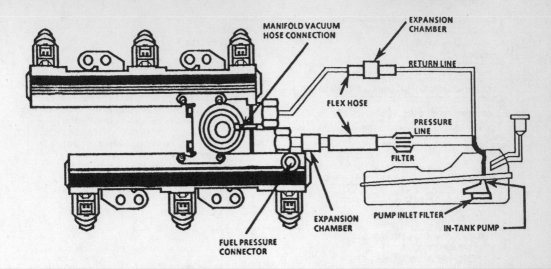

Fuel system diagram — 2.8L and 3.1L with MFI

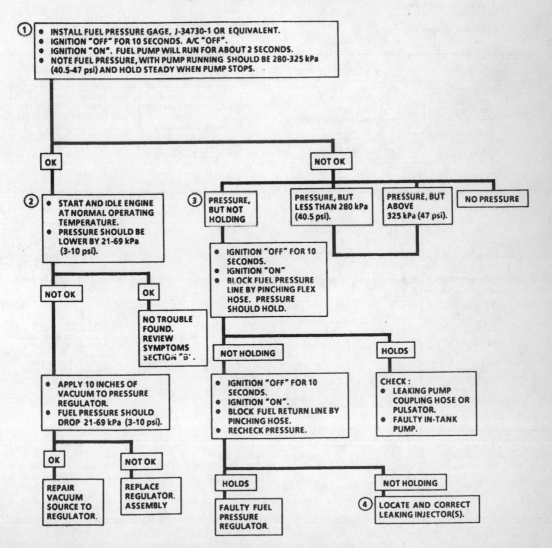

① INSTALL FUEL PRESSURE GAGE, J-34730-1 OR EQUIVALENT.
- IGNITION "OFF" FOR 10 SECONDS. A/C "OFF".
- IGNITION "ON". FUEL PUMP WILL RUN FOR ABOUT 2 SECONDS.
- NOTE FUEL PRESSURE, WITH PUMP RUNNING SHOULD BE 280-325 kPa (40.5-47 psi) AND HOLD STEADY WHEN PUMP STOPS.

OK

NOT OK

②
- START AND IDLE ENGINE AT NORMAL OPERATING TEMPERATURE.
- PRESSURE SHOULD BE LOWER BY 21-69 kPa (3-10 psi).

③ PRESSURE, BUT NOT HOLDING

PRESSURE, BUT LESS THAN 280 kPa (40.5 psi).

PRESSURE, BUT ABOVE 325 kPa (47 psi).

NO PRESSURE

NOT OK

OK

NO TROUBLE FOUND. REVIEW SYMPTOMS SECTION "B".

- IGNITION "OFF" FOR 10 SECONDS.
- IGNITION "ON"
- BLOCK FUEL PRESSURE LINE BY PINCHING FLEX HOSE. PRESSURE SHOULD HOLD.

NOT HOLDING

HOLDS

- APPLY 10 INCHES OF VACUUM TO PRESSURE REGULATOR.
- FUEL PRESSURE SHOULD DROP 21-69 kPa (3-10 psi).

- IGNITION "OFF" FOR 10 SECONDS.
- IGNITION "ON".
- BLOCK FUEL RETURN LINE BY PINCHING HOSE.
- RECHECK PRESSURE.

CHECK:
- LEAKING PUMP COUPLING HOSE OR PULSATOR.
- FAULTY IN-TANK PUMP.

OK

NOT OK

HOLDS

NOT HOLDING

REPAIR VACUUM SOURCE TO REGULATOR.

REPLACE REGULATOR. ASSEMBLY

FAULTY FUEL PRESSURE REGULATOR.

④ LOCATE AND CORRECT LEAKING INJECTOR(S).

Fuel system diagnosis chart, 2.3L Quad 4 — Part 1

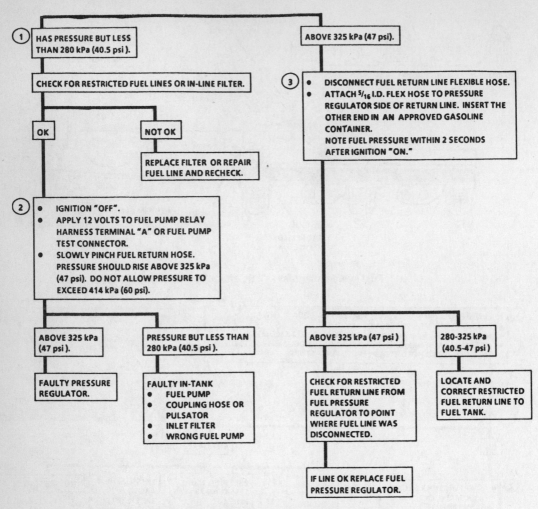

① HAS PRESSURE BUT LESS THAN 280 kPa (40.5 psi).

CHECK FOR RESTRICTED FUEL LINES OR IN-LINE FILTER.

OK

NOT OK

REPLACE FILTER OR REPAIR FUEL LINE AND RECHECK.

② • IGNITION "OFF".
• APPLY 12 VOLTS TO FUEL PUMP RELAY HARNESS TERMINAL "A" OR FUEL PUMP TEST CONNECTOR.
• SLOWLY PINCH FUEL RETURN HOSE. PRESSURE SHOULD RISE ABOVE 325 kPa (47 psi). DO NOT ALLOW PRESSURE TO EXCEED 414 kPa (60 psi).

ABOVE 325 kPa (47 psi).

PRESSURE BUT LESS THAN 280 kPa (40.5 psi).

FAULTY PRESSURE REGULATOR.

FAULTY IN-TANK
• FUEL PUMP
• COUPLING HOSE OR PULSATOR
• INLET FILTER
• WRONG FUEL PUMP

ABOVE 325 kPa (47 psi).

③ • DISCONNECT FUEL RETURN LINE FLEXIBLE HOSE.
• ATTACH 5/16 I.D. FLEX HOSE TO PRESSURE REGULATOR SIDE OF RETURN LINE. INSERT THE OTHER END IN AN APPROVED GASOLINE CONTAINER.
NOTE FUEL PRESSURE WITHIN 2 SECONDS AFTER IGNITION "ON."

ABOVE 325 kPa (47 psi)

280-325 kPa (40.5-47 psi)

CHECK FOR RESTRICTED FUEL RETURN LINE FROM FUEL PRESSURE REGULATOR TO POINT WHERE FUEL LINE WAS DISCONNECTED.

LOCATE AND CORRECT RESTRICTED FUEL RETURN LINE TO FUEL TANK.

IF LINE OK REPLACE FUEL PRESSURE REGULATOR.

Fuel system diagnosis chart, 2.3L Quad 4 — Part 2

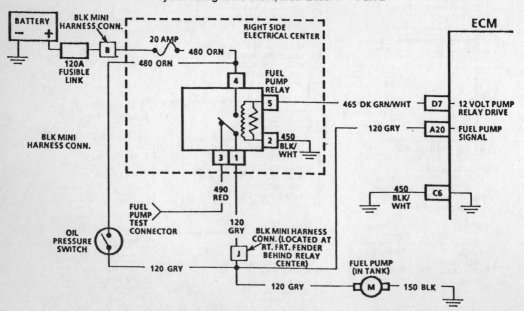

Fuel pump wiring schematic — 2.8L and 3.1L with MFI

A pressure regulator maintains 41–47 psi (280– 325 kPa) in the fuel line to the injectors and the excess fuel is fed back to the tank. On MFI systems, a fuel accumulator is used to dampen the hydraulic line hammer in the system created when all injectors open simultaneously.

The Manifold Air Flow Sensor is used to measure the mass of air that is drawn into the engine cylinders. It is located in the air cleaner assembly and consists of a heated film which measures the mass of air, rather than just the volume. A resistor is used to measure the temperature of the incoming air and the air mass sensor maintains the temperature of the film at 75 degrees above ambient temperature. As the ambient (outside) air temperature rises, more energy is required to maintain the heated film at the higher temperature and the control unit uses this difference in required energy to calculate the mass of the incoming air. The control unit uses this information to determine the duration of fuel injection pulse, timing and EGR.

The throttle body incorporates an idle air control (IAC) that provides for a bypass channel through which air can flow. It consists of an orifice and pintle which is controlled by the ECM through a stopper motor. The IAC provides air flow for idle and allows additional air during cold start until the engine reaches operating temperature. As the engine temperature rises, the opening through which air passes is slowly closed.

The Throttle Position Sensor (TPS) provides the control unit with information on throttle position, in order to determine injector pulse width and hence correct mixture. The TPS is connected to the throttle shaft on the throttle body and consists of a potentiometer with one end connected to a 5 volt source from the ECM and the other to ground. A third wire is connected to the ECM to measure the voltage output from the TPS which changes as the throttle valve angle is changed (accelerator pedal moves). At the closed throttle position, the output is low; as the throttle valve opens, the output increases to wide open throttle (WOT). The TPS can be misadjusted open, shorted, or loose and, if it is out of adjustment, the idle quality or WOT performance may be poor. A loose TPS can cause intermittent bursts of fuel from the injectors and an unstable idle because the ECM thinks the throttle is moving. This should cause a trouble code to be set. Once a trouble code is set, the ECM will use a preset value for TPS and some vehicle performance may return.

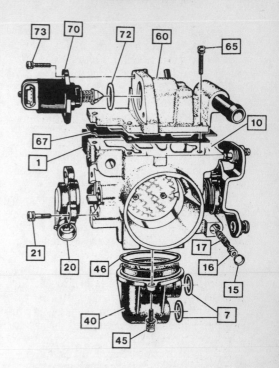

1. Flange gasket
7. Coolant line O-ring
10. Throttle body assembly
15. Idle stop screw plug
16. Idle stop screw
17. Spring
20. Throttle position sensor (TPS)
21. Screw
40. Coolant cover
45. Screw
46. O-ring
60. Idle air/vacuum signal housing assembly
65. Screw
67. Gasket
70. Idle air control valve (IAC)
72. O-ring
73. Screw

Throttle body assembly — 2.3L Quad 4

Throttle Body Assembly

REMOVAL AND INSTALLATION

2.3L QUAD 4 (VIN A, D)

NOTE: *The throttle body assembly can be removed from the intake plenum and replaced as a unit, but most components can be replaced without removing the throttle body. If replacing the throttle body, an eight digit part number is stamped on the bottom of the casting next to the coolant cover. This number is required to ensure the proper part is replaced. Each system uses different calibrations even though the throttle body looks identical.*

1. Disconnect the negative (–) battery cable. CAUTION: *To reduce the risk of fire and personal injury, it is necessary to relieve the fuel system pressure before servicing any fuel system component. If this procedure is not performed, fuel may be sprayed out of the connection under pressure. Always keep a dry chemical (Class B) fire extinguisher near the work area.*

2. **Fuel pressure relief procedures:**

a. Disconnect the negative (–) battery cable.

b. Loosen the fuel filler cap to relieve tank vapor pressure.

c. Connect a fuel pressure gauge J-34730-1 or equivalent to the fuel pressure relief connection at the fuel rail.

d. Wrap a shop towel around the fittings while connecting the gauge to prevent fuel spillage.

e. Install a bleed hose into an approved container and open the valve to bleed the system pressure. The system is safe for servicing.

3. Partially drain the radiator coolant.

4. Remove the air cleaner and duct.

5. Disconnect and mark the electrical and vacuum connections at the throttle body.

6. Remove the throttle cable and bracket from the throttle body and engine strut.

7. Remove the two throttle body retaining bolts and loosen the assembly from the intake manifold.

8. Disconnect and mark the throttle body coolant hoses.

9. Disconnect the cruise control and transaxle cables, if so equipped.

10. Remove the throttle body, gasket and O-rings.

To install:

1. Check all cavities for foreign material and clean if necessary. Clean all gasket mating surfaces. Do not damage aluminum castings.

2. Lubricate and install new coolant hose O-rings with antifreeze. Install the coolant lines.

3. Install the throttle, cruise and transaxle control cables.

4. Using a new gasket with NO sealer, position the throttle body-to-manifold and torque the retaining bolts to 19 ft. lbs. (26 Nm).

5. Install the throttle bracket and torque the nuts and bolts to 19 ft.

lbs. (26 Nm).

6. Connect the vacuum hoses, electrical connectors and install the air cleaner and duct.

7. Refill the radiator with engine coolant and connect the negative battery cable.

8. With the engine **OFF**, check to see if the throttle cables are free and working properly.

9. Reset the Idle Air Control (IAC) valve as follows:

a. Turn the ignition to the **ON** position with the engine **OFF**.

b. Ground the diagnostic test terminal for five seconds. At the ALDL (assembly line diagnostic link) under the instrument panel, place a jumper wire between the A and B terminal.

c. Remove the jumper wire.

d. Turn the ignition **OFF** for ten seconds.

e. Start the engine and check for proper idle operation.

2.8L and 3.1L V6 (VIN W, T)

CAUTION: *To reduce the risk of fire and personal injury, it is necessary to relieve the fuel system pressure before servicing any fuel system component. If this procedure is not performed, fuel may be sprayed out of the connection under pressure. Always keep a dry chemical (Class B) fire extinguisher near the work area.*

NOTE: *The throttle body assembly can be removed from the intake plenum and replaced as a unit, but most components can be replaced without removing the throttle body. If replacing the throttle body, an eight digit part number is stamped on the bottom of the casting next to the coolant cover. This number is required to ensure the proper part is replaced. Each system uses different calibrations even though the throttle body looks identical.*

1. **Fuel pressure relief procedures:**

a. Disconnect the negative (–) battery cable.

b. Loosen the fuel filler cap to relieve tank vapor pressure.

c. Connect a fuel pressure gauge J-34730-1 or equivalent to the fuel pressure relief connection at the fuel rail.

d. Wrap a shop towel around the fittings while connecting the gauge to prevent fuel spillage.

e. Install a bleed hose into an approved con-

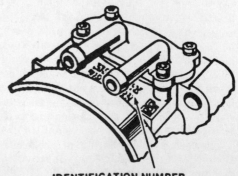

IDENTIFICATION NUMBER

Throttle body identification — MFI engines

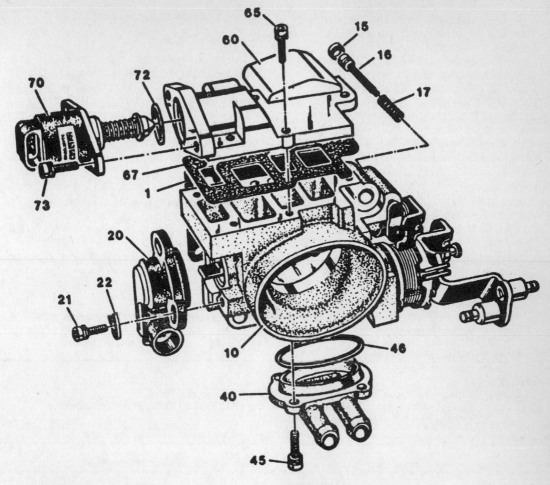

1. Flange gasket
10. Throttle body assembly
15. Idle stop screw plug
16. Idle stop screw assembly
17. Idle stop screw assembly spring
20. Throttle position sensor (TPS)
21. Screw
22. Retainer (adjustable TPS only)
40. Coolant cavity cover

45. Screw
46. Coolant cover O-ring
60. Idle air/vacuum signal housing
65. Screw
67. Gasket
70. Idle air control (IAC) valve
72. IAC O-ring
73. Screw

Throttle body — exploded view

tainer and open the valve to bleed the system pressure. The system is safe for servicing.

CAUTION: *When draining the coolant, keep in mind that cats and dogs are attracted by the ethylene glycol antifreeze, and are quite likely to drink any that is left in an uncovered container or in puddles on the ground. This will prove fatal in sufficient quantity. Always drain the coolant into a sealable container. Coolant should be reused unless it is contaminated or several years old.*

2. Partially drain the radiator to allow the coolant hoses at the throttle body to be removed.

3. Remove the air intake duct.

4. Disconnect the electrical connectors to the throttle body.

5. Note routing and remove the vacuum and coolant hoses.

6. Remove the throttle, transaxle and cruise control cables, if so equipped.

7. Remove the two throttle body retaining bolts and throttle body.

To install:

1. Clean all gasket surfaces with solvent and a gasket scraper.

2. Install the throttle body assembly with a new gasket and torque the retaining bolts to 18 ft. lbs. (25 Nm).

3. Install the throttle, transaxle and cruise control cables.

4. Connect the coolant and vacuum hoses to their original locations.

5. Refill the radiator with engine coolant.

6. Install the air intake duct and connect the negative battery cable.

NOTE: *Set the parking brake and block the wheels before starting the engine.*

7. Start the engine and shift the transaxle to the **DRIVE** position for automatic transxles and **NEUTRAL** position for manual transaxles.

8. Allow the engine to run for approximately seven minutes so the IAC valve pintle will return to its control position.

INJECTOR REPLACEMENT

2.3L QUAD 4, 2.8L and 3.1L V6

Use care in removing fuel injectors to prevent damage to the electrical connector pins on the injector and nozzle. The injector is serviced as a complete assembly only. Support the fuel rail to avoid damaging other components while removing the injector.

1. Disconnect the negative (–) battery cable.

2. Release the fuel system pressure as outlined in this chapter.

Step 1. If engine is at operating temperature, allow a 10 minute "cool down" period then connect fuel pressure gauge and injector tester.
1. Ignition "OFF".
2. Connect fuel pressure gauge and injector tester.
3. Ignition "ON".
4. Bleed off air in gauge. Repeat until all air is bled from gauge.

Step 2. Run test:
1. Ignition "OFF" for 10 seconds.
2. Ignition "ON". Record gauge pressure. (Pressure must hold steady, if not see the Fuel System diagnosis.
3. Turn injector on, by depressing button on injector tester, and note pressure at the instant the gauge needle stops.

Step 3.
1. Repeat step 2 on all injectors and record pressure drop on each. Retest injectors that appear faulty (Any injectors that have a 10 kPa difference, either more or less, in pressure from the average).

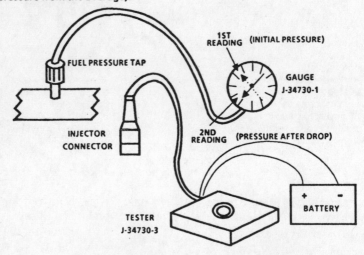

— EXAMPLE —

CYLINDER	1	2	3	4	5	6
1ST READING	225	225	225	225	225	225
2ND READING	100	100	100	90	100	115
AMOUNT OF DROP	125	125	125	135	125	110
	OK	OK	OK	FAULTY, RICH (TOO MUCH) (FUEL DROP)	OK	FAULTY, LEAN (TOO LITTLE) (FUEL DROP)

Fuel injector balance test — MFI

3. Remove the intake plenum assembly.

4. Remove the fuel rail assembly.

5. Remove the injector retaining clip and the injector.

To install:

NOTE: *Different fuel injectors are calibrated for different flow rates. The replacement injector may look the same but have different calibrations. When ordering replacement injectors, be sure identify the part number that is inscribed on the old injector.*

6. Remove the old O-rings from each end of the injector and install new O-rings to the injector.

7. Lubricate the new injector O-rings with engine oil and install the injector into the intake manifold.

8. Install new injector retaining clips with

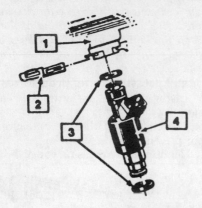

1. Fuel rail
2. Injector retainer clip
3. Injector O-ring seal
3. Injector assembly

Fuel injector — MFI

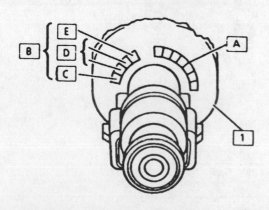

1. Fuel injector, top view
A. Part number
B. Build date
C. Month
D. Day
E. Year

MFI injector identification

the open end facing the injector electrical connection.

9. Install the injector into the fuel rail socket with the electrical connector facing outward. Push in far enough to engage the retaining clip with the machined slots of the rail socket.

10. Install the fuel rail assembly and temporarily connect the negative battery cable.

11. With the engine **OFF**, and the ignition **ON**, check for fuel leaks.

12. Disconnect the negative (–) battery cable.

13. Install the intake plenum and reconnect all wires, vacuum hoses and throttle cables to their original locations. Connect the negative battery cable.

NOTE: *Set the parking brake and block the wheels before starting the engine.*

14. Start the engine and shift the transaxle to the **DRIVE** position for automatic transaxles and **NEUTRAL** position for manual transaxles.

15. Allow the engine to run for approximately seven minutes so the IAC valve pintle will return to its control position.

Intake Manifold Plenum

REMOVAL AND INSTALLATION

2.3L QUAD 4 (VIN A, D)

Refer to the ''Intake Manifold'' section in Chapter 3.

2.8L and 3.1L V6 (VIN W, T)

The intake manifold plenum has to be removed to access the fuel rail and injectors.

1. Disconnect the negative (–) battery cable.

2. Remove and label the vacuum hoses.

3. Remove the EGR-to-plenum nuts.

4. Remove the two throttle body attaching bolts, throttle body and gasket.

5. Remove the throttle cable bracket, ignition wire shield, and plenum retaining bolts. Remove the intake plenum and gaskets.

NOTE: *Tap the edges of the plenum assembly with a rubber hammer to dislodge the gasket. Be careful not to damage the thin aluminum casting.*

To install:

1. Clean the gasket mating surfaces with solvent and a gasket scraper.

2. Install the intake plenum with new gaskets. Torque the plenum bolts to 16 ft. lbs. (21 Nm)

3. Install the ignition wire shield and throttle body. Torque the throttle body bolts to 18 ft. lbs. (25 Nm).

4. Install the EGR-to-plenum nuts, throttle cable bracket and vacuum hoses.

5. Install the negative (–) battery cable.

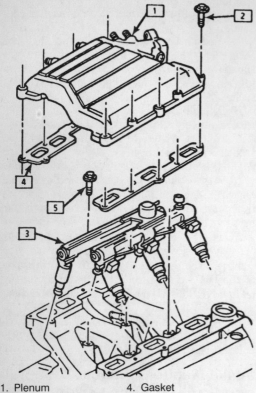

1. Plenum
2. Bolt
3. Fuel rail
4. Gasket
5. Bolt

Intake plenum removal — MFI

6. Set the parking brake and block the drive wheels. Start the engine and shift the transaxle into the **Drive** for automatic and **Neutral** for manual transaxles.

7. Allow the engine to run about seven minutes to return the IAC valve pintle to its control position.

Fuel Rail Assembly

REMOVAL AND INSTALLATION

2.3L QUAD 4 (VIN A, D)

NOTE: *An eight digit number is stamped on the side of the fuel rail. Refer to this number if servicing or parts replacement is required.*

1. Disconnect the negative (–) battery cable.

CAUTION: *To reduce the risk of fire and personal injury, it is necessary to relieve the fuel system pressure before servicing any fuel system component. If this procedure is not performed, fuel may be sprayed out of the connection under pressure. Always keep a dry chemical (Class B) fire extinguisher near the work area.*

2. **Fuel pressure relief procedures:**

a. Disconnect the negative (–) battery cable.

b. Loosen the fuel filler cap to relieve tank vapor pressure.

c. Connect a fuel pressure gauge J-34730-

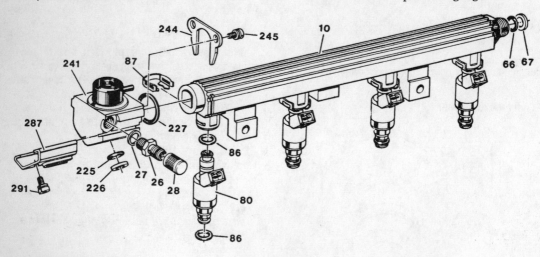

10. Fuel rail assembly
26. Fuel pressure connection
27. Fuel pressure connection seal
28. Fuel pressure connection cap
66. Fuel inlet tube seal
67. Seal retainer
80. Injector
86. O-ring injector seal
87. Injector retainer clip

225. Fuel return seal
226. Seal retainer
227. Seal
241. Pressure regulator assembly
244. Regulator retainer
245. Screw
287. Regulator retainer
291. Screw

Fuel rail assembly — 2.3L Quad 4

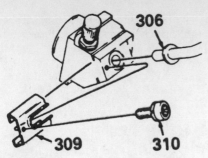

306. Fuel outlet pipe   310. Bolt–53 inch lbs.
309. Retainer

Fuel pipe removal – 2.3L Quad 4

1 or equivalent to the fuel pressure relief connection at the fuel rail.

d. Wrap a shop towel around the fittings while connecting the gauge to prevent fuel spillage.

e. Install a bleed hose into an approved container and open the valve to bleed the system pressure. The system is safe for servicing.

3. Remove the hoses at the front and side of the oil/air separator. Leave the vacuum hoses connected and remove the separator.

4. Remove the fuel pipe clamp bolt and pipe.

5. Disconnect the vacuum hose at pressure regulator.

6. Remove the fuel rail retaining bolts, lift the rail off of the cylinder head and disconnect the fuel injector electrical connectors.

7. Remove the fuel inlet pipe at the rail. Use a backup wrench on the fuel rail fitting to prevent damage to the rail.

8. Remove all fuel pipes and fuel rail assembly.

To install:

1. Apply a drop of engine oil and reconnect the fuel pipes-to-fuel rail. Torque the return pipe retainer screw to 53 inch lbs. and the inlet pipe to 22 ft. lbs. (30 Nm). Use a backup wrench on the fuel rail.

2. Position the fuel rail over the cylinder head and connect the injector connectors. Rotate the injectors to avoid stretching the wire harness.

3. Install the fuel rail and torque the retaining bolts to 19 ft. lbs. (26 Nm).

4. Connect the vacuum hoses and electrical connectors.

5. Install new fuel pipe O-rings and torque the front fitting to 20 ft. lbs. (27 Nm).

6. Install the fuel pipe clamp, oil/air separator and torque the separator bolts to 71 inch lbs. (8 Nm).

7. Tighten the fuel filler cap and connect

the negative battery cable.

8. Turn the ignition to the **ON** position for two seconds, then turn it to the **OFF** position for ten seconds, repeat step two and check for fuel leaks or odor. Repair if necessary before operating the vehicle.

2.8L and 3.1L V6 (VIN W, T)

The fuel rail assembly has an eight digit identification number stamped on the left side fuel rail. Refer to this number when servicing or parts replacement. The fuel rail is calibrated to the specific vehicle and replacement parts must have identical calibrations.

NOTE: *While servicing the fuel system for any reason, the system MUST be kept free of dirt and contamination. Fittings should be capped and hoses plugged. Replace any fuel system O-ring after the system has been opened.*

1. Disconnect the negative (–) battery cable.

2. Release the fuel system pressure as follows.

CAUTION: *To reduce the risk of fire and personal injury, it is necessary to relieve the fuel system pressure before servicing any fuel system component. If this procedure is not performed, fuel may be sprayed out of the connection under pressure. Always keep a dry chemical (Class B) fire extinguisher near the work area.*

a. Disconnect the negative (–) battery cable.

b. Loosen the fuel filler cap to relieve tank vapor pressure.

c. Connect a fuel pressure gauge J-34730-1 or equivalent to the fuel pressure relief connection at the fuel rail.

d. Wrap a shop towel around the fittings

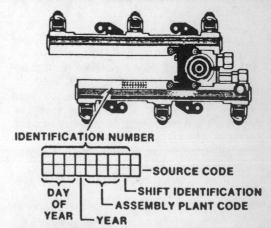

IDENTIFICATION NUMBER

DAY OF YEAR — SOURCE CODE, SHIFT IDENTIFICATION, ASSEMBLY PLANT CODE, YEAR

NOT ALL PRODUCTION INFORMATION MAY BE SHOWN

Fuel rail identification – MFI

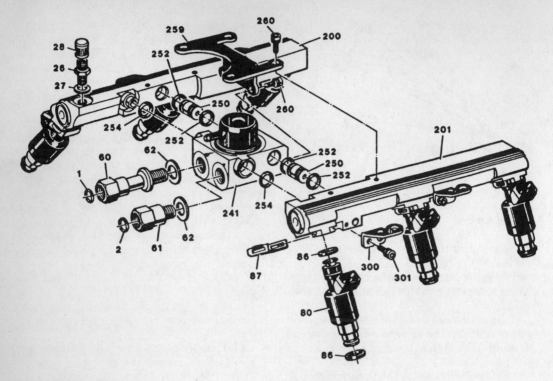

1. Fuel inlet line O-ring
2. Fuel return line O-ring 26. Fuel pressure connection assembly
27. Fuel pressure connection seal
28. Fuel pressure connection cap
60. Fuel inlet fitting
61. Fuel outlet fitting
62. Fuel fitting gasket
80. MPI Injector
86. Injector O-ring
87. Injector retainer clip

200. Left fuel rail
201. Right fuel rail
241. Pressure regulator assembly
250. Connector
252. Connector O-ring
254. Fuel return O-ring
259. Mounting bracket
260. Screw
300. Bracket
301. Screw

Fuel rail — exploded view

while connecting the gauge to prevent fuel spillage.

e. Install a bleed hose into an approved container and open the valve to bleed the system pressure. The system is safe for servicing.

3. Remove the intake manifold plenum assembly as previously outlined in this section.

4. Remove the fuel rail bracket bolts and fuel lines at the rail. Always use a backup wrench on the rail fittings to prevent turning. Remove the old O-rings.

5. Disconnect the vacuum hose from the fuel pressure regulator.

6. Remove the injector electrical connectors and fuel rail assembly.

WARNING: *Do NOT immerse any rubber or electrical components in cleaner or solvent.*

To install:

1. Clean the gasket mating surfaces with solvent and a gasket scraper.

2. Remove the old injector O-rings to re-

place with new ones.

3. Lubricate the new O-rings with engine oil.

4. Install the fuel rail assembly-to-manifold. Tilt the rail to install the injectors.

5. Torque the rail attaching bolts to 88 inch lbs. (10 Nm).

6. Connect the injector electrical connectors, vacuum hoses and install new O-rings to the fuel lines.

7. Install the fuel lines and torque the nuts to 17 ft. lbs. (23 Nm).

8. Temporarily connect the negative battery cable. With the engine **OFF** and the ignition key **ON** and check for fuel leaks.

9. Disconnect the negative (–) battery cable.

10. Install the intake manifold plenum and connect the negative battery cable.

11. Set the parking brake and block the drive wheels. Start the engine and shift the tran-

saxle into the **Drive** for automatic and **Neutral** for manual transaxles.

12. Allow the engine to run about seven minutes to return the IAC valve pintle to its control position.

Fuel Pressure Regulator

REMOVAL AND INSTALLATION

1. Disconnect the negative (–) battery cable. CAUTION: *To reduce the risk of fire and personal injury, it is necessary to relieve the fuel system pressure before servicing any fuel system component. If this procedure is not performed, fuel may be sprayed out of the connection under pressure. Always keep a dry chemical (Class B) fire extinguisher near the work area.*

2. **Fuel pressure relief procedures:**

a. Disconnect the negative (–) battery cable.

b. Loosen the fuel filler cap to relieve tank vapor pressure.

c. Connect a fuel pressure gauge J-34730-1 or equivalent to the fuel pressure relief connection at the fuel rail.

d. Wrap a shop towel around the fittings while connecting the gauge to prevent fuel spillage.

e. Install a bleed hose into an approved container and open the valve to bleed the system pressure. The system is safe for servicing.

3. Remove the intake plenum assembly as previously outlined in this chapter (V6 only).

4. Remove the fuel pressure regulator bracket attaching screws and mounting bracket.

5. Remove the right and left fuel rails with the fuel pressure regulator.

6. Remove the pressure regulator from the rails. Discard the old O-rings to replace with new. NEVER use old O-ring seals.

To install:

1. Lubricate the new O-rings with engine oil. Assembly the pressure regulator to the fuel rails with new O-rings. The fuel return O-ring is larger in diameter than the connector O-ring.

2. Install the rail connectors into the regulator base.

3. Install both rails to the regulator base (one rail for QUAD 4).

4. Install the pressure regulator bracket attaching screws and torque to 28 inch lbs. (3 Nm) (V6 only).

5. Install the fuel inlet and outlet. Torque both fittings to 30 ft. lbs. (40 Nm).

6. Temporarily connect the negative battery cable.

7. With the engine **OFF** and the ignition key **ON** and check for fuel leaks.

8. Disconnect the negative (–) battery cable.

9. Install the intake manifold plenum (V6) and connect the negative battery cable.

10. Set the parking brake and block the drive wheels. Start the engine and shift the transaxle into the **Drive** for automatic and **Neutral** for manual transaxles.

11. Allow the engine to run about seven minutes to return the IAC valve pintle to its control position.

Throttle Position Sensor (TPS)

The TPS is mounted on the side of the throttle body opposite the throttle lever assembly. The function of the TPS is to relay throttle valve position to the ECM (Electronic Control Module). The signal is needed to generate the proper injector controls (base pulse).

REMOVAL AND INSTALLATION

1. Disconnect the negative (–) battery cable.

2. Remove the electrical connector from the TP sensor.

3. Remove the two attaching screws and remove the sensor.

NOTE: *The throttle position sensor TPS is an electrical component and should not be immersed in any type of liquid solvent or cleaner.*

To install:

1. Position the TPS on the throttle body with the throttle valve normally closed. Install the sensor and rotate counter clockwise to align the mounting holes. Torque the two attaching screws to 18 inch lb. (2.0 Nm).

2. Connect the TPS electrical connector. Reconnect the negative (–) battery cable.

Idle Air Control (IAC) Valve

The Idle Air Control valve (IAC) is mounted on the throttle body assembly and provides a constant idle speed regardless of engine loads or driving conditions. The IAC valve controls the amount of air that enters the engine by the way of a ECM signal.

REMOVAL AND INSTALLATION

NOTE: *The IAC valve is flange mounted, with a dual taper and 10mm diameter pintle. If replacement is necessary, only an IAC valve with the correct part No. having the correct pintle shape and size may be used.*

1. Disconnect the negative (–) battery cable.

2. Remove the IAC valve electrical connector.

3. Remove the two attaching screws and the IAC valve.

WARNING: *Under no circumstances should the valve pintle be tampered with by hand,*

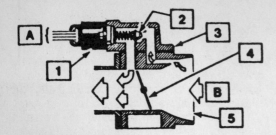

1. Valve assembly
2. Valve pintle
3. Idle air housing
4. Throttle valve
5. Throttle body assembly
A. Electrical input signal

Idle air control (IAC) valve — MFI

screwed or pushed in, or pulled out because damage may result. Do not soak the valve in any liquid cleaner or solvent, as damage may occur.

To install:

4. Lubricate the new O-ring seal with engine oil and install on the IAC valve.

5. Install the IAC valve to the throttle body.

6. Coat the two IAC valve attaching screws with thread locking compound and torque to 28 inch lb. (3.2 Nm).

7. Install the IAC electrical connector. Reconnect the negative (–) battery cable.

8. Start the engine and allow to reach operating temperature. Check the idle speed with a tachometer.

ADJUSTMENT

No adjustment of the IAC valve is required after installation. It will be reset by the ECM when the ignition is turned ON.

FUEL TANK

DRAINING

1. Disconnect the negative (–) battery cable. CAUTION: *To reduce the risk of fire and personal injury, always keep a dry chemical (Class B) fire extinguisher near the work area.*

2. Remove the fuel cap.

3. Raise the vehicle and support with jackstands.

4. Disconnect the filler vent hose from the tank.

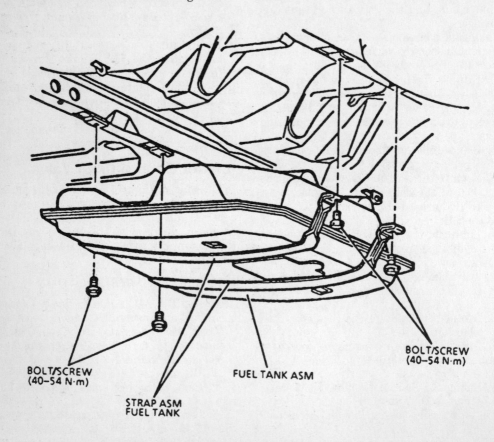

BOLT/SCREW
(40–54 N·m)

STRAP ASM
FUEL TANK

FUEL TANK ASM

BOLT/SCREW
(40–54 N·m)

Fuel tank and straps

CHILTON'S
FUEL ECONOMY
& TUNE-UP TIPS

55 WAYS TO IMPROVE FUEL ECONOMY

Tune-up • Spark Plug Diagnosis • Emission Controls

Fuel System • Cooling System • Tires and Wheels

General Maintenance

CHILTON'S FUEL ECONOMY & TUNE-UP TIPS

Fuel economy is important to everyone, no matter what kind of vehicle you drive. The maintenance-minded motorist can save both money and fuel using these tips and the periodic maintenance and tune-up procedures in this Repair and Tune-Up Guide.

There are more than 130,000,000 cars and trucks registered for private use in the United States. Each travels an average of 10-12,000 miles per year, and, and in total they consume close to 70 billion gallons of fuel each year. This represents nearly ⅔ of the oil imported by the United States each year. The Federal government's goal is to reduce consumption 10% by 1985. A variety of methods are either already in use or under serious consideration, and they all affect you driving and the cars you will drive. In addition to "down-sizing", the auto industry is using or investigating the use of electronic fuel delivery, electronic engine controls and alternative engines for use in smaller and lighter vehicles, among other alternatives to meet the federally mandated Corporate Average Fuel Economy (CAFE) of 27.5 mpg by 1985. The government, for its part, is considering rationing, mandatory driving curtailments and tax increases on motor vehicle fuel in an effort to reduce consumption. The government's goal of a 10% reduction could be realized — and further government regulation avoided — if every private vehicle could use just 1 less gallon of fuel per week.

How Much Can You Save?

Tests have proven that almost anyone can make at least a 10% reduction in fuel consumption through regular maintenance and tune-ups. When a major manufacturer of spark plugs sur-

TUNE-UP

1. Check the cylinder compression to be sure the engine will really benefit from a tune-up and that it is capable of producing good fuel economy. A tune-up will be wasted on an engine in poor mechanical condition.

2. Replace spark plugs regularly. New spark plugs alone can increase fuel economy 3%.

3. Be sure the spark plugs are the correct type (heat range) for your vehicle. See the Tune-Up Specifications.

Heat range refers to the spark plug's ability to conduct heat away from the firing end. It must conduct the heat away in an even pattern to avoid becoming a source of pre-ignition, yet it must also operate hot enough to burn off conductive deposits that could cause misfiring.

The heat range is usually indicated by a number on the spark plug, part of the manufacturer's designation for each individual spark plug. The numbers in bold-face indicate the heat range in each manufacturer's identification system.

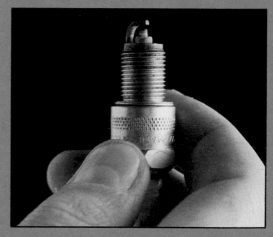

Periodically, check the spark plugs to be sure they are firing efficiently. They are excellent indicators of the internal condition of your engine.

On AC, Bosch (new), Champion, Fram/Autolite, Mopar, Motorcraft and Prestolite, a higher number indicates a hotter plug. On Bosch (old), NGK and Nippondenso, a higher number indicates a colder plug.

4. Make sure the spark plugs are properly gapped. See the Tune-Up Specifications in this book.

5. Be sure the spark plugs are firing efficiently. The illustrations on the next 2 pages show you how to "read" the firing end of the spark plug.

6. Check the ignition timing and set it to specifications. Tests show that almost all cars have incorrect ignition timing by more than 2°.

Manufacturer	Typical Designation
AC	R **45** TS
Bosch (old)	WA **145** T30
Bosch (new)	HR **8** Y
Champion	RBL **15** Y
Fram/Autolite	4**15**
Mopar	P-**62** PR
Motorcraft	BRF-**42**
NGK	BP **5** ES-15
Nippondenso	W **16** EP
Prestolite	14GR **5** 2A

veyed over 6,000 cars nationwide, they found that a tune-up, on cars that needed one, increased fuel economy over 11%. Replacing worn plugs alone, accounted for a 3% increase. The same test also revealed that 8 out of every 10 vehicles will have some maintenance deficiency that will directly affect fuel economy, emissions or performance. Most of this mileage-robbing neglect could be prevented with regular maintenance.

Modern engines require that all of the functioning systems operate properly for maximum efficiency. A malfunction anywhere wastes fuel. You can keep your vehicle running as efficiently and economically as possible, by being aware of your vehicle's operating and performance characteristics. If your vehicle suddenly develops performance or fuel economy problems it could be due to one or more of the following.

PROBLEM	POSSIBLE CAUSE
Engine Idles Rough	Ignition timing, idle mixture, vacuum leak or something amiss in the emission control system.
Hesitates on Acceleration	Dirty carburetor or fuel filter, improper accelerator pump setting, ignition timing or fouled spark plugs.
Starts Hard or Fails to Start	Worn spark plugs, improperly set automatic choke, ice (or water) in fuel system.
Stalls Frequently	Automatic choke improperly adjusted and possible dirty air filter or fuel filter.
Performs Sluggishly	Worn spark plugs, dirty fuel or air filter, ignition timing or automatic choke out of adjustment.

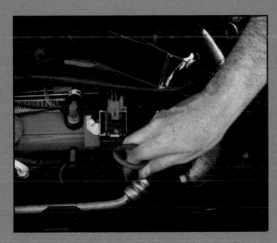

Check spark plug wires on conventional point type ignition for cracks by bending them in a loop around your finger.

Be sure that spark plug wires leading to adjacent cylinders do not run too close together. (Photo courtesy Champion Spark Plug Co.)

7. If your vehicle does not have electronic ignition, check the points, rotor and cap as specified.

8. Check the spark plug wires (used with conventional point-type ignitions) for cracks and burned or broken insulation by bending them in a loop around your finger. Cracked wires decrease fuel efficiency by failing to deliver full voltage to the spark plugs. One misfiring spark plug can cost you as much as 2 mpg.

9. Check the routing of the plug wires. Misfiring can be the result of spark plug leads to adjacent cylinders running parallel to each other and too close together. One wire tends to pick up voltage from the other causing it to fire "out of time".

10. Check all electrical and ignition circuits for voltage drop and resistance.

11. Check the distributor mechanical and/or vacuum advance mechanisms for proper functioning. The vacuum advance can be checked by twisting the distributor plate in the opposite direction of rotation. It should spring back when released.

12. Check and adjust the valve clearance on engines with mechanical lifters. The clearance should be slightly loose rather than too tight.

SPARK PLUG DIAGNOSIS

Normal

APPEARANCE: This plug is typical of one operating normally. The insulator nose varies from a light tan to grayish color with slight electrode wear. The presence of slight deposits is normal on used plugs and will have no adverse effect on engine performance. The spark plug heat range is correct for the engine and the engine is running normally.

CAUSE: Properly running engine.

RECOMMENDATION: Before reinstalling this plug, the electrodes should be cleaned and filed square. Set the gap to specifications. If the plug has been in service for more than 10-12,000 miles, the entire set should probably be replaced with a fresh set of the same heat range.

Oil Deposits

APPEARANCE: The firing end of the plug is covered with a wet, oily coating.

CAUSE: The problem is poor oil control. On high mileage engines, oil is leaking past the rings or valve guides into the combustion chamber. A common cause is also a plugged PCV valve, and a ruptured fuel pump diaphragm can also cause this condition. Oil fouled plugs such as these are often found in new or recently overhauled engines, before normal oil control is achieved, and can be cleaned and reinstalled.

RECOMMENDATION: A hotter spark plug may temporarily relieve the problem, but the engine is probably in need of work.

Incorrect Heat Range

APPEARANCE: The effects of high temperature on a spark plug are indicated by clean white, often blistered insulator. This can also be accompanied by excessive wear of the electrode, and the absence of deposits.

CAUSE: Check for the correct spark plug heat range. A plug which is too hot for the engine can result in overheating. A car operated mostly at high speeds can require a colder plug. Also check ignition timing, cooling system level, fuel mixture and leaking intake manifold.

RECOMMENDATION: If all ignition and engine adjustments are known to be correct, and no other malfunction exists, install spark plugs one heat range colder.

Photos Courtesy Fram Corporation

Carbon Deposits

APPEARANCE: Carbon fouling is easily identified by the presence of dry, soft, black, sooty deposits.

CAUSE: Changing the heat range can often lead to carbon fouling, as can prolonged slow, stop-and-start driving. If the heat range is correct, carbon fouling can be attributed to a rich fuel mixture, sticking choke, clogged air cleaner, worn breaker points, retarded timing or low compression. If only one or two plugs are carbon fouled, check for corroded or cracked wires on the affected plugs. Also look for cracks in the distributor cap between the towers of affected cylinders.

RECOMMENDATION: After the problem is corrected, these plugs can be cleaned and reinstalled if not worn severely.

MMT Fouled

APPEARANCE: Spark plugs fouled by MMT (Methycyclopentadienyl Maganese Tricarbonyl) have reddish, rusty appearance on the insulator and side electrode.

CAUSE: MMT is an anti-knock additive in gasoline used to replace lead. During the combustion process, the MMT leaves a reddish deposit on the insulator and side electrode.

RECOMMENDATION: No engine malfunction is indicated and the deposits will not affect plug performance any more than lead deposits (see Ash Deposits). MMT fouled plugs can be cleaned, regapped and reinstalled.

High Speed Glazing

APPEARANCE: Glazing appears as shiny coating on the plug, either yellow or tan in color.

CAUSE: During hard, fast acceleration, plug temperatures rise suddenly. Deposits from normal combustion have no chance to fluff-off; instead, they melt on the insulator forming an electrically conductive coating which causes misfiring.

RECOMMENDATION: Glazed plugs are not easily cleaned. They should be replaced with a fresh set of plugs of the correct heat range. If the condition recurs, using plugs with a heat range one step colder may cure the problem.

Ash (Lead) Deposits

APPEARANCE: Ash deposits are characterized by light brown or white colored deposits crusted on the side or center electrodes. In some cases it may give the plug a rusty appearance.

CAUSE: Ash deposits are normally derived from oil or fuel additives burned during normal combustion. Normally they are harmless, though excessive amounts can cause misfiring. If deposits are excessive in short mileage, the valve guides may be worn.

RECOMMENDATION: Ash-fouled plugs can be cleaned, gapped and reinstalled.

Detonation

APPEARANCE: Detonation is usually characterized by a broken plug insulator.

CAUSE: A portion of the fuel charge will begin to burn spontaneously, from the increased heat following ignition. The explosion that results applies extreme pressure to engine components, frequently damaging spark plugs and pistons.

Detonation can result by over-advanced ignition timing, inferior gasoline (low octane) lean air/fuel mixture, poor carburetion, engine lugging or an increase in compression ratio due to combustion chamber deposits or engine modification.

RECOMMENDATION: Replace the plugs after correcting the problem.

Photos Courtesy Champion Spark Plug Co.

EMISSION CONTROLS

13. Be aware of the general condition of the emission control system. It contributes to reduced pollution and should be serviced regularly to maintain efficient engine operation.

14. Check all vacuum lines for dried, cracked or brittle conditions. Something as simple as a leaking vacuum hose can cause poor performance and loss of economy.

15. Avoid tampering with the emission control system. Attempting to improve fuel econ-

FUEL SYSTEM

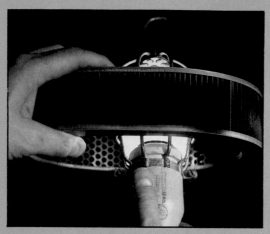

Check the air filter with a light behind it. If you can see light through the filter it can be reused.

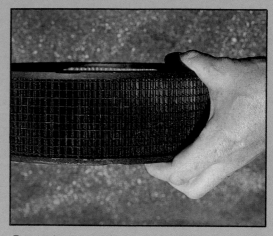

Extremely clogged filters should be discarded and replaced with a new one.

18. Replace the air filter regularly. A dirty air filter richens the air/fuel mixture and can increase fuel consumption as much as 10%. Tests show that ⅓ of all vehicles have air filters in need of replacement.

19. Replace the fuel filter at least as often as recommended.

20. Set the idle speed and carburetor mixture to specifications.

21. Check the automatic choke. A sticking or malfunctioning choke wastes gas.

22. During the summer months, adjust the automatic choke for a leaner mixture which will produce faster engine warm-ups.

COOLING SYSTEM

29. Be sure all accessory drive belts are in good condition. Check for cracks or wear.

30. Adjust all accessory drive belts to proper tension.

31. Check all hoses for swollen areas, worn spots, or loose clamps.

32. Check coolant level in the radiator or expansion tank.

33. Be sure the thermostat is operating properly. A stuck thermostat delays engine warm-up and a cold engine uses nearly twice as much fuel as a warm engine.

34. Drain and replace the engine coolant at least as often as recommended. Rust and scale

TIRES & WHEELS

38. Check the tire pressure often with a pencil type gauge. Tests by a major tire manufacturer show that 90% of all vehicles have at least 1 tire improperly inflated. Better mileage can be achieved by over-inflating tires, but never exceed the maximum inflation pressure on the side of the tire.

39. If possible, install radial tires. Radial tires deliver as much as ½ mpg more than bias belted tires.

40. Avoid installing super-wide tires. They only create extra rolling resistance and decrease fuel mileage. Stick to the manufacturer's recommendations.

41. Have the wheels properly balanced.

omy by tampering with emission controls is more likely to worsen fuel economy than improve it. Emission control changes on modern engines are not readily reversible.

16. Clean (or replace) the EGR valve and lines as recommended.

17. Be sure that all vacuum lines and hoses are reconnected properly after working under the hood. An unconnected or misrouted vacuum line can wreak havoc with engine performance.

23. Check for fuel leaks at the carburetor, fuel pump, fuel lines and fuel tank. Be sure all lines and connections are tight.

24. Periodically check the tightness of the carburetor and intake manifold attaching nuts and bolts. These are a common place for vacuum leaks to occur.

25. Clean the carburetor periodically and lubricate the linkage.

26. The condition of the tailpipe can be an excellent indicator of proper engine combustion. After a long drive at highway speeds, the inside of the tailpipe should be a light grey in color. Black or soot on the insides indicates an overly rich mixture.

27. Check the fuel pump pressure. The fuel pump may be supplying more fuel than the engine needs.

28. Use the proper grade of gasoline for your engine. Don't try to compensate for knocking or "pinging" by advancing the ignition timing. This practice will only increase plug temperature and the chances of detonation or pre-ignition with relatively little performance gain.

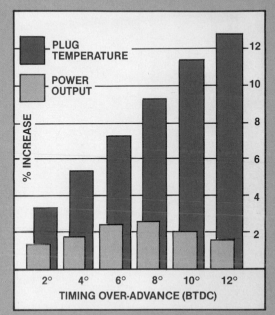

Increasing ignition timing past the specified setting results in a drastic increase in spark plug temperature with increased chance of detonation or preignition. Performance increase is considerably less. (Photo courtesy Champion Spark Plug Co.)

that form in the engine should be flushed out to allow the engine to operate at peak efficiency.

35. Clean the radiator of debris that can decrease cooling efficiency.

36. Install a flex-type or electric cooling fan, if you don't have a clutch type fan. Flex fans use curved plastic blades to push more air at low speeds when more cooling is needed; at high speeds the blades flatten out for less resistance. Electric fans only run when the engine temperature reaches a predetermined level.

37. Check the radiator cap for a worn or cracked gasket. If the cap does not seal properly, the cooling system will not function properly.

42. Be sure the front end is correctly aligned. A misaligned front end actually has wheels going in differed directions. The increased drag can reduce fuel economy by .3 mpg.

43. Correctly adjust the wheel bearings. Wheel bearings that are adjusted too tight increase rolling resistance.

Check tire pressures regularly with a reliable pocket type gauge. Be sure to check the pressure on a cold tire.

GENERAL MAINTENANCE

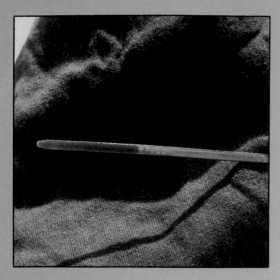

Check the fluid levels (particularly engine oil) on a regular basis. Be sure to check the oil for grit, water or other contamination.

A vacuum gauge is another excellent indicator of internal engine condition and can also be installed in the dash as a mileage indicator.

44. Periodically check the fluid levels in the engine, power steering pump, master cylinder, automatic transmission and drive axle.

45. Change the oil at the recommended interval and change the filter at every oil change. Dirty oil is thick and causes extra friction between moving parts, cutting efficiency and increasing wear. A worn engine requires more frequent tune-ups and gets progressively worse fuel economy. In general, use the lightest viscosity oil for the driving conditions you will encounter.

46. Use the recommended viscosity fluids in the transmission and axle.

47. Be sure the battery is fully charged for fast starts. A slow starting engine wastes fuel.

48. Be sure battery terminals are clean and tight.

49. Check the battery electrolyte level and add distilled water if necessary.

50. Check the exhaust system for crushed pipes, blockages and leaks.

51. Adjust the brakes. Dragging brakes or brakes that are not releasing create increased drag on the engine.

52. Install a vacuum gauge or miles-per-gallon gauge. These gauges visually indicate engine vacuum in the intake manifold. High vacuum = good mileage and low vacuum = poorer mileage. The gauge can also be an excellent indicator of internal engine conditions.

53. Be sure the clutch is properly adjusted. A slipping clutch wastes fuel.

54. Check and periodically lubricate the heat control valve in the exhaust manifold. A sticking or inoperative valve prevents engine warm-up and wastes gas.

55. Keep accurate records to check fuel economy over a period of time. A sudden drop in fuel economy may signal a need for tune-up or other maintenance.

5. Use a hand operated pump approved for gasoline to drain as much fuel as possible through the filler vent hose.

6. Reconnect the filler vent hose and tighten the clamp.

7. Install any removed lines, hoses and cap. Connect the negative battery cable.

REMOVAL AND INSTALLATION

1. Disconnect the negative (–) battery cable.

2. Drain the fuel tank.

3. Remove the fuel filler door assembly and disconnect the screw retaining the filler pipe-to-body bracket.

4. Raise the vehicle and support with jackstands.

5. Disconnect the tank level sender lead connector.

6. Support the tank with a transmission jack or equivalent. Remove the two tank retaining straps.

7. Lower the tank far enough to disconnect the ground lead and fuel hoses from the pump assembly.

8. Remove the tank from the vehicle slowly to ensure all connections and hoses have been disconnected.

9. Remove the fuel pump/level sender assembly using a locking cam tool J-24187 or equivalent.

To install:

1. Using a new fuel pump O-ring gasket, install the pump/sender assembly into the tank.

NOTE: *Do not twist the strainer when installing the pump/sender assembly. Make sure*

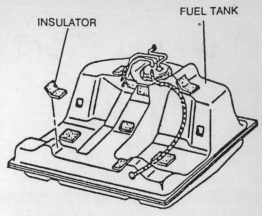

Fuel tank Insulator location

the strainer does not block the full travel of the float arm.

2. Place the tank on the jack.

3. Position the tank sound insulators in their original positions and raise the tank far enough to connect the electrical and hose connectors.

4. Raise the tank to the proper position and loosely install the retaining straps. Make sure the tank is in the proper position before tightening the retaining straps.

5. Torque the retaining straps to 26 ft. lbs. (35 Nm).

6. Connect the grounding strap and negative battery cable.

7. With the engine **OFF**, turn the ignition key to the **ON** position and check for fuel leaks at the tank.

Chassis Electrical

6

UNDERSTANDING AND TROUBLESHOOTING ELECTRICAL SYSTEMS

At the rate which both import and domestic manufacturers are incorporating electronic control systems into their production lines, it won't be long before every new vehicle is equipped with one or more on-board computer. These electronic components (with no moving parts) should theoretically last the life of the vehicle, provided nothing external happens to damage the circuits or memory chips.

While it is true that electronic components should never wear out, in the real world malfunctions do occur. It is also true that any computer-based system is extremely sensitive to electrical voltages and cannot tolerate careless or haphazard testing or service procedures. An inexperienced individual can literally do major damage looking for a minor problem by using the wrong kind of test equipment or connecting test leads or connectors with the ignition switch ON. When selecting test equipment, make sure the manufacturers instructions state that the tester is compatible with whatever type of electronic control system is being serviced. Read all instructions carefully and double check all test points before installing probes or making any test connections.

The following section outlines basic diagnosis techniques for dealing with computerized automotive control systems. Along with a general explanation of the various types of test equipment available to aid in servicing modern electronic automotive systems, basic repair techniques for wiring harnesses and connectors is given. Read the basic information before attempting any repairs or testing on any computerized system, to provide the background of information necessary to avoid the most common

and obvious mistakes that can cost both time and money. Although the replacement and testing procedures are simple in themselves, the systems are not, and unless one has a thorough understanding of all components and their function within a particular computerized control system, the logical test sequence these systems demand cannot be followed. Minor malfunctions can make a big difference, so it is important to know how each component affects the operation of the overall electronic system to find the ultimate cause of a problem without replacing good components unnecessarily. It is not enough to use the correct test equipment; the test equipment must be used correctly.

Safety Precautions

CAUTION: *Whenever working on or around any computer based microprocessor control system, always observe these general precautions to prevent the possibility of personal injury or damage to electronic components.*

• Never install or remove battery cables with the key **ON** or the engine running. Jumper cables should be connected with the key **OFF** to avoid power surges that can damage electronic control units. Engines equipped with computer controlled systems should avoid both giving and getting jump starts due to the possibility of serious damage to components from arcing in the engine compartment when connections are made with the ignition **ON**.

• Always remove the battery cables before charging the battery. Never use a high output charger on an installed battery or attempt to use any type of "hot shot" (24 volt) starting aid.

• Exercise care when inserting test probes into connectors to insure good connections without damaging the connector or spreading the pins. Always probe connectors from the rear (wire) side, NOT the pin side, to avoid accidental shorting of terminals during test procedures.

• Never remove or attach wiring harness connectors with the ignition switch **ON**, especially to an electronic control unit.

• Do not drop any components during service procedures and never apply 12 volts directly to any component (like a solenoid or relay) unless instructed specifically to do so. Some component electrical windings are designed to safely handle only 4 or 5 volts and can be destroyed in seconds if 12 volts are applied directly to the connector.

• Remove the electronic control unit if the vehicle is to be placed in an environment where temperatures exceed approximately 176°F (80°C), such as a paint spray booth or when arc or gas welding near the control unit location in the car.

• Disconnect the negative battery cable when are welding any part of the vehicle. The sudden surges of current may damage the electronic components.

ORGANIZED TROUBLESHOOTING

When diagnosing a specific problem, organized troubleshooting is a must. The complexity of a modern automobile demands that you approach any problem in a logical, organized manner. There are certain troubleshooting techniques that are standard:

1. Always check the fuses first. Establish when the problem occurs. Does the problem appear only under certain conditions? Were there any noises, odors, or other unusual symptoms?

2. Isolate the problem area. To do this, make some simple tests and observations; then eliminate the systems that are working properly. Check for obvious problems such as broken wires, dirty connections or split or disconnected vacuum hoses. Always check the obvious before assuming something complicated is the cause.

3. Test for problems systematically to determine the cause once the problem area is isolated. Are all the components functioning properly? Is there power going to electrical switches and motors? Is there vacuum at vacuum switches and/or actuators? Is there a mechanical problem such as bent linkage or loose mounting screws? Doing careful, systematic checks will often turn up most causes on the first inspection without wasting time checking components that have little or no relationship to the problem.

4. Test all repairs after the work is done to make sure that the problem is fixed. Some causes can be traced to more than one component, so a careful verification of repair work is important to pick up additional malfunctions that may cause a problem to reappear or a different problem to arise. A blown fuse, for example, is a simple problem that may require more than another fuse to repair. If you don't look for a problem that caused a fuse to blow, for example, a shorted wire may go undetected.

Experience has shown that most problems tend to be the result of a fairly simple and obvious cause, such as loose or corroded connectors or air leaks in the intake system; making careful inspection of components during testing essential to quick and accurate troubleshooting. Special, hand held computerized testers designed specifically for diagnosing the system are available from a variety of aftermarket sources, as well as from the vehicle manufacturer, but care should be taken that any test equipment being used is designed to diagnose that particular computer controlled system accurately without damaging the control unit (ECU) or components being tested.

NOTE: *Pinpointing the exact cause of trouble in an electrical system can sometimes only be accomplished by the use of special test equipment. The following describes commonly used test equipment and explains how to put it to best use in diagnosis. In addition to the information covered below, the manufacturer's instructions booklet provided with the tester should be read and clearly understood before attempting any test procedures.*

TEST EQUIPMENT

Jumper Wires

Jumper wires are simple, yet extremely valuable, pieces of test equipment. Jumper wires are merely wires that are used to bypass sections of a circuit. The simplest type of jumper wire is merely a length of multistrand wire with an alligator clip at each end. Jumper wires are usually fabricated from lengths of standard automotive wire and whatever type of connector (alligator clip, spade connector or pin connector) that is required for the particular vehicle being tested. The well equipped tool box will have several different styles of jumper wires in several different lengths. Some jumper wires are made with three or more terminals coming from a common splice for special purpose testing. In cramped, hard-to-reach areas it is advisable to have insulated boots over the jumper wire terminals in order to prevent accidental grounding, sparks, and possible fire, especially when testing fuel system components.

Jumper wires are used primarily to locate open electrical circuits, on either the ground (–) side of the circuit or on the hot (+) side. If an electrical component fails to operate, connect the jumper wire between the component and a good ground. If the component operates only with the jumper installed, the ground circuit is open. If the ground circuit is good, but the component does not operate, the circuit between the power feed and component is open. You can sometimes connect the jumper wire directly from the battery to the hot terminal of the component, but first make sure the component uses 12 volts in operation. Some electrical components, such as fuel injectors, are designed to operate on about 4 volts and running 12 volts directly to the injector terminals can burn out the wiring. By inserting an inline fuseholder between a set of test leads, a fused jumper wire can be used for bypassing open circuits. Use a 5 amp fuse to provide protection against voltage spikes. When in doubt, use a voltmeter to check the voltage input to the component and measure how much voltage is being applied normally. By moving the jumper wire successively back from the lamp toward the power source, you can isolate the area of the circuit where the open is located. When the component stops functioning, or the power is cut off, the open is in the segment of wire between the jumper and the point previously tested.

Never use jumpers made from wire that is of lighter gauge than used in the circuit under test. If the jumper wire is of too small gauge, it may overheat and possibly melt. Never use jumpers to bypass high resistance loads (such as motors) in a circuit. Bypassing resistances, in effect, creates a short circuit which may, in turn, cause damage and fire. Never use a jumper for anything other than temporary bypassing of components in a circuit.

12 Volt Test Light

The 12 volt test light is used to check circuits and components while electrical current is flowing through them. It is used for voltage and ground tests. Twelve volt test lights come in different styles but all have three main parts; a ground clip, a probe, and a light. The most commonly used 12 volt test lights have pick-type probes. To use a 12 volt test light, connect the ground clip to a good ground and probe wherever necessary with the pick. The pick should be sharp so that it can penetrate wire insulation to make contact with the wire, without making a large hole in the insulation. The wrap-around light is handy in hard to reach areas or where it is difficult to support a wire to push a probe pick into it. To use the wrap around light, hook the wire to probed with the hook and pull the trigger. A small pick will be forced through the wire insulation into the wire core.

Do not use a test light to probe electronic ig-nition spark plug or coil wires. Never use a pick-type test light to probe wiring on computer controlled systems unless specifically instructed to do so. Any wire insulation that is pierced by the test light probe should be taped and sealed with silicone after testing.

Like the jumper wire, the 12 volt test light is used to isolate opens in circuits. But, whereas the jumper wire is used to bypass the open to operate the load, the 12 volt test light is used to locate the presence of voltage in a circuit. If the test light glows, you know that there is power up to that point; if the 12 volt test light does not glow when its probe is inserted into the wire or connector, you know that there is an open circuit (no power). Move the test light in successive steps back toward the power source until the light in the handle does glow. When it does glow, the open is between the probe and point previously probed.

NOTE: *The test light does not detect that 12 volts (or any particular amount of voltage) is present; it only detects that some voltage is present. It is advisable before using the test light to touch its terminals across the battery posts to make sure the light is operating properly.*

Self-Powered Test Light

The self-powered test light usually contains a 1.5 volt penlight battery. One type of self-powered test light is similar in design to the 12 volt test light. This type has both the battery and the light in the handle and pick-type probe tip. The second type has the light toward the open tip, so that the light illuminates the contact point. The self-powered test light is dual purpose piece of test equipment. It can be used to test for either open or short circuits when power is isolated from the circuit (continuity test). A powered test light should not be used on any computer controlled system or component unless specifically instructed to do so. Many engine sensors can be destroyed by even this small amount of voltage applied directly to the terminals.

Open Circuit Testing

To use the self-powered test light to check for open circuits, first isolate the circuit from the vehicle's 12 volt power source by disconnecting the battery or wiring harness connector. Connect the test light ground clip to a good ground and probe sections of the circuit sequentially with the test light. (start from either end of the circuit). If the light is out, the open is between the probe and the circuit ground. If the light is on, the open is between the probe and end of the circuit toward the power source.

Short Circuit Testing

By isolating the circuit both from power and from ground, and using a self-powered test light, you can check for shorts to ground in the circuit. Isolate the circuit from power and ground. Connect the test light ground clip to a good ground and probe any easy-to-reach test point in the circuit. If the light comes on, there is a short somewhere in the circuit. To isolate the short, probe a test point at either end of the isolated circuit (the light should be on). Leave the test light probe connected and open connectors, switches, remove parts, etc., sequentially, until the light goes out. When the light goes out, the short is between the last circuit component opened and the previous circuit opened.

NOTE: *The 1.5 volt battery in the test light does not provide much current. A weak battery may not provide enough power to illuminate the test light even when a complete circuit is made (especially if there are high resistances in the circuit). Always make sure that the test battery is strong. To check the battery, briefly touch the ground clip to the probe; if the light glows brightly the battery is strong enough for testing. Never use a self-powered test light to perform checks for opens or shorts when power is applied to the electrical system under test. The 12 volt vehicle power will quickly burn out the 1.5 volt light bulb in the test light.*

Voltmeter

A voltmeter is used to measure voltage at any point in a circuit, or to measure the voltage drop across any part of a circuit. It can also be used to check continuity in a wire or circuit by indicating current flow from one end to the other. Voltmeters usually have various scales on the meter dial and a selector switch to allow the selection of different voltages. The voltmeter has a positive and a negative lead. To avoid damage to the meter, always connect the negative lead to the negative (–) side of circuit (to ground or nearest the ground side of the circuit) and connect the positive lead to the positive (+) side of the circuit (to the power source or the nearest power source). Note that the negative voltmeter lead will always be black and that the positive voltmeter will always be some color other than black (usually red). Depending on how the voltmeter is connected into the circuit, it has several uses.

A voltmeter can be connected either in parallel or in series with a circuit and it has a very high resistance to current flow. When connected in parallel, only a small amount of current will flow through the voltmeter current path; the rest will flow through the normal circuit current path and the circuit will work normally. When the voltmeter is connected in series with a circuit, only a small amount of current can flow through the circuit. The circuit will not work properly, but the voltmeter reading will show if the circuit is complete or not.

Available Voltage Measurement

Set the voltmeter selector switch to the 20V position and connect the meter negative lead to the negative post of the battery. Connect the positive meter lead to the positive post of the battery and turn the ignition switch ON to provide a load. Read the voltage on the meter or digital display. A well charged battery should register over 12 volts. If the meter reads below 11.5 volts, the battery power may be insufficient to operate the electrical system properly. This test determines voltage available from the battery and should be the first step in any electrical trouble diagnosis procedure. Many electrical problems, especially on computer controlled systems, can be caused by a low state of charge in the battery. Excessive corrosion at the battery cable terminals can cause a poor contact that will prevent proper charging and full battery current flow.

Normal battery voltage is 12 volts when fully charged. When the battery is supplying current to one or more circuits it is said to be "under load". When everything is off the electrical system is under a "no-load" condition. A fully charged battery may show about 12.5 volts at no load; will drop to 12 volts under medium load; and will drop even lower under heavy load. If the battery is partially discharged the voltage decrease under heavy load may be excessive, even though the battery shows 12 volts or more at no load. When allowed to discharge further, the battery's available voltage under load will decrease more severely. For this reason, it is important that the battery be fully charged during all testing procedures to avoid errors in diagnosis and incorrect test results.

Voltage Drop

When current flows through a resistance, the voltage beyond the resistance is reduced (the larger the current, the greater the reduction in voltage). When no current is flowing, there is no voltage drop because there is no current flow. All points in the circuit which are connected to the power source are at the same voltage as the power source. The total voltage drop always equals the total source voltage. In a long circuit with many connectors, a series of small, unwanted voltage drops due to corrosion at the connectors can add up to a total loss of voltage which impairs the operation of the normal loads in the circuit.

INDIRECT COMPUTATION OF VOLTAGE DROPS

1. Set the voltmeter selector switch to the 20 volt position.
2. Connect the meter negative lead to a good ground.
3. Probe all resistances in the circuit with the positive meter lead.
4. Operate the circuit in all modes and observe the voltage readings.

DIRECT MEASUREMENT OF VOLTAGE DROPS

1. Set the voltmeter switch to the 20 volt position.
2. Connect the voltmeter negative lead to the ground side of the resistance load to be measured.
3. Connect the positive lead to the positive side of the resistance or load to be measured.
4. Read the voltage drop directly on the 20 volt scale.

Too high a voltage indicates too high a resistance. If, for example, a blower motor runs too slowly, you can determine if there is too high a resistance in the resistor pack. By taking voltage drop readings in all parts of the circuit, you can isolate the problem. Too low a voltage drop indicates too low a resistance. If, for example, a blower motor runs too fast in the MED and/or LOW position, the problem can be isolated in the resistor pack by taking voltage drop readings in all parts of the circuit to locate a possibly shorted resistor. The maximum allowable voltage drop under load is critical, especially if there is more than one high resistance problem in a circuit because all voltage drops are cumulative. A small drop is normal due to the resistance of the conductors.

HIGH RESISTANCE TESTING

1. Set the voltmeter selector switch to the 4 volt position.
2. Connect the voltmeter positive lead to the positive post of the battery.
3. Turn on the headlights and heater blower to provide a load.
4. Probe various points in the circuit with the negative voltmeter lead.
5. Read the voltage drop on the 4 volt scale. Some average maximum allowable voltage drops are:

FUSE PANEL — 7 volts
IGNITION SWITCH — 5 volts
HEADLIGHT SWITCH — 7 volts
IGNITION COIL (+) — 5 volts
ANY OTHER LOAD — 1.3 volts

NOTE: *Voltage drops are all measured while a load is operating; without current flow, there will be no voltage drop.*

Ohmmeter

The ohmmeter is designed to read resistance (ohms) in a circuit or component. Although there are several different styles of ohmmeters, all will usually have a selector switch which permits the measurement of different ranges of resistance (usually the selector switch allows the multiplication of the meter reading by 10, 100, 1000 and 10,000). A calibration knob allows the meter to be set at zero for accurate measurement. Since all ohmmeters are powered by an internal battery (usually 9 volts), the ohmmeter can be used as a self-powered test light. When the ohmmeter is connected, current from the ohmmeter flows through the circuit or component being tested. Since the ohmmeter's internal resistance and voltage are known values, the amount of current flow through the meter depends on the resistance of the circuit or component being tested.

The ohmmeter can be used to perform continuity test for opens or shorts (either by observation of the meter needle or as a self-powered test light), and to read actual resistance in a circuit. It should be noted that the ohmmeter is used to check the resistance of a component or wire while there is no voltage applied to the circuit. Current flow from an outside voltage source (such as the vehicle battery) can damage the ohmmeter, so the circuit or component should be isolated from the vehicle electrical system before any testing is done. Since the ohmmeter uses its own voltage source, either lead can be connected to any test point.

NOTE: *When checking diodes or other solid state components, the ohmmeter leads can only be connected one way in order to measure current flow in a single direction. Make sure the positive (+) and negative (–) terminal connections are as described in the test procedures to verify the one-way diode operation.*

In using the meter for making continuity checks, do not be concerned with the actual resistance readings. Zero resistance, or any resistance readings, indicate continuity in the circuit. Infinite resistance indicates an open in the circuit. A high resistance reading where there should be none indicates a problem in the circuit. Checks for short circuits are made in the same manner as checks for open circuits except that the circuit must be isolated from both power and normal ground. Infinite resistance indicates no continuity to ground, while zero resistance indicates a dead short to ground.

RESISTANCE MEASUREMENT

The batteries in an ohmmeter will weaken with age and temperature, so the ohmmeter must be calibrated or "zeroed" before taking measurements. To zero the meter, place the selector switch in its lowest range and touch the two ohmmeter leads together. Turn the calibration knob until the meter needle is exactly on zero.

NOTE: *All analog (needle) type ohmmeters must be zeroed before use, but some digital ohmmeter models are automatically calibrated when the switch is turned on. Self-calibrating digital ohmmeters do not have an adjusting knob, but its a good idea to check for a zero readout before use by touching the leads together. All computer controlled systems require the use of a digital ohmmeter with at least 10 meagohms impedance for testing. Before any test procedures are attempted, make sure the ohmmeter used is compatible with the electrical system or damage to the on-board computer could result.*

To measure resistance, first isolate the circuit from the vehicle power source by disconnecting the battery cables or the harness connector. Make sure the key is OFF when disconnecting any components or the battery. Where necessary, also isolate at least one side of the circuit to be checked to avoid reading parallel resistances. Parallel circuit resistances will always give a lower reading than the actual resistance of either of the branches. When measuring the resistance of parallel circuits, the total resistance will always be lower than the smallest resistance in the circuit. Connect the meter leads to both sides of the circuit (wire or component) and read the actual measured ohms on the meter scale. Make sure the selector switch is set to the proper ohm scale for the circuit being tested to avoid misreading the ohmmeter test value.

WARNING: *Never use an ohmmeter with power applied to the circuit. Like the self-powered test light, the ohmmeter is designed to operate on its own power supply. The normal 12 volt automotive electrical system current could damage the meter!*

Ammeters

An ammeter measures the amount of current flowing through a circuit in units called amperes or amps. Amperes are units of electron flow which indicate how fast the electrons are flowing through the circuit. Since Ohms Law dictates that current flow in a circuit is equal to the circuit voltage divided by the total circuit resistance, increasing voltage also increases the current level (amps). Likewise, any decrease in resistance will increase the amount of amps in a circuit. At normal operating voltage, most circuits have a characteristic amount of amperes, called "current draw" which can be measured using an ammeter. By referring to a specified current draw rating, measuring the amperes, and comparing the two values, one can determine what is happening within the circuit to aid in diagnosis. An open circuit, for example, will not allow any current to flow so the ammeter reading will be zero. More current flows through a heavily loaded circuit or when the charging system is operating.

An ammeter is always connected in series with the circuit being tested. All of the current that normally flows through the circuit must also flow through the ammeter; if there is any other path for the current to follow, the ammeter reading will not be accurate. The ammeter itself has very little resistance to current flow and therefore will not affect the circuit, but it will measure current draw only when the circuit is closed and electricity is flowing. Excessive current draw can blow fuses and drain the battery, while a reduced current draw can cause motors to run slowly, lights to dim and other components to not operate properly. The ammeter can help diagnose these conditions by locating the cause of the high or low reading.

Multimeters

Different combinations of test meters can be built into a single unit designed for specific tests. Some of the more common combination test devices are known as Volt/Amp testers, Tach/Dwell meters, or Digital Multimeters. The Volt/Amp tester is used for charging system, starting system or battery tests and consists of a voltmeter, an ammeter and a variable resistance carbon pile. The voltmeter will usually have at least two ranges for use with 6, 12 and 24 volt systems. The ammeter also has more than one range for testing various levels of battery loads and starter current draw and the carbon pile can be adjusted to offer different amounts of resistance. The Volt/Amp tester has heavy leads to carry large amounts of current and many later models have an inductive ammeter pickup that clamps around the wire to simplify test connections. On some models, the ammeter also has a zero-center scale to allow testing of charging and starting systems without switching leads or polarity. A digital multimeter is a voltmeter, ammeter and ohmmeter combined in an instrument which gives a digital readout. These are often used when testing solid state circuits because of their high input impedance (usually 10 megohms or more).

The tach/dwell meter combines a tachometer and a dwell (cam angle) meter and is a specialized kind of voltmeter. The tachometer scale is marked to show engine speed in rpm and the dwell scale is marked to show degrees of distributor shaft rotation. In most electronic ignition systems, dwell is determined by the control unit, but the dwell meter can also be used to check the duty cycle (operation) of some electronic engine control systems. Some tach/dwell meters are powered by an internal battery, while others take their power from the car battery in use. The battery powered testers usually require calibration much like an ohmmeter before testing.

Special Test Equipment

A variety of diagnostic tools are available to help troubleshoot and repair computerized engine control systems. The most sophisticated of these devices are the console type engine analyzers that usually occupy a garage service bay, but there are several types of aftermarket electronic testers available that will allow quick circuit tests of the engine control system by plugging directly into a special connector located in the engine compartment or under the dashboard. Several tool and equipment manufacturers offer simple, hand held testers that measure various circuit voltage levels on command to check all system components for proper operation. Although these testers usually cost about $300-500, consider that the average computer control unit (or ECM) can cost just as much and the money saved by not replacing perfectly good sensors or components in an attempt to correct a problem could justify the purchase price of a special diagnostic tester the first time it's used.

These computerized testers can allow quick and easy test measurements while the engine is operating or while the car is being driven. In addition, the on-board computer memory can be read to access any stored trouble codes; in effect allowing the computer to tell you where it hurts and aid trouble diagnosis by pinpointing exactly which circuit or component is malfunctioning. In the same manner, repairs can be tested to make sure the problem has been corrected. The biggest advantage these special testers have is their relatively easy hookups that minimize or eliminate the chances of making the wrong connections and getting false voltage readings or damaging the computer accidentally.

NOTE: *It should be remembered that these testers check voltage levels in circuits; they don't detect mechanical problems or failed components if the circuit voltage falls within the preprogrammed limits stored in the tester PROM unit. Also, most of the hand held testers are designed to work only on one or two systems made by a specific manufacturer.*

A variety of aftermarket testers are available to help diagnose different computerized control systems. Owatonna Tool Company (OTC), for example, markets a device called the OTC Monitor which plugs directly into the assembly line diagnostic link (ALDL). The OTC tester makes diagnosis a simple matter of pressing the correct buttons and, by changing the internal PROM or inserting a different diagnosis cartridge, it will work on any model from full size to subcompact, over a wide range of years. An adapter is supplied with the tester to allow connection to all types of ALDL links, regardless of the number of pin terminals used. By inserting an updated PROM into the OTC tester, it can be easily updated to diagnose any new modifications of computerized control systems.

Wiring Harnesses

The average automobile contains about $1/2$ mile of wiring, with hundreds of individual connections. To protect the many wires from damage and to keep them from becoming a confusing tangle, they are organized into bundles, enclosed in plastic or taped together and called wire harnesses. Different wiring harnesses serve different parts of the vehicle. Individual wires are color coded to help trace them through a harness where sections are hidden from view.

A loose or corroded connection or a replacement wire that is too small for the circuit will add extra resistance and an additional voltage drop to the circuit. A ten percent voltage drop can result in slow or erratic motor operation, for example, even though the circuit is complete. Automotive wiring or circuit conductors can be in any one of three forms:

1. Single strand wire
2. Multistrand wire
3. Printed circuitry

Single strand wire has a solid metal core and is usually used inside such components as alternators, motors, relays and other devices. Multistrand wire has a core made of many small strands of wire twisted together into a single conductor. Most of the wiring in an automotive electrical system is made up of multistrand wire, either as a single conductor or grouped together in a harness. All wiring is color coded on the insulator, either as a solid color or as a colored wire with an identification stripe. A printed circuit is a thin film of copper or other conductor that is printed on an insulator backing. Occasionally, a printed circuit is sandwiched between two sheets of plastic for more protection and flexibility. A complete printed circuit, consisting of conductors, insulating material and connectors for lamps or other components is called a printed circuit board. Printed circuitry is used in place of individual wires or harnesses in places where space is limited, such as behind instrument panels.

Wire Gauge

Since computer controlled automotive electrical systems are very sensitive to changes in resistance, the selection of properly sized wires is critical when systems are repaired. The wire gauge number is an expression of the cross section area of the conductor. The most common system for expressing wire size is the American Wire Gauge (AWG) system.

Wire cross section area is measured in circular mils. A mil is $1/1000$ in. (0.001 in.); a circular mil is the area of a circle one mil in diameter. For example, a conductor $1/4$ in. in diameter is 0.250 in. or 250 mils. The circular mil cross section area of the wire is 250 squared (250^2)or 62,500 circular mils. Imported car models usually use metric wire gauge designations, which is simply the cross section area of the conductor in square millimeters (mm^2).

Gauge numbers are assigned to conductors of various cross section areas. As gauge number increases, area decreases and the conductor becomes smaller. A 5 gauge conductor is smaller than a 1 gauge conductor and a 10 gauge is smaller than a 5 gauge. As the cross section area of a conductor decreases, resistance increases and so does the gauge number. A conductor with a higher gauge number will carry less current than a conductor with a lower gauge number.

NOTE: *Gauge wire size refers to the size of the conductor, not the size of the complete wire. It is possible to have two wires of the same gauge with different diameters because one may have thicker insulation than the other.*

12 volt automotive electrical systems generally use 10, 12, 14, 16 and 18 gauge wire. Main power distribution circuits and larger accessories usually use 10 and 12 gauge wire. Battery cables are usually 4 or 6 gauge, although 1 and 2 gauge wires are occasionally used. Wire length must also be considered when making repairs to a circuit. As conductor length increases, so does resistance. An 18 gauge wire, for example, can carry a 10 amp load for 10 feet without excessive voltage drop; however if a 15 foot wire is required for the same 10 amp load, it must be a 16 gauge wire.

An electrical schematic shows the electrical current paths when a circuit is operating properly. It is essential to understand how a circuit works before trying to figure out why it doesn't. Schematics break the entire electrical system down into individual circuits and show

only one particular circuit. In a schematic, no attempt is made to represent wiring and components as they physically appear on the vehicle; switches and other components are shown as simply as possible. Face views of harness connectors show the cavity or terminal locations in all multi-pin connectors to help locate test points.

If you need to backprobe a connector while it is on the component, the order of the terminals must be mentally reversed. The wire color code can help in this situation, as well as a keyway, lock tab or other reference mark.

NOTE: *Wiring diagrams are not included in this book. As automobiles have become more complex and available with longer option lists, wiring diagrams have grown in size and complexity. It has become almost impossible to provide a readable reproduction of a wiring diagram in a book this size. Information on ordering wiring diagrams from the vehicle manufacturer can be found in the owner's manual.*

WIRING REPAIR

Soldering is a quick, efficient method of joining metals permanently. Everyone who has the occasion to make wiring repairs should know how to solder. Electrical connections that are soldered are far less likely to come apart and will conduct electricity much better than connections that are only "pig-tailed" together. The most popular (and preferred) method of soldering is with an electrical soldering gun. Soldering irons are available in many sizes and wattage ratings. Irons with higher wattage ratings deliver higher temperatures and recover lost heat faster. A small soldering iron rated for no more than 50 watts is recommended, especially on electrical systems where excess heat can damage the components being soldered.

There are three ingredients necessary for successful soldering; proper flux, good solder and sufficient heat. A soldering flux is necessary to clean the metal of tarnish, prepare it for soldering and to enable the solder to spread into tiny crevices. When soldering, always use a resin flux or resin core solder which is non-corrosive and will not attract moisture once the job is finished. Other types of flux (acid core) will leave a residue that will attract moisture and cause the wires to corrode. Tin is a unique metal with a low melting point. In a molten state, it dissolves and alloys easily with many metals. Solder is made by mixing tin with lead. The most common proportions are 40/60, 50/50 and 60/40, with the percentage of tin listed first. Low priced solders usually contain less tin, making them very difficult for a beginner to use because more heat is required to melt the solder. A common solder is 40/60 which is well suited for all-around general use, but 60/40 melts easier, has more tin for a better joint and is preferred for electrical work.

Soldering Techniques

Successful soldering requires that the metals to be joined be heated to a temperature that will melt the solder — usually 360–460°F (182–238°C). Contrary to popular belief, the purpose of the soldering iron is not to melt the solder itself, but to heat the parts being soldered to a temperature high enough to melt the solder when it is touched to the work. Melting flux-cored solder on the soldering iron will usually destroy the effectiveness of the flux.

NOTE: *Soldering tips are made of copper for good heat conductivity, but must be "tinned" regularly for quick transference of heat to the project and to prevent the solder from sticking to the iron. To "tin" the iron, simply heat it and touch the flux-cored solder to the tip; the solder will flow over the hot tip. Wipe the excess off with a clean rag, but be careful as the iron will be hot.*

After some use, the tip may become pitted. If so, simply dress the tip smooth with a smooth file and "tin" the tip again. An old saying holds that "metals well cleaned are half soldered." Flux-cored solder will remove oxides but rust, bits of insulation and oil or grease must be removed with a wire brush or emery cloth. For maximum strength in soldered parts, the joint must start off clean and tight. Weak joints will result in gaps too wide for the solder to bridge.

If a separate soldering flux is used, it should be brushed or swabbed on only those areas that are to be soldered. Most solders contain a core of flux and separate fluxing is unnecessary. Hold the work to be soldered firmly. It is best to solder on a wooden board, because a metal vise will only rob the piece to be soldered of heat and make it difficult to melt the solder. Hold the soldering tip with the broadest face against the work to be soldered. Apply solder under the tip close to the work, using enough solder to give a heavy film between the iron and the piece being soldered, while moving slowly and making sure the solder melts properly. Keep the work level or the solder will run to the lowest part and favor the thicker parts, because these require more heat to melt the solder. If the soldering tip overheats (the solder coating on the face of the tip burns up), it should be retinned. Once the soldering is completed, let the soldered joint stand until cool. Tape and seal all soldered wire splices after the repair has cooled.

Wire Harness and Connectors

The on-board computer (ECM) wire harness electrically connects the control unit to the various solenoids, switches and sensors used by the control system. Most connectors in the engine compartment or otherwise exposed to the elements are protected against moisture and dirt which could create oxidation and deposits on the terminals. This protection is important because of the very low voltage and current levels used by the computer and sensors. All connectors have a lock which secures the male and female terminals together, with a secondary lock holding the seal and terminal into the connector. Both terminal locks must be released when disconnecting ECM connectors.

These special connectors are weather-proof and all repairs require the use of a special terminal and the tool required to service it. This tool is used to remove the pin and sleeve terminals. If removal is attempted with an ordinary pick, there is a good chance that the terminal will be bent or deformed. Unlike standard blade type terminals, these terminals cannot be straightened once they are bent. Make certain that the connectors are properly seated and all of the sealing rings in place when connecting leads. On some models, a hinge-type flap provides a backup or secondary locking feature for the terminals. Most secondary locks are used to improve the connector reliability by retaining the terminals if the small terminal lock tangs are not positioned properly.

Molded-on connectors require complete replacement of the connection. This means splicing a new connector assembly into the harness. All splices in on-board computer systems should be soldered to insure proper contact. Use care when probing the connections or replacing terminals in them as it is possible to short between opposite terminals. If this happens to the wrong terminal pair, it is possible to damage certain components. Always use jumper wires between connectors for circuit checking and never probe through weather-proof seals.

Open circuits are often difficult to locate by sight because corrosion or terminal misalignment are hidden by the connectors. Merely wiggling a connector on a sensor or in the wiring harness may correct the open circuit condition. This should always be considered when an open circuit or a failed sensor is indicated. Intermittent problems may also be caused by oxidized or loose connections. When using a circuit tester for diagnosis, always probe connections from the wire side. Be careful not to damage sealed connectors with test probes.

All wiring harnesses should be replaced with

identical parts, using the same gauge wire and connectors. When signal wires are spliced into a harness, use wire with high temperature insulation only. With the low voltage and current levels found in the system, it is important that the best possible connection at all wire splices be made by soldering the splices together. It is seldom necessary to replace a complete harness. If replacement is necessary, pay close attention to insure proper harness routing. Secure the harness with suitable plastic wire clamps to prevent vibrations from causing the harness to wear in spots or contact any hot components.

NOTE: *Weatherproof connectors cannot be replaced with standard connectors. Instructions are provided with replacement connector and terminal packages. Some wire harnesses have mounting indicators (usually pieces of colored tape) to mark where the harness is to be secured.*

In making wiring repairs, it's important that you always replace damaged wires with wires that are the same gauge as the wire being replaced. The heavier the wire, the smaller the gauge number. Wires are color-coded to aid in identification and whenever possible the same color coded wire should be used for replacement. A wire stripping and crimping tool is necessary to install solderless terminal connectors. Test all crimps by pulling on the wires; it should not be possible to pull the wires out of a good crimp.

Wires which are open, exposed or otherwise damaged are repaired by simple splicing. Where possible, if the wiring harness is accessible and the damaged place in the wire can be located, it is best to open the harness and check for all possible damage. In an inaccessible harness, the wire must be bypassed with a new insert, usually taped to the outside of the old harness.

When replacing fusible links, be sure to use fusible link wire, NOT ordinary automotive wire. Make sure the fusible segment is of the same gauge and construction as the one being replaced and double the stripped end when crimping the terminal connector for a good contact. The melted (open) fusible link segment of the wiring harness should be cut off as close to the harness as possible, then a new segment spliced in as described. In the case of a damaged fusible link that feeds two harness wires, the harness connections should be replaced with two fusible link wires so that each circuit will have its own separate protection.

NOTE: *Most of the problems caused in the wiring harness are due to bad ground connections. Always check all vehicle ground connections for corrosion or looseness before performing any power feed checks to eliminate the chance of a bad ground affecting the circuit.*

Repairing Hard Shell Connectors

Unlike molded connectors, the terminal contacts in hard shell connectors can be replaced. Weatherproof hard-shell connectors with the leads molded into the shell have non-replaceable terminal ends. Replacement usually involves the use of a special terminal removal tool that depress the locking tangs (barbs) on the connector terminal and allow the connector to be removed from the rear of the shell. The connector shell should be replaced if it shows any evidence of burning, melting, cracks, or breaks. Replace individual terminals that are burnt, corroded, distorted or loose.

NOTE: *The insulation crimp must be tight to prevent the insulation from sliding back on the wire when the wire is pulled. The insulation must be visibly compressed under the crimp tabs, and the ends of the crimp should be turned in for a firm grip on the insulation.*

The wire crimp must be made with all wire strands inside the crimp. The terminal must be fully compressed on the wire strands with the ends of the crimp tabs turned in to make a firm grip on the wire. Check all connections with an ohmmeter to insure a good contact. There should be no measurable resistance between the wire and the terminal when connected.

Fuse Link

The fuse link is a short length of special, Hypalon (high temperature) insulated wire, integral with the engine compartment wiring harness and should not be confused with standard wire. It is several wire gauges smaller than the circuit which it protects. Under no circumstances should a fuse link replacement repair be made using a length of standard wire cut from bulk stock or from another wiring harness.

To repair any blown fuse link use the following procedure:

1. Determine which circuit is damaged, its location and the cause of the open fuse link. If the damaged fuse link is one of three fed by a common No. 10 or 12 gauge feed wire, determine the specific affected circuit.

2. Disconnect the negative battery cable.

3. Cut the damaged fuse link from the wiring harness and discard it. If the fuse link is one of three circuits fed by a single feed wire, cut it out of the harness at each splice end and discard it.

4. Identify and procure the proper fuse link

and butt connectors for attaching the fuse link to the harness.

5. To repair any fuse link in a 3-link group with one feed:

a. After cutting the open link out of the harness, cut each of the remaining undamaged fuse links close to the feed wire weld.

b. Strip approximately 1/2 in. (13mm) of insulation from the detached ends of the two good fuse links, Then insert two wire ends into one end of a butt connector and carefully push one stripped end of the replacement fuse link into the same end of the butt connector and crimp all three firmly together.

NOTE: *Care must be taken when fitting the three fuse links into the butt connector as the internal diameter is a snug fit for three wires. Make sure to use a proper crimping tool. Pliers, side cutter, etc. will not apply the proper crimp to retain the wires and withstand a pull test.*

c. After crimping the butt connector to the three fuse links, cut the weld portion from the feed wire and strip approximately 1/2 in. (13mm) of insulation from the cut end. Insert the stripped end into the open end of the butt connector and crimp very firmly.

d. To attach the remaining end of the replacement fuse link, strip approximately 1/2 in. (13mm) of insulation from the wire end of the circuit from which the blown fuse link was removed, and firmly crimp a butt connector or equivalent to the stripped wire. Then, insert the end of the replacement link into the other end of the butt connector and crimp firmly.

e. Using rosin core solder with a consistency of 60 percent tin and 40 percent lead, solder the connectors and the wires at the repairs and insulate with electrical tape.

6. To replace any fuse link on a single circuit in a harness, cut out the damaged portion, strip approximately 1/2 in. (13mm) of insulation from the two wire ends and attach the appropriate replacement fuse link to the stripped wire ends with two proper size butt connectors. Solder the connectors and wires and insulate with tape.

7. To repair any fuse link which has an eyelet terminal on one end such as the charging circuit, cut off the open fuse link behind the weld, strip approximately 1/2 in. (13mm) of insulation from the cut end and attach the appropriate new eyelet fuse link to the cut stripped wire with an appropriate size butt connector. Solder the connectors and wires at the repair and insulate with tape.

8. Connect the negative battery cable to the battery and test the system for proper operation.

NOTE: *Do not mistake a resistor wire for a fuse link. The resistor wire is generally longer and has print stating, "Resistor-don't cut or splice".*

When attaching a single No. 16, 17, 18 or 20 gauge fuse link to a heavy gauge wire, always double the stripped wire end of the fuse link before inserting and crimping it into the butt connector for positive wire retention.

HEATING AND AIR CONDITIONING

Refer to Chapter 1 for discharging, evacuating and recharging of the A/C system.

Heater and Air Conditioning Blower Motor

REMOVAL AND INSTALLATION

1. Disconnect the negative terminal from the battery.

2. Disconnect the electrical connections from the blower motor and resistor.

3. Remove the plastic water shield from the right side of the cowl.

4. Remove the blower motor-to-chassis screws and the blower motor.

5. Remove the cage retaining nut and the cage (old style).

NOTE: *Some of the new style blower cages are plastic welded to the motor shaft. Use a hot knife to cut a slot in the cage shaft sleeve in three places. Cut through the plastic material from the dome to the end of the shaft until the cage splits from the shaft.*

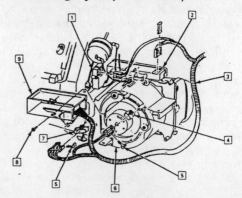

1. Temperature door motor
2. Vacuum solenoid box
3. Inst. panel harness
4. Connector
5. Retainer
6. Module
7. Resistor
8. 17 inch lbs
9. Convenience center

Heater blower motor and resistor

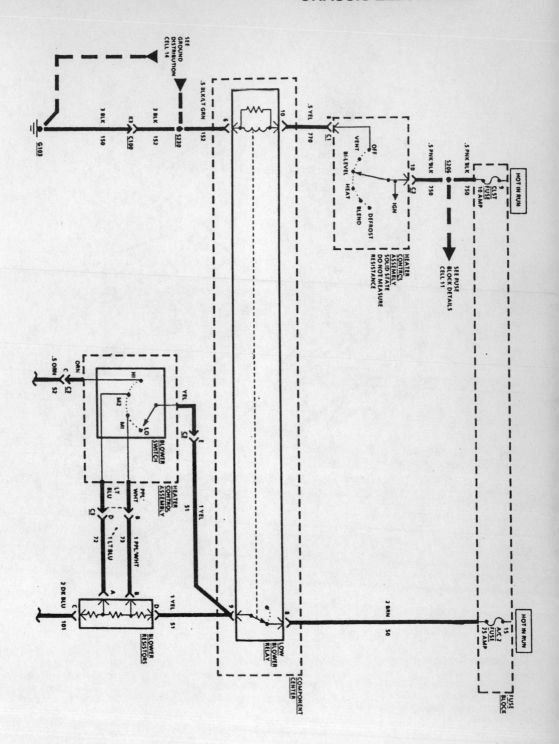

Blower motor wiring schematic

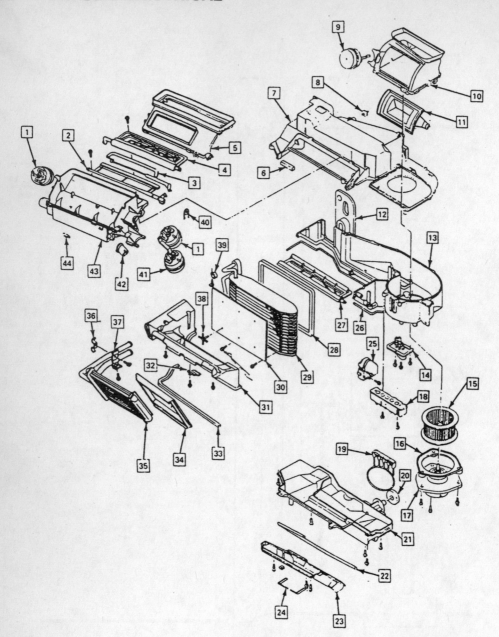

1. Vacuum actuator
2. Defroster valve
3. Inner and outer valve
4. Outer mode valve
5. Housing valce cover
6. Case seal
7. Upper and lower case
8. Case stud
9. Vacuum actuator
10. Air inlet case
11. Air inlet valve
12. Tube seal
13. Evaporator and blower lower case
14. Blower motor resistor
15. Blower motor fan

16. Gasket isolator
17. Fan and isolator motor
18. Vacuum electric solenoid
19. Vacuum harness
20. Drain seal
21. Core cover
22. Duct to core cover seal
23. Heater outlet duct
24. Duct seal
25. Electric actuator
26. Gasket
27. Temperature valve
28. Core evaporator seal
29. Evaporator core
30. Water core filter

31. Core shroud
32. Core heater clamp
33. Cover seal
34. Core heater seal
35. Heater core
36. Clamp
37. Support tube bracket
38. Filter retainer
39. Clamp
40. Torsion spring
41. Vacuum actuator
42. Side defog duct
43. Housing valve case
44. Label

Heater and air conditioning module — exploded view

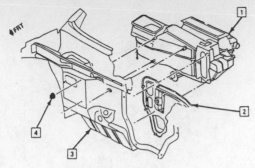

1. Module
2. Dash plate
3. Dash and toe panel
4. 89 inch lbs.

Heater and air conditioning module–to–firewall mounting

To install:

6. Install the cage on the new blower motor with the opening facing away from the motor.

7. Install the blower motor and screws. Install the sound insulator and connect the electrical leads to the motor and resistor.

8. Install the water shield to the cowl. Connect the negative battery cable.

Blower Resistor

The blower resistor is located behind the right hand side of the instrument panel mounted in the heater-A/C plenum. The lower RH side instrument panel sound insulator has to be removed to gain access.

Heater Core

REMOVAL AND INSTALLATION

CAUTION: *When draining the coolant, keep in mind that cats and dogs are attracted by the ethylene glycol antifreeze, and are quite likely to drink any that is left in an uncovered container or in puddles on the ground. This will prove fatal in sufficient quantity. Always drain the coolant into a sealable container. Coolant should be reused unless it is contaminated or several years old.*

1. Disconnect the negative battery cable.
2. Drain the cooling system.
3. Remove the upper firewall weatherstrip. Remove the upper cowl secondary panel.
4. Remove the heater hoses from the core. Cut the hoses to prevent damage to the core if they will not disconnect with slight force.
5. Inside the vehicle, remove the lower sound insulator panel. Remove the rear seat duct adapter. Blower shop air through the heater core to remove any excess coolant.
6. Remove the heater floor duct. Remove the heater core cover and remove the heater core.

To install:

1. Install the heater core, cover and attaching bolts. Install the rear seat duct adapter.

2. Install the lower right and left sound insulators and heater floor duct.

3. Attach the heater hoses to the core. Install the upper secondary cowl panel and weatherstrip.

4. Fill the cooling system and check for leaks. Connect the negative battery cable.

Control Head

REMOVAL AND INSTALLATION

Cutlass Supreme

1. Disconnect the negative (–) battery cable.

2. Remove the cluster trim plate-to-dash securing screws.

3. Tilt the top of the cluster trim plate downward releasing the clips that mount the bottom of the plate to the dash and remove the trim plate.

4. Remove the screws securing the accessory trim plate-to-dash.

5. Tilt the top of the accessory trim plate downward releasing the clips that mount the bottom of the plate-to-dash.

6. Remove the control assembly from the dash and disconnect the electrical connectors.

To install:

1. Install the control assembly and connect the electrical wiring-to-assembly.

2. Push the mounting clips into place, roll the top of the accessory trim plate upward into position and tighten screws.

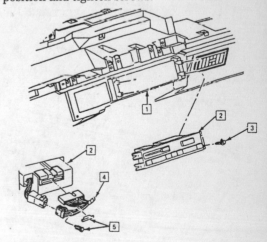

1. Instrument panel lower trim pad
2. Control assembly
3. Screw
4. Inst. panel harness
5. Connector retainer

Control head assembly – Cutlass Supreme

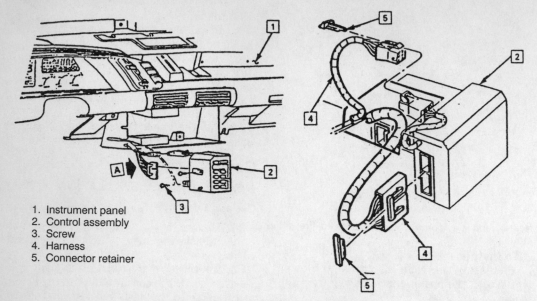

1. Instrument panel
2. Control assembly
3. Screw
4. Harness
5. Connector retainer

Control head assembly — Grand Prix

3. Push the mounting clips into place, roll the top of the cluster trim plate upward into position and tighten the screws.

4. Connect the negative battery cable and check operation.

Grand Prix

1. Disconnect the negative (–) battery cable.
2. Remove the lower left instrument panel pad.
3. Remove the control assembly trim plate.
4. Loosen the left securing screws, pull the assembly out and disconnect the electrical harness.

To install:

1. Connect the electrical harness and position the control assembly into the screws. Tighten the securing screws.

2. Install the control trim panel, lower left instrument panel pad and connect the negative battery cable.

Regal

1. Disconnect the negative (–) battery cable.
2. Remove the instrument panel trim plate.

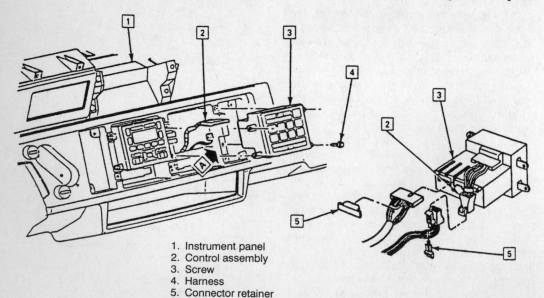

1. Instrument panel
2. Control assembly
3. Screw
4. Harness
5. Connector retainer

Control head assembly — Regal

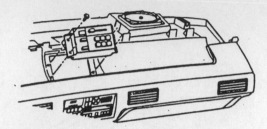

Control head assembly — Lumina

3. Remove the control assembly securing screws, control assembly and disconnect the electrical harness.

To install:

1. Connect the electrical harness, install the control assembly and tighten the securing screws.

2. Install the instrument panel trim plate, connect the negative battery cable and check for proper operation.

Lumina

1. Disconnect the negative (–) battery cable.

2. Remove the instrument cluster trim plate.

3. Remove the control assembly securing screws, control assembly and disconnect the electrical harness.

To install:

1. Install the control assembly, connect the electrical harness and tighten the securing screws.

2. Install the instrument panel trim plate, connect the negative battery cable and check for proper operation.

Evaporator Core
REMOVAL AND INSTALLATION

1. Disconnect the negative (–) battery cable.

2. Discharge the A/C system as outlined in chapter 1.

When draining the coolant, keep in mind that cats and dogs are attracted by the ethylene glycol antifreeze, and are quite likely to drink any that is left in an uncovered container or in puddles on the ground. This will prove fatal in sufficient quantity. Always drain the coolant into a sealable container. Coolant should be reused unless it is contaminated or several years old.

3. Drain the cooling system.

4. Remove the upper weatherstrip from the body.

5. Remove the lower and upper secondary cowl panels.

6. Remove the evaporator core block connection at the cowl.

7. Remove the heater hoses and blow out

the remaining coolant with shop air to prevent leakage into the passenger compartment when removing.

8. Remove the heater core cover and heater core as previously outlined in this chapter.

9. Remove the evaporator core cover and evaporator.

To install:

1. Install the evaporator and core cover.

2. Install the heater core and cover.

3. Connect the heater hoses and tighten the clamps.

4. Install the evaporator core block connectors.

5. Install the lower and upper secondary cowl panels.

6. Fill the cooling system with the specified engine coolant and check for leaks.

7. Evacuate, charge and leak test the A/C system as outlined in chapter 1.

8. Connect the negative battery cable and check for proper blower, A/C, heater and control functions.

RADIO
REMOVAL AND INSTALLATION

Lumina

1. Disconnect the negative (–) battery cable.

2. Remove the right instrument panel trim plate.

3. Remove the radio retaining bolts, disconnect electrical harness and remove the radio.

To install:

NOTE: *When installing the radio, do not pinch the wires or a short circuit to ground may happen and damage the radio.*

1. Connect the electrical harness to the back of the radio and tighten the retaining bolts.

2. Install the right side instrument panel trim plate and connect the negative battery cable.

Radio Controls

The Grand Prix, Cutlass Supreme and Regal are equipped with a remote radio receiver with the controls mounted in the instrument panel.

REMOVAL AND INSTALLATION

Grand Prix, Cutlass Supreme and Regal

1. Disconnect the negative (–) battery cable.

2. Remove the cluster trim plate.

3. Remove the control retaining bolts, disconnect the electrical harness and remove the radio control.

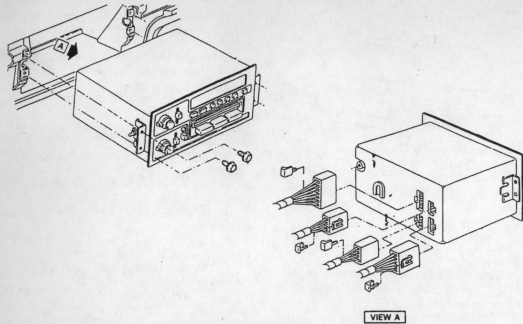

Radio assembly — Lumina

To install:

NOTE: *When installing the radio controls, do not pinch the wires or a short circuit to ground may happen and damage the radio.*

1. Connect the control electrical harness and tighten the control retaining bolts.

2. Install the cluster trim plate and reconnect the negative battery cable.

Radio Receiver

REMOVAL AND INSTALLATION

1. Disconnect the negative (−) battery cable.

2. Remove the right side sound insulator panel.

3. Remove the courtesy lamp and connector.

4. Remove the two receiver retaining bolts,

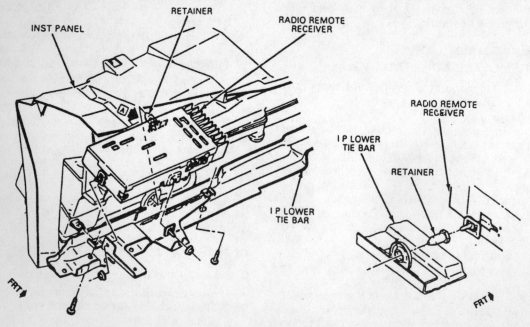

Radio remote receiver except Lumina

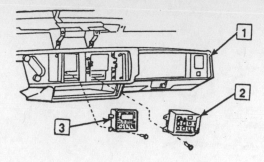

1. Inst. panel carrier
2. Heater and A/C control
3. Radio control

Radio controls — Regal

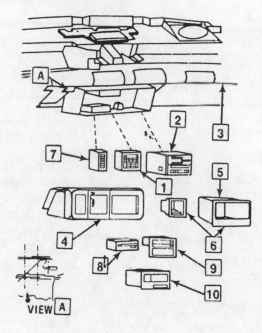

1. Radio
2. Cassette
3. Instrument panel carrier
4. Instrument panel trim plate
5. Storage compartment (without cassette)
6. Storage compartments (without radio and cassette)
7. A/C control unit
8. Cassette player
9. Cassette storage compartment
10. Instrument panel storage compartment

Radio controls — Grand Prix

disconnect the electrical harness and remove the receiver.

To install:

NOTE: *When installing the receiver assembly, do not pinch the wires or a short circuit to ground may happen and damage the radio.*

1. Connect the electrical harness, antenna cable and tighten the receiver retaining bolts.
2. Install the courtesy lamp and bolt.
3. Install the right side sound insulator panel and connect the negative battery cable.

Cassette/Equalizer/Compact Disc Player

REMOVAL AND INSTALLATION

1. Disconnect the negative (–) battery cable.
2. Remove the instrument panel accessory trim plate.
3. Remove the retaining bolts, pull unit out far enough to disconnect the electrical harness and remove the unit.

To install:

NOTE: *When installing the receiver assembly, do not pinch the wires or a short circuit to ground may happen and damage the radio.*

1. Connect the electrical harness and tighten the unit retaining bolts.
2. Install the instrument panel accessory plate and connect the negative battery cable.

WINDSHIELD WIPERS

Blade and Arm

REMOVAL AND INSTALLATION

1. Raise the hood and support.
2. Remove the protective cap and nut from the wiper arm.
3. Disconnect the washer hose from the arm.
4. Lift each wiper arm and insert a suitable pin or pop rivet completely through the two holes located next to the arm pivot.
5. Lift each arm off its transmission linkage shaft using a rocking motion.

To install:

1. Clean the metal shavings from the knurls of the shaft before installation.
2. Install the wiper arm onto the linkage shaft and adjust as follows.

 a. **Right Arm:** measure from the tip of the blade to the bottom edge of the glass. The measurement should be $9^1/_8$ in. (231mm).

 b. **Left Arm:** measure from the tip of the blade to the bottom edge of the glass. The measurement should be 2 in. (53mm).

3. Install the arm-to-shaft nut and torque to 25 ft. lbs. (34 Nm) and install the protective cap.
4. Connect the washer hose, close the hood and check for proper operation.

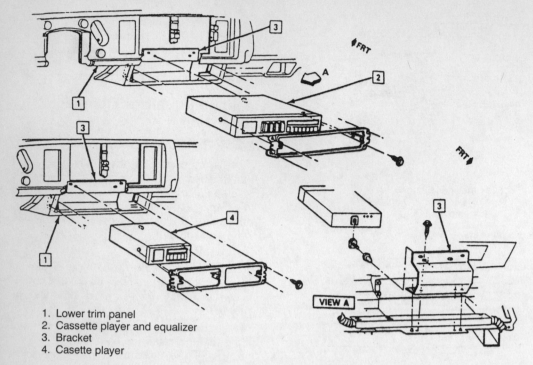

1. Lower trim panel
2. Cassette player and equalizer
3. Bracket
4. Casette player

Cassette player and equalizer

Wiper Module

REMOVAL AND INSTALLATION

1. Raise the hood and support.

2. Remove the protective cap and nut from the wiper arm.

3. Disconnect the washer hose from the arm.

4. Lift each wiper arm and insert a suitable pin or pop rivet completely through the two holes located next to the arm pivot.

5. Lift each arm off its transmission linkage shaft using a rocking motion.

6. Remove the lower reveal molding screws, lower the hood and remove the lower reveal molding.

7. Remove the air inlet panel screws, under-

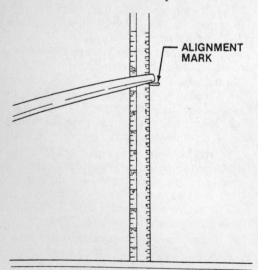

Right (passenger side) wiper arm measurement

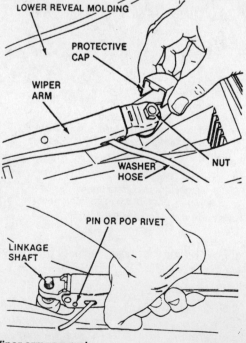

Wiper arm removal

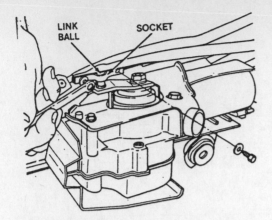

Removing socket from crank arm

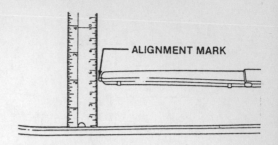

Left (driver side) wiper arm measurement

hood lamp switch and panel with the hood raised.

8. If the motor can run, place the crank arm in the inner wipe position as shown in the "Crank Arm Positioning" illustration in this section.

9. If the motor can not run, rotate the motor crank arm to the inner wipe position by applying a channel lock pliers against the top edge of the crank arm and lower jaw against the crank arm nut and turn the motor to the correct position before disassembly.

10. Remove the three bellcrank housing screws and lower the linkage from the module.

11. Remove the module assembly from the vehicle.

To install:

1. Install the module assembly into the vehicle.

2. Install the three bellcrank housing

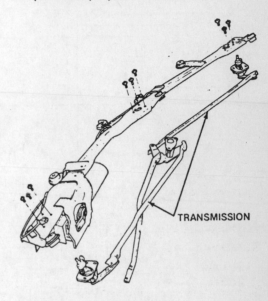

Wiper linkage to module

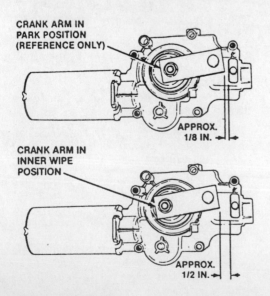

Crank arm positioning

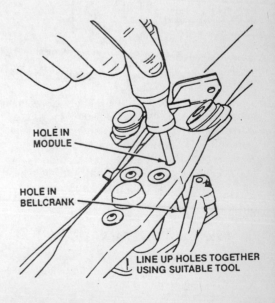

Module to bellcrank alignment

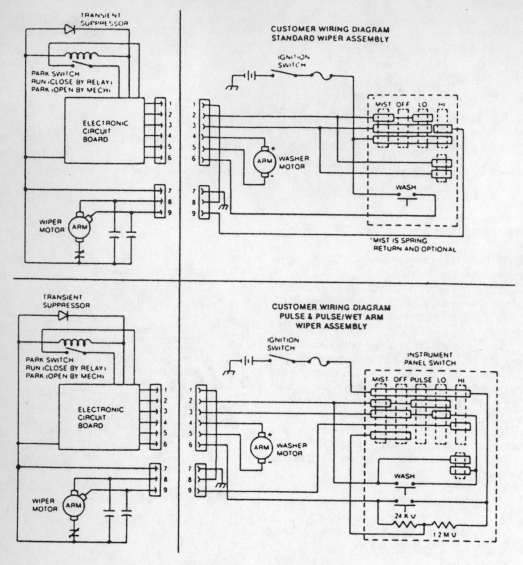

Windshield wiper circuit wiring

screws after lowering the linkage into the module.

3. Install the air inlet panel, underhood lamp switch and tighten the panel screws.

4. Install the lower reveal molding, wiper arm and cap. Connect the washer hose.

5. Adjust the wiper arm positioning as outlined earlier in the "Wiper Arm" section. Check each operation for proper installation.

Wiper Linkage

REMOVAL AND INSTALLATION

1. Disconnect the negative (–) battery cable.

2. Remove the wiper arm and module as previously outlined in this section.

3. Remove the two linkage socket screws and disconnect the sockets from the link ball.

4. Remove the right and left bellcrank

mounting screws and remove the linkage from the module.

To install:

1. Install the linkage to the module and tighten the bellcrank mounting screws.

NOTE: *The motor crank arm MUST be in the inner wiper position at this point. Refer to the illustration.*

2. Using a bolt or equivalent, line up the holes in the module and bellcrank as shown in the illustration.

3. Tighten the linkage socket screws while the alignment tool remains in place.

4. Install the module into the vehicle. Make sure the body seals are in the proper position.

5. Install the wiper arms and align the arms as outlined earlier in this section.

6. Connect the washer hose.

7. Run the wiper motor at HI and LO speeds with a wet and tacky windshield. Make sure the wiper **parks** properly.

Wiper Motor

REMOVAL AND INSTALLATION

1. Disconnect the negative battery cable.
2. Remove the washer hose, cap and retaining nut from each wiper arm. Remove the wiper arms from the vehicle.

3. Remove the screws retaining the cowl cover. Lower the hood partially and remove the cowl cover. Remove the air inlet panel.

4. Disconnect the wiring harness connectors at the wiper motor and the washer hose at the firewall.

5. Remove the 3 screws from the bellcrank housing and lower the wiper linkage.

6. Remove the wiper module assembly from the vehicle as outlined earlier. To remove the

NOTE: THE FOLLOWING PROCEDURES ASSUME THAT THE TECHNICIAN HAS CHECKED THE FOLLOWING BEFORE REMOVING THE WIPER MOTOR FROM THE VEHICLE:

1. CONTINUITY OF ALL HARNESS WIRES
2. WIPER MOTOR TO MODULE MOUNTING SCREWS TIGHT
3. FUSES

WIPER MOTOR BENCH TEST

ON A TEST BENCH, PERFORM THE FOLLOWING CHECKS IN THIS ORDER:

CHECK FOR WASHER PUMP OPERATION BEFORE REMOVING FROM VEHICLE. REMOVE COVER HARNESS CONNECTOR AND APPLY 12V(+) TO #4 TERMINAL OF WIRING HARNESS, GROUND #5 TERMINAL AS SHOWN.

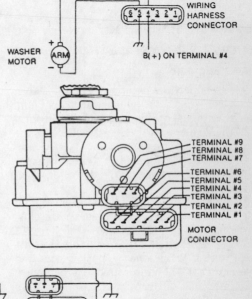

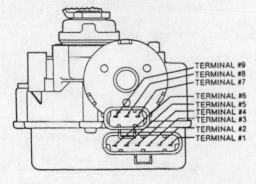

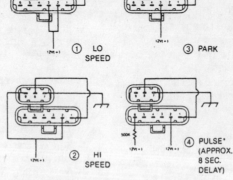

IF WIPER MOTOR FUNCTIONS IN ALL MODES, GO TO WIPER/WASHER SWITCH CHECK CHART, FIGURE 8C-14.

* IF A STANDARD TYPE MOTOR IS WIRED FOR THE PULSE CHECK, THE PARK RELAY WILL CLICK SHUT BUT THERE WILL BE NO OBSERVABLE MOTOR ACTION.

Wiper motor bench test

wiper motor from the module assembly, remove the 3 screw retaining the motor and remove the motor.

To install:

1. Attach the motor to the module assembly and install the module assembly in the vehicle.

2. Attach the bellcrank to module assembly and install the cowl cover, air inlet panel.

3. Attach the electrical connectors to the motor and attach the washer hose to the firewall. Install the wiper arms, nuts and caps. Torque the nuts to 25 ft. lbs. (34 Nm). Attach the washer hoses to the wiper arms.

4. Connect the negative battery cable.

INSTRUMENTS AND SWITCHES

Instrument Panel Pad

REMOVAL AND INSTALLATION

Cutlass Supreme

1. Disconnect the negative (–) battery cable.

2. Open the glove compartment door and lower the storage compartment by lifting out.

3. Remove the two screws from inside the glove compartment opening.

4. Remove the defroster grille, deflector and the two screws inside the defroster opening.

5. Remove the instrument cluster trim plate and the two screws at the sides of the cluster opening.

6. Lift up the pad and disconnect the daytime running lamp sensor, speaker wire and glove compartment lamp switch, if so equipped. Slide the pad off of the carrier.

To install:

1. Install the pad and connect the running lamp sensor, glove compartment switch and speaker wire.

2. Install the two screws at the cluster opening and the cluster trim plate.

3. Install the two screws at the defroster opening, defroster deflector and grille.

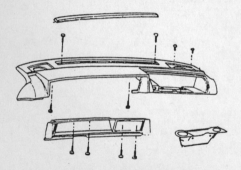

Instrument panel pad — Cutlass Supreme

4. Install the two screws at the glove compartment opening and lower the storage compartment into place. Connect the negative battery cable.

Regal

1. Disconnect the negative (–) battery cable.

2. Remove the speaker grilles by prying carefully and disconnect the daytime running lamp sensor connector.

3. Remove one screw under each speaker grille.

4. Remove the five screws under the lower edge of the panel pad.

5. Lift the front of the pad and pull rearward to release. Then lift up and out.

To install:

1. Install the pad and tighten the five lower edge screws.

2. Install the one screw under each speaker grille.

3. Connect the daytime running sensor and install the speaker grilles.

4. Connect the negative battery cable.

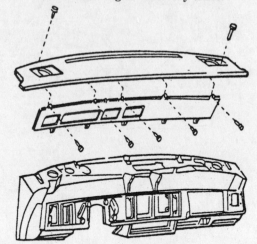

Instrument panel pad — Regal

Grand Prix

1. Disconnect the negative (–) battery cable.

2. Remove the two screws from the top of the cluster trim plate.

3. Remove the glove compartment and screws above the compartment.

4. Lift the front of the pad and pull rearward to release the clips.

5. Disconnect the speaker wire and daytime running lamp sensor, if so equipped.

To install:

1. Connect the speaker wire and daytime running sensor, if removed.

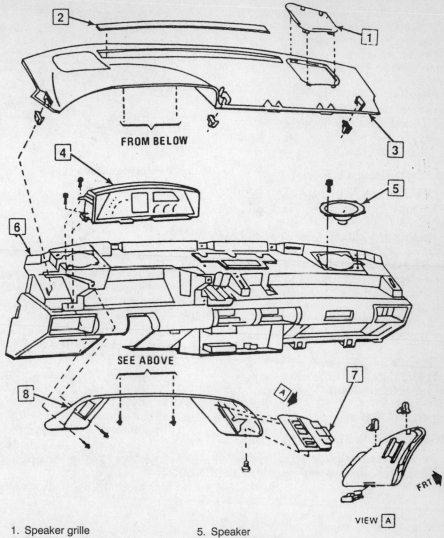

1. Speaker grille
2. Defroster grille
3. Instrument panel pad
4. Instrument cluster
5. Speaker
6. Instrument panel carrier
7. Switch assembly
8. Trim plate

Instrument panel pad and cluster — Grand Prix

2. Push the pad firmly toward the front of the vehicle to engage the clips. Push the pad down to engage the front clips.

3. Install the three screws, one in the glove compartment and the other two in the cluster trim plate.

4. Install the glove compartment and connect the negative battery cable.

Lumina

1. Disconnect the negative (–) battery cable and the daytime running lamp sensor, if so equipped.

2. Remove the screws under the instrument panel pad.

3. Remove the pad by lifting the front edge and pull rearward to release, then lift up and out.

To install:

1. Install the pad and retaining screws.

2. Connect the daytime running lamp sensor and negative battery cable.

Instrument Cluster

REMOVAL AND INSTALLATION

Cutlass Supreme

1. Disconnect the negative battery cable.

2. Remove the 5 screws retaining the clus-

ter trim plate. Pull the bottom of the trim plate out and remove it from the vehicle.

3. Remove the screws retaining the instrument cluster and remove the cluster from the instrument panel. Disconnect the electrical connectors.

To install:

1. Install the cluster to the instrument panel. Connect the electrical leads.

2. Install the cluster trim panel. Connect the negative battery cable.

Grand Prix, Regal and Lumina

1. Disconnect the negative battery cable.

2. Remove the instrument panel pad from the vehicle.

3. Remove the cluster trim plate and the four screws retaining the instrument cluster. Pull the cluster forward, disconnect the electrical connectors, PRNDL cable and remove the cluster from the vehicle.

To install:

1. Install the cluster to the instrument panel. Connect the electrical leads and PRNDL cable.

2. Install the upper panel pad.

3. Install the cluster trim panel.

4. Connect the negative battery cable.

Instrument Panel

REMOVAL AND INSTALLATION

1. Disconnect the negative (–) battery cable.

2. Remove the instrument panel pad and speakers.

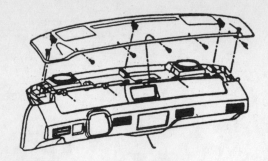

Instrument panel pad – Lumina

3. Remove the instrument cluster and glove compartment.

4. Remove the right sound insulator and ventilation system controls.

5. Remove the sound system controls unless they are mounted in the steering wheel.

6. Remove the light switches, cassette tape player or storage compartment.

7. Remove the ash tray and bracket.

8. Remove the ALDL (assembly line diagnostic link).

9. Remove the parking brake release handle, remote radio receiver and steering column trim cover. Disconnect the lower steering column.

10. Remove the seven panel retaining bolts, five at the top and two at the bottom.

11. Remove the two bolts from the steering column-to-panel carrier.

12. Remove the five bolts holding air duct.

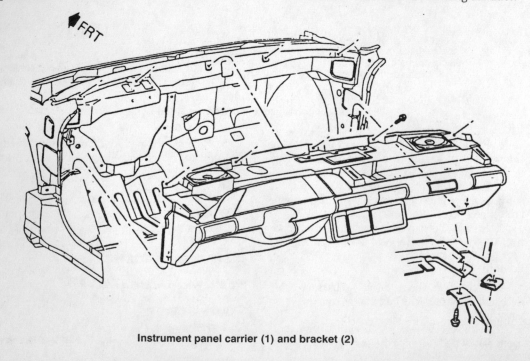

Instrument panel carrier (1) and bracket (2)

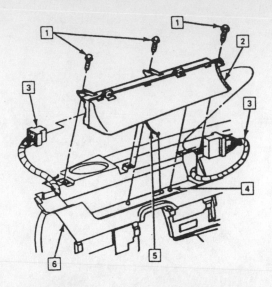

1. Screws
2. Cluster
3. Connector
4. Locating tab
5. P-R-N-D-L cable
6. Inst. panel carrier

Instrument cluster — Lumina

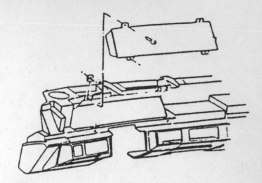

Instrument cluster — Cutlass Supreme

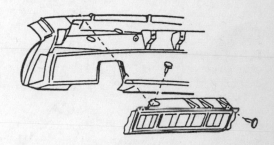

Instrument cluster — Regal

13. Remove the three nuts holding conduit, two above the glove compartment and one through the cassette opening.

14. Remove the wiring harness clips (nine).

15. Remove the instrument panel carrier by pulling the top out, then lift the panel up and out.

To install:

1. Install the panel into position.

2. Install the nine wire harness clips, three nuts-to-conduit and the five bolts-to-air duct.

3. Install the steering column-to-panel carrier retaining bolts.

4. Install the seven bolts retaining the panel carrier.

5. Install the steering column and trim cover.

6. Install the remote radio receiver, parking brake release handle and ALDL connector.

7. Install the ash tray and bracket.

8. Install the cassette player or storage compartment.

9. Install the light switches, sound system controls and ventilation system controls.

10. Install the right sound insulator, glove compartment and instrument cluster.

11. Install the speakers and instrument panel pad.

12. Connect the negative battery cable.

Console

REMOVAL AND INSTALLATION

Cutlass Supreme and Grand Prix

1. Disconnect the negative (–) battery cable.

2. Remove the shift handle snap ring by prying with a suitable pry bar.

3. Remove the shift handle, storage compartment and ash tray by lifting up and out.

4. Remove the trim plate and trip calculator, if so equipped.

5. Remove the arm rest, console wiring and electrical connectors.

6. Remove the front and rear console retaining screws and console.

To install:

1. Install the console and retaining screws.

2. Connect the electrical connectors and wiring.

3. Install the arm rest, trip calculator and trim plate.

4. Install the storage compartments, cassette holder and ash tray.

5. Install the shift handle and snap ring.

6. Connect the negative battery cable.

Lumina

1. Disconnect the negative (–) battery cable.

2. Apply the parking brake and shift the transaxle into neutral.

3. Remove the shift knob, trim plate and lamp socket from trim plate.

4. Remove the console-to-floor retaining screws and console.

To install:

1. Install the console and retaining screws.

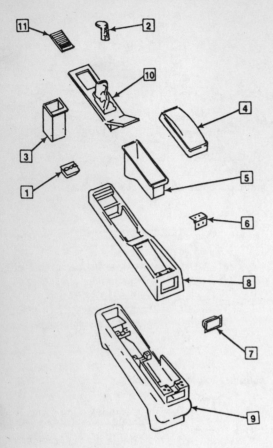

1. Holder
2. Shift knob
3. Cassette compartment
4. Door and arm rest
5. Compartment
6. Door hinge
7. Courtesy light
8. Upper panel
9. Lower panel
10. Cover plate
11. Sliding door

Console assembly — Cutlass Supreme

2. Install the storage compartments, lamp socket and trim plate.

3. Install the shift knob and connect the negative battery cable.

Windshield Wiper Switch

REMOVAL AND INSTALLATION

The windshield wiper switch is mounted on the right side of the instrument cluster, in Grand Prix models. In 1988 Cutlass Supreme, Regal and 1990 Lumina models, it is located on the left side of the instrument cluster in combination with the headlamp switch. In 1989 Cut-

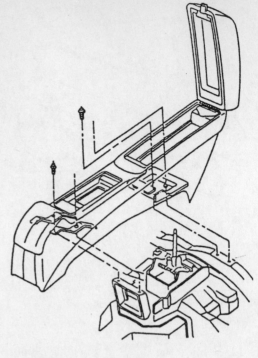

Console assembly — Lumina

lass Supreme and Regal models, the switch is located on the turn signal/combination switch.

1988 Models

1. Disconnect the negative battery cable.
2. Remove the screw retaining the switch panel to the instrument panel.
3. Remove the switch from the instrument panel by pulling the bottom out and releasing the top retaining clips.
4. Disconnect the electrical connector from the switch and remove it from the vehicle.
5. To install the switch, connect the electrical leads and push the switch into position.
6. Install the retaining screw. Connect the negative battery cable.

1989 Cutlass Supreme and Regal

1. Disconnect the negative (–) battery cable.
2. Remove the steering wheel horn pad, wheel retaining nut and steering wheel.
3. Remove the turn signal canceling cam assembly.
4. Remove the hazard knob and position the turn signal lever so that the housing cover screw can be removed through the opening in the switch. Remove the housing cover.
5. Remove the wire protector from the opening in the instrument panel bracket and separate the wires.
6. Disconnect the pivot and pulse switch con-

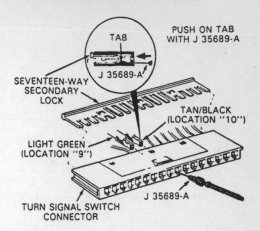

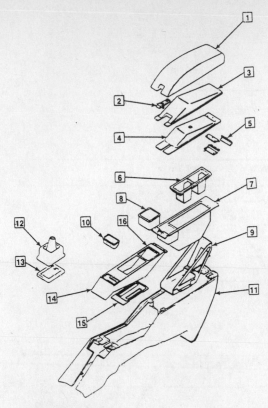

1. Door and arm rest
2. Button latch
3. Substrate
4. Arm rest inner door
5. Hinges (3 pieces)
6. Tape storage compartment
7. Console compartment
8. Cup holder
9. Bracket
10. Coin holder
11. Console assembly
12. Shifter boot
13. Boot retainer
14. Console trim plate
15. Trim plate – automatic trans.
16. Ash tray and lighter (with trip calculator)

Console assembly – Grand Prix

nector. Remove the pivot switch connector and pivot switch.

7. Remove the turn signal screws, signal connector and seventeen way secondary lock from the turn signal connector.

8. Remove the buzzer switch connectors from the turn signal connector using a terminal remover tool J–35689-A. Remove the turn signal switch from the column.

To install:

1. Install the turn signal switch assembly and wire protector.

2. Install the switch retaining screws and torque to 35 inch lbs. (4 Nm).

Removing terminals from the turn signal connector

3. Connect the buzzer switch wires to the turn signal connector (light green into location 9 and the tan/black wire into location 10).

4. Install the seventeen way secondary lock.

5. Install the pivot and pulse switch assembly.

6. Install the wiring protector around the instrument panel opening, covering all wires.

7. Install the steering column housing cover and torque the screws to 35 inch lbs. (4 Nm).

8. Install the hazard knob and lubricate the bottom side of the canceling cam with lithium grease.

9. Install the steering wheel and torque the shaft nut to 30 ft. lbs. (41 Nm).

10. Connect the negative battery cable and check steering column operations.

Rear Defogger Switch

The rear defogger switch is located in the heater control head. Refer to the "Control Head" procedures in this chapter.

Headlight Switch

REMOVAL AND INSTALLATION

Cutlass Supreme, Regal and Lumina

1. Disconnect the negative battery cable.

2. Remove the instrument cluster trim plate.

3. Remove the 4 screws retaining the switch and remove the switch from the instrument panel.

4. Disconnect the electrical connector from the switch and remove the switch.

5. To install the switch, connect the electrical connector and install the switch in the instrument panel.

6. Install the cluster trim plate.

7. Connect the negative battery cable.

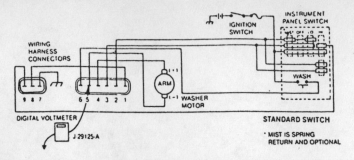

Testing Standard W/S Wiper/Washer Switch

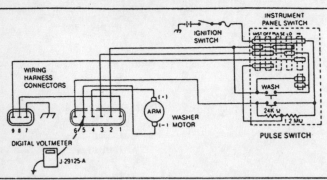

Testing Pulse W/S Wiper/Washer Switch

PROCEDURE		SWITCH MODE	TERMINAL #	MIST	OFF	PULSE	LO	HI †	WASH
DISCONNECT WIRING HARNESS FROM WIPER MOTOR AND PERFORM THE SWITCH TESTS LISTED IN THIS CHART. USE A DIGITAL VOLTMETER WITH IGNITION SWITCH ON.		PULSE	1	C	C	C	C	C	C
			2	B(+)	—	B(+)	B(+)	—	*B(+)
			3	B(+)	B(+)	—	B(+)	—	*B(+)
			4	—	—	—	—	—	—
			5	—	—	—	—	—	—
			6	10-12V	10-12V	10-12V	10-12V	10-12V	B(+)
			7	GROUND	GROUND	GROUND	GROUND	GROUND	GROUND
			8	C	C	C	C	C	C
			9	—	—	—	—	B(+)	—
		STANDARD	1		C		C	C	C
			2		—		B(+)	—	*B(+)
			3		B(+)		B(+)	—	*B(+)
			4		—		—	—	—
			5		—		—	—	—
			6		—		—	—	B(+)
			7		GROUND		GROUND	GROUND	GROUND
			8		C		C	C	C
			9		—		—	B(+)	—

C = CONTINUITY   † TERMINALS #2 & #3 CONNECTED TOGETHER.   *EXCEPT ON HI.

Windshield wiper switch testing

Grand Prix

1. Disconnect the negative battery cable.
2. Remove the screw retaining the headlight switch to the instrument panel.
3. Pull the top of the switch out to release the lower retaining clips and remove it from the instrument panel.

4. Disconnect the electrical connector and remove the switch from the vehicle.
5. To install the switch, connect the electrical connector and install the switch in the instrument panel.
6. Connect the negative battery cable.

Clock

The clock in an integral part of the radio assembly in the Lumina and the radio controls in the remaining models. The unit must be removed and serviced by a qualified radio repair service if the clock portion the the radio is inoperative.

Setting

1. Press the SET button. The set indicator light will appear.
2. Press the SCAN button and hold until the correct hours appear.
3. Press the SET button. The set indicator light will appear.
4. Press the SEEK button and hold until the correct minute appear.
5. Press the upper knob to recall the station or time.

Back-Up Light Switch

REMOVAL AND INSTALLATION

Manual

1. Disconnect the negative (–) battery cable and back-up light switch connector.
2. Remove the switch located on top of the transaxle with the proper size box wrench.
3. Apply thread locking compound to the switch threads and torque to 80 inch lbs. (9 Nm). Reconnect the negative battery cable.

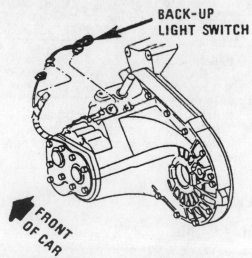

Back-up light switch — manual transaxle

Automatic

1. Disconnect the negative (–) battery cable.
2. Place the transaxle in the **NEUTRAL** position.
3. Raise the vehicle and support with jackstands.

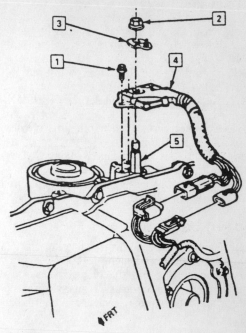

1. 18 ft. lbs.
2. 15 ft. lbs.
3. Shift lever
4. Neutral switch/back-up switch
5. Selector shaft

The back-up light switch is located on top of the automatic transaxle

4. Disconnect the switch electrical connector and remove the retaining clips.
5. Lower the vehicle and remove the vacuum hoses and electrical connectors from the cruise control servo, if so equipped.
6. Remove the shift lever at the transaxle. Do NOT disconnect the lever from the cable. Remove the two retaining bolts and switch.

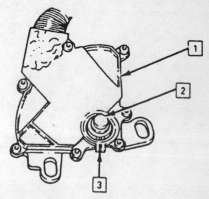

1. Back-up switch
2. Selector shaft
3. Align inner notch with outer notch

Automatic transaxle back-up switch adjustment

To install:

1. Align the notch (groove) on the inner sleeve with the notch on the switch body. Install the switch and torque the retaining bolts to 18 ft. lbs. (25 Nm).

2. Install the shift lever and torque the nut to 15 ft. lbs. (20 Nm).

3. Raise the vehicle and support with jackstands.

4. Connect the switch connector, harness clips and lower the vehicle.

5. Install the cruise control servo, if removed.

6. Connect the negative battery cable and check for proper operation.

Speed Sensor

An electronic speed sensor is used in place of a conventional speedometer cable. The speed sensor is mounted in the transaxle case tail shaft section. The automatic transaxle incorporates a speed sensor and governor in one assembly.

REMOVAL AND INSTALLATION

Manual

1. Disconnect the negative (–) battery cable.

2. Disconnect the speed sensor electrical connector, remove the bolt and retainer and sensor assembly from the transaxle housing.

3. Install the sensor and torque the retaining bolt to 84 inch lbs. (9 Nm).

4. Connect the sensor electrical connector and the negative battery cable.

Automatic

1. Disconnect the negative (–) battery cable.

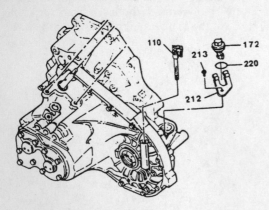

110. Transmission fluid level indicator
172. Speedo signal assembly
212. Speedo signal assembly retainer
213. Bolt
220. Seal

Speed sensor location — manual transaxle

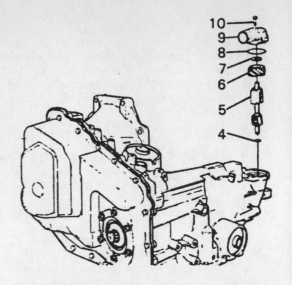

4. Oil seal ring
5. Governor assembly
6. Speedometer drive gear
7. Speedo gear thrust bearing
8. Governor cover O-ring
9. Governor cover
10. Screw

Speed sensor and governor location — automatic transaxle

2. Raise the vehicle and support with jackstands.

3. Remove the speed sensor wire connector at the transaxle.

4. Remove the two bolts attaching the sensor housing cover, cover and gasket.

5. Remove the spring washer, washers, magnet, coil assembly and O-ring as an assembly.

To install:

1. Install the spring washer, washers, magnet, coil assembly and O-ring as an assembly.

2. Install the cover, gasket and bolts.

3. Reconnect the sensor wire connector.

4. Lower the vehicle and connect the negative battery cable.

LIGHTING

Headlights

REMOVAL AND INSTALLATION

Bulb

CAUTION: *Halogen bulbs contain a gas under pressure. Handling the bulbs incorrectly could cause it to shatter into flying glass fragments. Do NOT leave the light switch ON and allow the bulb to cool before removal. Handle the bulb only by the base, avoid touching the glass.*

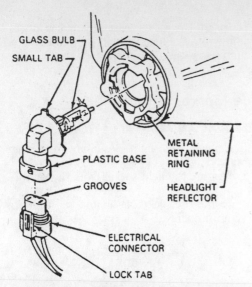

Headlight bulb replacement

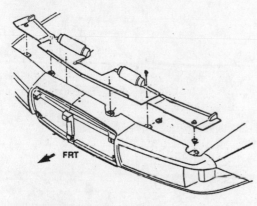

Headlight housing panel — Regal

1. Open the hood and support.
2. Remove the wire connector from the light bulb and turn the bulb out of the headlight assembly.
3. Install the bulb, connect the wiring and close the hood.

Light Assembly

1. Disconnect the negative (–) battery cable.
2. Open the hood and support.
3. Remove the headlight cover assembly (Regal only).
4. Remove the headlight assembly screws, pull assembly forward and turn the socket counterclockwise to remove.
5. Remove the bulb from the socket.
6. Turn the new bulb into the socket and the connect wire.
7. Install the assembly into position and tighten the retaining screws. Close the hood and connect the negative battery cable.

Front Turn Signal and Parking Lights

REMOVAL AND INSTALLATION

Lumina

1. Disconnect the negative (–) battery cable.
2. Raise the hood and remove the grille assembly as outlined in Chapter 10.
3. Remove the retaining screw and turn signal assembly.
4. Install the signal assembly, retaining screws, grille and connect the negative battery cable.

Regal

1. Disconnect the negative (–) battery cable.
2. Raise the hood and support safely.
3. Remove the cover over the headlights by turning the knob and folding back.
4. Remove the three light housing nuts and remove the sockets from the housing.
5. Install the sockets, housing, three nuts and install the headlight cover.
6. Connect the negative battery cable and lower the hood.

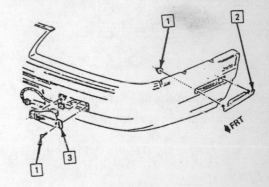

1. 18 inch lbs.
2. Reflector
3. Turn signal lamp

Turn signal light — Grand Prix

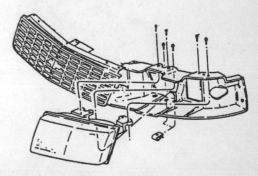

Headlight assembly — Lumina

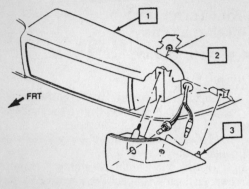

FRT

1. Headlamp housing panel
2. Nut
3. Locating pin

Park, turn and marker light — Regal

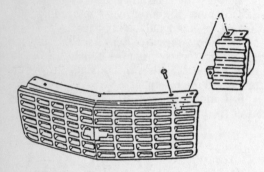

Turn signal light — Lumina

Grand Prix and Cutlass Supreme

1. Disconnect the negative (–) battery cable.
2. Remove the two screws at the top of the assembly and pull the assembly forward.
3. Disconnect the electrical connector by opening the tab.
4. Remove the bulb and socket assembly.

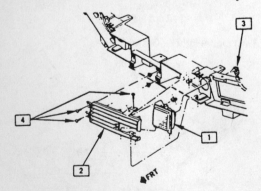

FRT

1. Light assembly
2. Grille
3. Bulb and socket
4. Bolts

Turn signal light — Cutlass Supreme

5. Install the socket assembly, position the assembly into the housing and tighten the two retaining screws. Connect the negative battery cable.

Side Marker Lights

REMOVAL AND INSTALLATION

1. Remove the light assembly retaining screws and light.
2. Remove the light socket from the assembly.
3. Install the socket, assembly and tighten the retaining screws.

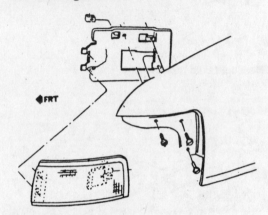

FRT

Side marker light — Cutlass Supreme

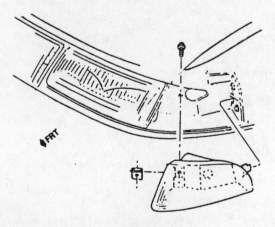

FRT

Side marker light — Lumina

Rear Turn Signal/Stop/Reverse Lights

REMOVAL AND INSTALLATION

NOTE: *Take care to prevent water leaks if the sealing surfaces around the tail light assembly is disturbed. Damaged gaskets must be replaced by using body caulking compound or equivalent in the critical areas.*

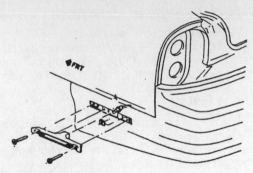

Rear side marker light

1. Disconnect the negative (–) battery cable.
2. Open the rear luggage compartment.
3. Remove the three carpet retaining clips and fold the carpet forward.
4. Remove the bulb sockets from the light assembly.
5. Remove the light assembly retaining nuts and remove the assembly.

NOTE: *The light assembly may not come right out because the gasket is holding it in place. Pry very gently on all corners equally and push the assembly out of the rear light cavity. When the assembly starts to move, cut the gasket with a knife.*

To install:
1. Install the light assembly with a new gasket and tighten the retaining nuts.
2. Install the light sockets into their proper location.
3. Install the carpeting and retaining clips.
4. Close the luggage compartment and connect the negative battery cable.

Fog Lights

REMOVAL AND INSTALLATION

Grand Prix

1. Disconnect the negative (–) battery cable.
2. Open the hood and support.

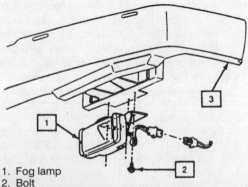

1. Fog lamp
2. Bolt
3. Impact bar

Regal fog light

3. Remove the three rear light cover retaining screws.
4. Remove the one bolt holding the cover-to-headlight housing panel.
5. Remove the cover by sliding it out from under the bolt.
6. Disconnect the electrical connector by opening the tabs and remove the bulb/socket assembly.
7. Remove the one bolt at the top rear of the fog light, if replacing assembly.

To install:
1. Install the light assembly and make sure the guide pins on the bottom are aligned with the holes.
2. Install the one bolt, bulb/socket and electrical connector.
3. Install the light cover and tighten the one bolt.

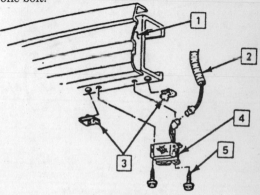

1. Bumper
2. Wiring harness
3. J-nuts
4. Fog lamp
5. Bolts

Cutlass Supreme fog lights

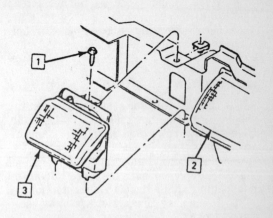

1. 89 inch lbs.
2. Headlight
3. Foglight

Grand Prix fog light

4. Install the three screws and close the hood.

5. Connect the negative battery cable.

Cutlass Supreme and Regal

1. Disconnect the negative (–) battery cable and the fog light electrical connector.

2. Remove the two retaining bolts and light assembly.

3. Install the light assembly, retaining bolts and connect the electrical connector. Connect the negative battery cable.

Horns

POOR HORN TONE

1. Poor horn tone — tighten the bolts in the mounting area.

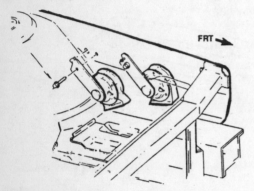

FRT →

Horn location — left front inner fender

2. Low pitched moan — Sounds like "mooing" caused by the current too high. Refer to the following **Adjustment** procedures.

3. Weak tone — current too low, correct poor connections, ground, or adjust as follows.

4. Weak stained tone — remove foreign object in the horn.

5. Harsh vibration — bend bracket so horn is not touching any sheet medal.

ADJUSTMENT

The current draw for a horn while operating should be 4.5–5.5 amperes at 11.5–12.5 volts. High current (more than 20 amperes) indicates an overheated winding or shorted horn; replace the horn if this condition exists. A current reading of 18 amperes means the contact points are not opening; adjust the horn current as follows.

1. To increase current — turn the adjusting screw clockwise.

2. To decrease current — turn the adjusting screw counterclockwise.

3. Current adjustments should be made 1/4 turn (90°) at a time.

REMOVAL AND INSTALLATION

There are two horn assemblies installed at the left front inner fender. Remove the electrical connector and retaining bolt. Install the horn and torque the bolt to 12 ft. lbs. (15 Nm).

Horn Relay

The horn relay is located under the right side electrical center in the forward light electrical center (underhood). To remove the relay, pull it straight out of the center.

TRAILER WIRING

Wiring the car for towing is fairly easy. There are a number of good wiring kits available and these should be used, rather than trying to design your own. All trailers will need brake lights and turn signals as well as tail lights and side marker lights. Most states require extra marker lights for overly wide trailers. Also, most states have recently required back-up lights for trailers, and most trailer manufacturers have been building trailers with back-up lights for several years.

Additionally, some Class I, most Class II and just about all Class III trailers will have electric brakes.

Add to this number an accessories wire, to operate trailer internal equipment or to charge the trailer's battery, and you can have as many as seven wires in the harness.

Determine the equipment on your trailer and buy the wiring kit necessary. The kit will contain all the wires needed, plus a plug adapter set which included the female plug, mounted on the bumper or hitch, and the male plug, wired into, or plugged into the trailer harness.

When installing the kit, follow the manufacturer's instructions. The color coding of the wires is standard throughout the industry.

One point to note: some domestic vehicles, and most imported vehicles, have separate turn signals. On most domestic vehicles, the brake lights and rear turn signals operate with the same bulb. For those vehicles with separate turn signals, you can purchase an isolation unit so that the brake lights won't blink whenever the turn signals are operated, or, you can go to your local electronics supply house and buy four diodes to wire in series with the brake and turn signal bulbs. Diodes will isolate the brake and turn signals. The choice is yours. The isolation units are simple and quick to install, but far more expensive than the diodes. The diodes, however, require more work to install properly, since they require the cutting of each bulb's wire and soldering in place of the diode.

One final point, the best kits are those with a spring loaded cover on the vehicle mounted socket. This cover prevents dirt and moisture from corroding the terminals. Never let the vehicle socket hang loosely; always mount it securely to the bumper or hitch.

CIRCUIT PROTECTION

Fuses

Main Fuse Block

The main fuse block is located in the underside of the instrument panel behind the glove compartment. Remove the access cover in the glove compartment to access the fuse block. The fuse block uses miniaturized fuses, designed for increased circuit protection and

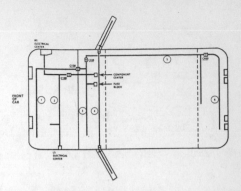

Electrical center location

greater reliability. Various convenience connectors, which snap-lock into the fuse block, add to the serviceability of this unit.

Component Center

The component center is located under the instrument panel, on the right side next to the fuse block. The component center houses circuit breakers, relays, chime module and hazard flasher.

Right Side Electrical Center

The right side electrical center is located on the right side inner fender in the engine compartment. The center houses a variety of fuses, fusible links and relays. The center can be serviced by removing the cover and remove the appropriate component.

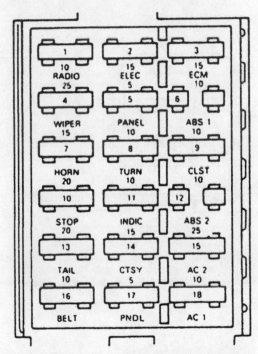

The instrument panel fuse block is located behind the glove compartment door.

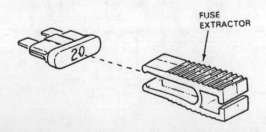

Fuse removal

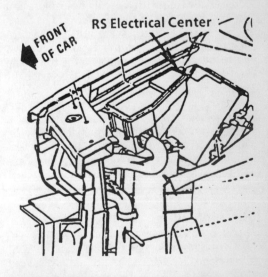

Fuse location — forward lamp center and location of horn relay

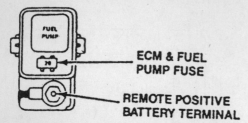

ECM & FUEL PUMP FUSE

REMOTE POSITIVE BATTERY TERMINAL

Fuse location — left underhood electrical center

Left Side Electrical Center

The left side electrical center is located on the left inner fender behind the battery. The center houses the remote positive battery terminal, fuel pump relay and the ECM/fuel pump fuse. The remote positive battery terminal is used for jump starting only.

Forward Lamp Center

The forward lamp center is located on the front right inner fender in front of the ECM unit. The center houses the fog light fuse, forward lamp relays and the horn relay.

Anti-lock Brake (ABS) Electrical Center

The ABS electrical center is used only with vehicles equipped with anti-lock brake systems. The center is located between the shock tower and the battery. The ABS center houses the ABS fuses, fusible links and relays.

The fuses can be removed by grasping the middle of the fuse with a needle nose pliers and pulling straight out of the fuse block. The fuses can be tested while they are still in the fuse block. Insert a fuse tester or a point type test light into the two metal tangs on the top of the fuse. With the ignition key ON, the test light should light at both metal tangs.

When replacing fuses, only use the correct amperage replacement fuse. Each fuse has a number stamped on the top which indicates the amperage rating. Damage to the electrical system may result if the incorrect fuses are used.

Fusible Links

Fusible links are sections of wire, with special insulation, designed to melt under electrical overload. Replacements are simply spliced into the wire. The wires are located at the starter solenoid terminal, right and left side electrical center in the engine compartment.

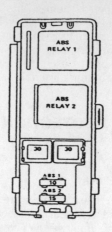

Fuse location — ABS electrical center located between the shock tower and the battery

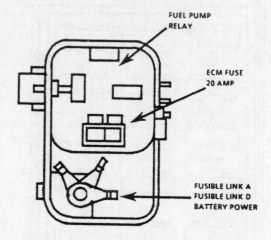

FUEL PUMP RELAY

ECM FUSE 20 AMP

FUSIBLE LINK A
FUSIBLE LINK D
BATTERY POWER

Fusible links located in the left side electrical center

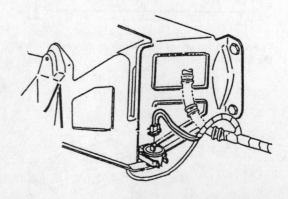

Turn signal flasher — right side of steering column bracket

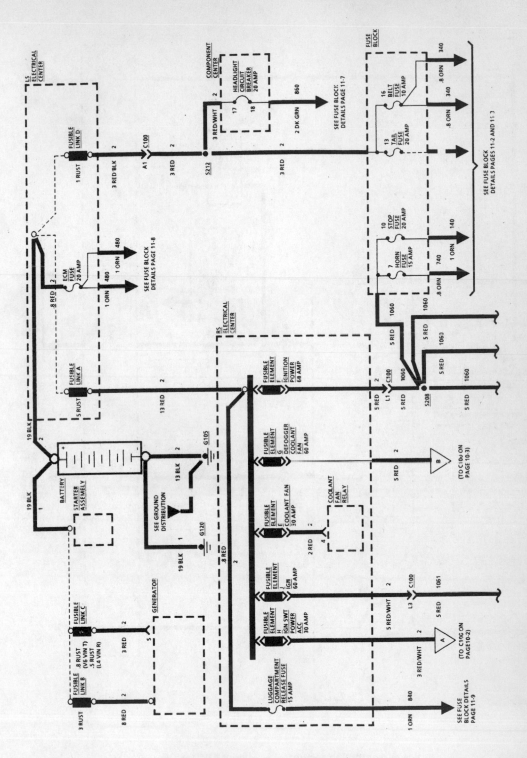

Power distribution schematic — without ABS

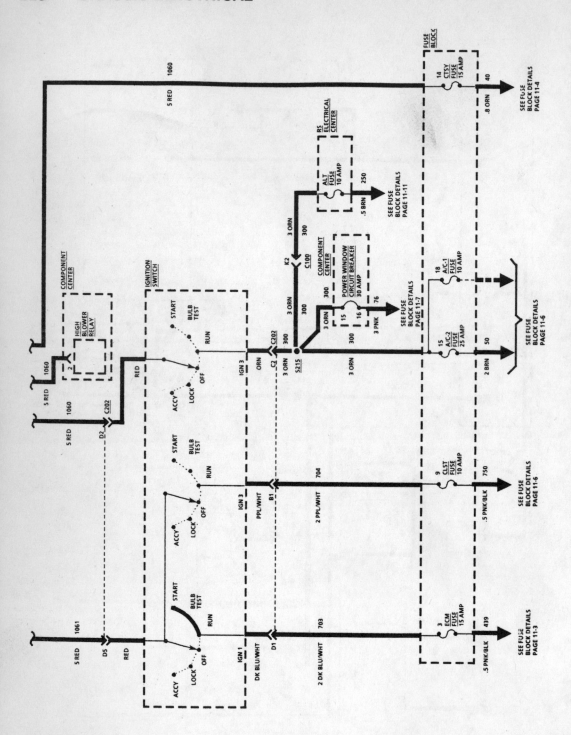

Power distribution schematic — without ABS (continued)

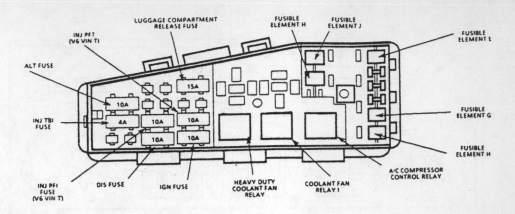

Fusible links located in the right side underhood electrical center

FUSIBLE LINK LOCATION, COLOR AND FUNCTION

• Link A – LS electrical center, rust, power to RS electrical center.
• Link B – starter motor, rust, power to alternator.
• Link C – starter motor, rust, power to alternator.
• Link D – LS electrical center, rust, power to fuse block/component center.
• Link E – RS electrical center, cooling fan. 30 amp

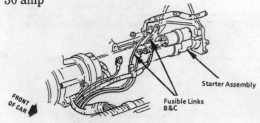

Fusible links located at starter motor

• Link F – RS electrical center, ignition power. 60 amp
• Link G – RS electrical center, defogger/coolant fan. 60 amp
• Link H – RS electrical center, ignition accessory power. 30 amp
• Link J – RS electrical center, ignition. 60 amp
• Link K – ABS electrical center, pump motor. 30 amp
• Link L – ABS electrical center, brake valve. 30 amp
• Link X – LS electrical center, power to ABS power center.

GM PART NO.	RATING	COLOR
12004003	3 AMP	VIOLET
12004005	5 AMP	TAN
12004006	7.5 AMP	BROWN
12004007	10 AMP	RED
12004008	15 AMP	LIGHT BLUE
12004009	20 AMP	YELLOW
12004010	25 AMP	WHITE

Fuse color coding

• Link Y – LS electrical center, power to ABS power center.

Circuit Breakers

Various circuit breakers are used throughout the electrical system. The breakers are designed to "trip" when an overload is placed on the system. The breaker automatically resets when the overload is removed. The breakers are located within the and component center located behind the instrument panel.

Flashers

REMOVAL AND INSTALLATION

Turn Signal

The turn signal flasher is mounted in a clip on the right side of the steering column support bracket.

Hazard

The hazard flasher is located in the component center, under the instrument panel, on the right side.

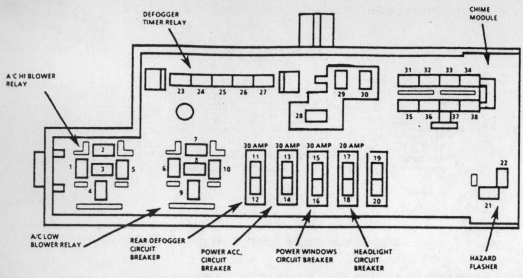

Circuit breakers located in component center

Troubleshooting Basic Windshield Wiper Problems

Problem	Cause	Solution
Electric Wipers		
Wipers do not operate— Wiper motor heats up or hums	• Internal motor defect • Bent or damaged linkage • Arms improperly installed on linking pivots	• Replace motor • Repair or replace linkage • Position linkage in park and reinstall wiper arms
Wipers do not operate— No current to motor	• Fuse or circuit breaker blown • Loose, open or broken wiring • Defective switch • Defective or corroded terminals • No ground circuit for motor or switch	• Replace fuse or circuit breaker • Repair wiring and connections • Replace switch • Replace or clean terminals • Repair ground circuits
Wipers do not operate— Motor runs	• Linkage disconnected or broken	• Connect wiper linkage or replace broken linkage
Vacuum Wipers		
Wipers do not operate	• Control switch or cable inoperative • Loss of engine vacuum to wiper motor (broken hoses, low engine vacuum, defective vacuum/fuel pump) • Linkage broken or disconnected • Defective wiper motor	• Repair or replace switch or cable • Check vacuum lines, engine vacuum and fuel pump • Repair linkage • Replace wiper motor
Wipers stop on engine acceleration	• Leaking vacuum hoses • Dry windshield • Oversize wiper blades • Defective vacuum/fuel pump	• Repair or replace hoses • Wet windshield with washers • Replace with proper size wiper blades • Replace pump

Troubleshooting Basic Turn Signal and Flasher Problems

Most problems in the turn signals or flasher system can be reduced to defective flashers or bulbs, which are easily replaced. Occasionally, problems in the turn signals are traced to the switch in the steering column, which will require professional service.

F = Front   R = Rear   ● = Lights off   ○ = Lights on

Problem		Solution
Turn signals light, but do not flash		• Replace the flasher
No turn signals light on either side		• Check the fuse. Replace if defective. • Check the flasher by substitution • Check for open circuit, short circuit or poor ground
Both turn signals on one side don't work		• Check for bad bulbs • Check for bad ground in both housings
One turn signal light on one side doesn't work		• Check and/or replace bulb • Check for corrosion in socket. Clean contacts. • Check for poor ground at socket
Turn signal flashes too fast or too slow		• Check any bulb on the side flashing too fast. A heavy-duty bulb is probably installed in place of a regular bulb. • Check the bulb flashing too slow. A standard bulb was probably installed in place of a heavy-duty bulb. • Check for loose connections or corrosion at the bulb socket
Indicator lights don't work in either direction		• Check if the turn signals are working • Check the dash indicator lights • Check the flasher by substitution

One indicator light doesn't light		• On systems with 1 dash indicator: See if the lights work on the same side. Often the filaments have been reversed in systems combining stoplights with taillights and turn signals.
		  Check the flasher by substitution
		• On systems with 2 indicators: Check the bulbs on the same side
		  Check the indicator light bulb
		  Check the flasher by substitution

Troubleshooting Basic Lighting Problems

Problem	Cause	Solution
Lights		
One or more lights don't work, but others do	• Defective bulb(s) • Blown fuse(s) • Dirty fuse clips or light sockets • Poor ground circuit	• Replace bulb(s) • Replace fuse(s) • Clean connections • Run ground wire from light socket housing to car frame
Lights burn out quickly	• Incorrect voltage regulator setting or defective regulator • Poor battery/alternator connections	• Replace voltage regulator • Check battery/alternator connections
Lights go dim	• Low/discharged battery • Alternator not charging • Corroded sockets or connections • Low voltage output	• Check battery • Check drive belt tension; repair or replace alternator • Clean bulb and socket contacts and connections • Replace voltage regulator
Lights flicker	• Loose connection • Poor ground • Circuit breaker operating (short circuit)	• Tighten all connections • Run ground wire from light housing to car frame • Check connections and look for bare wires
Lights "flare"—Some flare is normal on acceleration—if excessive, see "Lights Burn Out Quickly"	• High voltage setting	• Replace voltage regulator
Lights glare—approaching drivers are blinded	• Lights adjusted too high • Rear springs or shocks sagging • Rear tires soft	• Have headlights aimed • Check rear springs/shocks • Check/correct rear tire pressure
Turn Signals		
Turn signals don't work in either direction	• Blown fuse • Defective flasher • Loose connection	• Replace fuse • Replace flasher • Check/tighten all connections
Right (or left) turn signal only won't work	• Bulb burned out • Right (or left) indicator bulb burned out • Short circuit	• Replace bulb • Check/replace indicator bulb • Check/repair wiring
Flasher rate too slow or too fast	• Incorrect wattage bulb • Incorrect flasher	• Flasher bulb • Replace flasher (use a variable load flasher if you pull a trailer)
Indicator lights do not flash (burn steadily)	• Burned out bulb • Defective flasher	• Replace bulb • Replace flasher
Indicator lights do not light at all	• Burned out indicator bulb • Defective flasher	• Replace indicator bulb • Replace flasher

Troubleshooting Basic Dash Gauge Problems

Problem	Cause	Solution
Coolant Temperature Gauge		
Gauge reads erratically or not at all	• Loose or dirty connections • Defective sending unit • Defective gauge	• Clean/tighten connections • Bi-metal gauge: remove the wire from the sending unit. Ground the wire for an instant. If the gauge registers, replace the sending unit. • Magnetic gauge: disconnect the wire at the sending unit. With ignition ON gauge should register COLD. Ground the wire; gauge should register HOT.
Ammeter Gauge—Turn Headlights ON (do not start engine). Note reaction		
Ammeter shows charge Ammeter shows discharge Ammeter does not move	• Connections reversed on gauge • Ammeter is OK • Loose connections or faulty wiring • Defective gauge	• Reinstall connections • Nothing • Check/correct wiring • Replace gauge
Oil Pressure Gauge		
Gauge does not register or is inaccurate	• On mechanical gauge, Bourdon tube may be bent or kinked • Low oil pressure • Defective gauge • Defective wiring • Defective sending unit	• Check tube for kinks or bends preventing oil from reaching the gauge • Remove sending unit. Idle the engine briefly. If no oil flows from sending unit hole, problem is in engine. • Remove the wire from the sending unit and ground it for an instant with the ignition ON. A good gauge will go to the top of the scale. • Check the wiring to the gauge. If it's OK and the gauge doesn't register when grounded, replace the gauge. • If the wiring is OK and the gauge functions when grounded, replace the sending unit
All Gauges		
All gauges do not operate	• Blown fuse • Defective instrument regulator	• Replace fuse • Replace instrument voltage regulator
All gauges read low or erratically	• Defective or dirty instrument voltage regulator	• Clean contacts or replace
All gauges pegged	• Loss of ground between instrument voltage regulator and car • Defective instrument regulator	• Check ground • Replace regulator
Warning Lights		
Light(s) do not come on when ignition is ON, but engine is not started	• Defective bulb • Defective wire • Defective sending unit	• Replace bulb • Check wire from light to sending unit • Disconnect the wire from the sending unit and ground it. Replace the sending unit if the light comes on with the ignition ON.
Light comes on with engine running	• Problem in individual system • Defective sending unit	• Check system • Check sending unit (see above)

Troubleshooting the Heater

Problem	Cause	Solution
Blower motor will not turn at any speed	• Blown fuse • Loose connection • Defective ground • Faulty switch • Faulty motor • Faulty resistor	• Replace fuse • Inspect and tighten • Clean and tighten • Replace switch • Replace motor • Replace resistor
Blower motor turns at one speed only	• Faulty switch • Faulty resistor	• Replace switch • Replace resistor
Blower motor turns but does not circulate air	• Intake blocked • Fan not secured to the motor shaft	• Clean intake • Tighten security
Heater will not heat	• Coolant does not reach proper temperature • Heater core blocked internally • Heater core air-bound • Blend-air door not in proper position	• Check and replace thermostat if necessary • Flush or replace core if necessary • Purge air from core • Adjust cable
Heater will not defrost	• Control cable adjustment incorrect • Defroster hose damaged	• Adjust control cable • Replace defroster hose

MANUAL TRANSAXLE

Identification

NOTE: *General Motors, as of early 1990 has changed the names of their transaxles. The former THM 125C 3-speed automatic is changed to THM 3T40, the 440-T4 4-speed automatic is changed to THM 4T60 and the HM-282 5-speed manual is changed to 5TM40.*

The Cutlass Supreme and Grand Prix are available with the HM–282 (5TM40) Muncie 5–speed manual transaxle. The transaxle has an identification tag and stamp on the exterior case. The information on the tag will assist in servicing and ordering parts.

Adjustments

The shift control and cables are preset at the factory, requiring no adjustments. The clutch is a hydraulically actuated system that is self-adjusting. No periodic adjustments are needed.

Back-up Light Switch

REMOVAL AND INSTALLATION

1. Disconnect the negative (–) battery cable and back-up light switch connector.

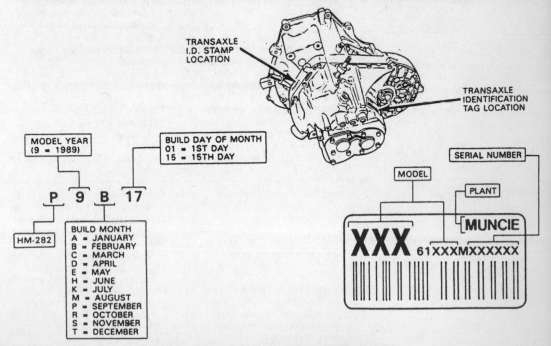

HM–282 (5–speed) manual transaxle identification

Troubleshooting the Manual Transmission

Problem	Cause	Solution
Transmission shifts hard	• Clutch adjustment incorrect • Clutch linkage or cable binding • Shift rail binding	• Adjust clutch • Lubricate or repair as necessary • Check for mispositioned selector arm roll pin, loose cover bolts, worn shift rail bores, worn shift rail, distorted oil seal, or extension housing not aligned with case. Repair as necessary.
	• Internal bind in transmission caused by shift forks, selector plates, or synchronizer assemblies • Clutch housing misalignment • Incorrect lubricant • Block rings and/or cone seats worn	• Remove, dissemble and inspect transmission. Replace worn or damaged components as necessary. • Check runout at rear face of clutch housing • Drain and refill transmission • Blocking ring to gear clutch tooth face clearance must be 0.030 inch or greater. If clearance is correct it may still be necessary to inspect blocking rings and cone seats for excessive wear. Repair as necessary.
Gear clash when shifting from one gear to another	• Clutch adjustment incorrect • Clutch linkage or cable binding • Clutch housing misalignment • Lubricant level low or incorrect lubricant • Gearshift components, or synchronizer assemblies worn or damaged	• Adjust clutch • Lubricate or repair as necessary • Check runout at rear of clutch housing • Drain and refill transmission and check for lubricant leaks if level was low. Repair as necessary. • Remove, disassemble and inspect transmission. Replace worn or damaged components as necessary.
Transmission noisy	• Lubricant level low or incorrect lubricant • Clutch housing-to-engine, or transmission-to-clutch housing bolts loose • Dirt, chips, foreign material in transmission • Gearshift mechanism, transmission gears, or bearing components worn or damaged • Clutch housing misalignment	• Drain and refill transmission. If lubricant level was low, check for leaks and repair as necessary. • Check and correct bolt torque as necessary • Drain, flush, and refill transmission • Remove, disassemble and inspect transmission. Replace worn or damaged components as necessary. • Check runout at rear face of clutch housing
Jumps out of gear	• Clutch housing misalignment • Gearshift lever loose • Offset lever nylon insert worn or lever attaching nut loose • Gearshift mechanism, shift forks, selector plates, interlock plate, selector arm, shift rail, detent plugs, springs or shift cover worn or damaged • Clutch shaft or roller bearings worn or damaged	• Check runout at rear face of clutch housing • Check lever for worn fork. Tighten loose attaching bolts. • Remove gearshift lever and check for loose offset lever nut or worn insert. Repair or replace as necessary. • Remove, disassemble and inspect transmission cover assembly. Replace worn or damaged components as necessary. • Replace clutch shaft or roller bearings as necessary

Troubleshooting the Manual Transmission

Problem	Cause	Solution
Jumps out of gear (cont.)	• Gear teeth worn or tapered, synchronizer assemblies worn or damaged, excessive end play caused by worn thrust washers or output shaft gears	• Remove, disassemble, and inspect transmission. Replace worn or damaged components as necessary.
	• Pilot bushing worn	• Replace pilot bushing
Will not shift into one gear	• Gearshift selector plates, interlock plate, or selector arm, worn, damaged, or incorrectly assembled	• Remove, disassemble, and inspect transmission cover assembly. Repair or replace components as necessary.
	• Shift rail detent plunger worn, spring broken, or plug loose	• Tighten plug or replace worn or damaged components as necessary
	• Gearshift lever worn or damaged	• Replace gearshift lever
	• Synchronizer sleeves or hubs, damaged or worn	• Remove, disassemble and inspect transmission. Replace worn or damaged components.
Locked in one gear—cannot be shifted out	• Shift rail(s) worn or broken, shifter fork bent, setscrew loose, center detent plug missing or worn	• Inspect and replace worn or damaged parts
	• Broken gear teeth on countershaft gear, clutch shaft, or reverse idler gear	• Inspect and replace damaged part
	Gearshift lever broken or worn, shift mechanism in cover incorrectly assembled or broken, worn damaged gear train components	• Disassemble transmission. Replace damaged parts or assemble correctly.

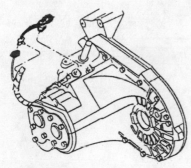

Back-up light switch

2. Remove the switch located on top of the transaxle with the proper size box wrench.

3. Apply thread locking compound to the switch threads and torque to 80 inch lbs. (9 Nm). Reconnect the negative battery cable.

Frame Assembly

REMOVAL AND INSTALLATION

1. Disconnect the negative (–) battery cable and remove the air cleaner assembly.

2. Install the engine support fixture J-28467-A.

3. Raise the vehicle and support with jackstands.

4. Position jackstands under the engine for support.

5. Remove the front wheel assemblies.

6. Disconnect the intermediate shaft from the steering gear stub shaft.

7. Remove the power steering hose bracket from the frame.

8. Remove the steering gear from the frame and support.

9. Remove the lower ball joints from the lower control arms.

10. Disconnect the engine and transaxle mounts.

11. Support the frame assembly and remove the frame-to-body mounting bolts.

12. Remove the frame assembly with the lower control arms and stabilizer shaft attached. Work the frame downward toward the rear of the vehicle.

13. Remove all loose frame hardware from the body.

To install:

1. Lubricate the frame insulators with rubber lubricant before installation.

2. Install the lower and upper insulators, retainers and spacers.

3. Install the transaxle mounting bracket, lower control arms and stabilizer shaft, if removed.

4. With an assistant, position the frame-to-body and hand tighten the retaining bolts.

5. Align the frame-to-body by inserting two

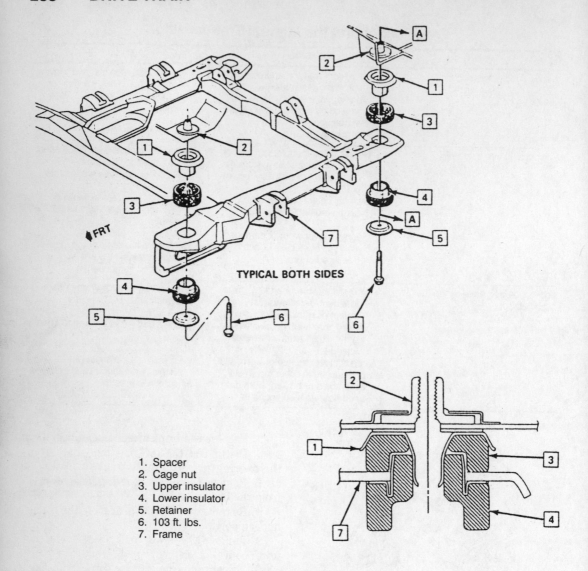

1. Spacer
2. Cage nut
3. Upper insulator
4. Lower insulator
5. Retainer
6. 103 ft. lbs.
7. Frame

Frame assembly

0.74 inch (19mm) diameter by 8.0 inch (203mm) long pins in the alignment holes on the right side of the frame.

6. Torque the frame-to-body retaining bolts to 103 ft. lbs. (140 Nm).

7. Reconnect the engine and transaxle mounts.

8. Install the lower ball joints and steering gear.

9. Install the hoses and brackets.

10. Install the intermediate shaft-to-steering stub shaft.

11. Install the front wheels and torque the lug nuts to 100 ft. lbs. (136 Nm).

12. Lower the vehicle and remove the engine support fixture.

13. Install the air cleaner and connect the negative battery cable.

14. Have a qualified alignment technician check the front end alignment.

Transaxle Assembly

REMOVAL AND INSTALLATION

NOTE: *Before preforming any manual transaxle removal procedures, the clutch master cylinder pushrod MUST be disconnected from the clutch pedal and the connection in the hydraulic line must be separated using tool No. J-36221. Permanent damage may occur to the actuator if the clutch pedal is depressed while the system is not resisted by clutch loads. Also, the pushrod bushing must be replaced once it has been disconnected from the master cylinder.*

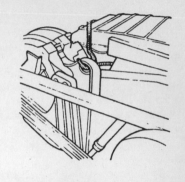

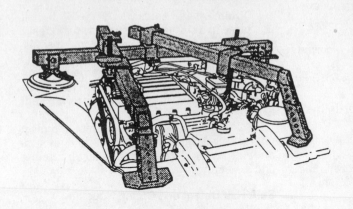

Engine support fixture

1. Disconnect the negative (–) battery cable and remove the air cleaner assembly.

2. Install the engine support fixture tool J-28467-A along with the support leg.

3. Remove the clutch actuator from the transaxle.

4. Remove the electrical connectors from the back-up switch.

5. Remove the shift and select and cables from the transaxle case.

6. Remove the exhaust crossover pipe at the left exhaust manifold.

7. Remove the EGR tube from the crossover.

8. Loosen the bolts and swing the crossover upward to gain clearance to the top transaxle bolts.

9. Remove the two upper transaxle-to-engine bolts and studs. Leave one lower mounting stud attached to hold the assembly in place.

10. Raise the vehicle and support with jackstands.

11. Drain the transaxle fluid into a pan.

12. Remove the four clutch housing cover screws.

13. Remove the front wheels and both wheelhouse splash shields.

14. Remove the power steering lines from the frame, rack and pinion heat shield and rack and pinion from the frame. Do NOT disconnect the steering hoses.

15. Remove the right and left ball joints at the steering knuckle.

16. Remove the transaxle upper mount retaining bolts and lower engine mount nuts.

17. Remove the frame-to-body retaining bolts.

18. Remove the frame from the vehicle as outlined in this section.

19. Disconnect both drive axles from the transaxle and support to the body with wire.

20. Remove the starter motor.

21. Securely support the transaxle case for removal.

22. Remove the remaining transaxle-to-engine retaining bolts and transaxle.

To install:

1. Install the transaxle and lower retaining bolts.

2. Install the starter motor and drive axles.

3. Install the frame assembly and retaining bolts as outlined in this section.

4. Install the engine mount retaining nuts and upper transaxle retaining bolt. Torque the transaxle-to-engine bolts to 55 ft. lbs. (75 Nm).

5. Install both ball joints-to-steering knuckle.

6. Install the power steering assembly, heat shield and hose brackets.

7. Install the wheelhouse splash shields and front wheels. Torque the lug nuts to 100 ft. lbs. (136 Nm).

8. Install the transaxle drain plug, clutch housing cover and lower the vehicle.

9. Connect the back-up light switch and speed sensor wiring.

10. Install the two upper transaxle mounting bolts and studs. Torque the bolts and studs to 55 ft. lbs. (75 Nm).

11. Install the crossover pipe, EGR pipe and tighten the retaining nuts.

12. Install the shift and select cables-to-transaxle.

13. Connect the clutch actuator-to-transaxle.

14. Install the air cleaner assembly and remove the engine support fixture.

15. Refill the transaxle to the proper fluid level with manual transaxle oil No. 12345349 or equivalent.

16. Check each procedure for proper installation and completion of repair.

17. Connect the negative battery cable.

Overhaul

DISASSEMBLY

External Mounts and Linkage

1. Remove the transaxle from the vehicle and place in a suitable holding fixture. Refer to the "Manual Transaxle" removal and installation procedures in this chapter.

2. Remove the shift lever nut, do not allow the lever to move during removal of nut. Use a $3/8$ inch drive wrench to hold the external shift lever.

3. Remove the washer, lever, retainer, pivot pin and pivot, bolts and bracket, fluid level indicator and the electronic speedometer retainer and assembly.

Shift Rail Detent and Clutch Housing

1. Remove the clutch disengage bearing.

2. Remove the detent holder cover by puncturing the cover in the middle and prying off.

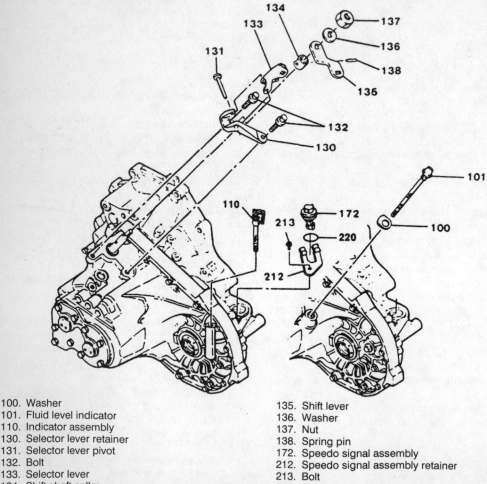

100. Washer
101. Fluid level indicator
110. Indicator assembly
130. Selector lever retainer
131. Selector lever pivot
132. Bolt
133. Selector lever
134. Shift shaft collar

135. Shift lever
136. Washer
137. Nut
138. Spring pin
172. Speedo signal assembly
212. Speedo signal assembly retainer
213. Bolt
220. Seal

External linkage mounting

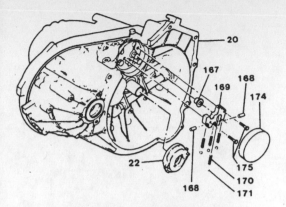

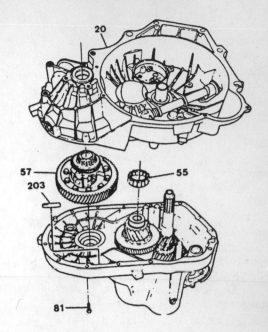

20. Clutch and differential housing
22. Clutch disengage bearing
167. Reverse shift rail bearing
168. Interlock pins
169. Detent holder
170. Detent springs
171. Detent balls
174. Detent holder cover
175. Bolts

Shift rail detent in clutch housing

20. Clutch and differential case
55. Output bearing
57. Differential assembly
81. Bolt
203. Magnet

Clutch housing

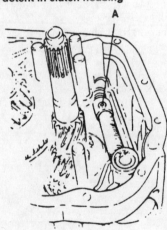

A. LOCATION OF PIN

Shift shaft pin

3. Remove the detent holder bolts, holder, detent, springs and interlock pins.
4. Remove the detent balls and bushing.

Shift Shaft Detent in Transaxle Housing

1. Remove the detent cover snapring, cover, screw and outer spring seat and the 5th/reverse bias spring/inner spring seat.

Transaxle Case and Clutch Housing Separation

1. Remove the fifteen clutch housing retaining bolts.
2. Transaxle must be in neutral. Remove

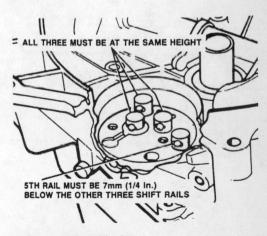

ALL THREE MUST BE AT THE SAME HEIGHT

5TH RAIL MUST BE 7mm (1/4 In.)
BELOW THE OTHER THREE SHIFT RAILS

Detent neutral positioning

the clutch housing by gently tapping the housing with a rubber hammer.
3. Remove the differential gear assembly, magnet and bearing.

Shift Shaft Components

1. Remove the shift shaft pin using a punch.
2. Remove the shift shaft assembly consisting of the shaft, rollers, 1st/2nd bias spring and shift and reverse lever.

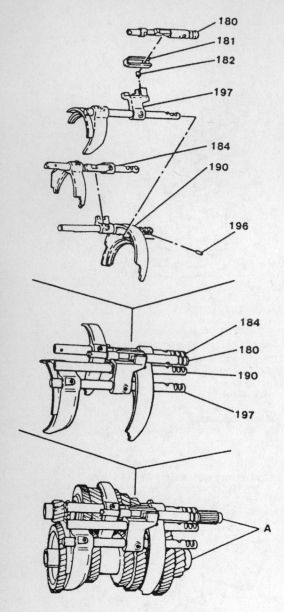

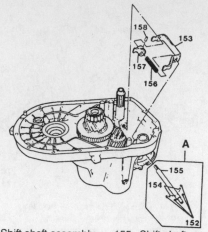

A. Shift shaft assembly
152. Shift shaft rollers
153. Reverse lever
154. Shift shaft pins
155. Shift shaft
156. 1–2 bias spring
157. Shift lever
158. Lever retainer pin

Shift shaft components

Gear Clusters

1. Using tool J-36182-1 and J-361821-2, position in a hydraulic press.

2. Position the transaxle case and gear cluster assembly in the press. Align the shift rail and shaft pilots to the fixture.

3. Position tool J-36185 on the shaft support bearings and pilots. Using the press, separate the shaft and gear clusters from the transaxle case.

Gear Clusters and Shift Rails

1. Remove the 1-2 shift rail assembly and lock pin.

A. Gear cluster and shift rail assembly
180. Reverse rail
181. Shift gate
182. Roller
184. 3rd–4th rail
190. 1st–2nd rail
196. Interlock pin
197. 5th rail

Shift shaft components

Gear Cluster Support Components

1. Engage the gear cluster in 4th (A) and reverse (B) by pushing down on the gear rails.

2. Remove the nine bearing retainer cover bolts and cover. Using tool J-36031, remove the bearing retainer Hex bolts and selective shim.

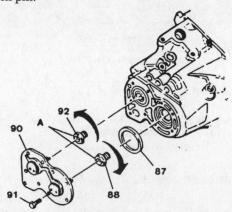

A. Use tool J–36031 or equivalent
87. Selective shim
88. Retainer (clockwise rotation)
90. End plate
91. Bolt
92. Retainer (Counterclockwise rotation)

Gear cluster supports

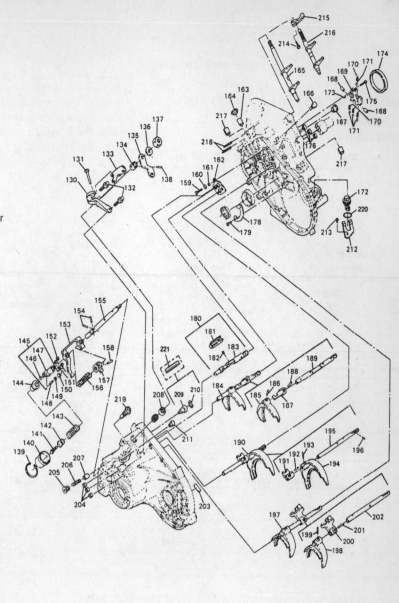

130. Selector lever retainer
131. Selector lever pin
132. Bolt
133. Selector lever
134. Shift shaft collar
135. Shift lever
136. Washer
137. Nut
138. Spring pin
139. Snapring
140. Shift shaft cover
141. Bolt/screw
142. Outer 5th spring seat
143. Spring
144. Inner 5th spring seat
145. Detent lever
146. Detent pin retainer
147. Detent lever
148. Detent lever pin
149. Detent lever spacer
150. Detent lever roller
151. Detent pin retainer
152. Detent roller (4)
153. Reverse lever
154. Detent lever roller (2)
155. Shift shaft
156. 3rd/4th bias spring
157. Shift lever
158. Roll pin
159. Bolt/screw
160. Flat washer (3)
161. Spacer (3)
162. Shift interlock plate
163. Outer clutch fork bushing
164. Clutch fork seal
165. Clutch fork shaft
166. Breather assembly
167. Reverse shift rail bushing
168. Interlock pin (2)
169. Detent holder
170. Detent spring (4)
171. Detent ball (4)
172. Speedometer signal assembly
173. Spring pin
174. Detent holder cover
175. Bolt/screw
176. Shift rail bushing (3)
178. Output bearing race retainer
179. Bolt/screw
180. Reverse shift rail
181. 5th/rev shift gate

182. Gear disengage roller
183. Reverse shift shaft
184. 3rd/4th shift rail
185. 3rd/4th shift fork
186. Fork retainer pin
187. 3rd/4th select lever
188. Lever retainer pin
189. 3rd/4th shift shaft
190. 1st/2nd shift rail
191. 1st/2nd select lever
192. Lever retainer pin
193. Fork retainer pin
194. 1st/2nd shift fork

195. 1st/2nd shift shaft
196. Lock pin
197. 5th shift rail
198. 5th shift fork
199. Fork retainer pin
200. 5th shift lever
201. Lever retainer pin
202. 5th shift shaft
203. Magnet clip
204. Shift rail plug (3)
205. Bolt/screw
206. Sliding sleeve spring
207. Sliding sleeve

Shift mechanisms

2. Remove the 3-4 shift rail assembly.

3. Remove the 5th shift rail assembly and reverse assembly.

4. Remove the shift gate and disengage roller.

UNIT DISASSEMBLY AND REPAIR

Input Shaft

DISASSEMBLY

1. **Important!** identify the blocker ring for the 3rd gear and 4th gear blocker ring. DO NOT MIX.

2. Remove the input shaft snapring before using the press.

3. Remove 4th and 5th gears, bearings, race, blocker ring, synchronizer and gear using an arbor press.

4. Remove the 3rd gear bearing.

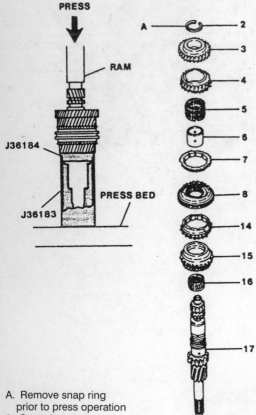

A. Remove snap ring
   prior to press operation
2. Snap ring
3. 5th gear
4. 4th gear
5. Bearing 4th
6. Race
7. Blocking ring 4th
8. 3rd–4th synchronizer
14. Blocking ring 3rd
15. 3rd gear
17. Input shaft

Input shaft assembly

INSPECTION

1. Clean all parts with solvent and blow dry with compressed air.

2. Inspect; input shaft splines for cracks or wear, gear teeth for scuffed, nicked, burred or broken teeth, bearings for roughness of rotation, burred or pitted conditions and bearing races for scoring, wear or overheating. Inspect the synchronizers for scuffs, nicks, burrs or scor-

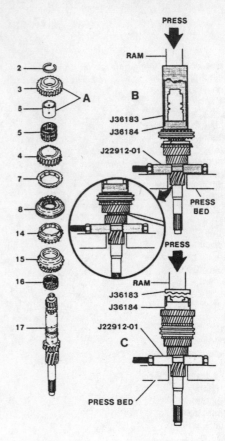

A. 5th gear and bearing race require heating prior to installation
B. Start press operation of 3rd–4th gear synchronizer; do not contact blocking ring. Lift gears with probe to engage blocking ring. Continue press operation
C. Press 5th gear
2. Snap ring
3. 5th gear
4. 4th gear
5. Bearing, 4th gear
6. Bearing race, 4th gear
7. Blocking ring, 4th gear
8. 3rd–4th synchronizer assembly
14. Blocking ring, 3rd gear
15. 3rd gear
16. Bearing, 3rd gear
17. Input shaft.

Input shaft reassembly

ing. If any condition exist for any component, restore or replace the component. It is much easier to replace worn components while the transaxle is disassembled than when it is in the vehicle.

ASSEMBLY

1. Install the input bearing, 3rd gear with the cone up and blocker ring.

2. **Important:** when pressing the 3-4 synchronizer assembly use the following:

　a. Start pressing the 3-4 synchro, STOP, before tang engages.

　b. Lift and rotate the gears into the synchro tangs.

　c. Continue to press until seated. Make sure all metal shavings are removed.

3. Install the 3-4 synchro using tool J-22912-01, J-36183, J-36184 and a press. The side marked 3RD gear and small OD groove of the sleeve goes toward the 3rd gear.

4. Install the bearing race and the bearing.

5. Install the blocker ring, then the 4th gear with the cone down and then the 5th gear using the press. The 5th gear should be flat side down.

6. Install the new snapring.

Output Shaft

DISASSEMBLY

1. **Important:** identify the blocker ring for 5th gear, ring for 2nd gear and ring for 1st gear. DO NOT MIX.

DIMENSION A
- SELECTED SHIM CAN BE 0.03 mm (0.001 IN.) ABOVE OR 0.12 mm (0.004 IN.) BELOW THE END PLATE MOUNTING SURFACE

PART NO.	DIM. A mm (IN.)
14092067	4.54 (0.179)
14092068	4.64 (0.183)
14092069	4.74 (0.187)
14092070	4.84 (0.191)
14092071	4.94 (0.194)
14092072	5.04 (0.198)
14092073	5.14 (0.202)

END PLATE MOUNTING SURFACE

Output shaft selective shim

2. Remove the 5th/reverse synchronizer assembly using tool J-22912-01 and a press.

3. Remove the blocker ring, 5th gear, bearing, thrust washer and ball.

4. Remove the snapring.

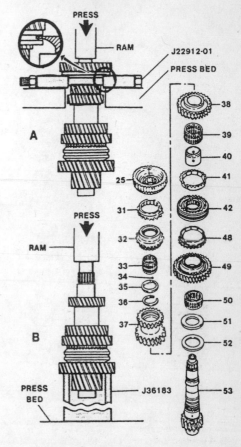

A. Install J–22912–01 in sleeve groove or on gear face only
B. Remove snap ring prior to press operation. Mount 1st gear on J–36183
25. Reverse gear/ 5th gear synchronizer
31. Blocking ring 5th gear
32. 5th gear
33. 5th gear bearing
34. Thrust washer positioning ball
35. Thrust washer
36. Snap ring
37. 3rd–4th gear cluster
38. 2nd gear
39. 2nd gear bearing
40. 2nd gear bearing race
41. Blocking ring 2nd gear
42. 1st–2nd synchronizer assembly
48. Blocking ring 1st gear
49. 1st gear
50. 1st gear bearing
51. Thrust bearing
52. Thrust washer
53. Output shaft

Output shaft assembly

5. Remove the 1st gear, bearing, caged thrust bearing and thrust washer using tool J-36183 and a press. The 2nd gear, bearing, race, 1-2 synchro and blocker rings will press off with the 1st gear.

INSPECTION

1. Clean all parts with solvent and blow dry with compressed air.

2. Inspect the output shaft for spline wear, cracks or excessive wear, gear teeth for scuffed,

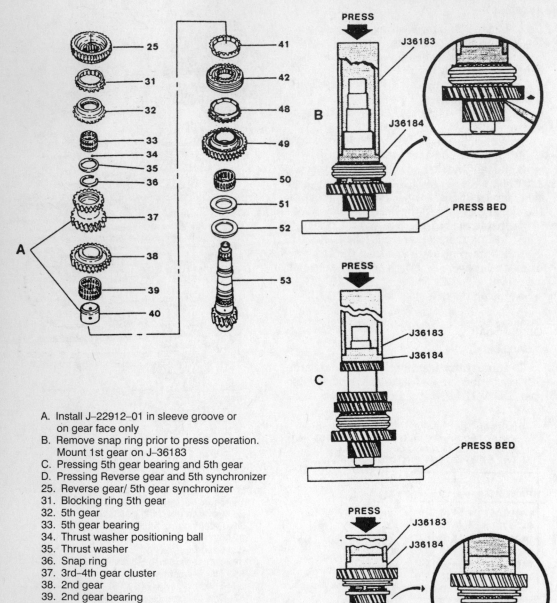

A. Install J–22912–01 in sleeve groove or on gear face only
B. Remove snap ring prior to press operation. Mount 1st gear on J–36183
C. Pressing 5th gear bearing and 5th gear
D. Pressing Reverse gear and 5th synchronizer
25. Reverse gear/ 5th gear synchronizer
31. Blocking ring 5th gear
32. 5th gear
33. 5th gear bearing
34. Thrust washer positioning ball
35. Thrust washer
36. Snap ring
37. 3rd–4th gear cluster
38. 2nd gear
39. 2nd gear bearing
40. 2nd gear bearing race
41. Blocking ring 2nd gear
42. 1st–2nd synchronizer assembly
48. Blocking ring 1st gear
49. 1st gear
50. 1st gear bearing
51. Thrust bearing
52. Thrust washer
53. Output shaft

Output shaft reassembly

nicked, burred or broken teeth and bearings for roughness, burred or pitted conditions. If scuffed, nicked, burred or scored conditions can not be removed with fine crocus cloth or soft stone, replace the component.

ASSEMBLY

1. Install the thrust washer with the chamfer down, caged thrust bearing with the needles down, 1st gear bearing, 1st gear with the cone up and the blocker ring.

2. **Important:** when pressing the 1-2 synchronizer assembly, start the press operation and STOP before tangs engages. Lift and rotate gears to engage the blocker ring tangs. Continue to press until seated and make sure all metal shavings are removed.

3. Install the 1-2 synchro using tool J-36183 and a press. The side marked 1ST and small OD groove goes toward the 1st gear.

4. Install the 2nd gear bearing race, bearing and 2nd gear with the cone down.

5. Install the 3-4 gear cluster using tool J-36183 and a press. Position the large OD gear down.

6. Install the new snapring, thrust washer positioning ball retained with petroleum jelly and the slotted thrust washer. Align the ID slot with ball.

7. Install the 5th gear bearing and the 5th gear with the cone up. Install the blocker ring.

8. **Important:** when pressing on the reverse gear and 5th synchro, start the press operation and STOP before tangs engage. Lift and rotate the 5th gear and blocker ring (thrust washer must stay down) until the tangs engage.

9. Install the 5th/reverse gear synchro assembly using tool J-36183 and a press.

Transaxle Case

DISASSEMBLY

NOTE: *Remove bearings and bushings only when there is evidence of damage and the component can not be reused.*

1. Remove snapring, plug, screw, spring and sliding sleeve.

2. Remove bushing using tool J-36034 and J-36190.

3. Remove detent lever, bushing and seal using a small pry bar.

4. Remove the shift shaft seal using tool J-36027.

5. Remove the axle seal, outer race, plugs, input shaft support bearing and the output shaft support bearing.

6. Remove the three shift rail bushing using tool J-36029, the reverse shift rail bush-

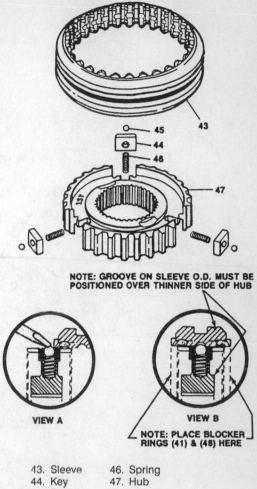

NOTE: GROOVE ON SLEEVE O.D. MUST BE POSITIONED OVER THINNER SIDE OF HUB

VIEW A   VIEW B

NOTE: PLACE BLOCKER RINGS (41) & (48) HERE

43. Sleeve	46. Spring
44. Key	47. Hub
45. Ball	

1st and 2nd synchronizer assembly

ing by driving down and removing through the back-up light switch hole.

ASSEMBLE

1. Install the shift shaft bearing and seal using tool J-36189 and J-36190.

2. Install the three shift rail bushing using tool J-36029.

3. Install the reverse rail bushing using tool J-36030 and J-36190.

4. Install the differential carrier outer race, axle seal and plugs.

5. Install detent lever bushings, sliding sleeve bushing using tools J-36039 and J-36034.

6. Install detent lever, sleeve, spring and screw tightened to 32 ft. lbs. (44 Nm).

7. Install plug, snapring and stud with the chamfer end out torqued to 15 ft. lbs. (21 Nm).

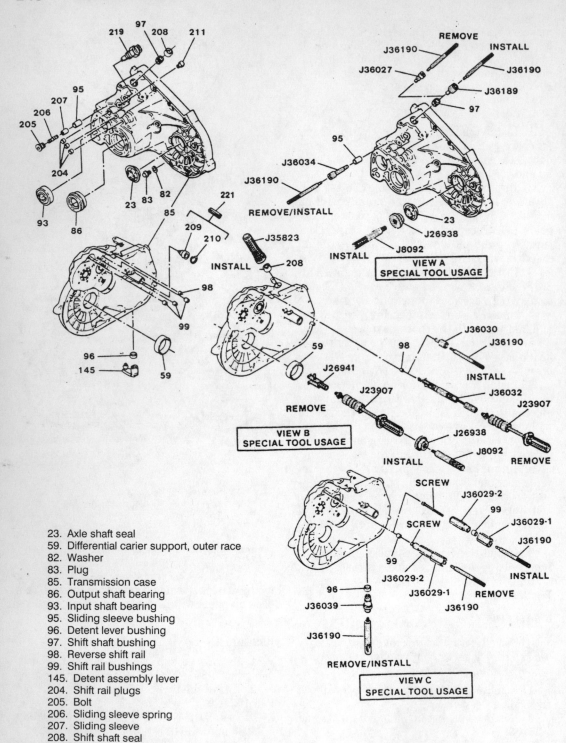

23. Axle shaft seal
59. Differential carier support, outer race
82. Washer
83. Plug
85. Transmission case
86. Output shaft bearing
93. Input shaft bearing
95. Sliding sleeve bushing
96. Detent lever bushing
97. Shift shaft bushing
98. Reverse shift rail
99. Shift rail bushings
145. Detent assembly lever
204. Shift rail plugs
205. Bolt
206. Sliding sleeve spring
207. Sliding sleeve
208. Shift shaft seal
209. Plug (some models)
210. Snap ring (some models)
211. Stud
219. Back-up lamp switch assembly
221. Spring pin (some models)

Transaxle case components

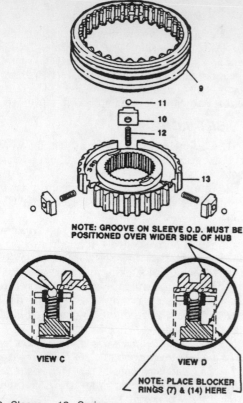

NOTE: GROOVE ON SLEEVE O.D. MUST BE POSITIONED OVER WIDER SIDE OF HUB

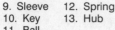

VIEW C

VIEW D

NOTE: PLACE BLOCKER RINGS (7) & (14) HERE

9. Sleeve	12. Spring
10. Key	13. Hub
11. Ball	

3rd and 4th synchronizer assembly

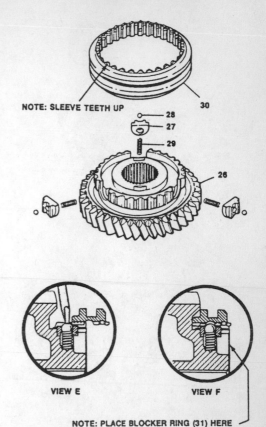

NOTE: SLEEVE TEETH UP

VIEW E

VIEW F

NOTE: PLACE BLOCKER RING (31) HERE

26. Reverse gear	29. Spring
27. Key	30. Sleeve
28. Ball	

5th gear assembly

Synchronizers

DISASSEMBLY

1. Place 1-2, 3-4, and 5th-reverse synchronizers in a separate shop towel. Wrap the assemblies and press against the inner hub.

2. Clean with solvent and blow dry with compressed air.

3. Inspect assemblies for worn or broken gear teeth, worn or broken keys and distorted or cracked balls and springs. If scuffed, nicked or burred condition can not be corrected with a soft stone or crocus cloth, replace the component.

ASSEMBLY

1. 1st-2nd gear synchro.
2. 3rd-4th gear synchro.
3. 5th gear synchro.

DIFFERENTIAL DISASSEMBLY

1. Remove the side bearing using a tool No. J-22888 and a puller leg kit.

2. Remove the ten ring gear retaining bolts and gear.

3. Using a screwdriver, pry off the speedometer drive gear. Do NOT use the old speedometer drive gear again.

4. Drive out the lock and cross pin.

5. Remove the pinion gears and thrust washers. Remove the side gears and thrust washers. Refer to the "Differential" assembly exploded view in the beginning of this section.

DIFFERENTIAL ASSEMBLY

NOTE: *Before assembling the shafts, apply a coat of specified lubricant to the thrust washers, all gears and washers.*

1. Install the two side gears on the differential case together with the thrust washers.

2. Position the two thrust washers and pinion gears opposite of each other. Install them in their positions by turning the side gears.

3. Insert the cross pin and make sure the gear backlash is within the rated range of 0.03–0.08mm.

4. Install the lock pin and stake it when the correct backlash is achieved.

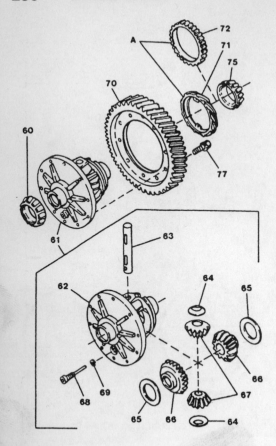

A. Electronic speedo gear requires heating prior to installation. Mechanical speedo gear requires heating (hot tap water) prior to installation.
60. Differential bearing
61. Differential carrier assembly
62. Carrier
63. Cross differential pin
64. Pinion gear thrust washer
65. Side gear thrust washer
66. Differential side gear
67. Differential pinion gear
68. Screw
69. Lock washer
70. Differential ring gear
71. Mechanical speedo gear
72. Electronic speedo gear
75. Differential bearing
77. Bolt

Differential assembly

5. Heat the speedometer drive gear to about 203°F (95°C) with a hot oil dryer or equivalent. Install the gear on the differential.

6. Install the ring gear onto the differential case and install the ten new bolts. Torque the bolts to 73-79 ft. lbs. (98-107 Nm) in a diagonal sequence.

7. Install the side bearings on the differential case using an arbor press.

Halfshaft (Drive Axle)

The halfshaft assemblies used on these cars are flexible units consisting of an inner Tri-Pot joint and an outer Constant Velocity (CV) joint. The inner joint is completely flexible, capable of up and down, in and out movement. The outer joint is only capable of up and down movement.

NOISE DIAGNOSIS

1. Clicking noise in turn: inspect for worn or damaged outer CV-joint and outer dust boots.

2. Clunk when accelerating from coast to drive: inspect for worn or damaged outer CV-joint.

3. Shudder or vibration during acceleration: inspect for excessive joint angle, excessive toe, incorrect trim height, worn or damaged outer CV-joint and sticking spider assembly.

4. Vibration at highway speeds: inspect for out of balance rear tires or wheels, out of round tires or wheels, worn outer CV-joint and binding or tight joint.

NOTE: *Some vehicles use a GRAY boot on the halfshaft axle joints. Use boot protector J-33162 on these boots. All other boots are made of thermoplastic material BLACK and require use of a boot protector.*

REMOVAL AND INSTALLATION

CAUTION: *Use care when removing the halfshaft. Tri-pot joints can be damaged if the drive axle is over-extended. It is important to handle the halfshaft in a manner to prevent over-extending.*

1. Disconnect the negative (–) battery cable.

2. Raise the car and support with jackstands. Remove the wheel and tire.

3. Remove the brake calipers, bracket assemblies and hang out of the way with wire.

4. Remove the brake rotors.

5. Remove the four hub/bearing retaining bolts and hub.

6. Remove the ABS sensor mounting bolt and position the sensor out of the way, if equipped with ABS brakes.

7. Place a drain pan under the transaxle.

8. **RIGHT** using a axle shaft removing tool J-33008 or equivalent, separate the halfshaft from the transaxle.

9. **LEFT** using a suitable pry bar, separate the halfshaft from the transaxle. Pry on the frame and the groove provided on the inner joint.

10. Separate the halfshaft from the bearing assembly, if not removed.

To install:

1. Install the halfshaft/bearing assembly through the knuckle and into the transaxle

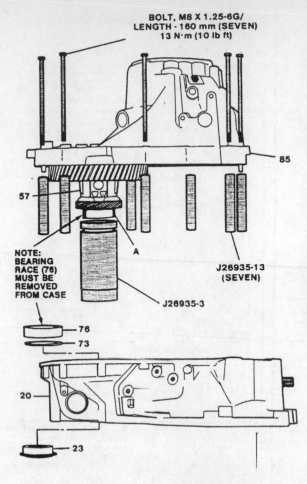

BOLT, M8 X 1.25-6G/
LENGTH - 160 mm (SEVEN)
13 N·m (10 lb ft)

NOTE:
BEARING
RACE (76)
MUST BE
REMOVED
FROM CASE

J26935-13
(SEVEN)

J26935-3

13 N·m (10 lb ft) (SEVEN)

DIM U

DIMENSION U
— DETERMINE LARGEST SHIM WITHOUT BINDING
— USE SHIM TWO SIZES LARGER

SHIM PART NO.	DIM U mm (IN.)	COLOR	STRIPES
14082132	0.30 (0.012)	ORANGE	1
14082133	0.35 (0.014)	ORANGE	2
14082134	0.40 (0.016)	ORANGE	3
14082135	0.45 (0.018)	ORANGE	4
14082136	0.50 (0.020)	YELLOW	1
14082137	0.55 (0.022)	YELLOW	2
14082138	0.60 (0.024)	YELLOW	3
14082139	0.65 (0.026)	YELLOW	4
14082140	0.70 (0.028)	WHITE	1
14082141	0.75 (0.030)	WHITE	2
14082142	0.80 (0.031)	WHITE	3
14082143	0.85 (0.033)	WHITE	4
14082144	0.90 (0.035)	GREEN	1
14082145	0.95 (0.037)	GREEN	2
14082146	1.00 (0.039)	GREEN	3
14082147	1.05 (0.041)	GREEN	4
14082148	1.10 (0.043)	BLUE	1
14082149	1.15 (0.045)	BLUE	2
14082150	1.20 (0.047)	BLUE	3
14082151	1.25 (0.049)	BLUE	4
14082152	1.30 (0.051)	RED	1

A. Bearing cup must be installed over bearing
20. Clutch and differential housing
23. Drive axle seal
57. Gear and differential assembly
73. Selective shim
76. Differential bearing race
85. Transmission case

Differential shim selection

until the retaining clip engages. Do NOT over-extend the inner joint.

2. Install the ABS sensor.

3. Torque the bearing assembly retaining bolts to 52 ft. lbs. (70 Nm).

4. Remove the drain pan and install a new halfshaft nut and washer.

5. Install the rotor, brake caliper and wheel assemblies. Torque the lug nuts to 100 ft. lbs. (136 Nm).

6. Lower the vehicle and torque the half-shaft axle nut to 184 ft. lbs. (250 Nm).

7. Add the necessary amount of transaxle fluid and connect the negative battery cable.

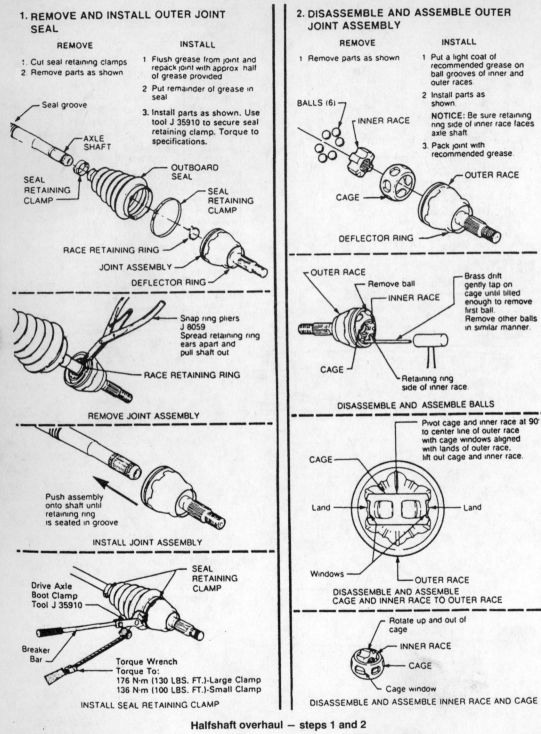

1. REMOVE AND INSTALL OUTER JOINT SEAL

REMOVE

1. Cut seal retaining clamps
2. Remove parts as shown

INSTALL

1. Flush grease from joint and repack joint with approx half of grease provided
2. Put remainder of grease in seal
3. Install parts as shown. Use tool J 35910 to secure seal retaining clamp. Torque to specifications.

- Seal groove
- AXLE SHAFT
- SEAL RETAINING CLAMP
- OUTBOARD SEAL
- SEAL RETAINING CLAMP
- RACE RETAINING RING
- JOINT ASSEMBLY
- DEFLECTOR RING

Snap ring pliers J 8059
Spread retaining ring ears apart and pull shaft out

- RACE RETAINING RING

REMOVE JOINT ASSEMBLY

Push assembly onto shaft until retaining ring is seated in groove

INSTALL JOINT ASSEMBLY

- SEAL RETAINING CLAMP
- Drive Axle Boot Clamp Tool J 35910
- Breaker Bar
- Torque Wrench
- Torque To:
  176 N·m (130 LBS. FT.)-Large Clamp
  136 N·m (100 LBS. FT.)-Small Clamp

INSTALL SEAL RETAINING CLAMP

2. DISASSEMBLE AND ASSEMBLE OUTER JOINT ASSEMBLY

REMOVE

1. Remove parts as shown

INSTALL

1. Put a light coat of recommended grease on ball grooves of inner and outer races.
2. Install parts as shown.

NOTICE: Be sure retaining ring side of inner race faces axle shaft.
3. Pack joint with recommended grease.

- BALLS (6)
- INNER RACE
- CAGE
- OUTER RACE
- DEFLECTOR RING

- OUTER RACE
- Remove ball
- INNER RACE
- Brass drift gently tap on cage until tilted enough to remove first ball. Remove other balls in similar manner.
- CAGE
- Retaining ring side of inner race.

DISASSEMBLE AND ASSEMBLE BALLS

- CAGE
- Land
- Windows
- Land
- OUTER RACE

Pivot cage and inner race at 90° to center line of outer race with cage windows aligned with lands of outer race, lift out cage and inner race.

DISASSEMBLE AND ASSEMBLE CAGE AND INNER RACE TO OUTER RACE

- Rotate up and out of cage
- INNER RACE
- CAGE
- Cage window

DISASSEMBLE AND ASSEMBLE INNER RACE AND CAGE

Halfshaft overhaul — steps 1 and 2

HALFSHAFT OVERHAUL

Outer Joint Boot

1. Cut and remove the boot retaining clamps with wire cutters.

2. Remove the race retaining ring with snapring pliers. Remove the joint and boot as-

sembly from the axle shaft. Refer to Step 1 of the CV–joint procedures.

3. Flush the grease from the joint and repack the boot with half of the grease provided with the new boot.

4. Install the new boot and clamps first. Second, install the joint and snap the race re-

3. REMOVE AND INSTALL INNER TRI-POT SEAL

REMOVE	INSTALL
1. Cut seal retaining clamps.	1. Flush grease from housing and repack housing with approx. half of grease furnished with new seal.
2. Remove parts as shown.	2. Put remainder of grease in seal.
	3. Install parts as shown. Use tool J 35910 to secure seal retaining clamp. Torque to specifications.

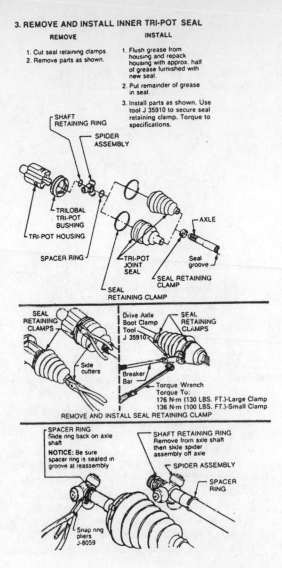

REMOVE AND INSTALL SEAL RETAINING CLAMP

Torque Wrench
Torque To:
176 N·m (130 LBS. FT.)-Large Clamp
136 N·m (100 LBS. FT.)-Small Clamp

Halfshaft overhaul — step 3

taining ring into place. Put the remainder of the grease into the joint.

5. Using an axle seal clamp tool J-35910 and a torque wrench, torque the small clamp to 100 ft. lbs. (136 Nm). Torque the large clamp to 130 ft. lbs. (176 Nm).

Outer Joint Assembly

1. Remove the large boot clamp and joint assembly from the axle as previously mentioned. Clean out the grease from the joint to aid in disassembly.

2. Use a brass drift to gently tap on the cage until tilted enough to remove the first ball. Remove the other balls in a similar manner.

3. Pivot the cage and inner race at 90° to the center line of the outer race with the cage

windows aligned with the lands of the outer race. Lift the cage out with the inner race. Refer to Step 2 of the CV-joint procedures.

4. Rotate the inner race up and out of the cage as in Step 2. Clean all parts with solvent and blow dry with compressed air.

To install:

5. Lightly coat the ball grooves with the provided CV grease.

6. Install the inner race into the cage, cage into the outer race and balls into the cage as removed.

7. Refill the joint with half the grease provided. Install the boot and clamps. Install the joint onto the axle. Fill the joint with the remaining grease and torque the clamps as in the previous procedure.

Inner Tri-Pot Boot

1. Cut the clamps from the boot.

2. Remove the axle from the Tri-Pot housing as in Step 3.

3. Remove the spider assembly from the axle by removing the shaft retaining snaprings.

4. Clean all metal parts with solvent and blow dry with compressed air.

To install:

5. Refill the housing with half of the grease provided with the new boot. Install the boot and clamps first, then the spider and snapring assembly onto the axle.

6. Position the axle into the Tri-Pot housing. Install the remaining grease into the joint.

7. Using a seal clamp tool J-35910 or equivalent, torque the small clamp to 100 ft. lbs. (136 Nm) and torque the large clamp to 130 ft. lbs. (176 Nm) as in Step 3. Side cutters can be used the tighten the boot clamps, but care must be used so not to cut the new clamps.

Intermediate Shaft Manual Transaxle Only

REMOVAL AND INSTALLATION

CAUTION: *Use care when removing the halfshaft. Tri-pot joints can be damaged if the drive axle is over-extended. It is important to handle the halfshaft in a manner to prevent over-extending.*

1. Disconnect the negative (–) battery cable.

2. Raise the car and support with jackstands. Remove the right wheel and tire.

3. Position a drain pan under the transaxle.

4. Remove the right halfshaft assembly as previously outlined in this section.

5. Remove the housing-to-bracket bolts, bracket and housing-to-transaxle bolts.

6. Carefully disengage the intermediate axle shaft from the transaxle and remove the shaft.

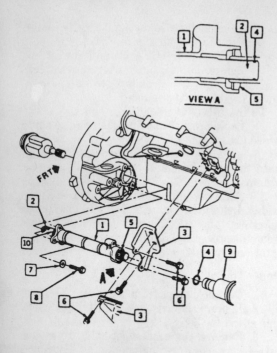

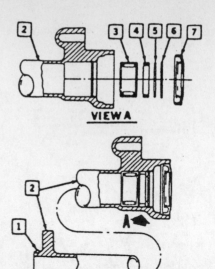

1. O-ring
2. Housing
3. Roller bearing
4. Spacer
5. Washer
6. Snap ring
7. Lip seal

1. Intermediate shaft assembly
2. Intermediate axle shaft
3. Bracket
4. Axle shaft retaining ring
5. Lip seal
6. Bolt
7. Washer
8. Bolt
9. Right drive axle
10. O-ring

Intermediate shaft — HM–282 manual only

Intermediate shaft bearing removal

To install:

1. Install the intermediate shaft into position and lock the shaft into the transaxle.

2. Install the housing-to-transaxle bolts and torque to 18 ft. lbs. (25 Nm).

3. Install the bracket-to-engine block bolts and torque to 37 ft. lbs. (50 Nm).

4. Install the housing-to-bracket bolts and torque to 37 ft. lbs. (50 Nm).

5. Coat the splines of the intermediate shaft with chassis grease and install the right halfshaft assembly as previously outlined in this section.

6. Install the front wheels and torque the lug nuts to 100 ft. lbs. (136 Nm).

7. Lower the vehicle and refill the transaxle to the proper levelk.

8. Connect the negative battery cable and recheck all procedures to ensure complete repair.

Intermediate Shaft Bearing

REMOVAL AND INSTALLATION

1. Remove the intermediate shaft from the vehicle as previously outlined.

2. Remove the seal, snapring and washer from the housing.

3. Press the spacer and bearing from the housing using a driver handle and bearing remover tools J-8592 and J-8810.

To install:

1. Press the bearing into the housing support, using a press and a bearing installer J-36379 or equivalent.

2. Install the spacer, washer and snapring.

3. Install the seal into the housing using a seal installer tool J-23771 or equivalent.

4. Install the intermediate shaft into the vehicle.

CLUTCH

The clutch system consists of a driving member (flywheel and clutch cover), a driven member (clutch disc and input shaft) and a operating member (hydraulic system and release bearing).

CAUTION: *The clutch driven disc contain asbestos, which has been determined to be a cancer causing agent. Never clean the clutch surfaces with compressed air! Avoid inhaling any dust from any clutch surface! When cleaning clutch surfaces, use a commercially available brake cleaning fluid.*

Adjustments

The clutch operating system consists of a hydraulic master cylinder, slave cylinder (actua-

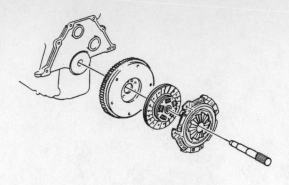

Aligning the clutch driven plate splines

tor) and fluid lines. This system is adjusted automatically, requiring no periodic service.

Driven Disc and Pressure Plate

REMOVAL AND INSTALLATION

WARNING: *Before preforming any manual transaxle removal procedures, the clutch master cylinder pushrod MUST be disconnected from the clutch pedal and the actuator must be separated from the transaxle. Permanent damage may occur to the actuator if the clutch pedal is depressed while the system is not resisted by clutch loads. Also, the pushrod bushing must be replaced once it has been disconnected from the master cylinder.*

1. Disconnect the negative (–) battery cable.
2. Remove the sound insulator from inside the vehicle and disconnect the clutch master cylinder pushrod from the clutch pedal.
3. Remove the two actuator retaining nuts from the transaxle and remove actuator. Position to the side and support.
4. Remove the transaxle assembly from the vehicle as outlined earlier in this chapter.
5. Mark the position of the clutch cover to the flywheel, if using old clutch cover.
6. Loosen the cover retaining bolts one turn at a time until all the spring pressure is released.
7. Support the clutch cover and remove all the bolts.
8. Remove the clutch cover and driven disc. Do not disassembly the clutch cover, if damaged replace entire unit.
9. Inspect the clutch cover and flywheel for scoring, warpage and excessive wear. Replace the clutch cover and resurface the flywheel if damaged.
NOTE: *While the transaxle is out of the vehicle, it is a good practice to replace the clutch cover, driven disc and release bearing. Also, the flywheel should be resurfaced or replaced when replacing the clutch assembly.*

Removing the transaxle is not an easy job, especially if it has to be done twice.
10. Clean the clutch cover and flywheel surfaces with solvent and light sandpaper if installing the used parts.
To install:
1. Position the clutch disc and cover onto the flywheel mating surface. The raised hub and springs should face away from the flywheel. The disc may be marked "Flywheel Side", meaning the stamp faces the flywheel.
2. Loosely install the clutch cover retaining bolts. Do NOT tighten at this time.
3. Support the clutch disc using a clutch alignment tool J-35822 or equivalent. This tool is needed to align the clutch disc to the flywheel so when the transaxle is installed, the input splines will align with the flywheel pilot bearing.
4. With the clutch alignment tool installed, torque the clutch cover-to-flywheel bolts to 6 ft. lbs. (21 Nm). Remove the alignment tool.
5. Replace the release bearing if needed. Lightly lubricate the clutch fork ends which contact the bearing and the inner recess of the release bearing with chassis grease.
6. Make sure the release bearing and fork move freely on the fork shaft.
7. Tie the actuator lever to the studs to hold the release bearing in place.
NOTE: *The clutch actuator lever must NOT move toward the flywheel until the transaxle is bolted to the engine.*
8. Install the transaxle assembly.
9. Remove the actuator lever tie. Inspect the actuator pushrod for the bushing and replace if missing.
10. Install the actuator-to-transaxle, making sure the bushing is centered in the pocket of the internal lever in the housing.
11. Install the actuator retaining nuts and tighten evenly to draw the actuator to the transaxle. Torque the nuts to 18 ft. lbs. (25 Nm).
12. Install a new bushing in the master cylinder pushrod and lubricate before installation.
13. Install the master cylinder pushrod to the clutch pedal.
14. Press the clutch pedal down several times to assure normal operation.
15. Install the sound insulator and negative battery cable.

Master Cylinder, Actuator and Reservoir

REMOVAL AND INSTALLATION

NOTE: *The factory hydraulic system is serviced as a single assembly. Replacement hydraulic assemblies are pre-filled with fluid and do not require bleeding. Individual com-*

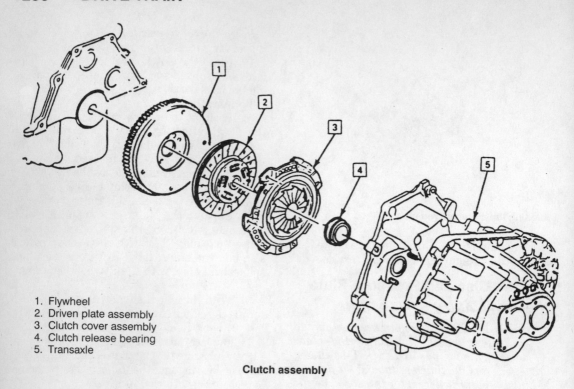

1. Flywheel
2. Driven plate assembly
3. Clutch cover assembly
4. Clutch release bearing
5. Transaxle

Clutch assembly

Troubleshooting Basic Clutch Problems

Problem	Cause
Excessive clutch noise	Throwout bearing noises are more audible at the lower end of pedal travel. The usual causes are: • Riding the clutch • Too little pedal free-play • Lack of bearing lubrication A bad clutch shaft pilot bearing will make a high pitched squeal, when the clutch is disengaged and the transmission is in gear or within the first 2″ of pedal travel. The bearing must be replaced. Noise from the clutch linkage is a clicking or snapping that can be heard or felt as the pedal is moved completely up or down. This usually requires lubrication. Transmitted engine noises are amplified by the clutch housing and heard in the passenger compartment. They are usually the result of insufficient pedal free-play and can be changed by manipulating the clutch pedal.
Clutch slips (the car does not move as it should when the clutch is engaged)	This is usually most noticeable when pulling away from a standing start. A severe test is to start the engine, apply the brakes, shift into high gear and SLOWLY release the clutch pedal. A healthy clutch will stall the engine. If it slips it may be due to: • A worn pressure plate or clutch plate • Oil soaked clutch plate • Insufficient pedal free-play
Clutch drags or fails to release	The clutch disc and some transmission gears spin briefly after clutch disengagement. Under normal conditions in average temperatures, 3 seconds is maximum spin-time. Failure to release properly can be caused by: • Too light transmission lubricant or low lubricant level • Improperly adjusted clutch linkage
Low clutch life	Low clutch life is usually a result of poor driving habits or heavy duty use. Riding the clutch, pulling heavy loads, holding the car on a grade with the clutch instead of the brakes and rapid clutch engagement all contribute to low clutch life.

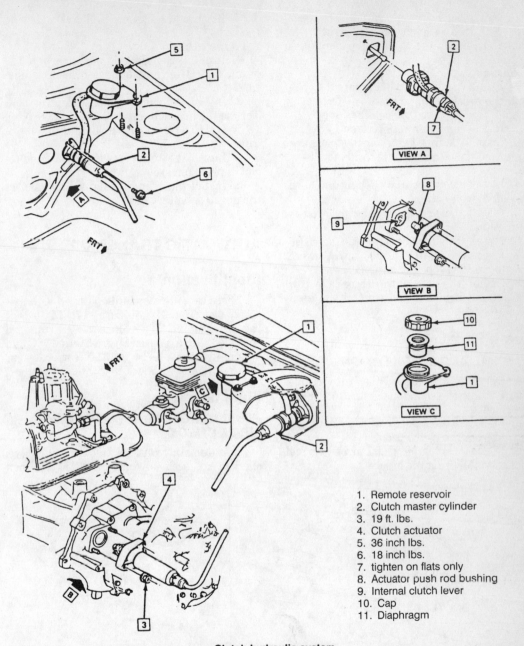

1. Remote reservoir
2. Clutch master cylinder
3. 19 ft. lbs.
4. Clutch actuator
5. 36 inch lbs.
6. 18 inch lbs.
7. tighten on flats only
8. Actuator push rod bushing
9. Internal clutch lever
10. Cap
11. Diaphragm

Clutch hydraulic system

ponents of the system are not available separately. Check with an aftermarket part supplier to see if individual components can be purchased separately.

1. Disconnect the negative (–) battery cable.
2. Remove the sound insulator inside the vehicle and disconnect the master cylinder pushrod at the clutch pedal.
3. Remove the left upper secondary cowl panel.
4. Remove the two master cylinder reservoir-to-strut tower retaining nuts.

5. Remove the anti-rotation screw located next to the master cylinder flange at the pedal support plate.
6. Using wrench flats on the front end of the master cylinder body, twist the cylinder counterclockwise to release the twist lock attachment-to-plate. Do NOT torque on the hose connection on top of the cylinder body, damage may occur.
7. Remove the two actuator-to-transaxle retaining nuts and actuator assembly.
8. Pull the master cylinder with the

pushrod attached forward out of the pedal plate. Lift the reservoir off the strut tower studs and remove the three components as a complete assembly.

To install:

1. Install the master cylinder into the opening in the pedal plate and rotate 45° degrees by applying torque on the wrench flats only.

2. Install the anti-rotation screw.

3. Install the fluid reservoir-to-strut tower and torque the retaining nuts to 36 inch lbs. (4 Nm).

4. Install a new pushrod bushing and lubricate before installation.

5. Install the master cylinder pushrod-to-clutch pedal.

6. Install the clutch actuator-to-transaxle.

7. Press the clutch pedal down several times to ensure proper operation.

8. Install the left upper secondary cowl panel, sound insulator and connect the negative battery cable.

Clutch Pedal

REMOVAL AND INSTALLATION

1. Disconnect the negative (–) battery cable.

2. Remove the sound insulator from inside the vehicle.

3. Remove the clutch master cylinder pushrod from the clutch pedal.

4. Remove the clutch pedal pivot bolt and pedal assembly from the bracket.

5. Remove the spacers and bushing from the pedal.

To install:

1. Install the spacer and bushings onto the pedal. Lubricate the bushings before installation.

2. Install the clutch pedal and pivot bolt. Torque the bolt and nut to 23 ft. lbs. (31 Nm).

3. Install a new pushrod bushing and lubricate.

4. Install the master cylinder pushrod-to-clutch pedal pin groove.

5. Install the sound insulator and connect the negative battery cable.

AUTOMATIC TRANSAXLE

Identification

These cars are standard-equipped with a 4-speed overdrive Hydra-Matic 440-T4, except the 2.5L Lumina. The 2.5L Lumina is standard equipped with a 3-speed Hydra-Matic 125C and optional with a 440-T4. All the transaxles are fully automatic with lockup torque converters.

Fluid Change

FLUID RECOMMENDATION AND LEVEL CHECK

The automatic transaxle fluid level should be checked at each engine oil change. When

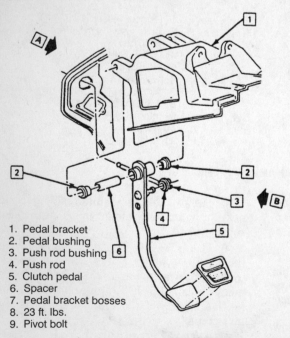

1. Pedal bracket
2. Pedal bushing
3. Push rod bushing
4. Push rod
5. Clutch pedal
6. Spacer
7. Pedal bracket bosses
8. 23 ft. lbs.
9. Pivot bolt

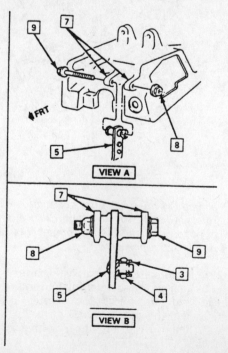

Clutch pedal assembly

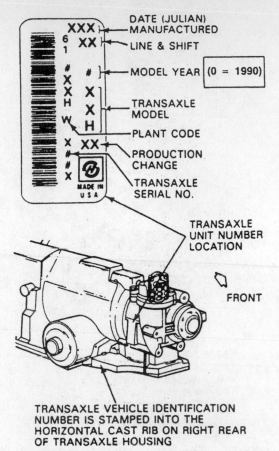

DATE (JULIAN) MANUFACTURED

LINE & SHIFT

MODEL YEAR (0 = 1990)

TRANSAXLE MODEL

PLANT CODE

PRODUCTION CHANGE

TRANSAXLE SERIAL NO.

TRANSAXLE UNIT NUMBER LOCATION

FRONT

TRANSAXLE VEHICLE IDENTIFICATION NUMBER IS STAMPED INTO THE HORIZONTAL CAST RIB ON RIGHT REAR OF TRANSAXLE HOUSING

Transaxle identification — 4–speed overdrive TH 440–T4

adding or changing the automatic transaxle fluid use only fluid labeled Dexron®II.

1. Set the parking brake and start the engine with the transaxle in "P" (Park).

2. With the service brakes applied, move the shift lever through all the gear ranges, ending in "P" (Park).

NOTE: *The fluid level must be checked with the engine running at slow idle, the car level and the fluid at least at room temperature. The correct fluid level cannot be read if you have just driven the car for a long time at high speed, city traffic in hot weather or if the car has been pulling a trailer. In these cases, wait at least 30 minutes for the fluid to cool down.*

3. Remove the dipstick located at the rear end of the engine compartment, wipe it clean, then push it back in until the cap seats.

4. Pull the dipstick out and read the fluid level. The level should be in the cross-hatched area of the dipstick.

5. Add fluid using a long plastic funnel in the dipstick tube. Keep in mind that it only takes one pint of fluid to raise the level from "ADD" to "FULL" with a hot transaxle.

WARNING: *Damage to the automatic transaxle may result if the fluid level is above the "FULL" mark. Remove excess fluid by threading a small rubber hose into the dipstick tube and pump the fluid out with a syphon pump.*

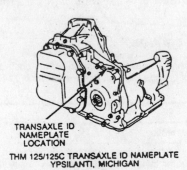

TRANSAXLE ID NAMEPLATE LOCATION

THM 125/125C TRANSAXLE ID NAMEPLATE YPSILANTI, MICHIGAN

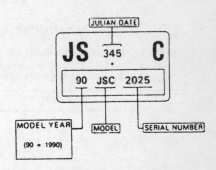

JULIAN DATE

JS   345   C

90 JSC 2025

MODEL YEAR (90 = 1990)   MODEL   SERIAL NUMBER

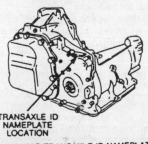

TRANSAXLE ID NAMEPLATE LOCATION

THM 125/125C TRANSAXLE ID NAMEPLATE WINDSOR, CANADA

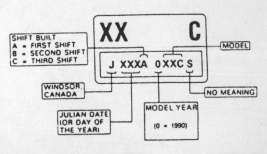

SHIFT BUILT
A = FIRST SHIFT
B = SECOND SHIFT
C = THIRD SHIFT

XX   C

MODEL

J XXXA 0XXC S

WINDSOR, CANADA

NO MEANING

JULIAN DATE (OR DAY OF THE YEAR)

MODEL YEAR (0 = 1990)

Transaxle identification — 3–speed TH–125C

FLUID DRAIN AND REFILL

According to General Motors, under normal operating conditions the automatic transmission fluid only needs to be changed every 100,000 miles unless one or more of the following driving conditions is encountered. In the following cases the fluid and filter should be changed every 15,000 miles:

a. Driving in heavy traffic when the outside temperature reaches 90°F.

b. Driving regularly in hilly or mountainous areas.

c. Towing a trailer.

d. Using a vehicle as a taxi or police car or for delivery purposes.

Remember, these are factory recommendations and are considered to be minimum. You must determine a change interval which fits your driving habits. If your vehicle is never subjected to these conditions, a 100,000 mile change interval is adequate. If you are a normal driver, a two-year/30,000 mile interval will be more than sufficient to maintain the long life for which your automatic transaxle was designed.

NOTE: *Use only fluid labeled Dexron®II. Use of other fluids could cause erratic shifting and transaxle damage.*

1. Raise the vehicle and support it safely with jackstands.

2. Disconnect the negative (–) battery cable.

3. Remove the bottom pan bolts.

4. Loosen the rear bolts about four turns.

5. Carefully pry the oil pan loose and allow the fluid to drain.

6. Remove the remaining bolts, the pan, and the gasket or RTV sealant. Discard the old gasket.

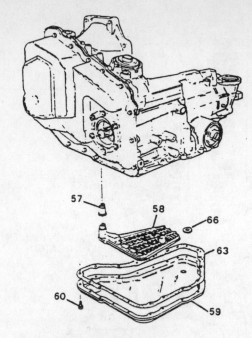

57. Oil filter seal assembly
58. Oil filter assembly
59. Transmission oil pan
60. Special screw (M8 x 1.25 x 16.0)
63. Pan gasket
66. Magnetic chip collector

Fluid pan and filter assembly

Transmission Fluid Indications

The appearance and odor of the transmission fluid can give valuable clues to the overall condition of the transmission. Always note the appearance of the fluid when you check the fluid level or change the fluid. Rub a small amount of fluid between your fingers to feel for grit and smell the fluid on the dipstick.

If the fluid appears:	It indicates:
Clear and red colored	• Normal operation
Discolored (extremely dark red or brownish) or smells burned	• Band or clutch pack failure, usually caused by an overheated transmission. Hauling very heavy loads with insufficient power or failure to change the fluid, often result in overheating. Do not confuse this appearance with newer fluids that have a darker red color and a strong odor (though not a burned odor).
Foamy or aerated (light in color and full of bubbles)	• The level is too high (gear train is churning oil) • An internal air leak (air is mixing with the fluid). Have the transmission checked professionally.
Solid residue in the fluid	• Defective bands, clutch pack or bearings. Bits of band material or metal abrasives are clinging to the dipstick. Have the transmission checked professionally.
Varnish coating on the dipstick	• The transmission fluid is overheating

1 FLUID LEVEL INDICATOR (125C)
2 LEVEL TO BE IN CROSS-HATCHED AREA ON
   FLUID LEVEL INDICATOR BLADE. CHECK AT
   OPERATING TEMPERATURE.
3 COLD LEVEL ENGINE OFF

1 FLUID LEVEL INDICATOR (440-T4)
2 LEVEL TO BE IN CROSS-HATCHED AREA ON
   FLUID LEVEL INDICATOR BLADE. CHECK AT
   OPERATING TEMPERATURE.
3 COLD LEVEL ENGINE OFF

Fluid level indicators

7. Clean the pan with solvent and dry it thoroughly, with compressed air.

8. Remove the filter and O-ring seal.

9. Install a new transaxle filter and O-ring seal, locating the filter against the dipstick stop.

NOTE: *Always replace the filter with a new one. Do not attempt to clean the old one.*

10. Install a new gasket or RTV sealant then tighten the pan bolts to 12 ft. lbs. (15 Nm).

11. Lower the car and add about 4 quarts of Dexron® II transmission fluid.

12. Start the engine and let idle. Block the wheels and apply the parking brake.

13. At idle, move the shift lever through the ranges. With the lever in "PARK", check the fluid level and add as necessary. The drain and refill capacity is 6 quarts.

NOTE: *The transmission fluid currently being used may appear to be darker and have a strong odor. This is normal and not a sign of required maintenance or transmission failure.*

Adjustments

CONTROL CABLE

1. Disconnect the negative (–) battery cable.

2. Lift up the locking button at the transaxle and cable bracket.

3. Place the transaxle shift lever in the **Neutral** position. This position can be found by ro-

Troubleshooting Basic Automatic Transmission Problems

Problem	Cause	Solution
Fluid leakage	• Defective pan gasket	• Replace gasket or tighten pan bolts
	• Loose filler tube	• Tighten tube nut
	• Loose extension housing to transmission case	• Tighten bolts
	• Converter housing area leakage	• Have transmission checked professionally
Fluid flows out the oil filler tube	• High fluid level	• Check and correct fluid level
	• Breather vent clogged	• Open breather vent
	• Clogged oil filter or screen	• Replace filter or clean screen (change fluid also)
	• Internal fluid leakage	• Have transmission checked professionally
Transmission overheats (this is usually accompanied by a strong burned odor to the fluid)	• Low fluid level	• Check and correct fluid level
	• Fluid cooler lines clogged	• Drain and refill transmission. If this doesn't cure the problem, have cooler lines cleared or replaced.
	• Heavy pulling or hauling with insufficient cooling	• Install a transmission oil cooler
	• Faulty oil pump, internal slippage	• Have transmission checked professionally
Buzzing or whining noise	• Low fluid level	• Check and correct fluid level
	• Defective torque converter, scored gears	• Have transmission checked professionally
No forward or reverse gears or slippage in one or more gears	• Low fluid level	• Check and correct fluid level
	• Defective vacuum or linkage controls, internal clutch or band failure	• Have unit checked professionally
Delayed or erratic shift	• Low fluid level	• Check and correct fluid level
	• Broken vacuum lines	• Repair or replace lines
	• Internal malfunction	• Have transmission checked professionally

Lockup Torque Converter Service Diagnosis

Problem	Cause	Solution
No lockup	• Faulty oil pump • Sticking governor valve • Valve body malfunction 　(a) Stuck switch valve 　(b) Stuck lockup valve 　(c) Stuck fail-safe valve • Failed locking clutch • Leaking turbine hub seal • Faulty input shaft or seal ring	• Replace oil pump • Repair or replace as necessary • Repair or replace valve body or its internal components as necessary • Replace torque converter • Replace torque converter • Repair or replace as necessary
Will not unlock	• Sticking governor valve • Valve body malfunction 　(a) Stuck switch valve 　(b) Stuck lockup valve 　(c) Stuck fail-safe valve	• Repair or replace as necessary • Repair or replace valve body or its internal components as necessary
Stays locked up at too low a speed in direct	• Sticking governor valve • Valve body malfunction 　(a) Stuck switch valve 　(b) Stuck lockup valve 　(c) Stuck fail-safe valve	• Repair or replace as necessary • Repair or replace valve body or its internal components as necessary
Locks up or drags in low or second	• Faulty oil pump • Valve body malfunction 　(a) Stuck switch valve 　(b) Stuck fail-safe valve	• Replace oil pump • Repair or replace valve body or its internal components as necessary
Sluggish or stalls in reverse	• Faulty oil pump • Plugged cooler, cooler lines or fittings • Valve body malfunction 　(a) Stuck switch valve 　(b) Faulty input shaft or seal ring	• Replace oil pump as necessary • Flush or replace cooler and flush lines and fittings • Repair or replace valve body or its internal components as necessary
Loud chatter during lockup engagement (cold)	• Faulty torque converter • Failed locking clutch • Leaking turbine hub seal	• Replace torque converter • Replace torque converter • Replace torque converter
Vibration or shudder during lockup engagement	• Faulty oil pump • Valve body malfunction • Faulty torque converter • Engine needs tune-up	• Repair or replace oil pump as necessary • Repair or replace valve body or its internal components as necessary • Replace torque converter • Tune engine
Vibration after lockup engagement	• Faulty torque converter • Exhaust system strikes underbody • Engine needs tune-up • Throttle linkage misadjusted	• Replace torque converter • Align exhaust system • Tune engine • Adjust throttle linkage
Vibration when revved in neutral Overheating: oil blows out of dip stick tube or pump seal	• Torque converter out of balance • Plugged cooler, cooler lines or fittings • Stuck switch valve	• Replace torque converter • Flush or replace cooler and flush lines and fittings • Repair switch valve in valve body or replace valve body
Shudder after lockup engagement	• Faulty oil pump • Plugged cooler, cooler lines or fittings • Valve body malfunction • Faulty torque converter • Fail locking clutch • Exhaust system strikes underbody • Engine needs tune-up • Throttle linkage misadjusted	• Replace oil pump • Flush or replace cooler and flush lines and fittings • Repair or replace valve body or its internal components as necessary • Replace torque converter • Replace torque converter • Align exhaust system • Tune engine • Adjust throttle linkage

tating the selector shaft/shift lever clockwise from **Park** through **Reverse** to **Neutral**.

4. Place the shift control inside the vehicle to the **Neutral** position.

5. Push down the locking button at the cable bracket and connect the negative battery cable.

PARK/LOCK CONTROL CABLE

1. Disconnect the negative (–) battery cable.

2. With the shift lever in the **Park** position and the key in the **Lock** position, make sure that the shifter cannot be moved to another position. The key should be removable from the column.

3. With the key in the **Run** position and the shifter in the **Neutral** position, the key should NOT turn to the **Lock** position.

4. Adjust the cable by pulling up the cable connector lock at the shifter.

5. If the key cannot be removed in the **Park** position, snap the connector lock button to the up position and move the cable connector nose rearward until the key can be removed from the ignition.

6. Snap the lock button down and recheck operation and connect the negative battery cable.

THROTTLE VALVE (TV) LINKAGE

1. Disconnect the negative (–) battery cable.

2. Pull on the upper end of the TV cable. It should travel a short distance with light resistance caused by a small spring on the TV lever.

3. The cable should go to the zero position when the upper end of the cable is released.

4. Verify that the TV cable is installed properly in the throttle lever and the slider is in the non-adjusted position as shown in the illustration.

5. With the engine **NOT** running, rotate the throttle lever to the full travel position (throttle body stop).

6. Depress and hold the adjustment button, pull the cable conduit out until the slider hits against the adjustment and release the button.

7. Repeat the adjustment.

Back-Up/Neutral Safety Switch

REMOVAL AND INSTALLATION

1. Disconnect the negative (–) battery cable.

2. Place the transaxle in the **NEUTRAL** position.

3. Raise the vehicle and support with jackstands.

4. Disconnect the switch electrical connector and remove the retaining clips.

5. Lower the vehicle and remove the

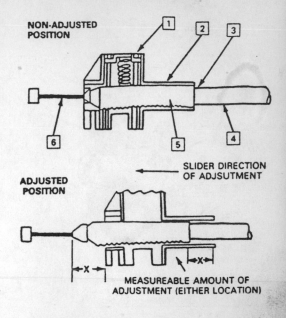

1. Readjustment button
2. Fitting
3. Slider against fitting; full non-adjusted position
4. Conduit
5. Slider
6. To throttle lever

TV cable adjustment

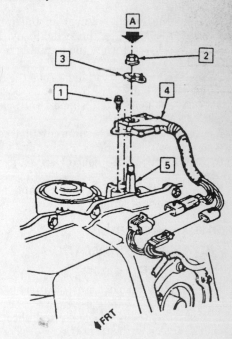

1. 18 ft. lbs.	4. Neutral switch
2. 15 ft. lbs.	5. Shaft
3. Lever	6. 80 inch lbs.

Back-up light/neutral switch

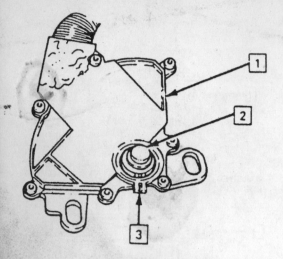

1. Switch
2. Selector shaft
3. Align inner notch with outer notch

Back-up light/neutral switch alignment

vacuum hoses and electrical connectors from the cruise control servo, if so equipped.

6. Remove the shift lever at the transaxle. Do NOT disconnect the lever from the cable. Remove the two retaining bolts and switch.

To install:

1. Align the notch (groove) on the inner sleeve with the notch on the switch body. Install the switch and torque the retaining bolts to 18 ft. lbs. (25 Nm).

2. Install the shift lever and torque the nut to 15 ft. lbs. (20 Nm).

3. Raise the vehicle and support with jackstands.

4. Connect the switch connector, harness clips and lower the vehicle.

5. Install the cruise control servo, if removed.

6. Connect the negative battery cable and check for proper operation.

Transaxle Assembly

REMOVAL AND INSTALLATION

Hydra-Matic 125C (3-speed)

1. Disconnect the negative (–) battery cable and remove the air cleaner assembly.

2. Remove the shift control and throttle valve (TV) cables at the transaxle.

3. Remove the throttle cable bracket and brake booster hose.

4. Remove the engine torque struts, left torque strut bracket and oil cooler lines at the transaxle.

5. Install the engine support fixture tool J-28467-A and J-36462.

6. Raise the vehicle and support with jack-stands.

7. Remove the front wheels, splash shields, calipers and rotors. Support the caliper to the frame witth wire.

8. Remove the front halfshafts (axle) assemblies as outlined in this chapter.

9. Disconnect both ball joints and tie rod ends from the strut assemblies. For further assistance, refer to Chapter 8.

10. Remove the engine oil filter.

11. Remove the A/C compressor and support out of the way. Do NOT disconnect the refrigerant lines.

12. Remove the rack and pinion heat shield and electrical connector.

13. Remove the rack and pinion assembly and wire to the exhaust for support.

14. Remove the power steering hoses-to-frame bracket.

15. Remove the engine and transaxle mounts at the frame.

16. Support the frame with jackstands at each end, remove the frame bolts and frame. Refer to the "Frame" section in this chapter.

17. Remove the torque converter cover and bolts.

18. Remove the starter bolts and support out of the way.

19. Remove the ground cable from the transaxle case.

20. Remove the fluid fill tube bolt and transaxle mount bracket.

21. Lower the vehicle.

22. Remove the fill tube.

23. Using the engine support fixture, lower the left side of the engine about four inches.

24. Raise the vehicle, support with jackstands and install a transaxle jack.

25. Remove the transaxle-to-engine bolts and transaxle.

To install:

1. The transaxle oil cooler lines should be flushed with a converter flush kit J-35944 or equivalent.

2. Lubricate the torque converter pilot hub with chassis grease.

NOTE: *Make sure the torque converter is properly seated in the oil pump drive. Damage to the transaxle may occur if converter is not seated completely.*

3. Position the transaxle into the vehicle and torque the transaxle-to-engine bolts to 55 ft. lbs. (75 Nm).

4. Install the transaxle mount bracket and lower the vehicle.

5. Using the engine support fixture, raise the engine into the proper position.

6. Install the fluid fill tube.

7. With an assistant, position and support

the frame under the vehicle. Install the frame bolts and torque to 103 ft. lbs. (140 Nm).

8. Remove the frame supports and lower the vehicle.

9. Position the engine and transaxle into the frame mounts. Remove the engine support fixture.

10. Raise the vehicle, install the torque converter-to-flywheel bolts and torque to 44 ft. lbs. (60 Nm). Install the torque converter cover.

11. Install the starter motor and transaxle ground cable.

12. Install the ball joints and tie rods.

13. Install the halfshaft (axle) assemblies, rotors and calipers.

14. Install the rack and pinion, lines-to-frame and heat shields.

15. Install the A/C compressor.

16. Install the engine oil filter and refill to the proper level.

17. Lower the vehicle.

18. Install the throttle cable bracket, torque strut bracket and torque strut.

19. Install the transaxle oil cooler lines-to-transaxle.

20. Install the shift control and TV cables.

21. Connect the negative battery cable, install the air cleaner and recheck each operation to ensure completion of repair.

22. Adjust the shift linkage and TV cable. Check the engine and transaxle oil levels.

23. Start the engine and check for fluid leaks.

Hydra-Matic 440-T4 (4-speed)

1. Disconnect the negative (–) battery cable and remove the air cleaner assembly.

2. Install the engine support fixture tool J-28467-A and J-36462.

3. Remove the shift control and throttle valve (TV) cables at the transaxle.

4. Remove the throttle cable bracket and brake booster hose.

5. Remove the crossover pipe-to-left exhaust manifold, EGR tube at crossover and crossover-to-exhaust pipe bolts.

6. Loosen the crossover-to-right manifold and swing the crossover upward to gain clearance to the top bell housing bolts.

7. Remove the four upper bell housing bolts.

8. Remove the TCC electrical connector, neutral start switch electrical connector and vacuum modulator hose at the transaxle.

9. Raise the vehicle and support with jackstands.

10. Remove the vehicle speed sensor electrical connector.

11. Remove the front wheels, splash shields, calipers and rotors. Support the caliper to the frame with wire.

12. Remove the front halfshafts (axle) assemblies as outlined in this chapter.

13. Disconnect both ball joints and tie rod ends from the strut assemblies. For further assistance, refer to Chapter 8.

14. Remove the rack and pinion heat shield and electrical connector.

15. Remove the rack and pinion assembly and wire to the exhaust for support.

16. Remove the power steering hoses-to-frame bracket, if so equipped.

17. Remove the engine and transaxle mounts at the frame.

18. Support the frame with jackstands at each end, remove the frame bolts and frame. Refer to the "Frame" section in this chapter.

19. Remove the torque converter cover and bolts.

20. Remove the transaxle oil cooler lines, support bracket and torque converter cover.

21. Remove the starter bolts and support out of the way.

22. Remove the ground cable from the transaxle case.

23. Support the transaxle with jackstands.

24. Remove the fluid fill tube bolt and transaxle mount bracket.

25. Remove the transaxle-to-engine bolts and transaxle.

To install:

1. The transaxle oil cooler lines should be flushed with a converter flush kit J-35944 or equivalent.

2. Lubricate the torque converter pilot hub with chassis grease.

NOTE: *Make sure the torque converter is properly seated in the oil pump drive. Damage to the transaxle may occur if converter is not seated completely.*

3. Position the transaxle into the vehicle and torque the transaxle-to-engine bolts to 55 ft. lbs. (75 Nm).

4. Install the transaxle mount bracket.

5. Install the torque converter-to-flywheel bolts and torque to 44 ft. lbs. (60 Nm).

6. Install the starter motor, halfshafts (axles) and torque converter cover.

7. Connect the oil cooler lines and support bracket.

8. Install the frame assembly and retaining bolts. Torque the bolts to 103 ft. lbs. (140 Nm).

9. Install the lower engine mount retaining nuts and upper transaxle mount retaining nuts.

10. Install the ball joints-to-steering knuckle and rack and pinion assembly-to-frame.

11. Install the power steering heat shield and cooler lines-to-frame.

12. Install the wheel house splash shields.

13. Install the rotor, calipers and front wheels. Torque the lug nuts to 100 ft. lbs. (136 Nm).

14. Install the vehicle speed sensor and lower the vehicle.

15. Connect the back-up/neutral switch.

16. Connect the modulator hose and TCC electrical connector.

17. Install the four upper bell housing bolts and torque to 55 ft. lbs. (75 Nm).

18. Install the crossover pipe to its proper position.

19. Install the crossover pipe-to-right and left manifolds.

20. Install the EGR tube-to-crossover.

21. Connect the TV and shift control cables.

22. Remove the engine support fixture J-28467-A and J-36462.

23. Connect the negative battery cable and install the air cleaner.

24. Adjust the fluid level, TV and shift cables.

25. Recheck all procedures for completion of repair. Start the engine and check for fluid leaks.

Halfshafts

REMOVAL AND INSTALLATION

CAUTION: *Use care when removing the halfshaft. Tri-pot joints can be damaged if the drive axle is over-extended. It is important to handle the halfshaft in a manner to prevent over-extending.*

1. Disconnect the negative (–) battery cable.
2. Raise the car and support with jackstands. Remove the wheel and tire.
3. Remove the brake calipers, bracket assemblies and hang out of the way with wire.
4. Remove the brake rotors.
5. Remove the four hub/bearing retaining bolts and hub.
6. Remove the ABS sensor mounting bolt and position the sensor out of the way, if equipped with ABS brakes.
7. Place a drain pan under the transaxle.
8. **RIGHT** using a axle shaft removing tool J-33008 or equivalent, separate the halfshaft from the transaxle.
9. **LEFT** using a suitable pry bar, separate the halfshaft from the transaxle. Pry on the frame and the groove provided on the inner joint.
10. Separate the halfshaft from the bearing assembly, if not removed.

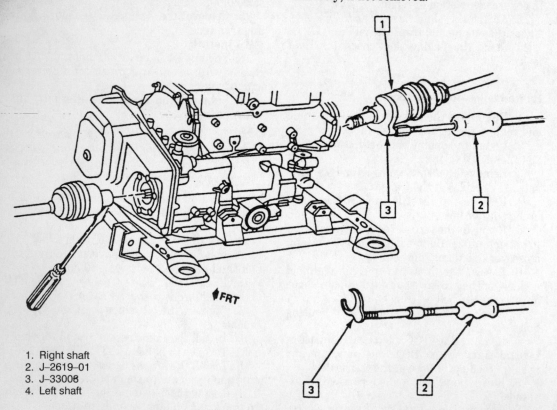

1. Right shaft
2. J–2619–01
3. J–33008
4. Left shaft

Halfshaft removal

To install:

1. Install the halfshaft/bearing assembly through the knuckle and into the transaxle until the retaining clip engages. Do NOT over-extend the inner joint.

2. Install the ABS sensor.

3. Torque the bearing assembly retaining bolts to 52 ft. lbs. (70 Nm).

4. Remove the drain pan and install a new halfshaft nut and washer.

5. Install the rotor, brake caliper and wheel assemblies. Torque the lug nuts to 100 ft. lbs. (136 Nm).

6. Lower the vehicle and torque the half-shaft axle nut to 184 ft. lbs. (250 Nm).

7. Add the necessary amount of transaxle fluid and connect the negative battery cable.

OVERHAUL

Refer to the "Halfshaft" overhaul procedures in the Manual Transaxle section in this chapter.

Suspension and Steering

8

FRONT SUSPENSION

CAUTION: *Some brake pads contain asbestos, which has been determined to be a cancer causing agent. Never clean the brake surfaces with compressed air! Avoid inhaling any dust from any brake surface! When cleaning brake surfaces, use a commercially available brake cleaning fluid.*

Strut Cartridge

REMOVAL AND INSTALLATION

The front MacPherson strut assembly does NOT have to be removed from the vehicle to remove the strut cartridge.

CAUTION: *Do NOT remove the strut cartridge nut without compressing the coil spring first. This procedure MUST be followed because it keeps the coil spring compressed. Use care to support the strut assembly adequately because the coil spring is under heavy load, if released too quickly per-*

sonal injury could result. Never remove the center strut nuts unless the spring is compressed with a MacPherson Strut Spring Compressor tool J-26584 or equivalent.

NOTE: *The vehicle weight can be used when the strut assembly is still in the vehicle and only the strut cartridge is going to be replaced.*

1. Disconnect the negative (–) battery cable.
2. Scribe the strut mount cover plate-to-body to ensure proper camber adjustment.
3. Remove the three strut mount cover plate retaining nuts and cover.
4. Remove the strut shaft nut using a No. 50 Torx® bit.
5. Remove the strut mount bushing by prying with a suitable pry bar.
6. Remove the jounce bumper retainer using a jounce bumper spanner wrench tool J-35670. Remove the jounce bumper by attaching the strut extension rod J-35668. Compress the shaft down into the cartridge. Remove the extension rod and pull out the jounce bumper.
7. Remove the strut cartridge closure nut by attaching the strut extension rod and re-extending the shaft. Remove the extension rod

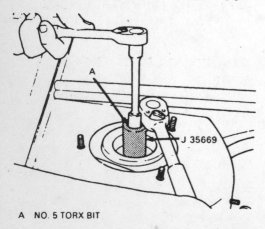

A NO. 5 TORX BIT

Shaft nut removal

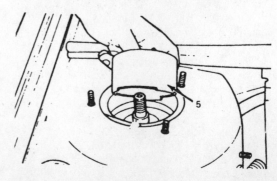

Strut mount bushing (5) removal

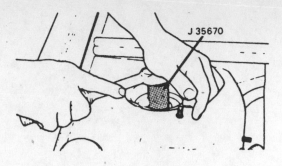

Jounce bumper retainer removal

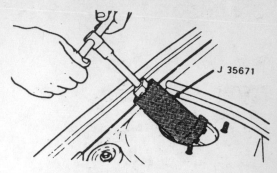

Strut closure nut removal

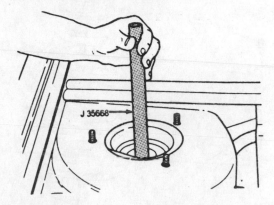

Use special tool shown to compress shaft down into cartridge

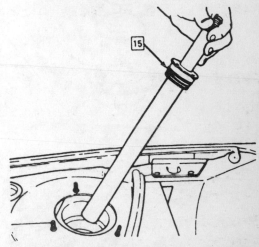

Strut cartridge. Tighten the retainer (15) to 82 ft. lbs.

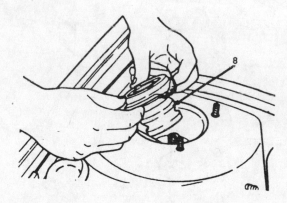

Jounce bumper (8) removal

and unscrew the closure nut using a strut cap nut wrench J-35671 or equivalent.

8. Remove the strut cartridge and oil from the strut tube using a suction device.

To install:

1. Install the self contained replacement cartridge using the strut cap nut wrench J-35671 or equivalent. The cartridge does not need oil added unless specified. If oil is not supplied with the cartridge, add the specified amount of hydraulic jack oil.

2. Install the jounce bumper and retainer.

3. Install the strut mount bushing. Use a soap solution to lubricate the bushing during installation.

4. Install the strut shaft nut and torque to 72 ft. lbs. (98 Nm).

5. Align the scribed marks from the strut cover-to-body. Install the strut cover plate and nuts. Torque the nuts to 17 ft. lbs. (24 Nm).

6. Connect the negative (–) battery cable and check for proper suspension operation.

MacPherson Strut/Knuckle Assembly

REMOVAL AND INSTALLATION

CAUTION: *Do NOT remove the strut cartridge nut without compressing the coil spring first. This procedure MUST be followed because it keeps the coil spring compressed. Use care to support the strut assembly adequately because the coil spring is under heavy load, if released too quickly personal injury could result. Never remove the center strut nuts unless the spring is compressed with a MacPherson Strut Spring*

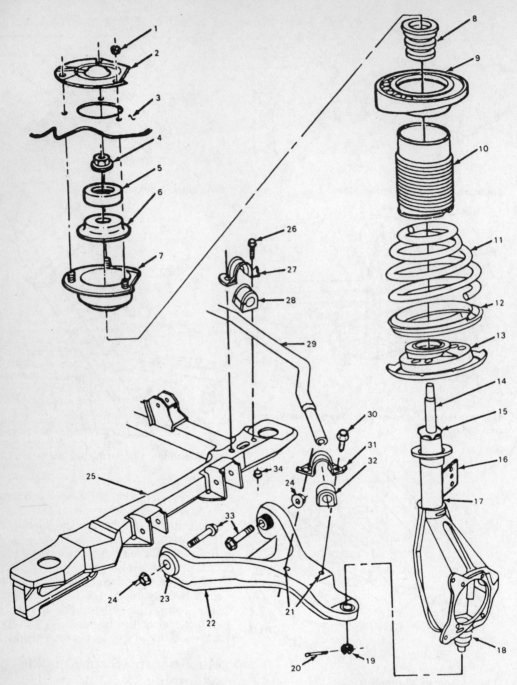

1. 17 ft. lbs.
2. Strut mount cover plate
3. Shock tower
4. 72 ft. lbs
5. Upper strut mount bushing
6. Bumper retainer
7. Strut mount
8. Bumper
9. Upper spring insulator
10. Dust shield
11. Spring
12. Lower spring insulator

13. Spring seat and bearing
14. Strut cartridge shaft
15. 82 ft. lbs.
16. Spring plate
17. Knuckle/strut assembly
18. Suspension ball joint
19. Castle nut
20. Cotter pin
21. Weld studs
22. Lower control arm
23. Lower control arm bushing

24. 72 ft. lbs.
25. Frame assembly
26. Insulator clamp bolt
27. Clamp
28. Stabilizer shaft insulator
29. Stabilizer shaft
30. 35 ft. lbs.
31. Clamp
32. Stabilizer shaft insulator
33. Lower control arm through bolt
34. 35 ft. lbs.

Front suspension — exploded view

Troubleshooting Basic Steering and Suspension Problems

Problem	Cause	Solution
Hard steering (steering wheel is hard to turn)	• Low or uneven tire pressure • Loose power steering pump drive belt • Low or incorrect power steering fluid • Incorrect front end alignment • Defective power steering pump • Bent or poorly lubricated front end parts	• Inflate tires to correct pressure • Adjust belt • Add fluid as necessary • Have front end alignment checked/adjusted • Check pump • Lubricate and/or replace defective parts
Loose steering (too much play in the steering wheel)	• Loose wheel bearings • Loose or worn steering linkage • Faulty shocks • Worn ball joints	• Adjust wheel bearings • Replace worn parts • Replace shocks • Replace ball joints
Car veers or wanders (car pulls to one side with hands off the steering wheel)	• Incorrect tire pressure • Improper front end alignment • Loose wheel bearings • Loose or bent front end components • Faulty shocks	• Inflate tires to correct pressure • Have front end alignment checked/adjusted • Adjust wheel bearings • Replace worn components • Replace shocks
Wheel oscillation or vibration transmitted through steering wheel	• Improper tire pressures • Tires out of balance • Loose wheel bearings • Improper front end alignment • Worn or bent front end components	• Inflate tires to correct pressure • Have tires balanced • Adjust wheel bearings • Have front end alignment checked/adjusted • Replace worn parts
Uneven tire wear	• Incorrect tire pressure • Front end out of alignment • Tires out of balance	• Inflate tires to correct pressure • Have front end alignment checked/adjusted • Have tires balanced

Compressor tool J-26584 or equivalent. The vehicle weight can be used when the strut assembly is still in the vehicle and only the strut cartridge is going to be replaced.

1. Disconnect the negative (–) battery cable.

2. Loosen the cover plate bolts.

3. Loosen the wheel nuts. Raise and safely support the vehicle.

4. Remove the wheel assembly. Remove the brake caliper and bracket assembly, hang the caliper aside. DO NOT hang the caliper by the brake lines.

5. Remove the brake rotor. Remove the hub and bearing attaching bolts.

6. Remove the halfshaft. Remove the tie rod attaching nut. Using tool J-35917 or equivalent, separate the tie rod from the steering knuckle.

7. Remove the lower ball joint attaching nut and separate the lower ball from the lower control arm.

8. Remove the hub and bearing attaching bolts and hub assembly.

9. Remove the cover plate bolts and remove the strut from the vehicle.

To install:

1. Install the strut mount cover plate, tighten the nuts after lowering the vehicle. Install the lower ball joint and torque to 81 inch lbs. (10 Nm) plus an additional 120° (2 flats) turn until the cotter pin hole is lined up.

2. Install the tie rod and torque to 40 ft. lbs. (54 Nm) to line up the cotter pin hole.

3. Install the halfshaft and install the hub and bearing-to-knuckle attaching bolts, tighten to 52 ft. lbs. (70 Nm).

4. Install the brake rotor and caliper assembly.

5. Install the wheel assembly, tighten the wheel lug nuts to 100 ft. lbs. (136 Nm).

6. Lower the vehicle, tighten the strut cover bolts to 17 ft. lbs. (24 Nm) and tighten the wheel nuts.

7. Connect the negative (–) battery cable.

OVERHAUL

CAUTION: *Do NOT remove the strut cartridge nut without compressing the coil spring first. This procedure MUST be followed because it keeps the coil spring com-*

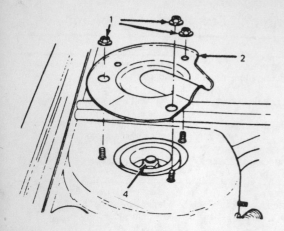

Front MacPherson strut cover plate. Tighten the three small nuts to 19 ft. lbs. and the center shaft nut to 74 ft. lbs.

pressed. Use care to support the strut assembly adequately because the coil spring is under heavy load, if released too quickly personal injury could result. Never remove the center strut nuts unless the spring is compressed with a MacPherson Strut Spring Compressor tool J-26584 or equivalent. The vehicle weight can be used when the strut assembly is still in the vehicle and only the strut cartridge is going to be replaced.

Disassembly

1. Remove the MacPherson strut assembly as outlined in this section.

2. Mount the strut assembly in a strut compressing tool J-34013-A and J-34013-88. Compress the spring using the forcing screw. Release the spring tension enough to remove the spring insulator.

3. Using a Torx® bit and a strut shaft nut remover tool J-35669, remove the strut shaft nut. Make sure there is no spring tension on the shaft.

4. Release all spring tension and remove the spring and insulator. Remove any component needed to perform repair.

Assembly

1. Inspect all components for wear and damage.

2. Install the spring seat and bearing.

3. Install the lower spring insulator. The lower spring coil end must be visible between the step and the first retention tab of the insulator.

4. Install the spring, dust shield and jounce bumper.

5. Install the upper spring insulator. The

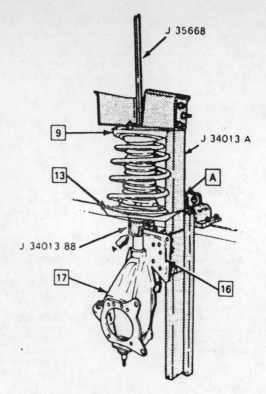

A. Compressor forcing screw
9. Upper strut mount
13. Lower seat and bearing
16. Spring plate
17. Knuckle/strut assembly

MacPherson strut spring compressor

upper spring coil end must be between the step and location mark on the insulator.

6. Install the jounce bumper retainer-to-strut mount using a jounce bumper spanner tool J-35670 or equivalent.

7. Align the strut cartridge shaft with a strut extension rod tool J-35668.

8. Install the strut mount and the upper strut mount bushing.

9. Compress the strut assembly using the strut spring compressor tool J-34013-A and J-34013-88.

10. Install the shaft nut using the strut rod installer and Torx® bit. Torque the shaft nut to 72 ft. lbs. (98 Nm).

11. Install the MacPherson strut assembly into the vehicle as outlined in this section.

Coil Spring

REMOVAL AND INSTALLATION

Refer to the "MacPherson Strut" overhaul procedures for coil spring removal and installation.

Lower Ball Joint

REMOVAL AND INSTALLATION

1. Disconnect the negative (–) battery cable.
2. Raise the vehicle and support with jack-stands.
3. Remove the front wheels, ball joint heat shield and lower ball joint cotter pin.
4. Remove the ball joint nut.
5. Loosen but do NOT remove the stabilizer shaft bushing assembly bolts.

WARNING: *Do NOT damage the halfshaft boots when drilling out the ball joint rivets.*

6. Remove the ball joint from the strut/knuckle assembly using a ball joint/tie rod puller J-35917 or equivalent.
7. Drill out the ball joint rivets and remove the ball joint from the knuckle. Refer to the instructions in the ball joint replacement kit.

To install:

1. Install the lower ball joint into the strut/knuckle assembly.
2. Install the four ball joint bolts and nuts in the kit and torque to specifications.
3. Install the ball joint-to-lower control arm. Install a new ball joint nut and torque to 89 inch lbs. (10 Nm) plus an additional 120° (2 flats) plus enough to align the cotter pin hole. Do NOT overtighten.
4. Install a new cotter pin and bend over.
5. Torque the stabilizer shaft bolts to 35 ft. lbs. (47 Nm).
6. Install the ball joint heat shield, front wheels and lower the vehicle.
7. Connect the negative (–) battery and check for proper suspension operation.

Lower Control Arm

REMOVAL AND INSTALLATION

1. Disconnect the negative (–) battery cable.
2. Raise the vehicle and support with jack-stands.
3. Remove the front wheels.
4. Remove the stabilizer shaft-to-lower control arm insulator bracket bolts.
5. Remove the lower ball joint cotter pin and nut.
6. Using a ball joint/tie rod puller J-35917 or equivalent, separate the ball joint from the control arm.
7. Remove the lower control arm-to-frame bolts and control arm. Be careful not to damage the halfshaft boots.

To install:

1. Install the lower control arm and bolts as shown in the illustration. Do NOT tighten at this time.
2. Install the ball joint-to-control arm and install the nut. Torque the new ball joint nut to

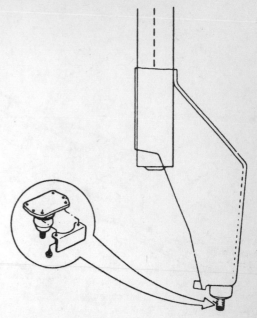

Front lower ball joint

89 inch lbs. (10 Nm) plus an additional 120° (2 flats) plus enough to align the cotter pin hole. Do NOT overtighten!

3. Install a new cotter pin and bent over.
4. Install the stabilizer shaft-to-lower control arm bracket and torque to 35 ft. lbs. (47 Nm).
5. Install the front wheels and torque the lug nuts to 100 ft. lbs. (136 Nm).
6. Lower the vehicle and connect the negative (–) battery cable.
7. Check for proper suspension operation before moving the vehicle.

Hub/Bearing Assembly

These cars are equipped with sealed hub and bearing assemblies. The hub and bearing assemblies are non-serviceable. If the assembly is damaged, the complete unit must be replaced. Refer to the "Sealed Wheel Bearing Diagnosis Chart" in Chapter 1.

CAUTION: *Some brake pads contain asbestos, which has been determined to be a cancer causing agent. Never clean the brake surfaces with compressed air! Avoid inhaling any dust from any brake surface! When cleaning brake surfaces, use a commercially available brake cleaning fluid.*

REMOVAL AND INSTALLATION

1. Disconnect the negative (–) battery cable.
2. Loosen the halfshaft nut and washer one turn. Do NOT remove the nut at this time.
3. Raise the vehicle and support with jack-stands.

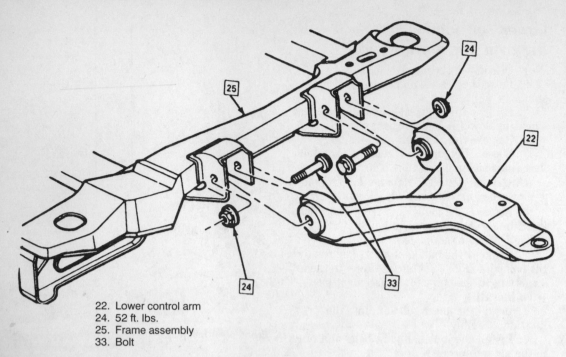

22. Lower control arm
24. 52 ft. lbs.
25. Frame assembly
33. Bolt

Front lower control arm

4. Remove the front wheel, caliper, bracket and rotor.
5. Remove the halfshaft nut and washer.
6. Loosen the four hub/bearing-to-knuckle attaching bolts.
7. Using a front hub spindle removing tool J-28733-A or equivalent, push the halfshaft splines back out of the hub/bearing assembly.
8. Protect the halfshaft boots from damage during removal. Remove the hub/bearing attaching bolts and hub/bearing.

To install:

1. Install the hub/bearing assembly onto the halfshaft splines. Install the four attaching bolts and torque to 52 ft. lbs. (70 Nm).
2. Install a new halfshaft nut and washer. Do NOT tighten the nut at this time.
3. Install the rotor, caliper and bracket.
4. Install the front wheel and torque the lug nut to 100 ft. lbs. (135 Nm).
5. Lower the vehicle.
6. Torque the halfshaft nut to 184 ft. lbs. (250 Nm). Connect the negative (–) battery cable.

Stabilizer Shaft and Insulators

REMOVAL AND INSTALLATION

1. Disconnect the negative (–) battery cable.
2. Raise the vehicle and support with jackstands.
3. Remove the front wheel.
4. Move the steering shaft dust seal for

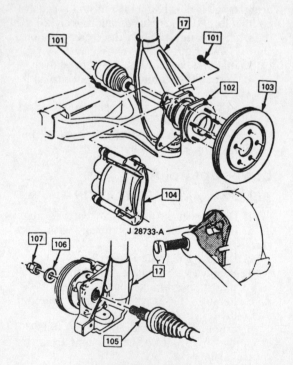

17. Knuckle/strut assembly
101. 52 ft. lbs.
102. Hub and bearing assembly
103. Rotor
104. Caliper and bracket
105. Drive axle
106. Washer
107. 184 ft. lbs

Front hub and bearing assembly

access to the pinch bolt. Refer to the "Rack and Pinion" section in this chapter.

5. Remove the pinch bolt from the lower intermediate steering shaft.

6. Loosen all the stabilizer insulator clamp attaching nuts and bolts.

7. Place a jackstand under the center of the rear frame crossmember.

8. Loosen the two front frame-to-body bolts (four turns only).

9. Remove the two rear frame-to-body bolts and lower the rear of the frame just enough to gain access to remove the stabilizer shaft.

10. Remove the insulators and clamps from the frame and control arms. Pull the stabilizer shaft rearward, swing down and remove from the left side of the vehicle.

To install:

1. Install the stabilizer shaft through the left side of the vehicle.

2. Coat the new insulators with rubber lubricant.

3. Loosely install the clamps-to-control arms and clamps-to-frame.

4. Raise the frame into position while guiding the steering gear into place.

5. Install new frame-to-body bolts and torque to 103 ft. lbs. (140 Nm).

6. Remove the frame jackstand.

7. Torque the stabilizer clamps-to-frame and control arms to 35 ft. lbs. (47 Nm).

8. Install the steering gear pinch bolt and dust seal.

9. Install the front wheels and torque the lug nuts to 100 ft. lbs. (136 Nm).

10. Check for completion of repair and lower the vehicle.

11. Connect the negative (–) battery cable.

Front End Alignment

NOTE: *The do-it-yourself mechanic should not attempt to perform any wheel alignment procedures. Expensive alignment tools are needed and would not be cost efficient to purchase these tools. The wheel alignment should be performed by a certified alignment technician using the proper alignment tools.*

Adjustment

A four wheel alignment should be performed whenever any adjustments are made to the front end. Align the vehicle in the following order; rear wheel camber, rear wheel toe and tracking, front wheel camber and toe.

Camber

1. Remove the strut cover plate nuts and strut cover plate.

2. Lift the front of the vehicle to the point that the strut studs clear the strut tower and cover the strut with a towel.

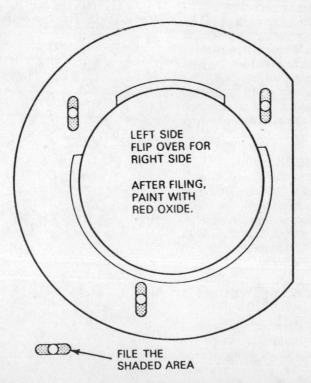

LEFT SIDE
FLIP OVER FOR
RIGHT SIDE

AFTER FILING,
PAINT WITH
RED OXIDE.

FILE THE
SHADED AREA

Front strut alignment template

Wheel Alignment Specifications

Years	Caster (deg.)		Camber (deg.)		Toe-in (in.)
	Range	Pref.	Range	Pref.	
Cutlass Supreme					
1988	1½P to 2½P	2P	³/₁₆P to 1³/₁₆P	¹¹/₁₆P	0
1989–90	1⁵/₁₆P to 2⁵/₁₆P	1¹³/₁₆P	³/₁₆P to 1³/₁₆P	¹¹/₁₆P	0
Grand Prix					
1988	1½P to 2½P	2P	³/₁₆P to 1³/₁₆P	¹¹/₁₆P	0
1989–90	1⁵/₁₆P to 2⁵/₁₆P	1¹³/₁₆P	³/₁₆P to 1³/₁₆P	¹¹/₁₆P	0
Regal					
1989–90	1½P to 2½P	2P	³/₁₆P to 1³/₁₆P	¹¹/₁₆P	0
Lumina					
1990	1½P to 2½P	2P	³/₁₆P to 1³/₁₆P	¹¹/₁₆P	0

3. Using a strut alignment template J–36892, mark and file the three holes to the specified amount. Do not exceed 0.2 inch (5mm).

4. Paint the exposed metal with primer and body paint.

5. Lower the vehicle and guide the strut studs into the slotted holes.

6. Install the strut cover plate, nuts and set camber to specifications. Tighten the strut nuts to 17 ft. lbs. (24 Nm).

Toe

1. Remove the rack and pinion seal clamp and make sure the seal does not twist.

2. With the wheels in the straight ahead position, loosen the jam nuts on the tie rods. Rotate the inner tie rod to obtain toe angle.

3. Check the number of threads on each side and make sure they are about equal.

4. Tighten the jam nuts to 46 ft. lbs. (62 Nm). Install the seal clamps.

The caster angle is not adjustable.

REAR SUSPENSION

The rear suspension features a lightweight composite fiberglass mono-leaf transverse spring. Each wheel is mounted to a tri-link independent suspension system. The three links consist of an inverted U channel trailing arm and tubular front and rear rods.

Transverse Spring Assembly
REMOVAL AND INSTALLATION

CAUTION: *Do NOT disconnect any rear suspension components until the transverse spring has been compressed using a rear spring compressor tool J-35778 or equivalent. Failure to follow this procedure may result in personal injury.*

NOTE: *Do not use any corrosive cleaning agents, silicone lubricants, engine degreasers, solvents, etc. on or near the fiberglass rear transverse spring. These materials may cause extensive spring damage.*

1. Disconnect the negative (–) battery cable.

2. Raise the vehicle and support with jackstands.

3. Remove the jack pad in the middle of the spring.

4. Remove the spring retention plates and the right trailing arm at the knuckle.

5. Separate the rear leaf spring compressor tool J-35778 from the center shank and hang

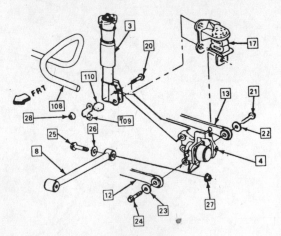

3. Rear strut	23. Washer
4. Knuckle assembly	24. 157 ft. lbs
8. Trailing arm	25. Bolt
12. Front rod	26. Washer
13. Rear rod	27. 192 ft. lbs
17. Auxilary spring	28. 133 ft. lbs.
20. Bolt	108. Stabilizer shaft
21. 157 ft. lbs.	109. Stabilizer shaft bracket
22. Washer	110. Insulator

Rear tri-link suspension system

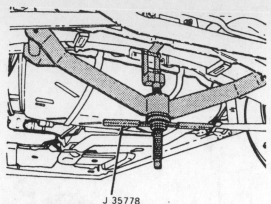

J 35778
Transverse spring compressor

the center shank of the tool at the spring center.

NOTE: *Attach the center shank of the compressor from the front side of the vehicle only.*

6. Install the compressor body to the center shank and spring. Important, always center the spring on the rollers of the spring compressor.

7. Fully compress the spring using the spring compressor tool J-35778.

8. Slide the spring to the left side. It may be necessary to pry the spring to the left using a pry bar against the right knuckle. When prying, do not damage any components.

9. Relax the spring to provide removal clearance from the right side and remove the spring.

To install:

1. Using the spring compressor tool, compress the spring and install it through the left knuckle. Slide towards the left side as far as possible and raise the right side of the spring as far as possible.

2. Compress the spring fully and install it into right knuckle.

NOTE: *The rear spring retention plates are designed with tabs one end. The tabs must be aligned with the support assembly to prevent damage to the fuel tank.*

3. Center the spring to align the holes for the spring retention plate bolts.

4. Install the spring retention plates and bolts. Do NOT tighten at this time.

5. Position the trailing arm and install the bolt. Torque the bolt to 192 ft. lbs. (260 Nm).

6. Remove the spring compressor tool J-35778.

7. Torque the spring retention plate bolts to 15 ft. lbs. (20 Nm).

8. Install the jack pads and torque the bolts to 18 ft. lbs. (25 Nm).

9. Install the wheels and torque the lug nuts to 100 ft. lbs. (136 Nm).

10. Lower the vehicle and connect the negative (–) battery cable.

Strut Assembly

REMOVAL AND INSTALLATION

1. Disconnect the negative (–) battery cable.

2. Raise the vehicle and support with jackstands.

3. Remove the rear wheel assembly.

4. Scribe the strut-to-knuckle for proper installation.

5. Remove the auxiliary spring, if so equipped.

6. Remove the jack pad.

7. Install a rear leaf spring compressor tool J-35778 or equivalent. Refer the the "Transverse Spring" procedures in this section.

8. Fully compress the spring, but do NOT remove the retention plates or the spring.

9. Remove the two strut-to-body bolts.

10. Remove the brake hose from the strut.

11. Remove the strut and auxiliary spring upper bracket from the knuckle.

To install:

1. Position the strut to the body and knuckle bracket.

2. Install the strut-to-body bolts and torque to 34 ft. lbs. (46 Nm).

3. Install the strut-to-knuckle, align the scribe marks and torque the bolts to 133 ft. lbs. (180 Nm).

4. Install the brake hose bracket and remove the spring compressing tool.

5. Install the jack pad and torque the bolts to 18 ft. lbs. (25 Nm).

6. Install the auxiliary spring, if so equipped.

7. Install the wheel and torque the lug nuts to 100 ft. lbs. (136 Nm).

8. Lower the vehicle and connect the negative (–) battery cable.

OVERHAUL

The rear strut assembly is not serviceable. The assembly is replaced as a complete unit.

Knuckle

REMOVAL AND INSTALLATION

1. Disconnect the negative (–) battery cable.

2. Raise the vehicle and support with jackstands.

3. Remove the rear wheels and scribe the strut-to-knuckle.

4. Remove the jack pad and install the rear leaf spring compressor tool J-35778 as outlined in the "Transverse Spring" procedures in this chapter.

5. Fully compress the spring but do not remove the spring or retention plates.

6. Remove the auxiliary spring, if so

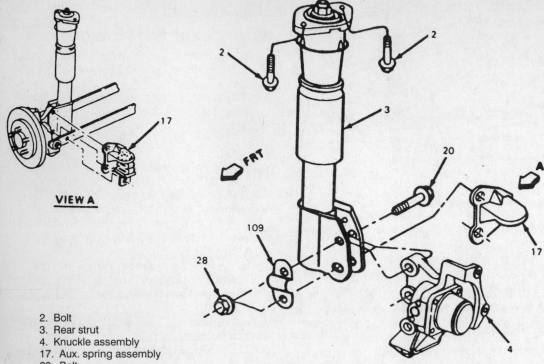

VIEW A

2. Bolt
3. Rear strut
4. Knuckle assembly
17. Aux. spring assembly
20. Bolt
28. Nut–133 ft. lbs.
109. Stabilizer shaft bracket

Strut and auxiliary spring assembly

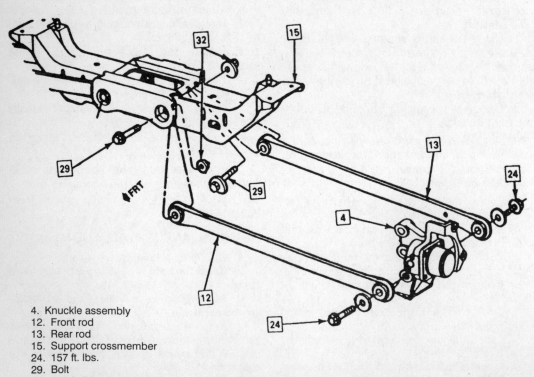

4. Knuckle assembly
12. Front rod
13. Rear rod
15. Support crossmember
24. 157 ft. lbs.
29. Bolt
32. 140 ft. lbs.

Knuckle and suspension rods

equipped. If not equipped, remove the rod -to-knuckle bolt.

7. Remove the front rod-to-knuckle.

8. Remove the brake hose bracket, caliper and rotor. Do not allow the caliper to hang by the brake hose.

9. Remove the hub and bearing assembly, trailing arm and the strut/upper auxiliary spring bracket from the knuckle. Remove the knuckle.

To install:

1. Install the knuckle and position it to the strut/upper auxiliary spring bracket. Hand start the bolts, but do not tighten.

2. Install the front rod and trailing arm-to-knuckle. Hand tighten the bolts.

3. Torque the trailing arm bolt and nut to 192 ft. lbs. (260 Nm).

4. Install the hub/bearing assembly and torque the bolts to 52 ft. lbs. (70 Nm).

5. Install the rotor and caliper.

6. Align the scribe marks to ensure proper alignment. Torque the strut-to-knuckle attaching bolts to 133 ft. lbs. (180 Nm).

7. Remove the rear leaf spring compressor.

8. Install the jack pad, auxiliary spring (if equipped) and rod-to-knuckle bolt. Apply thread locking compound to the knuckle bolts.

9. Torque the rod-to-knuckle bolts to 66 ft. lbs. (90 Nm) plus 120°.

10. Install the rear wheels and torque the lug nuts to 100 ft. lbs. (136 Nm).

11. Check for completion of repair, lower the vehicle and connect the negative (–) battery cable.

Tri-Link Suspension Assembly

REMOVAL AND INSTALLATION

Trailing Arm

1. Raise the vehicle and support with jackstands.

2. Remove the trailing arm-to-knuckle nut and bolt.

3. Remove the trailing arm-to-body nut, bolt and arm.

To install:

1. Install the trailing arm, bolts and nuts.

2. Torque the arm-to-knuckle bolt to 192 ft. lbs. (260 Nm) and the arm-to-body bolt to 48 ft. lbs. (65 Nm).

3. Lower the vehicle and recheck all repair procedures.

Rear Rod

1. Raise the vehicle and support with jackstands.

2. Remove the rear wheels.

3. Remove the auxiliary spring, if so

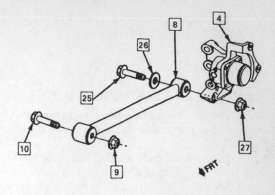

4. Knuckle assembly
8. Trailing arm
9. 48 ft. lbs
10. Bolt

25. Bolt
26. Washer
27. 192 ft. lbs.

Trailing arm

equipped. If not equipped, remove the rod-to-knuckle bolt.

4. Remove the lower auxiliary spring bracket at the rod, if so equipped.

5. Scribe the toe adjusting cam, remove the rod-to-crossmember bolt and rod.

To install:

1. Install the rod, push the bolt through the rod bushing and install the adjusting cam in its original location. Do not tighten at this time.

2. Install the lower auxiliary spring bracket-to-rod, if so equipped. Torque the nut to 133 ft. lbs. (180 Nm).

3. Install the rod-to-knuckle with thread locking compound. Do not tighten.

4. Install the rear wheels and lower the vehicle.

5. Torque the rod-to-crossmember bolt to 66 ft. lbs. (90 Nm) plus 120°.

6. Have a qualified alignment technician adjust the rear toe.

Front Rod

1. Raise the vehicle and support with jackstands.

2. Remove the rear wheels.

3. Remove the rod-to-knuckle bolt and exhaust pipe heat shield.

4. Lower and support the fuel tank just enough for access to the bolt at the frame.

5. Remove the rod-to-frame bolt and rod.

To install:

1. Install the rod, bolt and nut. Do not tighten at this time.

2. Apply thread locking compound to the rod-to-knuckle bolt.

3. Torque the rod-to-frame and rod-to-knuckle bolts to 66 ft. lbs. (90 Nm) plus 120°.

4. Reposition the fuel tank.

5. Install the exhaust pipe heat shield, rear wheels and lower the vehicle.

Stabilizer Shaft

REMOVAL AND INSTALLATION

1. Disconnect the negative (–) battery cable.
2. Raise the vehicle and support with jackstands.
3. Remove the right and left stabilizer shaft link bolts and open the brackets to remove the insulators.
4. Remove the right and left strut-to-knuckle-to-stabilizer shaft nuts. Do NOT remove the strut-to-knuckle bolts.
5. Remove the stabilizer shaft by prying the shaft on one side for clearance at the strut.

To install:

1. Install the stabilizer shaft by prying the shaft on one side for clearance at the strut.
2. Install the insulator brackets-to-stabilizer shaft-to-knuckle bolts. Do NOT tighten at this time.
3. Install the right and left stabilizer shaft link bolts.
4. Torque the link bolts to 40 ft. lbs. (54 Nm) and the knuckle bolts to 133 ft. lbs. (180 Nm).
5. Check for completion of repair, connect the negative (–) battery cable and lower the vehicle.

Hub/Bearing Assembly

These cars are equipped with sealed hub and bearing assemblies. The hub and bearing assemblies are non-serviceable. If the assembly is damaged, the complete unit must be replaced. Refer to the "Sealed Wheel Bearing Diagnosis Chart" in Chapter 1.

CAUTION: *Some brake pads contain asbestos, which has been determined to be a cancer causing agent. Never clean the brake surfaces with compressed air! Avoid inhaling any dust from any brake surface! When cleaning brake surfaces, use a commercially available brake cleaning fluid.*

REMOVAL AND INSTALLATION

1. Disconnect the negative (–) battery cable.
2. Raise the vehicle and support with jackstands.
3. Remove the rear wheel, caliper, bracket and rotor.
4. Loosen the four hub/bearing-to-knuckle attaching bolts.
5. Remove the hub/bearing assembly.

To install:

1. Install the hub/bearing assembly onto the knuckle. Install the four attaching bolts and torque to 52 ft. lbs. (70 Nm).
2. Install the rotor, caliper and bracket.
3. Install the rear wheel and torque the lug nut to 100 ft. lbs. (135 Nm).

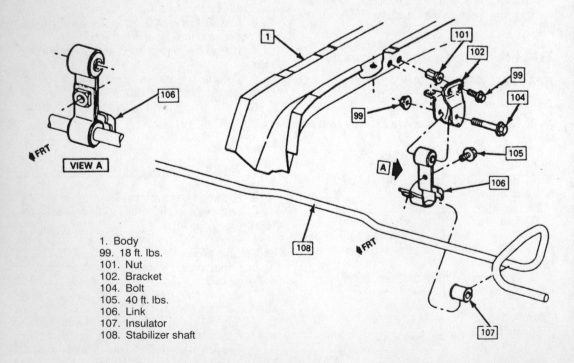

1. Body
99. 18 ft. lbs.
101. Nut
102. Bracket
104. Bolt
105. 40 ft. lbs.
106. Link
107. Insulator
108. Stabilizer shaft

Rear stabilizer shaft

4. Lower the vehicle and connect the negative (–) battery cable.

Rear Wheel Alignment

NOTE: *The do-it-yourself mechanic should not attempt to perform any wheel alignment procedures. Expensive alignment tools are needed and would not be cost efficient to pur-chase these tools. The wheel alignment should be performed by a certified alignment technician using the proper alignment tools.*

A four wheel alignment should be performed whenever any adjustments are made to the front end. Align the vehicle in the following order; rear wheel camber, rear wheel toe and tracking, front wheel camber and toe.

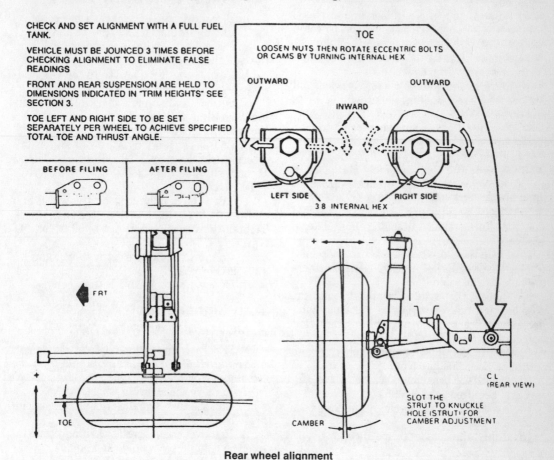

Rear wheel alignment

Rear Wheel Alignment Specifications

Years	Models	Camber (deg.)		Toe-in (in.)
		Range	Pref.	
1988	Cutlass Supreme	$7/16$N to $9/16$P	$1/16$P	$1/8$ out
	Grand Prix	$1/8$N to $7/8$P	$3/8$P	$1/8$ out
	Regal	$7/16$N to $9/16$P	$1/16$P	$1/8$ out
1989	Cutlass Supreme	0 to 1P	$1/2$P	$7/64$ out
	Grand Prix	0 to 1P	$1/2$P	$7/64$ out
	Regal	$7/16$N to $9/16$P	$1/16$P	$1/8$ out
1990	Lumina	$1/8$N to $7/8$P	$3/8$P	0
	Cutlass Supreme	$5/64$N to $7/64$P	$3/32$P	$7/64$ out
	Grand Prix	0 to 1P	$1/2$P	$7/64$ out
	Regal	$7/16$N to $9/16$P	$1/16$P	$1/8$ out

CAMBER

1. Raise and safely support the vehicle and remove the rear wheel assembly.

2. Support the suspension under the rear knuckle and hub with a jackstand.

3. Thread tool J–37098 or equivalent into the auxiliary spring assembly and tighten to hold the assembly in a compressed state, if so equipped.

4. Remove the brake caliper and support. Remove the rotor, brake hose bracket bolt and scribe the strut-to-knuckle for reassembly.

5. Remove the strut bolts at the body and let the assembly drop down.

6. Remove the stabilizer shaft bracket and remove the strut-to-knuckle attaching bolts and nuts.

7. Remove the rear auxiliary spring-to-rear lateral link attaching bolt and nut and the auxiliary spring.

8. Remove the strut assembly and place in a vise. At the lower strut-to-knuckle attaching hole, file the hole lateral (oblong).

9. Place the auxiliary spring in a vise and file the lower strut attaching hole lateral (oblong).

10. Place the stabilizer bracket in a vise and file the lower stabilizer bracket-to-strut attaching hole lateral (oblong).

11. Install the strut assembly-to-knuckle, auxiliary spring-to-rear lateral link and stabilizer shaft bracket. Do not tighten the strut bolts at this time.

12. Install the upper strut-to-body nuts and torque to 34 ft. lbs. (46 Nm).

13. Install the brake hose bracket, rotor, caliper and remove tool J–37098.

14. Install the wheel assembly and lower the vehicle.

15. Adjust the camber to specifications.

TOE

1. Loosen the inboard cam nuts at the rear support rod.

2. Rotate the cam to obtain the proper toe angle.

3. Align to specifications and torque the cam nuts to 140 ft. lbs. (190 Nm).

CASTER

The rear caster angle is non-adjustable.

STEERING

The power rack and pinion steering system has a rotary control valve which directs hydraulic fluid coming from the steering pump to one side or the other side of the rack piston. The piston converts hydraulic pressure to linear force which moves the rack right or left. When power assist is not available, manual control is maintained; however, more steering effort is needed. A vane type steering pump provides hydraulic pressure for steering assist.

Steering Wheel

REMOVAL AND INSTALLATION

1. Disconnect the negative battery cable.

2. Remove the horn pad and retainer.

3. Disconnect the horn electrical lead from the canceling cam tower.

4. Turn the ignition switch to the **ON** position.

5. Scribe an alignment mark on the steering wheel hub in line with the slash mark on the steering shaft.

6. Loosen the steering shaft nut and install steering wheel puller J–185903 or equivalent. Remove the steering wheel.

To install:

1. Align the matchmarks on the wheel hub and shaft and install the steering wheel. Tighten the steering shaft nut to 30 ft. lbs. (41 Nm).

2. Connect the horn electrical lead and install the horn pad.

3. Connect the negative battery cable.

Turn Signal Switch

REMOVAL AND INSTALLATION

NOTE: *Tool No. J–35689–A or equivalent, is required to remove the terminals from the connector on the turn signal switch.*

1. Remove the steering wheel.

2. Pull the turn signal canceling cam assembly from the steering shaft.

3. Remove the hazard warning knob-to-steering column screw and the knob.

NOTE: *Before removing the turn signal assembly, position the turn signal lever so the*

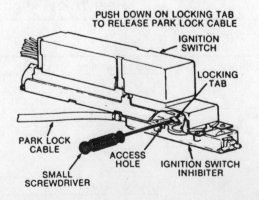

Park lock cable removal

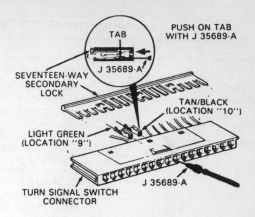

Turn signal switch terminals

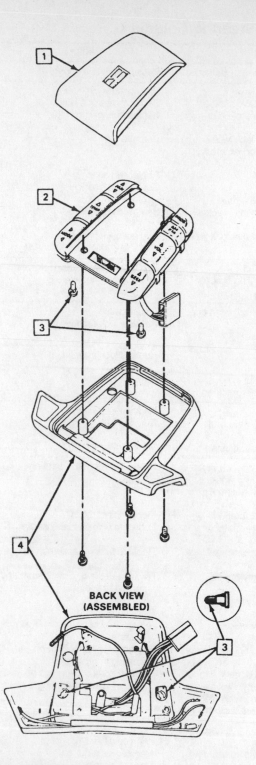

1. Horn pad
2. Steeering wheel control assembly
3. Backlight bulbs
4. Horn pad (back)

Steering wheel with radio and temperature controls

turn signal assembly to steering column screws can all be removed.

4. Remove the column housing cover-to-column housing bowl screw and the cover.

NOTE: *If equipped with cruise control, disconnect the cruise control electrical connector.*

5. Remove the turn signal lever-to-pivot assembly screw and the lever; one screw is in the front and one is in the rear.

6. Using the terminal remover tool No. J–35689–A or equivalent, disconnect and label the wires **F** and **G** on the connector at the buzzer switch assembly from the turn signal switch electrical harness connector.

7. Remove the turn signal switch-to-steering column screws and the switch.

To install:

1. Install the turn signal switch to the steering column, torque the turn signal switch-to-steering column screws to 35 inch lbs. (4 Nm).

2. Install the electrical connectors and install the turn signal lever to the pivot assembly. Install the hazard flasher knob. Install the cancelling cam.

3. Install the steering wheel and column cover. Connect the negative battery cable.

Ignition Switch/Lock

REMOVAL AND INSTALLATION

1. Disconnect the negative terminal from the battery. Remove the left side lower trim panel.

2. Remove the steering column-to-support screws and lower the steering column.

3. Disconnect the dimmer switch and turn signal switch connectors.

4. Remove the wiring harness-to-firewall nuts.

5. Remove the steering column-to-steering

Troubleshooting the Steering Column

Problem	Cause	Solution
Will not lock	• Lockbolt spring broken or defective	• Replace lock bolt spring
High effort (required to turn ignition key and lock cylinder)	• Lock cylinder defective • Ignition switch defective • Rack preload spring broken or deformed • Burr on lock sector, lock rack, housing, support or remote rod coupling • Bent sector shaft • Defective lock rack • Remote rod bent, deformed • Ignition switch mounting bracket bent • Distorted coupling slot in lock rack (tilt column)	• Replace lock cylinder • Replace ignition switch • Replace preload spring • Remove burr • Replace shaft • Replace lock rack • Replace rod • Straighten or replace • Replace lock rack
Will stick in "start"	• Remote rod deformed • Ignition switch mounting bracket bent	• Straighten or replace • Straighten or replace
Key cannot be removed in "off-lock"	• Ignition switch is not adjusted correctly • Defective lock cylinder	• Adjust switch • Replace lock cylinder
Lock cylinder can be removed without depressing retainer	• Lock cylinder with defective retainer • Burr over retainer slot in housing cover or on cylinder retainer	• Replace lock cylinder • Remove burr
High effort on lock cylinder between "off" and "off-lock"	• Distorted lock rack • Burr on tang of shift gate (automatic column) • Gearshift linkage not adjusted	• Replace lock rack • Remove burr • Adjust linkage
Noise in column	• One click when in "off-lock" position and the steering wheel is moved (all except automatic column) • Coupling bolts not tightened • Lack of grease on bearings or bearing surfaces • Upper shaft bearing worn or broken • Lower shaft bearing worn or broken • Column not correctly aligned • Coupling pulled apart • Broken coupling lower joint • Steering shaft snap ring not seated • Shroud loose on shift bowl. Housing loose on jacket—will be noticed with ignition in "off-lock" and when torque is applied to steering wheel.	• Normal—lock bolt is seating • Tighten pinch bolts • Lubricate with chassis grease • Replace bearing assembly • Replace bearing. Check shaft and replace if scored. • Align column • Replace coupling • Repair or replace joint and align column • Replace ring. Check for proper seating in groove. • Position shroud over lugs on shift bowl. Tighten mounting screws.
High steering shaft effort	• Column misaligned • Defective upper or lower bearing • Tight steering shaft universal joint • Flash on I.D. of shift tube at plastic joint (tilt column only) • Upper or lower bearing seized	• Align column • Replace as required • Repair or replace • Replace shift tube • Replace bearings
Lash in mounted column assembly	• Column mounting bracket bolts loose • Broken weld nuts on column jacket • Column capsule bracket sheared	• Tighten bolts • Replace column jacket • Replace bracket assembly

Troubleshooting the Steering Column (cont.)

Problem	Cause	Solution
Lash in mounted column assembly (cont.)	• Column bracket to column jacket mounting bolts loose	• Tighten to specified torque
	• Loose lock shoes in housing (tilt column only)	• Replace shoes
	• Loose pivot pins (tilt column only)	• Replace pivot pins and support
	• Loose lock shoe pin (tilt column only)	• Replace pin and housing
	• Loose support screws (tilt column only)	• Tighten screws
Housing loose (tilt column only)	• Excessive clearance between holes in support or housing and pivot pin diameters	• Replace pivot pins and support
	• Housing support-screws loose	• Tighten screws
Steering wheel loose—every other tilt position (tilt column only)	• Loose fit between lock shoe and lock shoe pivot pin	• Replace lock shoes and pivot pin
Steering column not locking in any tilt position (tilt column only)	• Lock shoe seized on pivot pin	• Replace lock shoes and pin
	• Lock shoe grooves have burrs or are filled with foreign material	• Clean or replace lock shoes
	• Lock shoe springs weak or broken	• Replace springs
Noise when tilting column (tilt column only)	• Upper tilt bumpers worn	• Replace tilt bumper
	• Tilt spring rubbing in housing	• Lubricate with chassis grease
One click when in "off-lock" position and the steering wheel is moved	• Seating of lock bolt	• None. Click is normal characteristic sound produced by lock bolt as it seats.
High shift effort (automatic and tilt column only)	• Column not correctly aligned	• Align column
	• Lower bearing not aligned correctly	• Assemble correctly
	• Lack of grease on seal or lower bearing areas	• Lubricate with chassis grease
Improper transmission shifting— automatic and tilt column only	• Sheared shift tube joint	• Replace shift tube
	• Improper transmission gearshift linkage adjustment	• Adjust linkage
	• Loose lower shift lever	• Replace shift tube

Troubleshooting the Ignition Switch

Problem	Cause	Solution
Ignition switch electrically inoperative	• Loose or defective switch connector	• Tighten or replace connector
	• Feed wire open (fusible link)	• Repair or replace
	• Defective ignition switch	• Replace ignition switch
Engine will not crank	• Ignition switch not adjusted properly	• Adjust switch
Ignition switch wil not actuate mechanically	• Defective ignition switch	• Replace switch
	• Defective lock sector	• Replace lock sector
	• Defective remote rod	• Replace remote rod
Ignition switch cannot be adjusted correctly	• Remote rod deformed	• Repair, straighten or replace

Troubleshooting the Turn Signal Switch

Problem	Cause	Solution
Turn signal will not cancel	• Loose switch mounting screws • Switch or anchor bosses broken • Broken, missing or out of position detent, or cancelling spring	• Tighten screws • Replace switch • Reposition springs or replace switch as required
Turn signal difficult to operate	• Turn signal lever loose • Switch yoke broken or distorted • Loose or misplaced springs • Foreign parts and/or materials in switch • Switch mounted loosely	• Tighten mounting screws • Replace switch • Reposition springs or replace switch • Remove foreign parts and/or material • Tighten mounting screws
Turn signal will not indicate lane change	• Broken lane change pressure pad or spring hanger • Broken, missing or misplaced lane change spring • Jammed wires	• Replace switch • Replace or reposition as required • Loosen mounting screws, reposition wires and retighten screws
Turn signal will not stay in turn position	• Foreign material or loose parts impeding movement of switch yoke • Defective switch	• Remove material and/or parts • Replace switch
Hazard switch cannot be pulled out	• Foreign material between hazard support cancelling leg and yoke	• Remove foreign material. No foreign material impeding function of hazard switch—replace turn signal switch.
No turn signal lights	• Inoperative turn signal flasher • Defective or blown fuse • Loose chassis to column harness connector • Disconnect column to chassis connector. Connect new switch to chassis and operate switch by hand. If vehicle lights now operate normally, signal switch is inoperative • If vehicle lights do not operate, check chassis wiring for opens, grounds, etc.	• Replace turn signal flasher • Replace fuse • Connect securely • Replace signal switch • Repair chassis wiring as required
Instrument panel turn indicator lights on but not flashing	• Burned out or damaged front or rear turn signal bulb • If vehicle lights do not operate, check light sockets for high resistance connections, the chassis wiring for opens, grounds, etc. • Inoperative flasher • Loose chassis to column harness connection • Inoperative turn signal switch • To determine if turn signal switch is defective, substitute new switch into circuit and operate switch by hand. If the vehicle's lights operate normally, signal switch is inoperative.	• Replace bulb • Repair chassis wiring as required • Replace flasher • Connect securely • Replace turn signal switch • Replace turn signal switch
Stop light not on when turn indicated	• Loose column to chassis connection • Disconnect column to chassis connector. Connect new switch into system without removing old.	• Connect securely • Replace signal switch

Troubleshooting the Turn Signal Switch (cont.)

Problem	Cause	Solution
Stop light not on when turn indicated (cont.)	Operate switch by hand. If brake lights work with switch in the turn position, signal switch is defective.	
	• If brake lights do not work, check connector to stop light sockets for grounds, opens, etc.	• Repair connector to stop light circuits using service manual as guide
Turn indicator panel lights not flashing	• Burned out bulbs • High resistance to ground at bulb socket	• Replace bulbs • Replace socket
	• Opens, ground in wiring harness from front turn signal bulb socket to indicator lights	• Locate and repair as required
Turn signal lights flash very slowly	• High resistance ground at light sockets	• Repair high resistance grounds at light sockets
	• Incorrect capacity turn signal flasher or bulb	• Replace turn signal flasher or bulb
	• If flashing rate is still extremely slow, check chassis wiring harness from the connector to light sockets for high resistance	• Locate and repair as required
	• Loose chassis to column harness connection	• Connect securely
	• Disconnect column to chassis connector. Connect new switch into system without removing old. Operate switch by hand. If flashing occurs at normal rate, the signal switch is defective.	• Replace turn signal switch
Hazard signal lights will not flash—turn signal functions normally	• Blow fuse • Inoperative hazard warning flasher	• Replace fuse • Replace hazard warning flasher in fuse panel
	• Loose chassis-to-column harness connection	• Conect securely
	• Disconnect column to chassis connector. Connect new switch into system without removing old. Depress the hazard warning lights. If they now work normally, turn signal switch is defective.	• Replace turn signal switch
	• If lights do not flash, check wiring harness "K" lead for open between hazard flasher and connector. If open, fuse block is defective	• Repair or replace brown wire or connector as required

Troubleshooting the Manual Steering Gear

Problem	Cause	Solution
Hard or erratic steering	• Incorrect tire pressure	• Inflate tires to recommended pressures
	• Insufficient or incorrect lubrication	• Lubricate as required (refer to Maintenance Section)
	• Suspension, or steering linkage parts damaged or misaligned	• Repair or replace parts as necessary
	• Improper front wheel alignment	• Adjust incorrect wheel alignment angles
	• Incorrect steering gear adjustment	• Adjust steering gear
	• Sagging springs	• Replace springs
Play or looseness in steering	• Steering wheel loose	• Inspect shaft spines and repair as necessary. Tighten attaching nut and stake in place.
	• Steering linkage or attaching parts loose or worn	• Tighten, adjust, or replace faulty components
	• Pitman arm loose	• Inspect shaft splines and repair as necessary. Tighten attaching nut and stake in place
	• Steering gear attaching bolts loose	• Tighten bolts
	• Loose or worn wheel bearings	• Adjust or replace bearings
	• Steering gear adjustment incorrect or parts badly worn	• Adjust gear or replace defective parts
Wheel shimmy or tramp	• Improper tire pressure	• Inflate tires to recommended pressures
	• Wheels, tires, or brake rotors out-of-balance or out-of-round	• Inspect and replace or balance parts
	• Inoperative, worn, or loose shock absorbers or mounting parts	• Repair or replace shocks or mountings
	• Loose or worn steering or suspension parts	• Tighten or replace as necessary
	• Loose or worn wheel bearings	• Adjust or replace bearings
	• Incorrect steering gear adjustments	• Adjust steering gear
	• Incorrect front wheel alignment	• Correct front wheel alignment
Tire wear	• Improper tire pressure	• Inflate tires to recommended pressures
	• Failure to rotate tires	• Rotate tires
	• Brakes grabbing	• Adjust or repair brakes
	• Incorrect front wheel alignment	• Align incorrect angles
	• Broken or damaged steering and suspension parts	• Repair or replace defective parts
	• Wheel runout	• Replace faulty wheel
	• Excessive speed on turns	• Make driver aware of conditions
Vehicle leads to one side	• Improper tire pressures	• Inflate tires to recommended pressures
	• Front tires with uneven tread depth, wear pattern, or different cord design (i.e., one bias ply and one belted or radial tire on front wheels)	• Install tires of same cord construction and reasonably even tread depth, design, and wear pattern
	• Incorrect front wheel alignment	• Align incorrect angles
	• Brakes dragging	• Adjust or repair brakes
	• Pulling due to uneven tire construction	• Replace faulty tire

Troubleshooting the Power Steering Gear

Problem	Cause	Solution
Hissing noise in steering gear	• There is some noise in all power steering systems. One of the most common is a hissing sound most evident at standstill parking. There is no relationship between this noise and performance of the steering. Hiss may be expected when steering wheel is at end of travel or when slowly turning at standstill.	• Slight hiss is normal and in no way affects steering. Do not replace valve unless hiss is extremely objectionable. A replacement valve will also exhibit slight noise and is not always a cure. Investigate clearance around flexible coupling rivets. Be sure steering shaft and gear are aligned so flexible coupling rotates in a flat plane and is not distorted as shaft rotates. Any metal-to-metal contacts through flexible coupling will transmit valve hiss into passenger compartment through the steering column.
Rattle or chuckle noise in steering gear	• Gear loose on frame	• Check gear-to-frame mounting screws. Tighten screws to 88 N·m (65 foot pounds) torque.
	• Steering linkage looseness	• Check linkage pivot points for wear. Replace if necessary.
	• Pressure hose touching other parts of car	• Adjust hose position. Do not bend tubing by hand.
	• Loose pitman shaft over center adjustment	• Adjust to specifications
	NOTE: A slight rattle may occur on turns because of increased clearance off the "high point." This is normal and clearance must not be reduced below specified limits to eliminate this slight rattle.	
	• Loose pitman arm	• Tighten pitman arm nut to specifications
Squawk noise in steering gear when turning or recovering from a turn	• Damper O-ring on valve spool cut	• Replace damper O-ring
Poor return of steering wheel to center	• Tires not properly inflated	• Inflate to specified pressure
	• Lack of lubrication in linkage and ball joints	• Lube linkage and ball joints
	• Lower coupling flange rubbing against steering gear adjuster plug	• Loosen pinch bolt and assemble properly
	• Steering gear to column misalignment	• Align steering column
	• Improper front wheel alignment	• Check and adjust as necessary
	• Steering linkage binding	• Replace pivots
	• Ball joints binding	• Replace ball joints
	• Steering wheel rubbing against housing	• Align housing
	• Tight or frozen steering shaft bearings	• Replace bearings
	• Sticking or plugged valve spool	• Remove and clean or replace valve
	• Steering gear adjustments over specifications	• Check adjustment with gear out of car. Adjust as required.
	• Kink in return hose	• Replace hose
Car leads to one side or the other (keep in mind road condition and wind. Test car in both directions on flat road)	• Front end misaligned	• Adjust to specifications
	• Unbalanced steering gear valve	• Replace valve
	NOTE: If this is cause, steering effort will be very light in direction of lead and normal or heavier in opposite direction	

Troubleshooting the Power Steering Gear (cont.)

Problem	Cause	Solution
Momentary increase in effort when turning wheel fast to right or left	• Low oil level • Pump belt slipping • High internal leakage	• Add power steering fluid as required • Tighten or replace belt • Check pump pressure. (See pressure test)
Steering wheel surges or jerks when turning with engine running especially during parking	• Low oil level • Loose pump belt • Steering linkage hitting engine oil pan at full turn • Insufficient pump pressure • Pump flow control valve sticking	• Fill as required • Adjust tension to specification • Correct clearance • Check pump pressure. (See pressure test). Replace relief valve if defective. • Inspect for varnish or damage, replace if necessary
Excessive wheel kickback or loose steering	• Air in system • Steering gear loose on frame • Steering linkage joints worn enough to be loose • Worn poppet valve • Loose thrust bearing preload adjustment • Excessive overcenter lash	• Add oil to pump reservoir and bleed by operating steering. Check hose connectors for proper torque and adjust as required. • Tighten attaching screws to specified torque • Replace loose pivots • Replace poppet valve • Adjust to specification with gear out of vehicle • Adjust to specification with gear out of car
Hard steering or lack of assist	• Loose pump belt • Low oil level **NOTE:** Low oil level will also result in excessive pump noise • Steering gear to column misalignment • Lower coupling flange rubbing against steering gear adjuster plug • Tires not properly inflated	• Adjust belt tension to specification • Fill to proper level. If excessively low, check all lines and joints for evidence of external leakage. Tighten loose connectors. • Align steering column • Loosen pinch bolt and assemble properly • Inflate to recommended pressure
Foamy milky power steering fluid, low fluid level and possible low pressure	• Air in the fluid, and loss of fluid due to internal pump leakage causing overflow	• Check for leak and correct. Bleed system. Extremely cold temperatures will cause system aeriation should the oil level be low. If oil level is correct and pump still foams, remove pump from vehicle and separate reservoir from housing. Check welsh plug and housing for cracks. If plug is loose or housing is cracked, replace housing.
Low pressure due to steering pump	• Flow control valve stuck or inoperative • Pressure plate not flat against cam ring	• Remove burrs or dirt or replace. Flush system. • Correct
Low pressure due to steering gear	• Pressure loss in cylinder due to worn piston ring or badly worn housing bore • Leakage at valve rings, valve body-to-worm seal	• Remove gear from car for disassembly and inspection of ring and housing bore • Remove gear from car for disassembly and replace seals

Troubleshooting the Power Steering Pump

Problem	Cause	Solution
Chirp noise in steering pump	• Loose belt	• Adjust belt tension to specification
Belt squeal (particularly noticeable at full wheel travel and stand still parking)	• Loose belt	• Adjust belt tension to specification
Growl noise in steering pump	• Excessive back pressure in hoses or steering gear caused by restriction	• Locate restriction and correct. Replace part if necessary.
Growl noise in steering pump (particularly noticeable at stand still parking)	• Scored pressure plates, thrust plate or rotor • Extreme wear of cam ring	• Replace parts and flush system • Replace parts
Groan noise in steering pump	• Low oil level • Air in the oil. Poor pressure hose connection.	• Fill reservoir to proper level • Tighten connector to specified torque. Bleed system by operating steering from right to left—full turn.
Rattle noise in steering pump	• Vanes not installed properly • Vanes sticking in rotor slots	• Install properly • Free up by removing burrs, varnish, or dirt
Swish noise in steering pump	• Defective flow control valve	• Replace part
Whine noise in steering pump	• Pump shaft bearing scored	• Replace housing and shaft. Flush system.
Hard steering or lack of assist	• Loose pump belt • Low oil level in reservoir **NOTE:** Low oil level will also result in excessive pump noise • Steering gear to column misalignment • Lower coupling flange rubbing against steering gear adjuster plug • Tires not properly inflated	• Adjust belt tension to specification • Fill to proper level. If excessively low, check all lines and joints for evidence of external leakage. Tighten loose connectors. • Align steering column • Loosen pinch bolt and assemble properly • Inflate to recommended pressure
Foaming milky power steering fluid, low fluid level and possible low pressure	• Air in the fluid, and loss of fluid due to internal pump leakage causing overflow	• Check for leaks and correct. Bleed system. Extremely cold temperatures will cause system aeriation should the oil level be low. If oil level is correct and pump still foams, remove pump from vehicle and separate reservoir from body. Check welsh plug and body for cracks. If plug is loose or body is cracked, replace body.
Low pump pressure	• Flow control valve stuck or inoperative • Pressure plate not flat against cam ring	• Remove burrs or dirt or replace. Flush system. • Correct
Momentary increase in effort when turning wheel fast to right or left	• Low oil level in pump • Pump belt slipping • High internal leakage	• Add power steering fluid as required • Tighten or replace belt • Check pump pressure. (See pressure test)
Steering wheel surges or jerks when turning with engine running especially during parking	• Low oil level • Loose pump belt • Steering linkage hitting engine oil pan at full turn • Insufficient pump pressure	• Fill as required • Adjust tension to specification • Correct clearance • Check pump pressure. (See pressure test). Replace flow control valve if defective.

Troubleshooting the Power Steering Pump (cont.)

Problem	Cause	Solution
Steering wheel surges or jerks when turning with engine running especially during parking (cont.)	• Sticking flow control valve	• Inspect for varnish or damage, replace if necessary
Excessive wheel kickback or loose steering	• Air in system	• Add oil to pump reservoir and bleed by operating steering. Check hose connectors for proper torque and adjust as required.
Low pump pressure	• Extreme wear of cam ring • Scored pressure plate, thrust plate, or rotor • Vanes not installed properly • Vanes sticking in rotor slots • Cracked or broken thrust or pressure plate	• Replace parts. Flush system. • Replace parts. Flush system. • Install properly • Freeup by removing burrs, varnish, or dirt • Replace part

gear bolt and the steering column from the vehicle.

6. Remove the combination switch.

7. Place the lock cylinder in the **RUN** position.

8. Remove the steering shaft assembly and turn signal switch housing as an assembly.

9. Using the Terminal Remover tool No. J–35689–A or equivalent, disconnect and label the wires **F** and **G** on the connector at the buzzer switch assembly from the turn signal switch electrical harness connector.

10. With the lock cylinder in the **RUN** position, remove the buzzer switch.

11. Place the lock cylinder in the **ACCESSORY** position, remove the lock cylinder retaining screw and the lock cylinder.

12. Remove the dimmer switch nut/bolt, the dimmer switch and actuator rod.

13. Remove the dimmer switch mounting stud (the mounting nut was mounted to it).

14. Remove the ignition switch-to-steering column screws and the ignition switch.

15. Remove the lock bolt screws and the lock bolt.

16. Remove the switch actuator rack and ignition switch.

17. Remove the steering shaft lock and spring.

To install:

1. To install the lock bolt, lubricate it with lithium grease and install the lock bolt, spring and retaining plate.

2. Lubricate the teeth on the switch actuator rack, install the rack and the ignition switch

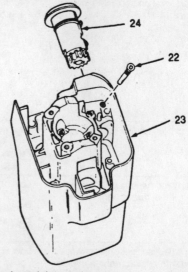

22. Lock retaining screw
23. Jacket and bowl assembly
24. Steering column lock cylinder set

Ignition lock cylinder removal

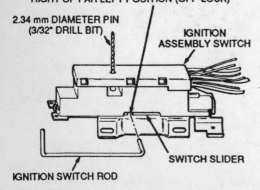

PLACE SWITCH SLIDER ON DETENT TO THE
RIGHT OF FAR LEFT POSITION (OFF-LOCK)

2.34 mm DIAMETER PIN
(3/32" DRILL BIT)

IGNITION
ASSEMBLY SWITCH

SWITCH SLIDER

IGNITION SWITCH ROD

Ignition switch alignment

through the opening in the steering bolt until it rests on the retaining plate.

3. Install the steering column lock cylinder set by holding the barrel of the lock cylinder, inserting the key and turning the key to the **ACCESSORY** position.

4. Install the lock set in the steering column while holding the rack against the lock plate.

5. Install the lock retaining screw. Insert the key in the lock cylinder and turn the lock cylinder to the **START** position and the rack will extend.

6. Center the slotted holes on the ignition switch mounting plate and install the ignition switch mounting screw and nut.

7. Install the dimmer switch and actuator rod into the center slot on the switch mounting plate.

8. Install the buzzer switch and turn the lock cylinder to the **RUN** position. Push the switch in until it is bottomed out with the plastic tab that covers the lock retaining screw.

9. Install the steering shaft and turn signal housing as an assembly.

10. Install the turn signal switch. Install the steering wheel to the column, torque the steering shaft nut to 30 ft. lbs. (41 Nm).

11. Install the steering column in the vehicle. Connect all electrical leads. Install the lower trim panels.

12. Connect the negative battery cable.

Steering Column

REMOVAL AND INSTALLATION

1. Disconnect the negative battery cable.

2. Remove the lower left hand trim panel below the steering column.

3. Push the top of the intermediate shaft seal down for access to the intermediate shaft seal coupling.

4. Remove the intermediate shaft coupling pinch bolt.

5. Disconnect the shift indicator cable end and casing from the column.

NOTE: *If the vehicle is equipped with park lock, disconnect the park lock cable from the column.*

6. Disconnect the shift cable from the ball stud on the shift lever.

7. Remove the lower column bolts first and then remove the upper bolts. Lower the column to the seat.

8. Disconnect the electrical connectors and remove the column from the vehicle.

To install:

1. Install the column into the vehicle and loosely install the column bolts. Install the in-

termediate shaft pinch bolt and tighten it to 35 ft. lbs. (48 Nm).

2. Connect the electrical connector and all the shift cables. Connect the park lock cable, if equipped.

3. Tighten the steering column mounting bolts to 18 ft. lbs. (25 Nm).

4. Reposition the intermediate shaft seal and install the trim panel.

5. Connect the negative battery cable.

Steering Linkage

REMOVAL AND INSTALLATION

Outer Tie Rod Ends

1. Disconnect the negative (−) battery cable.

2. Remove the cotter pin and hex slotted nut from the outer tie rod assembly.

3. Loosen the jam nut and remove the tie rod from the steering knuckle using a steering linkage removing tool J-35917 or equivalent.

4. Holding the inner tie rod stationary, count the amount of turns to remove the outer tie rod.

To install:

1. Lubricate the inner rod threads with anti-seize compound and install the outer tie rod the same amount of turns that it took to remove.

2. Install the outer tie rod-to-knuckle and install the slotted nut. Torque the nut to 35 ft. lbs. (50 Nm) and to 45 ft. lbs. (60 Nm) maximum to align the cotter pin slot. Do NOT back off to align the cotter pin.

3. Install a new cotter pin and bend over. Torque the jam nut to 50 ft. lbs. (70 Nm) and connect the negative battery cable.

NOTE: *The do-it-yourself mechanic should not attempt to perform any wheel alignment procedures. Expensive alignment tools are needed and would not be cost efficient to purchase these tools. The wheel alignment should be performed by a certified alignment technician using the proper alignment tools.*

4. Have a qualified alignment technician adjust the toe angle.

Inner Tie Rod End

1. Disconnect the negative (−) battery cable.

2. Remove the rack and pinion assembly from the vehicle as outlined in this chapter.

3. Remove the outer tie rod end as previously outlined.

4. Remove the jam nut, boot clamps and boot. Use side cutters to cut the boot clamps.

5. Remove the shock dampener from the inner tie rod and slide back on the rack.

NOTE: *Do not let the rack slide out of the rack housing while the tie rods are moved.*

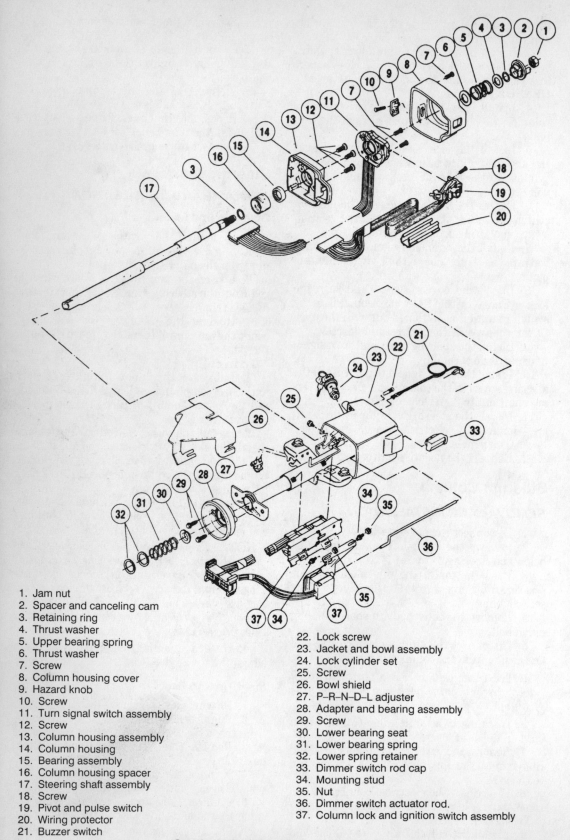

1. Jam nut
2. Spacer and canceling cam
3. Retaining ring
4. Thrust washer
5. Upper bearing spring
6. Thrust washer
7. Screw
8. Column housing cover
9. Hazard knob
10. Screw
11. Turn signal switch assembly
12. Screw
13. Column housing assembly
14. Column housing
15. Bearing assembly
16. Column housing spacer
17. Steering shaft assembly
18. Screw
19. Pivot and pulse switch
20. Wiring protector
21. Buzzer switch
22. Lock screw
23. Jacket and bowl assembly
24. Lock cylinder set
25. Screw
26. Bowl shield
27. P–R–N–D–L adjuster
28. Adapter and bearing assembly
29. Screw
30. Lower bearing seat
31. Lower bearing spring
32. Lower spring retainer
33. Dimmer switch rod cap
34. Mounting stud
35. Nut
36. Dimmer switch actuator rod.
37. Column lock and ignition switch assembly

Standard steering column — exploded view

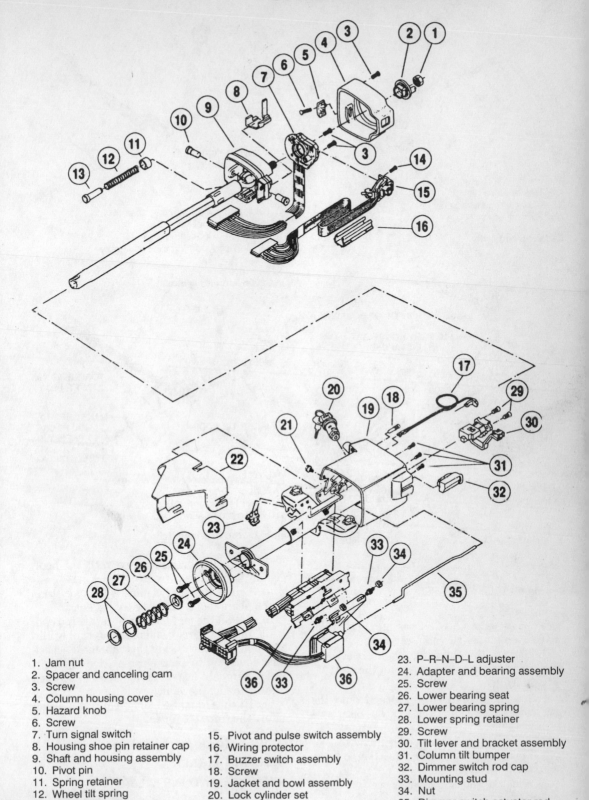

1. Jam nut
2. Spacer and canceling cam
3. Screw
4. Column housing cover
5. Hazard knob
6. Screw
7. Turn signal switch
8. Housing shoe pin retainer cap
9. Shaft and housing assembly
10. Pivot pin
11. Spring retainer
12. Wheel tilt spring
13. Tilt spring guide
14. Screw

15. Pivot and pulse switch assembly
16. Wiring protector
17. Buzzer switch assembly
18. Screw
19. Jacket and bowl assembly
20. Lock cylinder set
21. Screw
22. Bowl shield

23. P–R–N–D–L adjuster
24. Adapter and bearing assembly
25. Screw
26. Lower bearing seat
27. Lower bearing spring
28. Lower spring retainer
29. Screw
30. Tilt lever and bracket assembly
31. Column tilt bumper
32. Dimmer switch rod cap
33. Mounting stud
34. Nut
35. Dimmer switch actuator rod
36. Ignition switch assembly

Tilt steering column — exploded view

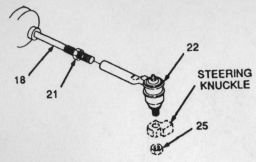

18. Inner tie rod assembly
21. Hex jam nut
22. Outer tie rod assembly
25. Slotted hex nut

Outer tie rod end

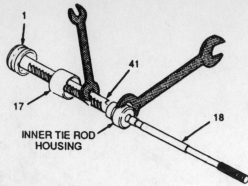

1. Rack and pinion housing assembly
17. Shock damper ring
18. Inner tie rod assembly
41. Piston and steering rack assembly

Inner tie rod end removal

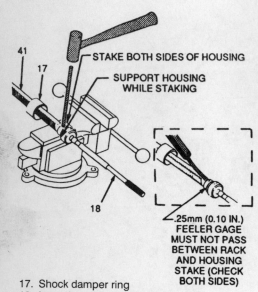

17. Shock damper ring
18. Inner tie rod assembly
41. Piston and steering rack assembly

Staking the inner tie rod end

6. Place suitable wrenches on the flats of the rack and inner tie rod assemblies.

7. Rotate the housing counterclockwise until the inner rod separates from the rack.

To install:

1. Install the inner tie rod end onto the rack and torque to 70 ft. lbs. (95 Nm) with suitable wrenches.

2. Support the rack assembly in a vise.

3. Stake both sides of the inner tie rod housing to the flats on the rack.

4. Slide the shock dampener over the housing until it engages.

5. Install the boot and new boot clamps. Do NOT tighten the clamps at this time.

6. Apply grease to the inner tie rod, housing and boot.

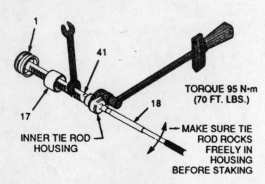

1. Rack and pinion housing assembly
17. Shock damper ring
18. Inner tie rod assembly
41. Piston and steering rack assembly

Inner tie rod end installation

7. Align the breather tube with the boot, making sure it is not twisted.

8. Crimp the boot clamps with a keystone clamp pliers tool J-22610 or equivalent.

9. Install the jam nut and outer tie rod end.

10. Install the rack and pinion assembly into the vehicle as outlined in this chapter. Recheck each operation to ensure completion of repair. Make sure all fasteners have been torqued before moving the vehicle.

11. Have a qualified alignment technician adjust the front toe angle.

Power Rack and Pinion Steering Gear

REMOVAL AND INSTALLATION

1. Disconnect the negative (–) battery cable.

2. Raise the vehicle and support with jackstands. Remove the front wheels.

3. Remove the intermediate shaft lower pinch bolt at the steering gear (end of the steer-

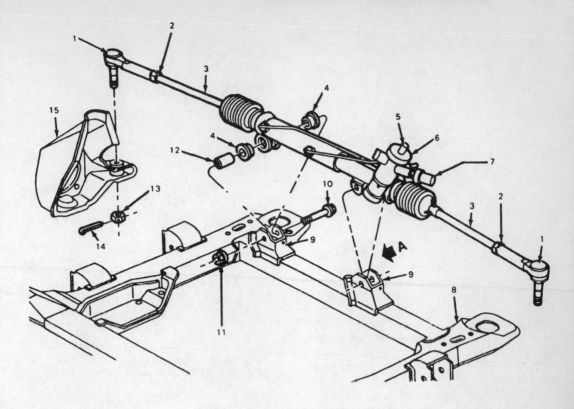

1. Tie rod end
2. Jam nut
3. Inner tie rod
4. Bushing
5. Stub shaft
6. Steering gear
7. Idle speed power steering switch
8. Frame
9. Steering gear mount
10. Bolt
11. Nut–59 ft. lbs.
12. Sleeve
13. Castle nut
14. Cotter pin
15. Knuckle/strut assembly
16. Heat shield
17. Screw

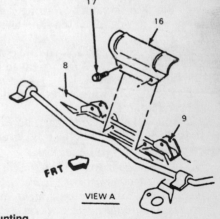

Power rack and pinion mounting

ing column shaft). Remove the intermediate shaft from the stub shaft.

NOTE: *Failure to disconnect the intermediate shaft from the rack and pinion stub shaft may result in damage to the steering gear. This damage may cause a loss of steering control and personal injury.*

4. Remove both tie rod ends from the knuckle using a tie rod puller tool J-35917 or equivalent.
5. Support the vehicle body with jackstands so that the frame assembly can be lowered.

NOTE: *Do NOT lower the frame too far, engine components near the firewall may be damaged.*

6. Remove the rear frame bolts and lower the rear of the frame up to five inches (128mm).
7. Remove the heat shield, pipe retaining clip and the fluid pipes from the rack assembly. Use flare nut wrenches to remove the fluid pipes.
8. Remove the rack mounting bolts, nuts

and rack assembly. Remove the rack assembly out through the left wheel opening.

To install:

1. Install the rack assembly through the left wheel opening.

2. Install the mounting bolts and nuts. Torque the bolts to 59 ft. lbs. (80 Nm).

3. Install the fluid pipes with new O-rings. Torque the fittings to 20 ft. lbs. (27 Nm) using flare nut wrenches.

4. Install the pipe retaining clips and heat shield.

5. Raise the frame and install the rear bolts. Torque the rear bolts to 103 ft. lbs. (140 Nm).

6. Install the tie rod ends, nut and cotter pin. Torque the nuts to 40 ft. lbs. (54 Nm). Always use a new cotter pin.

7. Install the intermediate shaft-to-stub shaft. Torque the lower pinch bolt to 40 ft. lbs. (54 Nm).

8. Install the front wheels, lower the vehicle and fill the steering pump with GM steering fluid or its equivalent.

9. Bleed the power steering system as follows.

a. With the engine OFF and the wheels **OFF** the ground. Turn the steering wheel all the way to the left, add steering fluid to the **COLD** mark on the level indicator.

b. Bleed the system by turning the wheels from side to side. Keep the fluid level at the **COLD** mark.

c. Start the engine and add fluid if necessary. Turn the wheels from right to left and add fluid if necessary.

d. Return the wheels to the center position and lower the vehicle.

e. Allow the engine to warn up, road test the vehicle and recheck the fluid level.

10. Inspect the system for leaks.

NOTE: *The do-it-yourself mechanic should not attempt to perform any wheel alignment procedures. Expensive alignment tools are needed and would not be cost efficient to purchase these tools. The wheel alignment should be performed by a certified alignment technician using the proper alignment tools.*

11. Have a qualified alignment technician adjust the front toe angle.

ADJUSTMENT

Rack Bearing Preload Adjustment

1. Make the adjustment with the front wheels raised and centered. Make sure to check the returnability of the steering wheel to center after the adjustment.

2. Loosen the adjuster plug lock nut and turn the adjuster plug clockwise until it bot-

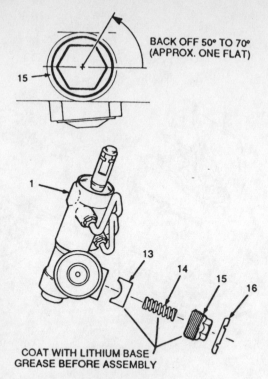

BACK OFF 50° TO 70° (APPROX. ONE FLAT)

COAT WITH LITHIUM BASE GREASE BEFORE ASSEMBLY

1. Rack and pinion housing
13. Rack bearing
14. Adjuster spring
15. Adjuster plug
16. Adjuster plug lock nut

Rack bearing adjustment

toms in the housing, then back off 50 to 70 degrees (about one flat).

3. Torque the lock nut to adjuster plug to 50 ft. lbs. (70 Nm). Hold the adjuster plug in place while tightening.

OVERHAUL

The rack and pinion assembly is a serviceable unit, but is not economically practical for the do-it-yourself mechanic to overhaul the power steering gear. A remanufactured unit can be purchased from a dealer or local parts distributor for a fraction of the cost of a new unit.

Power Steering Pump

REMOVAL AND INSTALLATION

2.5L L4 Lumina

1. Disconnect the negative (–) battery cable.

2. Raise the vehicle and support with jackstands.

3. Place a drain pan under the pump and remove the inlet and outlet lines from the pump.

4. Lower the vehicle.

5. Remove the ECM heat shield cover and

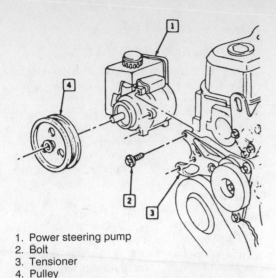

1. Power steering pump
2. Bolt
3. Tensioner
4. Pulley

Power steering pump — Lumina

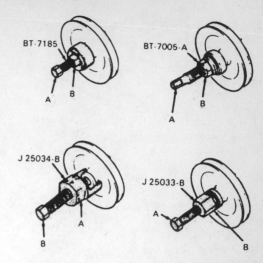

Power steering pump pulley removal and installation tools

serpentine belt by loosening the automatic tensioner as outlined in Chapter 1.

6. Remove the three pump retaining bolts and pump.

To install:

1. Install the pump and bolts. Torque the retaining bolts to 20 ft. lbs. (27 Nm).

2. Install the serpentine belt, ECM heat shield and raise the vehicle supported with jackstands.

3. Install the inlet and outlet hoses to the pump.

4. Lower the vehicle and connect the negative battery cable.

5. Bleed the system as follows.

a. With the engine OFF and the wheels **OFF** the ground. Turn the steering wheel all the way to the left, add steering fluid to the **COLD** mark on the level indicator.

b. Bleed the system by turning the wheels from side to side. Keep the fluid level at the **COLD** mark.

c. Start the engine and add fluid if necessary. Turn the wheels from right to left and add fluid if necessary.

d. Return the wheels to the center position and lower the vehicle.

e. Allow the engine to warm up, road test the vehicle and recheck the fluid level.

6. Inspect the system for leaks.

2.8L and 3.1L V6 (VIN W, T)

1. Disconnect the negative (–) battery cable.

2. Place a drain pan under the steering pump and remove the inlet and outlet hoses at the pump with flare nut wrenches. Do not damage the hose fittings.

3. Remove the serpentine belt from the pulleys by loosening the automatic belt tensioner as outlined in Chapter 1.

4. Remove the three pump mounting bolts and the pump.

5. Remove the pump reservoir as follows.

a. Using a suitable pry bar, remove the retaining clips from the reservoir.

b. Separate the reservoir from the pump.

c. Install the reservoir to the pump with a new O-ring seal and install the retaining clip. Make sure the tabs are fully engaged on the pump.

6. Remove the pump pulley using a power steering pump pulley removing tool J-25034-B or equivalent.

To install:

1. Install the reservoir and pulley to the pump.

2. Install the pump and retaining bolts. Torque the retaining bolts to 18 ft. lbs. (25 Nm).

3. Install the serpentine belt and ECM heat shield.

4. Install the inlet and outlet hoses using new O-rings, if so equipped.

5. Fill the reservoir with power steering fluid and connect the negative battery cable.

6. Bleed the system as follows.

a. With the engine OFF and the wheels **OFF** the ground. Turn the steering wheel all the way to the left, add steering fluid to the **COLD** mark on the level indicator.

b. Bleed the system by turning the wheels from side to side. Keep the fluid level at the **COLD** mark.

c. Start the engine and add fluid if necessary. Turn the wheels from right to left and add fluid if necessary.

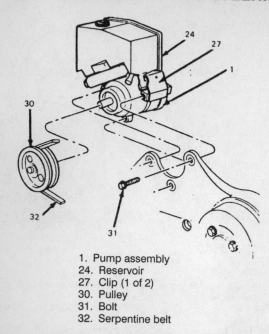

1. Pump assembly
24. Reservoir
27. Clip (1 of 2)
30. Pulley
31. Bolt
32. Serpentine belt

Power steering pump — 2.8L and 3.1L engines

d. Return the wheels to the center position and lower the vehicle.

e. Allow the engine to warn up, road test the vehicle and recheck the fluid level.

7. Check the system for leaks, road test and recheck the fluid level.

OVERHAUL

The power steering pump assembly is a serviceable unit, but is not economically practical for the do-it-yourself mechanic to overhaul the steering pump. A remanufactured unit can be purchased from a dealer or local parts distributor for a fraction of the cost of a new unit.

Power Steering Hoses

REMOVAL AND INSTALLATION

1. Disconnect the negative (–) battery cable.
2. Raise the vehicle and support with jackstands.
3. Place a drain pan under the steering gear. Remove the inlet and outlet hoses from the steering gear using flare nut wrenches.
4. Remove the hose clamp from the frame.
5. Remove the inlet and outlet hoses from the steering pump.

To install:
1. Replace the O-rings if necessary.
2. Install the hoses-to-steering pump, do NOT tighten at this time.
3. Install the hoses-to-steering gear and torque all fittings, using flare nut wrenches, to 20 ft. lbs. (27 Nm).
4. Install the hose clamp-to-frame and connect the negative battery cable.
5. Refill the pump reservoir with power steering fluid and bleed the system as follows

a. With the engine OFF and the wheels OFF the ground. Turn the steering wheel all the way to the left, add steering fluid to the COLD mark on the level indicator.

b. Bleed the system by turning the wheels from side to side. Keep the fluid level at the COLD mark.

c. Start the engine and add fluid if necessary. Turn the wheels from right to left and add fluid if necessary.

d. Return the wheels to the center position and lower the vehicle.

e. Allow the engine to warn up, road test the vehicle and recheck the fluid level.

6. Check the system for leaks, road test and recheck the fluid level.

BRAKE SYSTEM
BASIC OPERATING PRINCIPLES

Standard Brake System

Hydraulic systems are used to actuate the brakes of all automobiles. The system transports the power required to force the frictional surfaces of the braking system together from the pedal to the individual brake units at each wheel. A hydraulic system is used for two reasons.

First, fluid under pressure can be carried to all parts of an automobile by small pipes and flexible hoses without taking up a significant amount of room or posing routing problems.

Second, a great mechanical advantage can be given to the brake pedal end of the system, and the foot pressure required to actuate the brakes can be reduced by making the surface area of the master cylinder pistons smaller than that of any of the pistons in the wheel cylinders or calipers.

The standard master cylinder consists of a fluid reservoir, double cylinder and piston assembly and internal proportioning valves. Double type master cylinders are designed to diagonally separate the left rear and right front from the right rear and left front braking systems hydraulically in case of a leak.

Steel lines carry the brake fluid to a point on the vehicle's frame near each of the vehicle's wheels. The fluid is then carried to the front and rear calipers by flexible tubes in order to allow for suspension and steering movements.

In disc brake systems, the cylinders are part of the calipers. One cylinder in each caliper is used to force the brake pads against the disc.

All pistons employ some type of seal, usually made of rubber, to minimize fluid leakage. A rubber dust boot seals the outer end of the cyl-inder against dust and dirt. The boot fits around the outer end of the piston on disc brake calipers.

The standard hydraulic system operates as follows: When at rest, the entire system, from the piston(s) in the master cylinder to those in the wheel calipers, is full of brake fluid. Upon application of the brake pedal, fluid trapped in front of the master cylinder piston(s) is forced through the lines to the wheel calipers. Here, it forces the pistons outward. The motion of the pistons is opposed by spring seals, in disc brakes.

Upon release of the brake pedal, a spring located inside the master cylinder immediately returns the master cylinder pistons to the normal position. The pistons contain check valves and the master cylinder has compensating ports drilled in it. These are uncovered as the pistons reach their normal position. The piston check valves allow fluid to flow toward the calipers as the pistons withdraw. Then, as the return springs force the brake pads into the released position, the excess fluid flows through the compensating ports into the reservoir. It is during the time the pedal is in the released position that any fluid that has leaked out of the system will be replaced through the compensating ports.

Dual circuit master cylinders employ two pistons, located one behind the other, in the same cylinder. The primary piston is actuated directly by mechanical linkage from the brake pedal through the power booster. The secondary piston is actuated by fluid trapped between the two pistons. If a leak develops in front of the secondary piston, it moves forward until it bottoms against the front of the master cylinder, and the fluid trapped between the pistons will operate the rear brakes. If the rear brakes develop a leak, the primary piston will

Troubleshooting the Brake System

Problem	Cause	Solution
Low brake pedal (excessive pedal travel required for braking action.)	• Excessive clearance between rear linings and drums caused by inoperative automatic adjusters	• Make 10 to 15 alternate forward and reverse brake stops to adjust brakes. If brake pedal does not come up, repair or replace adjuster parts as necessary.
	• Worn rear brakelining	• Inspect and replace lining if worn beyond minimum thickness specification
	• Bent, distorted brakeshoes, front or rear	• Replace brakeshoes in axle sets
	• Air in hydraulic system	• Remove air from system. Refer to Brake Bleeding.
Low brake pedal (pedal may go to floor with steady pressure applied.)	• Fluid leak in hydraulic system	• Fill master cylinder to fill line; have helper apply brakes and check calipers, wheel cylinders, differential valve tubes, hoses and fittings for leaks. Repair or replace as necessary.
	• Air in hydraulic system	• Remove air from system. Refer to Brake Bleeding.
	• Incorrect or non-recommended brake fluid (fluid evaporates at below normal temp).	• Flush hydraulic system with clean brake fluid. Refill with correct-type fluid.
	• Master cylinder piston seals worn, or master cylinder bore is scored, worn or corroded	• Repair or replace master cylinder
Low brake pedal (pedal goes to floor on first application—o.k. on subsequent applications.)	• Disc brake pads sticking on abutment surfaces of anchor plate. Caused by a build-up of dirt, rust, or corrosion on abutment surfaces	• Clean abutment surfaces
Fading brake pedal (pedal height decreases with steady pressure applied.)	• Fluid leak in hydraulic system	• Fill master cylinder reservoirs to fill mark, have helper apply brakes, check calipers, wheel cylinders, differential valve, tubes, hoses, and fittings for fluid leaks. Repair or replace parts as necessary.
	• Master cylinder piston seals worn, or master cylinder bore is scored, worn or corroded	• Repair or replace master cylinder
Decreasing brake pedal travel (pedal travel required for braking action decreases and may be accompanied by a hard pedal.)	• Caliper or wheel cylinder pistons sticking or seized	• Repair or replace the calipers, or wheel cylinders
	• Master cylinder compensator ports blocked (preventing fluid return to reservoirs) or pistons sticking or seized in master cylinder bore	• Repair or replace the master cylinder
	• Power brake unit binding internally	• Test unit according to the following procedure: (a) Shift transmission into neutral and start engine (b) Increase engine speed to 1500 rpm, close throttle and fully depress brake pedal (c) Slow release brake pedal and stop engine (d) Have helper remove vacuum check valve and hose from power unit. Observe for backward movement of brake pedal. (e) If the pedal moves backward, the power unit has an internal bind—replace power unit

Troubleshooting the Brake System (cont.)

Problem	Cause	Solution
Spongy brake pedal (pedal has abnormally soft, springy, spongy feel when depressed.)	• Air in hydraulic system	• Remove air from system. Refer to Brake Bleeding.
	• Brakeshoes bent or distorted	• Replace brakeshoes
	• Brakelining not yet seated with drums and rotors	• Burnish brakes
	• Rear drum brakes not properly adjusted	• Adjust brakes
Hard brake pedal (excessive pedal pressure required to stop vehicle. May be accompanied by brake fade.)	• Loose or leaking power brake unit vacuum hose	• Tighten connections or replace leaking hose
	• Incorrect or poor quality brakelining	• Replace with lining in axle sets
	• Bent, broken, distorted brakeshoes	• Replace brakeshoes
	• Calipers binding or dragging on mounting pins. Rear brakeshoes dragging on support plate.	• Replace mounting pins and bushings. Clean rust or burrs from rear brake support plate ledges and lubricate ledges with molydisulfide grease. **NOTE:** If ledges are deeply grooved or scored, do not attempt to sand or grind them smooth—replace support plate.
	• Caliper, wheel cylinder, or master cylinder pistons sticking or seized	• Repair or replace parts as necessary
	• Power brake unit vacuum check valve malfunction	• Test valve according to the following procedure: (a) Start engine, increase engine speed to 1500 rpm, close throttle and immediately stop engine (b) Wait at least 90 seconds then depress brake pedal (c) If brakes are not vacuum assisted for 2 or more applications, check valve is faulty
	• Power brake unit has internal bind	• Test unit according to the following procedure: (a) With engine stopped, apply brakes several times to exhaust all vacuum in system (b) Shift transmission into neutral, depress brake pedal and start engine (c) If pedal height decreases with foot pressure and less pressure is required to hold pedal in applied position, power unit vacuum system is operating normally. Test power unit. If power unit exhibits a bind condition, replace the power unit.
	• Master cylinder compensator ports (at bottom of reservoirs) blocked by dirt, scale, rust, or have small burrs (blocked ports prevent fluid return to reservoirs).	• Repair or replace master cylinder **CAUTION:** Do not attempt to clean blocked ports with wire, pencils, or similar implements. Use compressed air only.
	• Brake hoses, tubes, fittings clogged or restricted	• Use compressed air to check or unclog parts. Replace any damaged parts.
	• Brake fluid contaminated with improper fluids (motor oil, transmission fluid, causing rubber components to swell and stick in bores	• Replace all rubber components, combination valve and hoses. Flush entire brake system with DOT 3 brake fluid or equivalent.
	• Low engine vacuum	• Adjust or repair engine

Troubleshooting the Brake System (cont.)

Problem	Cause	Solution
Grabbing brakes (severe reaction to brake pedal pressure.)	• Brakelining(s) contaminated by grease or brake fluid	• Determine and correct cause of contamination and replace brakeshoes in axle sets
	• Parking brake cables incorrectly adjusted or seized	• Adjust cables. Replace seized cables.
	• Incorrect brakelining or lining loose on brakeshoes	• Replace brakeshoes in axle sets
	• Caliper anchor plate bolts loose	• Tighten bolts
	• Rear brakeshoes binding on support plate ledges	• Clean and lubricate ledges. Replace support plate(s) if ledges are deeply grooved. Do not attempt to smooth ledges by grinding.
	• Incorrect or missing power brake reaction disc	• Install correct disc
	• Rear brake support plates loose	• Tighten mounting bolts
Dragging brakes (slow or incomplete release of brakes)	• Brake pedal binding at pivot	• Loosen and lubricate
	• Power brake unit has internal bind	• Inspect for internal bind. Replace unit if internal bind exists.
	• Parking brake cables incorrrectly adjusted or seized	• Adjust cables. Replace seized cables.
	• Rear brakeshoe return springs weak or broken	• Replace return springs. Replace brakeshoe if necessary in axle sets.
	• Automatic adjusters malfunctioning	• Repair or replace adjuster parts as required
	• Caliper, wheel cylinder or master cylinder pistons sticking or seized	• Repair or replace parts as necessary
	• Master cylinder compensating ports blocked (fluid does not return to reservoirs).	• Use compressed air to clear ports. Do not use wire, pencils, or similar objects to open blocked ports.
Vehicle moves to one side when brakes are applied	• Incorrect front tire pressure	• Inflate to recommended cold (reduced load) inflation pressure
	• Worn or damaged wheel bearings	• Replace worn or damaged bearings
	• Brakelining on one side contaminated	• Determine and correct cause of contamination and replace brakelining in axle sets
	• Brakeshoes on one side bent, distorted, or lining loose on shoe	• Replace brakeshoes in axle sets
	• Support plate bent or loose on one side	• Tighten or replace support plate
	• Brakelining not yet seated with drums or rotors	• Burnish brakelining
	• Caliper anchor plate loose on one side	• Tighten anchor plate bolts
	• Caliper piston sticking or seized	• Repair or replace caliper
	• Brakelinings water soaked	• Drive vehicle with brakes lightly applied to dry linings
	• Loose suspension component attaching or mounting bolts	• Tighten suspension bolts. Replace worn suspension components.
	• Brake combination valve failure	• Replace combination valve
Chatter or shudder when brakes are applied (pedal pulsation and roughness may also occur.)	• Brakeshoes distorted, bent, contaminated, or worn	• Replace brakeshoes in axle sets
	• Caliper anchor plate or support plate loose	• Tighten mounting bolts
	• Excessive thickness variation of rotor(s)	• Refinish or replace rotors in axle sets
Noisy brakes (squealing, clicking, scraping sound when brakes are applied.)	• Bent, broken, distorted brakeshoes	• Replace brakeshoes in axle sets
	• Excessive rust on outer edge of rotor braking surface	• Remove rust

Troubleshooting the Brake System (cont.)

Problem	Cause	Solution
Noisy brakes (squealing, clicking, scraping sound when brakes are applied.) (cont.)	• Brakelining worn out—shoes contacting drum of rotor	• Replace brakeshoes and lining in axle sets. Refinish or replace drums or rotors.
	• Broken or loose holdown or return springs	• Replace parts as necessary
	• Rough or dry drum brake support plate ledges	• Lubricate support plate ledges
	• Cracked, grooved, or scored rotor(s) or drum(s)	• Replace rotor(s) or drum(s). Replace brakeshoes and lining in axle sets if necessary.
	• Incorrect brakelining and/or shoes (front or rear).	• Install specified shoe and lining assemblies
Pulsating brake pedal	• Out of round drums or excessive lateral runout in disc brake rotor(s)	• Refinish or replace drums, re-index rotors or replace

move forward until direct contact with the secondary piston takes place, and it will force the secondary piston to actuate the front brakes. In either case, the brake pedal moves farther when the brakes are applied, and less braking power is available.

All dual circuit systems use a switch to warn the driver when only half of the brake system is operational. This switch is located in a valve body which is mounted on the firewall or the frame below the master cylinder. A hydraulic piston receives pressure from both circuits, each circuit's pressure being applied to one end of the piston. When the pressures are in balance, the piston remains stationary. When one circuit has a leak, however, the greater pressure in that circuit during application of the brakes will push the piston to one side, closing the switch and activating the brake warning light.

In disc brake systems, the proportioning valves are designed to provide better front to rear braking balance with heavy application. The valve is used when more front apply force is needed to obtain normal braking pressure.

Warning lights may be tested by depressing the brake pedal and holding it while opening one of the wheel cylinder bleeder screws. If this does not cause the light to go on, substitute a new lamp, make continuity checks, and, finally, replace the switch as necessary.

The hydraulic system may be checked for leaks by applying pressure to the pedal gradually and steadily. If the pedal sinks very slowly to the floor, the system has a leak. This is not to be confused with a springy or spongy feel due to the compression of air within the lines. If the system leaks, there will be a gradual change in the position of the pedal with a constant pressure.

Check for leaks along all lines and at wheel cylinders. If no external leaks are apparent, the problem is inside the master cylinder.

Anti-Lock Brake System
BASIC OPERATING PRINCIPLES

All of these cars (except Lumina) have the option of an Anti-lock Braking System (ABS). The Delco Moraine ABS (DM ABS – III) operates on all four wheels. The system is designed to reduce the tendency of a wheel to loose traction while braking, thus loosing control of the vehicle. The system operates in the same fashion as a standard braking systems until a speed sensor determines a lose of traction. At this time, the microprocessor (controller) adjusts brake pressure to both front and/or both rear wheels independently. The driver can control the vehicle more efficiently while the wheels are turning under heavy braking, wet or slippery road conditions.

The main components of the ABS system are the Powermaster III hydraulic booster/master cylinder, electric pump assembly, fluid accumulator, pressure switch, front and rear solenoids, fluid reservoir, four wheels speed sensors, remote proportioning valve and controller assembly.

The ABS controller monitors the speed of each wheel to determine if any wheel is approaching lock-up. If a lock-up condition is detected, the controller pulses the appropriate solenoids in the Powermaster III to adjust brake pressure for maximum stopping control without wheel lock-up. The controller assembly is located under the front passenger seat in a protective plastic case. The assembly is not serviceable and must be replaced as a complete unit.

The pressure inside the system is maintained in combination by the electric pump motor and the accumulator. The accumulator is pre-

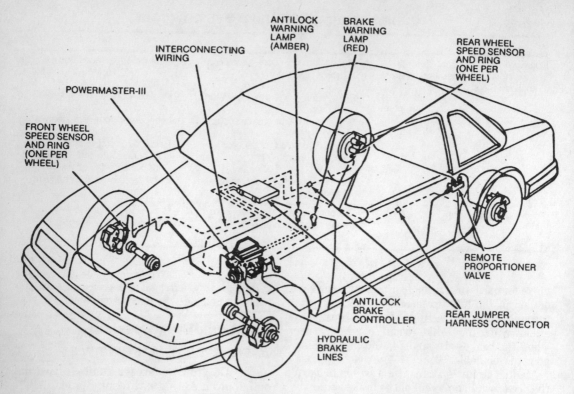

INTERCONNECTING WIRING

ANTILOCK WARNING LAMP (AMBER)

BRAKE WARNING LAMP (RED)

REAR WHEEL SPEED SENSOR AND RING (ONE PER WHEEL)

POWERMASTER-III

FRONT WHEEL SPEED SENSOR AND RING (ONE PER WHEEL)

REMOTE PROPORTIONER VALVE

ANTILOCK BRAKE CONTROLLER

REAR JUMPER HARNESS CONNECTOR

HYDRAULIC BRAKE LINES

Anti-lock brake system (ABS)

charged at a pressure of 1,200 psi and the pump maintains system pressure at approximately 2,700 psi. Upon braking, the pressure is modulated by three solenoid assemblies, two in the front and one in the rear. The solenoids operate according to signals from the ABS controller assembly.

Disc Brakes

BASIC OPERATING PRINCIPLES

Instead of the traditional expanding brakes that press outward against a circular drum, disc brake systems utilize a disc (rotor) with brake pads positioned on either side of it. Braking effect is achieved in a manner similar to the way you would squeeze a spinning phonograph record between your fingers. The disc (rotor) is a casting with cooling fins between the two braking surfaces. This enables air to circulate between the braking surfaces making them less sensitive to heat buildup and more resistant to fade. Dirt and water do not affect braking action since contaminants are thrown off by the centrifugal action of the rotor or scraped off the by the pads. Also, the equal clamping action of the two brake pads tends to ensure uniform, straight line stops. Disc brakes are inherently self-adjusting. There are three general types of disc brake:

1. A fixed caliper.
2. A floating caliper.
3. A sliding caliper.

The fixed caliper design uses two pistons mounted on either side of the rotor (in each side of the caliper). The caliper is mounted rigidly and does not move.

The sliding and floating designs are quite similar. In fact, these two types are often lumped together. In both designs, the pad on the inside of the rotor is moved into contact with the rotor by hydraulic force. The caliper, which is not held in a fixed position, moves slightly, bringing the outside pad into contact with the rotor. There are various methods of attaching floating calipers. Some pivot at the bottom or top, and some slide on mounting bolts. In any event, the end result is the same. The "W" body vehicles utilize the sliding caliper configuration, front and rear.

BRAKING SYSTEMS

Adjustments

STOPLAMP SWITCH

1. Disconnect the negative (–) battery cable.
2. Remove the left side sound insulator panel.

3. Depress the brake pedal as far as possible and hold.

4. Using a stiff wire with a hooked end, gently pull on the switch set lever and listen for an audible click. If there is NO click, release the brake pedal and repeat the steps. Also, if a click is not heard, the switch may be defective. Connect the negative battery cable.

Stoplamp Switch

REMOVAL AND INSTALLATION

1. Disconnect the negative (–) battery cable.
2. Remove the three fasteners from the left side insulator panel.
3. Slide the steering shaft protective cover towards the cowl.
4. Remove the vacuum hose at the cruise control cut off switch, if so equipped.
5. Remove the stoplamp switch-to-steering column bracket retaining pin.
6. Disconnect the electrical connector.
7. Push the switch arm to the left and towards the cowl to disconnect switch-to-pedal arm. Release the snap clip and remove the switch.

To install:

1. Install the switch and push up until it is seated into the top snap clip.
2. Install the electrical connectors.

3. Connect the switch to the pedal.
4. Install the switch-to-steering column retaining pin.
5. Install the vacuum hose if equipped with cruise control.
6. Install the steering shaft protective sleeve.
7. Adjust the stoplamp switch as previously outlined in this section.
8. Install the left sound insulator, connect the negative battery cable and check switch operation.

Master Cylinder

REMOVAL AND INSTALLATION

Standard System

NOTE: *Always use a proper size flare nut wrench when removing and installing the brake lines. Failure to use the proper wrench may cause damage to the line fittings.*

1. Disconnect the negative (–) battery cable and fluid level sensor at the master cylinder.
2. Using a flare nut wrench, remove and plug the brake lines from the master cylinder. Plug the lines to prevent fluid loss and contamination.
3. Remove the two master cylinder-to-brake power booster retaining nuts and master cylinder.

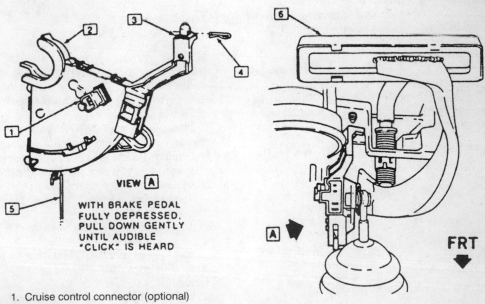

VIEW **A**

WITH BRAKE PEDAL
FULLY DEPRESSED,
PULL DOWN GENTLY
UNTIL AUDIBLE
"CLICK" IS HEARD

A ▶

FRT ▼

1. Cruise control connector (optional)
2. Switch
3. Wave washer
4. Retainer clip
5. Wire hook
6. Brake pedal

Stoplamp switch adjustment

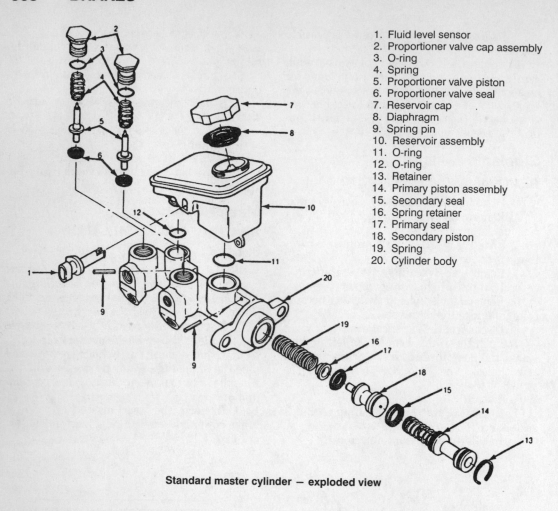

1. Fluid level sensor
2. Proportioner valve cap assembly
3. O-ring
4. Spring
5. Proportioner valve piston
6. Proportioner valve seal
7. Reservoir cap
8. Diaphragm
9. Spring pin
10. Reservoir assembly
11. O-ring
12. O-ring
13. Retainer
14. Primary piston assembly
15. Secondary seal
16. Spring retainer
17. Primary seal
18. Secondary piston
19. Spring
20. Cylinder body

Standard master cylinder — exploded view

To install:

1. Install the master cylinder and torque the retaining nuts to 20 ft. lbs. (27 Nm).

2. Install the brake lines and torque to 15 ft. lbs. (20 Nm), using a flare nut wrench.

3. Connect the fluid level sensor electrical wire.

4. Fill the master cylinder to the proper level with **NEW** brake fluid meeting DOT 3 specifications.

5. Bleed the system as outlined in this section.

6. Connect the negative battery cable and recheck the fluid level.

7. Do NOT move the vehicle until a firm brake pedal is felt.

Anti-Lock Brake System (ABS)

1. Disconnect the negative (–) battery cable.

2. **Depressurize the ABS brake system as follows.**

a. With the ignition key OFF, firmly apply and release the brake pedal a minimum of 40 times.

b. A noticeable change in the pedal feel will occur when the accumulator is completely discharged (a hard pedal).

c. Do **NOT** turn the ignition key ON after depressurizing the system unless instructed to do so.

3. Disconnect the three Powermaster III electrical connectors and move out of the way.

4. Remove and plug the three metal brake lines using flare nut wrenches. Plug the lines to prevent fluid loss and contamination.

5. Remove the hair pin clip from inside the vehicle at the brake pedal.

6. Remove the two ABS unit-to-cowl retaining nuts.

7. Remove the ABS unit. Make sure none of the electrical connectors are still connected.

To install:

1. Lightly lubricate the entire outer surface of the pushrod with silicone grease.

2. Position the ABS unit into the vehicle. Loosely install the retaining nuts and pushrod.

3. Install the pushrod hair pin clip and torque the two retaining nuts to 15–25 ft. lbs. (20–34 Nm).

4. Install the three brake pipes using flare

nut wrenches. Torque the pipes to 15 ft. lbs. (20 Nm).

5. Install the ABS unit electrical connectors.

6. Adjust the stoplamp switch as outlined in this chapter.

7. Bleed the ABS system as outlined in the "ABS Bleeding" procedures in this chapter. Reconnect the negative battery cable.

OVERHAUL

Standard System

DISASSEMBLY

1. Remove the master cylinder assembly from the vehicle.

2. Remove the reservoir cap and diaphragm. Empty the fluid out of the reservoir.

3. Remove the fluid level sensor with a needle noise pliers on the other side of the sensor and push through the reservoir. Remove the proportioning valve assemblies (2 through 6).

4. Remove the retainer (13) while depressing the primary piston.

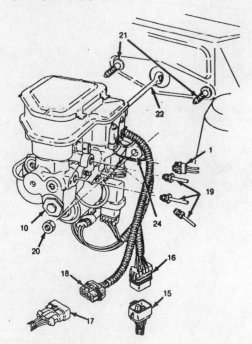

1. 2–pin electrical connector
10. Powermaster III
15. Vehicle 7–pin connector
16. 7–pin connector
17. Vehicle 10–pin connector
18. 10–pin connector
19. Brake pipe
20. Nuts
21. Cowl bracket stud
22. Pushrod
24. Mounting bracket

ABS unit removal

5. Apply low pressure unlubricated compressed air into the upper outlet port at the blind end of the bore to remove the primary and secondary piston, spring and spring retainer.

6. Inspect the cylinder bore for scoring or corrosion. No abrasives should be used in the bore.

ASSEMBLY

1. Clean all parts in denatured alcohol and dry with unlubricated compressed air.

2. Lubricate the seals and spring retainers with clean (new) DOT 3 brake fluid.

3. Install the spring and secondary piston (15 thru 18) into the bore.

4. Install the primary piston (14) and retainer (13) while depressing the primary piston.

5. Install the proportioning valves and fluid level sensor.

6. Install the master cylinder, diaphragm and reservoir cap.

7. Fill the reservoir to the **MAX** level and bleed the system as outlined in this section.

COMPONENT REPLACEMENT

Anti-Lock Brake System

ACCUMULATOR

The accumulator is a nitrogen charged pressure vessel which holds the brake fluid under high pressure. The accumulator can not be repaired and must be replaced as an assembly.

1. Disconnect the negative (–) battery cable.

2. Depressurize the ABS system as follows.

a. With the ignition key OFF, firmly apply and release the brake pedal a minimum of 40 times.

b. A noticeable change in the pedal feel will occur when the accumulator is completely discharged (a hard pedal).

c. Do **NOT** turn the ignition key ON after depressurizing the system unless instructed to do so.

3. Remove the accumulator (28) by turning the hex nut on the end of the accumulator with a 17mm socket. The unit can be removed by sliding out from beneath the ABS unit, towards the left front wheel well.

4. Remove the O-ring seal from the accumulator.

To install:

1. Lightly lubricate the new O-ring seal and install it on the accumulator.

2. Install the accumulator (28) and torque the unit to 23–36 ft. lbs. (31–35 Nm).

3. Bleed the system as outlined in the "ABS Bleeding" procedures in this chapter.

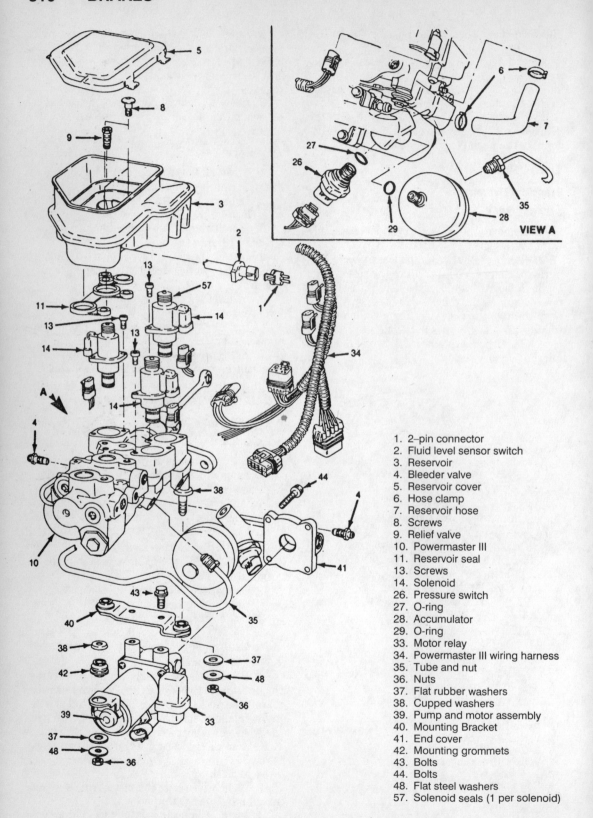

1. 2–pin connector
2. Fluid level sensor switch
3. Reservoir
4. Bleeder valve
5. Reservoir cover
6. Hose clamp
7. Reservoir hose
8. Screws
9. Relief valve
10. Powermaster III
11. Reservoir seal
13. Screws
14. Solenoid
26. Pressure switch
27. O-ring
28. Accumulator
29. O-ring
33. Motor relay
34. Powermaster III wiring harness
35. Tube and nut
36. Nuts
37. Flat rubber washers
38. Cupped washers
39. Pump and motor assembly
40. Mounting Bracket
41. End cover
42. Mounting grommets
43. Bolts
44. Bolts
48. Flat steel washers
57. Solenoid seals (1 per solenoid)

VIEW A

Powermaster III (ABS) — exploded view

RESERVIR

1. Disconnect the negative (–) battery cable.

2. Depressurize the ABS system as follows.

 a. With the ignition key OFF, firmly apply and release the brake pedal a minimum of 40 times.

 b. A noticeable change in the pedal feel will occur when the accumulator is completely discharged (a hard pedal).

 c. Do **NOT** turn the ignition key ON after depressurizing the system unless instructed to do so.

3. Remove the cover from the reservoir and remove the brake fluid.

4. Disconnect and remove the fluid level sensor.

5. To gain better access, loosen but do not remove the ABS unit-to-cowl attaching nuts. Pull the ABS unit forward.

6. Place rags around the body and engine components under the ABS unit.

7. Remove the upper reservoir hose clamp and disconnect the hose from the reservoir.

8. Remove the three reservoir mounting screws. Lift the rear of the reservoir up and carefully pull away from under the secondary dash. Use care not to damage solenoids and O-rings.

To install:

1. Check all reservoir components for damage and replace if necessary.

2. Make sure all the solenoid seals are in good condition and proper location before installing the reservoir.

3. Install the reservoir seal and reservoir. Make sure the seals are in proper position.

4. Install the three reservoir retaining screws and torque to 45 inch lbs. (5 Nm).

5. Install the reservoir hose and clamp.

6. Torque the ABS unit-to-cowl retaining nuts to 25 ft. lbs. (34 Nm).

7. Refill the reservoir with DOT 3 clean brake fluid and install the reservoir cover.

8. Adjust the stoplamp switch as outlined in this chapter.

9. Bleed the ABS system as outlined in the "ABS Bleeding" procedures in this chapter.

Fluid Reservoir

REMOVAL AND INSTALLATION

Standard System

1. Remove the master cylinder assembly from the vehicle.

2. Clamp the flange on the master cylinder body into a vise.

3. Drive out the spring pins (9) using a suitable 1/8 inch punch.

4. Pull the reservoir straight out of the cylinder body.

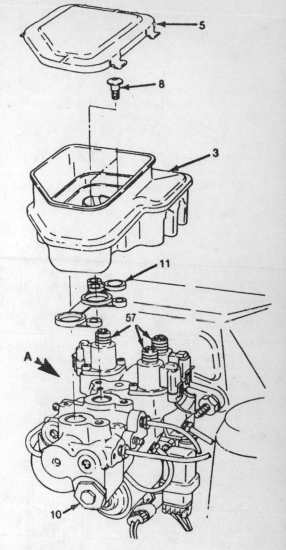

3. Reservoir
5. Reservoir cover
8. Screws
10. Powermaster III
11. Reservoir seal
57. Solenoid seals (1 per solenoid)

ABS reservoir removal

5. Remove the O-rings from the reservoir to replace with new.

To install:

1. Clean the reservoir with denatured alcohol and compressed air.

2. Lubricate and install new O-rings with clean DOT 3 brake fluid.

3. Seat the reservoir into the cylinder body by pressing straight in.

4. Drive the spring pins into the body to retain the reservoir.

5. Install the master cylinder and bleed the brake system.

Power Brake Booster

REMOVAL AND INSTALLATION

Standard System

1. Disconnect the negative (–) battery cable.
2. From inside the engine compartment, remove the secondary dash panels. The panels around the booster assembly.
3. Remove the booster grommet bolt and grommet
4. Remove the master cylinder from the power booster.
5. Scribe a mark on the front and rear booster covers in case the two covers get separated during removal.

NOTE: *When disconnecting the pushrod from the brake pedal, the brake pedal must be kept stationary or damage to the brake switch may result.*

6. Disconnect the brake pushrod from the brake pedal.
7. Unlock the booster from the front of the dash as follows.

a. Install a booster holding tool J-22805-01 to the master cylinder mounting studs.

b. Torque the stud nuts to 28 ft. lbs. (38 Nm).

c. Use a suitable pry bar to pry the locking tab on the booster out of the locking notch on the mounting flange.

d. At the same time, turn the booster counterclockwise with a large wrench on the booster holding tool.

e. Do NOT attempt to remove the booster until the pushrod has been disconnected from the brake pedal.

To install:

1. Lubricate the inside and outside diameters of the grommet and front housing seal with silicone grease before installation.
2. Install the booster by turning the booster holding tool clockwise until the locking flanges are engaged. Make sure the locking tab is fully seated to prevent rotation of the booster.
3. Install the booster pushrod to the brake pedal.
4. Install the master cylinder, booster grommet and secondary dash panel.
5. Connect the negative battery cable and bleed the system if the fluid pipes were disconnected from the master cylinder.

Proportioning Valves

REMOVAL AND INSTALLATION

Standard System

The proportioning valves are located in the master cylinder assembly. Refer to the "Master Cylinder" overhaul section and illustration in this chapter for service procedures.

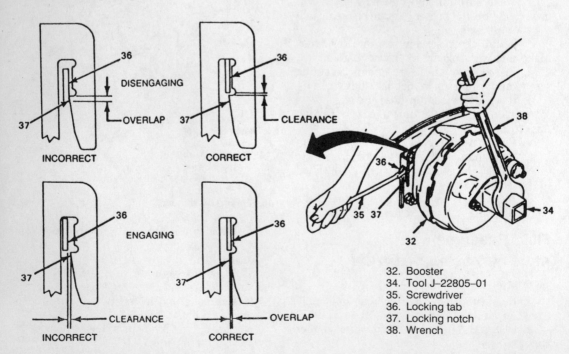

32. Booster
34. Tool J–22805–01
35. Screwdriver
36. Locking tab
37. Locking notch
38. Wrench

Power brake booster removal

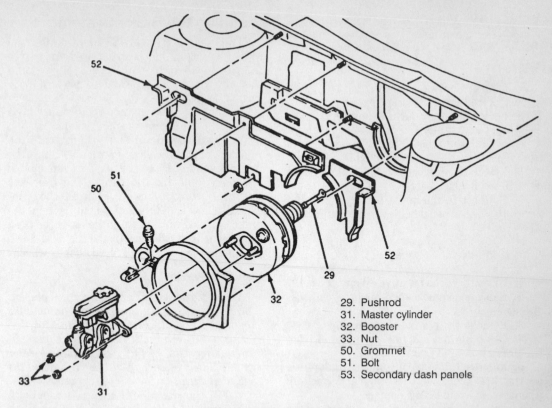

29. Pushrod
31. Master cylinder
32. Booster
33. Nut
50. Grommet
51. Bolt
53. Secondary dash panels

Power booster assembly

Anti-Lock Brake System

There is a remote proportioning valve located in the rear of the vehicle. Remove the three brake pipe fittings with a flare nut wrench only. The valve is not serviceable and must be replaced as a complete unit.

Brake hoses

REMOVAL AND INSTALLATION

Front

1. Disconnect the negative (–) battery cable.
2. Raise the vehicle and support with jackstands.
3. Remove the front wheel assembly.
4. Clean all dirt and foreign material from the brake hose and fitting.
5. Remove brake pipe from the brake hose at the bracket. Use flare nut and back-up wrenches to avoid fitting damage.
6. Remove the brake hose retainer at the mounting bracket.
7. Remove the hose from the bracket.
8. Remove the inlet fitting at the caliper, bolt and two copper washers.
   To install:
1. Using new copper washers, install the inlet-to-caliper. Torque the bolt to 30 ft. lbs. (40 Nm).

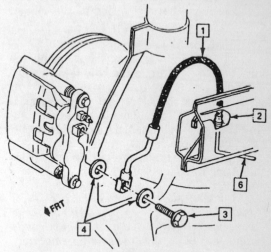

1. Hose
2. Bracket
3. 32 ft. lbs.
4. Washer
6. Brake pipe

Front brake hose – rear similar

2. With the vehicle weight on the suspension, install the brake hose-to-bracket and install the hose retainer. Make sure there are NO kinks in the hose.

3. Install the brake pipe-to-hose and torque the fitting to 15 ft. lbs. (20 Nm).

CAUTION: *Make sure the hose is NOT kinked or touching any part of the frame or suspension after installation. These conditions may cause the hose to fail prematurely.*

4. Check the hose after turning the steering wheel extreme right and then extreme left. If the hose is tight or touching anything, make the proper adjustments.

5. Install the wheel assembly and torque the lug nuts to 100 ft. lbs. (135 Nm).

6. Lower the vehicle and bleed the system as outlined in this chapter.

7. Connect the negative battery cable and pump the brake pedal before moving the vehicle.

Rear

1. Disconnect the negative (–) battery cable.

2. Raise the vehicle and support with jackstands.

3. Remove the rear wheel assembly.

4. Clean all dirt and foreign material from the brake hose and fitting.

5. Remove brake pipe from the brake hose at the bracket. Use flare nut and back-up wrenches to avoid fitting damage.

6. Remove the brake hose retainer at the mounting bracket.

7. Remove the hose from the bracket.

8. Remove the inlet fitting at the caliper, bolt and two copper washers.

To install:

1. Using new copper washers, install the inlet-to-caliper. Torque the bolt to 30 ft. lbs. (40 Nm).

2. With the vehicle weight on the suspension, install the brake hose-to-bracket and install the hose retainer. Make sure there is NO kinks in the hose.

3. Install the brake pipe-to-hose and torque the fitting to 15 ft. lbs. (20 Nm).

CAUTION: *Make sure the hose is NOT kinked or touching any part of the frame or suspension after installation. These conditions may cause the hose to fail prematurely.*

4. Check the hose after turning the steering wheel extreme right and then extreme left. If the hose is tight or touching anything, make the proper adjustments.

5. Install the wheel assembly and torque the lug nuts to 100 ft. lbs. (135 Nm).

6. Lower the vehicle and bleed the system as outlined in this chapter.

7. Connect the negative battery cable and pump the brake pedal before moving the vehicle.

Bleeding the Brake System

The brake system MUST be bled after the hydraulic system has been serviced. Air enters the system when components are removed and this air has to be removed to prevent poor system performance.

The time required to bleed the system can be reduced by removing as much air as possible before installing the master cylinder onto the vehicle. This is called bench bleeding the master cylinder. Place the master cylinder in a vise or holding fixture, run tubing from the fluid pipe fittings to the reservoir, fill the cylinder with DOT 3 brake fluid and pump the brake pushrod until most of the air is removed from the master cylinder. Install the master cylinder onto the vehicle and bleed all four wheels.

Standard System

NOTE: *Care MUST be taken to prevent brake fluid from contacting any automotive paint surface. Brake fluid can stain or dissolve paint finishes if not removed immediately. Clean the surface with soap and water immediately after the fluid has contacted the painted surface.*

1. Fill the master cylinder reservoir with brake fluid and keep the reservoir at least half full during the bleeding operation.

2. If the master cylinder has air in the bore, it must be removed before bleeding the calipers. Bleed the master cylinder as follows:

   a. Disconnect the forward brake pipe at the master cylinder.

   b. Fill the reservoir until fluid begins to flow from the forward pipe connector port.

   c. Reconnect the forward brake pipe and tighten.

   d. Depress the brake pedal slowly one time and hold. Loosen the forward brake pipe and purge the air from the bore. Tighten the brake pipe, wait 15 seconds and repeat until all air is removed.

   e. When the air is removed from the forward brake pipe, repeat the same procedures for the rear brake pipe.

3. Bleed the calipers in the following order, (right front, right rear, left rear, left front).

4. Install a box end wrench over the bleeder valve and connect a clear tube onto the valve. Place the other end of the tube into a container of new brake fluid. The end of the tube must be submerged in brake fluid.

5. Depress the brake pedal slowly one time and hold. Loosen the bleeder valve to purge the air from the caliper. Close the valve and release the pedal. Repeat the procedure until all air is removed from the brake fluid.

6. Do NOT pump the brake pedal rapidly,

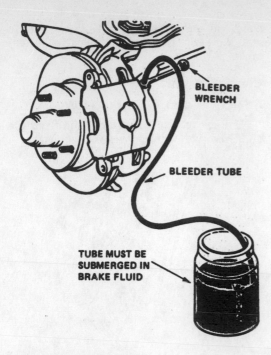

BLEEDER WRENCH

BLEEDER TUBE

TUBE MUST BE SUBMERGED IN BRAKE FLUID

Bleeding the brake system

this causes the air to brake up and make bleeding difficult.

7. After the calipers have been bled, check the brake pedal for sponginess and the **BRAKE** warning lamp for low fluid level.

8. Repeat the bleeding operation if a spongy pedal is felt and fill the reservoir to the **MAX** line.

Bleeding the Anti-Lock Brake System

CAUTION: *Use only clean DOT 3 brake fluid from a sealed container in the anti-lock brake system. Any other type of fluid may cause severe damage to the internal components causing brake failure and personal injury.*

1. Make sure the vehicle ignition is **OFF**.
2. Disconnect the negative (–) battery cable.
3. Depressurize the ABS system as follows.

a. With the ignition key OFF, firmly apply and release the brake pedal a minimum of 40 times.

b. A noticeable change in the pedal feel will occur when the accumulator is completely discharged (a hard pedal).

c. Do **NOT** turn the ignition key ON after depressurizing the system unless instructed to do so.

4. Clean and remove the reservoir cap.
5. Fill the reservoir with DOT 3 brake fluid.
6. Raise the vehicle and support with jackstands.

7. Bleed the right front wheel by attaching a clean hose to the bleeder valve and submerge the other end into a container of partially filled brake fluid.

8. Open the valve and slowly depress the brake pedal.

9. Tap lightly on the brake caliper with a rubber mallet to dislodge the air bubbles.

10. Close the valve and release the brake pedal. Repeat until all air is removed.

11. Repeat Steps 7–10 on the left front wheel.

12. Connect the negative battery cable and turn the ignition key to the **RUN** position without starting the vehicle. Allow the pump to run to pressurize the accumulator.

13. Bleed the right rear brake by installing a bleeder hose and container, open the valve, with the ignition **ON** slowly depress the pedal part way until the fluid begins to flow from the bleeder valve and allow the fluid to flow for 15 seconds.

14. Close the valve and release the brake pedal.

15. Fill the reservoir with fluid to one inch below the FULL mark.

16. Repeat Steps 13–16 for the left rear wheel.

17. Lower the vehicle and bleed the Powermaster III isolation valves (at the master cylinder) as follows.

a. Attach a clear hose and container to the Powermaster inboard bleeder valves.

b. With the ignition in the **ON** position, apply the pedal, slowly open the valve and allow fluid to flow until no air bubbles are seen.

c. Close the valve and repeat the steps to the outboard bleeder valve until no air bubbles are present.

18. Bleed the accumulator as follows.

a. Turn the ignition key to the **OFF** position, depressurize the system and wait two minutes to allow the air to settle.

b. Remove the reservoir cover and check the fluid level. Add if necessary.

c. Install the reservoir cap.

d. Turn the ignition key to the **RUN** position, but do not start the engine.

e. When the pump has stopped, depress the brake pedal and repeat the **OFF/RUN** procedures ten times to cycle the solenoids.

19. Apply the brake pedal and note the pedal feel and travel.

20. If the pedal feels firm and smooth without excessive travel, the system is properly bled. Connect the negative battery cable if not done so.

FRONT DISC BRAKES

CAUTION: *Some brake pads contain asbestos, which has been determined to be a cancer causing agent. Never clean the brake surfaces with compressed air! Avoid inhaling any dust from any brake surface! When cleaning brake surfaces, use a commercially available brake cleaning fluid.*

Brake Pads

INSPECTION

The pad thickness should be inspected every time that the wheels are removed. Pad thickness can be checked by looking down through the inspection hole in the top of the caliper. If the thickness of the pad is worn to within 0.030 inch. (0.76mm) of the rivet at either end of the pad, all the pads should be replaced. A thermal material is sandwiched between the lining and backing. Don't include this material when determining the lining thickness. This is the factory recommended measurement. Your state's automobile inspection laws may be different.

NOTE: *Always replace all pads on both front wheels at the same time. Failure to do so will result in uneven braking action and premature wear.*

REMOVAL AND INSTALLATION

1. Disconnect the negative (–) battery cable.
2. Raise the vehicle and support with jackstands.
3. Remove the wheel and tire assembly.
4. Remove the two caliper mounting bolts, caliper and hang from the suspension with a piece of wire. Do not hang by the brake hose.
5. Using a suitable pry bar, lift up the outboard pad retaining spring so that it will clear the center lug.
6. Remove the inboard pad by unsnapping the pad from the pistons.

To install:

1. Remove about ²/3 of the fluid from the brake reservoir with a syringe or equivalent.
2. Install the inboard pad-to-caliper pistons. Bottom the pistons in the caliper bore using a C-clamp and the inboard brake pad.
3. Make sure both inboard pad tangs are inside the piston cavity.
4. Install the outboard pad by snapping the pad retainer spring over the housing center lug and into the housing slot.
5. Make sure both pads remain free of grease or oil. The wear sensor should be at the trailing edge of the pad during rotation.
6. Install the caliper assembly, wheels assembly and lower the vehicle.
7. Fill the master cylinder to the **FULL**

mark and apply the brake pedal three times to seat the pads. Connect the negative battery cable.

Brake Caliper

REMOVAL AND INSTALLATION

1. Remove ²/3 of the brake fluid from the brake reservoir using a syringe or equivalent.

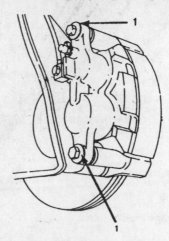

Front caliper mounting bolts (1)

2. Raise the vehicle and support with jackstands.
3. Mark the relationship of the wheel-to-hub and bearing assembly.
4. Remove the tire and wheel. Install two lug nuts to retain the rotor.
5. If the caliper is going to be removed, disconnect and plug the brake hose.
6. Remove the caliper mounting bolts and pull the caliper from the mounting bracket and rotor. Support the caliper with wire if not removing.

To install:

1. Inspect the bolt boots and support bushings for cuts or damage, replace if necessary.
2. Install the caliper over the rotor into the mounting bracket. Make sure the bolt boots are in place.
3. Lubricate the entire shaft of the mounting bolts and cavities with silicone grease.
4. Install the mounting bolts and torque to 79 ft. lbs. (107 Nm).
5. Install the brake hose, using new copper washers and torque to 32 ft. lbs. (44 Nm).
6. Remove the two wheel lugs, install the wheels and torque the lug nuts to 100 ft. lbs. (136 Nm).
7. Lower the vehicle.
8. Fill the master cylinder and bleed the calipers as outlined in the "Brake System Bleeding" procedures in this chapter.

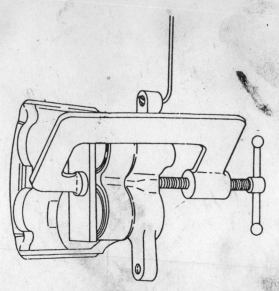

Compressing the front caliper pistons

9. Check for hydraulic leaks. Pump the brake pedal a few times before moving the vehicle.

OVERHAUL

Disassembly

1. Remove the caliper assembly from the vehicle as outlined earlier in this chapter.

CAUTION: *Do NOT place fingers in front of the pistons in an attempt to catch or protect*

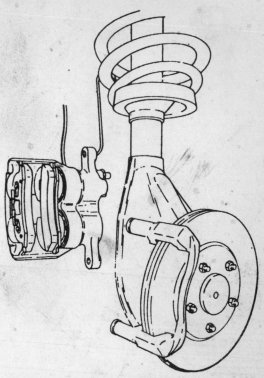

Supporting the caliper from the spring to prevent hose damage

them when applying compressed air. This could result in personal injury.

2. Remove the caliper pistons with compressed air into the caliper inlet hole.

3. If both pistons do not come out at the same time, use a piece of wood to back up the other piston until it starts moving.

4. Remove the boots with a non-metal prying tool.

5. Remove the piston seals using a seal pick.

Assembly

1. Loosen the brake bleeder valve. If the valve breaks off, the caliper will have to be replaced.

2. Inspect the caliper bores, pistons and mounting threads for scoring or excessive wear.

3. Use crocus cloth to polish out light corrosion from the piston and bore.

4. Clean all parts with denatured alcohol and dry with unlubricated air.

5. Tighten the bleeder valve.

6. Lubricate the new piston seals and bore with clean brake fluid.

7. Install the new seals and make sure they are not twisted.

8. Lubricate the piston bore.

9. Push the pistons into the bore and install the boots.

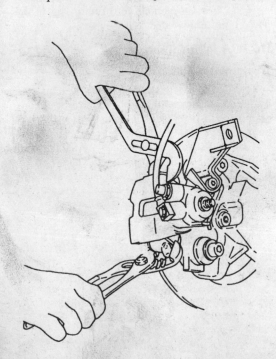

Compressing caliper piston for removal

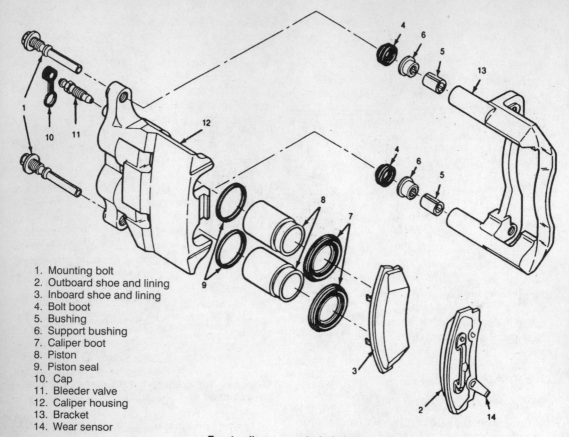

1. Mounting bolt
2. Outboard shoe and lining
3. Inboard shoe and lining
4. Bolt boot
5. Bushing
6. Support bushing
7. Caliper boot
8. Piston
9. Piston seal
10. Cap
11. Bleeder valve
12. Caliper housing
13. Bracket
14. Wear sensor

Front caliper — exploded view

10. Install the caliper onto the vehicle.

11. Install the front wheel and bleed the brake system as outlined in the "Bleeding the Brake System" section in this chapter.

Brake Rotor

REMOVAL AND INSTALLATION

CAUTION: *Some brake pads contain asbestos, which has been determined to be a cancer causing agent. Never clean the brake surfaces with compressed air! Avoid inhaling any dust from any brake surface! When cleaning brake surfaces, use a commercially available brake cleaning fluid.*

1. Raise the vehicle and support with jackstands.

2. Remove the wheel and tire assembly.

3. Remove the brake caliper and support with a wire to the surrounding body.

4. Remove the rotor assembly.

To install:

1. Install the brake rotor over the hub assembly.

2. Install the brake caliper as outlined in this chapter.

3. Install the wheel and tire assembly.

Torque the lug nuts to 100 ft. lbs. (136 Nm).

4. Lower the vehicle and pump the brake pedal before moving.

ROTOR INSPECTION

Thickness Variation Check

The thickness variation can be checked by measuring the thickness of the rotor at four or more points. All of the measurements must be made at the same distance from the edge of the rotor. A rotor the varies by more than 0.0005 inch (0.013mm) can cause a pulsation in the brake pedal. If these measurement are excessive, the rotor should be refinished or replaced.

Lateral Runout Check

1. Remove the caliper and hang from the body with a piece of wire. Install two inverted lug nuts to retain the rotor.

2. Install a dial indicator to the steering knuckle so that the indicator button contacts the rotor about 1 inch from the rotor edge.

3. Zero the dial indicator.

4. Move the rotor one complete revolution and observe the total indicated runout.

5. If the rotor runout exceeds 0.0015 inch

(0.040mm) have the rotor refinished or replaced.

Refinishing Brake Rotors

All brake rotors have a minimum thickness dimension cast onto them. Do NOT use a brake rotor that will not meet minimum thickness specifications in the "Brake Specifications" chart at the end of this chapter.

Accurate control of rotor tolerances is necessary for proper brake performance and safety. Machining of the rotor should be done by a qualified machine shop with the proper machining equipment.

The optimum speed for refinishing the rotor surface is a spindle speed of 200 rpm. Crossfeed for rough cutting should range from 0.010–0.006 inch (0.254–0.152mm) per revolution. The finish cuts should be made at crossfeeds no greater than 0.002 inch (0.051mm) per revolution.

REAR DISC BRAKES

CAUTION: *Some brake pads contain asbestos, which has been determined to be a cancer causing agent. Never clean the brake surfaces with compressed air! Avoid inhaling any dust from any brake surface! When cleaning brake surfaces, use a commercially available brake cleaning fluid.*

Brake Pads

INSPECTION

The pad thickness should be inspected every time that the wheels are removed. Pad thickness can be checked by looking down through the inspection hole in the top of the caliper. If the thickness of the pad is worn to within 0.030 inch. (0.76mm) of the rivet at either end of the pad, all the pads should be replaced. A thermal material is sandwiched between the lining and backing. Don't include this material when determining the lining thickness. This is the factory recommended measurement. Your state's automobile inspection laws may be different.

NOTE: *Always replace all pads on both rear wheels at the same time. Failure to do so will result in uneven braking action and premature wear.*

REMOVAL AND INSTALLATION

1. Raise the vehicle and support with jackstands.
2. Remove the rear wheels assemblies.
3. Remove the rear caliper and hang by the suspension with a piece of wire to prevent brake hose damage. Refer to the "Caliper" removal procedures in this section for assistance.
4. Using a suitable pry bar, disengage the buttons on the outboard pad from the holes in the caliper housing.
5. Press in on the edge of the inboard pad and tilt outward to release the pad from the pad retainer.
6. Remove the two way check valve from the end of the caliper piston using a small pry bar.

To install:
WARNING: *Do NOT allow pliers to contact the actuator screw. Protect the piston so the contact surface does not get damaged.*

1. Bottom the piston into the caliper bore by positioning a twelve inch adjustable pliers over the caliper housing and piston surface.
2. Lubricate a new two way check valve and install it into the end of the piston.
3. Install the inboard brake pad. Engage the pad edge in the retainer tabs closest to the caliper bridge. Press down and snap the tabs at the open side of the caliper. The wear sensor should be at the leading edge of the pad during wheel rotation. The back of the pad must lay flat against the piston. The button on the back of the pad must engage the D-shaped notch in the piston.
NOTE: *If the piston will not align or retract into the bore. Turn the piston clockwise using a piston turning tool J-7624 or equivalent.*
4. Install the outboard brake pad. Snap the pad retainer spring into the slots in the caliper housing. The back of the pad must lay flat against the caliper.
5. Install the caliper onto the mounting bracket as outlined in this section.
6. Apply force at least three times to the brake pedal to seat the brake pads before moving the vehicle.
7. Install the rear wheels and torque the lug nuts to 100 ft. lbs. (136 Nm).
8. Lower the vehicle and check for fluid leaks.

Brake Caliper

REMOVAL AND INSTALLATION

1. Remove 2/3 of the brake fluid from the reservoir with a syringe.
2. Raise the vehicle and support with jackstands.
3. Remove the rear wheel assembly and install two lug nuts to retain the rotor.
4. Remove the brake shield assembly.
5. Loosen the tension on the parking brake cable at the equalizer.
6. Remove the parking cable and return spring from the lever.

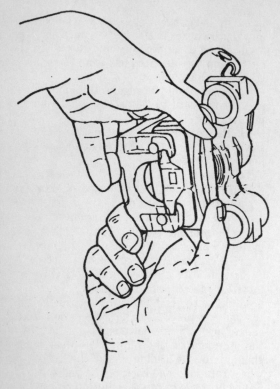

Compressing caliper piston for removal

7. Hold the cable lever and remove the lock nut, lever and seal.

8. Push the piston into the caliper bore using two adjustable pliers over the inboard pad tabs.

WARNING: *Do NOT allow pliers to contact the actuator screw. Protect the piston so the contact surface does not get damaged.*

9. Reinstall the lever seal with the sealing bead against the caliper housing, lever and lock nut.

10. Remove and plug the brake hose inlet fitting only if the caliper is going to be removed from the vehicle.

11. Remove the bolt and bracket to gain access to the upper mounting bolt.

12. Remove the caliper mounting bolts, caliper and hang from the suspension with a piece of wire to prevent brake hose damage.

To install:

1. Inspect all brake parts for damage and deterioration. Replace any parts if necessary.

2. Push the caliper sleeves inward.

3. Install the caliper-to-mounting bracket. Torque the mounting bolts to 92 ft. lbs. (125 Nm).

4. Install the bracket and bolt after the mounting bolts have been torqued.

5. Install the brake hose inlet with new copper washers if removed. Torque the hose bolt to 32 ft. lbs. (44 Nm).

6. Remove the lock nut, lever and seal. Lubricate the lever seal and lever shaft.

7. Install the seal and lever with the lever facing down.

8. Hold the lever back against the stop and torque the lock nut to 35 ft. lbs. (47 Nm).

9. Install the return spring and parking brake cable. Adjust the cable as outlined in the "Parking Brake Cable Adjustment" procedures in this chapter.

10. Install the brake shield and rear wheel assembly. Torque the lug nuts to 100 ft. lbs. (136 Nm).

11. Lower the vehicle.

12. Fill the brake reservoir with DOT 3 brake fluid.

13. Bleed the caliper if removed from the vehicle. Refer to the "Brake System Bleeding" procedures in this chapter.

14. Inspect the brake system for fluid leaks.

15. Apply the brake pedal three times to seat the brake pads before moving the vehicle.

OVERHAUL

Disassembly

1. Remove the caliper assembly from the vehicle as previously outlined.

2. Remove the sleeve and bolt boots. Check the boots and bolts for damage and corrosion.

3. Remove the brake pad retainer from the end of the piston by rotating the retainer until the inside tabs line up with the notches in the piston.

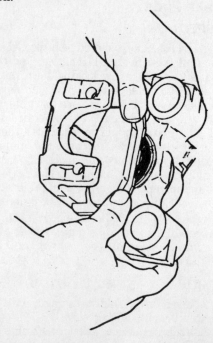

Installing rear outboard pad

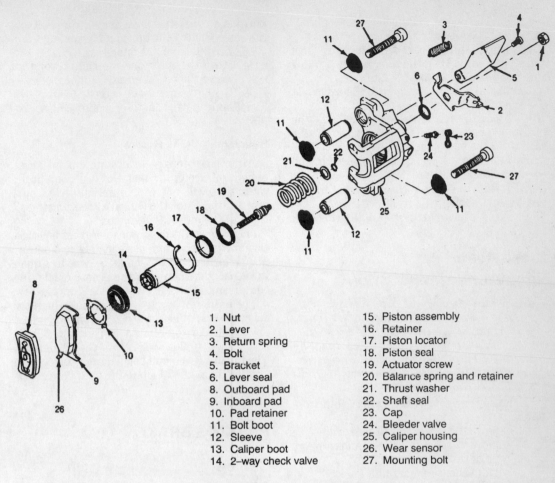

1. Nut
2. Lever
3. Return spring
4. Bolt
5. Bracket
6. Lever seal
8. Outboard pad
9. Inboard pad
10. Pad retainer
11. Bolt boot
12. Sleeve
13. Caliper boot
14. 2–way check valve
15. Piston assembly
16. Retainer
17. Piston locator
18. Piston seal
19. Actuator screw
20. Balance spring and retainer
21. Thrust washer
22. Shaft seal
23. Cap
24. Bleeder valve
25. Caliper housing
26. Wear sensor
27. Mounting bolt

Rear caliper — exploded view

4. Remove the lock nut, lever and seal from the caliper.

5. Remove the piston by using a wrench to rotate the actuator screw to work the piston out of the caliper bore.

6. Remove the balance spring and actuator screw.

7. Remove the shaft seal, thrust washer and boot.

8. Remove the retainer using ring pliers and a piston locator.

9. Remove the piston seal using a non-metal seal pick.

10. Remove the bleeder valve. If the valve breaks, the caliper will have to be replaced.

Assembly

1. Inspect all parts for damage and replace if necessary.

2. Clean all parts in denatured alcohol and dry with unlubricated shop air.

3. Install the bleeder valve and torque to 116 inch lbs. (13 Nm).

4. Install the bracket and bolt.

5. Lubricate the new piston seals with clean brake fluid and install into the caliper bore. Make sure they are not twisted.

6. Lubricate the piston locating tool J-36627, do NOT install the piston.

7. Install the thrust washer on the actuator screw with the copper side towards the piston.

8. Lubricate the shaft seal and install it on the actuator screw.

9. Install the actuator into the piston assembly.

10. Install the balance spring and retainer into the piston.

11. After all the components are lubricated and installed into the piston, install the piston into the bore. Push the piston into the bore so that the locator is past the retainer groove in the caliper bore.

12. Install the retainer using retainer ring pliers.

13. Install the boot onto the piston with the inside lip of the boot in the piston groove and the boot fold is towards the end of the piston. Push the piston to the bottom of the bore.

14. Lubricate and install the lever seal over the end of the actuator screw.

15. Install the lever and rotate away from the stop slightly. Hold the lever while torquing the lock nut to 32 ft. lbs. (44 Nm).

16. Install the pad retainer in the groove at the end of the piston.

17. Align the inside retainer tabs with the piston notches. Rotate the retainer so that the tabs enter the piston groove.

18. Lubricate with silicone grease and install the sleeve and bolt boots.

19. Install the caliper assembly and torque the retaining bolts to 92 ft. lbs. (125 Nm).

20. Bleed the brake system as outlined in this chapter.

Brake Rotor

REMOVAL AND INSTALLATION

CAUTION: *Some brake pads contain asbestos, which has been determined to be a cancer causing agent. Never clean the brake surfaces with compressed air! Avoid inhaling any dust from any brake surface! When cleaning brake surfaces, use a commercially available brake cleaning fluid.*

1. Raise the vehicle and support with jackstands.

2. Remove the wheel and tire assembly.

3. Remove the brake caliper and support with a wire to the surrounding body.

4. Remove the rotor assembly.

To install:

1. Install the brake rotor over the hub assembly.

2. Install the brake caliper as outlined in this chapter.

3. Install the wheel and tire assembly. Torque the lug nuts to 100 ft. lbs. (136 Nm).

4. Lower the vehicle and pump the brake pedal before moving.

ROTOR INSPECTION

Thickness Variation Check

The thickness variation can be checked by measuring the thickness of the rotor at four or more points. All of the measurements must be made at the same distance from the edge of the rotor. A rotor the varies by more than 0.0005 inch (0.013mm) can cause a pulsation in the brake pedal. If these measurement are excessive, the rotor should be refinished or replaced.

Lateral Runout Check

1. Remove the caliper and hang from the body with a piece of wire. Install two inverted lug nuts to retain the rotor.

2. Install a dial indicator to the steering knuckle so that the indicator button contacts the rotor about 1 inch from the rotor edge.

3. Zero the dial indicator.

4. Move the rotor one complete revolution and observe the total indicated runout.

5. If the rotor runout exceeds 0.0015 inch (0.040mm) have the rotor refinished or replaced.

Refinishing Brake Rotors

All brake rotors have a minimum thickness dimension cast onto them. Do NOT use a brake rotor that will not meet minimum thickness specifications in the "Brake Specifications" chart at the end of this chapter.

Accurate control of rotor tolerances is necessary for proper brake performance and safety. Machining of the rotor should be done by a qualified machine shop with the proper machining equipment.

The optimum speed for refinishing the rotor surface is a spindle speed of 200 rpm. Crossfeed for rough cutting should range from 0.010–0.006 inch (0.254–0.152mm) per revolution. The finish cuts should be made at crossfeeds no greater than 0.002 inch (0.051mm) per revolution.

PARKING BRAKE

Cables

REMOVAL AND INSTALLATION

Front Cable

1. Raise the vehicle and support with jackstands.

2. Loosen the equalizer under the drivers side door.

3. Remove the front cable from the left rear cable at the retainer.

4. Remove the nut at the underbody bracket.

5. Remove the clip from underbody.

6. Lower the vehicle.

7. Remove the cable from the parking brake lever assembly using a brake cable release tool J-37043 or equivalent.

To install:

1. Install the cable to the parking brake lever assembly.

2. Raise the vehicle and support with jackstands.

3. Install the clip-to-underbody and the nut at the underbody bracket.

4. Install the front cable-to-left rear cable at the retainer.

5. Adjust the cable as outlined in this section.

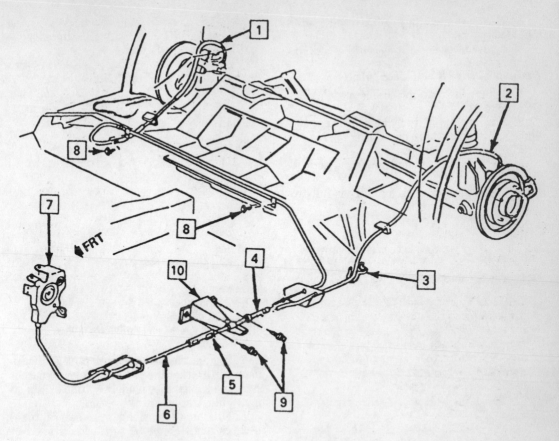

1. Right rear cable
2. Left rear cable
3. Support
4. Equalizer
5. Connector
6. Front cable
7. Parking brake lever assembly
8. 54 inch lbs.
9. 116 inch lbs.
10. Bracket

Parking brake cable routing

6. Lower the vehicle and check operation.

Left Rear Cable

1. Raise the vehicle and support with jack-stands.

2. Remove the spring from the equalizer under the drivers door and equalizer.

3. Remove the left rear cable from the front cable at the retainer.

4. Remove the cable retainer and cable from the caliper parking lever bracket using a cable release tool J-37043 or equivalent.

To install:

1. Install the cable-to-bracket and cable support.

2. Install the cable-to-brake lever and cable retainer.

3. Install the left rear cable-to-front cable with the retainer.

4. Install the equalizer and spring.

5. Adjust the parking brake as outlined in this chapter.

6. Lower the vehicle and check operation.

Right Rear Cable

1. Raise the vehicle and support with jack-stands.

2. Remove the spring from the equalizer under the drivers door and equalizer.

3. Remove the cable from the underbody bracket using a cable release tool J-37043 or equivalent.

4. Remove the bolts from the clips above the fuel tank.

5. Remove the cable retainer and cable from the caliper parking lever bracket using a cable release tool J-37043 or equivalent.

To install:

1. Position the cable above the fuel tank.

2. Install the cable-to-bracket and cable support.

3. Install the cable-to-brake lever and cable retainer.

4. Install the clips above the fuel tank.

5. Install the cable-to-underbody brackets.

6. Install the equalizer and spring.

7. Adjust the parking brake as outlined in this chapter.

8. Lower the vehicle and check operation.

PARKING BRAKE ADJUSTMENT

1. Apply the parking brake pedal three times with heavy force.

2. Do not apply the main brake pedal during this step. Fully apply and release the parking brake three times.

3. Raise the vehicle and support with jackstands.

4. Make sure the parking brake is fully released.

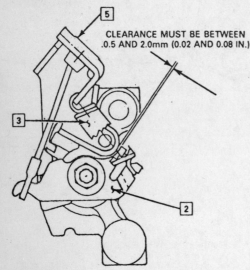

CLEARANCE MUST BE BETWEEN .0.5 AND 2.0mm (0.02 AND 0.08 IN.)

2. Lever
3. Return spring
5. Bracket

Parking brake adjustment

5. Remove the rear wheel assemblies and install two lug nuts to retain the rotors.

6. The parking brake levers at the calipers should be against the lever stop on the caliper housing. If not against the stops, check the cables for binding.

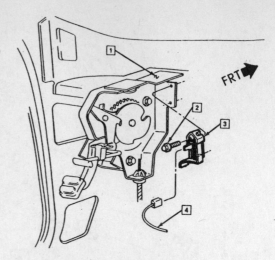

1. Parking brake lever assembly
2. Screw
3. Switch
4. Electrical harness

Parking brake lever and switch assembly

7. Tighten the parking brake cable at the adjuster until either the right or left lever reaches the dimensions shown in the "Cable Adjustment" illustration in this section.

8. Operate the parking brake several times to check adjustments. A firm pedal should be present.

9. Remove the two wheel lugs, install the rear wheels and lower the vehicle.

Parking Brake Cables

REMOVAL AND INSTALLATION

1. Disconnect the negative (–) battery cable.

2. Raise the vehicle and support with jackstands.

3. Loosen the parking brake cable equalizer under the drivers door.

4. Remove the front cable from the rear cable.

5. Remove the nut from the underbody bracket.

Brake Specifications

All specifications in inches

| Years | Models | Master Cylinder Bore | Brake Disc | | Minimum Lining Thickness | |
			Minimum Thickness	Maximum Run-out	Front	Rear
1988	All	0.945	F 0.972 R 0.429	0.003	3/32	3/32
1989–90	All	0.945	F 0.972 R 0.429	0.004	3/32	3/32

6. Lower the vehicle partially and remove the lower door sill trim plate.

7. Remove the drivers side sound insulator panel.

8. Fold the carpeting back and disconnect the electrical connector from the parking brake switch.

9. Remove the two release handle-to-instrument panel tie bar screws.

10. Remove the four lever assembly-to-body mounting bolts.

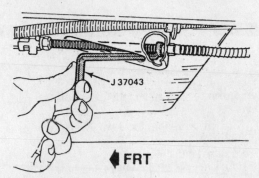

Parking brake cable release tool

11. Remove the cable from the ratcheting gear.

12. Remove the cable from the lever assembly using the cable release tool J-37043 or equivalent.

13. Remove the lever assembly from the vehicle.

To install:

1. Install the lever assembly and attach the cable to the mounting and ratcheting gear.

2. Install the four mounting bolts and torque to 18 ft. lbs. (25 Nm).

3. Install the two release handle-to-instrument panel tie bar screws.

4. Connect the parking brake switch and negative battery cable.

5. Reinstall the carpeting, sound insulator and lower door sill trim plate.

6. Raise the vehicle and support with jackstands.

7. Install the nut-to-underbody bracket and front cable-to-rear cable.

8. Adjust the parking brake cable as outlined in this chapter.

9. Lower the vehicle and check for proper operation.

Body

10

EXTERIOR

Body

You can repair most minor auto body damage yourself. Minor damage usually falls into one of several categories: (1) small scratches and dings in the paint that can be repaired with out the use of body filler, (2) deep scratches and dents that require body filler, but do not require pulling, or hammering metal back into shape and (3) rust-out repairs. The repair sequences illustrated in this chapter are typical of these types of repairs. If you want to get involved in more complicated repairs including pulling or hammering sheet metal back into shape, you will probably need more detailed instructions. Chilton's Minor Auto Body Repair, 2nd Edition is a comprehensive guide to repairing auto body damage yourself.

TOOLS AND SUPPLIES

The list of tools and equipment you may need to fix minor body damage ranges from very basic hand tools to a wide assortment of specialized body tools. Most minor scratches, dings and rust holes can be fixed using an electric drill, wire wheel or grinder attachment, half-round plastic file, sanding block, various grades of sandpaper (#36, which is coarse through #600, which is fine) in both wet and dry types, auto body plastic, primer, touch-up paint, spreaders, newspaper and masking tape.

Most manufacturers of auto body repair products began supplying materials to professionals. Their knowledge of the best, most-used products has been translated into body repair kits for the do-it-yourselfer. Kits are available from a number of manufacturers and contain the necessary materials in the required amounts for the repair identified on the package.

Kits are available for a wide variety of uses, including:
- Rusted out metal
- All purpose kit for dents and holes
- Fiberglass repair kit
- Epoxy kit for restyling

Kits offer the advantage of buying what you need for the job. There is little waste and little chance of materials going bad from not being used. The same manufacturers also merchandise all of the individual products used - spreaders, dent pullers, fiberglass cloth, polyester resin, cream hardener, body filler, body files, sandpaper, sanding discs and holders, primer, spray paint, etc.

CAUTION: *Most of the products you will be using contain harmful chemicals, so be extremely careful. Always read the complete label before opening the containers. When you put them away for future use, be sure they are out of children's reach!*

Most auto body repair kits contain all the materials you need to do the job right in the kit. So, if you have a small rust spot or dent you want to fix, check the contents of the kit before you run out and buy any additional tools.

Doors

REMOVAL AND INSTALLATION

1. Mark the location of the door hinge straps on the door.
2. Remove the rubber conduit and electrical connections from the door.
3. Remove the body side check link screw (door slider).
4. With an assistant, support the door with a jack.
5. Remove the hinge pin bolts.

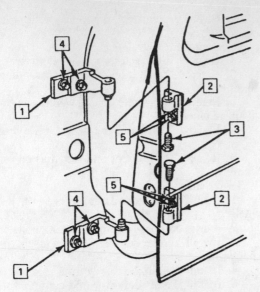

1. Body side hinge
2. Door side hinge
3. 53 inch lbs.
4. 34 inch lbs.
5. 20 ft. lbs.

Door hinge attachment

6. Remove the door from the hinges with an assistant.

To install:

1. Position the door over the hinges with an assistant and floor jack.

2. Apply Loktite® to the hinge bolts and install the door. Torque the bolts to 62 inch lbs. (7 Nm).

3. Make sure the door is in proper alignment with the frame and striker. If the door is not in alignment, refer to door alignment in this section.

4. Install the body side check link screw, electrical wiring and conduit, if so equipped.

DOOR ALIGNMENT

Adjust the up and down, in and out by loosening the four hinge-to-door retaining bolts and move to the desired position. An assistant is recommended to perform this procedure. Torque the bolts to 18 ft. lbs. (24 Nm).

Hood

REMOVAL AND INSTALLATION

NOTE: *Always remove the hood assembly with an assistant present. Cover the entire area with well padded blankets to prevent damage to the painted surfaces. The hood is heavy and may cause severe damage if not removed carefully.*

Mark the hood hinge for proper installation and place covers over the front fenders and lower windshield to prevent damage. With an

assistant, remove the hinge-to-hood bolts and lift the hood clear of the vehicle.

To install, position the hood onto the hinges and loosely install the hinge bolts. Align the hood-to-body and torque the hinge bolts to 20 ft. lbs. (27 Nm).

Trunk Lid

REMOVAL AND INSTALLATION

NOTE: *Always remove the trunk lid assembly with an assistant present. Cover the entire area with well padded blankets to prevent damage to the painted surfaces. The trunk lid is heavy and may cause severe damage if not removed carefully.*

1. Disconnect the negative (–) battery cable and electrical connectors to the trunk lid, if so equipped.

2. Tie a string to the wire harness assembly

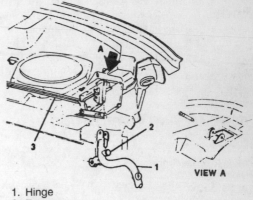

VIEW A

1. Hinge
2. Bumper
3. Torque rods

Trunk lid hinge positioning

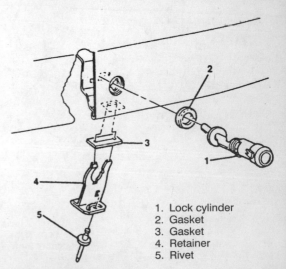

1. Lock cylinder
2. Gasket
3. Gasket
4. Retainer
5. Rivet

Trunk lid lock cylinder

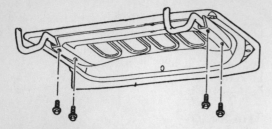

Trunk lid removal

and pull the wire out of the lid. Allow enough string so that when the lid is removed, the wire can be threaded through upon installation.

3. With an assistant, remove the four trunk lid retaining bolts and trunk lid.

To install:

1. With an assistant, install the trunk lid over the hinges.

2. Install the four retaining bolts and torque to 18 ft. lbs. (25 Nm).

3. Pull the string through the lid until the wire harness is through the inner lid. Reconnect the wiring harnesses, if so equipped.

4. Connect the negative (–) battery cable.

5. Align the trunk lid by moving the lid to the proper position and tighten the hinge bolts.

Bumpers

REMOVAL AND INSTALLATION

Front

CUTLASS SUPREME

1. Disconnect the negative (–) battery cable.

2. Raise the vehicle and support with jackstands.

3. Remove the air deflector.

4. Remove the fascia-to-wheelwell screws.

5. Remove the fascia-to-body retaining nuts.

6. Remove the upper and lower fascia-to-body retainers.

7. Remove the bumper-to-body retaining bolts.

8. Remove the bumper and fascia as an assembly.

To install:

1. Install the bumper assembly onto the vehicle.

2. Install bumper-to-body retaining bolts.

3. Install the upper and lower fascia-to-body retainers.

4. Install the fascia-to-body nuts.

5. Install the air deflector and connect the negative (–) battery cable.

REGAL

1. Disconnect the negative (–) battery cable.

2. Raise the vehicle and support with jackstands.

3. Remove the chrome strip bracket, air deflector and center push retainers.

4. Remove the fascia-to-wheelwell screws.

5. Remove the upper and lower fascia-to-body retaining nuts (right and left).

6. Remove the bumper guards.

7. Remove the lower fascia-to-bumper nuts (center).

8. Unplug the top fascia retaining tabs.

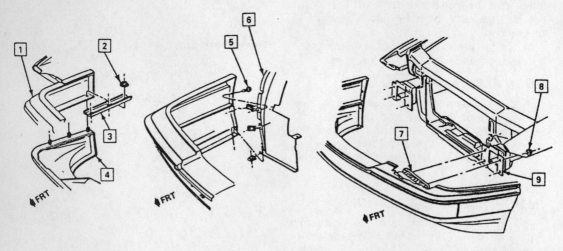

1. Upper fascia	4. Lower fascia	7. Mounting bracket
2. 45 inch lbs	5. 14 inch lbs	8. 18 ft. lbs.
3. Reinforcement	6. Inner fender liner	9. Bumper mounting bracket

Front bumper — Regal

9. Remove the bumper-to-body bolts and bumper assembly.

To install:

1. Install the bumper and fascia assembly.
2. Install the top fascia retaining tabs.
3. Install the bumper-to-body bolts.
4. Install the lower fascia-to-bumper nuts (center).
5. Install the bumper guards.
6. Install the upper and lower fascia-to-bumper nuts (right and left).
7. Install the fascia-to-wheelwell screws.

8. Install the center push retainers, air deflector, chrome strip bracket and connect the negative (–) battery cable.

LUMINA

1. Disconnect the negative (–) battery cable.
2. Raise the vehicle and support with jackstands.
3. Remove the valance panels.
4. Remove the fascia-to-fender nuts.
5. Remove the bumper-to-body nuts.
6. Remove the assembly from the vehicle.

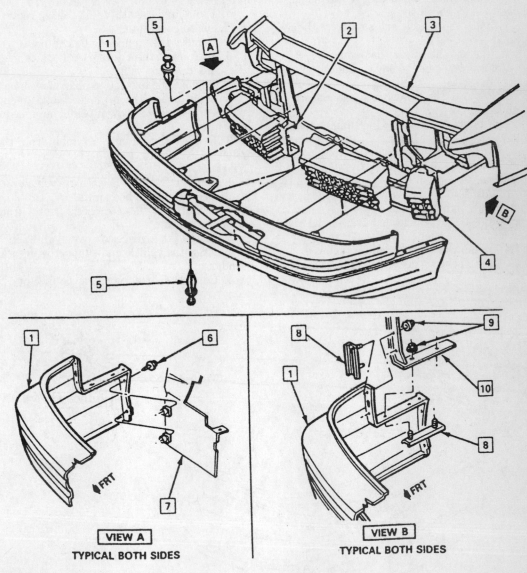

VIEW A
TYPICAL BOTH SIDES

VIEW B
TYPICAL BOTH SIDES

1. Fascia
2. Impact bar
3. Body
4. Energy absorber
5. Push-on retainer

6. 18 inch lbs.
7. Fender liner
8. Reinforcement
9. 45 inch lbs.
10. Fender

Front bumper — Cutlass Supreme

To install:

1. Position the bumper assembly onto the body and install the bumper-to-body nuts. Torque the nuts to 18 ft. lbs. (24 Nm).

2. Install the fascia-to-body nuts.

3. Install the bumper-to-body nuts.

4. Install the valance panels and connect the negative (–) battery cable.

GRAND PRIX

1. Disconnect the negative (–) battery cable.

2. Raise the hood and remove the top fascia bolts.

3. Raise the vehicle and support with jack-stands.

4. Remove the turn signal lamps.

5. Remove the front valance-to-fascia bolts.

6. Remove the fender-to-fascia screws on both sides.

7. Remove the right and left reinforcement and fascia-to-fender bolts.

8. Remove the vacuum tank if in the way.

9. Remove the fascia from the vehicle.

To install:

1. Position the fascia onto the vehicle and install the top bolts finger tight.

2. Raise the vehicle and install the right and left fascia-to-fender bolts.

3. Install the vacuum tank if removed.

4. Install the fender-to-fascia bolts on both sides.

5. Install the valance panel, turn signal lamps and lower the vehicle.

6. Tighten the top fascia bolts and connect the negative (–) battery cable.

Rear Bumper

CUTLASS SUPREME

1. Disconnect the negative (–) battery cable.

2. Raise the vehicle and support with jack-stands.

3. Remove the splash shield-to-upper and lower fascia screws.

4. From underneath the vehicle, remove the fascia-to-body nuts.

5. Remove the bumper-to-body nuts.

6. Disconnect the side marker lamp connections and lower the vehicle.

7. Remove the luggage compartment liner.

8. From inside the luggage compartment, remove the fascia-to-body nuts and bumper-to-body nuts.

9. Remove the bumper assembly from the vehicle.

To install:

1. Position the bumper onto the vehicle and install the bumper-to-body nuts.

2. Install the fascia-to-body nuts from inside the vehicle.

3. Install the luggage compartment liner.

4. Raise the vehicle and support with jack-stands.

5. Connect side marker lamp connectors.

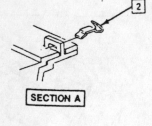

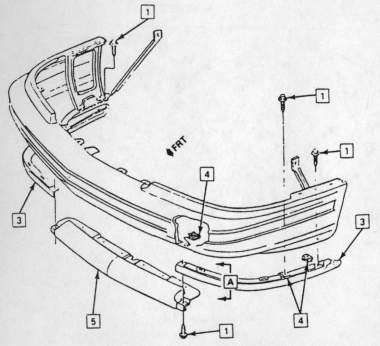

1. 45 inch lbs.
2. Retainer
3. Outer valance panel
4. J–nut
5. Center valance panel

Front bumper — Lumina

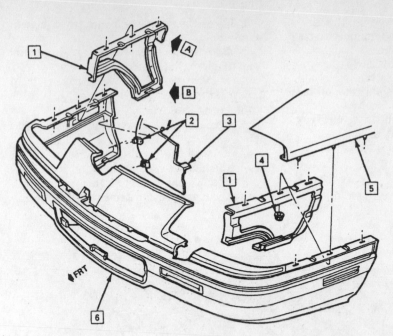

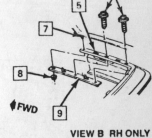

1. Reinforcement
2. Body nut
3. Fender liner
4. 90 inch lbs.
5. Fender
6. Fascia

Front bumper — Grand Prix

6. Install the bumper-to-body nuts from underneath the vehicle.

7. Install the fascia-to-body nuts from underneath the vehicle.

8. Install the upper and lower fascia-to-splash shield screws.

9. Lower the vehicle and connect the negative (–) battery cable.

REGAL

1. Disconnect the negative (–) battery cable.

2. Remove the splash shield screws on both sides.

3. Remove the fascia-to-body screws from inside the luggage compartment.

4. Remove the bumper-to-body nuts and bumper.

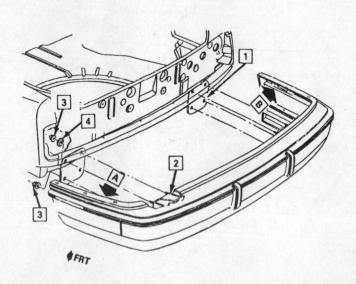

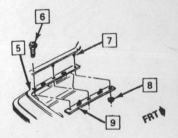

1. Rear end panel
2. Impact bar
3. 18 ft. lbs.
4. Washer
5. Rear fascia
6. Sealing screw
7. Rear quarter panel
8. 45 inch lbs.
9. Fascia reinforcement

VIEW A LH ONLY

Rear bumper — Regal

To install:

1. Install the fascia and bumper-to-body nuts.

2. Install the screws inside the luggage compartment.

3. Install the splash shield screws on both sides.

4. Install the fascia-to-body screws from inside the luggage compartment.

5. Connect the negative (–) battery cable.

LUMINA

1. Disconnect the negative (–) battery cable.

2. Raise the vehicle and support with jack-stands.

3. Remove the fascia-to-quarter panel nuts from underneath the vehicle.

4. Remove the bumper-to-body nuts from underneath the vehicle.

5. Lower the vehicle.

6. Remove the luggage compartment trim panel.

7. Remove the fascia-to-body screws from inside the luggage compartment.

8. Remove the bumper-to-body nuts from inside the luggage compartment and bumper.

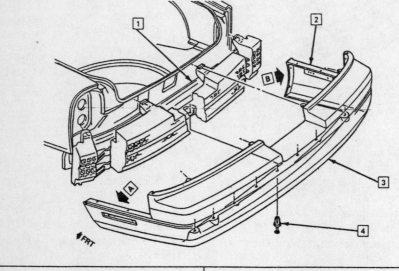

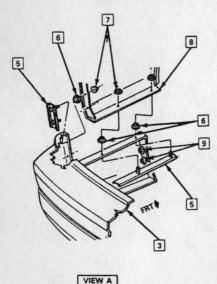

| VIEW A | VIEW B |

1. Impact bar
2. Energy absorber
3. Fascia

4. Retainer
5. Reinforcement
6. Push-on nut

7. 89 inch lbs.
8. Body quarter panel
9. 18 inch lbs.

Rear bumper — Cutlass Supreme

To install:

1. Position the bumper onto the vehicle.

2. Install the bumper-to-body nuts from inside the luggage compartment.

3. Install the fascia-to-quarter panel screws from inside the luggage compartment.

4. Install the luggage compartment trim panel.

5. Raise the vehicle and support with jackstands.

6. Install the bumper-to-body nuts from underneath the vehicle.

7. Lower the vehicle and connect the negative (–) battery cable.

GRAND PRIX

1. Disconnect the negative (–) battery cable.

2. Remove luggage compartment liner.

3. Remove the two right side and one left

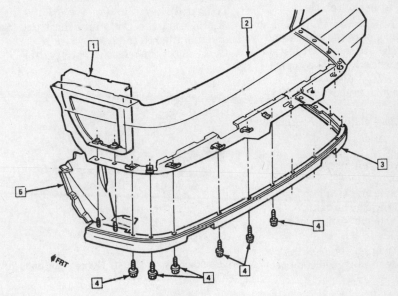

1. Reinforcement
2. Fascia
3. Valance panel
4. 54 inch lbs.
5. Splash shield

Rear bumper — Grand Prix

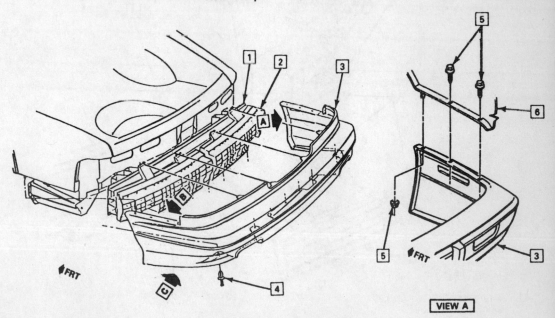

4. Retainer
5. 89 inch lbs.
6. Quarter panel

1. Impact bar
2. Energy absorber
3. Fascia

Rear bumper — Lumina

side fascia-to-body nuts from inside the luggage compartment.

4. Raise the vehicle and support with jack-stands.

5. Remove the right and left inner fenders.

6. Remove the two left and one right fascia-to-body nuts from underneath the vehicle.

7. Remove the lower reinforcement and fascia-to-body bolts.

8. Remove the retainers.

9. Remove the license plate lamp electrical connector and bumper from the vehicle.

To install:

1. Position the bumper onto the vehicle and finger tighten the two right and one left fascia-to-body nuts from inside the luggage compartment.

2. Raise the vehicle and support with jack-stands.

3. Connect the license plate lamp connector.

4. Install the retainers.

5. Install the lower reinforcement and fascia-to-body nuts.

6. Install the one right and two left fascia-to-body nuts from underneath the vehicle.

7. Install the right and left fender liners.

8. Lower the vehicle.

9. Tighten the two right and one left fascia-to-body nuts from inside the luggage compartment.

10. Install the luggage compartment liner and connect the negative (–) battery cable.

Grille

REMOVAL AND INSTALLATION

1. Disconnect the negative (–) battery cable.

2. Remove the grille retaining screws at the fascia.

3. Remove the grille assembly from the vehicle.

To install:

1. Position the grille into the front fascia and install the retaining screws.

2. Connect the negative battery cable.

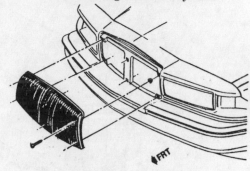

Grille assembly — Regal. Tighten the bolts to 18 inch lbs.

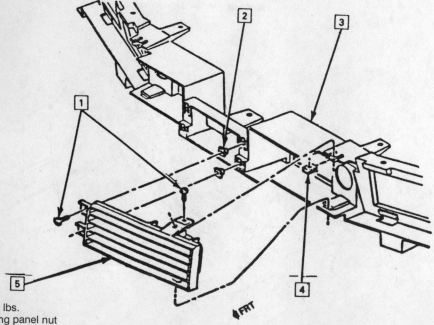

1. 18 inch lbs.
2. Mounting panel nut
3. Headlamp housing panel
4. Radiator grille nut
5. Grille

Grille assembly — Cutlass Supreme

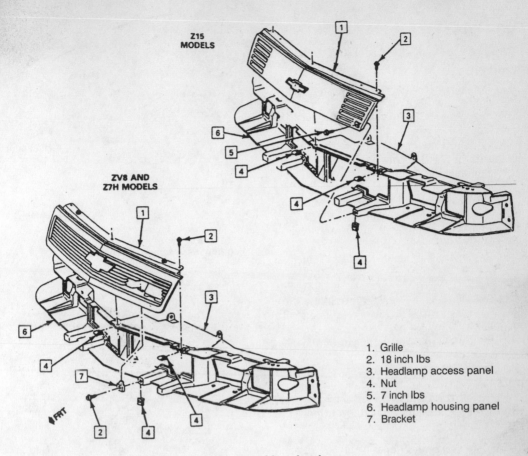

Z15
MODELS

ZV8 AND
Z7H MODELS

FRT

1. Grille
2. 18 inch lbs
3. Headlamp access panel
4. Nut
5. 7 inch lbs
6. Headlamp housing panel
7. Bracket

Grille assembly — Lumina

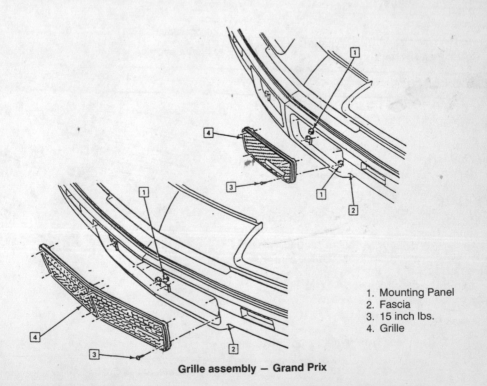

1. Mounting Panel
2. Fascia
3. 15 inch lbs.
4. Grille

Grille assembly — Grand Prix

Fog Lights

REMOVAL AND INSTALLATION

Grand Prix

1. Disconnect the negative (–) battery cable.
2. Open the hood and remove the three screws holding the cover over the rear of the lights.
3. Remove the one bolt holding the cover to the headlight housing panel.
4. Remove the cover by sliding out from under the bolt.
5. Disconnect the light electrical connector.
6. Remove the bulb socket.
7. Remove the one bolt at the top rear of the assembly.
8. Remove the assembly from the vehicle, if replacing.

To install:

1. Install the light assembly making sure the guide pins on the bottom are aligned with the holes.
2. Install the one bolt, bulb/socket and electrical connector.
3. Install the cover under the bolt and tighten.
4. Install the three cover retaining screws, connect the negative battery cable and close the hood.

Cutlass Supreme and Regal

1. Disconnect the negative (–) battery cable and the fog light connector.
2. Remove the two retaining bolts under the front bumper.
3. Install the assembly, retaining bolts and connect the negative battery cable.

Outside Mirrors

REMOVAL AND INSTALLATION

Manual

1. Remove the door trim panel as outlined in this chapter.
2. Remove the three mirror-to-door retaining nuts, mirror and filler.

To install:

1. Install the filler, mirror and retaining nuts.
2. Torque the retaining nuts in sequence to 80 inch lbs. (9 Nm). Torque sequence; center, top then bottom.
3. Install the door trim panel as outlined in this chapter.

Electric and Remote

1. Remove the door trim panel as outlined in this chapter.
2. Remove the water deflector.

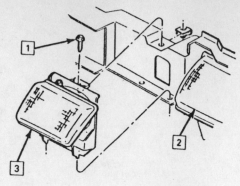

1. 89 inch lbs.
2. Headlight
3. Foglight

Fog light assembly — Grand Prix

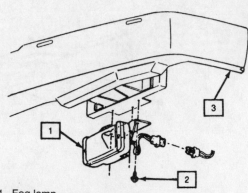

1. Fog lamp
2. Bolt
3. Impact bar

Fog light assembly — Regal

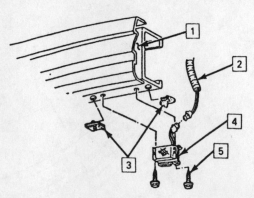

1. Bumper
2. Wiring harness
3. J-nuts
4. Fog lamp
5. 89 inch lbs.

Fog light assembly — Cutlass Supreme

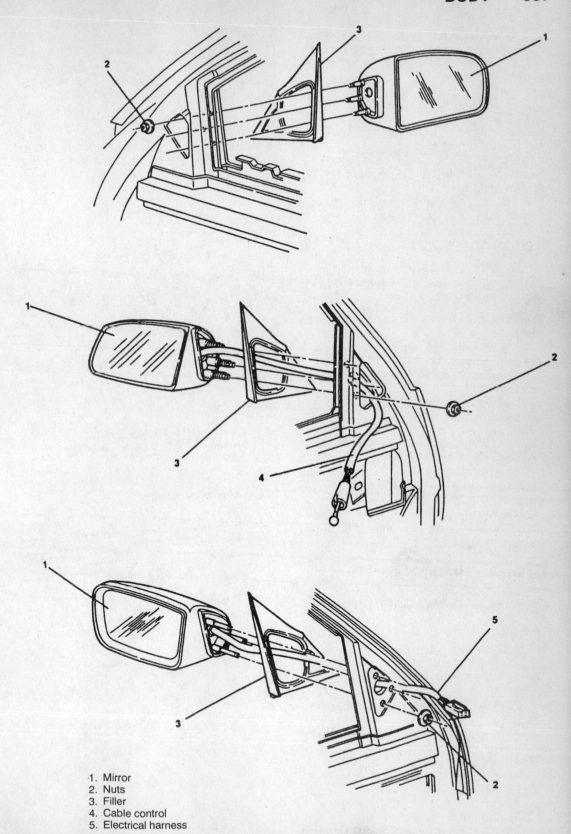

1. Mirror
2. Nuts
3. Filler
4. Cable control
5. Electrical harness

Outside mirrors

3. Remove the remote control cable or electrical connector from the inner panel.

4. Remove the three mirror-to-door retaining nuts, mirror and filler.

To install:

1. Install the filler, mirror and retaining nuts.

2. Install the control cable or electrical connector to the inner panel.

3. Torque the retaining nuts in sequence to 80 inch lbs. (9 Nm). Torque sequence; center, top then bottom.

4. Install the water deflector and door trim panel as outlined in this chapter.

MIRROR GLASS REPLACEMENT

CAUTION: *Wear gloves and safety glasses to prevent personal injury when removing broken mirror glass.*

NOTE: *1. Place masking or duct tape over the entire mirror glass.*

2. Cover the painted surfaces of the vehicle to prevent damage to the paint surfaces.

3. Break the mirror face with a small hammer.

4. Remove all pieces of mirror glass from the frame.

5. Clean all adhesive from the mirror frame with solvent.

To install:

1. Remove the paper backing from the back side of the new mirror to expose the adhesive.

2. Center the mirror in the frame and press firmly to ensure the adhesion of the mirror glass-to-frame.

Antenna

REMOVAL AND INSTALLATION

Fixed

1. Remove the antenna mast from the antenna lead.

2. Remove the nut from the top of the quarter panel.

3. Remove the luggage compartment side trim panel.

4. Remove the antenna securing bracket from the quarter panel.

5. Disconnect the antenna lead and remove the antenna assembly.

To install:

1. Install the bracket, nut and bolt.

2. Install the antenna and lead.

3. Install the nut to the top of the quarter panel.

4. Install the mast-to-antenna lead.

Power

The power antenna may be replaced separately from the motor. The mast should be cleaned when it becomes dirty, but do not lubricate.

1. With the antenna in the **DOWN** position, remove the antenna mast nut.

NOTE: *Do NOT pull the antenna mast up by hand. Clean the bottom the contact spring with contact cleaner and set aside to be reused.*

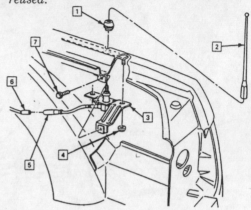

1. Nut	5. Antenna lead
2. Antenna	6. Antenna lead to radio
3. Bracket	7. 54 inch lbs.
4. Nut	

Fixed antenna mounting

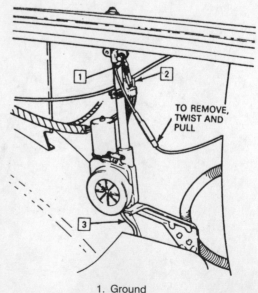

1. Ground
2. Relay
3. Drain tube

Power antenna mounting

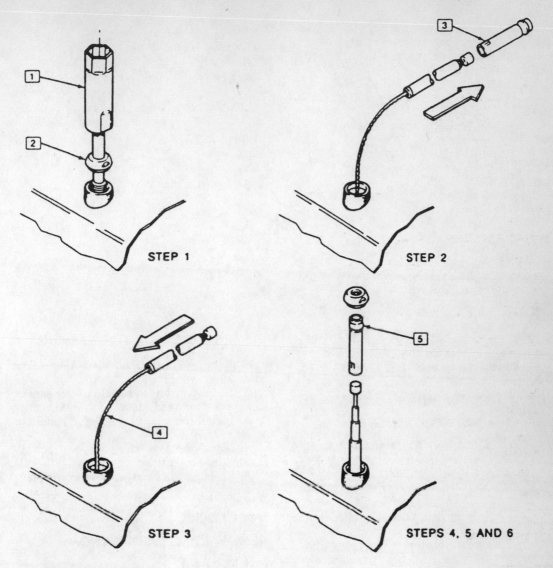

STEP 1

STEP 2

STEP 3

STEPS 4, 5 AND 6

1. Socket
2. Antenna mast nut
3. Contact spring
4. Serrated side of cable must face antenna
5. Flanged end

Power antenna replacement

2. With the ignition key in the **ON** position, turn the radio **ON** to raise the antenna out of the motor.

To install:

1. Insert the plastic cable into the housing and stop when about 12 inches of resistance if felt.

2. The serrated side of the cable MUST face the antenna motor. Activate the motor to the down position until the plastic cable retracts into the housing.

3. If the cable do NOT retract into the housing, rotate the cable until the cable is pulled into the housing while the motor is operating.

4. Install the contact spring to the antenna. Make sure the flanged end of the contact spring faces upward.

5. Install the antenna nut and cycle the antenna several times to check operation.

6. Remove the luggage compartment side trim panel if the entire antenna assembly has to be replaced.

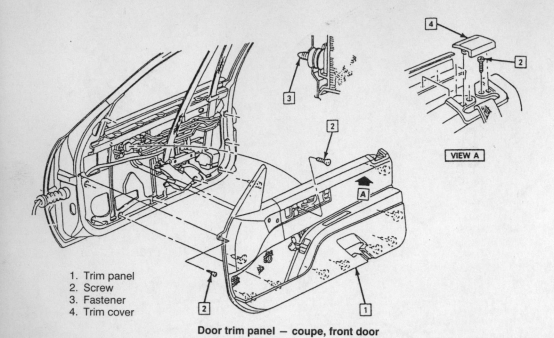

1. Trim panel
2. Screw
3. Fastener
4. Trim cover

VIEW A

Door trim panel — coupe, front door

INTERIOR

Door Trim Panels

REMOVAL AND INSTALLATION

NOTE: *Use a door trim panel and garnish clip remover tool J-24595-C or equivalent to remove the door trim panel. Failure to use this tool may cause damage to the retaining clips, panel backing and door.*

1. Remove the door latch trim plate (coupe and sedan front doors).

2. Remove the ashtray (sedan rear doors).

3. Remove the seat belt retractor cover (coupe and sedan front doors). Use the door trim panel removing tool J-24595-C to release the clip retainers.

4. Remove the door lock trim plate and the power window switch, if so equipped.

5. Remove the window regulator handle by removing the inner retaining clip, if so equipped.

6. Remove the remote mirror control, if so equipped.

7. Remove the trim panel retaining screws.

8. Remove the door trim panel using the door trim panel removing tool J-24595-C or equivalent.

9. Disconnect all electrical and remote mirror controls.

To install:

1. Install the wiring harnesses through the openings in the panel, if so equipped.

2. Position the trim panel to the door and align the clips. Press the trim panel to the door until all the clips are fully engaged. Align all the holes before engaging the clips.

3. Install the screws, remote mirror control and inside door handle bezel, if so equipped.

4. Install the window regulator handle or power window switch.

5. Install the door trim plate, seat belt retractor cover or ashtray.

6. Check each operation for completion of repair.

Door Locks

REMOVAL AND INSTALLATION

Lock Module

2-Door Coupe

1. Disconnect the negative (–) battery cable.

2. Remove the door trim panel as outlined in this section.

3. Loosen the water deflector to gain access to the lock module.

4. Remove the screw and nut securing the cover assembly to the door.

5. Remove the door handle cover assembly.

6. Remove the lock cylinder-to-lock rod and outside handle-to-lock rod.

7. Remove the screws securing the lock assembly to the door.

8. Using a 3/16 inch drill bit, drill out the rivets securing the lock module to the door.

9. Disconnect the power lock electrical connector and remove the lock module.

To install:

1. Install the lock module through the access hole in the door inner panel.

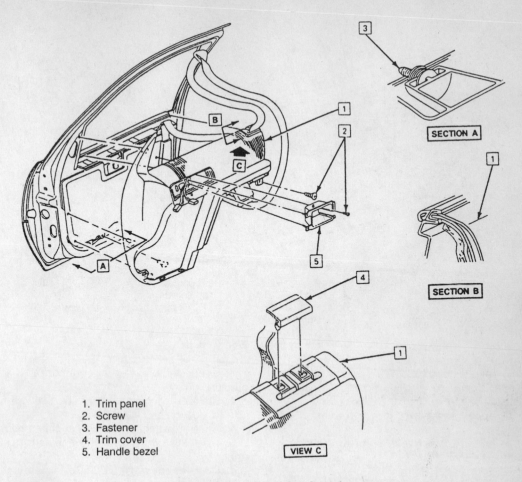

SECTION A

SECTION B

VIEW C

1. Trim panel
2. Screw
3. Fastener
4. Trim cover
5. Handle bezel

Door trim panel — sedan, front door

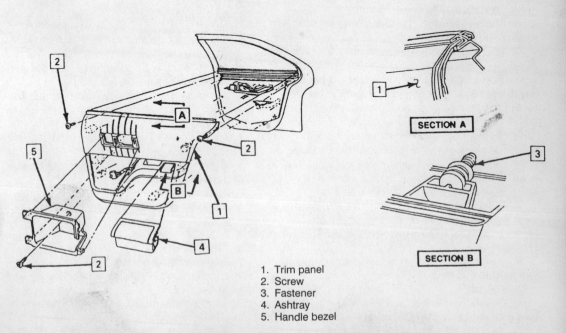

SECTION A

SECTION B

1. Trim panel
2. Screw
3. Fastener
4. Ashtray
5. Handle bezel

Door trim panel — sedan, rear door

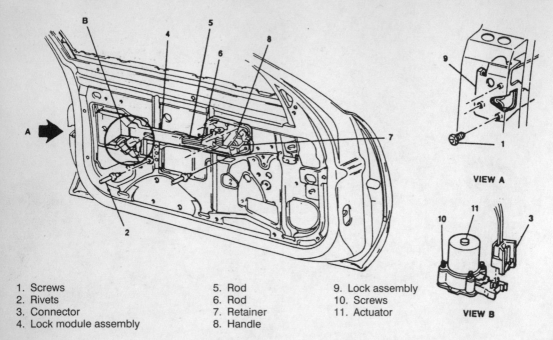

1. Screws
2. Rivets
3. Connector
4. Lock module assembly

5. Rod
6. Rod
7. Retainer
8. Handle

9. Lock assembly
10. Screws
11. Actuator

VIEW A

VIEW B

Door lock system — 2-door coupe

2. Install the lock assembly screws at a 90 degree angle to prevent cross threading. Torque the screws to 62 inch lbs. (7 Nm).

3. Install the power lock connector, if so equipped.

4. Install the rivets securing the lock module-to-door. Use $3/16$ in. × $1/4$ in. peel type rivets.

5. Install the outside handle and lock cylinder lock rods. Check the locking operation before going any further.

6. Install the door handle cover, retaining screws and nuts.

7. Install the water deflector and door trim panel.

8. Connect the negative battery cable and check all door operations for completion of repair.

4-DOOR SEDAN

1. Disconnect the negative (–) battery cable.

2. Remove the door trim panel and water deflector.

3. Remove the lock cylinder lock rod.

4. Remove the retaining screws and rivets. Drill the rivets out with a $3/16$ inch drill bit.

5. Disconnect the power lock connector, if so equipped.

6. Remove the lock module and disconnect the handle lock rod.

To install:

1. Position the lock module onto the door and connect the handle lock rod.

2. Install the screws at a 90 degree angle to prevent cross threading.

3. Connect the power lock connector, if so equipped.

4. Install the lock module rivets. Use $3/16$ in. × $1/4$ in. peel type rivets.

5. Check the door operations at this time.

6. Install the water deflector and door trim panel.

7. Connect the negative battery cable and recheck door operations.

Lock Cylinder

2-DOOR COUPE

1. Disconnect the negative (–) battery cable.

2. Remove the door handle cover.

3. Remove the lock cylinder-to-lock rod.

4. Remove the anti-theft shield.

5. Remove the lock cylinder from the door.

To install:

1. Install the lock cylinder, anti-theft shield and shield retaining screw.

2. Connect the cylinder lock rod and handle cover assembly.

3. Check all door operations.

4. Connect the negative battery cable.

4-DOOR SEDAN

1. Disconnect the negative (–) battery cable.

2. Remove the door trim panel and water deflector. Refer to the appropriate section in this chapter.

3. Using a small flat pry bar, remove the lock cylinder retainer.

4. Disconnect the cylinder lock rod and remove the lock cylinder and gasket.

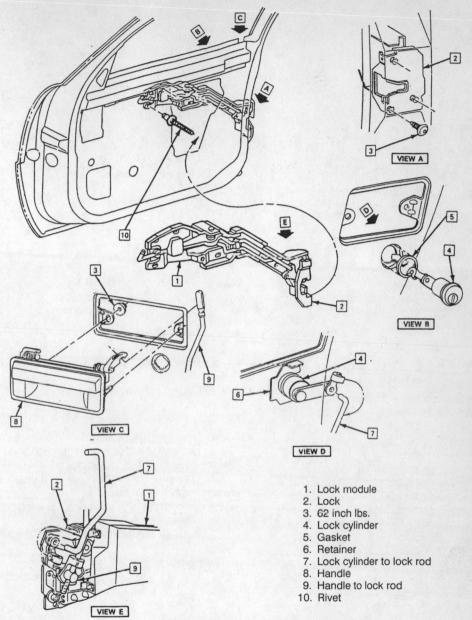

1. Lock module
2. Lock
3. 62 inch lbs.
4. Lock cylinder
5. Gasket
6. Retainer
7. Lock cylinder to lock rod
8. Handle
9. Handle to lock rod
10. Rivet

Door lock system — 4-door sedan, front. (Rear similar)

To install:

1. Install the cylinder and gasket.
2. Connect the cylinder lock rod and install the retainer with a small flat pry bar.
3. Check all door operations at this time.
4. Install the trim panel and water deflector.
5. Connect the negative battery cable.

Power Lock Actuator

The optional power door lock system has motor actuators in each door. The system is activated by a control switch on each front door. All locks are activated when any switch is pushed up or down. Each actuator has an internal circuit breaker which may require one to three minutes to reset after service.

2-DOOR COUPE

1. Disconnect the negative (−) battery cable.
2. Remove the door trim panel and water deflector as outlined in this chapter.
3. Remove the two actuator retaining screws located at opposite corners.
4. Disconnect the electrical connector and linkage.
5. Remove the actuator through the access hole.

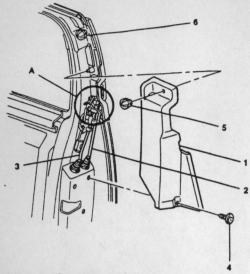

1. Cover assembly
2. Lock cylinder to lock rod
3. Outer handle to lock rod
4. Screw
5. Nut
6. Nut
7. Anti-theft shield
8. Screw
9. Lock cylinder

VIEW A

Door lock cylinder at handle — 2-door coupe

To install:

1. Install the actuator linkage, electrical connector and retaining screws.

2. Check for proper operation by cycling the system.

1. Actuator
2. Lock module
3. Rivet
4. Connector
5. Clip

VIEW A

Power lock actuator — 4-door sedan

3. Install the water deflector and trim panel.

4. Connect the negative battery cable.

4-DOOR SEDAN

1. Disconnect the negative (–) battery cable.

2. Remove the door trim panel and water deflector as outlined in this chapter.

3. Using a $\frac{3}{16}$ inch drill bit, drill out the actuator retaining rivets.

4. Disconnect the electrical connector and linkage rod.

5. Remove the actuator through the access hole.

To install:

1. Install the actuator linkage, electrical connector and retaining rivets or screws.

2. Check for proper operation by cycling the system.

3. Install the water deflector and trim panel.

4. Connect the negative battery cable.

Door Glass

REMOVAL AND INSTALLATION

Front

1. Disconnect the negative (–) battery cable.

2. Remove the door trim panel and water deflector as outlined in this chapter.

3. Remove the inner belt sealing strip and front window guide retainer.

4. Raise the window half way and push on the rear guide retainer with a flat pry bar to

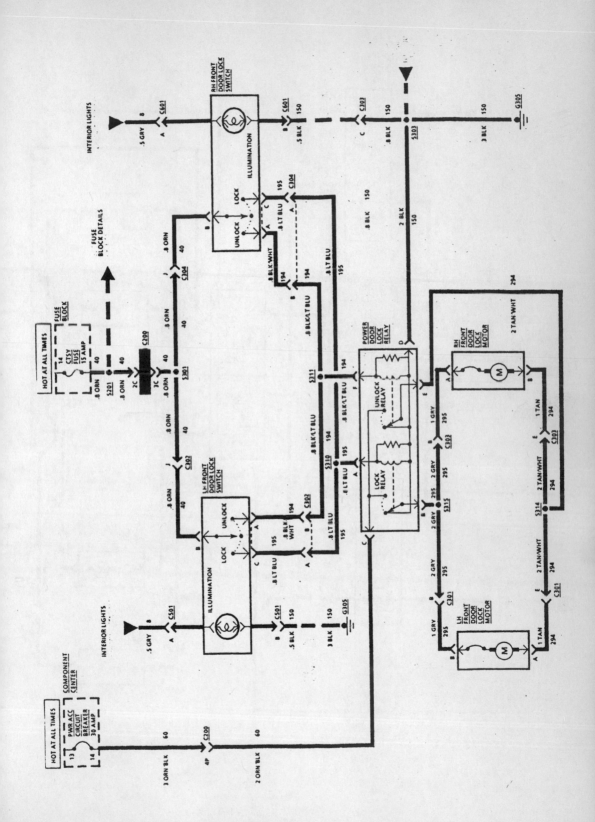

Power door lock wiring — 2-door coupe

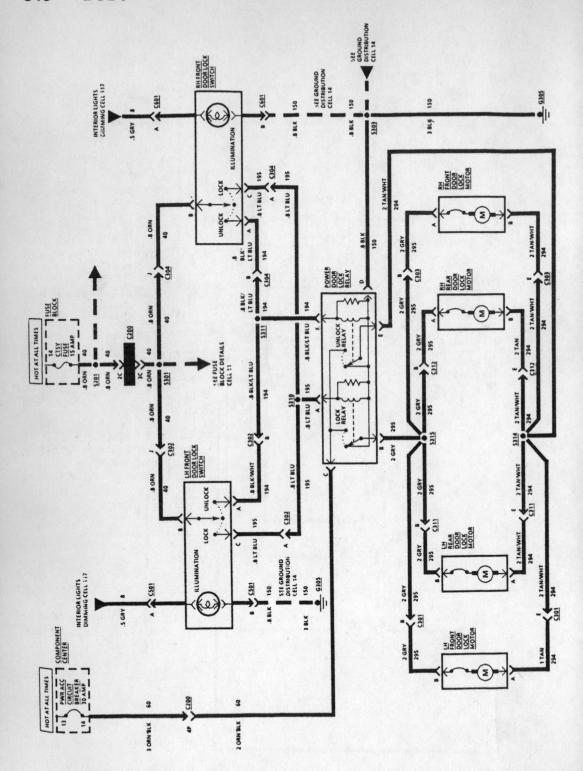

Power door lock wiring — 4-door sedan

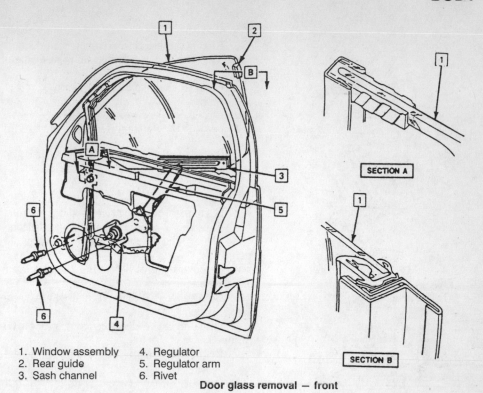

1. Window assembly
2. Rear guide
3. Sash channel
4. Regulator
5. Regulator arm
6. Rivet

SECTION A

SECTION B

Door glass removal — front

disengage the rear run channel. Lift the glass up and to the inboard side of the door frame.

To install:

1. Install the glass into the regulator arm roller and sash channel.

2. Lower the glass half way and pull rearward to engage the rear guide retainer-to-run channel.

3. Install the front window guide retainer by lowering the glass to about three inches above the belt line and locate the retainer on the door.

4. Check for proper window and door operation at this time.

5. **Adjust the door glass as follows.**

a. With the trim panel and water deflector removed, loosen the front window guide retainer bolts.

b. Cycle the glass to the full DOWN position.

c. Finger tighten the top retainer bolt and torque the bottom bolt to 53 inch lbs. (6 Nm).

d. Run the glass up to one inch from the full-up position and torque the top bolt to 53 inch lbs. (6 Nm).

e. Recheck the glass for proper operation without binding.

6. Install the inner belt sealing strip, water deflector and trim panel.

7. Connect the negative battery cable and check for proper door operation.

Rear

1. Disconnect the negative (–) battery cable.

2. Remove the door trim panel and water deflector as outlined in this chapter.

3. Remove the inner and outer belt sealing strip.

4. Remove the nuts securing the regulator sash-to-glass and place a wedge between the division channel and door outer panel.

5. Mask the outboard side of the division channel with protective tape and lower the glass to the bottom of the door.

6. Remove the front portion of the glass channel from the front door frame.

7. Make sure the glass is disengaged from the division channel and lift the glass upward and outboard of the door frame.

To install:

1. Install the glass to the door from the outboard side.

2. Install the front portion of the window channel-to-door frame by lowering the glass to the bottom.

3. Install the rear guide-to-division channel. Torque the nuts to 80 inch lbs. (9 Nm).

4. Remove the wedge and masking tape.

5. Check the window for proper operation.

6. Install the outer and inner belt sealing strips.

7. Install the water deflector and trim panel.

8. Connect the negative battery cable.

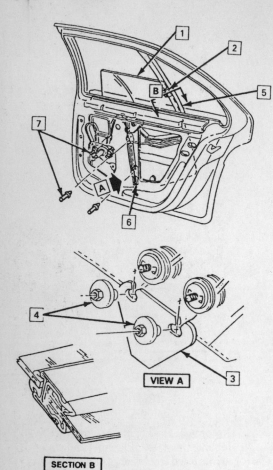

VIEW A

SECTION B

1. Window assembly
2. Rear guide
3. Regulator sash
4. 80 inch lbs.
5. Division channel
6. Regulator
7. Rivet

Door glass removal — rear

Window Regulator and Electric Motor

REMOVAL AND INSTALLATION

Front

1. Disconnect the negative (–) battery cable.
2. Tape the window in the full-up position.
3. Remove the door trim panel and water deflector.
4. Using a $1/4$ inch drill bit, drill out the regulator rivets.
5. Remove the regulator by disengaging the regulator arm from the sash channel.
6. Disconnect the electrical connectors, if so equipped.
7. If removing the electric motor, drill out the rivets using a $1/4$ inch drill bit.

To install:
1. Install the regulator through the access hole and attach the regulator arm-to-sash channel.
2. Connect the electrical connectors.
3. Install $1/4$ in. $\times$ $1/2$ in. rivets to retain the regulator. Check for proper operation.
4. Install the water deflector and trim panel.
5. Connect the negative battery cable and remove the tape.

Rear

1. Disconnect the negative (–) battery cable.
2. Tape the window in the full-up position.
3. Remove the door trim panel and water deflector.
4. Remove the nuts securing the regulator sash-to-glass.
5. Using a $1/4$ inch drill bit, drill out the regulator rivets.
6. Disconnect the electrical connectors, if so equipped.
7. Remove the regulator through the access hole.
8. If removing the electric motor, drill out the rivets using a $1/4$ inch drill bit.

To install:
1. Install the electric motor and regulator through the access hole.
2. Connect the electrical connectors.
3. Install $1/4$ in. $\times$ $1/2$ in. rivets to retain the regulator. Check for proper operation.
4. Install the retaining nuts and torque to 80 inch lbs. (9 Nm).
5. Install the water deflector and trim panel.
6. Connect the negative battery cable and remove the tape.

Inside Rear View Mirror

REMOVAL AND INSTALLATION

The rearview mirror is attached to a support which is secured to the windshield glass. A service replacement windshield glass has the support bonded to the glass assembly. To install a detached mirror support or install a new part, use the following procedures to complete the service.

1. Locate the support position at the center of the glass 3 inches from the top of the glass to the top of the support.
2. Circle the location on the outside of the glass with a wax pencil or crayon. Draw a large circle around the support circle.
3. Clean the area within the circle with household cleaner and dry with a clean towel. Repeat the procedures using rubbing alcohol.
4. Sand the bonding surface of the support

CHILTON'S
AUTO BODY
REPAIR TIPS

**Tools and Materials • Step-by-Step Illustrated Procedures
How To Repair Dents, Scratches and Rust Holes
Spray Painting and Refinishing Tips**

With a little practice, basic body repair procedures can be mastered by any do-it-yourself mechanic. The step-by-step repairs shown here can be applied to almost any type of auto body repair.

TOOLS & MATERIALS

You may already have basic tools, such as hammers and electric drills. Other tools unique to body repair — body hammers, grinding attachments, sanding blocks, dent puller, half-round plastic file and plastic spreaders — are relatively inexpensive and can be obtained wherever auto parts or auto body repair parts are sold. Portable air compressors and paint spray guns can be purchased or rented.

Auto Body Repair Kits

The best and most often used products are available to the do-it-yourselfer in kit form, from major manufacturers of auto body repair products. The same manufacturers also merchandise the individual products for use by pros.

Kits are available to make a wide variety of repairs, including holes, dents and scratches and fiberglass, and offer the advantage of buying the materials you'll need for the job. There is little waste or chance of materials going bad from not being used. Many kits may also contain basic body-working tools such as body files, sanding blocks and spreaders. Check the contents of the kit before buying your tools.

BODY REPAIR TIPS

Safety

Many of the products associated with auto body repair and refinishing contain toxic chemicals. Read all labels before opening containers and store them in a safe place and manner.

• Wear eye protection (safety goggles) when using power tools or when performing any operation that involves the removal of any type of material.

• Wear lung protection (disposable mask or respirator) when grinding, sanding or painting.

Sanding

1 Sand off paint before using a dent puller. When using a non-adhesive sanding disc, cover the back of the disc with an overlapping layer or two of masking tape and trim the edges. The disc will last considerably longer.

2 Use the circular motion of the sanding disc to grind *into* the edge of the repair. Grinding or sanding away from the jagged edge will only tear the sandpaper.

3 Use the palm of your hand flat on the panel to detect high and low spots. Do not use your fingertips. Slide your hand slowly back and forth.

WORKING WITH BODY FILLER

Mixing The Filler

Cleanliness and proper mixing and application are extremely important. Use a clean piece of plastic or glass or a disposable artist's palette to mix body filler.

1 Allow plenty of time and follow directions. No useful purpose will be served by adding more hardener to make it cure (set-up) faster. Less hardener means more curing time, but the mixture dries harder; more hardener means less curing time but a softer mixture.

2 Both the hardener and the filler should be thoroughly kneaded or stirred before mixing. Hardener should be a solid paste and dispense like thin toothpaste. Body filler should be smooth, and free of lumps or thick spots.

Getting the proper amount of hardener in the filler is the trickiest part of preparing the filler. Use the same amount of hardener in cold or warm weather. For contour filler (thick coats), a bead of hardener twice the diameter of the filler is about right. There's about a 15% margin on either side, but, if in doubt use less hardener.

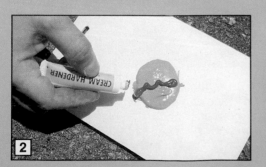

3 Mix the body filler and hardener by wiping across the mixing surface, picking the mixture up and wiping it again. Colder weather requires longer mixing times. Do not mix in a circular motion; this will trap air bubbles which will become holes in the cured filler.

Applying The Filler

1 For best results, filler should not be applied over ¼″ thick.

Apply the filler in several coats. Build it up to above the level of the repair surface so that it can be sanded or grated down.

The first coat of filler must be pressed on with a firm wiping motion.

Apply the filler in one direction only. Working the filler back and forth will either pull it off the metal or trap air bubbles.

REPAIRING DENTS

Before you start, take a few minutes to study the damaged area. Try to visualize the shape of the panel before it was damaged. If the damage is on the left fender, look at the right fender and use it as a guide. If there is access to the panel from behind, you can reshape it with a body hammer. If not, you'll have to use a dent puller. Go slowly and work the metal a little at a time. Get the panel as straight as possible before applying filler.

1 This dent is typical of one that can be pulled out or hammered out from behind. Remove the headlight cover, headlight assembly and turn signal housing.

2 Drill a series of holes ½ the size of the end of the dent puller along the stress line. Make some trial pulls and assess the results. If necessary, drill more holes and try again. Do not hurry.

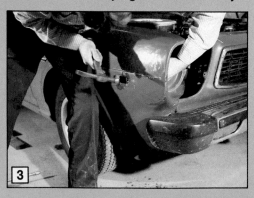

3 If possible, use a body hammer and block to shape the metal back to its original contours. Get the metal back as close to its original shape as possible. Don't depend on body filler to fill dents.

4 Using an 80-grit grinding disc on an electric drill, grind the paint from the surrounding area down to bare metal. Use a new grinding pad to prevent heat buildup that will warp metal.

5 The area should look like this when you're finished grinding. Knock the drill holes in and tape over small openings to keep plastic filler out.

6 Mix the body filler (see Body Repair Tips). Spread the body filler evenly over the entire area (see Body Repair Tips). Be sure to cover the area completely.

7 Let the body filler dry until the surface can just be scratched with your fingernail. Knock the high spots from the body filler with a body file ("Cheesegrater"). Check frequently with the palm of your hand for high and low spots.

8 Check to be sure that trim pieces that will be installed later will fit exactly. Sand the area with 40-grit paper.

9 If you wind up with low spots, you may have to apply another layer of filler.

10 Knock the high spots off with 40-grit paper. When you are satisfied with the contours of the repair, apply a thin coat of filler to cover pin holes and scratches.

11 Block sand the area with 40-grit paper to a smooth finish. Pay particular attention to body lines and ridges that must be well-defined.

12 Sand the area with 400 paper and then finish with a scuff pad. The finished repair is ready for priming and painting (see Painting Tips).

Materials and photos courtesy of Ritt Jones Auto Body, Prospect Park, PA.

REPAIRING RUST HOLES

There are many ways to repair rust holes. The fiberglass cloth kit shown here is one of the most cost efficient for the owner because it provides a strong repair that resists cracking and moisture and is relatively easy to use. It can be used on large and small holes (with or without backing) and can be applied over contoured areas. Remember, however, that short of replacing an entire panel, no repair is a guarantee that the rust will not return.

1 Remove any trim that will be in the way. Clean away all loose debris. Cut away all the rusted metal. But be sure to leave enough metal to retain the contour or body shape.

2 Grind away all traces of rust with a 24-grit grinding disc. Be sure to grind back 3-4 inches from the edge of the hole down to bare metal and be sure all traces of paint, primer and rust are removed.

3 Block sand the area with 80 or 100 grit sandpaper to get a clear, shiny surface and feathered paint edge. Tap the edges of the hole inward with a ball peen hammer.

4 If you are going to use release film, cut a piece about 2-3″ larger than the area you have sanded. Place the film over the repair and mark the sanded area on the film. Avoid any unnecessary wrinkling of the film.

5 Cut 2 pieces of fiberglass matte to match the shape of the repair. One piece should be about 1″ smaller than the sanded area and the second piece should be 1″ smaller than the first. Mix enough filler and hardener to saturate the fiberglass material (see Body Repair Tips).

6 Lay the release sheet on a flat surface and spread an even layer of filler, large enough to cover the repair. Lay the smaller piece of fiberglass cloth in the center of the sheet and spread another layer of filler over the fiberglass cloth. Repeat the operation for the larger piece of cloth.

7 Place the repair material over the repair area, with the release film facing outward. Use a spreader and work from the center outward to smooth the material, following the body contours. Be sure to remove all air bubbles.

8 Wait until the repair has dried tack-free and peel off the release sheet. The ideal working temperature is 60°-90° F. Cooler or warmer temperatures or high humidity may require additional curing time. Wait longer, if in doubt.

9 Sand and feather-edge the entire area. The initial sanding can be done with a sanding disc on an electric drill if care is used. Finish the sanding with a block sander. Low spots can be filled with body filler; this may require several applications.

10 When the filler can just be scratched with a fingernail, knock the high spots down with a body file and smooth the entire area with 80-grit. Feather the filled areas into the surrounding areas.

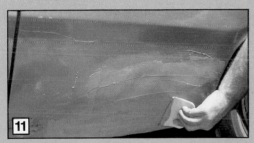

11 When the area is sanded smooth, mix some topcoat and hardener and apply it directly with a spreader. This will give a smooth finish and prevent the glass matte from showing through the paint.

12 Block sand the topcoat smooth with finishing sandpaper (200 grit), and 400 grit. The repair is ready for masking, priming and painting (see Painting Tips).

Materials and photos courtesy Marson Corporation, Chelsea, Massachusetts

PAINTING TIPS

Preparation

1 SANDING — Use a 400 or 600 grit wet or dry sandpaper. Wet-sand the area with a 1/4 sheet of sandpaper soaked in clean water. Keep the paper wet while sanding. Sand the area until the repaired area tapers into the original finish.

2 CLEANING — Wash the area to be painted thoroughly with water and a clean rag. Rinse it thoroughly and wipe the surface dry until you're sure it's completely free of dirt, dust, fingerprints, wax, detergent or other foreign matter.

3 MASKING — Protect any areas you don't want to overspray by covering them with masking tape and newspaper. Be careful not get fingerprints on the area to be painted.

4 PRIMING — All exposed metal should be primed before painting. Primer protects the metal and provides an excellent surface for paint adhesion. When the primer is dry, wet-sand the area again with 600 grit wet-sandpaper. Clean the area again after sanding.

Painting Techniques

Paint applied from either a spray gun or a spray can (for small areas) will provide good results. Experiment on an old piece of metal to get the right combination before you begin painting.

SPRAYING VISCOSITY (SPRAY GUN ONLY) — Paint should be thinned to spraying viscosity according to the directions on the can. Use only the recommended thinner or reducer and the same amount of reduction regardless of temperature.

AIR PRESSURE (SPRAY GUN ONLY) — This is extremely important. Be sure you are using the proper recommended pressure.

TEMPERATURE — The surface to be painted should be approximately the same temperature as the surrounding air. Applying warm paint to a cold surface, or vice versa, will completely upset the paint characteristics.

THICKNESS — Spray with smooth strokes. In general, the thicker the coat of paint, the longer the drying time. Apply several thin coats about 30 seconds apart. The paint should remain wet long enough to flow out and no longer; heavier coats will only produce sags or wrinkles. Spray a light (fog) coat, followed by heavier color coats.

DISTANCE — The ideal spraying distance is 8"-12" from the gun or can to the surface. Shorter distances will produce ripples, while greater distances will result in orange peel, dry film and poor color match and loss of material due to overspray.

OVERLAPPING — The gun or can should be kept at right angles to the surface at all times. Work to a wet edge at an even speed, using a 50% overlap and direct the center of the spray at the lower or nearest edge of the previous stroke.

RUBBING OUT (BLENDING) FRESH PAINT — Let the paint dry thoroughly. Runs or imperfections can be sanded out, primed and repainted.

Don't be in too big a hurry to remove the masking. This only produces paint ridges. When the finish has dried for at least a week, apply a small amount of fine grade rubbing compound with a clean, wet cloth. Use lots of water and blend the new paint with the surrounding area.

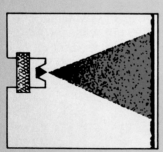

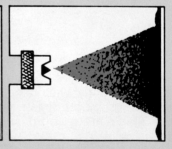

WRONG

Thin coat. Stroke too fast, not enough overlap, gun too far away.

CORRECT

Medium coat. Proper distance, good stroke, proper overlap.

WRONG

Heavy coat. Stroke too slow, too much overlap, gun too close.

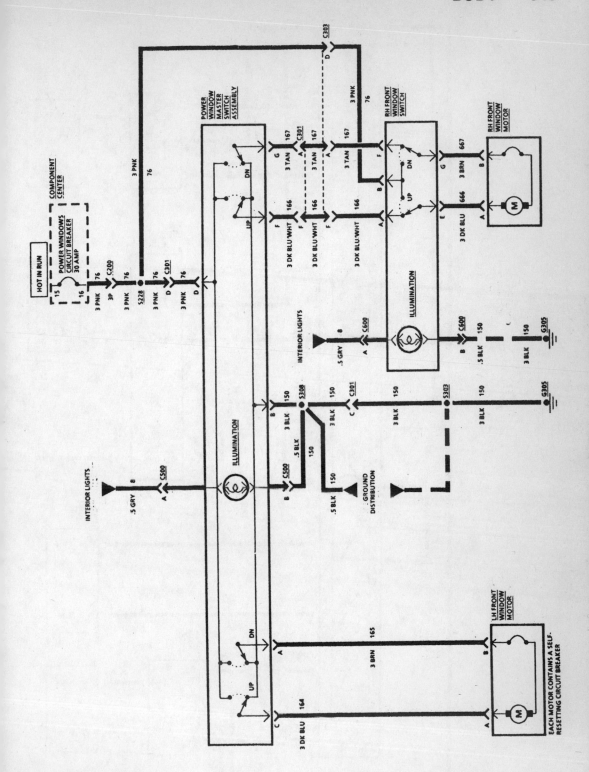

Power window wiring — 2-door

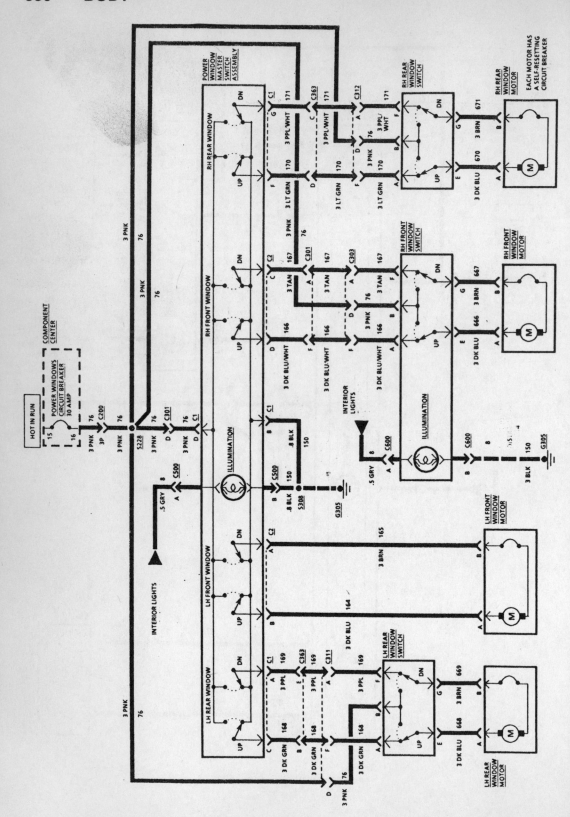

Power window wiring — 4-door

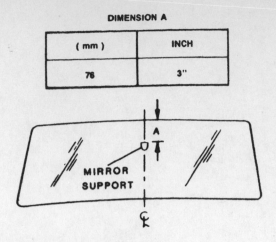

DIMENSION A

(mm)	INCH
76	3"

MIRROR SUPPORT

Rear view mirror support location

with fine grit (320–360) emery cloth or sandpaper. If the original support is being used, remove the old adhesive with rubbing alcohol and a clean towel.

5. Apply the adhesive as outlined in the kit instructions.

6. Position the support to the marked location with the rounded end UP.

7. Press the support to the glass for 30-60 seconds. Excessive adhesive can be removed after five minutes with rubbing alcohol.

CAUTION: *Do NOT apply excessive pressure to the windshield glass. The glass may break, causing personal injury.*

Seats

REMOVAL AND INSTALLATION

Front

1. Operate the seat to the full-forward position (full-forward and full-up if six way power seat).

2. Remove the track covers and front anchor bolts.

3. Operate the seat to the full-rearward position.

4. Remove the rear anchor bolts.

5. Disconnect the electrical connectors (six way power seats).

6. With an assistant, lift the seat out of the vehicle making sure the spacer washers remain in place.

NOTE: *Be careful not to damage the interior and painted surfaces when removing the seat assemblies.*

To install:

1. With an assistant, install the seat assembly into place and make sure the spacer washers are located between the floor pan and seat tracks.

2. Connect the electrical connectors (six way power seats).

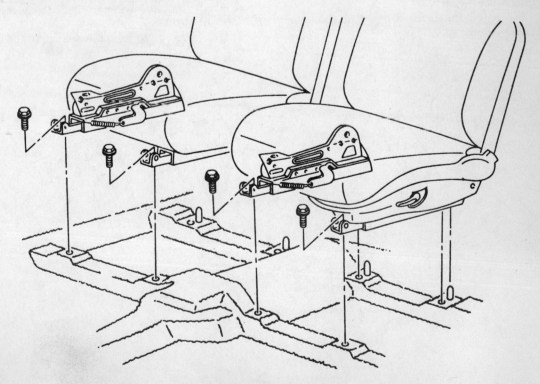

Front seat attachment

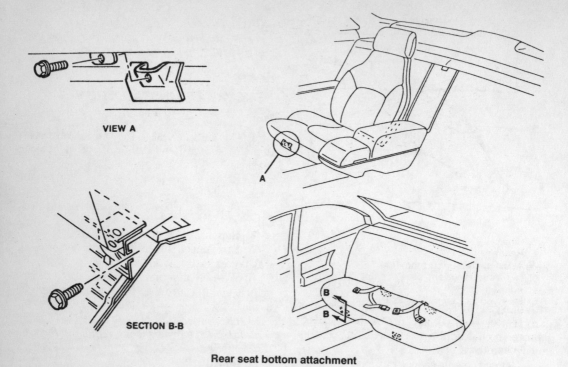

VIEW A

SECTION B-B

Rear seat bottom attachment

3. Install the rear anchor bolts and torque to 15 ft. lbs. (20 Nm).

4. Operate the seat to the full-forward position.

5. Install the front anchor bolts and torque to 20 ft. lbs. (27 Nm).

6. Install the track covers and check for proper operation.

Rear

1. Remove the two bolts at the base of the seat bottom (one bolt for buckets).

2. Remove the seat bottom by lifting up and pulling out.

3. At the bottom of the seatback, remove the two or four anchor nuts.

4. Grasp the bottom of the seatback and

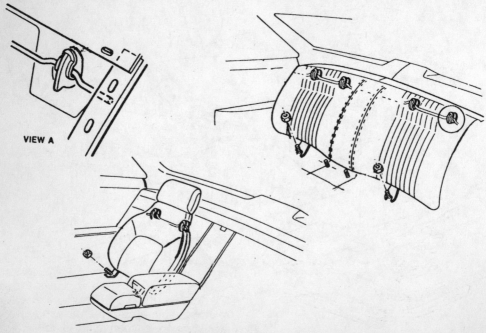

VIEW A

Rear seat support attachments. Arrows indicate offsets in seatback

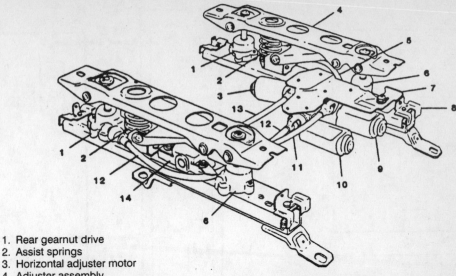

1. Rear gearnut drive
2. Assist springs
3. Horizontal adjuster motor
4. Adjuster assembly
5. Rear vertical gearnut assembly
6. Front gearnut drive
7. Motor support bracket
8. Lower channel stop
9. Front vertical gearnut motor

10. Rear vertical gearnut motor
11. Front vertical drive cable
12. Rear vertical drive cable
13. Horizontal drive cable
14. Horizontal adjustor drive

Six-way power seat assembly

swing upward to disengage the offsets on the upper frame bar. Then lift the seat and remove.

To install:

1. Slide the seatback into place and make sure the offsets are engaged to the seatback.

2. Install the retaining nuts and torque to 20 ft. lbs. (27 Nm).

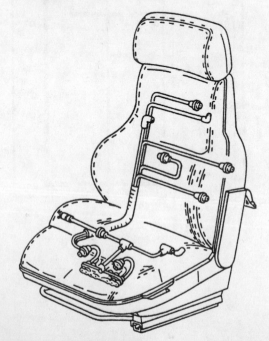

Pneumatic seat hose routing

3. Install the seat bottom into position and torque the retaining bolts to 20 ft. lbs. (27 Nm).

Head Rest

REMOVAL AND INSTALLATION

1. Fabricate a head rest removing tool as shown in the "Head Rest Removal" illustration in this section.

2. Raise the head rest to the full-up position.

3. Insert the spring clip release tool down into the left head rest shaft.

4. Push the head rest and tool down at the same time to disengage the detent from the tab.

5. Lift the head rest out after the detent has been released.

To install:

1. Install the shafts into the guides.

2. Push the head rest into the full-down position.

3. Raise the head rest to ensure the detent is properly seated.

Power Seat Motors

The six-way power seat adjusters are actuated by three 12V, reversible permanent magnet motors with built in circuit breakers. The motors drive the front and rear vertical gearnuts and a horizontal actuator. When the adjusters are at their limit of travel, an overload relay provides stall torque so the motors

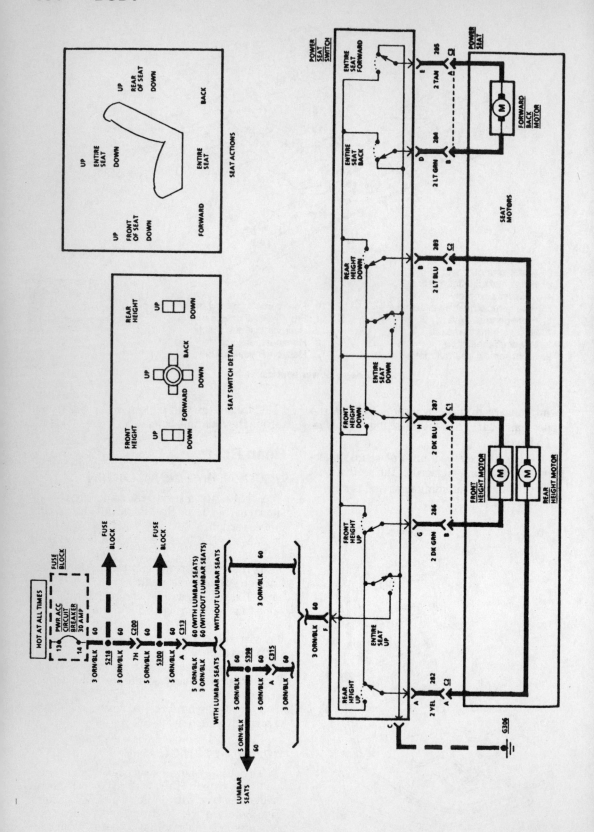

Power seat wiring

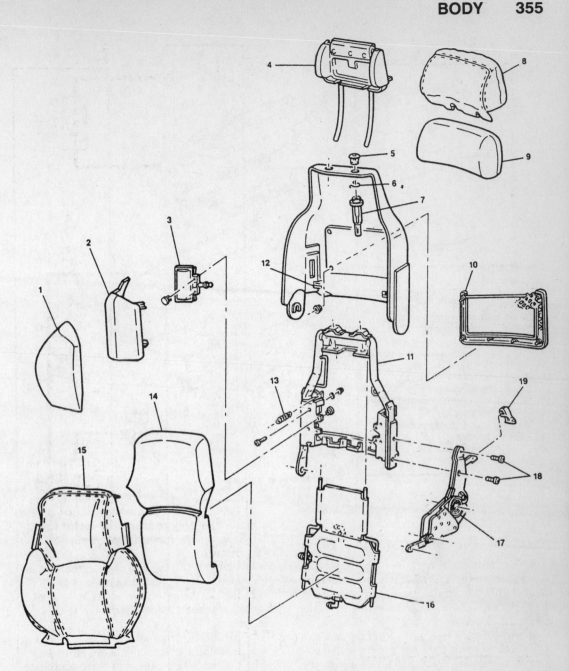

1. Wing pad
2. Outer wing
3. Wing pneumatic bladder
4. Head restraint
5. Seatback collar trim
6. Seatback collar trim retainer clip
7. Head restraint guide tube
8. Head restraint cover
9. Head restraint pad
10. Map pocket assembly

11. Seatback frame
12. Seatback trim panel lower guide channel
13. Wing return spring
14. Seatback pad
15. Seatback cover
16. Seatback pneumatic bladder assembly
17. Recliner mechanism
18. Recliner mechanism upper attaching bolts
19. Inertial lock release lever knob

Pneumatic seat support

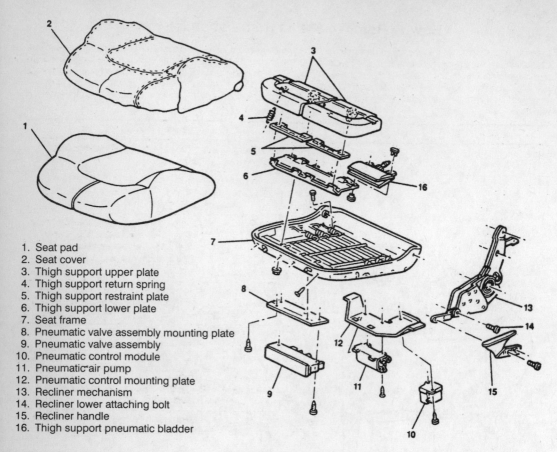

1. Seat pad
2. Seat cover
3. Thigh support upper plate
4. Thigh support return spring
5. Thigh support restraint plate
6. Thigh support lower plate
7. Seat frame
8. Pneumatic valve assembly mounting plate
9. Pneumatic valve assembly
10. Pneumatic control module
11. Pneumatic air pump
12. Pneumatic control mounting plate
13. Recliner mechanism
14. Recliner lower attaching bolt
15. Recliner handle
16. Thigh support pneumatic bladder

Pneumatic seat bottom

are not overloaded. Each motor can be serviced as a separate unit.

REMOVAL AND INSTALLATION

1. Disconnect the negative (–) battery cable.
2. Remove the seat assembly from the vehicle as outlined in this chapter.
3. Remove the adjuster assembly from the seat.
4. Remove the feed wires from the motor.
5. Remove the nuts securing the front of the motor support bracket-to-inboard adjuster. Partially withdraw the assembly from the adjuster and gearnut drives.
6. Remove the drive cables from the motor. Completely disassemble the support bracket with the motors attached.

7. Grind off the peened over ends of the grommet assembly securing the motor-to-support. Separate the motor from the support.

To install:

1. Drill out the top end of the grommet assembly using an $\frac{3}{16}$ inch drill bit.
2. Install the grommet assembly-to-motor support bracket. Secure the motor with a $\frac{3}{16}$ in. rivet.
3. Install the drive cables.
4. Install the motor-to-inboard adjuster.
5. Connect the motor feed wires and negative battery cable.
6. Install the adjuster assembly-to-seat bottom.
7. With an assistant, install the seat and check for proper operation.

How to Remove Stains from Fabric Interior

For rest results, spots and stains should be removed as soon as possible. Never use gasoline, lacquer thinner, acetone, nail polish remover or bleach. Use a 3' x 3" piece of cheesecloth. Squeeze most of the liquid from the fabric and wipe the stained fabric from the outside of the stain toward the center with a lifting motion. Turn the cheesecloth as soon as one side becomes soiled. When using water to remove a stain, be sure to wash the entire section after the spot has been removed to avoid water stains. Encrusted spots can be broken up with a dull knife and vacuumed before removing the stain.

Type of Stain	How to Remove It
Surface spots	Brush the spots out with a small hand brush or use a commercial preparation such as K2R to lift the stain.
Mildew	Clean around the mildew with warm suds. Rinse in cold water and soak the mildew area in a solution of 1 part table salt and 2 parts water. Wash with upholstery cleaner.
Water stains	Water stains in fabric materials can be removed with a solution made from 1 cup of table salt dissolved in 1 quart of water. Vigorously scrub the solution into the stain and rinse with clear water. Water stains in nylon or other synthetic fabrics should be removed with a commercial type spot remover.
Chewing gum, tar, crayons, shoe polish (greasy stains)	Do not use a cleaner that will soften gum or tar. Harden the deposit with an ice cube and scrape away as much as possible with a dull knife. Moisten the remainder with cleaning fluid and scrub clean.
Ice cream, candy	Most candy has a sugar base and can be removed with a cloth wrung out in warm water. Oily candy, after cleaning with warm water, should be cleaned with upholstery cleaner. Rinse with warm water and clean the remainder with cleaning fluid.
Wine, alcohol, egg, milk, soft drink (non-greasy stains)	Do not use soap. Scrub the stain with a cloth wrung out in warm water. Remove the remainder with cleaning fluid.
Grease, oil, lipstick, butter and related stains	Use a spot remover to avoid leaving a ring. Work from the outisde of the stain to the center and dry with a clean cloth when the spot is gone.
Headliners (cloth)	Mix a solution of warm water and foam upholstery cleaner to give thick suds. Use only foam—liquid may streak or spot. Clean the entire headliner in one operation using a circular motion with a natural sponge.
Headliner (vinyl)	Use a vinyl cleaner with a sponge and wipe clean with a dry cloth.
Seats and door panels	Mix 1 pint upholstery cleaner in 1 gallon of water. Do not soak the fabric around the buttons.
Leather or vinyl fabric	Use a multi-purpose cleaner full strength and a stiff brush. Let stand 2 minutes and scrub thoroughly. Wipe with a clean, soft rag.
Nylon or synthetic fabrics	For normal stains, use the same procedures you would for washing cloth upholstery. If the fabric is extremely dirty, use a multi-purpose cleaner full strength with a stiff scrub brush. Scrub thoroughly in all directions and wipe with a cotton towel or soft rag.

Mechanic's Data

11

General Conversion Table

Multiply By	To Convert	To	
LENGTH			
2.54	Inches	Centimeters	.3937
25.4	Inches	Millimeters	.03937
30.48	Feet	Centimeters	.0328
.304	Feet	Meters	3.28
.914	Yards	Meters	1.094
1.609	Miles	Kilometers	.621
VOLUME			
.473	Pints	Liters	2.11
.946	Quarts	Liters	1.06
3.785	Gallons	Liters	.264
.164	Cubic inches	Liters	61.02
16.39	Cubic inches	Cubic cms.	.061
28.32	Cubic feet	Liters	.0353
MASS (Weight)			
28.35	Ounces	Grams	.035
.4536	Pounds	Kilograms	2.20
—	To obtain	From	Multiply by

Multiply By	To Convert	To	
AREA			
6.45	Square inches	Square cms.	.155
.836	Square yds.	Square meters	1.196
FORCE			
4.448	Pounds	Newtons	.225
.138	Ft. lbs.	Kilogram/meters	7.23
1.356	Ft. lbs.	Newton-meters	.737
.113	In. lbs.	Newton-meters	8.844
PRESSURE			
.068	Psi	Atmospheres	14.7
6.89	Psi	Kilopascals	.145
OTHER			
1.104	Horsepower (DIN)	Horsepower (SAE)	.9861
.746	Horsepower (SAE)	Kilowatts (KW)	1.34
1.609	Mph	Km/h	.621
.425	Mpg	Km/L	2.35
—	To obtain	From	Multiply by

Tap Drill Sizes

National Coarse or U.S.S.

Screw & Tap Size	Threads Per Inch	Use Drill Number
No. 5	40	39
No. 6	32	36
No. 8	32	29
No. 10	24	25
No. 12	24	17
1/4	20	8
5/16	18	F
3/8	16	5/16
7/16	14	U
1/2	13	27/64
9/16	12	31/64
5/8	11	17/32
3/4	10	21/32
7/8	9	49/64

National Coarse or U.S.S.

Screw & Tap Size	Threads Per Inch	Use Drill Number
1	8	7/8
1 1/8	7	63/64
1 1/4	7	1 7/64
1 1/2	6	1 11/32

National Fine or S.A.E.

Screw & Tap Size	Threads Per Inch	Use Drill Number
No. 5	44	37
No. 6	40	33
No. 8	36	29
No. 10	32	21

National Fine or S.A.E.

Screw & Tap Size	Threads Per Inch	Use Drill Number
No. 12	28	15
1/4	28	3
6/16	24	1
3/8	28	Q
7/16	20	W
1/2	20	29/64
9/16	18	33/64
5/8	18	37/64
3/4	16	11/16
7/8	14	13/16
1 1/8	12	1 3/64
1 1/4	12	1 11/64
1 1/2	12	1 27/64

Drill Sizes In Decimal Equivalents

Inch	Decimal	Wire	Letter	mm
1/64	.0156			.39
	.0157			.4
	.0160	78		
	.0165			.42
	.0173			.44
	.0177			.45
	.0180	77		
	.0181			.46
	.0189			.48
	.0197			.5
	.0200	76		
	.0210	75		
	.0217			.55
	.0225	74		
	.0236			.6
	.0240	73		
	.0250	72		
	.0256			.65
	.0260	71		
	.0276			.7
	.0280	70		
	.0292	69		
	.0295			.75
	.0310	68		
1/32	.0312			.79
	.0315			.8
	.0320	67		
	.0330	66		
	.0335			.85
	.0350	65		
	.0354			.9
	.0360	64		
	.0370	63		
	.0374			.95
	.0380	62		
	.0390	61		
	.0394			1.0
	.0400	60		
	.0410	59		
	.0413			1.05
	.0420	58		
	.0430	57		
	.0433			1.1
	.0453			1.15
3/64	.0465	56		
	.0469			1.19
	.0472			1.2
	.0492			1.25
	.0512			1.3
	.0520	55		
	.0531			1.35
	.0550	54		
	.0551			1.4
	.0571			1.45
	.0591			1.5
	.0595	53		
	.0610			1.55
1/16	.0625			1.59
	.0630			1.6
	.0635	52		
	.0650			1.65
	.0669			1.7
	.0670	51		
	.0689			1.75
	.0700	50		
	.0709			1.8
	.0728			1.85
	.0730	49		
	.0748			1.9
	.0760	48		
5/64	.0768			1.95
	.0781			1.98
	.0785	47		
	.0787			2.0
	.0807			2.05
	.0810	46		
	.0820	45		
	.0827			2.1
	.0846			2.15
	.0860	44		
	.0866			2.2
	.0886			2.25
	.0890	43		
	.0906			2.3
	.0925			2.35
3/32	.0935	42		
	.0938			2.38
	.0945			2.4
	.0960	41		
	.0965			2.45
	.0980	40		
	.0981			2.5
	.0995	39		
	.1015	38		
	.1024			2.6
	.1040	37		
	.1063			2.7
	.1065	36		
	.1083			2.75
7/64	.1094			2.77
	.1100	35		
	.1102			2.8
	.1110	34		
	.1130	33		
	.1142			2.9
	.1160	32		
	.1181			3.0
	.1200	31		
	.1220			3.1
1/8	.1250			3.17
	.1260			3.2
	.1280			3.25
	.1285	30		
	.1299			3.3
	.1339			3.4
	.1360	29		
	.1378			3.5
	.1405	28		
9/64	.1406			3.57
	.1417			3.6
	.1440	27		
	.1457			3.7
	.1470	26		
	.1476			3.75
	.1495	25		
	.1496			3.8
	.1520	24		
	.1535			3.9
	.1540	23		
5/32	.1562			3.96
	.1570	22		
	.1575			4.0
	.1590	21		
	.1610	20		
	.1614			4.1
	.1654			4.2
	.1660	19		
	.1673			4.25
	.1693			4.3
	.1695	18		
11/64	.1719			4.36
	.1730	17		
	.1732			4.4
	.1770	16		
	.1772			4.5
	.1800	15		
	.1811			4.6
	.1820	14		
	.1850	13		
	.1850			4.7
	.1870			4.75
3/16	.1875			4.76
	.1890			4.8
	.1890	12		
	.1910	11		
	.1929			4.9
	.1935	10		
	.1960	9		
	.1969			5.0
	.1990	8		
	.2008			5.1
	.2010	7		
13/64	.2031			5.16
	.2040	6		
	.2047			5.2
	.2055	5		
	.2067			5.25
	.2087			5.3
	.2090	4		
	.2126			5.4
	.2130	3		
	.2165			5.5
7/32	2188			5.55
	.2205			5.6
	.2210	2		
	.2244			5.7
	.2264			5.75
	.2280	1		
	.2283			5.8
	.2323			5.9
	.2340		A	
15/64	.2344			5.95
	.2362			6.0
	.2380		B	
	.2402			6.1
	.2420		C	
	.2441			6.2
	.2460		D	
	.2461			6.25
	.2480			6.3
1/4	.2500		E	6.35
	.2520			6.
	.2559			6.5
	.2570		F	
	.2598			6.6
	.2610		G	
	.2638			6.7
17/64	.2656			6.74
	.2657			6.75
	.2660		H	
	.2677			6.8
	.2717			6.9
	.2720		I	
	.2756			7.0
	.2770		J	
	.2795			7.1
	.2810		K	
9/32	.2812			7.14
	.2835			7.2
	.2854			7.25
	.2874			7.3
	.2900		L	
	.2913			7.4
	.2950		M	
	.2953			7.5
19/64	.2969			7.54
	.2992			7.6
	.3020		N	
	.3031			7.7
	.3051			7.75
	.3071			7.8
	.3110			7.9
	.3125			7.93
5/16	.3150			8.0
	.3160		O	
	.3189			8.1
	.3228			8.2
	.3230		P	
	.3248			8.25
	.3268			8.3
21/64	.3281			8.33
	.3307			8.4
	.3320		Q	
	.3346			8.5
	.3386			8.6
	.3390		R	
	.3425			8.7
11/32	.3438			8.73
	.3445			8.75
	.3465			8.8
	.3480		S	
	.3504			8.9
	.3543			9.0
	.3580		T	
	.3583			9.1
23/64	.3594			9.12
	.3622			9.2
	.3642			9.25
	.3661			9.3
	.3680		U	
	.3701			9.4
	.3740			9.5
3/8	.3750			9.52
	.3770		V	
	.3780			9.6
	.3819			9.7
	.3839			9.75
	.3858			9.8
	.3860		W	
	.3898			9.9
25/64	.3906			9.92
	.3937			10.0
	.3970		X	
	.4040		Y	
13/32	.4062			10.31
	.4130		Z	
	.4134			10.5
27/64	.4219			10.71
	.4331			11.0
7/16	.4375			11.11
	.4528			11.5
29/64	.4531			11.51
15/32	.4688			11.90
	.4724			12.0
31/64	.4844			12.30
	.4921			12.5
1/2	.5000			12.70
	.5118			13.0
33/64	.5156			13.09
17/32	.5312			13.49
	.5315			13.5
35/64	.5469			13.89
	.5512			14.0
9/16	.5625			14.28
	.5709			14.5
37/64	.5781			14.68
	.5906			15.0
19/32	.5938			15.08
39/64	.6094			15.47
	.6102			15.5
5/8	.6250			15.87
	.6299			16.0
41/64	.6406			16.27
	.6496			16.5
21/32	.6562			16.66
	.6693			17.0
43/64	.6719			17.06
11/16	.6875			17.46
	.6890			17.5
45/64	.7031			17.85
	.7087			18.0
23/32	.7188			18.25
	.7283			18.5
47/64	.7344			18.65
	.7480			19.0
3/4	.7500			19.05
49/64	.7656			19.44
	.7677			19.5
25/32	.7812			19.84
	.7874			20.0
51/64	.7969			20.24
	.8071			20.5
13/16	.8125			20.63
	.8268			21.0
53/64	.8281			21.03
27/32	.8438			21.43
	.8465			21.5
55/64	.8594			21.82
	.8661			22.0
7/8	.8750			22.22
	.8858			22.5
57/64	.8906			22.62
	.9055			23.0
29/32	.9062			23.01
59/64	.9219			23.41
	.9252			23.5
15/16	.9375			23.81
	.9449			24.0
61/64	.9531			24.2
	.9646			24.5
31/32	.9688			24.6
	.9843			25.0
63/64	.9844			25.0
1	1.0000			25.4

AIR/FUEL RATIO: The ratio of air to gasoline by weight in the fuel mixture drawn into the engine.

AIR INJECTION: One method of reducing harmful exhaust emissions by injecting air into each of the exhaust ports of an engine. The fresh air entering the hot exhaust manifold causes any remaining fuel to be burned before it can exit the tailpipe.

ALTERNATOR: A device used for converting mechanical energy into electrical energy.

AMMETER: An instrument, calibrated in amperes, used to measure the flow of an electrical current in a circuit. Ammeters are always connected in series with the circuit being tested.

AMPERE: The rate of flow of electrical current present when one volt of electrical pressure is applied against one ohm of electrical resistance.

ANALOG COMPUTER: Any microprocessor that uses similar (analogous) electrical signals to make its calculations.

ARMATURE: A laminated, soft iron core wrapped by a wire that converts electrical energy to mechanical energy as in a motor or relay. When rotated in a magnetic field, it changes mechanical energy into electrical energy as in a generator.

ATMOSPHERIC PRESSURE: The pressure on the Earth's surface caused by the weight of the air in the atmosphere. At sea level, this pressure is 14.7 psi at 32°F (101 kPa at 0°C).

ATOMIZATION: The breaking down of a liquid into a fine mist that can be suspended in air.

AXIAL PLAY: Movement parallel to a shaft or bearing bore.

BACKFIRE: The sudden combustion of gases in the intake or exhaust system that results in a loud explosion.

BACKLASH: The clearance or play between two parts, such as meshed gears.

BACKPRESSURE: Restrictions in the exhaust system that slow the exit of exhaust gases from the combustion chamber.

BAKELITE: A heat resistant, plastic insulator material commonly used in printed circuit boards and transistorized components.

BALL BEARING: A bearing made up of hardened inner and outer races between which hardened steel balls roll.

BALLAST RESISTOR: A resistor in the primary ignition circuit that lowers voltage after the engine is started to reduce wear on ignition components.

BEARING: A friction reducing, supportive device usually located between a stationary part and a moving part.

BIMETAL TEMPERATURE SENSOR: Any sensor or switch made of two dissimilar types of metal that bend when heated or cooled due to the different expansion rates of the alloys. These types of sensors usually function as an on/off switch.

BLOWBY: Combustion gases, composed of water vapor and unburned fuel, that leak past the piston rings into the crankcase during normal engine operation. These gases are removed by the PCV system to prevent the buildup of harmful acids in the crankcase.

BRAKE PAD: A brake shoe and lining assembly used with disc brakes.

BRAKE SHOE: The backing for the brake lining. The term is, however, usually applied to the assembly of the brake backing and lining.

BUSHING: A liner, usually removable, for a bearing; an anti-friction liner used in place of a bearing.

BYPASS: System used to bypass ballast resistor during engine cranking to increase voltage supplied to the coil.

CALIPER: A hydraulically activated device in a disc brake system, which is mounted straddling the brake rotor (disc). The caliper contains at least one piston and two brake pads. Hydraulic pressure on the piston(s) forces the pads against the rotor.

CAMSHAFT: A shaft in the engine on which are the lobes (cams) which operate the valves. The camshaft is driven by the crankshaft, via a belt, chain or gears, at one half the crankshaft speed.

CAPACITOR: A device which stores an electrical charge.

CARBON MONOXIDE (CO): A colorless, odorless gas given off as a normal byproduct of combustion. It is poisonous and extremely dangerous in confined areas, building up slowly to toxic levels without warning if adequate ventilation is not available.

CARBURETOR: A device, usually mounted on the intake manifold of an engine, which mixes the air and fuel in the proper proportion to allow even combustion.

CATALYTIC CONVERTER: A device installed in the exhaust system, like a muffler, that converts harmful byproducts of combustion into carbon dioxide and water vapor by means of a heat-producing chemical reaction.

CENTRIFUGAL ADVANCE: A mechanical method of advancing the spark timing by using flyweights in the distributor that react to centrifugal force generated by the distributor shaft rotation.

CHECK VALVE: Any one-way valve installed to permit the flow of air, fuel or vacuum in one direction only.

CHOKE: A device, usually a moveable valve, placed in the intake path of a carburetor to restrict the flow of air.

CIRCUIT: Any unbroken path through which an electrical current can flow. Also used to describe fuel flow in some instances.

CIRCUIT BREAKER: A switch which protects an electrical circuit from overload by opening the circuit when the current flow exceeds a predetermined level. Some circuit breakers must be reset manually, while most reset automatically

COIL (IGNITION): A transformer in the ignition circuit which steps up the voltage provided to the spark plugs.

COMBINATION MANIFOLD: An assembly which includes both the intake and exhaust manifolds in one casting.

COMBINATION VALVE: A device used in some fuel systems that routes fuel vapors to a charcoal storage canister instead of venting them into the atmosphere. The valve relieves fuel tank pressure and allows fresh air into the tank as the fuel level drops to prevent a vapor lock situation.

COMPRESSION RATIO: The comparison of the total volume of the cylinder and combustion chamber with the piston at BDC and the piston at TDC.

CONDENSER: 1. An electrical device which acts to store an electrical charge, preventing voltage surges.
2. A radiator-like device in the air conditioning system in which refrigerant gas condenses into a liquid, giving off heat.

CONDUCTOR: Any material through which an electrical current can be transmitted easily.

CONTINUITY: Continuous or complete circuit. Can be checked with an ohmmeter.

COUNTERSHAFT: An intermediate shaft which is rotated by a mainshaft and transmits, in turn, that rotation to a working part.

CRANKCASE: The lower part of an engine in which the crankshaft and related parts operate.

CRANKSHAFT: The main driving shaft of an engine which receives reciprocating motion from the pistons and converts it to rotary motion.

CYLINDER: In an engine, the round hole in the engine block in which the piston(s) ride.

CYLINDER BLOCK: The main structural member of an engine in which is found the cylinders, crankshaft and other principal parts.

CYLINDER HEAD: The detachable portion of the engine, fastened, usually, to the top of the cylinder block, containing all or most of the combustion chambers. On overhead valve engines, it contains the valves and their operating parts. On overhead cam engines, it contains the camshaft as well.

DEAD CENTER: The extreme top or bottom of the piston stroke.

DETONATION: An unwanted explosion of the air/fuel mixture in the combustion chamber caused by excess heat and compression, advanced timing, or an overly lean mixture. Also referred to as "ping".

DIAPHRAGM: A thin, flexible wall separating two cavities, such as in a vacuum advance unit.

DIESELING: A condition in which hot spots in the combustion chamber cause the engine to run on after the key is turned off.

DIFFERENTIAL: A geared assembly which allows the transmission of motion between drive axles, giving one axle the ability to turn faster than the other.

DIODE: An electrical device that will allow current to flow in one direction only.

DISC BRAKE: A hydraulic braking assembly consisting of a brake disc, or rotor, mounted on an axle, and a caliper assembly containing, usually two brake pads which are activated by hydraulic pressure. The pads are forced against the sides of the disc, creating friction which slows the vehicle.

DISTRIBUTOR: A mechanically driven device on an engine which is responsible for electrically firing the spark plug at a predetermined point of the piston stroke.

DOWEL PIN: A pin, inserted in mating holes in two different parts allowing those parts to maintain a fixed relationship.

DRUM BRAKE: A braking system which consists of two brake shoes and one or two wheel cylinders, mounted on a fixed backing plate, and a brake drum, mounted on an axle, which revolves around the assembly. Hydraulic action applied to the wheel cylinders forces the shoes outward against the drum, creating friction, slowing the vehicle.

DWELL: The rate, measured in degrees of shaft rotation, at which an electrical circuit cycles on and off.

ELECTRONIC CONTROL UNIT (ECU): Ignition module, module, amplifier or igniter. See Module for definition.

ELECTRONIC IGNITION: A system in which the timing and firing of the spark plugs is controlled by an electronic control unit, usually called a module. These systems have no points or condenser.

ENDPLAY: The measured amount of axial movement in a shaft.

ENGINE: A device that converts heat into mechanical energy.

EXHAUST MANIFOLD: A set of cast passages or pipes which conduct exhaust gases from the engine.

FEELER GAUGE: A blade, usually metal, of precisely predetermined thickness, used to measure the clearance between two parts. These blades usually are available in sets of assorted thicknesses.

F-HEAD: An engine configuration in which the intake valves are in the cylinder head, while the camshaft and exhaust valves are located in the cylinder block. The camshaft operates the intake valves via lifters and pushrods, while it operates the exhaust valves directly.

FIRING ORDER: The order in which combustion occurs in the cylinders of an engine. Also the order in which spark is distributed to the plugs by the distributor.

FLATHEAD: An engine configuration in which the camshaft and all the valves are located in the cylinder block.

FLOODING: The presence of too much fuel in the intake manifold and combustion chamber which prevents the air/fuel mixture from firing, thereby causing a no-start situation.

FLYWHEEL: A disc shaped part bolted to the rear end of the crankshaft. Around the outer perimeter is affixed the ring gear. The starter drive engages the ring gear, turning the flywheel, which rotates the crankshaft, imparting the initial starting motion to the engine.

FOOT POUND (ft.lb. or sometimes, ft. lbs.): The amount of energy or work needed to raise an item weighing one pound, a distance of one foot.

FUSE: A protective device in a circuit which prevents circuit overload by breaking the circuit when a specific amperage is present. The device is constructed around a strip or wire of a lower amperage rating than the circuit it is designed to protect. When an amperage higher than that stamped on the fuse is present in the circuit, the strip or wire melts, opening the circuit.

GEAR RATIO: The ratio between the number of teeth on meshing gears.

GENERATOR: A device which converts mechanical energy into electrical energy.

HEAT RANGE: The measure of a spark plug's ability to dissipate heat from its firing end. The higher the heat range, the hotter the plug fires.

HUB: The center part of a wheel or gear.

HYDROCARBON (HC): Any chemical compound made up of hydrogen and carbon. A major pollutant formed by the engine as a byproduct of combustion.

HYDROMETER: An instrument used to measure the specific gravity of a solution.

INCH POUND (in.lb. or sometimes, in. lbs.): One twelfth of a foot pound.

INDUCTION: A means of transferring electrical energy in the form of a magnetic field. Principle used in the ignition coil to increase voltage.

INJECTION PUMP: A device, usually mechanically operated, which meters and delivers fuel under pressure to the fuel injector.

INJECTOR: A device which receives metered fuel under relatively low pressure and is activated to inject the fuel into the engine under relatively high pressure at a predetermined time.

INPUT SHAFT: The shaft to which torque is applied, usually carrying the driving gear or gears.

INTAKE MANIFOLD: A casting of passages or pipes used to conduct air or a fuel/air mixture to the cylinders.

JOURNAL: The bearing surface within which a shaft operates.

KEY: A small block usually fitted in a notch between a shaft and a hub to prevent slippage of the two parts.

MANIFOLD: A casting of passages or set of pipes which connect the cylinders to an inlet or outlet source.

MANIFOLD VACUUM: Low pressure in an engine intake manifold formed just below the throttle plates. Manifold vacuum is highest at idle and drops under acceleration.

MASTER CYLINDER: The primary fluid pressurizing device in a hydraulic system. In automotive use, it is found in brake and hydraulic clutch systems and is pedal activated, either directly or, in a power brake system, through the power booster.

MODULE: Electronic control unit, amplifier or igniter of solid state or integrated design which controls the current flow in the ignition primary circuit based on input from the pickup coil. When the module opens the primary circuit, the high secondary voltage is induced in the coil.

NEEDLE BEARING: A bearing which consists of a number (usually a large number) of long, thin rollers.

OHM:(Ω) The unit used to measure the resistance of conductor to electrical flow. One ohm is the amount of resistance that limits current flow to one ampere in a circuit with one volt of pressure.

OHMMETER: An instrument used for measuring the resistance, in ohms, in an electrical circuit.

OUTPUT SHAFT: The shaft which transmits torque from a device, such as a transmission.

OVERDRIVE: A gear assembly which produces more shaft revolutions than that transmitted to it.

OVERHEAD CAMSHAFT (OHC): An engine configuration in which the camshaft is mounted on top of the cylinder head and operates the valves either directly or by means of rocker arms.

OVERHEAD VALVE (OHV): An engine configuration in which all of the valves are located in the cylinder head and the camshaft is located in the cylinder block. The camshaft operates the valves via lifters and pushrods.

OXIDES OF NITROGEN (NOx): Chemical compounds of nitrogen produced as a byproduct of combustion. They combine with hydrocarbons to produce smog.

OXYGEN SENSOR: Used with the feedback system to sense the presence of oxygen in the exhaust gas and signal the computer which can reference the voltage signal to an air/fuel ratio.

PINION: The smaller of two meshing gears.

PISTON RING: An open ended ring which fits into a groove on the outer diameter of the piston. Its chief function is to form a seal between the piston and cylinder wall. Most automotive pistons have three rings: two for compression sealing; one for oil sealing.

PRELOAD: A predetermined load placed on a bearing during assembly or by adjustment.

PRIMARY CIRCUIT: Is the low voltage side of the ignition system which consists of the ignition switch, ballast resistor or resistance wire, bypass, coil, electronic control unit and pick-up coil as well as the connecting wires and harnesses.

PRESS FIT: The mating of two parts under pressure, due to the inner diameter of one being smaller than the outer diameter of the other, or vice versa; an interference fit.

RACE: The surface on the inner or outer ring of a bearing on which the balls, needles or rollers move.

REGULATOR: A device which maintains the amperage and/or voltage levels of a circuit at predetermined values.

RELAY: A switch which automatically opens and/or closes a circuit.

RESISTANCE: The opposition to the flow of current through a circuit or electrical device, and is measured in ohms. Resistance is equal to the voltage divided by the amperage.

RESISTOR: A device, usually made of wire, which offers a preset amount of resistance in an electrical circuit.

RING GEAR: The name given to a ring-shaped gear attached to a differential case, or affixed to a flywheel or as part a planetary gear set.

ROLLER BEARING: A bearing made up of hardened inner and outer races between which hardened steel rollers move.

ROTOR: 1. The disc-shaped part of a disc brake assembly, upon which the brake pads bear; also called, brake disc.
2. The device mounted atop the distributor shaft, which passes current to the distributor cap tower contacts.

SECONDARY CIRCUIT: The high voltage side of the ignition system, usually above 20,000 volts. The secondary includes the ignition coil, coil wire, distributor cap and rotor, spark plug wires and spark plugs.

SENDING UNIT: A mechanical, electrical, hydraulic or electromagnetic device which transmits information to a gauge.

SENSOR: Any device designed to measure engine operating conditions or ambient pressures and temperatures. Usually electronic in nature and designed to send a voltage signal to an on-board computer, some sensors may operate as a simple on/off switch or they may provide a variable voltage signal (like a potentiometer) as conditions or measured parameters change.

SHIM: Spacers of precise, predetermined thickness used between parts to establish a proper working relationship.

SLAVE CYLINDER: In automotive use, a device in the hydraulic clutch system which is activated by hydraulic force, disengaging the clutch.

SOLENOID: A coil used to produce a magnetic field, the effect of which is to produce work.

SPARK PLUG: A device screwed into the combustion chamber of a spark ignition engine. The basic construction is a conductive core inside of a ceramic insulator, mounted in an outer conductive base. An electrical charge from the spark plug wire travels along the conductive core and jumps a preset air gap to a grounding point or points at the end of the conductive base. The resultant spark ignites the fuel/air mixture in the combustion chamber.

SPLINES: Ridges machined or cast onto the outer diameter of a shaft or inner diameter of a bore to enable parts to mate without rotation.

TACHOMETER: A device used to measure the rotary speed of an engine, shaft, gear, etc., usually in rotations per minute.

THERMOSTAT: A valve, located in the cooling system of an engine, which is closed when cold and opens gradually in response to engine heating, controlling the temperature of the coolant and rate of coolant flow.

TOP DEAD CENTER (TDC): The point at which the piston reaches the top of its travel on the compression stroke.

TORQUE: The twisting force applied to an object.

TORQUE CONVERTER: A turbine used to transmit power from a driving member to a driven member via hydraulic action, providing changes in drive ratio and torque. In automotive use, it links the driveplate at the rear of the engine to the automatic transmission.

TRANSDUCER: A device used to change a force into an electrical signal.

TRANSISTOR: A semi-conductor component which can be actuated by a small voltage to perform an electrical switching function.

TUNE-UP: A regular maintenance function, usually associated with the replacement and adjustment of parts and components in the electrical and fuel systems of a vehicle for the purpose of attaining optimum performance.

TURBOCHARGER: An exhaust driven pump which compresses intake air and forces it into the combustion chambers at higher than atmospheric pressures. The increased air pressure allows more fuel to be burned and results in increased horsepower being produced.

VACUUM ADVANCE: A device which advances the ignition timing in response to increased engine vacuum.

VACUUM GAUGE: An instrument used to measure the presence of vacuum in a chamber.

VALVE: A device which control the pressure, direction of flow or rate of flow of a liquid or gas.

VALVE CLEARANCE: The measured gap between the end of the valve stem and the rocker arm, cam lobe or follower that activates the valve.

VISCOSITY: The rating of a liquid's internal resistance to flow.

VOLTMETER: An instrument used for measuring electrical force in units called volts. Voltmeters are always connected parallel with the circuit being tested.

WHEEL CYLINDER: Found in the automotive drum brake assembly, it is a device, actuated by hydraulic pressure, which, through internal pistons, pushes the brake shoes outward against the drums.

A: Ampere

AC: Alternating current

A/C: Air conditioning

A-h: Ampere hour

AT: Automatic transmission

ATDC: After top dead center

μA: Microampere

bbl: Barrel

BDC: Bottom dead center

bhp: Brake horsepower

BTDC: Before top dead center

BTU: British thermal unit

C: Celsius (Centigrade)

CCA: Cold cranking amps

cd: Candela

cm^2: Square centimeter

cm^3, cc: Cubic centimeter

CO: Carbon monoxide

CO_2: Carbon dioxide

cu.in., in^3: Cubic inch

CV: Constant velocity

Cyl.: Cylinder

DC: Direct current

ECM: Electronic control module

EFE: Early fuel evaporation

EFI: Electronic fuel injection

EGR: Exhaust gas recirculation

Exh.: Exhaust

F: Fahrenheit

F: Farad

pF: Picofarad

μF: Microfarad

FI: Fuel injection

ft.lb., ft. lb.,ft. lbs.: foot pound(s)

gal: Gallon

g: Gram

HC: Hydrocarbon

HEI: High energy ignition

HO: High output

hp: Horsepower

Hyd.: Hydraulic

Hz: Hertz

ID: Inside diameter

in.lb; in. lb.; in. lbs.: inch pound(s)

Int.: Intake

K: Kelvin

kg: Kilogram

kHz: Kilohertz

km: Kilometer

km/h: Kilometers per hour

$k\Omega$: Kilohm

kPa: Kilopascal

kV: Kilovolt

kW: Kilowatt

l: Liter

l/s: Liters per second

m: Meter

mA: Milliampere

mg: Milligram

mHz: Megahertz

mm: Millimeter

mm^2: Square millimeter

m^3: Cubic meter

$M\Omega$: Megohm

m/s: Meters per second

MT: Manual transmission

mV: Millivolt

μm: Micrometer

N: Newton

N-m: Newton meter

NOx: Nitrous oxide

OD: Outside diameter

OHC: Over head camshaft

OHV: Over head valve

Ω: Ohm

PCV: Positive crankcase ventilation

psi: Pounds per square inch

pts: Pints

qts: Quarts

rpm: Rotations per minute

rps: Rotations per second

R-12: A refrigerant gas (Freon)

SAE: Society of Automotive Engineers

SO_2: Sulfur dioxide

T: Ton

t: Megagram

TBI: Throttle Body Injection

TPS: Throttle Position Sensor

V: 1. Volt; 2. Venturi

μV: Microvolt

W: Watt

∞: Infinity

<: Less than

>: Greater than

CHILTON'S REPAIR MANUAL MODEL INDEX
Car and truck model names are listed in alphabetical and numerical order

Part No.	Model	Repair Manual Title
6980	Accord	Honda 1973-88
7747	Aerostar	Ford Aerostar 1986-90
7165	Alliance	Renault 1975-85
7199	AMX	AMC 1975-86
7163	Aries	Chrysler Front Wheel Drive 1981-88
7041	Arrow	Champ/Arrow/Sapporo 1978-83
7032	Arrow Pick-Ups	D-50/Arrow Pick-Up 1979-81
6637	Aspen	Aspen/Volare 1976-80
6935	Astre	GM Subcompact 1971-80
7750	Astro	Chevrolet Astro/GMC Safari 1985-90
6934	A100, 200, 300	Dodge/Plymouth Vans 1967-88
5807	Barracuda	Barracuda/Challenger 1965-72
6844	Bavaria	BMW 1970-88
5796	Beetle	Volkswagen 1949-71
6837	Beetle	Volkswagen 1970-81
7135	Bel Air	Chevrolet 1968-88
5821	Belvedere	Roadrunner/Satellite/Belvedere/GTX 1968-73
7849	Beretta	Chevrolet Corsica and Beretta 1988
7317	Berlinetta	Camaro 1982-88
7135	Biscayne	Chevrolet 1968-88
6931	Blazer	Blazer/Jimmy 1969-82
7383	Blazer	Chevy S-10 Blazer/GMC S-15 Jimmy 1982-87
7027	Bobcat	Pinto/Bobcat 1971-80
7308	Bonneville	Buick/Olds/Pontiac 1975-87
6982	BRAT	Subaru 1970-88
7042	Brava	Fiat 1969-81
7140	Bronco	Ford Bronco 1966-86
7829	Bronco	Ford Pick-Ups and Bronco 1987-88
7408	Bronco II	Ford Ranger/Bronco II 1983-88
7135	Brookwood	Chevrolet 1968-88
6326	Brougham 1975-75	Valiant/Duster 1968-76
6934	B100, 150, 200, 250, 300, 350	Dodge/Plymouth Vans 1967-88
7197	B210	Datsun 1200/210/Nissan Sentra 1973-88
7659	B1600, 1800, 2000, 2200, 2600	Mazda Trucks 1971-89
6840	Caballero	Chevrolet Mid-Size 1964-88
7657	Calais	Calais, Grand Am, Skylark, Somerset 1985-86
6735	Camaro	Camaro 1967-81
7317	Camaro	Camaro 1982-88
7740	Camry	Toyota Camry 1983-88
6695	Capri, Capri II	Capri 1970-77
6963	Capri	Mustang/Capri/Merkur 1979-88
7135	Caprice	Chevrolet 1968-88
7482	Caravan	Dodge Caravan/Plymouth Voyager 1984-89
7163	Caravelle	Chrysler Front Wheel Drive 1981-88
7036	Carina	Toyota Corolla/Carina/Tercel/Starlet 1970-87
7308	Catalina	Buick/Olds/Pontiac 1975-90
7059	Cavalier	Cavalier, Skyhawk, Cimarron, 2000 1982-88
7309	Celebrity	Celebrity, Century, Ciera, 6000 1982-88
7043	Celica	Toyota Celica/Supra 1971-87
8058	Celica	Toyota Celica/Supra 1986-90
7309	Century FWD	Celebrity, Century, Ciera, 6000 1982-88
7307	Century RWD	Century/Regal 1975-87
5807	Challenger 1965-72	Barracuda/Challenger 1965-72
7037	Challenger 1977-83	Colt/Challenger/Vista/Conquest 1971-88
7041	Champ	Champ/Arrow/Sapporo 1978-83
6486	Charger	Dodge Charger 1967-70
6845	Charger 2.2	Omni/Horizon/Rampage 1978-88

Part No.	Model	Repair Manual Title
6739	Cherokee 1974-83	Jeep Wagoneer, Commando, Cherokee, Truck 1957-86
7939	Cherokee 1984-89	Jeep Wagoneer, Comanche, Cherokee 1984-89
6840	Chevelle	Chevrolet Mid-Size 1964-88
6836	Chevette	Chevette/T-1000 1976-88
6841	Chevy II	Chevy II/Nova 1962-79
7309	Ciera	Celebrity, Century, Ciera, 6000 1982-88
7059	Cimarron	Cavalier, Skyhawk, Cimarron, 2000 1982-88
7049	Citation	GM X-Body 1980-85
6980	Civic	Honda 1973-88
6817	CJ-2A, 3A, 3B, 5, 6, 7	Jeep 1945-87
8034	CJ-5, 6, 7	Jeep 1971-90
6842	Colony Park	Ford/Mercury/Lincoln 1968-88
7037	Colt	Colt/Challenger/Vista/Conquest 1971-88
6634	Comet	Maverick/Comet 1971-77
7939	Comanche	Jeep Wagoneer, Comanche, Cherokee 1984-89
6739	Commando	Jeep Wagoneer, Commando, Cherokee, Truck 1957-86
6842	Commuter	Ford/Mercury/Lincoln 1968-88
7199	Concord	AMC 1975-86
7037	Conquest	Colt/Challenger/Vista/Conquest 1971-88
6696	Continental 1982-85	Ford/Mercury/Lincoln Mid-Size 1971-85
7814	Continental 1982-87	Thunderbird, Cougar, Continental 1980-87
7830	Continental 1988-89	Taurus/Sable/Continental 1986-89
7583	Cordia	Mitsubishi 1983-89
5795	Corolla 1968-70	Toyota 1966-70
7036	Corolla	Toyota Corolla/Carina/Tercel/Starlet 1970-87
5795	Corona	Toyota 1966-70
7004	Corona	Toyota Corona/Crown/Cressida/Mk.II/Van 1970-87
6962	Corrado	VW Front Wheel Drive 1974-90
7849	Corsica	Chevrolet Corsica and Beretta 1988
6576	Corvette	Corvette 1953-62
6843	Corvette	Corvette 1963-86
6542	Cougar	Mustang/Cougar 1965-73
6696	Cougar	Ford/Mercury/Lincoln Mid-Size 1971-85
7814	Cougar	Thunderbird, Cougar, Continental 1980-87
6842	Country Sedan	Ford/Mercury/Lincoln 1968-88
6842	Country Squire	Ford/Mercury/Lincoln 1968-88
6983	Courier	Ford Courier 1972-82
7004	Cressida	Toyota Corona/Crown/Cressida/Mk.II/Van 1970-87
5795	Crown	Toyota 1966-70
7004	Crown	Toyota Corona/Crown/Cressida/Mk.II/Van 1970-87
6842	Crown Victoria	Ford/Mercury/Lincoln 1968-88
6980	CRX	Honda 1973-88
6842	Custom	Ford/Mercury/Lincoln 1968-88
6326	Custom	Valiant/Duster 1968-76
6842	Custom 500	Ford/Mercury/Lincoln 1968-88
7950	Cutlass FWD	Lumina/Grand Prix/Cutlass/Regal 1988-90
6933	Cutlass RWD	Cutlass 1970-87
7309	Cutlass Ciera	Celebrity, Century, Ciera, 6000 1982-88
6936	C-10, 20, 30	Chevrolet/GMC Pick-Ups & Suburban 1970-87

Chilton's Repair Manuals are available at your local retailer or by mailing a check or money order for **$14.95** per book plus **$3.50** for 1st book and **$.50** for each additional book to cover postage and handling to:

Chilton Book Company
Dept. DM
Radnor, PA 19089

NOTE: When ordering be sure to include your name & address, book part No. & title.

CHILTON'S REPAIR MANUAL MODEL INDEX
Car and truck model names are listed in alphabetical and numerical order

Part No.	Model	Repair Manual Title
8055	C-15, 25, 35	Chevrolet/GMC Pick-Ups & Suburban 1988-90
6324	Dart	Dart/Demon 1968-76
6962	Dasher	VW Front Wheel Drive 1974-90
5790	Datsun Pickups	Datsun 1961-72
6816	Datsun Pickups	Datsun Pick-Ups and Pathfinder 1970-89
7163	Daytona	Chrysler Front Wheel Drive 1981-88
6486	Daytona Charger	Dodge Charger 1967-70
6324	Demon	Dart/Demon 1968-76
7462	deVille	Cadillac 1967-89
7587	deVille	GM C-Body 1985
6817	DJ-3B	Jeep 1945-87
7040	DL	Volvo 1970-88
6326	Duster	Valiant/Duster 1968-76
7032	D-50	D-50/Arrow Pick-Ups 1979-81
7459	D100, 150, 200, 250, 300, 350	Dodge/Plymouth Trucks 1967-88
7199	Eagle	AMC 1975-86
7163	E-Class	Chrysler Front Wheel Drive 1981-88
6840	El Camino	Chevrolet Mid-Size 1964-88
7462	Eldorado	Cadillac 1967-89
7308	Electra	Buick/Olds/Pontiac 1975-90
7587	Electra	GM C-Body 1985
6696	Elite	Ford/Mercury/Lincoln Mid-Size 1971-85
7165	Encore	Renault 1975-85
7055	Escort	Ford/Mercury Front Wheel Drive 1981-87
7059	Eurosport	Cavalier, Skyhawk, Cimarron, 2000 1982-88
7760	Excel	Hyundai 1986-90
7163	Executive Sedan	Chrysler Front Wheel Drive 1981-88
7055	EXP	Ford/Mercury Front Wheel Drive 1981-87
6849	E-100, 150, 200, 250, 300, 350	Ford Vans 1961-88
6320	Fairlane	Fairlane/Torino 1962-75
6965	Fairmont	Fairmont/Zephyr 1978-83
5796	Fastback	Volkswagen 1949-71
6837	Fastback	Volkswagen 1970-81
6739	FC-150, 170	Jeep Wagoneer, Commando, Cherokee, Truck 1957-86
6982	FF-1	Subaru 1970-88
7571	Fiero	Pontiac Fiero 1984-88
6846	Fiesta	Fiesta 1978-80
5996	Firebird	Firebird 1967-81
7345	Firebird	Firebird 1982-90
7059	Firenza	Cavalier, Skyhawk, Cimarron, 2000 1982-88
7462	Fleetwood	Cadillac 1967-89
7587	Fleetwood	GM C-Body 1985
7829	F-Super Duty	Ford Pick-Ups and Bronco 1987-88
7165	Fuego	Renault 1975-85
6552	Fury	Plymouth 1968-76
7196	F-10	Datsun/Nissan F-10, 310, Stanza, Pulsar 1976-88
6933	F-85	Cutlass 1970-87
6913	F-100, 150, 200, 250, 300, 350	Ford Pick-Ups 1965-86
7829	F-150, 250, 350	Ford Pick-Ups and Bronco 1987-88
7583	Galant	Mitsubishi 1983-89
6842	Galaxie	Ford/Mercury/Lincoln 1968-88
7040	GL	Volvo 1970-88
6739	Gladiator	Jeep Wagoneer, Commando, Cherokee, Truck 1962-86
6981	GLC	Mazda 1978-89
7040	GLE	Volvo 1970-88
7040	GLT	Volvo 1970-88
7593	Golf	VW Front Wheel Drive 1974-90
7165	Gordini	Renault 1975-85
6937	Granada	Granada/Monarch 1975-82
6552	Gran Coupe	Plymouth 1968-76
6552	Gran Fury	Plymouth 1968-76
6842	Gran Marquis	Ford/Mercury/Lincoln 1968-88
6552	Gran Sedan	Plymouth 1968-76
6696	Gran Torino	Ford/Mercury/Lincoln Mid-Size 1971-85
1972-76		
7346	Grand Am	Pontiac Mid-Size 1974-83
7657	Grand Am	Calais, Grand Am, Skylark, Somerset 1985-86
7346	Grand LeMans	Pontiac Mid-Size 1974-83
7346	Grand Prix	Pontiac Mid-Size 1974-83
7950	Grand Prix FWD	Lumina/Grand Prix/Cutlass/Regal 1988-90
7308	Grand Safari	Buick/Olds/Pontiac 1975-87
7308	Grand Ville	Buick/Olds/Pontiac 1975-87
6739	Grand Wagoneer	Jeep Wagoneer, Commando, Cherokee, Truck 1957-86
7199	Gremlin	AMC 1975-86
6575	GT	Opel 1971-75
7593	GTI	VW Front Wheel Drive 1974-90
5905	GTO 1968-73	Tempest/GTO/LeMans 1968-73
7346	GTO 1974	Pontiac Mid-Size 1974-83
5821	GTX	Roadrunner/Satellite/Belvedere/GTX 1968-73
5910	GT6	Triumph 1969-73
6542	G.T.350, 500	Mustang/Cougar 1965-73
6930	G-10, 20, 30	Chevy/GMC Vans 1967-86
6930	G-1500, 2500, 3500	Chevy/GMC Vans 1967-86
8040	G-10, 20, 30	Chevy/GMC Vans 1987-90
8040	G-1500, 2500, 3500	Chevy/GMC Vans 1987-90
5795	Hi-Lux	Toyota 1966-70
6845	Horizon	Omni/Horizon/Rampage 1978-88
7199	Hornet	AMC 1975-86
7135	Impala	Chevrolet 1968-88
7317	IROC-Z	Camaro 1982-88
6739	Jeepster	Jeep Wagoneer, Commando, Cherokee, Truck 1957-86
7593	Jetta	VW Front Wheel Drive 1974-90
6931	Jimmy	Blazer/Jimmy 1969-82
7383	Jimmy	Chevy S-10 Blazer/GMC S-15 Jimmy 1982-87
6739	J-10, 20	Jeep Wagoneer, Commando, Cherokee, Truck 1957-86
6739	J-100, 200, 300	Jeep Wagoneer, Commando, Cherokee, Truck 1957-86
6575	Kadett	Opel 1971-75
7199	Kammback	AMC 1975-86
5796	Karmann Ghia	Volkswagen 1949-71
6837	Karmann Ghia	Volkswagen 1970-81
7135	Kingswood	Chevrolet 1968-88
6931	K-5	Blazer/Jimmy 1969-82
6936	K-10, 20, 30	Chevy/GMC Pick-Ups & Suburban 1970-87
6936	K-1500, 2500, 3500	Chevy/GMC Pick-Ups & Suburban 1970-87
8055	K-10, 20, 30	Chevy/GMC Pick-Ups & Suburban 1988-90
8055	K-1500, 2500, 3500	Chevy/GMC Pick-Ups & Suburban 1988-90
6840	Laguna	Chevrolet Mid-Size 1964-88
7041	Lancer	Champ/Arrow/Sapporo 1977-83
5795	Land Cruiser	Toyota 1966-70
7035	Land Cruiser	Toyota Trucks 1970-88
7163	Laser	Chrysler Front Wheel Drive 1981-88
7163	LeBaron	Chrysler Front Wheel Drive 1981-88
7165	LeCar	Renault 1975-85

Chilton's Repair Manuals are available at your local retailer or by mailing a check or money order for **$14.95** per book plus **$3.50** for 1st book and **$.50** for each additional book to cover postage and handling to:

Chilton Book Company
Dept. DM
Radnor, PA 19089

NOTE: When ordering be sure to include your name & address, book part No. & title.

CHILTON'S REPAIR MANUAL MODEL INDEX
Car and truck model names are listed in alphabetical and numerical order

Part No.	Model	Repair Manual Title	Part No.	Model	Repair Manual Title
6817	4×4-63	Jeep 1981-87	6932	300ZX	Datsun Z & ZX 1970-87
6817	4-73	Jeep 1981-87	5982	304	Peugeot 1970-74
6817	4×4-73	Jeep 1981-87	5790	310	Datsun 1961-72
6817	4-75	Jeep 1981-87	7196	310	Datsun/Nissan F-10, 310, Stanza,
7035	4Runner	Toyota Trucks 1970-88			Pulsar 1977-88
6982	4wd Wagon	Subaru 1970-88	5790	311	Datsun 1961-72
6982	4wd Coupe	Subaru 1970-88	6844	318i, 320i	BMW 1970-88
6933	4-4-2 1970-80	Cutlass 1970-87	6981	323	Mazda 1978-89
6817	6-63	Jeep 1981-87	6844	325E, 325ES, 325i,	BMW 1970-88
6809	6.9	Mercedes-Benz 1974-84		325iS, 325iX	
7308	88	Buick/Olds/Pontiac 1975-90	6809	380SEC, 380SEL,	Mercedes-Benz 1974-84
7308	98	Buick/Olds/Pontiac 1975-90		380SL, 380SLC	
7587	98 Regency	GM C-Body 1985	5907	350SL	Mercedes-Benz 1968-73
5902	100LS, 100GL	Audi 1970-73	7163	400	Chrysler Front Wheel Drive 1981-88
6529	122, 122S	Volvo 1956-69	5790	410	Datsun 1961-72
7042	124	Fiat 1969-81	5790	411	Datsun 1961-72
7042	128	Fiat 1969-81	7081	411, 412	Volkswagen 1970-81
7042	131	Fiat 1969-81	6809	450SE, 450SEL, 450	Mercedes-Benz 1974-84
6529	142	Volvo 1956-69		SEL 6.9	
7040	142	Volvo 1970-88	6809	450SL, 450SLC	Mercedes-Benz 1974-84
6529	144	Volvo 1956-69	5907	450SLC	Mercedes-Benz 1968-73
7040	144	Volvo 1970-88	6809	500SEC, 500SEL	Mercedes-Benz 1974-84
0529	145	Volvo 1956-69	5982	504	Peugeot 1970-74
7040	145	Volvo 1970-88	5790	510	Datsun 1961-72
6529	164	Volvo 1956-69	7170	510	Nissan 200SX, 240SX, 510, 610,
7040	164	Volvo 1970-88			710, 810, Maxima 1973-88
6065	190C	Mercedes-Benz 1959-70	6816	520	Datsun/Nissan Pick-Ups and Path-
6809	190D	Mercedes-Benz 1974-84			finder 1970-89
6065	190DC	Mercedes-Benz 1959-70	6844	524TD	BMW 1970-88
6809	190E	Mercedes-Benz 1974-84	6844	525i	BMW 1970-88
6065	200, 200D	Mercedes-Benz 1959-70	6844	528e	BMW 1970-88
7170	200SX	Nissan 200SX, 240SX, 510, 610,	6844	528i	BMW 1970-88
		710, 810, Maxima 1973-88	6844	530i	BMW 1970-88
7197	210	Datsun 1200, 210, Nissan Sentra	6844	533i	BMW 1970-88
		1971-88	6844	535i, 535iS	BMW 1970-88
6065	220B, 220D, 220Sb,	Mercedes-Benz 1959-70	6980	600	Honda 1973-88
	220SEb		7163	600	Chrysler Front Wheel Drive 1981-88
5907	220/8 1968-73	Mercedes-Benz 1968-73	7170	610	Nissan 200SX, 240SX, 510, 610,
6809	230 1974-78	Mercedes-Benz 1974-84			710, 810, Maxima 1973-88
6065	230S, 230SL	Mercedes-Benz 1959-70	6816	620	Datsun/Nissan Pick-Ups and Path-
5907	230/8	Mercedes-Benz 1968-73			finder 1970-89
6809	240D	Mercedes-Benz 1974-84	6981	626	Mazda 1978-89
7170	240SX	Nissan 200SX, 240SX, 510, 610,	6844	630 CSi	BMW 1970-88
		710, 810, Maxima 1973-88	6844	633 CSi	BMW 1970-88
6932	240Z	Datsun Z & ZX 1970-87	6844	635CSi	BMW 1970-88
7040	242, 244, 245	Volvo 1970-88	7170	710	Nissan 200SX, 240SX, 510, 610,
5907	250C	Mercedes-Benz 1968-73			710, 810, Maxima 1973-88
6065	250S, 250SE,	Mercedes-Benz 1959-70	6816	720	Datsun/Nissan Pick-Ups and Path-
	250SL				finder 1970-89
5907	250/8	Mercedes-Benz 1968-73	6844	733i	BMW 1970-88
6932	260Z	Datsun Z & ZX 1970-87	6844	735i	BMW 1970-88
7040	262, 264, 265	Volvo 1970-88	7040	760, 760GLE	Volvo 1970-88
5907	280	Mercedes-Benz 1968-73	7040	780	Volvo 1970-88
6809	280	Mercedes-Benz 1974-84	6981	808	Mazda 1978-89
5907	280C	Mercedes-Benz 1968-73	7170	810	Nissan 200SX, 240SX, 510, 610,
6809	280C, 280CE, 280E	Mercedes-Benz 1974-84			710, 810, Maxima 1973-88
6065	280S, 280SE	Mercedes-Benz 1959-70	7042	850	Fiat 1969-81
5907	280SE, 280S/8,	Mercedes-Benz 1968-73	7572	900, 900 Turbo	SAAB 900 1976-85
	280SE/8		7048	924	Porsche 924/928 1976-81
6809	280SEL, 280SEL/8,	Mercedes-Benz 1974-84	7048	928	Porsche 924/928 1976-81
	280SL		6981	929	Mazda 1978-89
6932	280Z, 280ZX	Datsun Z & ZX 1970-87	6836	1000	Chevette/1000 1976-88
6065	300CD, 300D,	Mercedes-Benz 1959-70	6780	1100	MG 1961-81
	300SD, 300SE		5790	1200	Datsun 1961-72
5907	300SEL 3.5,	Mercedes-Benz 1968-73	7197	1200	Datsun 1200, 210, Nissan Sentra
	300SEL 4.5				1973-88
5907	300SEL 6.3,	Mercedes-Benz 1968-73	6982	1400GL, 1400DL,	Subaru 1970-88
	300SEL/8			1400GF	
6809	300TD	Mercedes-Benz 1974-84	5790	1500	Datsun 1961-72

Chilton's Repair Manuals are available at your local retailer or by mailing a check or money order for **$14.95** per book plus **$3.50** for 1st book and **$.50** for each additional book to cover postage and handling to:

Chilton Book Company
Dept. DM
Radnor, PA 19089

NOTE: When ordering be sure to include your name & address, book part No. & title.

CHILTON'S REPAIR MANUAL MODEL INDEX
Car and truck model names are listed in alphabetical and numerical order

Part No.	Model	Repair Manual Title	Part No.	Model	Repair Manual Title
5905	LeMans	Tempest/GTO/LeMans 1968-73	5790	Patrol	Datsun 1961-72
7346	LeMans	Pontiac Mid-Size 1974-83	6934	PB100, 150, 200,	Dodge/Plymouth Vans 1967-88
7308	LeSabre	Buick/Olds/Pontiac 1975-87		250, 300, 350	
6842	Lincoln	Ford/Mercury/Lincoln 1968-88	5982	Peugeot	Peugeot 1970-74
7055	LN-7	Ford/Mercury Front Wheel Drive 1981-87	7049	Phoenix	GM X-Body 1980-85
			7027	Pinto	Pinto/Bobcat 1971-80
6842	LTD	Ford/Mercury/Lincoln 1968-88	6554	Polara	Dodge 1968-77
6696	LTD II	Ford/Mercury/Lincoln Mid-Size 1971-85	7583	Precis	Mitsubishi 1983-89
			6980	Prelude	Honda 1973-88
7950	Lumina	Lumina/Grand Prix/Cutlass/Regal 1988-90	7658	Prizm	Chevrolet Nova/GEO Prizm 1985-89
			8012	Probe	Ford Probe 1989
6815	LUV	Chevrolet LUV 1972-81	7660	Pulsar	Datsun/Nissan F-10, 310, Stanza, Pulsar 1976-88
6575	Luxus	Opel 1971-75			
7055	Lynx	Ford/Mercury Front Wheel Drive 1981-87	6529	PV-444	Volvo 1956-69
			6529	PV-544	Volvo 1956-69
6844	L6	BMW 1970-88	6529	P-1800	Volvo 1956-69
6844	L7	BMW 1970-88	7593	Quantum	VW Front Wheel Drive 1974-87
6542	Mach I	Mustang/Cougar 1965-73	7593	Rabbit	VW Front Wheel Drive 1974-87
6812	Mach I Ghia	Mustang II 1974-78	7593	Rabbit Pickup	VW Front Wheel Drive 1974-87
6840	Malibu	Chevrolet Mid-Size 1964-88	6575	Rallye	Opel 1971-75
6575	Manta	Opel 1971-75	7459	Ramcharger	Dodge/Plymouth Trucks 1967-88
6696	Mark IV, V, VI, VII	Ford/Mercury/Lincoln Mid-Size 1971-85	6845	Rampage	Omni/Horizon/Rampage 1978-88
			6320	Rancho	Fairlane/Torino 1962-70
7814	Mark VII	Thunderbird, Cougar, Continental 1980-87	6696	Ranchero	Ford/Mercury/Lincoln Mid-Size 1971-85
6842	Marquis	Ford/Mercury/Lincoln 1968-88	6842	Ranch Wagon	Ford/Mercury/Lincoln 1968-88
6696	Marquis	Ford/Mercury/Lincoln Mid-Size 1971-85	7338	Ranger Pickup	Ford Ranger/Bronco II 1983-88
			7307	Regal RWD	Century/Regal 1975-87
7199	Matador	AMC 1975-86	7950	Regal FWD 1988-90	Lumina/Grand Prix/Cutlass/Regal 1988-90
6634	Maverick	Maverick/Comet 1970-77			
6817	Maverick	Jeep 1945-87	7163	Reliant	Chrysler Front Wheel Drive 1981-88
7170	Maxima	Nissan 200SX, 240SX, 510, 610, 710, 810, Maxima 1973-88	5821	Roadrunner	Roadrunner/Satellite/Belvedere/GTX 1968-73
6842	Mercury	Ford/Mercury/Lincoln 1968-88	7659	Rotary Pick-Up	Mazda Trucks 1971-89
6963	Merkur	Mustang/Capri/Merkur 1979-88	6981	RX-7	Mazda 1978-89
6780	MGB, MGB-GT, MGC-GT	MG 1961-81	7165	R-12, 15, 17, 18, 18i	Renault 1975-85
			7830	Sable	Taurus/Sable/Continental 1986-89
6780	Midget	MG 1961-81	7750	Safari	Chevrolet Astro/GMC Safari 1985-90
7583	Mighty Max	Mitsubishi 1983-89			
7583	Mirage	Mitsubishi 1983-89	7041	Sapporo	Champ/Arrow/Sapporo 1978-83
5795	Mk.II 1969-70	Toyota 1966-70	5821	Satellite	Roadrunner/Satellite/Belvedere/GTX 1968-73
7004	Mk.II 1970-76	Toyota Corona/Crown/Cressida/Mk.II/Van 1970-87	6326	Scamp	Valiant/Duster 1968-76
6554	Monaco	Dodge 1968-77	6845	Scamp	Omni/Horizon/Rampage 1978-88
6937	Monarch	Granada/Monarch 1975-82	6962	Scirocco	VW Front Wheel Drive 1974-90
6840	Monte Carlo	Chevrolet Mid-Size 1964-88	6936	Scottsdale	Chevrolet/GMC Pick-Ups & Suburban 1970-87
6696	Montego	Ford/Mercury/Lincoln Mid-Size 1971-85	8055	Scottsdale	Chevrolet/GMC Pick-Ups & Suburban 1988-90
6842	Monterey	Ford/Mercury/Lincoln 1968-88			
7583	Montero	Mitsubishi 1983-89	5912	Scout	International Scout 1967-73
6935	Monza 1975-80	GM Subcompact 1971-80	8034	Scrambler	Jeep 1971-90
6981	MPV	Mazda 1978-89	7197	Sentra	Datsun 1200, 210, Nissan Sentra 1973-88
6542	Mustang	Mustang/Cougar 1965-73			
6963	Mustang	Mustang/Capri/Merkur 1979-88	7462	Seville	Cadillac 1967-89
6812	Mustang II	Mustang II 1974-78	7163	Shadow	Chrysler Front Wheel Drive 1981-88
6981	MX6	Mazda 1978-89	6936	Siera	Chevrolet/GMC Pick-Ups & Suburban 1970-87
6844	M3, M6	BMW 1970-88			
7163	New Yorker	Chrysler Front Wheel Drive 1981-88	8055	Siera	Chevrolet/GMC Pick-Ups & Suburban 1988-90
6841	Nova	Chevy II/Nova 1962-79			
7658	Nova	Chevrolet Nova/GEO Prizm 1985-89	7583	Sigma	Mitsubishi 1983-89
7049	Omega	GM X-Body 1980-85	6326	Signet	Valiant/Duster 1968-76
6845	Omni	Omni/Horizon/Rampage 1978-88	6936	Silverado	Chevrolet/GMC Pick-Ups & Suburban 1970-87
6575	Opel	Opel 1971-75			
7199	Pacer	AMC 1975-86	8055	Silverado	Chevrolet/GMC Pick-Ups & Suburban 1988-90
7587	Park Avenue	GM C-Body 1985			
6842	Park Lane	Ford/Mercury/Lincoln 1968-88	6935	Skyhawk	GM Subcompact 1971-80
6962	Passat	VW Front Wheel Drive 1974-90	7059	Skyhawk	Cavalier, Skyhawk, Cimarron, 2000 1982-88
6816	Pathfinder	Datsun/Nissan Pick-Ups and Pathfinder 1970-89	7049	Skylark	GM X-Body 1980-85

Chilton's Repair Manuals are available at your local retailer or by mailing a check or money order for **$14.95** per book plus **$3.50** for 1st book and **$.50** for each additional book to cover postage and handling to:

Chilton Book Company
Dept. DM
Radnor, PA 19089

NOTE: When ordering be sure to include your name & address, book part No. & title.